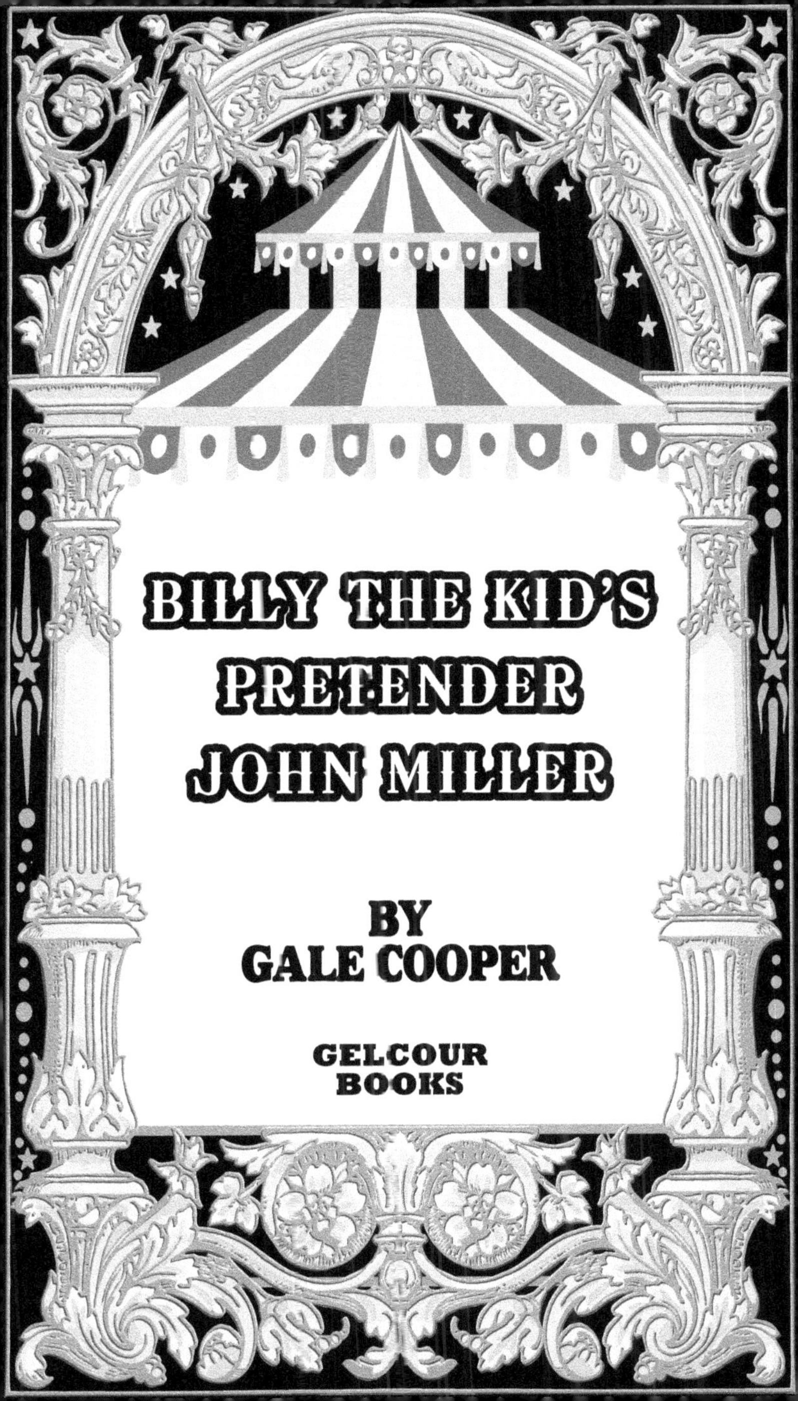

BILLY THE KID'S PRETENDER JOHN MILLER

BY
GALE COOPER

GELCOUR
BOOKS

COVER CREDITS:

Cover and book design by Gale Cooper

Photo of John Miller, courtesy of Sunstone Press, Santa Fe, New Mexico, from their 1993 *Whatever Happened to Billy the Kid?* book by Helen Airy, was the basis for the adaptation.

OTHER BILLY THE KID BOOKS BY GALE COOPER

THE HISTORY

BILLY AND PAULITA: THE SAGA OF BILLY THE KID, PAULITA MAXWELL, AND THE SANTA FE RING

BILLY THE KID'S WRITINGS, WORDS, AND WIT

THE LOST PARDON OF BILLY THE KID: AN ANALYSIS FACTORING IN THE SANTA FE RING, GOVERNOR LEW WALLACE'S DILEMMA, AND A TERRITORY IN REBELLION~

THE SANTA FE RING VERSUS BILLY THE KID: THE MAKING OF AN AMERICAN MONSTER

THE CORONER'S JURY REPORT OF BILLY THE KID: THE INQUEST THAT SEALED THE FAME OF BILLY BONNEY AND PAT GARRETT

THE HOAXES

CRACKING THE BILLY THE KID CASE HOAX: THE STRANGE PLOT TO EXHUME BILLY THE KID, CONVICT SHERIFF PAT GARRETT OF MURDER, AND BECOME PRESIDENT OF THE UNITED STATES

THE COLD CASE BILLY THE KID MEGAHOAX: THE PLOT TO STEAL BILLY THE KID'S IDENTITY AND DEFAME SHERIFF PAT GARRETT AS A MURDERER

CRACKING THE BILLY THE KID IMPOSTER HOAX OF BRUSHY BILL ROBERTS

THE "BILLY THE KID'S BAD BUCKS" HOAX: FAKING BILLY BONNEY AS A WILLIAM BROCKWAY GANG COUNTERFEITER

BLANDINA SEGALE, THE NUN WHO RODE ON BILLY THE KID: SLEUTHING A FOISTED FRONTIER FABLE

For the real Billy Bonney

and

For random man, William Hudspeth;
now part of his history,
and still awaiting justice

FIRST EDITION

ISBN: 978-1-949626-16-2 HARDCOVER
ISBN: 978-1-949626-17-9 PAPERBACK
LIBRARY OF CONGRESS CONTROL NUMBER:
2019937142

GELCOUR BOOKS
ALBUQUERQUE, NEW MEXICO

ORDERING THIS BOOK:
Amazon.com, BarnesandNoble.com, bookstores

WEBSITE:
GaleCooperBillytheKidBooks.com

YOUTUBE
"Gale Cooper's Real Billy the Kid"

Printed in the United States of America
on acid free paper

CONTENTS

PART I:
THE BILLY THE KID CIRCUS

CHAPTER 1:
STEALING HISTORY

CHAPTER 2:
IMPASSABLE HURDLES

CHAPTER 3:
THE WITNESSES AND THE DEATH SCENE

CHAPTER 4:
MORE HISTORICAL RECORDS HURDLES

PART II:
THE REAL BILLY BONNEY

CHAPTER 1:
HISTORY OF BILLY BONNEY

CHAPTER 2:
REAL BILLY BONNEY IN HIS OWN WORDS

PART III:
JOHN MILLER'S BILLY THE KID IMPOSTER HOAX

CHAPTER 1:
JOHN MILLER'S BID TO BE BILLY THE KID

CHAPTER 2:
MASQUERADING JOHN MILLER AS BILLY THE KID

PART IV:
THE "BILLY THE KID CASE" HOAX AND JOHN MILLER

CHAPTER 1:
THE "BILLY THE KID CASE" FORENSIC DNA HOAX

CHAPTER 2:
THE "BILLY THE KID CASE" HOAX'S FAKED DEATH SCENE

CHAPTER 3:
"BILLY THE KID CASE" HOAX'S LEGAL FILINGS

CHAPTER 4:
"BILLY THE KID CASE" HOAX TV PROGRAM WITH FAKE DEATH SCENE

CHAPTER 5:
"BILLY THE KID CASE" HOAX FAKE FORENSICS WITH DR. HENRY LEE

CHAPTER 6:
ILLEGALLY EXHUMING JOHN MILLER AND WILLIAM HUDSPETH FOR A MEDIA CIRCUS

PART V: THE COLD CASE BILLY THE KID MEGAHOAX AND JOHN MILLER

CHAPTER 1: DEAD JOHN MILLER JOINS A MEGAHOAX

CHAPTER 2: COLLECTED CLOWNS FAKING DEATH SCENE DOUBTS

CHAPTER 3: FAKING NO INQUEST

CHAPTER 4: RETURN OF THE FAKE FORENSICS

CHAPTER 5: RETURN OF THE "BILLY THE KID CASE'S" JOHN MILLER EXHUMATION FAKERY

PART VI: SUMMARY AND CONCLUSIONS

CHAPTER 1: WILLIAM HUDSPETH GOT THE LAST WORD

PREFACE

I tell you what. After Billy Bonney was killed by Pat Garrett he just kept on getting more famous as Billy the Kid, the likes of which made old-timers real jealous by the 1930's when Billy coulda still been alive, cept for being killed young in 1881. So them with nothing better to do, and feeling the chill up their spine of knowing they'd be forgittable after their big day with the grim reaper, come up with a scheme that made bout as much sense as a pup chasing his tail: they said they was Billy the Kid.

Now if you was somebody, it follows like ducklings trailing their momma, that you'd know what happened in your life as that somebody. Well, they didn't, for the simple reason that they wasn't Billy, and the history books wasn't written yet for stocking up on Billy's lines, like some actor acting a part. So they mostly was just scratching their seat and airing their lungs. I admit that some worked harder at it then others. This here book is bout a fella named John Miller, who was so lazy that he just got his wife and a few neighbors to say he was Billy. Now it don't take much in the brains department to recognize that this don't get you remembered by nobody. And he pretty much wasn't. He did get him an author long after he crossed the great divide, but she wasn't inclined either to waste sweat either.

That woulda been the end of the story, cept in 2003 there came the biggest gang of history rustlers that's ever been seen. They called theirselves "Billy the Kid Case" investigators set on proving that Pat never did kill Billy. And like fancying up an old nag with a new saddle, they said they'd prove it with highfalutin DNA. But they had to get DNA from somewheres. And the author of this here book stopped them in their tracks from digging up Billy and his momma for their highjinks. So as quick as you can say Billy the Kid, these crooks realized that nobody was protecting old John Miller's bones. So they dug him up to look like they was investigating something. And old John finally made the news.

This here author tells why all this made as much sense as a chicken running around without its head. And with me being fictional myself, it all seems kinda familiar.

Vern Blanton Johnson, Jr.
Lincoln, Lincoln County, New Mexico

AUTHOR'S FOREWORD

All the Billy the Kid imposter hoaxes of the 20th century are ridiculous because of contorted fakery trying to escape the documented fatal shooting of Billy Bonney by Sheriff Pat Garrett on July 14, 1881. From delusional and exhibitionistic pretenders to their profiteering authors, they were an unpalatable bunch, exploiting public ignorance and foisting antiquated outlaw mythology of "Billy the Kid," mouthed as pseudo-memories.

These hoaxes were resuscitated in the 21st century. In district courts, I have blocked their sham DNA forensics attempting exhumations of Billy Bonney and his mother. I wrote debunking books: 2010's *Billy the Kid's Pretenders: Brushy Bill and John Miller;* 2014's *Cracking the Billy the Kid Case Hoax: The Strange Plot to Exhume Billy the Kid, Convict Sheriff Pat Garrett of Murder, and Become President of the United States*; 2017's *Blandina Segale: The Nun Who Rode on Billy the Kid;* 2019's *The Cold Case Billy the Kid Megahoax: The Plot to Steal Billy the Kid's Identity and Defame Sheriff Pat Garrett as a Murderer;* and 2019's *Cracking the Billy the Kid Imposter Hoax of Brushy Bill Roberts.* The common denominator of all these hoaxes, besides lying about actual history, was labor-intensive trickery.

Old-timer Billy the Kid pretender, John Miller, was different. He skimmed a few fictionalized books from the 1920's, used fables circulating about the Kid's outlawry, sewed himself a hat like in Billy's tintype, and hinted to associates about being Billy.

What justifies writing about him at all, is that, 66 years after his 1937 death, he became key to the gigantic "Billy the Kid Case" hoax. Blocked by me from Billy's and his mother's graves, the perpetrators were desperate for DNA of any Billy the Kid claimant for this profiteering publicity stunt. So, shielded by New Mexico's corrupt governor backing the hoax, its perpetrators dug up John Miller for no reason other than TV cameras, and destroyed his remains for meaningless DNA extractions. This criminality was topped-off by grave-robbing his underground neighbor, random man, William Hudspeth, for more bones.

So this is a tale of non-entity, John Miller, who, after death, had the potential to topple New Mexico's then 139 year old racketeering Santa Fe Ring. I wanted to give him the chance.

Gale Cooper, M.D.
Sandia Park, New Mexico

METHODOLOGY

PRIMARY DOCUMENTS: For readers' reference, primary documents are presented; with italics for handwriting, two column newsprint for articles, and in distinctive font for books.

COMMENTARY: Author's notes and responses are provided in boldface; boldface is also used to highlight important claims by hoaxers; underlings and italics are added for emphasis; page numbers are given for cited text in books, or to refer back to pages in this book itself; and the "Appendix" and "Bibliography" are annotated.

ACKNOWLEDGMENTS

Overriding is my debt to Billy Bonney, whose cause, courage, intelligence, and joie de vivre are my inspiration.

Historical bedrock is from books by Frederick Nolan on Billy the Kid, the Lincoln County War, and John Henry Tunstall. As valuable is Leon Metz's Pat Garrett biography and Jerry (Richard) Weddle's book on Billy Bonney's early adolescence.

Hoaxbusting appreciation goes to brave journalist, Jay Miller, who acted as my open records proxy in my early dangerous days of exposing Governor Bill Richardson's "Billy the Kid Case" hoax.

Collections used were at the Las Cruces, New Mexico State University Library's Rio Grande Historical Collections' Herman B. Weisner Papers, ca. 1957-1992 and Blazer Family Papers, 1864-1965; the Albuquerque, University of New Mexico Center for Southwest Studies, University Library, Catron Papers; the State of New Mexico Office of Cultural Affairs Historic Preservation Division; the Office of the New Mexico State Historian; the Silver City Museum and Library; the Midland, Texas Nita Stewart and J. Evetts Haley Memorial Library and Historical Center; the Canyon, Texas Panhandle-Plains Historical Museum; and the Morgantown, West Virginia & Regional History Center at West Virginia University Libraries' Stephen B. Elkins Papers.

Collections used for William Bonney's and Lew Wallace's documents were the Santa Fe, New Mexico, Fray Angélico Chávez Historical Library; and the Indianapolis, Indiana Historical Society's Lew and Wallace Collection.

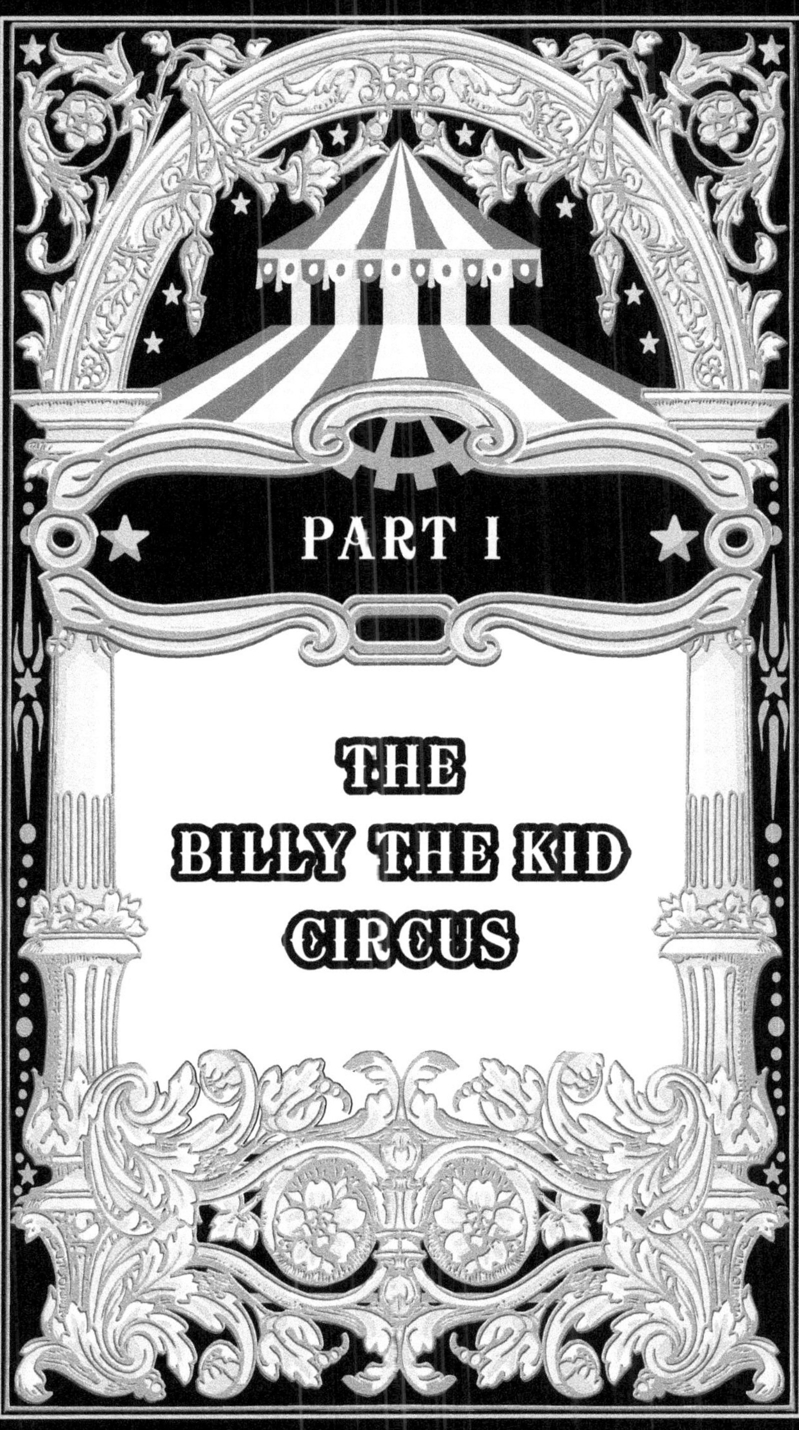

PART I

THE BILLY THE KID CIRCUS

CHAPTER 1
STEALING HISTORY

SEND IN THE CLOWNS

In the real world, Sheriff Pat Garrett fatally shot William Bonney aka Billy the Kid near midnight on July 14, 1881 in Fort Sumner, New Mexico Territory.

In the imaginary world of Billy the Kid pretenders, Pat Garrett killed an innocent victim instead, and they survived to old age. As circus impresario P.T. said, "Clowns are the pegs on which the circus is hung." And those old-timer clowns became the pegs on which later profiteering clowns hung their own hoaxes.

The modern clowns, seeking media circuses, embellished the old clowns' acts by making-up that Garrett was the Kid's friend and accomplice in his jailbreak killing of his two deputy guards, before becoming the killer of the innocent victim as grave-filler for Billy's grave! And it would all be proved by fake DNA forensics. That means, from the get-go, pretender and hoaxer tales made world-famous lawman Pat Garrett a world-class criminal, who garnered fame, but deserved infamy.

Other pretender and hoaxer prerequisites followed. The historically certain killing of Billy the Kid, with its Coroner's Jury Report and profuse witnesses, had to be denied. Tales had to be invented for the fake death scenes.

But nothing that parade of buffoons juggled around could hide that they were nothing but clowns, hoping for a three-ring circus around themselves under a fictional big top of their own creation.

As Stephen Sondheim, the creator of 1973's musical "A Little Night Music," said in a 2008 interview about his lyrics for "Send in the Clowns": "The song could have been called 'Send in the Fools" ... Well, a synonym for fools is clowns."

So this is the tale of the Billy the Kid pretender who was obviously both a fool and a clown: John Miller.

THE MOST PATHETIC CLOWN OF ALL

This book exposes the Billy the Kid pretender named John Miller. Differing from other imposters in the second quarter of the 20th century - like Oliver "Brushy Bill" Roberts - he put little effort into his hoax, and knew no Billy the Kid history. And the only apparent profit he sought was impressing his wife, adopted son, and a his acquaintances with his clowning antics.

Dead by 1937, he got an equally lethargic author named Helen Airy, for her 1993 book, *Whatever Happened to Billy the Kid?*, She kept secret that his 1850 birth had made him almost a decade older than real Billy Bonney - and no kid.

But dead John Miller got caught up in a huge media circus ten years after Airy's book, with the 2003 advent of the "Billy the Kid Case" hoax: the most elaborate historic-forensic fraud ever perpetrated. Perpetrated by New Mexico's corrupt Governor, Bill Richardson, as self-promotion and apparent pay-to-play to a major political donor, its intent was to fake DNA matchings from graves of the Kid and his mother to proclaim "Brushy Bill" Roberts as Billy the Kid. But after I blocked those meaningless exhumations in courts, the hoaxers were desperate for any DNA claim for their tabloid-level TV documentaries and fake news press.

That was when John Miller reappeared to public notice, because his was the only grave vulnerable backhoeing for a publicity stunt. His 2005, illegal, Arizona exhumation transformed him from having no connection to Billy the Kid history, to becoming a clowning side-show to Billy Bonney's non-ending fame.

THE GROWTH OF THE OUTLAW MYTH

Old-timer Billy the Kid imposters, like John Miller, gave themselves away by performing Billy with the antiquated outlaw mythology from his day - which he himself would have abhorred.

Real Billy's true story had started with that faked history. Even his moniker, "Billy the Kid," was created by his enemies to vilify him as their outlaw-murderer creation. The time was the 1870's, when New Mexico Territory was in the throes of grass-roots uprisings against the land-grabbing political cabal of the deadly Santa Fe Ring: the real outlaws covering-up their villainy.

In 1872, legislators in Santa Fe rose up against the increasing Ring stranglehold, and were suppressed by the Ringite Governor.

In 1876, to the southwest, was the Grant County Rebellion, with citizens writing a "Declaration of Independence" and trying to secede and join Arizona Territory to escape the Ring. From 1875 to 1877, Ring atrocities escalated to the north, in the Colfax County War, with assassination of the anti-Ring leader and with citizens' futile exposés to Ring-biased President Rutherford B. Hayes. The culminating defeat was the 1878 Lincoln County War, where Ring-beholden troops illegally enabled citizens' murders, and Billy Bonney emerged as a grass-roots hero and future threat with his bi-cultural links eliciting a future Hispanic uprising.

The result was Billy's outlawing by the Ring, magnified by his 1879 pardon bargain with Governor Lew Wallace, who disreputably reneged under Ring pressure, and concealed his moral failure by self-justifying articles adding to the outlaw myth of Billy the Kid. By 1882, Sheriff Pat Garrett capitalized on his fame for killing Billy the year before by publishing his own outlaw myth book. That mold was not broken by the scholarly historians of the latter half of the 20th century, who merely plastered new findings onto that antique armature.

It has taken my research, analyses, and books to restore Billy Bonney to his freedom fighter glory, along with his compatriots, in that period when democracy was destroyed by Ring infiltration of all public offices, and by its terrorism of malicious prosecutions, massacres, assassinations, and military suppression. The Ring's victor's option of writing history hid that history. So, of course, the imposters were ignorant of real Billy Bonney and his cause.

In John Miller's case, he was even ignorant of the Lincoln County War. And important for the forensic DNA hoax that elevated him, he did not claim Billy's mother as his own - making the intended maternal DNA matching meaningless.

ENTRY OF HISTORICAL PARASITES

The peculiar side-effect of Billy Bonney's posthumous fame was the emergence of mentally disturbed, attention-seeking old men, in the second quarter of the 20th century, who claimed to be him. Since Billy was fatally shot on July 14, 1881 by Pat Garrett, that necessitated these imposters' second fabrication: accusing Pat Garrett of killing the wrong man and covering it up.

This was also the period in which fascination for Billy's story was so insatiable that his old-timer contemporaries got their own mundane life stories published in books, simply by adding him.

Thus, some Billy the Kid impersonators likewise attracted hoaxing profiteering authors.

The problem the fabricating historical parasites faced was insurmountable: scholarly history books about Billy Bonney's life had not yet been written. There was only the antiquated outlaw mythology. So cribbing fake fables was the imposters' undoing. But their salvation was an equally benighted public, unable to distinguish hoaxes from truth, and eager for tales of Billy the Kid.

THE "BRUSHY BILL" HOAX AND JOHN MILLER

The most famous pretender was Oliver Pleasant "Brushy Bill" Roberts, who was promoted by a traveling salesman and attorney imposter named William V. Morrison, who coached him with available sources; unsuccessfully sought the Billy the Kid pardon for him from New Mexico's modern governor; and co-wrote a 1955 book, *Alias Billy the Kid*, that created "Brushy's" duped followers. That hoax was recycled by W.C. Jameson and Frederick Bean for their 1998 book: *The Return of the Outlaw Billy the Kid.*

"Brushy's" success inspired Helen Airy, for her 1993 John Miller book: *Whatever Happened to Billy the Kid?* Miller reappeared in 2003's "Billy the Kid Case" hoax, to fuel their TV documentaries' exhumation franchise faking forensic DNA investigations of old pretenders.

THE "BILLY THE KID" CASE HOAX

The "Billy the Kid Case," covertly backing "Brushy Bill," was a murder case against Pat Garrett, intending to prove his "guilt" at killing the innocent victim by faking DNA matchings from exhumations. I halted that hoax in courts and by exposé books.

THE "COLD CASE BILLY THE KID" MEGAHOAX

In 2018, "Brushy Bill"-backing author, W.C. Jameson, worked with past "Billy the Kid Case" hoaxers to unite their fakery with "Brushy Bill's" for his book: *Cold Case Billy the Kid: Investigating History's Mysteries.* To cast doubt on the recorded history, he even included John Miller as a death scene survivor possibility. His book's pernicious result was bringing back the three-ring circus of both hoaxes under the same big top.

CHAPTER 2
IMPASSABLE HURDLES

THE CORONER'S JURY REPORT

The original Spanish July 15, 1881 Coroner's Jury Report proved Billy Bonney's death. **[Figure: 1]**

It confirmed the Report's proper filing with the District Attorney of the First Judicial District, William Breeden: "To the District Attorney of the First Judicial District of the Territory of New Mexico, Greetings."

It presented the proper action of San Miguel County Justice of the Peace Alejandro Segura, as *ex officio* coroner: "[I]mmediately upon receiving said information [of a murder in Fort Sumner] I proceeded to the said place and named Milnor Rudulph, Jose Silva, Antonio Sevedra, Pedro Antonio Lucero, Lorenzo Jaramillo and Sabal Gutierres a jury to investigate the case."

The body was identified: "/The jury] found the body of William Bonney alias "Kid" with a shot in the left breast."

The eye-witness was interviewed: "[The Jurymen]examined the evidence of Pedro Maxwell [Peter Maxwell, owner of Fort Sumner], which evidence is as follows: "I being in my bed in my room, at about midnight on the 14th day of July, Pat F. Garrett came into my room and sat down. William Bonney came in and got close to my bed with a gun in his hand and asked me "who is it" and then Pat F. Garrett fired two shots at the said William Bonney and the said William Bonney fell near my fire place and I went out of the room and when I came in again about three or four minutes after the shots the said William Bonney was dead."

The jurymen's verdict stated: "[T]he deed of said Garrett was justifiable homicide."

The conclusion was for reward: "[G]ratitude ... is due to the said Garrett for his deed and [he] is worthy of being rewarded."

THE TRANSLATED CORONER'S JURY REPORT

Territory of New Mexico) Precinct No. 27
County of San Miguel)

To the District Attorney of the First Judicial District of the Territory of New Mexico,

Greetings:

On this 15th day of July, A.D. 1881, I, the undersigned, Justice of the Peace of the above named precinct, received information that a murder had taken place in Fort Sumner, in said precinct, and immediately upon receiving said information I proceeded to the said place and named Milnor Rudulph, Jose Silva, Antonio Saavedra, Pedro Antonio Lucero, Lorenzo Jaramillo and Sabal Gutierres a jury to investigate the case and the above jury convened in the home of Luz B. Maxwell and proceeded to a room in the said house where they found the body of William Bonney alias "Kid" with a shot in the left breast and having examined the body they examined the evidence of Pedro Maxwell, which evidence is as follows:

"I being in my bed in my room, at about midnight on the 14th day of July, Pat F. Garrett came into my room and sat at the end on my bed to talk with me. A little while after Garrett sat down, William Bonney came in and got close to my bed with a gun in his hand and asked me "Who is it Who is it?" and then Pat F. Garrett fired two shots at the said William Bonney and the said Bonney fell near my fire place and I went out of the room and when I came in again about three or four minutes after the shots the said Bonney was dead."

The jury has found the following verdict:

We the jury unanimously find that William Bonney has been killed by a bullet in the left breast in the region of the heart, the same having been fired from a pistol in the hand of Pat F. Garrett, and our verdict is that the act of said Garrett was justifiable homicide and we are unanimous in the opinion that the gratitude of all the community is due to the said Garrett for his deed and is worthy of being rewarded.

M. Rudulph, President
Anto. Saavedra
Pedro Anto. Lucero
Jose Silva (X)
Sabal Gutierrez (X)
Lorenzo Jaramillo (X)

All which information I put at your disposal.

Alejandro Segura Justice of the Peace

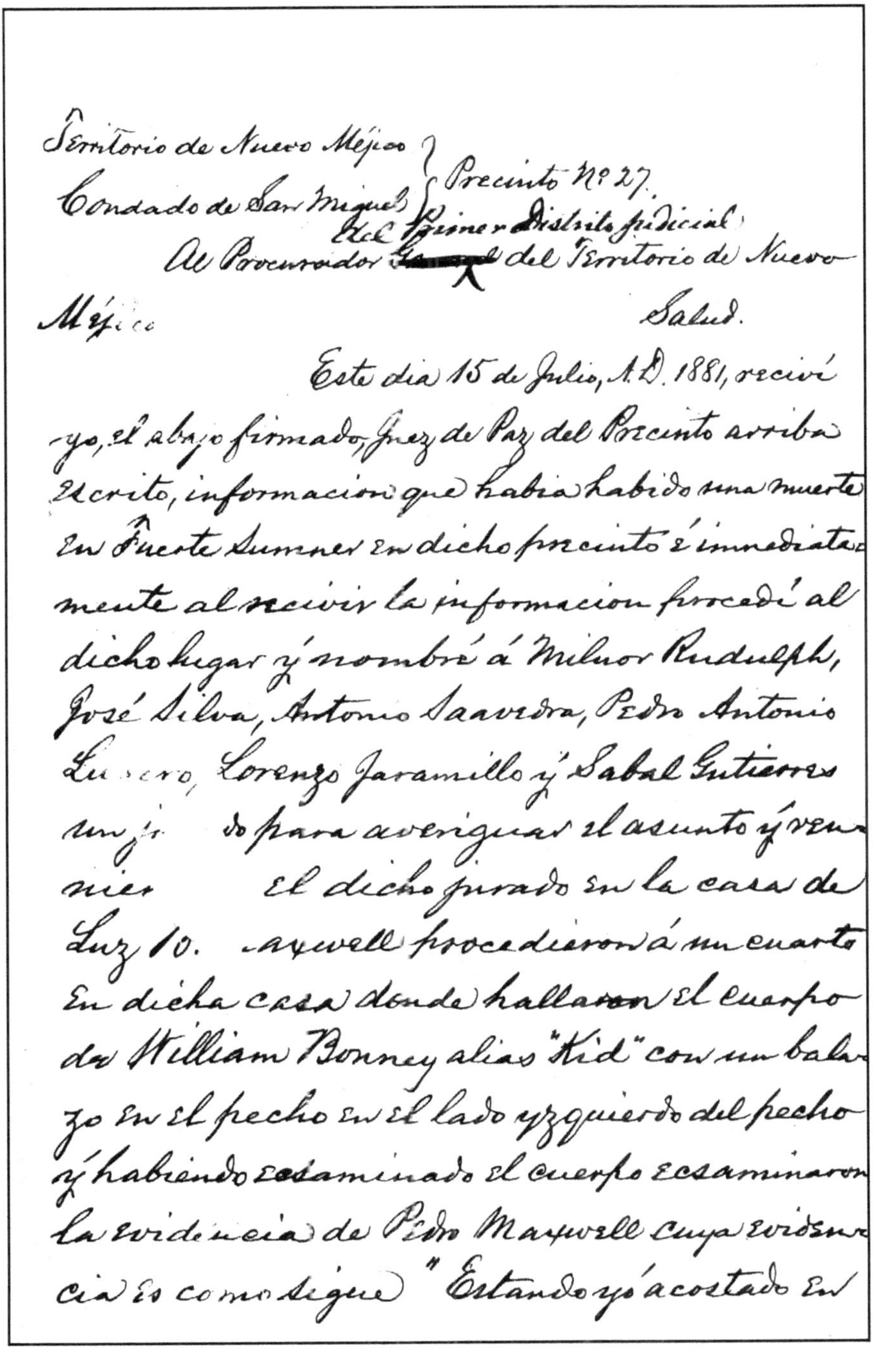

Territorio de Nuevo Méjico } Precinto No. 27.
Condado de San Miguel } Del Primer Distrito Judicial

Al Procurador General del Territorio de Nuevo Méjico

Salud.

Este dia 15 de Julio, A.D. 1881, recivé yo, el abajo firmado, Juez de Paz del Precinto arriba escrito, informacion que habia habido una muerte en Fuerte Sumner en dicho precinto é immediatamente al recivir la informacion procedé al dicho lugar y nombré á Milnor Rudulph, José Silva, Antonio Saavedra, Pedro Antonio Lucero, Lorenzo Jaramillo y Sabal Gutierres un jurado para averiguar el asunto y venier El dicho jurado en la casa de Luz B. Maxwell procedieron á un cuarto en dicha casa donde hallaron el cuerpo de William Bonney alias "Kid" con un balazo en el pecho en el lado yzquierdo del pecho y habiendo ecsaminado el cuerpo ecsaminaron la evidencia de Pedro Maxwell cuya evidencia es como sigue " Estando yo acostado en

FIGURE: 1. Original Spanish Coroner's Jury Report of July 15, 1881 for William H. Bonney aka Kid (Courtesy of the Indiana Historical Society, Lew Wallace Collection)

mi cama en mi cuarto a cosa de media noche el dia 14 de Julio entró á mi cuarto Pat. F. Garrett y se sentó en la orilla de mi cama á platicar conmigo. A poco rato que Garrett se sentó entró William Bonney y se arrimó á mi cama con una pistola en la mano y me preguntó "Who is it? Who is it?" y Entónces Pat. F. Garrett le tiró dos balazos á dicho William Bonney y se cayó el dicho Bonney en un lado de mi fogon y yo salí del cuarto. Cuando volví á Entrar yá en tres ó cuatro minutos despues de los balazos Estaba muerto dicho Bonney."

El jurado há hallado el siguiente dictámen "Nosotros los del jurado unanimente hallamos que William Bonney há sido muerto por un balazo en el pecho yzquierdo en la region del corazon tirado de una pistola en la mano de Pat. F. Garrett y nuestro dictámen es que el hecho de dicho Garrett fué homicidio justificable y estamos unánimes en opinion que la gratitud de toda la comunidad es devida á dicho Garrett por su hecho y que es digno de ser recompensado."

W. A. [illegible]
Presidente

Ant^o Salcedra
pedro Ant^o Lucero
Jose + Silba
Vidal + gutierrez
Lorenso + Jaramillo

Todo cuya información pongo á conocimiento de V.

Alejandro Segura
Jues de Paz

PAT GARRETT'S LETTER TO THE ACTING-GOVERNOR

On July 15, 1881, the day after killing Billy Bonney, Pat Garrett sent a letter, enclosing a copy of that day's Coroner's Jury Report, to Territorial Acting-Governor, William Ritch, confirming the killing and its circumstances.

The letter was quoted in July 23, 1881's Las Cruces *Rio Grande Republican* as "Kid the Killer Killed, Wm. Bonney alias Antrim, alias Billy the Kid, Fatally Meets Pat Garrett, the Lincoln County Sheriff." It stated: "Below is given Sheriff Garrett's report as made to Acting Governor Ritch which contains also the verdict of the coroner's jury [with English translation, but explaining: 'The verdict is given in Spanish in Garrett's report']." The article stated:

William Bonney, alias 'the Kid,' is dead. No report could have caused more general feeling of gratification than this, and when it was further announced that the faithful and brave Pat Garrett, he who had been the mainstay of law and order in Lincoln county, the chief reliance of the people in the dark days, when danger lurked at every hand, has accomplished the crowning feat of his life by bringing down the fierce and implacable foe single-handed, the sense of satisfaction was heightened to one of delight. The following is Sheriff Garrett's official report to the chief executive of the territory.

It is as follows. – Fort Sumner, N.M., July 15. - Fort Sumner, N.M., July 15, '81 - To his Excellency the Governor of New Mexico:

"I have the honor to inform your Excellency that I had received several communications from persons in and about Fort Sumner, what William Bonney, alias the Kid, had been there, or in that vicinity for some time.

"In view of these reports I deemed it my duty to go there, and ascertain if there was any truth in them or not, all the time doubting their accuracy; but on Monday, July 11, I left home, taking with me John W. Poe and T.L. McKinney, men in whose courage and sagacity I relied implicitly, and arrived just below Fort Sumner, on Wednesday, 13th [sic]. I remained concealed near the houses, until night, and then entered the fort about midnight, and went to Mr. P. Maxwell's room. I found him in bed, and had just commenced talking to him about the object of my visit at such an unusual hour, when a man entered the room in stockinged feet, with a pistol in one hand and a knife in the other. He came and placed his hand on the bed just beside me, and in a low whisper, "who is it?" (and repeated the question) he asked Mr. Maxwell.

I at once recognized the man, and knew he was the Kid. and reached behind me for my pistol, feeling almost certain of receiving a ball from his at the moment of my doing so, as I felt sure he had now recognized me, but fortunately he drew back from the bed at noticing my movement, and, although he had his pistol pointed at my breast, he delayed to fire, and asked me in Spanish, "Quien es? Quien es?" This gave me time to bring mine to bear on him, and the moment I did so I pulled the trigger and he received his death wound, for the ball struck him in the left breast and pierced his heart. He never spoke, but died in a minute. It was my desire to have been able to take him alive, but his coming upon me so suddenly and unexpectedly leads me to believe that he had seen me enter the room, or had been informed by someone of the fact; and that he came there armed with pistol and knife expressly to kill me if he could. Under that impression I had no alternative but to kill him or to suffer death at his hands.

I herewith annex a copy of the verdict rendered by the jury called in by the justice of the peace (ex officio coroner), the original of which is in the hands of the prosecuting attorney of the first judicial district."

(The verdict is given in Spanish in Garrett's report, and upon being translated is as follows:

"We the jury unanimously say that William Bonney came to his death by a wound in the breast in the region of the heart, fired from a pistol in the hand of Pat F. Garrett, and our decision is that the action of said Garrett, was justifiable homicide; and we are united in opinion that the gratitude of all the community is due to said Garrett for his action, and he deserves to be compensated."

(Signed) M. Rudulph, Foreman,
Antonio Savedra,
Pedro Antonio Lucero,
Sabal Gutierres,
Lorenzo Jaramillo

I am Governor, very respectfully your Excellency's obedient servant,

Pat F. Garrett

THE ISSUE OF NO CULPABILITY

Pat Garrett's letter of July 15, 1881 to Acting-Governor William Ritch confirmed that he had followed proper legal procedure and sent the original Coroner's Jury Report to the District Attorney for the First Judicial District, William Breeden, responsible for San Miguel County, in which was the homicide site of Fort Sumner. Garrett's letter to Ritch had stated: "I herewith annex a copy of the verdict rendered by the jury called in by the justice of the peace (*ex officio* coroner, meaning by virtue of his position or status), **the original of which is in the hands of the prosecuting attorney of the first judicial district.**"

Breeden, also Territorial Attorney General, would have checked the verdict: "[O]ur verdict is that the action of said Garrett was justifiable homicide." That meant the killing as self-defense, as was subsequently confirmed by prosecutor Breeden's filing no murder charge against Garrett, and later by his assisting Acting-Governor Ritch in processing Garrett's reward payment. There were no grounds for a cold case murder accusation against Garrett.

ISSUES COMPLICATING GARRETT'S REWARD COLLECTION

Garrett's letter to Acting-Governor Ritch also initiated the process of collecting his reward. The Coroner's Jury Report had presented no problem with its conclusion stating: "[H]e deserves to be rewarded." But issuing the reward to him was complicated by two variables: its being a **private offer** by past-Governor Lew Wallace, and its **not being a dead-or-alive offer**.

The reward offer, published by Lew Wallace, in his own name, in December 22, 1880's *Las Vegas Daily Gazette*, and May 3, 1881's *Santa Fe Daily New Mexican*, had stated:

BILLY THE KID
$500 REWARD

I will pay $500 reward to any person or persons who will capture William Bonney, alias The Kid, and deliver him to any sheriff of New Mexico. Satisfactory proofs of identity will be required.

LEW. WALLACE,
Governor of New Mexico

Its stipulating capture and delivery "to any sheriff" meant alive. To cover that Bonney was now dead (i.e., not deliverable alive), Garrett's letter to Ritch had explained that killing had been the only option: "I had no alternative but to kill him or to suffer death at his hands." So death instead of capture presented no problem to all concerned in justifying the reward.

REWARD NEEDING LEGISLATIVE INTERVENTION

Acting-Governor William Ritch could not simply issue payment of Garrett's reward. He hesitated to use Territorial funds to cover Lew Wallace's private offer. And Wallace had left the Territory and his governorship in May of 1881.

So Ritch sought legal advice from the ideal person: William Breeden. Not only was he the proper prosecutor as District Attorney of the First Judicial District, who himself possessed the original of the Coroner's Jury Report, and who knew Garrett's killing had been in self-defense; but he was also the Territorial Attorney General, who could advise on the proper legal solution of conversion of a private reward to a Territorial one.

Garrett himself met with Ritch on July 20, 1881, as reported by the July 21, 1881 *Santa Fe Daily New Mexican.* Ritch was quoted as "willing to pay the amount, and was willing to do so," but made clear that the delaying issue was that proper procedure had to be followed first. The article stated:

> Yesterday afternoon Pat. Garrett; accompanied by Hon. T.B. Catron and Col. M. Brunswick, called upon acting-Governor Ritch in regard to the reward offered by ex-Governor Lew Wallace for the Kid. The reward was fixed at five hundred dollars, and the offer was published in the papers. Governor Ritch announced that he was willing to pay the amount, and would be glad to do so, but that he would have to look at the records first. He was not in the city when the offer was made, and had never received any notification of it, consequently did not know whether or not it was on record. In consequence of the state of affairs, the question of the reward was not settled.

Ritch recorded his consultation with Breeden in his July 21, 1881 *Executive Record Book 2* entry as: "In the matter of the application by Patrick F. Garrett for a reward claimed to have been offered May-1881 for the capture of Wm Bonney alias 'the Kid.' " It confirmed that Breeden agreed that the reward was a private offer, since Wallace had not filed it with his office or that of the Territorial Secretary [then Ritch himself], converting it to a Territorial offer. Breeden stated: "*In addition, we will add as fact that there was no record whatever in this [Attorney General's] office or at the Secretary's office of there having been a reward offered as set forth by Attorney General, nor was there any reward or file in said offices of a corresponding reward in any form.*" So the issue was converting Wallace's private reward to a Territorial reward.

Ritch's July 21, 1881 *Executive Record Book 2* entry transcribed Breeden's opinion; stating:

Executive Department
Territory of New Mexico
July 21st 1881

July 20th 1881 Pat F. Garret [sic- throughout] Sheriff of Lincoln County appeared and presented a bill for $500. claiming it as a reward offered on or about the 7th of May 1881 by the late Governor Lew Wallace, for the capture of said Bonny [sic, throughout].

As evidence of said offer having been made the affidavit of publication thereof made by Chas. H. Green [sic – Greene] the editor and manager of the Daily New Mexican was presented with said bill, as also was presented a statement of the proceedings and verdict of a coroner's jury at Fort Sumner in San Miguel County upon the body of the said Bonny, captured as aforesaid, and a statement of Garret directed to this office of his doings in the premises.

Upon examination of said papers it was deemed important that the opinion of the Attorney General be taken thereon and they were at once transmitted to that office. On the following day the papers with the opinion of Hon. Wm Breeden Attorney General were filed.

Said opinion is quite full. We quote the closing paragraphs as sufficient in this connection, to with

"The offer by the Governor, or the notice thereof, which is all there is to show such an offer, is as follows –

Billy the Kid
$500 Reward

"I will pay five hundred dollars reward to any person or persons, who will capture William Bonny, alias the Kid, and deliver him to any Sheriff of New Mexico. Satisfactory proof of identity will be required.

Lew Wallace
Governor of New Mexico

"This certainly appears to be the personal offer of Governor Wallace, and it seems he did nothing to indicate that it was intended as an executive act on behalf of, and to bind the Territory.

"If the reward should be paid, it is very probable that the Legislature would approve the payment if so desired, and that no objection would be raised, or that it will provide for its payment if it remained unpaid, at the next session thereof;

[AUTHOR'S NOTE: Breeden saw no problem with the Legislature's eventual approving of reward payment.]

but if the Governor [Ritch] should now direct the payment of the claim, he would doubtless expose himself to the charge of misappropriation of the Territorial funds, in case the Legislature should refuse to ratify or approve the payment."

[AUTHOR'S NOTE: So Breeden said if Ritch paid the reward himself *before proper procedure of legislative approval*, it could be criticized as misappropriating funds. Ritch next returned to presenting his own words.]

In addition we will add as a fact that there was no record whatsoever; either in this office or at the [Territorial] Secretary's office of there having been a reward offered as set forth by Attorney General, nor was there any record or file in said offices of a corresponding reward in any form.

[AUTHOR'S NOTE: Ritch confirmed that Wallace had not converted his reward offer into a Territorial offer.]

The opinion of the Attorney General appearing to be consistent with the law and the facts. Decision is rendered accordingly and the Governor [Ritch] declines to allow the reward at this time. <u>Believing however, that Mr Garret has an equitable claim against the Territory for said reward, the action at this office will simply be suspended until the case can properly be represented to the next Legislative Assembly</u>.

Ritch

Act Governor NM

[AUTHOR'S NOTE: Ritch confirmed that the reward was justified, but had to be converted to a Territorial reward, though that made a delay till the legislative meeting.]

REWARD GRANTED TO GARRETT BY THE LEGISLATURE

The Act granting Pat Garrett his reward made clear that only the conversion "technicality" had caused the delay. It stated:

AN ACT FOR THE RELIEF OF PAT. GARRETT

CONTENTS

SECTION 1. Authorizes payment of $500 reward for the arrest of "the Kid."

WHEREAS, The Governor of New Mexico did, on or about the 7th day of May, A.D., 1881, issue certain proclamation in words and figures as follows, to-wit:

"I will pay five hundred dollars reward to any person or persons who will capture William Bonney, alias 'The Kid,' and deliver him to any sheriff of New Mexico. Satisfactory proof of identity will be required."

(Signed) Lew. Wallace
Governor of New Mexico.

AND, WHEREAS, Pat. Garrett was at that time sheriff of Lincoln county, and did, on or about the month of August, 1881, in pursuance of the above reward, and by virtue of a warrant placed in his hands for the purpose, attempted to arrest said William Bonney, and in said attempt did kill said William Bonney at Fort Sumner, in the county of San Miguel, in the Territory of New Mexico, and wherefore, said Garrett is justly entitled to the above reward, and payment thereof has been refused upon a technicality. Therefore

Be it enacted by the Legislative Assembly of the Territory of New Mexico:

SECTION 1. The Territorial Auditor is hereby authorized to draw a warrant upon the Territorial Treasurer of the Territory of New Mexico, in favor of Pat. Garrett for the sum of five hundred dollars, payable out of any funds in the Territorial treasury not otherwise appropriated, in payment of the reward of five hundred dollars heretofore offered by his Excellency, Governor

Lew. Wallace, for the arrest of William Bonney, alias "The Kid."

SEC. 2. This act shall take effect and be in force from and after its passage.

Approved February 18, 1882.

LATER FINDING OF THE REPORT

After the Coroner's Jury Report fulfilled its uses, it was filed away by William Breeden. It was indirectly referenced in a 1935 book by a Frank M. King titled *Wranglin' the Past: Reminiscences of Frank M. King*, in the chapter titled "The Kid's Exit." King wrote that Garrett's letter to Acting-Governor William Ritch, which cited its copy, had recently been located in old files of the Secretary of State of New Mexico.

And the original William Bonney Coroner's Jury Report of July 15, 1881 - sent to William Breeden, as District Attorney of the First Judicial District, and also legally analyzed by him as Attorney General - was found in 1932 by a Harold Abbott, employed from 1931 to 1933 in Santa Fe in the State Land Office, when he discovered it in the basement of the state capitol. He made copies of it for himself and others, including his brother George. Harold died in 1937; George in 2006.

So George Abbott lived to see his brother's finding of the Coroner's Jury Report making the front page of November 30, 1950's *Alamogordo News* as "Sumner Jury Thought The Kid Had Been Killed." It stated:

Although the perennial controversy over whether the infamous Billy the Kid still lives, has again arisen, at least one Alamogordo man, Frank Phillips, 84, claims personal knowledge of his death in 1881 at the hands of the late Sheriff Pat Garrett, and George Abbott, also of Alamogordo has in his office at the Pioneer Abstract Co., a photostatic copy of the verdict of the coroner's jury which viewed the remains of the late Wm. Bonney

Some twenty years ago, when the late Harold Abbott, brother of George, was an employee of the state land office in Santa Fe, <u>he, with other employees, were going over some old records in the basement of the state capitol. There they ran across, in the San Miguel court records, the original</u>

copy of the coroner's jury, dated July 15, 1881, and written in Spanish. The document covered three pages of which they made photostatic copies.

As the reader will see from the document, translated below, the six men serving on the jury and the Justice of the Peace who empanneled them, seemed convinced that Wm. Bonney, known as "Kid," was quite dead, and that he had been killed by Pat Garrett.

The most recent controversy arose when a firm of El Paso lawyers appealed to Governor Mabry for a full pardon for Wm. Bonney, who claims that the man killed at Fort Sumner by Pat Garrett was another outlaw, and not the Kid at all; that the Kid left the country, assumed the name of ["Brushy Bill"] Roberts, and has lived in Old and New Mexico all this time.

The documentary evidence of the Kid's death is translated as follows:

Territory of New Mexico
San Miguel County
Precinct No. 27

To the attorney of the 1st Judicial district of the Territory of New Mexico:
Greetings: [The English Translation followed]

FROM BREEDEN TO HAROLD ABBOTT

One can trace the Coroner's Jury Report's storage in the state Capitol Buildings. First was William Breeden's Palace of the Governors office. Breeden apparently filed the Report in his capacity as District Attorney for the First Judicial District under San Miguel County court records, as he categorized this Fort Sumner killing in that county. As Attorney General also, his office was in rooms 5, 6, and 8, according to Clinton P. Anderson in his 1944 *New Mexico Historical Review* article titled "The Adobe Palace." (Anderson, Page 110) **[FIGURE: 2]** Anderson noted that Breeden kept that office till 1889. (Anderson, Page 112)

Next occupying Breeden's office area in that Palace of the Governors Capitol Building was the State Land Office's Commissioner.

A Jesse Nusbaum's 1909 journal recorded Palace of the Governor's rooms; being published in 1978 by Rosemary Nusbaum, as: *The City Different and the Palace, The Palace of the Governors: It's Role in Santa Fe History*. It stated that "the block of five rooms west of the Historical Society's quarters were occupied by Robert P. Ervin, Commissioner of Lands." (Nusbaum, 86)

Robert P. Ervin served as State Land Commissioner from 1907 to 1918. And though the Palace of the Governors was renovated from Breeden's period to the Ervin one, the general office location stayed the same. And apparently Breeden's old records were stored along with those of the State Land Office.

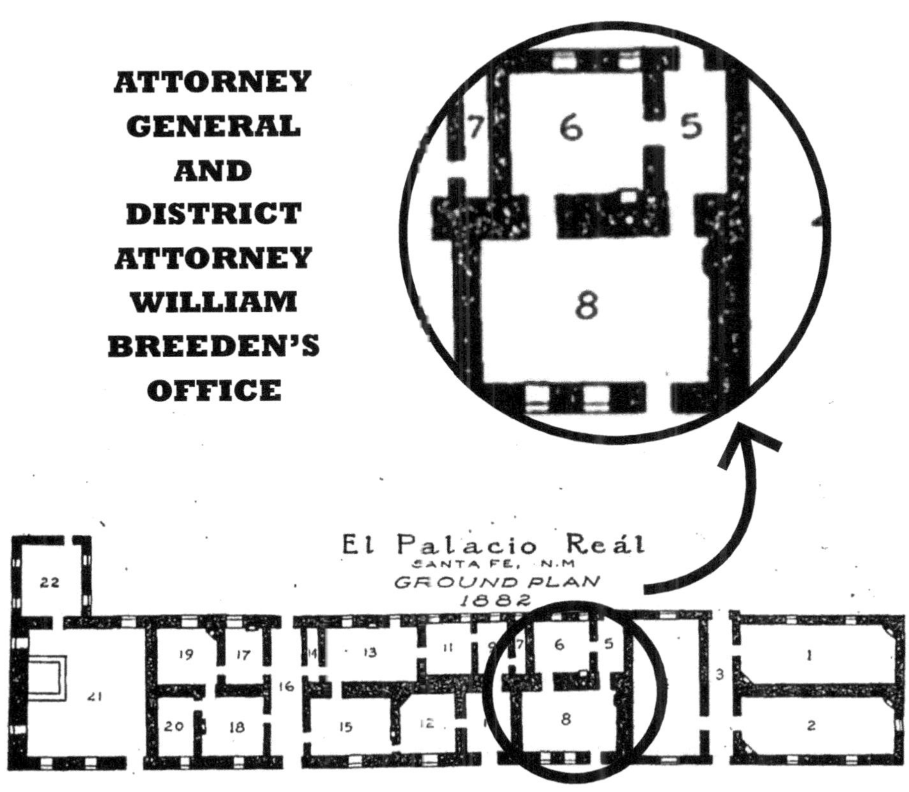

FIGURE: 2 Palace of the Governors in 1882, showing Attorney General William Breeden's office as rooms 5, 6, and 8. From Clinton P. Anderson's 1944 *New Mexico Historical Review*

The office's combined records joined the history of the Capitol Building's relocations. Harold Abbott had stated that in 1932 "he, with other employees, were going over some old records **in the basement of the state capitol**;" so those records presumably related to his Land Office job. But his finding of Breeden's "**San Miguel court records"** with them indicates that they had stayed together since their first Palace of the Governors storage.

But the Capitol Building in Harold Abbott's day was not the one after the Palace of the Governors. From 1850 to 1886 one was under construction, but ended up as the Territorial Courthouse.

In 1886, another building became the Capitol, replacing the Palace of the Governors, but burned down in six years, on May 12, 1892; though its archives were saved.

Then the Territorial Courthouse became the temporary Capitol Building until another was completed in 1900. That one was used for 66 years, until today's Capitol Building, "the Roundhouse," was dedicated in 1966. And the previous Capitol Building was renamed as the Bataan Memorial Building.

So by Harold Abbott's 1932 finding of the Coroner's Jury Report in the Capitol Building's basement (of the future Bataan Memorial Building), the old Palace of the Governors records might have been moved multiple times. Additionally, Frank M. King had reported in his 1935 book, *Wranglin' the Past*, that Garrett's July 15, 1881 letter to Ritch, with the Coroner's Jury Report copy, was found in old files of New Mexico's Secretary of State. And his offices were also in that Capitol Building, according to a 1932 article in the *Santa Fe New Mexican* titled "Call for Bids."

Demonstrated is that governmental personnel had done a good job in keeping San Miguel County legal records together. And the found Coroner's Jury Report proves their achievement!

GARRETT'S PROSECUTION IMMUNITY BY STATUTE OF LIMITATIONS FOR MURDER

Besides the Coroner's Jury Report absolving Pat Garrett of murder, there was a second hurdle for imposters and hoaxers claiming a "cold case" murder of the innocent victim existed against him: prosecution was blocked.

Even if Garrett had committed a murder, it was in 1881. And New Mexico Territory had a Statute of Limitations for murder prosecutions. The 1876 *Acts of the Legislative Assembly of the Territory of New Mexico* established a **10 year limitation on prosecution for murder** after the alleged crime. This appeared in the 1882's *The General Laws of New Mexico* Edited by L. Bradford Prince, under "Limitation of Criminal Actions, Acts of the Legislative Assembly of the Territory of New Mexico, Twenty-Second Session, Chapter 13. Section 1."

With the killing on July 14, 1881, the possibility of prosecution ended on July 14, 1891. That statute stayed in effect as (NMSA) 1953, 40A-1-8(3). It stated:

CHAPTER XIII.

AN ACT to provide the limitations of criminal actions.

CONTENTS

Sec. 1. Limitation; - murder, within ten years; 2d, manslaughter, six years; 3d, perjury and other felonies, three years; 4th, misdemeanors, two years; 5th, violation of revenue laws, three years

Sec. 2. Provides if defendant absconds or secretes himself the limitation shall not hold for that time.

Be it enacted by the Legislative Assembly of the Territory of New Mexico:

SECTION 1. No person shall hereafter be prosecuted, tried, or punished, in any court of this Territory; unless the indictment shall be found, or information filed therefore as hereinafter limited and provided.

First. For murder, within ten years from the time of the offence or act was committed.

Second. For manslaughter, or any other killing of a human being, except murder in the first degree, within six years from the time the offence was committed.

CHAPTER 3
THE WITNESSES AND THE DEATH SCENE

It took delusional disorders of Billy the Kid imposters, and sociopathic scorn of public intelligence by their hoaxing promoters, to claim that the most documented death in the Old West never happened. It was not only the Coroner's Jury Report that was an impassable hurdle. A huge number of people saw the corpse, besides the Report's witness, Peter Maxwell; and they documented their experience. In addition, the killing of Billy the Kid was a major media event, with national reporting.

PAT GARRETT WROTE A BOOK

The 1881 killing of Billy the Kid had viral fame, inspiring Pat Garrett to ally with his journalist boarder, Ashmun "Ash" Upson, to create his ghostwritten book, issued the following year: *The Authentic Life of Billy the Kid The Noted Desperado of the Southwest, Whose Deeds of Daring and Blood Made His Name a Terror in New Mexico, Arizona, and Northern Mexico.* Though it used that period's lurid dime novel style, and though the history of Billy Bonney had not yet been researched, so was fictionalized, both men knew Billy. Upson had been a border with his family in Silver City; and Garrett, having met him in 1878, when both spent time in Fort Sumner, certainly knew the specifics of his own tracking, capturing, jailing, and killing of him.

Garrett's lethality was undisputable, with his first killing of two of Billy's companions in his attempt to kill him. On December 19, 1880, he and his Texan posse ambushed Billy's group returning to Fort Sumner. Tom O'Folliard was fatally shot. In the morning of December 22, 1881, with Billy and his group attempting to escape the Territory and having spent the night in a rock line cabin at Stinking Springs, Charlie Bowdre emerged first wearing either Billy's hat, or one that looked like it, and was immediately killed by Garrett as mistaken for Billy. Only then did Garrett settle on capturing Billy for certain hanging trials.

As to his finally killing Billy, his book described his coming to Fort Sumner with his Deputies John William Poe and Thomas "Kip" McKinney; and, late that moonlit night of July 14, 1881, stationing them on the porch of the Maxwell family mansion, while he went inside to check with the town's owner, Peter Maxwell, in his dark bedroom. The book stated:

> I left Poe and McKinney at the end of the porch, and about twenty feet from the door of Pete's bedroom, while I myself entered it. I walked to the head of the bed and sat down near the pillow and beside Maxwell's head. I asked him as to the whereabouts of the Kid. He replied that the Kid had certainly been about, but he did not know whether he had left or not. At that moment, a man sprang quickly in the door, and looking back, called twice in Spanish, "Quien es? Quien es? (Who comes there?)" No one replied, and he came into the room. I could see he was bareheaded, and from his tred I could perceive he was either barefooted or in his stocking feet. He held a revolver in his right hand and a butcher knife in his left.
>
> He came directly towards me while I was sitting at the head of Maxwell's bed. Before he reached the bed, I whispered, "Who is it, Pete?" but received no reply for a moment. It struck me that it might be Pete's brother-in-law, Manuel Abreu, who had seen Poe and McKinney on the outside and wanted to know their business. The intruder came close to me, leaned both hands on the bed, his right almost touching my knee, and asked in a low tone "Who are they, Pete?" At the same instant Maxwell whispered to me, "That's him!"
>
> Simultaneously the Kid must have seen or felt the presence of a third person at the head of the bed. He raised quickly his pistol - a self-cocker - within a foot of my breast. Retreating rapidly across the room, he cried, "Quien es? Quien es? (Who is that? Who is that?)" All this happened more rapidly than it takes to tell it. As quick as possible I drew my revolver and fired, threw my body to one side, and fired again. The second shot was useless. The Kid fell dead at the first one. He never spoke.

A struggle or two, a little strangling sound as he gasped for breath, and the Kid was with his many victims. (Garrett, Pages 215-216)

Garrett's description matched Peter Maxwell's witness statement to the Coroner's Jury the next day: "I being in my bed in my room, at about midnight on the 14th day of July, Pat F. Garrett came into my room and sat down. William Bonney came in and got close to my bed with a gun in his hand and asked me "who is it" and then Pat F. Garrett fired two shots at the said William Bonney and the said William Bonney fell near my fire place and I went out of the room and when I came in again about three or four minutes after the shots the said William Bonney was dead."

DEPUTY POE WROTE A BOOK

John William Poe, a Kentucky-born and a past buffalo hunter, like Pat Garrett, was a Deputy U.S. Marshal and a Deputy Sheriff in Texas. In late 1880, he was hired by the Canadian River Cattlemen's Association to combat rustling centered in New Mexico, and had moved there to White Oaks. He was deputized by Garrett, who was then Lincoln County Sheriff and a Deputy U.S. Marshal, to hunt Billy Bonney following his April 28, 1881 jailbreak in Lincoln while awaiting hanging.

Poe was elected Lincoln County Sheriff the following year, serving until 1885; then did ranching and later moved to Roswell in the Territory, operating a store and founding both the Bank of Roswell and the Citizen's Bank of Roswell.

Poe's book, *The Death of Billy the Kid*, was first printed as a long article, *The Killing of Billy the Kid*, then as a booklet by an E.A. Brininstool in 1922 and 1923. It was published as a book by Houghton Mifflin in 1933. Though Poe had never met Billy until moments before the fateful encounter, he was the one who had urged Pat Garrett's recognizance of Fort Sumner because of Billy's rumored presence there. And his reporting of the shooting gives the multiple victim identifications that left Poe confident that Billy had been killed. His book stated:

It was probably not more than thirty seconds after Garrett had entered Maxwell's room, when my attention was attracted , from where I sat in the little gateway, to a man approaching me on the inside of and along the fence, some forty or fifty steps away. I observed that he was only partially dressed and was both bareheaded and barefooted, or rather, had only socks on his feet, and it seemed to me that he was fastening his trousers as he came toward me at a brisk walk.

As Maxwell's was the one place in Fort Sumner that I had considered above suspicion of harboring the Kid, I was entirely off my guard, the thought coming into my mind that the man approaching was either Maxwell or some guest of his ... He came on until he was almost within arm's-length of where I sat, before he saw me, as I was partially concealed from his view by the post of the gate.

Upon seeing me, he covered me with his six-shooter as quick as lightning, sprang onto the porch, calling out in Spanish, "Quien es" (Who is it?) – at the same time backing away from me toward the door through which only a few seconds before had passed, repeating his query, "Who is it?" in Spanish several times.

At this I stood up and advanced toward him, telling him not to be alarmed, that he should not be hurt; and still without the least suspicion that this was the very man we were looking for. As I moved toward him trying to reassure him, he backed up into the doorway of Maxwell's room, where he halted for a moment, his body concealed by the thick adobe wall at the side of the doorway, from whence he put out his head and asked in Spanish for the fourth or fifth time who I was. I was within a few feet of him when he disappeared into the room.

After this, and until after the shooting, I was unable to see what took place on account of the darkness of the room, but plainly heard what was said inside. An instant after the man left the door, I heard a voice inquire in a sharp tome, "Pete, who are those fellows on the outside?" An instant later a shot was fired in the room, followed immediately by what everyone within hearing distance thought were two other shots. However, there were only two shots fired, the third report, as we learned afterward, being caused by the rebound of the second bullet, which had struck the adobe wall and rebounded against the headboard of the wooden bedstead.

I heard a groan and one or two gasps from where I stood in the doorway, as of someone dying in the room. An instant later, Garrett came out ... He stood close by me to the wall at the side of the door ands said to me, "that was the Kid that came in there onto me, and I think I have got him." I said, "Pat, the Kid would not come to this place; you have shot the wrong man.

Upon my saying this, Garrett seemed to be in doubt himself as to whom he had shot, but quickly spoke up and said, "I am sure that was him, for I know his voice too well to be mistaken." This remark of Garrett's relieved me of considerable apprehension, as I had felt almost certain that someone whom we did not want had been killed.

A moment after Garrett came out of the door, Peter Maxwell rushed squarely onto me in frantic effort to get out of the room, and I certainly would have shot him but for Garrett's striking down my gun, saying, "Don't shoot Maxwell ..."

We afterwards discovered that the Kid had frequently been at his house after his escape from Lincoln, but Maxwell stood in such terror of him that he did not dare inform against him.

[Maxwell then got a candle from his mother's room and placed it on the window-sill from the outside.] This enabled us to get a view of the inside, where we saw a man lying stretched upon his back dead, in the middle of the room, with a six-shooter lying at his right hand and a butcher knife at his left. Upon examining the body, we found it to be that of Billy the Kid. Garrett's first shot had penetrated his breast just above the heart. (Poe, Pages 32-41)

Poe's description matched Pat Garrett's as well as the Coroner's Jury Report; which stated: "[The jury] found the body of William Bonney alias "Kid" with a shot in the left breast."

A.P. "PACO" ANAYA BURIED BILLY AND GOT A BOOK

A.P. "Paco" Anaya was a young Fort Sumner friend of Billy's. His 1991, posthumously printed memoir held the truth in his title: *I Buried Billy*. Anaya was one of the 200 Fort Sumner residents who held a candle-light vigil for Billy's body on the night of July 14-15, 1881, all having identified him. Real dead Billy ends the imposters' and "Billy the Kid Case" promulgators' hoaxes. Anaya wrote: "I, the writer, and my brother, Higinio Garcia, and several others of those that were there, dressed Billy with those clothes then we laid him on a high bed ... [A]nd on the next day we buried him." (Anaya, Page 132)

A TOWN IDENTIFIED THE BODY TOO

After his jailbreak on April 28, 1881, Billy had chosen Fort Sumner as a destination for two reasons: his secret young lover, Paulita Maxwell, was there; and he felt confident in the protection of the Maxwell family and Fort Sumner's over 200 residents, who had known him since early 1878, and would have been aware of his freedom fighter role. The response of the townspeople to this shocking killing in their midst, was described by John William Poe in his 1933 book, *The Death of Billy the Kid*. Once again, as an outsider, he was surprised. He quickly realized that this boy, who had been presented to him as a despicable outlaw-murderer, was beloved by the primarily Hispanic residents. Poe wrote:

> Within a short time after the shooting, quite a number of the native people gathered around, some of the bewailing the death of their friend, while several women pleaded for permission to take charge of the body, which we allowed them to do. They carried it across the yard to a carpenter shop, where it was laid out on a workbench, the women placing lighten candles around it according to their ideas of properly conducting a "wake" for the dead ...
>
> [The shooting] occurred at about midnight on the fourteenth of July, 1881. We spent the remainder of the night on the Maxwell premises, keeping constantly on our

guard, as we were expecting to be attacked by friends of the dead man. (Pages 41-42, 44)

So not only did the multiple townspeople identify Billy as the corpse in the night vigil, but they were infuriated enough to present a risk to his killers.

As an aside, the townspeople's response put in perspective the Coroner's Jury Report's statement: "[W]e are unanimous in the opinion that the gratitude of all the community is due to the said Garrett for his deed and is worthy of being rewarded." The Report was written by its President, Milnor Rudulph, the Postmaster of Sunnyside, seven miles north of Fort Sumner. Rudulph was a loyal Ringite who had helped Thomas Benton Catron and his Santa Fe Ring take over the Legislature in 1872 to block anti-Ring bills. Rudulph's actions contributed to the first of the Territorial, anti-Ring, freedom fights, which I named the 1872 Legislature Revolt. It took Ringite Governor Marsh Giddings's bringing the military into the Legislature's hall, to suppress the legislators, for the Ring to prevail, and for it to keep their biased judges in power to continue malicious prosecutions of their opponents. Bi-lingual, Rudulph wrote the Coroner's Jury Report in Spanish. The frightened juryman had no alternative but to sign his conclusion the day after Ring terrorism had invaded their once safe town.

DELUVINA MAXWELL WAS THERE TOO

A Navajo woman, purchased as a nine year old child slave by Lucien Bonaparte Maxwell, the owner of the two million acre Maxwell Land Grant and then Fort Sumner, was deeply attached to Billy Bonney. She laid wildflowers on his Fort Sumner grave for decades, until her own death.

Her own eye-witness confirmation of his being the corpse was given in a June 24, 1927 interview to historian, J. Evetts Haley, in Fort Sumner. She stated:

> I came here about [1869] and was here when Billy the Kid was killed. Billy the Kid was my compadre, my friend, poor Billy ... Pete Maxwell had told Billy he better go, as Pat Garrett was coming after him. Billy said he did not care, he was not afraid of Pat Garrett. The night he was killed Billy came in hungry, went down with a butcher

knife to get some meat at Pete Maxwell's ... After passing the men outside, he went into Maxwell's room where Garrett was and he shot him. The story is told that I was there and went in with a candle to see if Billy was dead. I did not do it. Pete took a candle and held it around in the window and Pat stood back in the dark where he could see in the room. When they saw he was dead, they both went in ...

Most of the native people (Mexicans) who lived in town went to his funeral ...

I did not see Billy the night after he was killed, **but I saw him the following morning.**

To be noted is that Deluvina's description matched that of John William Poe about Maxwell placing the candle, and the Hispanic residents' vigil to view the body.

THE PRESS WAS PROFUSE

There was also massive, front page, national press about the killing of Billy the Kid, with no reason to fabricate the event; and with Billy portrayed as a terrifying outlaw-murderer, whose death was a public relief. Already mentioned, has been the July 23, 1881's Las Cruces *Rio Grande Republican's* "Kid the Killer Killed, Wm. Bonney alias Antrim, alias Billy the Kid, Fatally Meets Pat Garrett, the Lincoln County Sheriff." which quoted from the Coroner's Jury Report itself.

Here are some Territorial examples:

On July 18, 1881, *The Las Vegas Daily Optic's* headline was: " 'The Kid' Killed! He Meets His Death at the Hands of Sheriff Pat Garrett, of Lincoln County." It gave identification of the body, as confirmed in the correctly cited Coroner's Jury Report: "An inquest was held on his body today [sic] and the verdict of the jury was 'justifiable homicide' and that Pat Garrett ought to receive the thanks of the whole community ... and that he is truly worthy of a handsome reward."

The July 21, 1881 *Santa Fe Daily New Mexican*, in "Garrett Exonerates Maxwell," confirmed Peter Maxwell as a witness to the shooting, and addressed rumors that he had hidden Billy the Kid in Fort Sumner before the killing. Garrett was quoted

"[H]e does not think that Maxwell was in with the Kid ... He says that Pete acknowledged that fear kept him from informing on the Kid."

The July 22, 1881 *Las Vegas Daily Gazette*, in "Words of Commendation and Encouragement," stated: "Immediately on the receipt of the news of the killing of Billy 'the Kid' by Sheriff Garrett, prominent citizens of Roswell and the lower Pecos wrote us giving particulars and expressing satisfaction. [One wrote] The words, 'God bless Pat Garrett for his good work' will escape many a lip, and people will never cease to love him for his great achievements."

Here are some national examples.

July 20, 1881's *The Chicago Daily Tribune* had "Account of the Manner in Which 'Billy the Kid' Was Killed, The Kid Killed;" stated: "[Garrett], who had taken advantage of the dim, uncertain light to get his weapon ready for use, brought it to bear on the Kid, shooting him through the heart at the first pull of the trigger. He died in two minutes without uttering a word. The [Las Vegas *Daily*] *Optic* to-night says of the affair: "Billy the Kid" was the terror not only of Lincoln County, but of the whole Territory; a young desperado who has long been noted as a bold thief, a cold-blooded murderer, having, perhaps, killed more men than any person of his age in the world ... All mankind rejoices ... It is now in order for Pat Garrett to be well rewarded for his services."

The Weekly Gazette (Colorado Springs Gazette) of July 23, 1881 had "Billy the Kid, At Last the Bullet Finds its Billet, New Mexico's Noted Outlaw Shot by a Sheriff." It stated: "The Gazette has positive information this morning from Fort Sumner of the death of 'Billy the Kid.' This noted desperado was killed at Fort Sumner on the Pecos river on the 14th by Pat Garrett, sheriff of Lincoln county."

One July 26, 1881, under "Champion Murderer," the *Fort Wayne Daily Gazette* stated: "The *Daily Optic* to-night give [sic] an interesting account of the killing of William Bonney, alias Billy the Kid, the noted desperado, at Fort Sumner on Thursday night."

That July 26, 1881 was also the *Savannah Morning News's* "Billy the Kid, A Youth With Nineteen Murders to His Account – The Inhabitants of New Mexico Overawed by a Boy of Twenty-One, Who Was Killed at Sight." It stated: "It is said that there was only one man in Lincoln county, Pat Garrett, who had the nerve to meet [Billy the Kid]. Pat was selected for this very purpose, and started on Billy's trail a few weeks ago, meeting with success ... as the telegraph informs us of Billy's death by his hands."

On August 10, 1881 *The New York Sun*, reprinted from the *St. Louis Globe-Democrat* "The Life of Billy the Kid. His Name Was Billy McCarthy, And He Was Born in New York."

That reprint was also in August 12, 1881's *The Lancaster Intelligencer* as "Billy the Kid, His Name Was Billy McCarthy and He was Born in New York, Murdering a Man at the Age of Sixteen – Made a Deputy Constable – Gen. Lew Wallace's Admiration for the Youthful Desperado, Under Sentence of Death – Killing Two Men in Thirty Seconds – The Kid Killed." It stated: "Billy the Kid was rapidly nearing the inevitable close of his blood-stained career ... Deputy Sheriff Pat Garrett with two companions started on his trail, swearing to capture or kill him or die trying ... Shortly before midnight Garrett went to Maxwell's, and had just seated himself in the dark on the side of Maxwell's bed when the door opened, and in walked the Kid ... [He] leveled his pistols, exclaiming: "Quien es? Quien es? But the delay of asking was fatal. Before the words were off his lips Pat Garrett's bullet was through his heart, and 'Billy the Kid,' the terror of New Mexico, lay a gasping, quivering corpse."

CHAPTER 4
MORE HISTORICAL RECORDS HURDLES

A MOUNTAIN OF RECORDS

Billy the Kid history fabricators picked an impossible period to hoax. It had a huge store of historical records generated by Billy and by the uprisings against the Santa Fe Ring. But for mid-20th century imposters, most were still undiscovered, and the scholarly history books were not yet written. That forced fabricating their life as Billy. Duped true-believers later ignored accumulating facts, and merely made conspiracy theories. And 21st century forensic fraudsters relied on public ignorance for their lying.

For validating truth, there existed Billy's extensive recorded words and writings, plus his contemporaries' autobiographical publications describing him in detail. An undisputed tintype of him at age 20 is famous. In addition, 1870's New Mexico Territory grass-roots uprisings against the Santa Fe Ring generated massive output of letters, petitions, exposés, newspaper articles court transcripts, a federal investigation with depositions and reports, a military court of inquiry, and Secret Service reports; all giving intimate details of Billy's world.

What did exist for imposters was history's junkyard: lurid dime novel-style publications cashing in on Billy the Kid mythology, and windbag oldsters spinning malarkey for self-aggrandizement, or trading hearsay and rumor for attention. Fortunately, for exposing the impersonators, their parroting of others' faking exposed their own. And even coaching of them by hoaxing authors from the few legitimate sources required their remembering a mind-boggling complexity and profusion of events. Their limited intelligence made that hard task unworkable.

Modern pretender promoters responded to this information hurdle by ignoring the historical record, or accusing historians of a conspiracy against them. In truth, these hoax promoters' relied on public ignorance of the facts which laid bare their fabrications.

ANTIQUATED SOURCES FOR HOAXING

It is important to take stock of sources available to the old-timer Billy the Kid malarkey spouters and imposters, to expose their scamming. John Miller seems to have read a few books. More flagrant was heavily coached "Brushy Bill" Roberts, with authors lying that he was illiterate and could not read-up on sources. Ergo, he must have been there as Billy the Kid!

AVAILABLE TO IMPOSTERS

Billy the Kid imposters in the second quarter of the 20th century knew about mythologized falsified fame of an outlaw boy named Billy the Kid, who murdered a man for each of his twenty-one years, and was killed by a Sheriff named Pat Garrett.

For more life details, there were just a few quasi-historical books. There was a 1927 reprint of Pat Garrett's 1882, ghost-written, dime novel-style *The Authentic Life of Billy the Kid The Noted Desperado of the Southwest, Whose Deeds of Daring and Blood Made His Name a Terror in New Mexico, Arizona, and Northern Mexico.* Adding minimally more was Walter Noble Burns's 1926 book, *The Saga of Billy the Kid,* based on Garrett's 1882 version. Robert N. Mullin and Maurice Garland Fulton were early researcher/writers, but no salvation for pretenders, who were left just with some historical names and a few big events.

To manufacture Billy himself, there were his pardon bargain letters with Governor Lew Wallace in the Lew Wallace Collection of the Indiana Historical Society at Indianapolis, with two more in personal possession of Wallace's grandson, Lew Wallace Jr. And known was his April 15, 1881 letter to Attorney Edgar Caypless, which existed only as a copy in New Mexico's Lincoln Museum.

And there were apparently available some pages of the 1879 Fort Stanton military Court of Inquiry for Commander N.A.M. Dudley, but lacking Billy Bonney's full testimony.

And because the historic town of Lincoln - site of the Lincoln County War Battle - has remained largely intact, it could be visited to fabricate past participation in events there. But lost for that trickery was the entire town of Fort Sumner, including the Maxwell family mansion in which Billy was killed, with only a few foundations of outlying buildings remaining. And the diagrams of the old fort seem to have been unavailable to the early hoaxers.

LATER SCHOLARLY HISTORY BOOKS

The imposters were dead by the renaissance in Billy the Kid scholarship in the second half of the 20th century. In 1957, William Keleher's *Violence in Lincoln County 1869-1881* published both the original and translated Coroner's Jury Report. The unsurpassed scholarly researcher of the period, Frederick Nolan, published his *The Life and Death of John Henry Tunstall* in 1965; *The Lincoln County War: A Documentary History* in 1992; and *The West of Billy the Kid* in 1998. Billy's early adolescence in Silver City, New Mexico Territory, and Bonita, Arizona Territory, were unavailable until 1993 with Jerry Weddle's book, *Antrim is My Stepfather's Name: The Boyhood of Billy the Kid.* Other modern historians were Joel Jacobsen in 1994 with *Such Men as Billy the Kid. The Lincoln County War Reconsidered*; Philip Rasch with his 1995 compendium, *Trailing Billy the Kid*; and Robert Utley, with his 1989 *Billy the Kid: A Short and Violent Life.*

My own 21st century books, using major historical collections and new interpretations, added understanding of the role of the Santa Fe Ring from its 1866 origin, to its bloody Territorial take-overs of the 1870's, and its continuation to the present. There are 2012's *Billy the Kid's Writings, Words, and Wit;* 2017's *The Lost Pardon of Billy the Kid: An Analysis Factoring in The Santa Fe Ring, Governor Lew Wallace's Dilemma, and a Territory in Rebellion*; and 2018's *The Santa Fe Ring: The Making of an American Monster.* And, in multiple books, I have made it my mission to expose the profiteering hoaxes, from early 20th century origins to the present, that ride on Billy the Kid's coattails.

There also exists the marriage record of Billy's mother and step-father by Reverend David F. McFarland, in his Santa Fe, First Presbyterian Church's entry of March 1, 1873 listed in the "*Ledger: Session Records 1867-1874. Marriages in Santa Fe New Mexico. Mr. William H. Antrim and Mrs. Catherine McCarty.*" Unpublished, it was unknown to the pretenders; so they had no clue about Billy's mother's name or brother, Josie, listed in it.

Pat Garrett himself got a major biographer, Leon Metz; whose *Pat Garrett: The Story of a Western Lawman* came out in 1974, and countered the defamation intrinsic in the pretender hoaxes based on Billy the Kid's not being killed by him on July 14, 1881.

And some of these later sources would reveal subsequent fakery, since the next generation of hoaxing authors surreptitiously used their new facts to fix-up the old scammers.

KEY FIGURES AND OFFICIAL DOCUMENTS

Furthering imposter discrediting, were key figures in Billy's life, along with a multitude of depositions, court transcripts, and daily notes - all exposing their hoaxing by their ignorance of them.

INVESTIGATOR FRANK WARNER ANGEL

The Frank Warner Angel depositions and reports on the murder of John Tunstall, the Lincoln County troubles, and corruption of public officials were discovered in 1956 by historian, Frederick Nolan. Attorney Angel, an energetic and observant chronicler, was sent in May of 1878 by President Rutherford B. Hayes, and via the Departments of Justice and the Interior, to investigate the February 18, 1878 murder of John Henry Tunstall, as well as Territorial corruption. He produced a prodigious amount of first-hand documentation, including Billy Bonney's own June 8, 1878 deposition.

So, left for posterity, were Angel's 39 depositions and reports: October 4, 1878's *In the Matter of the Examination of the Causes and Circumstances of the Death of John H. Tunstall a British Subject*; October 4, 1878's *In the Matter of the Lincoln County Troubles*; October 3, 1878's *In the Matter of the Investigation of the Charges Against S.B. Axtell Governor of New Mexico*; and October 2, 1878's *Examination of Charges against F. C. Godfroy, Indian Agent, Mescalero, N. M.*

Aware of the Santa Fe Ring, but obstructed in its exposure by the corrupt administration of President Rutherford B. Hayes, frustrated Angel provided incoming Territorial Governor Lew Wallace with a secret notebook listing people's Ring affiliations; some of which Billy himself would have known.

As to real Billy Bonney, like all victims of the Santa Fe Ring, he would have been fully aware of Angel as a ray of hope. And he knowingly risked his life to give his deposition to Angel to get justice for his assassinated and admired employer John Tunstall. And real Billy would have seen the eventual injustice that the Ring was left untouched; except for scapegoating removal of one lower-tier member: Governor Samuel Beach Axtell.

The imposters, of course, lacked any notion of the specifics of Ring atrocities, or of Billy's articulate deposition about them.

ATTORNEY IRA E. LEONARD

Billy's best friend in a high place was Attorney Ira E. Leonard, widow Susan McSween's attorney against past Commander N.A.M. Dudley for murdering her husband and arson of her home in the Lincoln County War Battle. Leonard, bravely took her case against Dudley right after the Ring murdered her first lawyer: Leonard's office-mate: Attorney Huston Chapman.

Leonard met Billy in March of 1879 when Billy was in his sham arrest in Lincoln for his Lew Wallace pardon bargain; and Leonard witnessed Billy's fulfilling that bargain by testifying in the April, 1879 Grand Jury against Attorney Huston Chapman's murderers. Reporting on Billy's behalf to Wallace in a letter of April 20, 1879, Leonard stated: "*I will tell you Gov. that the prosecuting officer of this Dist. [William Rynerson] is no friend to the enforcement of the law.* ***He is bent on going for the Kid & ... is proposed to destroy his testimony & influence.*** *He is bent on pushing him to the wall. He is a Dolan [Ring] man and is defending him by his conduct all he can.*"

Leonard also aided the prosecution at Dudley's Fort Stanton Court of Inquiry, and would have heard Billy risking his life while testifying devastatingly against that past Commander; and consequently became his loyal attorney into 1881.

During Leonard's 1879 litigation against Commander N.A.M. Dudley, he sustained a near assassination by the Ring. Billy, nearby in his Patrón house sham arrest for his pardon bargain, would have known about that April 25, 1879 attempt.

Leonard also continued to assist Billy's pardon hope, even facilitating a possible one from the Secret Service. He then represented him in his 1881 Mesilla hanging trial, getting Billy's federal indictment for the "Buckshot" Roberts killing quashed; but quitting after a likely Ring death threat; leaving Billy with Ring-biased court-appointed attorneys.

But this central advocate in Billy's life was unknown to the pretenders, except for token name-dropping.

COMMANDER NATHAN AUGUSTUS MONROE DUDLEY AND SUSAN McSWEEN

Comparable in magnitude to the Angel reports, is the Court of Inquiry for possible court martial for Fort Stanton's Commander N.A.M. Dudley. It has over a hundred testimonies of people involved in the Lincoln County War, including Billy's own, given on May 28th and 29th of 1879. Others speaking through time include the plaintiff herself, Alexander McSween's widow, Susan McSween, whose pivotal and courageous role in the post-war Lincoln County struggle was unknown to the pretenders. She would have seemed a heroine to Billy; and his testimony in the Dudley Court of Inquiry was on her behalf.

Billy's testimony, on his own anti-Ring initiative, in an honest court, would have achieved Dudley's court martial: Billy saw three of his white soldiers, likely officers, under order to shoot at least one volley at civilians, including Billy, escaping the burning McSween house. The imposters, of course, knew nothing of this.

SECRET SERVICE OPERATIVE AZARIAH WILD

Sent to New Mexico Territory from September to December of 1880 by the Secret Service, a Treasury Department branch, ostensibly to track counterfeiters, but, in fact, to eliminate anti-Ring Billy Bonney and remaining Regulators, New Orleans based Operative Azariah F. Wild, was one of 40 in the country. He wrote daily reports; thus, recording information about Billy Bonney in a format like the following; giving the date for the events documented, then the date on which he wrote the report:

U.S. Treasury Department
SECRET-SERVICE DIVISION

New Orleans **District**

James J. Brooks,
Chief U.S. Secret Service

Sir: I have the honor to submit the following, my report as *Chief* **Operative of this District for** *Monday* **the** *29th* **day of** *December,* **18** *79,* **written at** *New Orleans, Louisiana,* **and completed at** *9* **o'clock** *A* **M on the** *30th* **day of** *December,* **18** *79*

Wild was duped by Ringmen into believing that Billy Bonney headed a counterfeiting and rustling gang. So Wild helped Pat Garrett become both Sheriff of Lincoln County and a Deputy U.S. Marshal to track down Billy. But Billy's attorney, Ira Leonard, proposed to Wild that Billy would testify against the actual counterfeiters in exchange for a pardon. Billy even wrote a confirmation to Wild. On October 8, 1880, Wild described the offer:

> *I left Fort Stanton at 7 o'clock A.M. on the stage and reached Lincoln the County seat at 8:30 A.M. ... The object of my visit to Lincoln was to see Judge Ira Leonard ... In my report of October 5th ... I spoke of an outlaw whose name was Antrom alias Billy Bonney. During the Lincoln Co. War he killed men on the Indian Reservation for which he has been indicted in the territorial and the United States Court. Gov. Wallace has issued a proclamation granting immunity to those not indicted but as Antrom has been indicted the proclamation did not cover his (Antrom's) case and he (Antrom) has been in the mountains as an outlaw ever since a space of about two years time.*
>
> *Governor Wallace has since written Antrom's attorney on the subject saying he should be let go but has failed to put it on shape that satisfied Judge Leonard Antrom's attorney.*
>
> *It is believed and in fact is almost known that he (Antrom) is one of the leading members of this gang.*
>
> ***Antrom has recently written a letter to Judge Leonard which has been shown to me in confidence that leads me to believe that we can use Antrom in these cases provided Gov. Wallace will make good his written promises and the U.S. Attorney will allow the case pending in the U.S. Court to slumber and give him (Antrom) one more chance to reform.***
>
> *I have promised nothing and will not except to receive and propositions he Leonard and his client see fit to make and submit them to U.S. Attorney Barnes.*
>
> *Judge Leonard has written Antrom to meet him (Leonard) at once for consultation.*
>
> *The chances are that the conversation will take place within the next week I will report fully to you and submit whatever propositions they see fit to make to US. Attorney Barnes for such action as he deems proper to take.*

Ringites' interventions, however, made Wild decide to arrest Billy at the pardon meeting. Canny Billy, however, robbed the mail coach carrying Wild's reports, discovered Wild's fatal plan, and avoided the meeting. But he lost his second pardon chance.

The imposters were unaware of the Secret Service, of Azariah Wild, and of how close Billy actually came to getting his pardon. Obviously, Billy himself knew all that.

THE FRITZ INSURANCE POLICY CASE

The imposters were unaware of the Santa Fe Ring's malicious prosecution of Attorney Alexander McSween for embezzling - with fraudulent entanglement of John Tunstall by wrongly claiming a business partnership - in the case of life insurance recovery for Emil Fritz, the deceased original partner in Lincoln's mercantile monopoly called "The House." Billy was certainly aware, having almost shot corrupt Sheriff William Brady's deputies doing the property attachments for the case at Tunstall's store, and then being eye-witness to Brady's posseman murdering Tunstall with excuse of those attachments. All that was the subject of Billy's June 8, 1878 deposition to Frank Warner Angel, and was the precipitant to the Lincoln County War uprising against the Ring - unknown to the impersonators, and fully known to Billy Bonney who became the people's hero in the ensuing lost freedom fight.

SHERIFF WILLIAM BRADY

Lincoln County Sheriff William Brady was the Ring enforcer for the Fritz insurance policy case's fake embezzlement charge. Its documents still exist: the Action of Assumpsit to permit seizure of McSween's possessions, the Writ of Attachment (which falsely claimed a McSween-Tunstall partnership, making Tunstall's possessions seizeable also), and the inventory of items which Sheriff Brady attached. Billy, and the other Regulators, would have been aware of these machinations - and outraged.

As important, the case was part of a larger Ring scheme to kill Tunstall and McSween. Brady was such a danger to McSween, that Deputy Adolph Barrier - from McSween's arrest site in Las Vegas for the embezzling case - kept him in personal custody to protect him. After Barrier departed, and McSween was about to return to Lincoln for his Grand Jury trial, the Regulators - including Billy - knew Brady and his deputies would assassinate him that return day of April 1, 1878; since Brady had murdered Tunstall just 42 days earlier. So they ambushed Brady and his deputies. Brady and Deputy George Hindman died. (The killings of Brady and Hindman - as well as the Regulator killing of Tunstall murder posseman, Andrew "Buckshot" Roberts - constituted Billy's indictments for which he made the pardon bargain, then stood trial in 1881.) It was for the Brady killing that Billy got his hanging sentence in Mesilla on April 9, 1881.

The pretenders had no knowledge of Brady's role in the Lincoln County War, or the reason for Brady's ambush killing, or the Regulators existence, or Billy's reasonable mitigating defense that the ambush was done to save Alexander McSween's life.

A.P. "PACO" ANAYA

Young A.P. "Paco" Anaya was a Fort Sumner friend of Billy's. His 1991, posthumously printed memoir held the truth in his title: *I Buried Billy*. Anaya was one of the 200 Fort Sumner residents in a candle-light vigil for Billy's body on the night of July 14-15, 1881, all having identified him.

Real dead Billy, as confirmed by Anaya, ends the imposters' and "Billy the Kid Case" promulgators' hoaxes.

PAULITA MAXWELL

Unknown to the imposters was the romance of Billy and Paulita Maxwell, Billy's secret sweetheart in Fort Sumner. She was the daughter of deceased Lucien Bonaparte Maxwell, past owner of the 2 million acre Maxwell Land Grant and founder of Fort Sumner.

She was the motivation for his post-jailbreak return to Fort Sumner - and almost certain death - rather than escaping to Old Mexico. And he was killed in the Maxwell mansion by Pat Garrett's ambush in her brother's bedroom.

Their love story was confirmed in an unpublished letter by historian, Walter Noble Burns. On June 3, 1926, he wrote to Jim East, one of Pat Garrett's Stinking Springs possemen:

> *I also know that the Kid and Paulita were sweethearts - at least I heard that story on most good authority many times. But I was unable to write it frankly because my publishers were afraid any such statement might lay them open to a libel suit.*

THE SANTA FE RING

Pivotal to New Mexico Territory's 1870's history were the freedom fights against the rapaciously expanding Santa Fe Ring. Its Territorial "boss" was Thomas Benton Catron; his Washington, D.C. "co-boss" was Stephen Benton Elkins. Tunstall and McSween, aware of the Ring, would have informed Billy and Tunstall's other employees.

On April 27, 1877, writing to his family, Tunstall stated: "***Everything in New Mexico, that pays at all (you may say) is worked by a "ring."*** (Nolan, *Life and Death*, of *John Henry Tunstall*, Page. 213)

Alexander McSween's February 23, 1878 letter to just-murdered Tunstall's father, John Partridge; stated: "**[Tunstall] understood well from the U.S. Attorney [Catron] to the lowest magistrate that there was a combination and determination to keep down independence. This combination is known as the "Santa Fe Ring." To the branch of the Ring down here he had become particularly obnoxious owing to the fact that he was acquiring so much land, and because I aided him.**" (Nolan, *Documentary History of the Lincoln County War*, Pages 206-207)

The day before the start of the Lincoln County War Battle, and five days after outlaw John Kinney was used by Ringite Lincoln County Sheriff George Peppin for the massacre of McSween-side Hispanic residents of San Patricio, Billy wrote his July 13, 1878 "Regulator Manifesto" to Catron's brother-in-law, Edgar Walz, managing his Lincoln County Carrizozo cattle ranch, It stated: "*We are all aware that your brother-in-law,* ***T.B. Catron sustains the Murphy-Kinney party*** *... Steal from the poorest or richest American or Mexican, and the* ***full measure of the injury you do, shall be visited upon the property of Mr. Catron***."

On November 14, 1878, soon after arriving in the Territory as Governor, Lew Wallace wrote to his friend Absalom Markland: "***I came here, and found a "Ring" with a hand on the throat of the Territory. I refused to join them, and now they are proposing to fight me in the Senate. Ex Delegate Elkins is head-center in Washington.***

Billy's attorney, Ira Leonard, knowledgeable about the Ring, wrote to Lew Wallace on May 20, 1879 about "The House's" partners, Lawrence Murphy and James Dolan: "***They were a***

part and parcel of the Santa Fe Ring that has been so long an incubus on the government of this Territory."

Norman Cleaveland was a descendant of a Ring-fighting family in the Colfax County War. In his 1971 book, *The Morleys: Young Upstarts of the Southwest,* he wrote: "When my grandparents, William Raymond Morley and Ada McPherson Morley, pioneer New Mexicans, were in their twenties they were confronted with **an "establishment" known as the Santa Fe Ring.** By comparison, present-day establishments would rate rather as societies of butterfly collectors. (Cleaveland, p. viii)

The Santa Fe Ring is also in D.W. Meinig's 1998 *The Shaping of America: A Geographical Perspective on 500 Years of History, Volume 3: Transcontinental America 1850 - 1915.* Meinig wrote:

> In the 1870's anticipation of railroad connections to the East began to alter the prospects [in New Mexico] for profits and position. Slowly forming over the years, the "Santa Fe Ring" now emerged into full notoriety: "it was essentially a set of lawyers, politicians, and businessmen who united to run the territory and to make money of this particular region. Although located on the frontier, the ring reflected the corporative, monopolistic, and multiple enterprise tendencies of all American business after the Civil War. Its uniqueness lay in the fact that, rather than dealing with some manufactured item, they regarded land as their first medium of currency." "Land" meant litigation, and "down the trail from the states came ... an amazing number of lawyers" who, "still stumbling over their Spanish, would build their own political and economic empire out of the tangled heritage of land grants." And so, somewhat belatedly, a general repetition of the California situation got under way, and with the same general results: "eventually over 80 per cent of the Spanish grants went to American lawyers and settlers." Important differences were the presence in New Mexico of a much greater number of Hispanic peasants and communities well rooted on the land, the considerable resistance and violence generated by this American assault, and the sullen resentment created in an

increasingly constricted and impoverished people who felt they had been cheated out of much of their lands. In contrast to common representations it was not a case of vigorous, expanding society moving upon "a static culture," for "the Hispanos were still settling and conquering New Mexico, ever-extending their control" when the Anglos arrived. Here even more starkly than in California the conflict arose not just out of simple imperial position and crass chicanery but out of the clash of two fundamentally different sets of values, perceptions, and motivations. For ordinary Hispanos land was simply basic to a comfortable existence: "enough land to farm, enough pasture for stock, enough game to hunt, enough wood to burn, and enough material to build," all "to help one live as one ought to live" - including the continuity of such life generation after generation. Although operating to a great extent on tradition and custom, this was not the simple, "primitive" society most Anglos took it to be; it had its own laws relating to land and water, its own complexities of status, politics, and factions. To the Anglos land was a commodity to buy and sell, to exploit as quickly as possible, a means of profit and propellant of one's personal progress. Furthermore, "American land policy featured precise measurement and documentation, assumed individual ownership, and came out of a tradition that expected western land to be open for settlement." And it came out of eastern lands - out of the humid woodlands of Europe and America - and its assumptions about settlement and family farms, its rigid uniform rectangular survey system, its laws relating to water, cultivation, and seasonal use were incongruous with the needs and practices of Hispano farming and stock raising in the arid southwest. The most vulnerable parts of the Hispano system were the common lands, essential to the grazing economy, but often used without title, or held by a patrón who ultimately sold or lost his title, or by a community grant that was readily challenged under American law and likely to be declared by the courts to be public land subject to routine survey and sale. This process of Anglo encroachment went through several phases over several decades but reached an important victory in an early court approval of the Maxwell Grant, an infamous case wherein the original 97,000 acres was inflated to nearly 2 million covering a huge county-sized area of prime piedmont lands. Well before the owner had certain title to this baronial tract he sold it to London speculators, and once the country that had "seemed worthless to Kearny's soldiers" became "an item in the stock exchange and a topic of interest in a dozen investment houses in Europe," the invasion of New Mexico had taken on a new momentum.

SANTA FE RING SOURCE FOR BILLY THE KID IMPOSTERS

Unaware of the Ring's history, the imposters missed real Billy's world - with his anti-Ring cause and the Ring's outlaw myth campaign to kill him as "Billy the Kid." But for name-dropping, they, or their authors, seem to have used the 1927 edition of Pat Garrett's *The Authentic Life of Billy the Kid.*

In his original 1882 first edition, cautious Garrett did not name the dangerous Ring; but he stated: "It is not the intention here to discuss the merits of the imbroglio or to censure or uphold either one faction or the other, but merely to detail such events of the [Lincoln County] war as ... [Billy the Kid] took part in. The principles in this difficulty were on one side John S. Chisum, called the Cattle King of New Mexico, with Alexander A. McSween and John H. Tunstall as important allies. On the other side were the firm of Murphy & Dolan, merchants in Lincoln, the county seat, backed by nearly every small cattle owner in the Pecos Valley. **This latter faction was supported by Thomas B. Catron, United States Attorney for the Territory, a resident of Santa Fe, one of the eminent lawyers of the Territory, and a considerable owner in the Pecos region."** (Garrett, Page 52)

For the 1927 reprint of Garrett's book, annotating historian, Maurice Garland Fulton, added the Ring; writing: "Garrett is one of the few writers of the Lincoln County War who has had the frankness and courage to mention Catron's name in connection with it. [Catron] is the figure that looms up behind the Murphy and Dolan faction. As the president of the powerful First National Bank at Santa Fe, he furnished the money needed by Murphy and Dolan in their business, of course taking mortgages which at the close of the War gave him possession of their store and its stock of goods. Catron was also a cattle raiser, and in some sense a dominating figure in that industry in the western part of the county. **Besides all this he was a powerful member of the clique of politicians and business men called in those days the "Santa Fe Ring," which largely controlled the Territory of New Mexico**." (*The Authentic Life of Billy the Kid*, Fulton Note, Page 59)

THE BILLY BONNEY TINTYPE

Billy appears in the flesh, at about age 20, in a full-length tintype photograph, thought to have been taken in Fort Sumner; forcing any imposter to match-up physically, and yielding failure by mismatch.

Ignorance that tintypes were right-to-left reversed, left mimicking impersonators claiming *left-handedness*, since Billy's *right hand* his cocked over his Colt 44's butt. Imposters also seized naively on details: like Billy's right ear happening to be pushed down by his jaunty rightward tilt of his hat brim, by claiming deformities in their *left* (tintype-reversed) ear! Small hands were claimed by impersonators to go along with the fable that Billy escaped the Lincoln courthouse-jail by slipping off his handcuffs, when his actual hand, cocked beside his gun butt, looks muscular and normal-sized.

Most repugnant, however, were "experts"-for-hire who matched aged imposters, John Miller and "Brushy Bill" Roberts, to that tintype to fake Billy the Kid identity matchings for each of these men, who bore no resemblance to Billy.

And in 1989, a photo-analysis study done by the Lincoln County Heritage Trust, under famed anthropologist Clyde Snow, found no match of John Miller or of "Brushy Bill" to Billy Bonney's tintype.

PUBLIC IGNORANCE AS SALVATION

The old imposters, their scamming authors, and modern-day "Billy the Kid Case" and "Cold Case Billy the Kid" hoaxers got a hearing only because of public ignorance of Billy the Kid's complex history. That enabled those fraudsters to spin Billy the Kid tales based on the Santa Fe Ring's original outlaw mythology of Billy the Kid, which had proliferated as mainstream books and movies.

Unknown, to this day, is that the Lincoln County War was a freedom fight of poor Anglo homestead farmers and disenfranchised Hispanic people against the land grabbing Santa Fe Ring seeking cattle ranching and mercantile monopolies. Unknown, to this day, is Billy Bonney's bi-cultural and bi-lingual role in bridging those two victimized sub-cultures, and bringing in Mexican fighters from nearby towns of San Patricio and Picacho into that War's final battle. Unknown, to this day, was Billy's future risk to the Ring as a potential leader of another uprising (along with equally zealous Hispanics, like his best friend, Yginio Salazar). Unknown too was Billy's more immediate risk to the Ring by testifying against its terrorist assassins - unless he was eliminated first. Certainly unknown, except by an occasional dropped name, were almost all the other historical participants in that unsung period when New Mexicans were willing to risk their lives to fight for their democratic rights.

So Billy the Kid's massive fame and popularity, plus massive ignorance about him, added up to an ideally non-critical but receptive audience for old imposters and modern hoaxers. But the antique oblivion and meaningless misinformation relied on by all those clowns, is destined for failure and deserved ridicule, as the magnificent history of Billy Bonney and his compatriots becomes more commonly known. And juxtaposing the hoaxed claims of the imposters with known history ends their frauds.

And paralleling the exposure of Billy the Kid fakery, is righting the wrong done to famous lawman, Pat Garrett by the fraudsters, whose impersonations depended on claiming their own survival by fabricating that, by incompetent accident or by intent, he murdered an innocent victim enabling Billy the Kid's escape to long life, and kept it secret for personal profit.

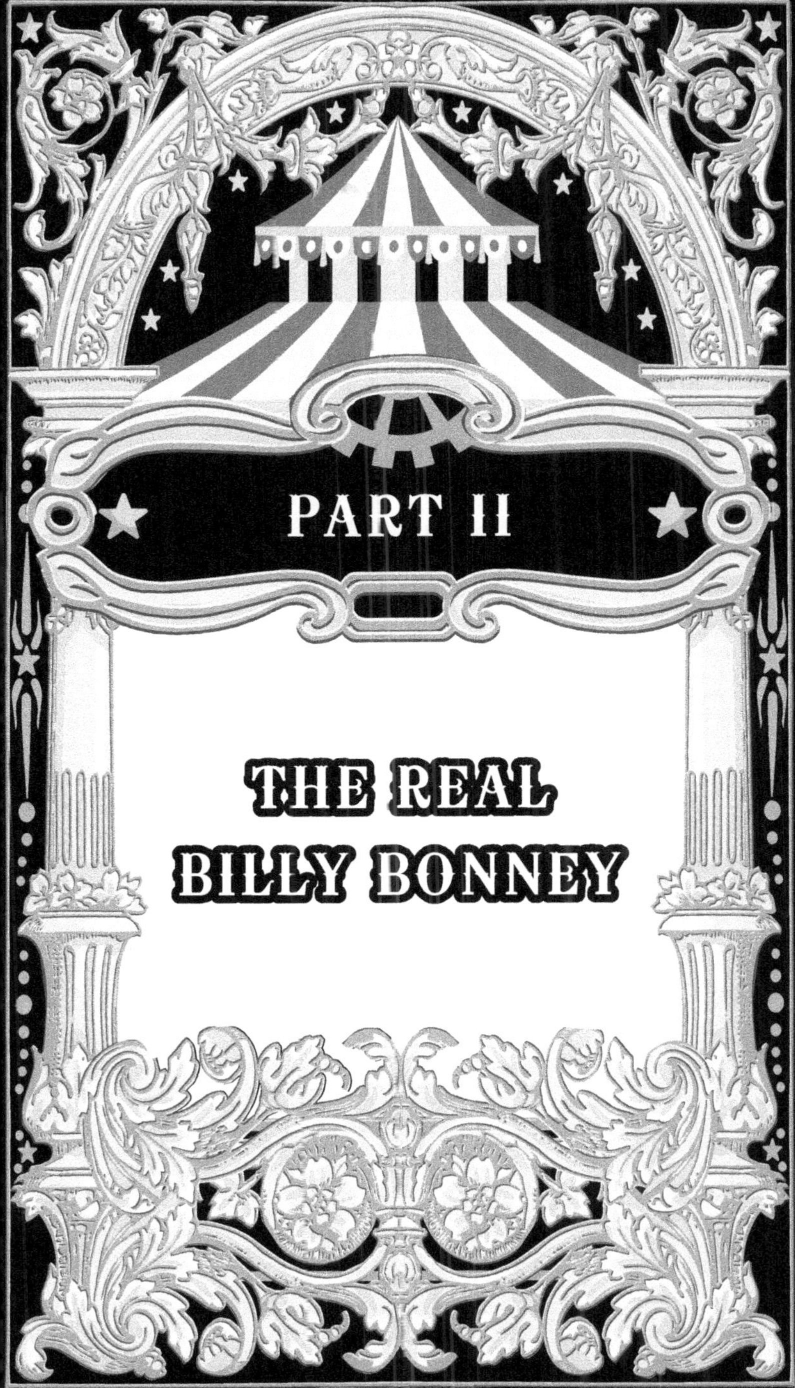

PART II

THE REAL BILLY BONNEY

CHAPTER 1
HISTORY OF BILLY BONNEY

THE REAL HISTORY

Central to debunking the misinformation in the Billy the Kid imposter hoaxes, is Billy Bonney's history. It is a complex, colorful, traumatic life of a brilliant, charismatic, teenaged, literate, bi-cultural resistance fighter against the Santa Fe Ring; fit amazingly into just 21 years. Most of it was unknown to his old-timer impersonators. All of it was a problem to the modern "Billy the Kid Case" and Cold Case Billy the Kid" hoaxers.

* * * * * * * * * * * * *

In a hot, full-mooned, New Mexico Territory night as bright as day, the 21 year old, homeless youth, Billy Bonney, with trusting stockinged feet, approached the porticoed, two story, Fort Sumner mansion of the Maxwell family, at about a quarter to mid-night.

That day, July 14, 1881, was the third anniversary of the Lincoln County War's start, which had left him branded as the outlaw, "Billy the Kid;" though, to himself, he was a freedom fighter: the last Regulator and that War's only participant to be convicted and sentenced to hanging.

That July night, he intended to cut a dinner steak from the side of beef hanging, at the patrón's generosity, on the mansion's north porch. But first he would check in, as requested, with that patrón and town owner, Peter Maxwell, at his south porch's corner bedroom.

Asleep in that mansion was Billy's secret lover, Maxwell's sister, Paulita, seventeen, and just pregnant with Billy's child. Also there, lived a never-emancipated Navajo slave, Deluvina; purchased, as a child, by Peter's and Paulita's fabulously wealthy, deceased father, Lucien Bonaparte Maxwell. Then, the family lived in Cimarron, a New Mexico Territory town in Colfax County, which Lucien had created on his and his wife's almost two million acre land grant; later named after himself.

That was before Lucien was cheated in the sale of that Maxwell Land Grant by unscrupulous lawyers, Thomas Benton Catron and Stephen Benton Elkins, who used their profits to propel their Santa Fe Ring. As Billy knew, that corrupt collusion of public officials still held New Mexico Territory in a stranglehold. As a hero in the failed Lincoln County War of 1878, Billy had fought that Ring. If Billy was thinking about his mortal danger, he knew its source was the Ring. If he thought about injustice, its focus would have been his promised pardon withheld by departed Territorial Governor Lew Wallace.

That July of 1881 day was 2½ months since Billy's jailbreak escape from his scheduled hanging on May 13th. He knew that Lincoln County Sheriff Pat Garrett would be in pursuit. Garrett had captured him on December 22, 1880 at Stinking Springs for his hanging trial. And in Billy's April 28, 1881 escape from Garrett's Lincoln jail, he had shot dead his deputy guards: James Bell and Robert Olinger. Garrett would kill him on sight.

When first tracking Billy in late 1880, Garrett had killed Billy's friends, Tom O'Folliard and Charlie Bowdre - missing Billy only by accident in two consecutive ambushes: at Fort Sumner and Stinking Springs. In fact, at the Stinking Springs capture of Billy and his companions, Garrett killed Bowdre by mistaking him for Billy: the prize for which the Ring had made Garrett a Sheriff.

To be near Paulita, Billy had recklessly chosen return to Fort Sumner, instead of fleeing to Old Mexico, the natural choice given his bi-culturalism. But he relied on the Maxwell family's protection, as well affection of the townspeople he had known since late 1877. It would take betrayal to bring his death.

Billy's life had been traumatic. Illegitimate, he was a second son, born on November 23, 1859, in New York City, as William Henry McCarty. Raised in Indiana with his brother, Josie, by his mother, Catherine, he became "Henry Antrim" after she married an Indiana man, William Henry Harrison Antrim, in 1873, after they relocated to New Mexico Territory. Antrim became a miner; and the family lived in Silver City. He was a rejecting father, evicting Billy at 14½ to homelessness when Catherine died of tuberculosis in 1874. But Billy's longing for a father remained, and he sometimes used the name "Antrim" for himself.

In Silver City's school, he learned Spencerian script. He also became fluent in Spanish; and, atypically, was equally comfortable in Anglo and Hispanic sub-cultures in those racist times. By 1975, 15½ year old Billy spent his last year in Silver City doing petty thievery, and butcher shop and hotel work; while altercations with local boys revealed his violent temperament.

By September, Silver City Sheriff, Harvey Whitehill arrested him for burglary, and laundry and revolver robbery; his adult accomplice having escaped. Facing ten years hard labor - the statutes making no provision for juveniles - he achieved his first dramatic escape: through the jail's chimney. He fled across the border to Arizona Territory's little town of Bonita.

In Arizona, as Henry Antrim, Billy again combined work - as a cook at a small hotel - with crime: stealing military blankets, saddles, and horses; while fatefully developing shootist skills. In 1876, incarcerated at local Fort Grant's guardhouse with his older, thieving accomplice, John Mackie, he escaped through a roof ventilation space. But he defiantly stayed in Bonita, relying on his rustling charges being dropped on a technicality, his first demonstration of risky behavior for his wish to have a "home."

On August 17, 1877, Billy's life again changed horrifically. His argument at Bonita's Atkins Cantina with a bullying blacksmith, Frank "Windy" Cahill, escalated to his fatally shooting that unknowably unarmed man. Billy escaped on a stolen horse. The Coroner's Jury declared him - as Henry Antrim - guilty of homicide, though in absentia; ignoring self-defense. So at 17½, Billy was almost hanged for murder. He escaped back to New Mexico Territory with an alias: William Henry Bonney - Billy Bonney. "Bonney" was likely his mother's maiden name.

In New Mexico Territory, by the next month of September, 1877, Billy attached himself to familiar sociopaths in Jessie Evans's murderous and rustling Santa Fe Ring-affiliated gang. And since all Ringites ended up immune to prosecution and profited financially, intelligent and energetic Billy, unknown to history, would have likely had a wealthy and long life.

But Billy had a conversion. He met kind, wealthy Englishman, John Henry Tunstall, a Ring competitor. By the next month, October of 1877, he left Jessie Evans's gang to become Tunstall's youngest ranch hand. Tunstall's men affectionately nick-named him "Kid." Tunstall became the lost father found; even gifting him, under the Homestead Act, with a ranch on the Peñasco River in partnership with another employee, half-Chickasaw Fred Waite. That was likely Billy's proudest and most optimistic moment.

Billy had stumbled into a noble cause: ending Ring oppression. His gunman skill now elevated him as a protector of the good. His hair-trigger temper became vehemence for justice. And the town of Lincoln, as well as Tunstall's ranch on the Feliz River, became home. But Billy's tragic destiny was unrelenting. After only 4½ months, this idyllic time ended with Tunstall's Ring murder.

Lincoln, site of the future Lincoln County War, had already sustained Ring abuses through mercantile monopoly of "The House": a huge, two-story adobe, general store run by its local Ring bosses, Emil Fritz, Lawrence Murphy, James Dolan, and John Riley for secret partner, Ring boss, Thomas Benton Catron. They bled cash-poor Mexicans and Anglo homesteaders with usurious credit. Redress was impossible, since law enforcement and courts were Ring-controlled. Terror reigned. In 1875, when rancher, Robert Casey, defeated Murphy in a Lincoln election, he was assassinated the same day. Three weeks later, Lincoln's anti-Ring, Mexican community leader, Juan Patrón, was shot by Riley; though accidentally surviving as a limping cripple.

Hope for change began in late 1876 with arrival in Lincoln of English merchant, John Henry Tunstall; persuaded to settle there by a resident attorney, Alexander McSween, a Ring opponent, but once legal counsel to "The House." Tunstall planned to defeat the Ring by fair mercantile and ranching competition.

But Tunstall's plans coincided with boss Catron's monopolistic thrust into Lincoln County: secretly owning a Pecos River cow camp fronted by "The House," and creating his Carrizozo Land and Cattle Company after taking dying Murphy's ranch in 1878.

By 1877, Tunstall built, just a quarter mile northeast of "The House," a general store and bank. And he began two cattle ranches to wrest from "The House" its beef and flour contracts to local Fort Stanton and Mescalero Indian Reservation. He even exposed Ringite Lincoln County Sheriff William Brady's embezzlement of tax money to buy rustled cattle for Catron's ranches. So Tunstall and McSween got on the Ring's hit list.

Ringmen preferred to kill with guise of legality. So they entangled Tunstall in fabricated criminality, starting with false prosecution of McSween, who was then attorney for the estate of "The House's" partner, Emil Fritz, who died intestate in 1874, but had two local siblings and a life insurance policy. The Ring seized on that policy. In 1877, McSween had successfully litigated to get its $10,000 proceeds from its withholding New York City insurance company, minus $3,000 to the collections firm – leaving

$7,000 minus his fees. Knowing that the House faced bankruptcy from Tunstall's competition, and would extort that sum from Fritz's local heirs, he retained it while seeking heirs in Germany.

In December of 1877, McSween left on business to St. Louis with his wife and with Tunstall's business associate, the cattle king, John Chisum, then also president of the bank in Tunstall's store. The Ring pounced, declaring McSween an absconding embezzler of the Fritz insurance money. Ring boss Catron, then U.S. Attorney, issued his arrest warrant for capture. Chisum was also jailed in retaliation for backing Tunstall. On February 4, 1878, McSween had his hearing in Mesilla under Ringite District Judge Warren Bristol (later Billy's hanging judge), who indicted him for embezzling; intending his incarceration and killing in Lincoln by its Ringite Sheriff, William Brady. McSween was saved by the honorable Deputy Sheriff, Adolph Barrier, from his Las Vegas, New Mexico, arrest site, who kept him in personal custody.

But Judge Bristol had set the Ring's traps for assassination of McSween and Tunstall. His indictment did two things. First, he set the bail at $8,000, with approval only by Ringite District Attorney William Rynerson; who refused all bondsmen to leave McSween open to Sheriff Brady's fatal custody at any time.

The second was Tunstall's trap. Bristol attached McSween's property to the sum of $10,000 - falsely deemed the embezzled total - to ensure the money if he was convicted at that April's Grand Jury. Then Bristol lied that Tunstall was in partnership with McSween, to attach Tunstall's property also. And Bristol empowered Sheriff Brady to do attachment inventories at their properties. The intent was harassment to provoke Tunstall and his men to violence to justify his killing in "self-defense."

But Tunstall merely said that any man's life was worth more than all he owned. Billy, with Tunstall three months, must have been overwhelmed by this novel idealism.

Tunstall's businesses had bankrupted "The House," making boss Catron emerge its mortgage owner. And the April Grand Jury would likely exonerate McSween. So the Ring acted urgently, using the embezzlement case's property attachment.

On February 18, 1878, when Tunstall sought to transfer his fine horses, which were immune to the attachment, from his Feliz River Ranch to Lincoln, Brady called it theft of attached property and sent his big posse of Deputies, Ring rustlers, and Jessie Evans's outlaw gang after him and his men, including Billy. Tunstall, becoming isolated, was murdered, his horse slain; with both corpses mutilated. This martyrdom, coupled with more Ring outrages, triggered the Lincoln County War.

Sheriff Brady refused to arrest the murderers. So anti-Ring Justice of the Peace John "Squire" Wilson issued warrants for James Dolan, Jessie Evans, and his other possemen. For service, he appointed Billy and Fred Waite as Deputy Constables under Town Constable Atanacio Martinez. Billy had already given Wilson an affidavit as to first-hand knowledge of the murderers. But Brady shielded them by putting Billy, Waite, and Martinez in Lincoln's pit jail. And he confiscated Billy's Winchester '73 carbine - likely a gift from Tunstall.

Next, "Squire" Wilson defied the Ring by deputizing Tunstall's foreman, Dick Brewer; who, in turn, made Tunstall's men, including now-released Billy, his possemen to serve those murder warrants. Billy, then 18, was still a lawman.

Meanwhile, Attorney Alexander McSween, in mortal danger from Brady and the Ring, went into hiding with Deputy Sheriff Barrier; mostly in the nearby Hispanic town of San Patricio.

By March of 1878, Dick Brewer's posse had captured Tunstall murder possemen, William "Buck" Morton and Frank Baker, who were shot attempting escape. Billy was in the firing group.

At that point, including "Windy" Cahill, Billy Bonney was now involved in three killings.

The Ring hit back. Ringite Governor Samuel Beach Axtell, by illegal proclamation, removed Wilson's Justice of the Peace powers to retroactively outlaw Dick Brewer's posse; then declared Sheriff William Brady to be Lincoln County's only law enforcer.

Enraged, Tunstall's men named themselves "Regulators" after pre-Revolutionary War freedom fighters. Included were Tunstall men - Billy; Fred Waite; John Middleton; Jim "Frenchie" French; farmer cousins, George and Frank Coe; and homesteader, Charlie Bowdre - and a John Chisum cattle detective, Frank MacNab. Dick Brewer was chosen as leader. Only one month after Tunstall died, Billy was being schooled in politics of revolution.

The Ring's next chance to assassinate McSween was April 1, 1878, when he returned to Lincoln for his Grand Jury embezzlement trial. That morning, to save him, Regulators with carbines, and Billy with only a revolver, ambushed Brady and his three deputies from behind an adobe corral wall at Tunstall's store. Brady and his Deputy George Hindman died. Recklessly, Billy, with Jim French, ran out to retrieve his confiscated

Winchester '73 carbine from Brady's body. Both got leg wounds from firing surviving deputy, Jacob Basil "Billy" Matthews. But Billy regained his symbol of father-figure Tunstall. (It is likely the carbine held in Billy's famous tintype two years hence.)

Three days later, on April 4, 1878, Deputy Dick Brewer, seeking stolen Tunstall horses, led Billy, John Middleton, Fred Waite, Frank Coe, George Coe, and Charlie Bowdre to Blazer's Mill - a privately owned, way station and grist mill within the Mescalero Indian Reservation. Accidently encountered was Tunstall murder posseman, Andrew "Buckshot" Roberts, for whom they had a warrant. Roberts fired his Winchester carbine at Bowdre, who shot him in the belly. Roberts's bullet had hit Bowdre's belt buckle, ricocheted, and wrenched George Coe's revolver, mutilating his trigger finger. Another Roberts shot hit Middleton's chest, though Middleton survived. Then Roberts killed Brewer, later dying himself from Bowdre's wound. Billy had not fired a shot. Roberts had demonstrably resisted arrest murderously, necessitating self- defense response. But Ring boss Catron, as U.S. Attorney, seized on this killing to file his federal indictment against the Regulators, including Billy, claiming the murder site was the Mescalero Reservation, under federal control.

Billy's murder involvement now totaled six men; though only "Windy" Cahill was demonstrably by his hand.

At the April, 1878, Lincoln County Grand Jury, McSween was exonerated for embezzling. He continued his anti-Ring fight backed by the Regulators, though they had never been paid; John Chisum having dishonestly reneged. Revolutionary fervor sufficed. And Billy, their hot-headed fearless zealot, was becoming an inspiration - with McSween as his new father substitute.

McSween's lawful tactic was seeking high-level intervention, since murder of a foreign citizen could elicit a Washington, D.C. investigation. He filed a complaint with the British ambassador and to President Rutherford B. Hayes, accusing U.S. officials of murdering Tunstall. In response, investigating attorney, Frank Warner Angel, was sent by the Departments of the Interior and Justice. Arriving May 4, 1878, Angel took 39 depositions. Billy, volunteering for one, entered the national stage.

Public optimism of Ring defeat further grew when the Lincoln County Commissioners appointed neutral John Copeland, as Sheriff replacing Brady. He even deputized Regulator, Josiah "Doc" Scurlock, to recover Tunstall's horses, stolen by the Ring.

Still a lawman, Billy was on Scurlock's posse. And Wilson, ignoring Axtell's proclamation, continued as Justice of the Peace.

Optimism was short-lived. New Regulator leader, Frank MacNab, was killed in ambush on April 28, 1878 by Ringite Seven Rivers rustlers. By May 28th, because John Copeland forgot to post his tax collecting bond, Governor Axtell, by another proclamation, removed him and appointed as Sheriff, Ringite George Peppin, Brady's deputy, present at Brady's killing.

War fervor built, with furious Regulators and Mexicans calling themselves "McSweens." Billy's affiliation with local, firebrand youth, Yginio Salazar, and Billy's closeness to Hispanic residents of nearby San Patricio and Picacho, had arguably brought them all into the McSween alliance. By April 30, 1878, McSweens were skirmishing with Ring partisans, known as "Murphy-Dolans."

McSween again hid, often in San Patricio. In revenge, Sheriff George Peppin, with John Kinney's Ring-rustler gang from Mesilla, on July 3, 1878 massacred residents and destroyed farm animals and property there. On July 13th, the "Regulator Manifesto" was sent to Catron's brother-in-law, then managing his Carrizozo cattle ranch, threatening retaliation against Catron himself. Signed only "Regulator," it was likely created by Billy.

The Lincoln County War's culminating Battle began the next day: July 14, 1878. McSween, with 60 men - Regulators and Hispanic residents of San Patricio and Picacho - occupied Lincoln. Reflecting McSween's intended peaceful victory was that his wife, Susan, and her sister with five children, remained in his double-winged house; along with the sister's attorney husband's law intern, Harvey Morris.

McSween's men took strategic positions in houses throughout the mile-long town, most of whose inhabitants had fled. When Seven Rivers and John Kinney outlaws joined James Dolan and Sheriff George Peppin, Billy; his friends, Yginio Salazar and Tom O'Folliard; and San Patricio men - José Chávez y Chávez, Ignacio Gonzales, Florencio Chávez, Francisco Zamora, and Vincente Romero - rushed to McSween's house, joining guard, Jim French.

Though Ring men occupied foothills south of Lincoln, they were held at bay for five days by shooting McSweens. Regulators were about to win. But McSween did not realize that Fort Stanton's new Commander, Lieutenant Colonel N.A.M. Dudley, was beholden to the Ring. McSween was also reassured by the Posse Comitatus Act, passed the month before in Washington, baring military intervention in civilian disputes.

On July 16th, Commander Dudley began his invention by sending to Lincoln, for "fact-finding," 9th Cavalry Private Berry Robinson, who was almost hit in the mutual gunfire. Next, on July 18th, James Dolan used Ringite Lincolnite, Saturnino Baca, to claim his wife and children were at risk from the McSweens.

The next day, July 19th, violating the Posse Comitatus Act, Dudley marched on Lincoln with 39 troops - white infantry, black 9th Cavalry, and white officers - two ambulances; a mountain howitzer cannon; and a Gatling machine-gun, that period's most awesome weapon. Panicked McSweens - except for those in his besieged house - fled north across the nearby Bonito River. Dudley himself threatened McSween with razing his house if any soldier was shot. He then left three soldiers there to inhibit its defenders' shooting from it, and ordered three more to accompany Sheriff Peppin as a shield. Next, by death threats, he forced Justice of the Peace Wilson to write arrest warrants for McSween and his men as attempting murder of Private Robinson to feign reason for his intervention. Then he encamped at the east side of Lincoln.

Backed by the participating troops, Sheriff Peppin's outlaw posseman set fire to McSween's house's west wing. His family was evacuated after Dudley refused McSween's wife's plea to save him.

By nightfall, the McSween house conflagration - worsened by an exploding keg of gunpowder for bullet-making - left all trapped in the east wing. At about 9 p.m., escape was attempted into fire-lit shooting Ringites. With Billy was law intern, Harvey Morris, whom he saw fatally shot. And before Billy escaped across the Bonito River, at the property's rear - to rescue by fellow Regulators - he witnessed Dudley's treasonous crime: three of his white soldiers, imbedded with the assailants, under orders, fired a volley at those escaping. Arguably, they had even killed Morris.

Shot dead were Alexander McSween, Francisco Zamora, and Vincente Romero. Yginio Salazar survived with two bullets in his back. Symbolizing horror, McSween's starving, yard chickens ate the eyeballs of his corpse Again was Ring murder and mutilation in Lincoln County to gain treacherous victory.

No one knew that Ring influence extended to Washington, D.C. Investigator Frank Warner Angel, after documenting crimes of Governor S.B. Axtell, U.S. Attorney Catron, and Sheriff Brady's posse, nevertheless concluded falsely in his report - likely under duress - that no U.S. officials were involved in Tunstall's murder. As part of the cover-up, Catron resigned as U.S. Attorney. And President Hayes scapegoated Governor Axtell, replacing him with

Civil War General Lew Wallace. But Angel secretly tried to get justice by writing for Wallace a notebook listing Ringites, and sending him an exposé on the Santa Fe Ring printed in 1877.

Though most Regulators fled the Territory, Billy stayed and carried out the Regulator Manifesto's guerrilla stock rustling with Tom O'Folliard and Charlie Bowdre - who had relocated to Fort Sumner with his wife Manuela. For his stolen stock, Billy used non-Ring outlets: Pat Coghlan in the western part of the Territory; and Dan Dedrick. Dedrick was a counterfeiter and rustler owner of Bosque Grande, a ranch 12 miles south of Fort Sumner. With his two brothers, he also owned a livery stable in White Oaks, a town about 45 miles northwest of Lincoln. Those brothers were another stock outlet for Billy. Billy also sold rustled horses in Tascosa, Texas; where he wrote a subsequently famous, bill of sale to friendly a doctor, Henry Hoyt, for an expensive sorrel horse - likely dead Sheriff Brady's. He also got money by gambling. He was again a homeless drifter. That would now be permanent.

Amidst public hope, on October 1, 1878, new Governor, Lew Wallace took office. A high-achieving elitist, he was the son of an Indiana governor; a Civil War Major General; an Abraham Lincoln murder trial prosecutor; author of best-selling novel, *The Fair God*; and was writing *Ben-Hur A Tale of the Christ*. He had sought an exotic ambassadorship, like to Turkey, not governorship of backwater New Mexico Territory. So, to dispatch quickly with Lincoln County "troubles" without confronting the Santa Fe Ring, he issued, a month after arriving, an Amnesty Proclamation; though excluding those already indicted. Billy had been indicted for the Brady, Hindman, and Roberts murders.

There were more sources of hope. The new Sheriff, George Kimbrell - having been appointed to replace Sheriff George Peppin who resigned - was anti-Ring. And McSween's intrepid widow, Susan, had brought to Lincoln Attorney Huston Chapman to charge Commander N.A.M. Dudley with the Lincoln County War Battle's murder of her husband and arson of her home.

In that atmosphere of legal scrutiny, James Dolan made peace overtures, first to Susan McSween, then to Billy - a proof of that teenager's Ring threat. Billy and his Hispanic compatriots could yield another uprising - as T.B. Catron feared.

The Billy-Dolan peace meeting was fatefully scheduled on the February 18, 1879 anniversary of Tunstall's murder. It ended in calamity. As James Dolan; Billy; Jessie Evans and Jessie's new gang member, Billy Campbell; and Billy's Regulator friends, Tom O'Folliard and Josiah "Doc" Scurlock, walked Lincoln's dark street after the meeting, they encountered Chapman. Dolan and Campbell fired at point-blank range, killing him, then igniting his clothing. Billy was again an eye-witness. And again there was murder and mutilation in Lincoln County.

Chapman's murder forced Governor Wallace to go to Lincoln - after procrastinating for five months after arriving. Once there, he avoided Ring confrontation, using the Ring's own concoction of vague "outlaws and rustlers" causing trouble. The Ring had given him a list of Regulators as "outlaws;" with Billy on it as "the Kid."

Focus on Billy - likely through Dolan - made Wallace put the astronomical reward of $1,000 on his head. Billy responded with his pardon plea, writing on March 13, 1879, to offer Wallace his eye-witness testimony against Chapman's murderers in exchange for annulling his Lincoln County War indictments. It was Billy's bold and calculated risk to negate Ring power over himself.

His articulate pardon plea letter, in his personalized Spencerian script, led to his March 17, 1879, nighttime meeting with Wallace in Justice of the Peace Wilson's Lincoln house. Evidence indicates that Wilson was covertly backing Billy's plea. And Billy believed Wallace agreed to his pardon bargain.

To avoid assassination before testifying, Billy requested from Wallace a sham arrest (He had already seen Ring assassinations of John Tunstall, Alexander McSween, Harvey Morris, Francisco Zamora, Vincente Romero, and Huston Chapman.) He was kept in the home of his Lincoln friend, Juan Patrón, the town Jailer. Wallace, housed next door, interviewed him and got his additional letter about Lincoln County War issues.

Billy fulfilled his pardon bargain the next month by testifying in the Grand jury. He got indictment of Chapman's killers, with James Dolan and Billy Campbell for first degree murder, and Jessie Evans as accessory. But Ringite District Attorney William Rynerson, colluding with Judge Bristol, had his trial venue for his indictments switched from Lincoln to Doña Ana County to guarantee a hanging verdict. Still Wallace issued no pardon.

By that April of 1879, Alexander McSween's widow, Susan, retained Attorney Ira Leonard, Chapman's office-mate from Las Vegas, to prosecute Dudley. So Dudley, under likely advisement from Catron, who had represented him for past court martials, got defamatory affidavits to diminish her credibility. And he requested a military Court of Inquiry, where judges would be biased, and where he would be defended by Catron's law firm member, Henry Waldo. And on April 25th, the Ring tried unsuccessfully to assassinate Ira Leonard to stop the case.

Wallace, having removed Dudley as Commander, testified against him in the 1879 Court of Inquiry, though without confronting the Ring. Billy testified also, for his own anti-Ring agenda. He devastatingly reported the three white soldiers firing a volley at him and escaping others: meaning officers; meaning under Dudley's orders; meaning violating the Posse Comitatus Act and justifying court martial, and even hanging. His courage made Ira Leonard take him as client.

By July of 1879, the biased Court of Inquiry exonerated Dudley. And Billy, with no pardon and imminent transport to Mesilla for a hanging trial, exited his bogus jailing.

The Ring recouped. By October of 1879, Susan McSween lost her civil trial against Dudley in Mesilla, to which her venue had been changed by Judge Bristol. That month, Bristol also voided James Dolan's Chapman murder indictment based on no witnesses daring to appear for a trial. Dolan, certain of immunity, had even taken over Tunstall's store. Tunstall's ranch property was given by the Ring to Dolan, Riley, and Rynerson; and Billy's Peñasco River ranch went to Jacob Basil "Billy" Matthews, head posseman for Tunstall's murder. And there was a more subtle Ring victory: Lew Wallace's humiliation in the Court of Inquiry made him shun Lincoln County "troubles" and Billy's pardon.

Billy's future killer, Patrick "Pat" Floyd Garrett, had arrived in New Mexico Territory's Fort Sumner in 1878. Born to an Alabama plantation family, relocated to Claiborne Parrish, Louisiana, when 9½ - and Billy was just born - he had even been willed a slave. After the Civil War, he drifted to Texas, where he possibly murdered a black man, before becoming a buffalo hunter from 1876 to 1878 with two partners and a kid named Joe Briscoe. Garrett murdered Briscoe, but claimed self-defense. He never met fellow buffalo hunter, John William Poe; but later, his, Poe's, and Billy's histories would merge on the night of July 14, 1881.

In Fort Sumner, tall Garrett met transient kid, Billy Bonney, gambling at Hargrove's or Beaver Smith's Saloons. They were given townspeople's nicknames, "Big Casino" and "Little Casino," for their poker playing and height discrepancies.

The original Fort Sumner was built in 1865 by the U.S. government on desert flatlands east of the Pecos River for soldiers guarding Bosque Redondo: a concentration camp for 3,500

Navajos and 400 Apaches, until their scandalous starvation caused release of the Navajos to their homeland in 1868; the Apaches having already escaped. In 1870, Fort Sumner was purchased by Lucien Bonaparte Maxwell, one of the Territory's richest men. Converting it into a town around its parade ground, and using its thousands of acres for sheep raising, he settled there with his wife, Luz Beaubien; daughters, including Paulita; and son, Peter. Retained was the military cemetery for his family. Eventually it received Billy's body, to lie beside Pat Garrett's earlier shooting victims: Billy's Regulator pals, Tom O'Folliard and Charlie Bowdre. Maxwell died in 1875, leaving the town to his wife and son, Peter; who became the family's ruin through mismanagement. But when Pat Garrett and Billy Bonney gambled there, Fort Sumner was still thriving.

Before buying Fort Sumner, Maxwell's wealth came from his marriage to Luz Beaubien, an heiress of the almost two million acre Beaubien-Miranda Land Grant, buying its shares from her siblings. In 1870, he then sold it as the Maxwell Land Grant. But he was cheated by his robber baron attorneys, Thomas Benton Catron and Steven Benton Elkins, who resold it for double the money. That profit fortified their Santa Fe Ring, as they enriched themselves with railroads, banks, and mines. Catron eventually owned six million acres - more than anyone in U.S. history. In the Lincoln County War period, he was Billy's lethal enemy, with the Ring branding him as the murderous outlaw "Billy the Kid" to justify killing him. By 1912's New Mexico statehood, Catron became one of the two first senators.

By 1878, before the Lincoln County War, Pat Garrett and Billy Bonney led separate lives, though connected by Fort Sumner's Gutierrez sisters: Juanita, Apolinaria, and Celsa. Billy befriended Celsa, married to her cousin, Saval Gutierrez, a Maxwell sheep herder. Billy's July 14, 1881 death walk would start at their house. Garrett married Juanita, who died soon after of a possible miscarriage. Two years later, in 1880, he married Apolinaria, with whom he would father eight children. It was a double marriage with his Fort Sumner, best friend, Maxwell's foreman, Barney Mason, later a spy assisting Garrett's capture of Billy.

In 1878, Garrett had been desperate for employment. At Fort Sumner, he drove a wagon for Peter Maxwell; helped a local hog raiser, Thomas "Kip" McKinney; and bartended at Hargrove's Saloon. Then came 1880 and the opportunity of his life. For Lincoln County's November election, the Ring needed a compatible

Sheriff. To qualify, Garrett moved with his wife, Apolinaria, to that county's town of Roswell; adding, as a boarder, an unemployed journalist named Ashmun "Ash" Upson. In 1882, Upson would ghostwrite Garrett's book about killing Billy the Kid.

By 1880, the Ring's outlaw myth propaganda had advertised Billy's gunman reputation. That almost succeeded in his killing on January 3, 1880 at Fort Sumner's Hargrove's Saloon. A Texan bounty hunter named Joe Grant tried to shoot him in the back. Saved by Grant's gun's misfiring, Billy retaliated fatally. Obvious self-defense, that killing was not legally pursued.

Billy was now linked to murders of seven men: Frank "Windy" Cahill, William Brady, George Hindman, Andrew "Buckshot" Roberts, William "Buck" Morton, Frank Baker, and Joe Grant.

That 1880, when his now-famous tintype photograph was taken in Fort Sumner, Billy may have heard first mythological whispers of his outlawry. The Ring was setting its legal trap for eliminating him. In addition to murderer and rustler, he would be declared a counterfeiter to bring in the Secret Service, a branch of the U.S. Treasury Department with funding and power to track him down. Catron's Lincoln County agent, James Dolan, initiated the investigation by reporting receipt of a counterfeit $100 bill in his Lincoln store. And Catron or Elkins were the likely contact to Secret Service Chief, James Brooks.

By September 11, 1880, Secret Service Special Operative Azariah Wild was sent to Lincoln. Dolan's received counterfeit bill, falsely linked to Billy, actually came from two youths, Billy Wilson and Tom Cooper, employed by the real counterfeiter, Dan Dedrick. But they occasionally rustled with Billy and his regulars: Tom O'Folliard, Charlie Bowdre, and a "Dirty Dave" Rudabaugh. Billy himself used Dedrick as an outlet for rustled stock, along with Dedrick's brothers at their White Oaks livery.

Gullible Operative Azariah Wild was led to believe by James Dolan and Catron's brother-in-law, Edgar Walz - then managing Catron's Carrizozo cattle ranch - that Billy was in the country's largest counterfeiting and rustling gang. In December of 1880, the *New York Sun*, with leaked Wild reports, featured Ring propaganda of Billy in: "Outlaws of New Mexico. The Exploits of a band headed by a New York Youth, War Against a Gang of Cattle Thieves, Murderers, and Counterfeiters." He was alias "the Kid." The Ring had launched his national outlaw myth.

The Ring's plot almost backfired when Wild was told by Attorney Ira Leonard that his client, Billy Bonney, would testify against the counterfeiters. On October 8, 1880, Wild wrote in his daily report to Chief James Brooks that he himself would arrange a pardon for Billy in exchange for that testimony. But Wild confided that pardon plan to his Ringite informers, who convinced him that Billy, staying in Fort Sumner, was the gang's leader! In his report for October 14, 1880, Wild wrote that he intended to arrest those desperados. By then, Billy was cautious. He held up the stagecoach with Wild's mail, read that report, and avoided apprehension by avoiding the meeting with Leonard and Wild. But another pardon was lost.

The Ring was determined to eliminate Billy. The next option was getting a Lincoln County Sheriff willing do it. The current Sheriff, George Kimbrell, who had assisted in Billy's sham arrest, was a McSween-side sympathizer. The Ring chose Pat Garrett. Secretly, Wild worked with him to form a dragnet to capture Billy and his "rustler-counterfeiter gang;" while, for the upcoming sheriff's election, Garrett was advertised as a law-and-order man to new gold-rush settlers in White Oaks, unaware of Lincoln County War issues, but a third of Lincoln County's voters.

In the November 2, 1880 election, Pat Garrett got 358 votes to Kimbrell's 141. Wild, convinced by his Ring contacts that Kimbrell protected the "Kid gang," also gave Garrett immediate Territorial power for the capture by appointing him Deputy U.S. Marshall. Unaware, Billy would have wrongly thought that Garret's lawman authority was limited to Lincoln County, not Fort Sumner's San Miguel County, where he stayed.

And unaware of his locally publicized "outlawry," Billy still brought stolen horses to the Dedrick's White Oaks livery. On November 22, 1880, a White Oaks posse ambushed him, Tom O'Folliard, Billy Wilson, Tom Pickett, and "Dirty" Dave Rudabaugh at nearby Coyote Spring, shooting dead two of their horses before Billy's group escaped. Five days later, that posse attacked them again at the way station ranch of "Whiskey" Jim Greathouse, 45 miles northeast of White Oaks; accidentally killing one of their own men, Jim Carlyle, but blaming Billy.

That accusation prompted Billy's only letter of 1880 to Governor Lew Wallace. On December 12th, he wrote, denying his outlawry and murdering of Jim Carlyle. He even described his Robin Hood role of seeking justice for the downtrodden. Wallace never answered. Instead, on December 22nd, he placed a

Las Vegas *Daily Gazette* notice: "Billy the Kid: $500 Reward." He would repeat it in the *Daily New Mexican* on May 3, 1881, after Billy's jailbreak. His betrayal of the pardon bargain was complete.

By December of 1880, dreadful days began for Billy. U.S. Marshall Pat Garrett, backed by Azariah Wild, had assembled Texan posses to ride after Billy, since New Mexicans, to whom he was an anti-Ring hero, refused. Garrett's first ambush was on December 19, 1880, when Billy, Tom O'Folliard, Charlie Bowdre, Billy Wilson, Tom Pickett, and Dave Rudabaugh rode into Fort Sumner. O'Folliard was shot dead. The rest escaped.

Billy's group tried to flee the Territory in a snowstorm; but stopped, about 16 miles from Fort Sumner, on December 21, 1880, at a rock-walled, windowless, shepherds' line cabin at Stinking Springs. There Garrett ambushed them the next morning, killing Charlie Bowdre, whom he mistook for Billy, his intended victim. The rest surrendered. It would be seven months before Garrett succeeded in his mission to kill Billy.

Garrett transported his prisoners by train, via Las Vegas, New Mexico, to the Santa Fe jail. Billy remained there from December 27, 1880 to March 28, 1881, because the Ring awaited completion of the railroad to Mesilla to impede any rescue. But he almost escaped by tunneling out with fellow prisoners.

From his cell, Billy wrote four unanswered letters to Wallace, in 1881, pleading for his pardon: writing on March 4th: "*I have done everything that I promised you I would, and you have done nothing that you promised me.*" On March 2nd, he had threatened: "*I have some letters which date back two years and there are Parties who are very anxious to get them but I will not dispose of them until I see you.*" Wallace never got over that audacity or his own guilt, reworking the pardon obsessively till the end of his life in vindictive fictionalized articles on the outlaw "Billy the Kid."

Billy's first Mesilla murder trial, under Ringite Judge Warren Bristol, began on March 30, 1881, with jurors unaware of Lincoln County War's issues, and without any Lincolnites daring to be witnesses for his defense. Attorney Ira Leonard represented him for past U.S. Attorney Catron's June 21, 1878 federal indictment, Case Number 411, the United States versus Charles Bowdre, Josiah Scurlock, Henry Brown, William Bonney alias Henry Antrim alias the Kid, John Middleton, Steven Stevens, John Scroggins, Frederick Waite, and George Coe for the murder of Andrew "Buckshot" Roberts. It was first because the Ringites likely considered it air-tight.

But, surprising everyone, Leonard got it quashed as invalid, since the federal government had no jurisdiction over Blazer's Mill, the murder site; because private property, like it, was under Territorial jurisdiction. Its being surrounded by the federally-controlled Mescalero Reservation was irrelevant.

Remaining were only the Brady and Hindman Territorial indictments; and, though Billy been firing in the group of Regulators, he had only a revolver lacking accurate range.

But, suddenly, Ira Leonard withdrew, likely after a Ring threat. That was disastrous for Billy. He got Ring-biased, court appointed attorney, Albert Jennings Fountain, who considered him an outlaw, along with co-counsel John D. Bail, a Ringite Catron friend.

On April 8th and 9th of 1881, was Billy's Brady murder trial. His Spanish-speaking jury, given no translator, heard only prosecution witnesses - including James Dolan. After Judge Bristol's biased instructions (with translator) made Billy's mere presence equal to firing the fatal shot, the jury found him guilty of first degree murder; its sole punishment being hanging. On April 13th, Judge Bristol set Billy's hanging date for May 13th, to limit time for appeal. Billy was to be hanged in Lincoln by its Sheriff, Pat Garrett.

From the Mesilla jail, Billy wrote to Attorney Edgar Caypless - conducting his replevin case against Stinking Springs posseman, Frank Stewart for stealing his racing mare at Stinking Springs - hoping to get money from her sale to pay for an appeal.

Ironically, the new Lincoln jail, where Billy was incarcerated to await hanging, was in the past "House," which Catron had sold to Lincoln County for its courthouse, with second floor as jail.

On April 21, 1881, Billy arrived to Sheriff Garrett's custody. For his 24 hour guard, Garrett deputized a White Oaks man, James Bell, and a Seven Rivers man, Bob Olinger. Garrett's further precaution was shackling Billy at wrists and ankles, with securing to a floor ring - all to guarantee his hanging death.

But on April 28th, with Garrett away collecting White Oaks's taxes, Billy escaped. He used a revolver from an accomplice's putting it in the outhouse, or by seizing Bell's. A likely accessory was caretaker, Gottfried Gauss: Tunstall's past cook, and witness to Ring's Lincoln County War atrocities. Billy shot Bell dead as the man fled down the jail's stairway to sound alarm.

Deputy Bob Olinger, across the street at the Wortley Hotel with jail prisoners, either heard the shot or was directed to the ambush. Billy was at the second-floor window, and killed him with his own Whitney double-barrel shotgun.

Billy then spent hours using a miner's pick, supplied by Gauss, to break his leg chain to enable riding; while gathered loyalist Lincoln townspeople, in passive resistance, did nothing to stop him. He finally rode away on a pony supplied by Gauss.

As of that April 28, 1881 escape, Billy was involved in the murder of nine men; James Bell and Robert Olinger adding to Frank "Windy" Cahill and Joe Grant as Billy's only provable killings.

Of the dead, Billy would have said that that Cahill's and Grant's killings were in self-defense; that he was a legal posseman at the group shooting of escaping arrested Tunstall murderers, William "Buck" Morton and Frank Baker; that his gun lacked range to hit Sheriff William Brady or Deputy George Hindman, and their killings by the Regulators were to save Alexander McSween from murder by them; that he had not shot Andrew "Buckshot" Roberts, a Tunstall murderer and murderer of Dick Brewer firing at his group, and killed solely by Charlie Bowdre in self defense; and that Deputy James Bell, after refusing to be tied, had tried to run for help, so was killed to save himself from unjust hanging (and Bell had been on the White Oaks posse, and possibly killed Jim Carlyle, then falsely accused him).

Only Seven Rivers rustler, Bob Olinger, would have been admittedly hated as being in each Lincoln County War period crime - Tunstall's murder, Frank MacNab's ambush murder, and the War's skirmishes and battle. Billy's rage was so great, that he smashed apart Olinger's shotgun to throw it on his corpse, delaying his own escape.

That count of nine killed men - with only four certain - remained as Billy's final true tally.

Billy's escape route was across the Capitan Mountains to the Las Tablas home of his friend, Yginio Salazar. He next went south, possibly intending to go to Old Mexico, and visited friendly rancher, John Meadows. But he reversed, going northeast to Fort Sumner and Paulita, where he hid in the Maxwell's sheep camps, confident of protection by the Maxwells and townspeople. He was unaware that Pat Garrett was paying Maxwell foreman, Barney Mason, as a spy, through Secret Service Agent Azariah Wild.

Garrett's two deputies for the pursuit of Billy to Fort Sumner - John William Poe and Thomas "Kip" McKinney - did not know Billy. Poe, a buffalo hunter, past Deputy U.S. Marshall in Texas, cattle detective, and recent White Oaks settler, had met Garrett during the Wild-assisted tracking of the "Kid gang." McKinney knew Garrett from their 1878, hog farming days.

Once in Fort Sumner, Garrett, doubting Billy's presence as too foolhardy, was urged by Poe to stay. On July 14, 1881, Poe, a stranger to the townspeople, did recognizance of the town; and also checked with Sunnyside postmaster, Milnor Rudulph, seven miles to its north. Poe became convinced Billy was nearby. That night, he, Garrett, and McKinney planned an ambush in Peter Maxwell's bedroom, with Maxwell as traitor. Unknown accomplices likely directed Billy to Maxwell's bedroom, where Garrett waited, with Poe and McKinney outside to kill Billy if he managed to escape through the door to the porch.

Near midnight, Billy proceeded from the converted barracks house of Celsa and Saval Gutierrez, carrying their butcher knife across the parade ground to cut a dinner steak in light of the almost-full huge moon, hovering at the horizon. He first went toward Maxwell's bedroom; but seeing Poe, asked in Spanish who he was, then entered.

Inside, to Maxwell, in bed as decoy, Billy asked again in Spanish who was there, possibly sensing Garrett in the darkness. Garrett then fired. Next, he fired wild. But the first shot was fatal. In terror, Maxwell ran out, almost getting shot by Poe, primed for back-up killing. Then Garrett returned to the room, with Poe and McKinney, and made sure Billy was dead.

The townspeople held a night vigil for Billy in their carpenter's shop. The Coroner's Jury, the next day on July 15, 1881, had as **President, Postmaster Milnor Rudulph, a loyal Ringite who had helped take over the Legislature in 1872 to block anti-Ring bills.** Bi-lingual, Rudulph wrote the Coroner's Jury Report in Spanish. The frightened juryman had no alternative but to sign his conclusion: "*[O]ur verdict is that the deed of said Garrett was justifiable homicide and we are unanimous in the opinion that the gratitude of all the community is due to the said Garrett for his deed and he is worthy of being rewarded.*"

Ring terrorism was now complete. Silence fell for a generation before any dared contradict the Santa Fe Ring's outlaw mythology of Billy the Kid.

BILLY BONNEY'S CHAMPIONS

In the 20th century, Billy Bonney's aging Lincoln County War period contemporaries finally felt safe enough to contradict the Santa Fe Ring's outlaw myth propaganda in print. They confirmed his brilliance, charisma, ease in both Anglo and Hispanic subcultures in those racist times, and fluency in Spanish. He had a zealot's fervor in the Lincoln County War, in which he was a freedom fighting soldier. And neither he, nor his champions, would have seen him as an outlaw. He was a deputized pursuer of John Tunstall's murderers, then a hunted risk to the Ring.

FRANK AND GEORGE COE

John Tunstall's employees, local Homestead Act farmers, cousins Frank and George Coe, 26 and 21 respectively, nick-named new, 17 year old ranch hand, Billy Bonney, as "Kid." By 1878, after Tunstall's murder, they became his fellow Regulators. After the lost Lincoln County War Battle, they fled to the Territory's northwest, near Farmington.

FRANK COE

As an old-timer, Frank Coe wrote about Billy in an unpublished letter to a William Steele Dean, dated August 3, 1926. He emphasized Billy's multiculturalism, and above-average height (5'6" was average), belying his mythologized "shortness": "[He was] 5ft 8in, weight 138 lb stood straight as an Indian, fine looking a lad as I ever met. He was a lady's man, the Mex girls were all crazy about him. He spoke their language well. He was a fine dancer, could go all their gaits and was one of them. He was a wonder, you would have been proud to know him."

On September 16, 1923, Frank Coe - like Billy, considering himself a Regulator soldier - gave a quote to the *El Paso Times*: "[Billy] was brave and reliable, one of the best soldiers we had. He never pushed his advice or opinions, but he had a wonderful presence of mind; the tighter the place the more he showed his cool nerve and quick brain."

Frank Coe also related Billy's shootist preoccupation: "He never seemed to care for money, except to buy cartridges with ... and he always used about 10 times as many as any one else."

GEORGE COE

In 1934, George Coe, Frank Coe's cousin and fellow farmer, published *Frontier Fighter: The Autobiography of George Coe Who Fought and Rode With Billy the Kid.* He described employer, John Tunstall's, paternal affection for Billy: "Tunstall seemed really devoted to the Kid. One day I was in Lincoln and I asked him about Billy. 'George, that's the finest lad I ever met," he said. "He's a revelation to me every day and would do anything to please me. I'm going to make a man out of that boy yet. He has it in him.' "

George Coe also emphasized Billy's charisma: "Billy came down to the Dick Brewer Ranch on the Ruidoso. He was the center of interest everywhere he went, and though heavily armed, he seemed as gentlemanly as a college-bred youth. He quickly became acquainted with everybody, and because of his humorous and pleasing personality grew to be a community favorite. In fact, Billy was so popular there wasn't enough of him to go around. He had a beautiful voice and sang like a bird. One of our special amusements was to get together every few nights and have singing. The thrill of those happy evenings still lingers - a pleasant memory - and tonight I would give a lot to live through one again. Frank Coe and I played the fiddles, and all of us danced, and here Billy, too, was in demand."

About Lincoln County War fighting, George Coe quoted Billy to show the boy's militant fervor in its freedom fighting: "As for ... giving up to that outfit, we'll die first." Billy himself exhibited that brave bellicosity in his March 20, 1879 pardon bargain letter to Governor Lew Wallace; writing: "*I am not afraid to die like a man fighting but I would not like to be killed like a dog unarmed.*"

George Coe gave a telling anecdote about Billy's teasing bravado which occurred around April 3, 1878 in the lead-up to the Lincoln County War Battle. It shows how this teenager inspired grown men, and foreshadowed Billy's undaunted and ironic press interviews which he gave after his capture and after his unjust Mesilla hanging trial: "We made a big bonfire, and sat around swapping lies and bragging ... Then we talked about riding into Lincoln and setting in short order all the difficulties that were troubling the people there. We were a brave band as we told it.

Our guns, which formed the most important part of our possessions, had been placed carelessly around against nearby trees. Billy sized up the situation and, looking for a little fun and excitement with an inexperienced bunch of greenhorns, he slipped about five or six cartridges out of his belt and tossed them into the fire. In less than a minute they began to go off, and such a mad dash for tall timber you have never seen ... I looked back as I ran, and there stood the Kid with his arms folded, perfectly unconcerned ... 'Well, you're a damn fine bunch of soldiers. Run like a bunch of coyotes and forget to take your guns. I just wanted to break you in a little before we met the enemy, and, boys, I'm sure proud of your nerve.' "

YGENIO SALAZAR

Quoted in Maurice Garland Fulton's 1926 *The Saga of Billy the Kid*, Billy's good friend, Ygenio Salazar stated: " 'Billy the Kid' ... was the bravest fellow I ever knew. All through the three-days' battle [sic – six day Lincoln County War Battle] he was as cool and cheerful as if he were playing a game instead of fighting for his life." (Fulton, Page 144)

GOTTFRIED GAUSS

German-born Gottfried Gauss, 56 at Billy's great escape from Lincoln's courthouse-jail, was part of Billy's Lincoln County history from that teenager's October of 1877 arrival as a John Tunstall ranch hand - when Gauss was Tunstall's cook - through the Lincoln County War period, and to Billy's 1881 jailbreak, when Gauss was the Lincoln courthouse-jail's caretaker and likely supplier of Billy's escape revolver.

Gauss's anti-Ring stance went back to 1876 when he was employed in the Ring's store called "The House," and was cheated out of his wages and profits from its brewery, which he ran.

Billy himself mentioned Gauss in his June 8, 1878 deposition to Washington Investigator Frank Warner Angel as being at Tunstall's Feliz River ranch before Tunstall's ambush-murder, as well as during an earlier intimidation of its ranch hands by Sheriff William Brady's possemen. Billy's transcriptionist wrote: "*The persons at the ranch were R. M. Brewer, John Middleton,*

***G. Gauss**, M. Martz, R.A. Widenmann, Henry Brown, F.T. Waite, W^{m} McClosky and this deponent.*" The night before Tunstall made his fatal return ride with his men and horses to Lincoln from that ranch, he assigned Gauss to stay. Thus, Gauss witnessed the arrival of Sheriff William Brady's posse, on its way to murder Tunstall. By shared traumas, he was Billy's steadfast friend.

On March 1, 1890, in an interview with the *Lincoln County Leader* about Billy's 1881 jailbreak, Gauss implied enabling by non-intervening Lincolnites, as well as his own sympathy for Billy. Gauss may even have directed Deputy Bob Olinger to the courthouse's east side, where Billy shot him. Gauss stated:

> I was crossing the yard behind the courthouse, when I heard a shot fired then a tussle upstairs in the courthouse, somebody hurrying downstairs, and deputy sheriff Bell emerging from the door running toward me. He ran right into my arms, expired the same moment, and I laid him down, dead. That I was in a hurry to secure assistance, or perhaps to save myself, everybody will believe.
>
> When I arrived at the garden gate leading to the street, in front of the courthouse, I saw the other deputy sheriff Olinger, coming out of the hotel opposite, with the four or five other county prisoners, where they had taken their dinner. I called to him to come quick. He did so, leaving his prisoners in front of the hotel. When he had come up close to me, and while I was standing not a yard apart, I told him that I was just after laying Bell dead on the ground in the yard behind. Before he could reply, he was struck by a well-directed shot fired from a window above us, and fell dead at my feet. I ran for my life to reach my room and safety, when Billy the Kid called to me: "Don't run, I wouldn't hurt you – I am alone, and master not only of the courthouse, but also of the town, for I will allow nobody to come near us." "You go," he said, "and saddle one of Judge (Ira) Leonard's horses, and I will clear out as soon as I have the shackles loosened from my legs." With a little prospecting pick I had thrown to him through the window he was working for at least an hour, and could not accomplish more than to free one leg. He came to the conclusion to wait a

better chance, tie one shackle to his waistbelt, and start out. Meanwhile I had saddled a small skittish pony belonging to Billy Burt (the county clerk), as there was no other horse available, and had also, by Billy's command, tied a pair of red blankets behind the saddle ...

When Billy went down the stairs at last, on passing the body of Bell he said, "I'm sorry I had to kill him but I couldn't help it."

On passing the body of Olinger he gave him a tip with his boot, saying, "You are not going to round me up again." And so Billy the Kid started out that evening, after he had shaken hands with everybody around and after having a little difficulty in mounting on account of the shackle on his leg, he went on his way rejoicing.

HENRY HOYT

Henry Hoyt was a 24 year old medical doctor, working as a mail rider, when he met Billy Bonney in Tascosa, Texas, three months after the lost Lincoln County War Battle. Billy and fellow Regulators, Charlie Bowdre and Tom O'Folliard, were selling horses, rustled in retaliation from Ringmen, as forewarned in Billy's "Regulator Manifesto" letter of July 13, 1878 to Catron's Carrizozo cattle ranch manager and brother-in-law, Edgar Walz.

Billy gifted Hoyt a horse, likely dead Sheriff William Brady's, writing a legally protective bill of sale, dated October 24, 1878.

Hoyt admired Billy's intelligence and bi-culturalism. In his autobiographical, 1929 book, *A Frontier Doctor*, he wrote: "After learning his history directly from himself and recognizing his many superior natural qualifications, I often urged him, while he was free and the going was good, to leave the country, settle in Mexico or South America, and begin all over again. He spoke Spanish like a native and although only a beardless boy was nevertheless a natural leader of men. With his poise, iron nerve, and all-around efficiency properly applied, he could have made a success anywhere."

JOHN P. MEADOWS

A cattle rancher living in New Mexico Territory from early 1880, John P. Meadows, when an old-timer, gave interviews to historians about having known Billy; and performed about it in an historical pageant called "Days of Billy the Kid in Story, Song and Dance" on February 26, 1931 in Roswell, New Mexico. Subsequently, he used his "Days of Billy the Kid" act for serialized newspaper accounts in the *Roswell Daily Record* on March 2nd, 3rd, and 4th of 1931.

That year, he also typed a 78 page manuscript with information about Billy. And from August 8, 1935 to June 25, 1936, the *Alamogordo News* printed almost forty reminiscence articles by him. These recollections are collected in a 2004 book titled *Pat Garrett and Billy the Kid as I Knew Them: Reminiscences of John P. Meadows*. It gives insight into how Billy inspired the older men. Meadows stated: "When he was rough, he was as rough as men ever get to be, yet he had a good streak in him."

E.C. "TEDDY BLUE" ABBOTT

E.C. "Teddy Blue" Abbott, a cowboy about Billy's age, roving through New Mexico Territory in 1878, and having merely heard of him, recorded Billy's atypical multi-culturalism.

It implied Billy could instigate a Hispanic revolt against the land-grabbing, Anglo, Santa Fe Ring minority. "Boss" Thomas Benton Catron himself confirmed that fear of uprisings in his February 10, 1913 *Washington Times* article stating, "Mexicans ... were perfectly equal to starting five new revolutions in five days." And Catron's anxiety connected to the Ring's mission to eliminate Billy by fabricating his outlaw myth.

In 1955, as an old-timer, "Teddy Blue" Abbott published *We Pointed Them North: Recollections of a Cowpuncher*. Open about his own racism, Abbott reported, as common knowledge, the existence of two sides, with Billy as the Mexican's hero, writing: "The Lincoln County troubles was still going on, and you had to be either for Billy the Kid or against him. It wasn't my fight ... it was the Mexicans that made a hero of him."

A.P. "PACO" ANAYA

A Fort Sumner friend of Billy's, three years younger, was A.P. "Paco" Anaya, whose posthumous manuscript about Billy was published in 1991 as *I Buried Billy*. In it, about Billy's bi-culturalism, Anaya stated: "Billy liked better to be with Hispanics than with Americans." (Anaya, Page 82)

CHAPTER 2
REAL BILLY BONNEY IN HIS OWN WORDS

SPEAKING THROUGH TIME

The real Billy Bonney was spectacularly brave, brilliant, and literate; and he left a big paper trail proving all that. His dull-witted imposters were left with an unattainable standard to mimic. And he certainly would not have referred to himself by the hated Santa Fe Ring moniker outlawing him for hanging as "Billy the Kid" - which his impersonators used for themselves.

The quantity of written and recorded records by Billy Bonney is incredible for a minor historical figure; explained, in part, by his anti-Ring political activism, which yielded his deposition and court testimonies. Additionally, his unusual charisma made people save his letters or documents.

So surviving were his 1878 affidavit and deposition on the murder of John Henry Tunstall, and his testimony in the 1879 military Court of Inquiry for possible court martial for Commander N.A.M. Dudley. His pardon bargain letters and interview with Governor Lew Wallace were retained by Wallace when he left the Territory, and were almost the only civilian documents Wallace kept. They ended up in his collected papers, donated to the Indiana Historical Society. Likewise, Dr. Henry Hoyt kept the Bill of Sale that Billy wrote out for him for a sorrel horse. And as big news in his day, Billy had press interviews.

Quotes of his clowning imposters exist, with devastating mismatch of their unschooled fractured grammar and ignorance of the contents of his known documents.

But the imposters' undoing was that they were impersonating a mythological, dime novel version of an outlaw: an uncouth, unschooled, mindlessly violent lout, as was expected by their second quarter of the 20th century audiences. The real Billy was beyond their conception.

AFFIDAVIT AND DEPUTIZING

A key factor Billy Bonney's history was his lawman status in pursuing John Tunstall's killers. On February 19, 1878, the day after Tunstall's murder, Billy and Tunstall's foreman, Dick Brewer, gave eye-witness affidavits to Lincoln Justice of the Peace John "Squire" Wilson, to enable his writing arrest warrants. It is the first time Billy's voice is publicly heard. He named Tunstall's killers as Sheriff Brady's possemen: "*James J. Dolan, Frank Baker, Jessie Evans, George Davis, A.H. Mills, W.S. Morton, [William] Moore, George Hindman, [Frank] Rivers, Pantaleon Gallegos, divers other persons unknown.*" It yielded Wilson's February 19th legal arrest warrants, stating:

Territory of New Mexico)
County of Lincoln)

Be it remembered that before the undersigned Justice of the Peace in and for the County and Territory aforesaid, personally came R.M. Brewer & ***W. Bonney*** *who being duly sworn according to law deposeth & saith that at the County and Territory aforesaid on the 18th day of February 1878 in and upon the [presence] of J.H. Tunstall, Robt A. Widenman[n], R.M. Brewer,* ***William Boney*** *[sic] & John Middleton, then and there in the Peace of the Territory an assault was made with divers deadly weapons to wit with Winchester Guns and Colts Revolvers, and divers other deadly weapons by James J. Dolan, Frank Baker, Jessie Evans, George Davis, A.H. Mills, W.S. Morton, [omitted first name] Moore, George Hindman, [Frank] Rivers, Pantaleon Gallegos, divers other persons unknown and did then and there as affiant believes wounded & killed J.H. Tunstall contrary to the statute in such case made and provided against the Peace & dignity of the Territory.*

R.M. Brewer
William Bonney.

After Sheriff Brady refused to serve them, Wilson concluded that "*there being then and there no officers to serve such warrant the undersigned as directed by law, in such cases specially empowered Richard H. Brewer to serve the same endorsing such deputation on said last mentioned warrant.*" Wilson wrote:

The Territory of New Mexico)
County of Lincoln)

I, John B. Wilson justice of the Peace in and for precinct № 1 Lincoln County, New Mexico, do hereby certify that on or about the 19th day of February 1878 ***W. Boney*** *[sic] and R.M. Brewer filed in my office affidavits charging John [James] J. Dolan, J. Conovair, Frank Baker, Jessie Evans, Tom Hill, George Davis, A. [Andrew] L. ["Buckshot"] Roberts, P. [Panteleon] Gallegos, T. Green, J. Awly, A.H. Mills, "Dutch Charley" proper name unknown, R.W. Beckwith, William Morton, [Deputy] George Hindman, J.B. Matthews and others with having murdered and killed one John H. Tunstall at the said County of Lincoln on or about the 18th day of February 1878, that on or about the 20th day of Feby 1878, I secured warrants on said affidavits for the arrest of the parties above named and directed the same to the Constable of for precinct № one in said County to wit: Atanacio Martines [Martinez].*

That on or about the 20th day of Feby 1878 said warrant was returned "not served" that on or about the said last mentioned day the undersigned issued an alias warrant for the apprehension of the above named persons, and there being then and there no officers to serve such warrant the undersigned as directed by law, in such cases specially empowered Richard H. Brewer to serve the same endorsing such deputation on said last mentioned warrant.

In testimony whereof I have hereinto set my hand at Lincoln Precinct № 1 Lincoln County, N. Mexico this 31st day of August 1878.

John Wilson, Justice of the Peace

This enabled Special Constable Dick Brewer to deputize Billy and Fred Waite as Deputy Constables under Lincoln Town Constable Atanacio Martinez to serve the warrants. To block the arresting, Sheriff William Brady then illegally locked them in Lincoln's pit jail, and confiscated Billy's Winchester '73 carbine.

DEPOSITION TO FRANK WARNER ANGEL

On June 8, 1878, Billy gave his eloquent eye-witness deposition, with characteristic meticulous attention to detail, on John Tunstall's murder, to Investigator for the Departments of Justice and the Interior, Frank Warner Angel, with Lincoln

Justice of the Peace John "Squire" Wilson, as witness. In it, Billy stated information unknown to the imposters: that he had a ranch on the Peñasco River along with another Tunstall employee, Fred Waite; that he knew about the injustice of the case against Tunstall; and that the horses being herded back to Lincoln were exempted from the case's attachments.

Lacking that still-undiscovered deposition, imposters had no knowledge of Tunstall's murder scene and its motive.

And proving his Regulator zeal to attain justice, Billy was risking his life by coming to Lincoln after Ringite Governor Samuel Beach Axtell's illegal proclamation outlawing the Regulators, and after receiving his own April Grand Jury indictments for Regulator killings in the Lincoln County War. He then signed the document, as witnessed by Angel and Wilson; which Angel's transcriptionist recorded as follows:

Territory of New Mexico)
County of Lincoln)
)

William H. Bonney was duly sworn, deposand says that he is a resident of said county, that on the 11th day of February A.D. 1878 he in company with Robt. A. Widenmann and Fred T. Waite went to the ranch of J. H. Tunstall on the Rio Feliz, that ***he and said Fred T. Waite at the time intended to go to the Rio Peñasco to take up a ranch*** *for the purpose of farming. That the cattle on the ranch of said J. H. Tunstall were throughout the County of Lincoln, known to be the property of said Tunstall; that on the 13th of February A.D. 1878 one J.B. Matthews claiming to be a Deputy Sheriff came to the ranch of said J.H. Tunstall in company with Jesse Evans, Frank Baker, Tom Hill and [Frank] Rivers, known outlaws who had been confined to the Lincoln County jail and had succeeded in making their escape, John Hurley, George Hindman, [Andrew] Roberts and an Indian aka Poncearo the latter said to be the murderer of Benaito Cruz, for the arrest of murderers of whom (Benaito Cruz) the Governor of this Territory offers a reward of $500. Before the arrival of said J.B. Matthews, deputy Sheriff, and his posse, having been informed that said deputy sheriff and posse were going to round up all the cattle and drive them off and kill the persons at the ranch, the persons at the ranch cut portholes into the walls of the house and filled sacks with earth, so that they, the persons at the ranch,* *should they be attacked or murder attempted, could defend themselves, this course being thought necessary* ***as the sheriffs posse was composed of murderers, outlaws, and desperate characters none of whom has any interest at stake in the County, nor being residents of said County****. That said Matthews when within about 50 yards of the house was called to stop and advance alone and state his business, that said Matthews after arriving at the ranch said that he had come to attach the cattle and property of A.A McSween, that* ***said Matthews was informed that A.A. McSween had no cattle or property there****, but that if he had he, said Matthews could take it. That said Matthews said that he thought some of the cattle belonging to R. M. Brewer whose cattle were also at the ranch of J.H. Tunstall, belonged to A.A. McSween, that said Matthews was told by said Brewer that he Matthews could round up the cattle and that he, Brewer, would help him. That said Matthews said that he would go back to Lincoln to get new instructions and if he came back to the ranch he would come back with one man. That said Matthews and his posse were then invited by R.M. Brewer to come to the house to get something to eat.*

Deponent further states that Robert A. Widenmann told R.M. Brewer and the others at the ranch, that he was going to arrest Frank Baker, Jesse Evans and Tom Hill said Widenmann having warrants for them. That said Widenmann was told by Brewer and the others at the ranch that the arrest could not be made because if it was made they, all the persons at the ranch would be killed and murdered by J.J. Dolan and their party. That said Evans advanced upon said Widenmann, said Evans swinging his gun and catching it cocked and pointed directly at said Widenmann. That said Jesse Evans asked said Widenmann whether he Widenmann, was hunting for him, Evans, to which Widenmann answered that if he was looking for him, he, Evans, would find it out. Evans also asked Widenmann whether he had a warrant for him; Widenmann answered that it was his (Widenmann's) business. Evans told Widenmann, that if he ever came to arrest him (Evans) he, Evans would pick Widenmann as the first man to shoot at, to which Widenmann answered that that was all right, that two could play at that game. That during the talking Frank Baker stood near said Widenmann, swinging his pistol on his finger, catching it full cocked pointed at said Widenmann.

The persons at the ranch were R. M. Brewer, John Middleton, G. Gayss [Gauss], M. Martz, R.A. Widenmann, Henry Brown, F.T.

Waite, Wm McClosky and this deponent. J.B. Matthews after eating started for Lincoln with John Hurley and Ponceano the rest of the party or posse saying they were going to the Rio Peñasco. Deponent started to Lincoln with Robert A. Widenmann and F.T. Waite and arrived at Lincoln the same evening and again left Lincoln on the next day, February the 14th in company with the above named persons, having heard that said Matthews was going back to the ranch of said J.H. Tunstall with a large party of men to take the cattle and deponent and Widenmann and Waite arrived at said ranch the same day.

Deponent states that on the road to Lincoln he heard said Matthews ask said Widenmann whether any resistance would be offered if he Matthews returned to take the cattle, to which said Widenmann answered that no resistance would be offered if the cattle were left at the ranch but if an attempt was made to drive the cattle to the Indian Agency and kill them for beef as he, said Matthews had been heard to say would be done, he, said Widenmann, would do all in his power to prevent this.

Deponent further says that on the night of the 17th of February A.D. 1878 J.H. Tunstall arrived at the ranch and informed all persons there that reliable information had reached him that J.B. Matthews was gathering a large party of outlaws and desperados as a posse and the said posse was coming to the ranch, the Mexicans in the party to gather up the cattle and the balance of the party to kill the persons at the ranch. It was thereupon decided that all persons at the ranch excepting G. Gauss, were to leave and Wm McClosky was that night sent to the Rio Peñasco to inform the posse who were camped there, that they could come over and round up the cattle, count them and leave a man there to take care of them and that Mr. Tunstall would also leave a man there to help round up and count the cattle and help take care of them, and said McClosky was also ordered to go to Martin Martz, who had left Tunstalls ranch when deponent, Widenmann and Waite returned to the town of Lincoln on the 13th of February and asked him said Martz to come to the ranch of said Tunstall and aid the sheriffs posse in rounding up and counting the cattle and to stay at the ranch and take care of the cattle.

Deponent left the ranch of said Tunstall in company with J.H. Tunstall, R.A. Widenmann, R.M. Brewer, John Middleton, F.T. Waite, said Tunstall, Widenmann, Brewer, Middleton and deponent driving the loose horses, Waite driving the wagon. Said Waite took the road for Lincoln with the wagon, the rest of the party taking the trail with the horses. ***Deponent says that all the horses which he and the party were driving, excepting 3 had been released by sheriff Brady at Lincoln that one of these 3 horses belonged to R.M. Brewer, and the other was traded by Brewer to Tunstall for one of the released horses.***

Deponent further says, that when he and the party has traveled to within about 3 miles from the Rio Ruidoso he and John Middleton were in drag in the rear of the balance of the party as just upon reaching the brow of a hill they saw a large party of men coming towards them from the rear at full speed and that he and Middleton at once rode forward to inform the balance of the party of the fact. Deponent had not more than barely reached Brewer and Widenmann who were some 200 or 300 yards to the left of the trail when the attacking party cleared the brow of the hill and commenced firing at him, Widenmann and Brewer. Deponent, Widenmann and Brewer rode over a hill towards another which was covered with large rocks and trees in order to defend themselves and make a stand. But the attacking party, undoubtedly seeing Tunstall, left off pursuing deponent and the two with him and turned back at the caño in which the trail was. Shortly afterwards we heard two or three separate and distinct shots and the remark was then made by Middleton that they, the attacking party must have killed Tunstall. Middleton had in the meantime joined deponent and Widenmann and Brewer. Deponent then made the rest of his way to Lincoln in company with Robt. A. Widenmann, Brewer, Waite and Middleton stopping on the Rio Ruidoso in order to get men to look for the body of J.H. Tunstall.

Deponent further says that neither he nor any of the party fired off either rifle or pistol and that neither he nor the parties with him fired a shot.

William H. Bonney

Sworn and subscribed before me this
eighth day of June A.D. 1878.

John B. Wilson
Justice of the Peace

"REGULATOR MANIFESTO"

On July 3, 1878, during the multiple skirmishes in the Lincoln County War, and leading to the final Battle, there occurred a retaliatory Santa Fe Ring massacre at anti-Ring San Patricio: the Hispanic community which was like bi-cultural Billy's second home. On July 13, 1878, ten days after it, Billy took action: challenging the Ring, in what I named the "Regulator Manifesto." It is the anti-Ring declaration of the Lincoln County War Battle, starting the next day. It is signed only "*Regulator*."

Existing as a copy, it was first attributed to Charles Bowdre by early historian, Maurice Garland Fulton, who claimed implausibly that its recipient, Ring head, T.B. Catron's, brother-in-law, Edgar Walz, recognized Bowdre's handwriting. But I believe it was Billy's production, either dictated to Bowdre, or wrongly attributed to him by Walz. And it heralds Billy's future retaliative guerrilla rustling from Ringites, like Catron and Walz. It stated:

In Camp, July 13, 1878.

Mr. Walz. Sir: - We are all aware that your brother-in-law, T.B. Catron sustains the Murphy-Kinney party, and take this method of informing you that if any property belonging to the residents of this county is stolen or destroyed, Mr. Catron's property will be dealt with as nearly as can be in the way in which the party he sustains deals with the property stolen or destroyed by them.

We returned Mr. Thornton the horses we took for the purpose of keeping the Murphy crowd from pursuing us with the promise that these horses should not again be used for that purpose. Now we know that the Tunstall estate cattle are pledged to Kinney and party. If they are taken, a similar number will be taken from your brother [in-law, Catron]. It is our object and efforts to protect property, but the man who plans destruction shall have destruction measured on him. Steal from the poorest or richest American or Mexican, and the full measure of the injury you do, shall be visited upon the property of Mr. Catron. This murderous band is harbored by you as your guest, and with the consent of Catron occupies your property.

Regulator

HOYT BILL OF SALE

After the lost Lincoln County War, refusing to leave the Territory, like most Regulators, Billy earned money by gambling and retaliatory rustling from Ringites, as threatened in his July 13, 1878 "Regulator Manifesto." His self-concept was not as a law-breaking rustler - as he later labeled Seven Rivers rustlers to Governor Lew Wallace in a March 23, 1879 interview.

Billy used non-Ring outlets for stock, and sold horses himself in Tascosa, Texas. There, on October 24, 1878, he "sold" to Dr. Henry Hoyt a sorrel horse - likely Sheriff William Brady's Dandy Dick, stolen from Catron's Carrizozo ranch. He priced it high for its bill of sale, which demonstrated legalese he had possibly learned from Alexander McSween; and with proper witnessing by saloon owners, James E. McMasters and George J. Howard. That skill would be used in 132 days to write his first pardon plea letter to Governor Lew Wallace.

Billy's abilities impressed Hoyt enough for him to keep the document. On April 27, 1929, Hoyt sent its copy to Lew Wallace Jr.; writing: "I am one of the very few men living who was well acquainted with that famous outlaw 'Billy the Kid' and for many years supposed I had the only specimen of his handwriting in existence [until learning about the Lew Wallace letters], **a Bill of Sale for a horse he presented me with, and wrote out himself,** to protect me should my ownership ever be questioned, a very important matter in that part of the world at that period. This paper I have preserved all these years."

The Hoyt Bill of Sale stated:

Tascoso Texas
Thursday Oct 24th 1878

Know all persons by these presents that I do hereby Sell and deliver to Henry F. Hoyt one Sorrel Horse Branded BB on left hip and other indistinct Branded on Shoulders for the sum of Seventyfive $ dollars in hand received
W HBonney

Witness
Jas. E. McMasters
Geo. J. Howard

LETTER OF MARCH 13, 1879 TO LEW WALLACE

On approximately March 13, 1879, Billy began his pardon plea to Governor Lew Wallace, offering eye-witness testimony against Ringite murderers of Attorney Huston Chapman on February 18, 1879 for an exchange, since Wallace's November 13, 1878 Amnesty Proclamation had excluded those indicted, like him. Noteworthy is that Billy asked to "*annuly*" - meaning annul - his indictments for the murders of William Brady, George Hindman, and Andrew "Buckshot" Roberts. That was correct: a pardon is post-sentencing; annulment is before. And Billy's ability to spell even "indicted," contrasts the pretenders' low literacy. He wrote:

To his Excellency the Governor.
General Lew. Wallace
Dear Sir I have heard that You will give one thousand $ dollars for my body which as I can understand it means alive as a witness. I know it is as a witness against those that murdered Mr. Chapman. if it was so as that I could appear at Court, I could give the desired information. but I have indictments against me for things that happened in the late Lincoln County War and am afraid to give up because my Enimies would Kill me. the day Mr. Chapman was murderded I was in Lincoln, at the request of good citizens to meet Mr. J.J. Dolan to meet as Friends. So as to be able to lay aside our arms and go to Work. I was present when Mr. Chapman was murderded and know who did it and if it were not for these indictments I would have made it clear before now. if it is in your power to Annully those indictments I hope you will do so so as to give me a chance to explain. please send me an annser telling me what you can do. You can send annser by bearer.

I have no wish to fight any more indeed I have not raised an arm since Your proclamation. as to my Character I refer to any of the Citizens, for the majority of them are my Friends and have been helping me all they could. I am called Kid Antrim but Antrim is my stepfathers name.

Waiting for an annser I remain
Your Obedient Servant
W.H. Bonney

LETTER OF MARCH 20, 1879 TO "SQUIRE" WILSON

Billy began a flurry of March 20, 1879 letters by writing to Justice of the Peace John "Squire" Wilson to check with Lew Wallace about his planned feigned arrest for his pardon bargain, since many of the men he was supposed to testify against for the Huston Chapman murder had escaped from their Fort Stanton imprisonment. He wrote from his safe-haven:

San Patricio
Thursday 20th 1879
Friend Wilson.
Please tell You know who that I do not know what to do, now as those Prisoners have escaped. So send word by bearer. a note through You it may be he has made different arrangements if not and he still wants it the same to Send :William Hudgins [Hudgens]: as Deputy, to the Junction tomorrow at three Oclock with some men you know to be all right. Send a note telling me what to do
WHBonney
P.S. do not send Soldiers

LETTER OF MARCH 20, 1879 TO LEW WALLACE

Wallace responded to Wilson with arrangements, and enclosed a vague "*note*" for Billy about their "*understanding.*" Billy responded with a precautionary scenario for his sham arrest:

San Patricio
Lincoln County
Thursday 20th 1879
General. Lew. Wallace:
Sir. I will keep the appointment I made. but be Sure and have men come that You can depend on I am not afraid to die like a man fighting but

I would not like to be killed like a dog unarmed. tell Kimbal [Kimbrell] to let his men be placed around the house and for him to come in alone: and he can arrest us. all I am afraid of is that in the Fort we might be poisoned or killed through a window at night. but You can arrange that all right. tell the Commanding Officer to watch)Let Goodwin(he would not hesitate to do anything there Will be danger on the road of Somebody Waylaying us to kill us on the road to the Fort. You will never catch those fellows on the road Watch Fritzes. Captain Bacas ranch and the Brewery they Will either go to Seven Rivers or to Jicarillo Mountains they will stay around close untill the scouting parties come in. give a spy a pair of glasses and let him get on the mountain back of Fritzes and watch and if they are there there will be provisions carried to them. it is not my place to advise you, but I am anxious to have them caught, and perhaps know how men hide from Soldiers, better than you. please excuse me for having so much to say

and I still remain Yours Truly

W H. Bonney

P.S.

I have changed my mind Send Kimbal [Kimbrell] to Gutieres just below San Patricio one mile, because Sanger and Ballard are or were great friends of Camels [Billy Campbell's] Ballard told me ~~today~~ yesterday to leave for you were doing everything to catch me. it was a blind to get me to leave tell Kimbal [Kimbrell] not to come before 3 oclock for I may not be there before

THE LEW WALLACE INTERVIEW

For his sham arrest in Lincoln, Lew Wallace and Billy were housed next door to each other; with Billy in his friend, jailor Juan Patrón's, house, and Wallace at José Montaño's. On March 23, 1879, Wallace interviewed Billy, asking nothing about the Lincoln County War. At this period, Wallace was also collecting information about Territorial outlawry, and Billy seems to have responded to that quest by telling him about the Santa Fe Ring's network of cattle rustlers, who fulfilled the beef contracts for Fort Stanton and the Mescalero Indian Reservation; which were held by the local Ring front, "The House," then controlled by James J. Dolan and John Riley. Noteworthy is Billy's vast fund of local information and geography. The notes stated:

William Bonney ("Kid")
relative to arrangement
with him.
Notes:

3-23-1879

<u>Statements by Kid, made Sunday night March 23, 1879</u>

1. There is a cattle trail beginning about 5 miles above Yellow Lake in a cañon, running a little west of north to Cisneza del Matcho (Mule Spring) and continuing around the point of the Capitan Mountains down toward Carrizozo in the direction of the Rio Grande. Frank Wheeler, Jake Owens and Dutch Chris are supposed to have used this trail taking a bunch of cattle over. Vansickle told K. so. They stopped and killed two beavers for Sam Corbett – hush money to Vansickle to whom they gave the beavers. Vansickle also said the Owens-Wheeler outfit mentioning "Chris" Ladbessor using this trail for about a year, but that lately their horses had given out, and of 140 head which they started to work they had only got through with 40. That now they were going to the Reservation to make a raid on the Indian horses to work on.

<u>The Rustlers.</u>

The "Rustlers," Kid says: were organized in Fort Stanton. Before they organized as "Rustlers" they had been with Peppin's posse. They came from Texas. Owens was conspicuous amongst them. ***They were organized before the burning of McSween's house****, and after that they went on their first trip down the county as far as the Coe's ranch and* ***thence to the Feliz where they took the Tunstall cattle.*** *From the Feliz they went to the Pecos, where some of them deserted, Owens amongst them. (Martin, known to Sam Corbett) was in charge of the Tunstall cattle, and was taken prisoner, and saw them kill one of their own party. On the same trip they burnt Lola Wise's house, and took some horses. Coe at the time was ranching at the house. On this trip they moved behind a body of soldiers, one company, and a company of Navajo Scouts. They moved in sight of the soldiers, taking horses, insulting women. Lorenzo Trujillo (Jus. Peder) Juan Trujillo, Jose M. Gutierres, Pancho Sanchez, Santos Tafoya, are witnesses against them. They stopped on Pecos at Seven Rivers. Collins, now at Silver City, was one of the outfit – nick-named the Prowler by the cowboys. At Seven Rivers. There joined them Gus Gildey (wanted at San Antonio for killing Mexicans) Gildey is carrying the mail now from Stockton to Seven Rivers – James Irvin and*

Reese Gobles, (rumored that their bodies were found in a drift down the Pecos) – Rustling Bob (found dead in the Pecos, killed by his own party) – John Selman (whereabouts unknown) came to Roswell while [Captain] Carroll was there –

The R's [Rustlers] stayed at Seven Rivers; which they left on their second trip via the Berenda for Fort Stanton. On their return back they killed Chavez boys and the crazy boy, Lorenzo – and the Sanchez boy, 14 years old. They also committed many robberies. They broke up after reaching the Pecos, promising to return when some more horses got fat.

Shedd's Ranch

The trail used going from Seven Rivers to Shedd's was round the S.W. part of the Guadalupe Mts. by a tank on the right hand of trail: from Shedd's the drives would be over to Las Cruces Jesse Evans, Frank Baker (killed) Jim [James] McDaniels (at Cruces, ranging between Cruces and El Paso) Reed at Shedd's bought cattle from them – also sold cattle to E.C. Priest, butcher in Cruces. "Big Mose" (at Cruces last heard from) and [blank], deserter from cavalry – (went to Arizona)

Mimbres

Used to be called Mormon City – situated 30 miles on the road to Cruces from Silver City south. A great many of what are known as "West Harden gang" are there. Among them Joe Olney, known in Mimbres as Joe Hill; he has a ranch in old Mexico somewheres near Coralitos. He makes trips up in this country: was at Penasco not long ago.

San Nicholas Spring

Is about 18 miles from Shedd's Ranch on the road to Tularosa, left hand road. There's a house at the spring and about 4 or 5 miles from it N.W. is another corral of brush and a spring, situated in a cañon. There Jim [James] McDaniels used to keep stolen Indian horses. McD. one of the Rio Grande posse. Kid says the latter is still used.

The Jones Family

Came from Texas. Used to keep saloon at Fort Griffin. The family consists of the father, Jim Jones, John Jones, boy about 10 years old, a girl about 13, and the mother. Marion Turner lives with the family, and he killed a Mexican man at Blazers Mill "just to see him kick." He had no cattle ***when the War started****. The Jones, John and Jim, killed a man named Riley, a partner of theirs, on the Penasco 3 or 4 years ago.*

THE "BILLIE" LETTER TO LEW WALLACE

On a likely March 24, 1879, Billy wrote a letter to Wallace about Lincoln County War events. It exists now as a one-page fragment, signed "Billie." I dated and authenticated it in my 2012 book, *Billy the Kid's Writings, Words, and Wit.* It stated:

... on the Pecos. All that I can remember are the So Called Dolan Outfit but they are all up here now. and on the Rio Grande this man Cris Moten I believe his name is he drove a herd of 80 head one Year ago last December in Company with Frank Wheeler Frank Baker deceased Jesse Evans George Davis alias Tom Jones. Tom Hill, his name in Texas being Tom Chelson also deceased, they drove the cattle to the Indian Reservation and sold them to John Riley and JJ Dolan. and the cattle were turned in for Beef for the Indians the Beckwith family made their boasts that they came to Seven Rivers a little over four years ago with one Milch Cow borrowed from John Chisum they had when I was there Year ago one thousand six hundred head of cattle. the male members of the family are Henry Beckwith and John Beckwith Robert Beckwith was killed the time McSween's house was burned. Charles [blank] Robert Olinger and Wallace Olinger are of the same gang. their cattle ranch is Situated at Rock Corral twelve miles below Seven Rivers on the Pecos. Paxton and Pierce are Still below them forty miles from Seven Rivers there are four of them Paxton: Pierce: Jim Raymers, and Buck Powel. they had when I seen them last about one thousand head of cattle: at Rocky Arroyo there is another Ranch belonging to [blank] Smith who Operated on the Penasco last year with the Jesse Evans gang those and the places I mentioned are all I know of this man Chris Moten at the time they stole those Cattle was in the employ of Dolan and Co. I afterwards Seen Some of the cattle at the Rinconada Bonita on the reservation those were the men we were in search of when we went to the Agency. the Beckwith family were attending to their own Business when this War started but G.W. Peppin told them that this was John Chisums War. and so they took a hand thinking they would lose their Cattle in case that he Chisum won the fight. this is all the information I can give you on this point

Yours Respectfully Billie

LOST GRAND JURY TESTIMONY

Billy fulfilled his side of the Lew Wallace pardon bargain by testifying against the murderers of Attorney Huston Chapman - James Dolan, Billy Campbell, and Jessie Evans - in the April 1879 Lincoln County Grand Jury. By doing that, he was also implicating the Santa Fe Ring and risking his life. His testimony achieved those men's murder indictments (James Dolan and Billy Campbell for murder; Jessie Evans for accessory to murder).

That testimony was confirmed in *The Grant County Herald* of May 10, 1879, as reprinted from the Mesilla *Thirty Four*: "At the recent term of court in Lincoln, about 200 indictments were found. Among them, Col. Dudley and George W. Peppin for burning McSween's house, **Dolan and Campbell for the Chapman murder, in which the Kid is the principal witness**."

TESTIMONY AGAINST N.A.M. DUDLEY

Proof of Billy Bonney's anti-Ring commitment was his testifying against past Fort Stanton Commander N.A.M. Dudley on May 28th and 29th, 1879, since it was not part of his pardon bargain, and it risked his life. But he was seeking justice for Dudley's illegal military intervention in the Lincoln County War Battle, enabling the murders of Billy's freedom fighting compatriots: Alexander McSween, Harvey Morris, Francisco Zamora, and Vincente Romero. Billy twice made the unprotected, nine mile trip from his Lincoln sham custody to the courtroom in the Fort Stanton Adjutant's office for his court appearances.

His Regulator zeal, plus his courage and intellectual brilliance, made him unshakable under Dudley's lawyer's abusive cross-examination. Billy's precise and devastating testimony alone should have yielded a court martial after this interchange: "*How many soldiers fired at you? ... Three ... How many shots did those soldiers fire, that you say shot from the Tunstall building? ... I could not swear to that on account of firing on all sides, I could not hear. I seen them fire one volley ... Were the soldiers which you say fired at you as you escaped from the McSween house on the evening of July 19th last, colored or white? ... White troops.*"

A volley meant the three soldiers fired in unison. That required Dudley's order. "White" meant they were officers. That directly linked Dudley to ordering his soldiers to murder civilians. That was his treasonous Posse Comitatus Act violation.

So dangerous was this evidence, that Dudley's lawyer's closing argument devoted a large part to a false attack on Billy.

Noteworthy, is that the Ring had already bestowed his outlaw moniker, "Billy the Kid," and Billy was still uncertain about it under questioning. His transcript stated:

WILLIAM BONNEY, a witness being duly sworn, testified as follows.

Q. by Recorder. What is your name and place of residence?

Answer. My name is William Bonney. I reside in Lincoln.

Q. by Recorder. Are you known or called Billy Kidd, also Antrim?

Answer. Yes Sir.

Q. by Recorder. Where were you on the 19th day of July last and what, if anything, did you see of the movements and actions of the troops in that city, state fully?

Answer. I was in the McSween house in Lincoln, and I saw soldiers come from the post with the sheriff's party, that is the sheriff's posse joined them a short distance below there, the McSween house. Soldiers passed on by and the men dropped off and surrounded the house, the sheriff's party. Shortly after, the soldiers came back with Peppin, passed the house twice afterwards. Three soldiers came and stood in front of the house, in front of the windows. Mr. McSween wrote a note to the officer in charge asking what the soldiers were placed there for. He replied saying that they had business there, that if a shot was fired over his camp, or at Peppin, or at any of his men, that he had no objection to blowing up, if he wanted, his own house. I read the note myself, he handed it to me to read. I saw nothing further of the soldiers until night. I was in the back part of the house. ***When I escaped from the house three soldiers fired at me from the Tunstall store, outside corner of the store.*** *That's all I know in regards to it.*

Q. by Recorder. Did the soldiers that stood in front of the windows have guns with them while there?

Answer. Yes Sir.

Q. by Recorder. Who escaped from the house with you and who was killed at the time, if you know, while attempting to make their escape?

Answer. Jose Chavez [Chávez y Chávez] escaped with me, Vincente Romero, Francisco Zamora and McSween.

Q. by Recorder. How many persons were killed in that fight that day, if you know, and who killed them, if you know?

Answer. I seen five killed, I could not swear to who killed them, I seen some of them that fired.

Q. by Recorder. Who did you see that fired?

Answer. Robt. Beckwith, John Hurley, John Jones, ***those three soldiers, I don't know their names.***

Q. by Recorder. Did you see any persons setting fire to the McSween house that day, if so, state who it was, if you know?

Answer. I did, Jack Long, and there was another man I did not recognize.

Recorder stated he had finished with the witness.
Cross examination.

Q. By Col. Dudley. What were you, and the others there with you, doing in McSween's house that day?

Answer. We came here with McSween.

Q. By Col. Dudley. Did you know, or had you not heard, that the sheriff was endeavoring to arrest yourself and others there with you at the time?

Answer. Yes Sir. I had heard so, I did not know.

Q. By Col. Dudley. Then were you not engaged in resisting the sheriff at the time you were in the house?

Objected to by Recorder. The Court has already ruled that nothing extraneous from the actual occurrence that took place, and Col. Dudley's actions in connection therewith, should be further inquired into ... it cannot be a matter of defense of Col. Dudley or justify his actions however much the parties may have been resisting the sheriff or civil authorities.

Lt. Col. Dudley, by his Counsel, states he does not deem it necessary to make reply to the objection.

Objection sustained.

Q. By Col. Dudley. In addition to the names you have given, are you also known as the "Kid?"

Answer. I have already answered that question, Yes Sir, I am, but not "Billy Kid" that I know of.

Q. By Col. Dudley. Were you not and were not the parties with you in the McSween house on the 19th day of July last and the days immediately preceding, engaged in firing at the sheriff's posse?

Court objects to the question.

Lt. Col. Dudley, by his Counsel, asks, does the Court intend to rule here, that after once gone into this matter of firing into the McSween house by the testimony of this witness, it is not permissible to show all the circumstances under which this firing took place ...

Court cleared and closed.

Court opened and its decision announced ...

The Court directs the case to proceed calling attention to its previous rulings which were deemed sufficient by explicit.

Q. By Col. Dudley. Whose name was signed to the note received by McSween in reply to the one previously sent by him to Col. Dudley?

Answer. Signed N.A.M. Dudley, did not say what rank, he received two notes, one had no name signed to it.

Q. By Col. Dudley. Are you as certain of everything else you have sworn to as you are to what you have sworn to in answer to the last proceeding question?

Answer. Yes Sir.

Q. By Col. Dudley. From which direction did Peppin come the first time the soldiers passed with him?

Answer. Passed up from the direction of where the soldiers camped, the first time I saw him.

Q. By Col. Dudley. What direction did he come from the second time?

Answer. From the direction of the [Wortley] hotel from the McSween house.

Q. By Col. Dudley. In what direction did you go upon your escape from the McSween house?

Answer. Ran towards the Tunstall store, was fired at, and there turned towards the river.

Q. By Col. Dudley. From what part of the McSween house did you make your escape?

Answer. The northeast corner of the house.

Q. By Col. Dudley. How many soldiers fired at you?

Answer. Three.

Q. By Col. Dudley. How many soldiers were with Peppin when he passed the McSween house each time, as you say?

Answer. Three.

Q. By Col. Dudley. The soldiers appeared to go in company of threes that day, did they not?

Answer. All that I ever saw appeared to be three in a crowd at a time after they passed the first time.

Q. By Col. Dudley. Who was killed first that day, Bob Beckwith or McSween men?

Answer. Harvey Morris, McSween man, was killed first.

Q. By Col. Dudley. How far is the Tunstall building from the McSween house?

Answer. I could not say how far, I never measured the distance. I should judge it to be 40 yards, between 30 and 40 yards.

Q. By Col. Dudley. How many shots did those soldiers fire, that you say shot from the Tunstall building?

Answer. I could not swear to that on account of firing on all sides, I could not hear. I seen them fire one volley.

Q. By Col. Dudley. What did they fire at?

Answer. Myself and Jose Chavez [Chávez y Chávez].

Q. By Col. Dudley. Did you not just now state in answer to the question who killed Zamora, Romero, Morris, and McSween that you did not know who killed them, but you saw Beckwith, John Jones, ***and three soldiers fire at them****?*

Answer. Yes Sir. I did.

Q. By Col. Dudley. Were these men, the McSween men, there with you ***when the volley was fired at you and Chavez by the soldiers****?*

Answer. Just a short ways behind us.

Q. By Col. Dudley. Were you looking back at them?

Answer. No Sir.

Q. By Col. Dudley. How then do you know they were just behind you then, or that they were in range of the volley?

Answer. Because there was a high fence behind, and a good many guns to keep them there. I could hear them speak.

Q. By Col. Dudley. How far were you from the soldiers when you saw them?

Answer. I could not swear exactly, between 30 and 40 yards.

Q. By Col. Dudley. Did you know either of the soldiers that were in front of the window of McSween's house that day? If so, give it.

Answer. No Sir, I am not acquainted with them.

Redirect.

Q. by Recorder. Explain whether all the men that were in the McSween house came out at the same time when McSween and the others were killed and the firing came from the soldiers and others?

Answer. Yes Sir, all came out at the same time. ***The firing was done by the soldiers until some had escaped.***

Recorder stated that he had finished with the witness.

Q. by Col. Dudley. How do you know if you were making your escape at the time and the men Zamora, Morris and McSween were behind you that they were killed at that time, is it not true that you did not know of their death or the death of either of them until afterwards?

Answer. I knew of the death of some of them, I did know of the death of one of them. I saw him lying down there.

Q. by Col. Dudley. Did you see any of the men last mentioned killed?

Answer. Yes Sir, I did, I seen Harvey Morris killed first, he was out in front of me.

Q. by Col. Dudley. Did you not then a moment ago swear that he was among those who were behind you and Jose Chavez [Chávez y Chávez] when you saw the soldiers deliver the volley?

Answer. No Sir, I didn't think I did. I misunderstood the question if I did. I said he was among them that was killed not behind me.

Witness then withdrew ...

In Billy's second day of testimony on May 29th, he confirmed that Dudley's white officers fired at escaping McSweens, including himself; and that visibility came from the burning McSween house that made the area "*almost light as day*." The transcript stated:

Q. by Court. Were the soldiers which you say fired at you as you escaped from the McSween house on the evening of July 19th last, colored or white?

Answer. White troops.

Q. by Court. Was it light enough so you could distinctly see the soldiers when they fired?

Answer. The house was burning. Made it almost light as day for a short distance all around.

LETTER OF DECEMBER 12,1880 TO LEW WALLACE

After Governor Lew Wallace betrayed the pardon bargain, Billy was publicly outlawed in lurid press. On December 12, 1880, he wrote to Wallace to deny a December 3, 1880 *Las Vegas Gazette* article by J.H. Koogler, titled "Desperadoe's Stronghold."

Billy's letter made clear that he did not consider himself an outlaw. He wrote: *"I noticed in the Las Vegas Gazette a piece which stated that, Billy "the" Kid, the name by which I am known in the Country was the captain of a Band of Outlaws who hold Forth at the Portales.* ***There is no such Organization in Existence. So the Gentleman must have drawn very heavily on his Imagination.***" In addition, the letter shows his self-assured legal knowledge, describing to Wallace that he considered the posse illegal, for lack of proper arrest warrants: *"I asked for their Papers [warrants] and they had none. So I concluded that it amounted to nothing more than a mob."*

By that December 12th, he had endured Secret Service pursuit, another lost pardon through a possible Secret Service bargain, two White Oaks posse ambushes, and a false murder accusation for Jim Carlyle. Seven days later, Garrett's posse would ambush Billy's group near Fort Sumner, killing Tom O'Folliard, intending to kill him. Ten days away was Billy's Stinking Springs capture, where Garrett would shoot dead Charlie Bowdre when mistaking him for Billy. Billy wrote:

Fort Sumner
Dec. 12th 1880
Gov. Lew Wallace
Dear Sir

I noticed in the Las Vegas Gazette a piece which stated that, Billy "the" Kid, the name by which I am known in the Country was the captain of a Band of Outlaws who hold Forth at the Portales. There is no such Organization in Existence. So the Gentleman must have drawn very heavily on his Imagination. *My business at the White Oaks at the time I was waylaid and my horse killed was to See Judge Leonard who has my case in hand. he had written me to come up, that he thought he could get Everything Straightened up I did not find him at the Oaks & Should have gone to Lincoln if I had met with no accident. After mine and Billie Wilsons horses were killed we both made our way to a Station, forty miles from the Oaks kept by Mr Greathouse. When I got up the next morning The house was Surrounded by an outfit led by one Carlyle, Who had come into the house and Demanded a Surrender. I asked for their Papers [warrants] and they had none. So I concluded that it amounted to nothing more than a mob and told Carlyle that he would have to Stay in the house and lead the way out that night. Soon after a* *note was brought in Stating that if Carlyle did not come out inside of five minutes they would Kill the Station Keeper)Greathouse) who had left the house and was with them. in a Short time a Shot was fired on the outside and Carlyle thinking Greathouse was Killed jumped through the window. breaking the Sash as he went and was killed by his own Party they think it was me trying to make my Escape. the Party then withdrew.*

they returned the next day and burned an old man named Spencer's house and Greathouses also

I made my way to this Place afoot and During my absence Deputy Sheriff Garrett Acting under Chisum's orders went to the Portales and found Nothing. on his way back he went by Mr Yerby's ranch and took a pair of mules of mine which I had left with Mr Bowdre who is in Charge of mr Yerby's cattle. he (Garrett) claimed that they were stolen and even if they were not he had no right to Confiscate any Outlaws property.

I had been at Sumner Since I left Lincoln making my living Gambling the mules were bought by me the truth of which I can prove by the best citizens around Sumner. J.S. Chisum is the man who got me into Trouble and was benefited Thousands by it and is now doing all he can against me There is no Doubt but what there is a great deal of Stealing going on in the Territory. and a great deal of the Property is taken across the [Staked] Plains as it is a good outlet but so far as my being at the head of a Band there is nothing of it in Several Instances I have recovered Stolen Property when there was no chance to get an Officer to do it.

one instance for Hugo Zuber Post office Puerto de Luna. another for Pablo Analla Same Place.

if Some impartial Party were to investigate this matter they would find it far Different from the impression put out by Chisum and his Tools.

Yours Respect

William Bonney

SANTA FE JAIL LETTER: JANUARY 1, 1881

After capture, Billy was kept in the Santa Fe jail, awaiting transport to Mesilla for his hanging trial. On January 1, 1881, four days after arriving, he wrote to Lew Wallace:

Santa Fe
Jan 1st 1881

Gov. Lew Wallace
Dear Sir
I would like to see you for a few moments if You can spare the time.
Yours Respect.
W.HBonney

SANTA FE JAIL LETTER: MARCH 2, 1881

On March 2, 1881, Billy sent his second jail letter, which Wallace considered "blackmail." Billy wrote:

Santa Fe Jail New Mex
March 2nd 1881
Gov. Lew Wallace
Dear Sir
I wish you would come down to the jail to see me. it will be to your interest to come and see me. ***I have some letters which date back two years, and there are Parties who are very anxious to get them but I shall not dispose of them until I see you. that is if you will come immediately***
Yours Respect
Wm H Bonney

SANTA FE JAIL LETTER: MARCH 4, 1881

On March 4, 1881, Billy wrote his third jail letter in tragic confirmation of the pardon's betrayal: "*I have done everything that I promised you I would, and You have done nothing that You promised me.*" Billy wrote:

Santa Fe. In jail.

March 4th 1881

Gov. Lew Wallace

Dear Sir

I wrote You a little note the day before yesterday but have received no annser. I Expect you have forgotten what you promised me, this Month two Years ago. but I have not, and I think You had ought to have come and seen me as I requested you to. ***I have done everything that I promised you I would, and You have done nothing that You promised me.***

I think when You think the matter over, You will come down and See me, and I can then Explain Everything to You.

Judge Leonard, Passed through here on his way East, in january and promised to come and See me on his way back. but he did not fulfill his Promise. it looks to me like I am getting left in the Cold. I am not treated right by [U.S. Marshal John] Sherman. he lets Every Stranger that comes to See me through Curiosity in to See me, but will not let a Single one of my friends in, not Even an Attorney.

I guess they mean to Send me up without giving me any Show. but they will have a nice time doing it. I am not entirely without friends.

I shall Expect to See you Sometime today

Patiently Waiting

I am Very truly Yours, Respect.

Wm H. Bonney.

SANTA FE JAIL LETTER: MARCH 27, 1881

On March 27, 1881, Billy wrote to Wallace for the last time, emphasizing the pardon bargain, possibly hoping that it would be issued after sentencing in the Mesilla trial. He wrote:

Santa Fe New Mexico

March 27th/81

Gov Lew Wallace

Dear Sir

for the last time I ask: Will you keep Your promise. I start below tomorrow. Send Annser by bearer.

Yours Respt

WBonney

LETTER TO ATTORNEY EDGAR CAYPLESS

After Billy's unjust hanging sentence for the Regulators' killing of Sheriff William Brady, handed down by Ringite Judge Warren Bristol on April 13, 1881, Billy wanted to appeal. Two days later, on April 15th, he wrote to Las Vegas attorney, Edgar Caypless, whom he had earlier hired on contingency to file his audacious replevin (rustling) suit for recovery of his bay mare from Pat Garrett's posseman, Frank Stewart, who had stolen her at Billy's Stinking Springs capture. Billy hoped to sell her to pay an appeal lawyer, with grounds that his Spanish-speaking jurymen had been deprived of a translator.

Caypless prevailed in the replevin case, but only after Billy's death; and he kept the mare's sales price as fee.

For his last known letter, Billy wrote:

Dear Sir. I would have written before this but could get no paper. My United States case was thrown out of court and I was rushed to trial on my Territorial charge. was convicted of murder in the first degree and am to be hanged on the 13th day of May. Mr. A.J. Fountain was appointed to defend me and has done the best he could for me. He is willing to carry the case further if I can raise the money to bear his expense. The mare is about all I can depend on at present so hope you will settle the case right away and give him the money you get for her. If you do not settle the matter with Scott Moore [to whom Frank Stewart sold the mare] and have to go to court about it either give him [Fountain] the mare or sell her at auction and give him the money. please do as he wishes in the matter. I know you will do the best you can for me in this. I shall be taken to Lincoln tomorrow. Please write and direct care of Garrett, sheriff. excuse bad writing. I have my handcuffs on. I remain as ever

Yours respectfully,
W.H. Bonney

NEWSPAPER INTERVIEWS

Billy Bonney's press interviews occurred after his Stinking Springs capture, and after his Mesilla hanging verdict. He was already nationally famous, and making ironic commentary like in his April 3, 1881's *Santa Fe Daily New Mexican's* "Something About the Kid": "At least two hundred men have been killed in Lincoln County during the past three years, but I did not kill all of them."

On December 27, 1880, the *Las Vegas Daily Gazette* published editor, Lucius "Lute" Wilcox's, article about the Stinking Springs capture and prisoner transport to Las Vegas, titled: 'The Kid. Interview with Billy Bonney The Best Known Man in New Mexico." Billy teased his outlaw myth; stating about onlookers: "Well, perhaps some of them will think me half man now; everyone seems to think I was some sort of animal." Wilcox wrote:

With its customary enterprise, the *Gazette* was the first paper to give the story of the capture of Billy Bonney, who has risen to notoriety under the sobriquet of "the Kid," Billy Wilson, Dave Rudabaugh and Tom Pickett. Just at this time everything of interest about the men is especially interesting, and after damning the men in general and "the Kid" in particular through the columns of this paper we considered it the correct thing to give them a show.

Through the kindness of [San Miguel County] Sheriff Romero, a representative of the *Gazette* was admitted to the jail yesterday morning.

Mike Cosgrove, the obliging mail contractor, who has met the boys frequently while on business down the Pecos, had just gone in with four large bundles. The doors at the entrance stood open, and the large crowd strained their necks to get a glimpse of the prisoners, who stood in the passageway like children waiting for a Christmas tree distribution. One by one the bundles were unpacked disclosing a good suit of clothes for each man. Mr. Cosgrove remarked that he wanted "to see the boys go away in style."

"Billy the Kid," and Billy Wilson who were shackled together stood patiently while a blacksmith took off their shackles and bracelets to allow them an opportunity to make a change of clothing. Both prisoners watched the operation which was to set them free for a short while, but Wilson scarcely raised his eyes, and spoke but once or twice to his compadres. **Bonney on the other hand, was light and chipper, and was very communicative, laughing, joking and chatting with the bystanders.**

"You appear to take it easy," the reporter said.

"Yes! What's the use of looking at the gloomy side of everything. The laugh's on me this time," he said. Then looking about the placita, he asked: "Is the jail at Santa Fe any better than this?"

This seemed to trouble him considerably, for as he explained, "this is a terrible place to put a fellow in." He put the same question to every one who came near him and when he learned that there was nothing better in store for him, he shrugged his shoulders and said something about putting up with what he had to.

He was the attraction of the show, and as he stood there, lightly kicking the toes of his boots on the stone pavement to keep his feet warm, one would scarcely mistrust that he was the hero of "Forty Thieves," romance which this paper has been running in serial form for six weeks or more.

"There was a big crowd gazing at me wasn't there?" he exclaimed, and then smiling continued: "Well perhaps some of them will think me half a man now; everyone seems to think I was some kind of an animal."

He did look human, indeed, but there was nothing very mannish about him in appearance, for he looked and acted like a mere boy. He is about five feet, eight or nine inches tall, slightly built and lithe, weighing about 140; a frank and open countenance, looking like a school boy, with the traditional silky fuzz on his upper lip, clear blue eyes, with a roguish snap about them, light hair and complexion. He is, in all, quite a handsome looking fellow, the only imperfection being two prominent front teeth, slightly protruding like a squirrels' teeth, and he has agreeable and winning ways.

On December 28, 1880, for the *Las Vegas Gazette*, from inside the train to Santa Fe, for "Interview with the Kid," Billy's steely self-control is evident when one realizes it was detained by a mob, either to lynch or to rescue him. The article stated:

> We saw him again at the depot when the crowd presented a really war like appearance. Standing by the car, out of one of the windows from which he was leaning, he talked freely with us of the whole affair:
>
> "I don't blame you for writing of me as you have. You have had to believe others' stories, but then **I don't know as anyone would believe anything good of me, anyway," he said. "I really wasn't the leader of any gang.** I was for Billy all the time. About that Portales business, I owned the ranch with Charlie Bowdre. I took it up and was holding it because I knew that at some time a stage line would run there, and I wanted to keep it for a station. **But I found that there were certain men who wouldn't let me live in the country and so I was going to leave.**
>
> We had all our grub in the house when they took us in, and we were going to a place six miles away in the morning to cook it and then light out. I haven't stolen any stock. I made my living by gambling, but that was the only way I could live. **They wouldn't let me settle down; if they had I wouldn't be here today," and he held up his right arm on which was the bracelet.**
>
> "Chisum got me into all this trouble and then wouldn't help me out. I went up to Lincoln to stand my trial on the warrant that was out for me, but the Territory took a change of venue to Dona Ana, and I knew I had no show, and so I skinned out ...
>
> If it had not been for the dead horse in the doorway I wouldn't be here in Las Vegas. I would have ridden out on my bay mare and taken my chances of escaping. But I couldn't ride over that for she would have jumped back **and I would have got it in the head**. We could have stayed in the house but there wouldn't have been anything gained by that for they would have starved us out. I thought it was better to come out and get a square meal - don't you?"
>
> The prospects of a fight exhilarated him, and he bitterly bemoaned being chained. "If I only had my Winchester, I'd lick the whole crowd" was his confident comment on the strength of the attacking party. He sighed and sighed again for the chance to take a hand in the fight and the burden of his desire was to be set free to fight on the side of his captors as soon as he should smell powder.
>
> As the train rolled out, he lifted his hat and invited us to call and see him in Santa Fe, calling out "*adios.*"

Billy's loyal attorney, Ira Leonard, protectively accompanied him on the train ride to Mesilla, via the Rincón depot. From there, they took the stagecoach ride to Las Cruces. With them were guards and prisoner, Billy Wilson, also transported to Mesilla. At Las Cruces, a crowd had gathered to see the famous outlaw, Billy the Kid. The arrival was covered in the April 3, 1881 *Santa Fe Daily New Mexican* in: "Something About the Kid." It stated:

An extract of a letter written by W.S. Fletcher from Mesilla to a gentleman in the city reads about as follows: Tony Neis and Francisco Chaves, deputy U.S. Marshals, arrived Thursday night with **Billy, the Kid,** and Billy Wilson. They met an ugly crowd at Rincon, where some threats were made, but Tony's crowd were too much for them. **At Las Cruces an impulsive mob gathered around the coach and someone asked which is "Billy the Kid." The Kid himself answered by placing his hand on Judge Leonard's shoulder and saying "this is the man."** The Kid weakened somewhat at Las Cruces, where he found quite a number of Lincoln County men, who were to appear against him as witnesses.

[AUTHOR'S NOTE: Billy had no defense witnesses. The prosecution had Ringites James Dolan, Saturnino Baca, and Sheriff William Brady's deputy, Billy Matthews; and subpoenaed Lincolnite, Isaac Ellis.]

He says at least two hundred men have been killed in Lincoln County during the past three years, but that he did not kill all of them. I think twenty murders can be charged against him. He was arraigned yesterday (Wednesday) before the United States court for the murder of Roberts, on the Mescalero Apache reservation, in 1878. Judge Leonard was assigned to his defense. Judge Newcomb gave notice that he had three other indictments for murder against him, and it looks as if he had no show to get off. His counsel asked today for time to send to Lincoln, which was granted, so that his trial will not commence for at least ten days. Billy Wilson's case is before the grand jury. He is charged with passing counterfeit money. He has retained Judge Thornton as his counsel. He seems to have friends here while the Kid has none.

No mails between Rincon and Doña Ana for the past week. Mosquitoes and flies abound and weather hot as blazes.

Billy's articulate response to the hanging verdict was in an April 16, 1881 article in the *Mesilla News*. He summarized Santa Fe Ring injustice: "I think it hard that I should be the only one to suffer the extreme penalty of the law." He called his court "mob law;" ending with facetious "personal advice": "If mob law is going to rule, better dismiss judge and sheriff and let all take chances alike." And he said sarcastically: "Advise persons never to engage in killing." About Lew Wallace's pardon, he said curtly: "Don't know that he will do it." The article stated:

> Well I had intended at one time not to say a word on my own behalf because persons would say, "Oh he lied." Newman, editor of the *Semi-Weekly*, gave me a rough deal; he created prejudice against me, and is trying to incite a mob to lynch me. He sent me a paper which showed it; I think it a dirty mean advantage to take of me, **considering my situation and knowing that I could not defend myself by word or act. But I suppose he thought he would give me a kick down hill.** Newman came to see me the other day. I refused to talk to him or tell him anything. But I believe the *News* is always willing to give its readers both sides of a question. **If mob law is going to rule, better dismiss judge and sheriff and let all take chances alike.** I expect to be lynched going to Lincoln. **Advise persons never to engage in killing.**
>
> **Considering the active part Governor Wallace took on our side and the friendly relations that existed between him and me, and the promise he made me, I think he ought to pardon me. Don't know that he will do it.** When I was arrested for that murder he let me out and gave me freedom of the town, and let me go about with my arms. When I got ready to leave Lincoln in June, 1879, I left. **I think it hard that I should be the only one to suffer the extreme penalty of the law.**

For his secret transport to Lincoln for hanging by Pat Garrett, to prevent his partisans' rescue, in darkness, on April 17, 1881, Billy was taken by wagon from the Mesilla jail. April 20, 1881's *Newman's Semi-Weekly* reported his departure, with Billy, as usual, joking:

On Saturday night about 10 o'clock Deputy U.S. marshal Robt. Ollinger [sic] with deputy sheriff David Wood and a posse of five men (Tom Williams, Billy Mathews [sic], John Kinney, D.M. Reade and W.A. Lockhart) started for Lincoln with Henry Antrim *alias* the Kid. The fact that they intended to leave at that time had been purposely concealed and the report circulated that they would not leave before the middle of the week in order to avoid any possibility of trouble, it having been rumored that the Kid's band would attempt a rescue. They stopped in front of our office while we talked to them, and we handed the Kid an addressed envelope with some paper and he said he would write some things he wanted to make public. **He appeared quite cheerful and remarked that he wanted to stay until their whiskey gave out, anyway.** Said he was sure that his guard would not hurt him unless a rescue should be attempted and he was certain that it would not be done, unless, perhaps, "those fellows at White Oaks come out to take me," meaning to kill him. **It was, he said, about a stand-off whether he was hanged or killed in the wagon ...** He was hand-cuffed to the back seat of the ambulance. Kinney sat beside him, Olinger on the seat facing him, Mathews on the seat facing Kinney, Lockhart driving, and Reade, Wood and Williams riding along on horseback on each side and behind. The whole party was armed to the teeth and anyone who knows the men of whom it was composed will admit that a rescues would be a hazardous undertaking. Kid was informed that if trouble should occur he would be shot first and the attacking party attended to afterwards.

CONCLUSION

The real Billy Bonney's high intelligence, literacy, and fund of knowledge,- proved by his own writings and recorded words - contrasts the mental dullness and ignorance of information of his imposters; and is their undoing.

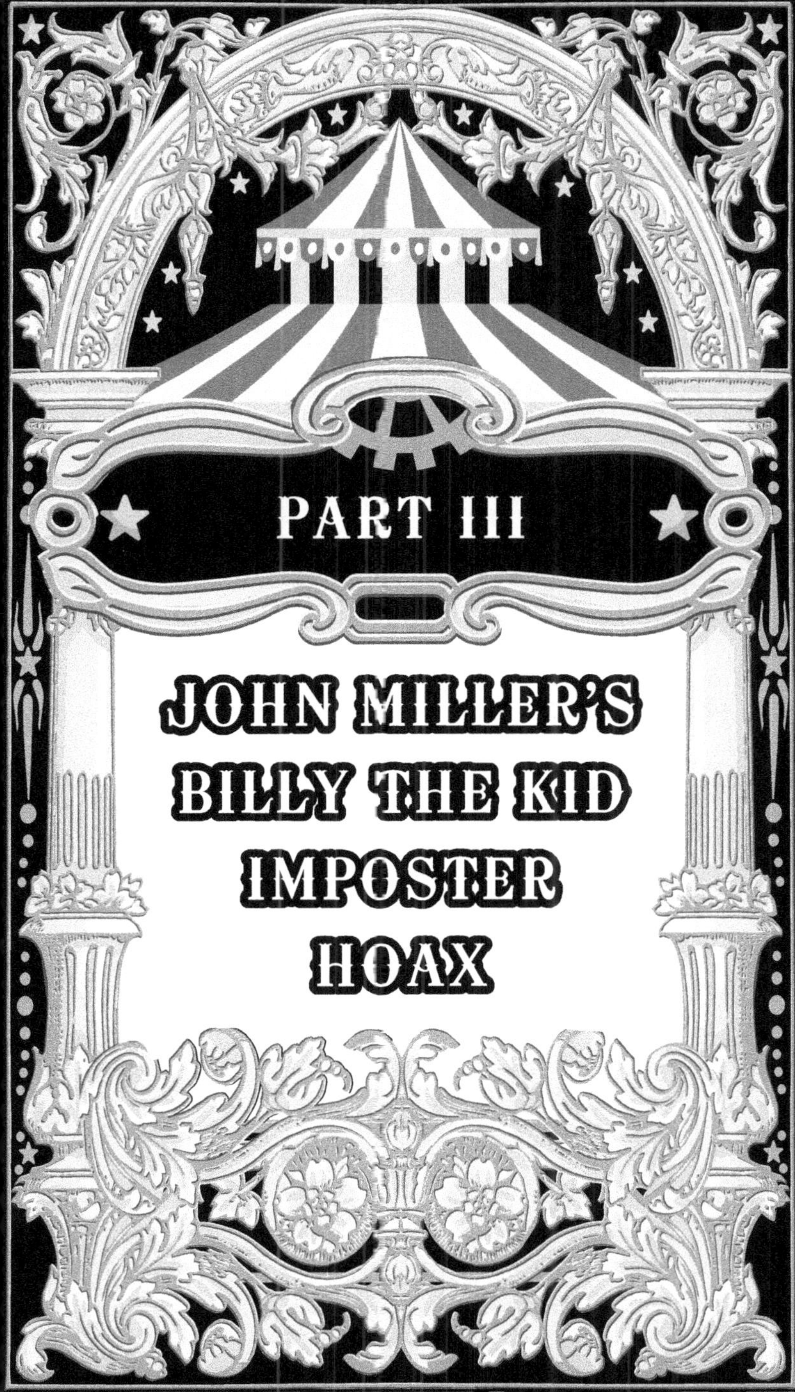
PART III
JOHN MILLER'S
BILLY THE KID
IMPOSTER
HOAX

CHAPTER 1
JOHN MILLER'S BID TO BE BILLY THE KID

A CLOWNING IMPOSTER

John Miller put so little effort into his Billy the Kid impersonation, that one wonders if he was just clowning around with those close to him. Since he left no writings, his claim comes only through those intimates, who were led by him to believe he was Billy. But they knew no Billy the Kid history themselves for fact-checking. It was a harmless gambit for reflected glory, with none of the venality that characterized other pretender hoaxes.

John Miller would have been rightly forgotten if he had not gotten an author in 1993: Helen Airy with her *Whatever Happened to Billy the Kid?* That was 56 years after his death on November 7, 1937 in the Arizona Pioneers' Home, in which he was placed at 87, following a disabling fall from a roof.

His November 8, 1937 *Prescott Evening Courier* obituary was titled: "Man Raised by Indians Passes." It gave his history, as he told it to his Arizona Pioneers' Home caretakers. It had no match whatsoever to Billy Bonney's, and made no claim of being Billy the Kid. Its details would subsequently be hidden by others promoting his imposter hoax. The obituary stated:

> John Miller, who was adopted as an infant or very young boy by an Indian tribe after one of his parents had been killed outright and the other burned to death as a sacrifice by the Indians, died at 6:30 p.m. Sunday in the Arizona Pioneers' Home.
>
> Despite the circumstances of his childhood he was hazy about exact facts of his life, though he believed he was born in December, 1850, at Fort Sill, which he said was in Texas though there is a Fort Sill also in Oklahoma.
>
> Miller did not know his parent's names, the date he entered this state but he believed it was a short time after the capture of Geronimo [September 4, 1886], or the tribe of Indians it was except

that it was not an Arizona tribe.

Though the Indians had meted his parents a most cruel death, he remembered them as always being kind to him, though indeed he had to live for long periods of time on nothing more than parched corn and shiver in the winter time in skins. But he did not regard such existence as a hard life necessarily because it was all he and the Indians with whom he lived knew.

One time the Indians painted him all up for some sort of ceremonial dance and some of the paint accidentally got into his eyes. It was of a nature that impaired his eyesight henceforth.

[AUTHOR'S NOTE: Even if Miller was fabricating this Indian background, his impaired eyesight alone cancels his Billy the Kid identity claim.]

At one time he was married , but whether it was to an Indian woman never was determined by those in charge of the pioneers' home. But his married life was short, for once when he was away the house caught fire and his wife was burned to death. He never did explain whether it was accidental.

[AUTHOR'S NOTE: Miller appears confused, since this was the death of his wife, Isadora, whom he married in about 1886, and who died in the fire on October 18, 1936, less than a year before his Pioneers' Home admission in 1937, according to Jim Johnson's 2006 book, *Billy the Kid: His Real Name Was ....* (Johnson, Page 6)]

On October 14 Miller fell at the home and broke his hip. That mishap hastened the end.

He entered the home last March 14 from Phoenix but had lived around Buckeye for a good many years and listed Ralph Watkins, secretary of the chamber of commerce there, as a friend. There are no known relatives.

The incidents about his life he remembered only hazily and as related here have been patched together from odds and ends of information told those at the home. He was not a man to make up stories about himself, however, consequently what he has told has been taken as truth.

Burial arrangements are being held in abeyance at the Hunter Mortuary.

This notice was followed by the November 9, 1937 *Prescott Evening Courier's* "Brief Items in the Daily Life of Prescott;" stating merely: "John Miller, Arizona pioneer who died here Sunday [November 7], will be buried Wednesday afternoon in Pioneers' cemetery in Miller Valley. Services are scheduled in the chapel of the Hunter Mortuary at 2 o'clock."

Besides no match to Billy the Kid history, there was worse. The Arizona Pioneers' Home got his birth date - presumably from him - as December of 1850. Unbeknownst to Miller, Billy Bonney was born nine years after him, on November 23, 1859. John Miller would have been no kid in the Lincoln County War period.

John Miller, obviously, merely belonged to his generation's old-timer windbags spouting attention-grabbing malarkey about being or knowing Billy the Kid.

THEN THE CIRCUS CAME TO TOWN

John Miller's body had laid a-mouldering in his Arizona Pioneers' Home Cemetery grave for 66 years when the "Billy the Kid Case" hoax media circus swung into action. His own fakery, coupled with Helen Airy's hoax, were based on the claim of Pat Garrett's shooting an innocent victim and Billy surviving. That was the premise of the imposter-based "Billy the Kid Case" hoax, starting in 2003, and becoming became desperate by 2005 for any bones whatsoever for its fake forensic DNA matchings, after I had blocked its clowns in district courts from exhuming Billy Bonney and his mother, Catherine Antrim.

So, in 2005, for fodder for their TV production company, these hoaxers illegally exhumed John Miller as a concession prize "Billy the Kid." Possibly they thought it would prime the media pump to facilitate their actual goal: digging up "Brushy Bill" Roberts and faking *him* as the Kid. It failed; and only corrupt political intervention saved the hoaxers from deserved felony convictions for desecration of human remains and grave-robbing.

I exposed their chicanery in my 2014 book, *Cracking the Billy the Kid Case Hoax: The Strange Plot to Exhume Billy the Kid, Convict Sheriff Pat Garrett of Murder, and Become President of the United States*; and in my 2019 book, *The Cold Case Billy the Kid Megahoax: The Plot to Steal Billy the Kid's Identity and Defame Sheriff Pat Garrett as a Murderer*.

But the hoaxers had given John Miller a place in their burgeoning imposter-backing hoax. Alternately, he was claimed by them to be the Kid by faked forensics; or was just used as an example that history was not as written, and Garrett may have shot someone other than Billy on July 14, 1881. But they had to hide that his fake death scene of an accidentally shot Indian friend did not match their fake death scene of Billy being purposefully shot by Garrett to play dead for the townspeople's vigil, while Garrett killed an innocent victim for grave-filler. This mismatch alone removed justification to exhume John Miller as their "Billy the Kid."

And, as will be seen, a random man, named William Hudspeth, made it into Billy the Kid history by mere coincidence of being buried beside John Miller's unmarked and uncertain grave, in one equally unmarked. So he too was dug up with bones stolen by the out-of-control "Billy the Kid Case" hoaxers, as possibly being "John Miller" himself - and leaving them unperturbed about having absconded with two subterranean "Billy the Kids."

CHAPTER 2
MASQUERADING JOHN MILLER AS BILLY THE KID

Author, Helen Airy, made little effort to costume her clown, John Miller, for her 1993 *Whatever Happened to Billy the Kid?* With her almost non-existent knowledge of Billy the Kid history, she relied on old-timer friends of Miller's merely recalling that he and his wife implied he was Billy the Kid. And the Millers' adopted Navajo son, Max Miller, believed it. (Page 14) That was Airy's lethargic hoaxlet. And she seemed unperturbed that nothing in his actual history matched Billy Bonney's.

THE BIRTH BARRIER

Age was John Miller's impassable obstacle. Being born in December of 1850, made him nine years older than Billy. As Billy, would have been older than "his" boss John Tunstall, who himself died at 24 in 1878. Miller would have been the same age as Pat Garrett. And no one would have called him "Kid;" which was transmogrified to the famous "Billy the Kid" moniker in outlaw myth press. In response, Helen Airy, hid that inconvenient truth.

And Miller's birthdate was easily available to Airy, being at the Arizona Pioneers' Home in Prescott where he was placed in March of 1937 - as she herself stated in her book. Miller died at 87, on November 7, 1937 of complicating pneumonia after falling in the Home and breaking his hip. He was buried in their Pioneers' Home Cemetery on November 9, 1937. (**Remember that fatal broken hip. It will figure dramatically in his fabricated inclusion in "Billy the Kid Case's" hoaxing.**)

In addition, John Miller claimed his birthplace as Fort Sill, Texas (which would have been Fort Sill, Oklahoma, at his birth date), to a Comanche mother - all unconnected to Billy Bonney – and unperturbing to Helen Airy.

FAKING GARRETT SHOOTING SURVIVAL

Apparently unaware of William Bonney's actual July 15, 1881 Coroner's Jury Report, which put an end to all imposter hoaxes, Helen Airy started her book with a tiny sly death scene: "It was near midnight on July 14, 1881, when Sheriff Pat Garrett shot someone in Pete Maxwell's darkened bedroom in the old officers' quarters in Fort Sumner, where Maxwell lived." (Page 9) Why that "someone" was not Billy is missing; though later, to John Miller, is attributed a tale of an accidental killing of an Indian-dressed-similarly death scene.

Airy added that there was a cover-up of the victim's identity. What made her think that? She said Garrett and a coroner's jury identified Billy, but there were "doubts." (Page 9) She mentions an unreferenced, unknown document, and says: "When he was asked to sign an affidavit that it was the Kid he had shot, Garrett refused to sign." (Page 9) She also malingers: "McKinney and Poe accused Garrett of shooting the wrong man" (Pages 9, 13) adding McKinney to her own distortion of John Poe's statement of initial identity concern in his 1933 book, *The Death of Billy the Kid*, explained by his not knowing Billy.

Airy concluded: "But all through the years since that night, there have been doubts that it really was Billy the Kid's body they buried the next day." (Page 9) Why doubts? Airy claimed unnamed people "saw Billy" after the death date **[meaningless hearsay]**; some Coroner's Jurymen signed with an X **[so what, they were illiterate]**; the Coroner's Jury Report "was never officially filed, as required by law" **[false]** (Page 27); and the corpse was seen by few people **[false]**. For witnesses, she listed Garrett and his deputies, "immediate family members" **[there were none]**, and added snidely: "supposedly, members of the coroner's jury" **[snideness is no argument]**. She adds: "Years afterward, there were warrants issued for the Kid's arrest" **[made-up]**. (Page 27) Her vague conspiracy theory is that T.B. Catron and the Santa Fe Ring "wanted to see Miller dead" for unstated reason. (Page 38) She concluded unconvincingly: "Surely there was reason to wonder" that Miller was Billy the Kid. (Page 27)

The rest of Helen Airy's 175 page book is about John Miller's irrelevant life after July 14, 1881; though little flash-backs of blighted Billy history are given - and prove nothing.

ROMANCE AND RESEMBLANCE

It appears that John Miller's hoax was a team effort with his wife, Isadora, "a dark-eyed Mexican girl." (Page 9) To friends and neighbors, she claimed that he, as "the Kid," had been shot "**some days before the shoot-out at Pete Maxwell's house**," - without elaboration - and she tended his wounds and hid him from "officers" in her Fort Sumner house's mattress. (Page 9) But, for unstated reason, the Santa Fe Ring of "unscrupulous and treacherous men" and Thomas Benton Catron was after him, as well as Governor Lew Wallace (actually gone from the Territory)." (Pages 11, 13)

Airy calls Isadora the widow of Charlie Bowdre, while admitting that the widow's actual name was Manuela (Page 12); and was unaware that she left Fort Sumner after her husband's killing by Garrett in 1880. Airy stated that Miller married Isadora on August 8, 18881. But debunking author, Jim Johnson, in his 2006 book, *Billy the Kid. His Real Name Was ...* stated that census reports show the marriage was in 1885 or 1886. (Johnson, Page 2)

But why should anyone think John Miller was Billy?

Airy says there were similarities: blue eyes, prominent front teeth, heavy eyebrows (which she says were like his mother's, though Miller claimed she was a Comanche Indian, not Catherine Antrim; and no authenticated picture of Catherine exists for eyebrow matching anyway). He had the pretenders' requisite small hands and thick wrists for shackle-slipping, a trick he did for friends, saying: "Billy the Kid could do that." (Pages 10, 144) Airy descended to the ridiculous, adding that Miller wore a hat like Billy's (from the tintype). That claim is more absurd than it appears, because the tintype hat was likely the photographer's prop. Called the "Carlsbad," it first appeared in 1880 as a peculiar, high crowned, short-brimmed style; and was definitely not for riding the range. Real Billy wore a sombrero. It seems that Miller sewed his version to posture as Billy. Airy preposterously added as a match that Miller carried a gun, had a very bad temper, and tended to point his rifle at people! (Page 11)

John Miller himself would strip to show friends twelve supposed bullet scars on his chest; though real Billy had just a thigh wound from Deputy Jacob Basil Matthews at the Regulators' Sheriff Brady ambush shooting. And no thigh wound is claimed in Miller's collection.

To back physical identity, Helen Airy gave photos of wax busts made by a sympathetic artist named Deborah Robinson, who stated: "I aged the sculpture [of Billy the Kid] to a man of about sixty years ... In my opinion, John Miller and Billy the Kid were the same person." (Pages 161-162) The sculptures demonstrate that, by revising Billy and Miller a resemblance can be faked.

Airy and sculptor Robinson appear unaware that, in 1989, the Lincoln County Heritage Trust: the Lincoln, New Mexico, museum which, at that time, housed the Billy the Kid tintype, did a photo-comparison study headed by world-famous forensic anthropologist, Clyde Snow, along with a Thomas G. Kyle of the Los Alamos National Laboratory, and historical experts. The tintype was compared to the over 150 alleged photographs of Billy the Kid, along with a control of 100 photographs of random men. Historian, Don Cline, in his unpublished 1988 *Brushy Bill Roberts: I Wasn't Billy the Kid*, referenced that study. It concluded no match to John Miller or to "Brushy Bill" Roberts. (Cline, Page 169)

Another Airy "proof" would have outraged real Billy. Miller's last shooting victim was a Mexican worker. (Pages 15, 19) Billy's bi-culturalism was famous. As cited above, "Teddy Blue" Abbott, a cowboy contemporary of Billy's, wrote in his 1955 book, *We Pointed Them North*: "The Lincoln County troubles was still going on, and you had to be either for Billy the Kid or against him. It wasn't my fight ... it was the Mexicans that made a hero of him." (See page 77 above) And as Henry Hoyt wrote in his 1929 book, *A Frontier Doctor*: "He spoke Spanish like a native."

FAKING HISTORY OF BILLY THE KID

Having presented nothing indicating that John Miller was Billy Bonney, Airy summarized her day's Billy the Kid history, as if connected to Miller. But there was no evidence that Miller had known any of it. And she did not reconcile it with Miller's known history of being raised by Indians after they killed his parents.

To her, Billy was a "gunslinger" (Page 19), and the Lincoln County War was the "bloodiest range war of them all." (Page 22) Tunstall and McSween were incorrectly called partners, and the strife was mercantile competition with the Murphy firm, backed by T.B. Catron (Page 22) - in a description apparently relying on Maurice Garland Fulton's note in Pat Garrett's 1927 edition of

The Authentic Life of Billy the Kid. (See pages 47-48 above) After Tunstall's murder, Billy and the Regulators merely seek "revenge." (Page 23) She made-up the Lincoln County War as a three day battle, with McSween's men surrounding a building with Sheriff Peppin's men; until Fort Stanton's Colonel Dudley forced McSween's men to flee in the night (Page 24) **[The flight was actually the morning of Dudley's arrival.]** For the burning building escape, Billy takes command in her fiction.

Unaware of Huston Chapman's murder, Billy's pardon bargain, or real Billy's letters, Airy has him writing to Governor Wallace about wanting justice done, and volunteering to tell a court about Lincoln County troubles. (Page 24) Unsure of what went wrong, she makes-up that people got tired of thinking about the Lincoln County War, so nothing came of testifying or pardon! (Page 24) She also made-up that "Billy the Kid was the only member of the Regulator gang who was not pardoned by Governor Wallace at the end of the Lincoln County War." (Page 147) **[No Regulators were pardoned.]**

In Airy's version, Billy became a cattle rustler tracked by Pat Garrett, and had a ranch for stolen cattle in Las Portales. (Page 24) That only proved that she used the December 22, 1880 *New York Sun* outlaw myth article titled: "Outlaws of New Mexico. The Exploits of a Band Headed by a New York Youth. The Mountain Fastness of the Kid and His Followers - War Against a Gang of Cattle Thieves and Murderers."

Airy mentioned the Stinking Springs capture and Santa Fe jailing, with Billy writing to Wallace that he had letters going back two years that certain parties wanted to see. (Page 25) That was lifted from a June 23, 1900 *The Indianapolis Press* article titled: "Gen. Wallace's Feud with Billy the Kid, When the General Was Governor of New Mexico and Billy Bonne Was the Most Dangerous Western Outlaw;" which stated: "He had been in jail a week when he addressed me: 'Governor, why haven't you come to see me?' I paid no attention to it. A few days later there was a second note: 'Governor, I have some papers you would not want to see displayed. Come to the jail.' " And it was in the June 8, 1902 *New York World Magazine* in "General Lew Wallace Writes a Romance of 'Billy the Kid' Most Famous Bandit of the Plains;" which stated: "Then the outlaw sent him a note. The note said: 'Come to the jail. I have some papers you would not want to see displayed.' "

For the Mesilla trial, she is unaware of the "Buckshot" Roberts case; and, for the Brady trial, makes-up that Judge

Bristol was controlled by the "Brady crowd" and "cowed the local Mexican jury." (Page 25) For the jailbreak, she had a gun in the privy scenario, with a slipped shackle striking Bell; and the shooting of Olinger with his own shotgun. (Page 26)

For the Fort Sumner death scene, she used "Brushy Bill's" version of being at a dance! But the victim is an Indian mistaken for Miller. She called conventional history "Garrett's version."

Then she tried to manufacture doubts. She says the Kid would not go into a darkened room; makes-up that Poe said Garrett was not a good enough shot to hit the Kid; makes-up that Poe and McKinney accused Garrett of shooting the wrong man; says people saw Billy after the death date; and makes-up that years after the death date rewards were offered for arrest of Billy. (Page 27) The coroner's jury is attacked as "hastily recruited," with illiterate signatures with an X, no one viewing the body, and no official report filed. (Page 27)

And she makes no attempt to reconcile the death scene with Miller's claim of being shot days before that event; so his attackers and their motives in his fable remain a mystery.

MILLER'S LIFE AFTER BILLY'S DEATH

Miller's irrelevant life with his wife is covered, as a rancher for over 30 years in McKinley County's Ramah, in northwestern New Mexico, originally a Mormon settlement, between the Zuni and the Ramah Navajo Indian Reservations, with Airy editorializing that he lived in fear that Catron and the Santa Fe Ring were after him. (Pages 38, 147) For a 1900 census for Valencia County, New Mexico Territory, he lied about his birth date, making it 1857. (Page 39) And in the 1910 census, he changed his age to 58. Airy states all this was to throw off people chasing him as Billy the Kid. (Page 39) In the 1900's he moved to Arizona with his wife, Isadora, living in Buckeye, where she died. (Page 154) Airy adds marriages to two Navajo women, living in Borrego Pass, and placement in the Prescott, Arizona Pioneers' Home. (Page 146)

According to Jim Johnson, after he fell off a roof, his placement was arranged on March 12, 1937, with arrival on March 14th. After breaking his right hip in the care facility, he died there, after complicating pneumonia, on November 7, 1937; being buried in their Pioneers' Home Cemetery.

FRIENDS SAY MILLER WAS BILLY

Having offered nothing to indicate that Miller was Billy the Kid, Helen Airy used Miller's friends' recollections, padding her book with details of their irrelevant lives. Most merely said he *told them or told others they knew* that he was Billy the Kid.

HERMAN TECKLENBURG

The oddest story-teller is a Herman Tecklenburg, who made-up that he knew John Miller in Fort Sumner as Billy the Kid; and was later his "most trusted friend." (Page 42)

On August 9, 1944, Tecklenburg, then a janitor, but claiming to have been a cowpuncher and Indian hunter, gave an interview for the *Gallup Independent*, to a Wesley Huff, titled: "Did Garrett Kill Billy the Kid? Herman Tecklenburg Says No; Billy Lived on Ranch at Ramah 35 Years Ago and Visited Him." Huff even tried to build a conspiracy theory of survival around Tecklenburg's fables. Tecklenburg's article, referenced by Airy (Page 43), stated:

Was Billy the Kid killed by Sheriff Pat Garrett in 1881 in Fort Sumner, or did he spend his later years on a ranch south of Ramah? Herman Tecklenburg can give you the answer as he knows it.

Tecklenburg, who has punched cattle, driven the mule freights and hunted Indians all over the southwest in the past 60 years knew Billy the Kid personally in his cowpunching days. He will tell you:

"They shot somebody over in Fort Sumner, and they buried him there and put an end to the hunt for Billy the Kid. But it wasn't Billy they shot.

"He and his Mexican wife escaped over into Old Mexico ... [Later] he was ranching down near Ramah. They all knew of him down there as Billy the Kid, but never spoke of it for fear of getting him in trouble. He was a prince. Big shots made him out to be an outlaw because they couldn't handle him.

"Down at Ramah he was known as John Miller."

[Walter Noble Burns's *Saga of Billy the Kid* is then used for the conventional killing scene.]

TWO THINGS about this shooting never have been explained.

First: Why was it that neither Poe nor McKinney recognized the Kid as he came toward the porch in the bright moonlight of that July night? Under the law of the Old West they would have shot the moment they recognized him as a matter of self preservation. But they thought he was a sheep herder.

[AUTHOR'S NOTE: Huff is unaware that McKinney and Poe and did not know Billy.]

Second: It was the nature of Billy the Kid to shoot first and ask questions afterwards. Yet he asked, "Quien es?" *three* times before ducking into Maxwell's room to ask still another question. Why? Was it a blunder by the Kid or was it really the Kid?

[AUTHOR'S NOTE: Huff is unaware it was an ambush, and Billy had no way of knowing if McKinney and Poe were just visitors. It would have been crazy to shoot random people for no reason. And Billy continued by asking Maxwell also. This is no indication he was not Billy. Nor is it any indication of why a non-Billy would ask the question.]

Herman Tecklenburg doesn't think it was Billy – not only because of these strange circumstances, but because he knows the man who lived in Ramah was the Billy of old, and his wife, Billy's Mexican sweetheart from Fort Sumner who he had known in his cowpunching days.

[Tecklenburg's history is given, with the claim that in 1869, when he was 14, he left Hanover, Germany, to come to America, where he was a cowpuncher.] It was in his cowpunching days that he became acquainted with Billy the Kid in Fort Sumner. The Kid had many friends there, and resentment ran high when outsiders came there to hunt the outlaw, for they knew him as a friend.

"Billy the Kid would kill and butcher a maverick and ride all night leaving cuts of it with the poor people so they could eat," Mr. Tecklenburg said. "That's how bad Billy the Kid was. He was no cattle thief.

"All they have to do is say something bad about Billy and I see red. I knew him as a friend and he was no cow thief or bad man.

"THIRTY-FIVE years ago [Billy the Kid visited him in Page.] Billy the Kid and Len Shumaker came in the house there and stayed with me over night. We traded horses and talked over old times ... [The Kid] and his wife were living on their ranch near Ramah and he went by the name of John Miller. He was 11 years older than me, and if he is still alive he's be about 85.

"He was a prince. Them was the kind of men who made the West. They did the fighting to bring civilization" ...

Mr. Tecklenburg said that Billy the Kid lived as John Miller at his Ramah ranch until about 25 years ago ... when he sold out and moved near to Phoenix. "

[Reporter Huff researched land records and found a John Miller with a cattle contract near Ramah, and a 1914 homestead deed with his wife, Isadora Miller.]

"I USED TO HEAR of the Kid through friends up to about ten years ago," Mr. Tecklenburg said, "but I don't know whether he is alive today or not. He had lots of friends all over the country. But there were a few who wanted him out of the way because they could not handle him. That's why they outlawed him and kept hounding him.

[AUTHOR'S NOTE: The total ignorance of Billy the Kid history is obvious.]

Mr. Tecklenburg chuckled. "If he is alive and sees this story I can just hear what he'll say – "They can't even leave me alone now when I'm old and worn out."

"He was a real man and there aren't many like him anywhere."

Jim Johnson, in his 2006 book, *Billy the Kid, His real Name Was ...* exposed Tecklenburg's lying through family records showing that he was born in Germany on June 9, 1869, and immigrated to the United States as a teenager, **arriving on June 5, 1884**. (Johnson, Page 4) Thus, in 1880 and 1881, he was in Germany, not in Fort Sumner as "Billy the Kid's friend."

FRANK BURRARD "BURT" CREASY

Frank Creasy, was a ranch hand of John Miller's. He alleged that Miller told him his history as Billy the Kid. It is Helen Airy's only sample of Miller's fabrications and demonstrates his total historical ignorance. But his alleged possession of a framed "pardon" hung in his ranch house, implies more extensive forged props than his self-made tintype hat.

The first part of Creasy's narrative had Miller's garbling from Pat Garrett's *The Authentic Life of Billy the Kid* or Walter Noble Burns's 1926 *The Saga of Billy the Kid*; stating: "[I]n 1871, when he was twelve years old ... [a] deputy sheriff apparently insulted Billy's mother for which Billy promptly shot him and fled to the hills." (Page 91) Garrett's and Burns's books stated: **"**When young Billy was about twelve years of age, he first imbrued his hand in human blood" [after an insult to his mother.]"

Creasy continued Miller's malarkey: "[B]illy made his next appearance in Arizona four years later in 1875, when he killed another man in a gunfight and later had a shoot-out with three Indians and a white man over a dispute in a horse trading deal. He killed all four ... [Then he appeared] in New Mexico during the famous Cattle War of the West, where he was arrested and thrown into Lincoln jail, from which he escaped, killing his guard and a deputy sheriff in the process." Creasy claimed that a

$10,000 reward was made for Billy, dead or alive. Then he segued to the death scene. (Page 92)

Creasy stated that it was in 1880 – not 1881 - when, in the company of an Indian boy who looked like him, Miller **went to Lincoln** to visit his Mexican sweetheart. Hearing that a side of beef hung next door, the Indian went there to steal some meat. "Pat Garrett, who was the marshal of Lincoln at the time, and a well known bounty hunter, heard that Billy was in town and along with two of his deputies laid in waiting near the side of beef. **When the Indian boy stepped up onto the veranda of the house, he was shot down by Pat Garrett, who had apparently mistaken him for Billy.**" Creasy added: "Billy [Miller] told me once that he and the Indian were dressed alike to confuse people. Pat Garrett was afraid of the reaction of townspeople and immediately buried the body. [And he collected the $10,000 reward.] (Page 92)

Creasy concluded: "Billy [Miller] hearing the shooting, and after finding out what happened he immediately left with the Mexican girl, whom he later married." (Page 92)

Important is not only the total misinformation - including the shooting in **Lincoln County's Lincoln town, instead of Fort Sumner**, 150 miles away in San Miguel County - but that totally ignorant Helen Airy thought it was correct!

Creasy then presented an elaborate fable, apparently from Miller; writing: "Billy was not heard of again until 1902, when he and six others held up a bank somewhere in Montana and got away with $8,000 ... The posse, however, closed in on them and five were shot and two got away ... Billy was badly wounded on the side and had to be seared with a red hot branding iron to stop the bleeding. I saw the scar of this wound myself [presumably on Miller]. Billy stood trial and bought his pardon for $4,0000 and I saw this pardon many times after it was framed and hung on the wall of Billy's ranch house. It was under the name of John Miller." (Page 92) And Miller gave him his 1880 Army Colt .45 revolver and holster, as the gun of Billy the Kid. (Page 95)

Creasy's fabrications inspired Helen Airy to a vehement crescendo of conspiracy theory hoaxing. She wrote: "To date, American historians maintain Sheriff Pat Garrett **killed Billy the Kid in Lincoln County, New Mexico.** But according to Creasy's account Garrett killed the wrong man, concealed the error and collected the reward ... For reasons unknown, historians in the United States failed to follow up on the leads Frank Creasy furnished about John Miller's claim that he was Billy the Kid." (Page 92)

BILL CROCKETT

Bill Crockett, speaking for Miller's adopted son Max Miller, his friend; stated: "I do believe John Miller was truly William Bonney, alias Billy the Kid ... Max told me many times that Miller had told him about the Lincoln County War and Pat Garrett, who Miller said was his good friend. Miller said there was a Mexican shot and buried in the coffin that was supposed to be the Kid." (Page 155) **[But Miller had told Frank Creasy that the victim was his Indian friend dressed like him.]**

Jim Johnson, in his 2006 book, *Billy the Kid: His Real Name Was ...* cited an interview of an 88 year old Eugene Lambson, a neighbor of the Miller's, in July of 1976. Lambson stated: "[T]here was the Crockett family, whose land adjoined the Miller land. All of the Crockett family will tell you that they knew John Miller was Billy the Kid." (Johnson, Page 4) Implied is Miller's coy publicizing of himself as Billy Bonney.

EUGENE LAMBSON

Helen Airy's other meaningless interviews with old-timers demonstrated that it was common in their day to fake personal knowledge of Billy the Kid and Pat Garrett for reflected glory.

An Apollas Boaz Lambson's son, Eugene Lambson, said, when he was a boy, his father knew John Miller in Ramah, and Miller "talked a lot about Billy the Kid, but never admitted he was Billy the Kid." And he once pointed a rifle at them before he recognized who they were. But he had no memory of Miller's tales. (Page 48)

But he did recall his father telling him he knew Pat Garrett too. And this made-up Pat Garrett told him that Billy the Kid was hiding in Pete Maxwell's house, so Garrett knocked on the door and a Mexican youth opened it, and Garrett shot him dead. Then he told Billy the Kid and his girlfriend "to pack up and leave Lincoln County forever." (Page 50) From this fakery, Helen Airy concluded absurdly that when John Miller and his wife went to

El Paso for supplies, they were actually socializing with Pat Garrett as friends! (Page 50)

Jim Johnson, in his 2006 book, *Billy the Kid: His Real Name Was* ... stated that Lambson's malarkey came from his July of 1976 interview about Garrett. Airy gave that quote:

> My father was a friend of Pat Garrett when Garrett was stationed at Holbrook, Arizona **[Garrett never was there]**, and my father was living seven miles south of the town ... Pat Garrett told me father about the night he was supposed to have shot the Kid at Fort Sumner. Pat Garrett, in company of his deputies, McKinney and Poe, learned the kid was in Fort Sumner, holed up in the house of Pete Maxwell. They sneaked up to the house in the dead of night, and Garrett knocked on the door. A Mexican youth with a gun in his hand answered the knock and queried, "Quien es?" Sheriff Garrett pushed the door open and fired. The Mexican youth fell dead, and Garrett told the Kid and his girl who was there with him, to pack and leave Lincoln County **[sic – Fort Sumner was in San Miguel County]** forever ... [Garrett let the Kid escape because] Garrett and the Kid were friends. (Page 50)

In the interview, Lambson added that after Miller's death a "stranger from Phoenix," searching for kin, told him that in "an old trunk, they found documents, letters, and other items which convinced them that John Miller was Billy the Kid." But Lambson never saw that trunk. (Johnson, Page 6)

Interestingly, imposter Oliver "Brushy Bill" Roberts also had a posthumously located trunk in which *he* had stored the items he had used for his Billy the Kid impersonation. It might be that John Miller also kept "tools of his trade."

ATHELING BOND

According to Helen Airy, an Atheling Bond claimed Miller was Billy the Kid because Miller's wife, adopted Navajo son, the son's children, and Herman Tecklenburg told him so. (Pages 56, 58) He recalled that Miller told stories of Billy the Kid's gun fights, and would show them his 12 "bullet hole" scars **[which real Billy did not have]**. (Page 57)

And Bond claimed Miller's Billy the Kid tales made him seem like the Kid himself. (Page 57) Bond also gave an example of Miller's first-person as Billy fables: "Bond said that Miller claimed Pat Garrett couldn't have shot the Kid in the chest. 'He wasn't a good enough shot,' Miller said. 'He would have had to shoot the Kid in the back.' " (Page 59)

Jim Johnson, in his 2006 book, *Billy the Kid: His Real Name Was* ... described Atheling Bond as another Miller neighbor, who was interviewed in 1978 at age 89. The quote provided portrays John Miller's clowning with vague impersonation, and his wife's backing him up. Obvious is ignorance of real history they all shared. Bond stated:

> John Miller liked to tell stories about Billy the Kid's gun fights, but he did not want us to think he, himself, was the Kid ... However, his wife, Isadora, who could not speak English, would tell us in Spanish that he was really Billy the Kid, and his name was not John Miller. She told us how Billy [Miller] was shot in Fort Sumner, and how she took care of his wounds, and when the officers came around her house looking for him, she hid him between two straw mattresses which she slid under the bed. (Johnson, Page 5)

GEORGIE CONLEY JACKSON

Georgie Jackson, who knew the Millers in her childhood, had a version that eliminated Miller as Billy by total mismatch; stating; "[Miller] was on the run with his wife ... [H]is mother was a Comanche Indian, and his father was a white man ... He lived in Texas with his mother and the Comanche Indians until he was grown ... Miller knew Billy the Kid and ran with him on some of his escapades. John Miller told us he had a horse stealing corral in a canyon in New Mexico. Most of John Miller's doings were horse stealing. He was taught by the Comanche Indians. He lived with them. He grew up there, not in New York." (Pages 143-144) But Airy ignores this negation of Miller as Billy.

Jim Johnson, in his 2006 book, *Billy the Kid: His Real Name Was ...* stated that Georgie Jackson was a Miller family friend. He stated that when interviewed she did not believe he was the Kid, but he seemed to be on the run. And she stated his mother was a Comanche and his father a white buffalo hunter. To her, he stated that he stole horses with Billy the Kid, and kept them in a corral in a New Mexico canyon. Demonstrated is a rare example of Miller's own hoaxing, with reading of outlaw myth press.

OTHER OLD-TIMERS' FABLES

Airy presents other meaningless old-timer reminiscences. A Blanche Lewis, as a child, was taken to the Millers and was frightened because John Miller talked about guns, had many on the wall. She said, "[He] told everyone he was Billy the Kid." (Page 60) This makes the only actual imposter claim by Miller himself.

In about 1883, an Emma Tietjen, one of Mormon Earnest Tietjen's wives, was frightened by some rough men who came to the house when she was alone, so she hit one over the head with a bowl of butter. Another told her she had hit Billy the Kid; though no one said he was John Miller. And nothing was done to her. To Airy, it proved Billy was alive in 1883, was chivalrous to women, and was John Miller! (Page 62)

A woman named Feliz Bustamante was a neighbor of the Millers and spent time in their home as a girl. And the Millers talked about Billy the Kid. (Page 72) Airy interjected that the Kid was basically good, and so was John Miller. (Pages 72-73)

An Andrew Vander Wagen was a missionary, and stated that John Miller was thinking of stealing his horse, but decided not to, and then attended his sermons. He thought both that Miller was Billy the Kid, and that he was "not right in the head" (Pages 77, 79) – the latter opinion being the only true statement Airy gleaned from her old folks' interviews.

A Joe Conley stated that Miller was critical of published Billy the Kid stories; saying: "[T]hey were wrong] and I ought to know because I was there." And he would do a "shackle-slipping" trick with rope-tied wrists. (Page 144) When Conley stated that Miller said he had been a horse thief and raided a town, Helen Airy interjected preposterously that this must refer to when he was in Lincoln County as the outlaw Billy the Kid. (Page 145)

A Miller neighbor named Joe Baxter had a son, a Carl Baxter, stated for Airy's book: "I believe that John Miller knew Billy the Kid." (Page 147) He gave an example of Miller's sly insertion of himself into the history, when he was reading to him from a Billy the Kid book. And Miller said: "That's a damn lie. There don't even know where the corral was." (Page 140) Carl Baxter also was shown a trunk by Miller, in which he had a revolver "with twenty-one notches." (Page 140) Twenty-one was the fictional number of Billy the Kid's victims. And this was the likely storage place of Miller's Billy the Kid props.

And an unnamed source added that Miller also knew John Chisum, and worked for "the Chisum brothers." (Page 146) To ignorant Airy, it was amazing that Miller knew that Chisum had brothers, missing the point that real Billy never worked for them.

A BUNCH OF FAKE DEATH SCENES

Jim Johnson, in his 2006 book, *Billy the Kid: His Real Name Was* ... summarized John Miller's death scene tales, which he stated had been recounted by his old-timer friends (though Johnson does not cite specific names). Adding to those presented by Helen Airy, they reflect either Miller's changing renditions, or garblings of them. Johnson wrote:

> It is said that Miller told different versions of the escape [death scene] to his friends. One version is that he was shot in the chest a week or so before July 14 and that Isadora was nursing him back to health when Garrett accidentally killed Mexican sheep herder in the Maxwell house. Another version is that Miller was shot by Garrett in the Maxwell house and played dead while Garrett inspected him. When he was carried away by his Mexican friends to be prepared for burial, they noticed signs of life and he was hidden and cared for by Isadora. Meanwhile, a Mexican who died a day earlier was placed in the casket and buried ... [and] Garrett supposedly never learned that Billy was not killed by him. (Johnson, Page 11)

CONCLUDING FAKERY

Pretending her nonsense was proof, Helen Airy launched a conspiracy theory that "the testimonies that Billy the Kid had escaped death in Fort Sumner [she forgot that Bernard Creasy said it was in Lincoln] were silenced [because] the myths surrounding Billy the Kid and Pat Garrett were too overwhelming." (Page 147)

She wildly fantasized that maybe Susan McSween, "Cattle Queen of the Pecos," helped Miller escape New Mexico; or got him money from John Tunstall's family. (Pages 159-160)

Without evidence, or even claiming John Miller said anything like her claim, Airy rhapsodized: "John Miller in his youth was known throughout the world as the brave young man who was called Billy the Kid, who in a bloody war known as the Lincoln County War, heroically took on the Santa Fe Ring conspiracy." (Page 148) And she bemoaned that people had made money from the story, but not John Miller, because he was forced to hide out from the Ring.

Airy's little "Afterward," adding hearsay claims by non-historical people So a woman whose father lived near Fort Sumner in the early 1900's said a Mexican he worked for told him he saw Billy the Kid in bullfights in Mexico after the death date. Someone from Albuquerque was told by a man who died in 1935 and said he worked for Pete Maxwell, that an Indian who died the night before the supposed shooting of Billy was buried as him. A man told his family that he was Billy the Kid's friend, and helped bury the body, and it was not Billy's. A granddaughter of Sheriff William Brady told someone that someone told her that Garrett had not killed Billy, but had killed a "wanderer" to let Billy escape. And George Coe was claimed as not believing Billy was shot, though he had no way of knowing. (Pages 162-163)

For press of post-death sightings, Airy presented tabloid-like *El Paso Times* articles from the 1920's to 1960's. For example, the Fort Sumner Billy the Kid grave is said to have been "marked by a rude cross, that was to prove to Billy's sister that he was still alive." (Page 165) **[But Billy had no sister. And he was dead!]**

Airy ended whimsically: "And so William Bonney, alias Billy the Kid, alias John Miller, alias The Old Man, alias Old Dad, died alone and was buried in the Arizona Pioneer [sic] Home

Cemetery in Prescott. But John Miller won the last round. He was not hanged by the lackeys of the Santa Fe Ring." (Page 148)

AN AMAZING OUTCOME

John Miller had no match whatsoever to Billy Bonney: by his birthdate; by his personal history; by his appearance, by his total ignorance of Billy's life; and by his promoter, Helen Airy's, failure to find any real evidence for his claim. His death on November 7, 1937 should have buried his hoaxlet with his corpse in his fittingly unmarked grave in the Arizona Pioneers' Home Cemetery.

But something unforeseeable happened. In 2003, the huge "Billy the Kid Case" hoax got him in its sights. First, it used his survival claim to fake that the Kid had not been killed in Fort Sumner on July 14, 1881. But, by 2005, that forensic scam, perpetrated by New Mexico's corrupt Governor, Bill Richardson, was blocked from exhumations by my litigations. That left John Miller's Arizona grave as the only one vulnerable to their grave-robbing for fake DNA forensics. So that occurred. And, in unchecked secrecy, the hoaxers also dug up the random man buried beside him: William Hudspeth. These were felonies, necessitating racketeering-like additional crimes for cover-up. So dead John Miller became a fantastic litmus test for imposter hoaxing. He was the scarlet letter badge of the dark clowns.

So, with the gallows humor of past "Saturday Night Live" writer, Jack Handy, one can capture these creepy clowns: "To me clowns aren't funny. In fact, they're kind of scary. I've wondered where this started and I think it does back to the circus, and a clown killed my dad." One needs just a small change to add John Miller or William Hudspeth: "To me clowns aren't funny. In fact, they're kind of scary. I've wondered where this started and I think it does back to the circus, and a clown dug up my dad."

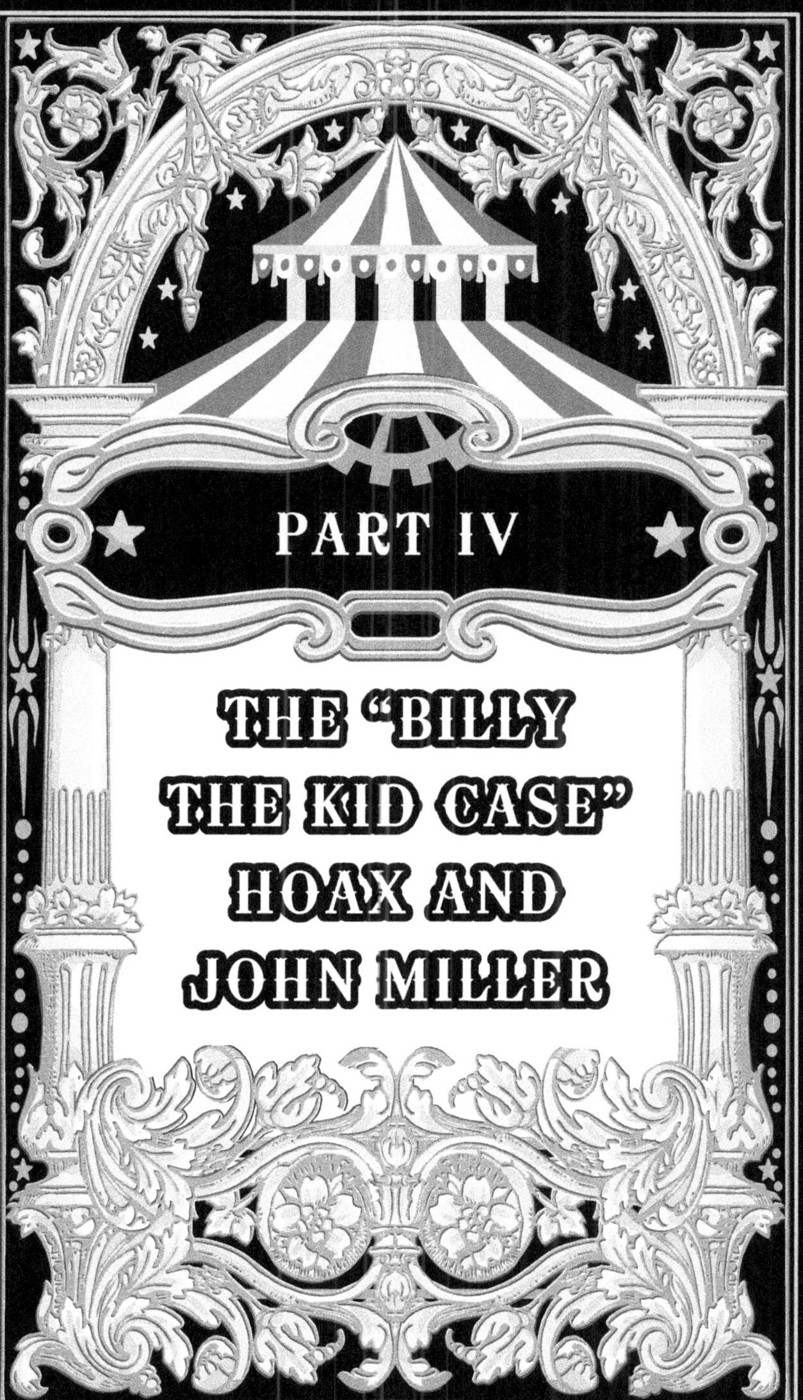

PART IV

THE "BILLY THE KID CASE" HOAX AND JOHN MILLER

CHAPTER 1
THE "BILLY THE KID CASE" FORENSIC DNA HOAX

HERE COME THE CLOWNS

The "Billy the Kid Case" hoax was arguably the most elaborate and most expensive historic-forensic hoax ever perpetrated. Spawned as a self-promoting media circus by corrupt New Mexico Governor Bill Richardson, it was also his apparent pay-to-play to his major political donor, who was a "Brushy"-believer. Its covert goal was to fake "Brushy Bill" Roberts as Billy the Kid. But to cast doubt on the Fort Sumner death scene, pretender John Miller was also rolled out by the hoax's hoard of creepy performing clowns.

This hoax modernized old-timer Billy the Kid imposters' death scene survival claims by alleging plans for DNA matchings from exhumations of Billy the Kid; his mother, Catherine Antrim; "Brushy Bill" Roberts;" and John Miller to prove that an innocent victim, not Billy Bonney, lay in the Fort Sumner grave. **This was just clowning around. In reality, no valid DNA existed from Billy's or his mother's graves for matchings, because their graves were just tourist markers; and New Mexico's Office of the Medical Investigator (OMI) had refused the hoaxers exhumation permits based on the graves being invalid for any DNA quest. So the clowns kept that secret.**

I exposed this massive hoax in my 2014 book, *Cracking the Billy the Kid Case Hoax: The Strange Plot to Exhume Billy the Kid, Convict Sheriff Pat Garrett of Murder, and Become President of the United States*; and in my 2019 book, *The Cold Case Billy the Kid Megahoax: The Plot To Steal Billy the Kid's Identity and Defame Sheriff Pat Garrett as a Murderer.*

And I litigated against the "Billy the Kid Case" hoaxers from 2003 to 2014; first to block their exhumations of Billy and his mother, then to expose their DNA frauds.

Theirs was a pretender hoax on an astronomical scale, appearing in national and international press and a TV documentary. It became Lincoln County Sheriff's Department murder Case 2003-274 filed against Pat Garrett, and was given its "Billy the Kid Case" name by its promulgators.

Of course, non-existence of Billy the Kid's DNA to match with anyone was a big problem. So required was a forensic expert who was a sociopathic profiteer like the perpetrators, and willing to fake claims and results. The perfect match was Dr. Henry Lee, scorned by colleagues as doing "show-biz" forensics: a clown who choose cases for their limelight. He belonged in their circus.

But all this chicanery reduced down to using a version of the old pretenders' innocent victim death scene, their denial of the Coroner's Jury Report of William Bonney, with some conspiracy theories thrown in about why real historians called them clowns. But to spare themselves head-on ridicule, "Billy the Kid Case" clowns presented their hoax as merely investigating if the pretenders had told the truth, while hiding that they were long debunked by wrong ages, and total historical ignorance.

CLOWNING THE "BILLY THE KID CASE" HOAX AS A DEATH SCENE ALTERNATIVE

The "Billy the Kid Case" hoax entered public awareness at a stratospheric level. On June 5, 2003, Governor Bill Richardson announced his scam in a front page *New York Times* article titled "122 Years Later, The Lawmen Are Still Chasing Billy the Kid." Its fake news reporter, Michael Janofsky, never researched that the "experts" were just Richardson's clowns: "Brushy"-believers and a few complicit lawmen.

So Janofsky wrote that Richardson was seeking **"evidence to a long-held alternative theory that Garrett shot someone other than the Kid and led a conspiracy to cover up his crime."** Listed lawmen were Lincoln County Sheriff Tom Sullivan, and his Deputy, Steve Sederwall, filing a murder case against Pat Garrett; as well as a Texas law firm for the case [**Attorney Bill Robins III, the "Brushy"-believer**]. Janofsky concluded that if "Brushy" was not a DNA match, they could check John Miller. But, at that point, Miller was just thrown in, and not seen as the key to the hoax's survival that he would become. The article stated:

LINCOLN, NEW MEXICO - For more than 120 years, Pat Garrett has enjoyed legendary status in the American West, a lawman on a par with Wyatt Earp, Bat Masterson, even Matt Dillon. As sheriff here in Lincoln County in 1881, Garrett is credited with shooting to death the notorious outlaw known as Billy the Kid, a killing that made Garrett a hero. For years, a patch bearing his likeness has adorned uniforms worn by sheriff"s deputies here.

But now, modern science is about to interrupt Garrett's fame in a way that some say could expose him as a liar who covered up a murder to save his own skin and reputation.

Officials in New Mexico and Texas are working out plans to exhume and conduct genetic tests on the bodies of a woman buried in New Mexico who was believed to be the Kid's mother and a Texas man known as Brushy Bill Roberts, who claimed to be the Kid and died in 1950 at the age of 90. If test results suggest that the two were related, it would add new evidence to a long-held alternative theory that Garrett shot someone other than the Kid and led a conspiracy to cover up his crime.

Such skepticism is hardly uncommon. Disputes over major events in the Old West have engaged historians almost since they happened. The debate over Billy the Kid is one of the longest-running.

Beyond renewing interest in the Kid saga, the possibility that testing could enlarge Garrett's reputation or destroy it has even caught the fancy of Gov. Bill Richardson of New Mexico, who has offered state aid for the investigation and a possible pardon that an earlier New Mexico governor had once promised the Kid for a murder he committed.

"The problem is, there's so much fairy tale with this story that it's hard to nail down the facts," said Steve Sederwall, the mayor of Capitan, N.M., who is working with Lincoln County's current sheriff, Tom Sullivan, to resolve the matter. "All we want is the truth, whatever it is. If the guy Garrett killed was Billy the Kid, that makes him a hero. If it wasn't, Garrett was a murderer, and we have egg on our face, big time."

No matter what the genetic testing may show - and it might not show much of anything - it is hard to overstate the prominence of Garrett and the Kid in Western lore, especially here in southeastern New Mexico where their lives converged during and after the gun battles for financial control of the region that were known as the Lincoln County War. The Kid's notoriety grew after he and friends on one side of the conflict killed several men in an ambush, including Garrett's predecessor, Sheriff William Brady. For that, the Kid was hunted down, captured by Garrett, found guilty of murder and taken to the Lincoln jail, where he was placed in shackles to await hanging. He was only 21.

Today the tiny town of Lincoln, population 38, is a memorial to what happened next. More than a dozen buildings, including one that housed the jail, have been preserved as a state monument that attracts as many as 35,000 visitors a year.

Historians generally agree that the Kid, born Henry McCarty and known at times as William H. Bonney, escaped after it became apparent that Gov. Lew Wallace had reneged on a promise to pardon him in exchange for information about another killing in the county war. On April 28, 1881, the Kid managed to get his hands on a gun, kill the two deputies assigned to watch him and leave the area on horseback.

But then the stories diverge, providing fuel for two major theories of where, when, and how the Kid's life ended.

The version embraced here and supported by numerous books and Garrett relatives is that the Kid made his way to a friend's ranch in Fort Sumner, about 100 miles northeast of Lincoln. The ranch owner, Pete Maxwell, was also a friend of Garrett and somehow got word to Garrett that the Kid was in the area. After arriving, Garrett posted two deputies at the door.

As the Kid approached on the night of July 13 [sic], he spoke a few words in Spanish to the deputies, who did not recognize him. But Garrett, waiting inside, knew the voice. When the Kid walked in, Garrett turned and shot him in the heart.

William F. Garrett of Alamogordo, N.M., who is Garrett's grand-nephew, said years of research, including conversations with his cousin Jarvis, the last of Garrett's eight children, convinced him there is "no question about it" that his great-uncle killed Billy the Kid at Maxwell's. Jarvis died in 1991 at the age of 86.

"He was hired to get the Kid, and he got the Kid," Mr. Garrett said in an interview. "uncle Pat was a person of integrity who did his job. He was a law abider, not a law breaker."

But just as the story of Garrett as hero has flourished over the years, so have others, including the tale of Brushy Bill of Hico, Tex. His trip to New Mexico in 1950 to seek the pardon he said he was denied nearly 70 years before gave new life to an alternative possibility, that Garrett had not killed the Kid at all, but a drifter friend of the Kid's named Billy Barlow.

This story holds that Garrett and the Kid may have been in cahoots for some reason and that Garrett had stashed a gun at the outhouse at the jail that the Kid used to kill the deputies and escape. Even if only part of that is true, it would strongly suggest that Garrett killed the wrong man.

Speaking with the same person as Garrett's great-nephew, Jannay P. Valdez,

curator of the Billy the Kid Museum in Canton, Tex., said he had no doubt that Garrett killed someone else and that Brushy Bill was the Kid. "I'm absolutely convinced," he said here on Monday after meeting with Mr. Sederwall to discuss theories and how to begin the kind of genetic testing that has been used to ascertain lineage of other historical figures like Thomas Jefferson and Jessie James. "I'd bank everything I have on it."

As longtime friends, Mr. Sederwall and Sheriff Sullivan decided they wanted to settle the matter once and for all but could do so only through scientific analysis. To justify the effort that would require much of their time and, perhaps at some point, taxpayer money, they needed an official reason. So in April, they opened the first-ever investigation into the murders of the two deputies shot in the Kid's escape, James W. Bell and Robert Olinger, to examine what happened at the jail and Maxwell's ranch.

[AUTHOR'S NOTE: Janofsky is parroting the hoax. The deputy murders and Garrett's killing of the Kid are unconnected, but the hoaxers made-up that Garrett helped the escape.]

As Mr. Sederwall said, "There's no statute of limitations on murder."

[AUTHOR'S NOTE: This announces the real murder case; but hidden is New Mexico's having had a Statute of Limitations.]

The goal now, he said, is to compare genetic evidence of Catherine Antrim, believed to be the Kid's mother, who died of tuberculosis in 1874 and is buried in Silver City, N.M., and of Brushy Bill, who lived out his life in Texas. A Dallas firm [sic Houston] has agreed to help, and a spokesman for governor Richardson said the state would assist by clearing legal hurdles to gain access to the mother's body.

The Kid was buried at Fort Sumner, N.M., although the whereabouts of the grave are uncertain; he has no known living relatives. Mr. Valdez said he had already secured permission to exhume the body of Brushy Bill, who is buried 20 miles from Hico in Hamilton, Texas.

But solving the mystery might not be so simple. For one thing, Mr. Valdez said he was certain that the woman buried in Silver City was but "a half aunt." And even if tests disqualify Brushy Bill as Billy the Kid, other "Kids" have emerged over the years, including a man named John Miller, who died in 1937 and is buried in Prescott, Ariz. Mr. Sederwall said that efforts would be made to exhume his body as well.

The investigators conceded that much is riding on their quest. Sheriff Sullivan, a tall, strapping man who carries a turquoise-handled

.357 magnum on his right hip, said he, like so many others in the West, revered Garrett for gunning down the Kid. The uniform patch with Garrett's likeness was his design. Now, the legend is threatened.

"I just want to get to the bottom of it," said Sheriff Sullivan, who is retiring next year. "My integrity's at stake. So's my department's. So's what we believe in and even New Mexico history. If Garrett shot someone other than the Kid, that makes him a murderer and he covered it up. He wouldn't be such a role model, then, and we'd have to take the patches off the uniforms."

On June 10, 2003, Richardson held a press conference with his collected clowns: Lincoln County's Sheriff Tom Sullivan and Deputy Steve Sederwall; De Baca County's Sheriff Gary Graves; Attorney for exhuming the mother, Sherry Tippett; and University of New Mexico professor Paul Hutton, appointed by Richardson as the hoax's "historical advisor." Richardson revealed that Lincoln County Sheriff's Department murder case against Pat Garrett had been flied as No. 2003-274. The press release promised use of forensic DNA to prove that the Kid deserved a pardon. It stated:

State of New Mexico
Office of the Governor

Bill Richardson
Governor
For immediate release
6/10/03

Contact: Billy Sparks
telephone number

GOVERNOR BILL RICHARDSON ANNOUNCES STATE SUPPORT OF BILLY THE KID INVESTIGATION

SANTA FE – Governor Bill Richardson today outlined how the state of New Mexico will support the investigation efforts to investigate the life and death of Billy the Kid.

Governor Richardson delivered the following remarks during a news conference today in the State Capitol:

This is an important day in the history of New Mexico and the American West. I am announcing my support and the support of the state of New Mexico for the investigation into the life and death of Henry McCarty, also known as William Bonney. To millions around the world, he was called Billy the Kid. How he captured the world's imagination is well worth exploring. His life, though ended at the age of 21, is part of what makes New Mexico and an American West, unique.

My goal is to shed new light on old history.

I am pleased to be joined here by Lincoln County Sheriff Tom Sullivan, Capitan Mayor Steve Sederwall, DeBaca County Sheriff Gary Grays [sic - Graves]. Grant County Attorney Sherry Tippett, University of New Mexico History Professor, Doctor Paul Hutton and State Police Major Tom Branch.

Let me tell you how this all came about.

Last month I was contacted by Lincoln County Sheriff, Tom Sullivan and Capitan Mayor, Steve Sederwall, to support reopening the case. Case number 2003-274 seeks to answer key questions that have lingered for over 120 years surrounding the life and the death of Billy the Kid.

This episode in the history of New Mexico and the history of the old west is both fact and legend and continues to stir the imagination and interest of people all over the world.

By utilizing modern forensic, DNA and crime scene techniques, the goal of the investigation is to get to the truth. In the process, the reputation of Pat Garrett, still a hero in Lincoln County law enforcement, hangs in the balance. **The question is did Sheriff Garrett kill Billy the Kid at Fort Sumner, New Mexico on July 14. 1881?**

This investigation will also seek to shed new light on the events surrounding the escape of Billy the Kid from the Lincoln County Jail on April 28, 1881. The shooting of Deputies J.W. Bell and Bob Olinger by Billy the Kid has never been officially investigated. Where did Billy get his gun and what really happened?

I have contacted the national Labs, Los Alamos and Sandia and have been assured that they will volunteer their support in this effort. Los Alamos Lab can assist us by providing ground penetrating radar, DNA expertise and technical forensic assistance. Sandia Labs will allow their experts to volunteer their time to help us uncover the facts.

The State Police will help supervise the investigation and crime scene analysis of the evidence uncovered in the investigation.

I **have also asked University of New Mexico Professor of History and Executive Director of the Western History Association, Doctor Paul Hutton, to serve as our historical advisor.** Dr. Hutton has served as President of the Western Writers of America and has won several national honors for his works on western history.

I intend to hold hearings at Fort Sumner, Lincoln, Silver City and Mesilla. I will appoint a defense counsel and a prosecutor to present the evidence. **[Never done.]**

As Governor, I will examine the events surrounding the alleged offer of a pardon to Billy the Kid by former New Mexico

> **Governor Lew Wallace. I will evaluate the evidence uncovered and make a decision.**
>
> There is no question that this story deserves our attention and that the history of New Mexico and the American West is important to all of us. If we can get to the truth we will. I have total confidence in the team you see here today to conduct a professional, honest and exhaustive investigation of the facts and report back to me and to the rest of the world what really happened here in New Mexico.
>
> The benefits to our state and to the history of the West far outweigh any cost we may incur. I expect the actual cost to be nominal. Just since this investigation was announced, it has sparked news articles about New Mexico and Lincoln County from New York to London to India. Getting to the truth is our goal. But, if this increases interest and tourism in our state, I couldn't be happier.
>
> I understand that Movie Producer Ron Howard has donated the cabin used in shooting his movie "The Missing", being shot in Santa Fe, to Silver City. The cabin is a replica of a Billy the Kid era home. The cabin will be delivered to Silver City this week.
>
> The potential benefit from this investigation to all of New Mexico is already being felt and is well worth the effort. #30#

But how did DNA connect to a pardon? **The mother's "DNA" (though there was none) would also be matched to "Brushy" (though he denied she was his mother, and the DNA to be used was mitochondrial, which is for *mother-child* identity matchings). A fake "match" was to "prove" "Brushy" was Billy the Kid; and, by extrapolation, the Fort Sumner grave held the innocent victim, making Pat Garrett his murderer.** And since there would be no real DNA anyway, any "matchings" wanted could be claimed.

But what about the pardon? Hoax Attorney, Bill Robins III, revealed the link in Grant County District Court in his January 5, 2004 "Pre-Hearing Brief" about digging up the mother: Catherine Antrim. His fakery began with stating that his client was dead Billy the Kid! (Note that a corpse cannot be a client.) Speaking for "Billy," Robins claimed DNA would prove that Garrett had not shot him, and he survived to lead a long and law-abiding life deserving pardon. So Robins wrote: "**Should the DNA extracted from Ms. Antrim confirm that one of the potential Kids ["Brushy Bill" or John Miller] was in fact Billy the Kid, undersigned counsel will be able to make an even stronger argument for pardon by citing to the long years of law abiding life.**"

CHAPTER 2 THE "BILLY THE KID CASE" HOAX'S FAKED DEATH SCENE

NEWLY INVENTED DEATH SCENES

The "Billy the Kid Case" hoax hinged on Sheriff's Departments' filings of a murder case against Pat Garrett to get legal justification to do exhumations to "prove" he murdered the innocent victim. So the documents required fabrication of a non-historical death scene. Possibly because "Brushy Bill's" and John Miller's death scenes were so silly, they were not used.

Made-up for the "Billy the Kid Case" hoax was a new death scene scenario: a non-historical bromance between Pat Garrett and Billy Bonney, with Pat first being complicit in Billy's jailbreak by giving him the revolver to murder his own Deputies, James Bell and Robert Olinger; then helping Billy escape again by purposefully killing the innocent victim in Fort Sumner as grave-filler. Of course, there was no shooting of Billy the Kid by Garrett. **It should be noted that this was a mismatch with "Brushy's" and John Miller's death scenes which had accidental innocent victim killings by Garrett intending to kill Billy, followed by his covering-up this murder by a rushed burial so he could get the Billy the Kid reward.**

But the hoaxers hit a wall. My litigation blocked their fake exhumations of Billy and his mother, so there was no way to fake DNA matches to claim the murdered innocent victim lay in the Fort Sumner grave. So, by 2004, the hoaxers secretly rewrote their hoax, with a Version II death scene so preposterous that it took the clowns' sociopathy to foist it on the public.

They claimed to have found the carpenter's bench on which shot Billy Bonney had been laid out. Of course, in Version I, the point was that *Billy was not shot*. But the hoaxers were now desperate for any DNA claim to continue their hoax and TV cameras. So now claimed was that shot Billy bled on the bench, leaving "blood DNA" to match with "Brushy" and John Miller. (It should be noted that neither clown claimed a death scene of being laid out on a carpenter's bench; so, obviously, "Billy's bench blood" was not even needed to cancel them out. So this was kept secret.)

But if there was shot Billy on the bench, it meant he was dead, and defaulted to conventional history. So they lied that "dead men don't bleed," and segued to the absurd scenario that Garrett shot Billy in a mutual plot, *so Billy could "play dead;"* then he murdered the innocent victim to substitute for Billy on the carpenter's bench (while Billy presumably painfully exited). And presumably the 200 townspeople doing the night vigil on Billy's corpse did not notice all this activity - or a new corpse!

In my books on this hoax, I debunked Version II, as more than just silly, by using forensic consultants. Confirmed was that dead men *do bleed*, because blood flows out from exit wounds from residual blood pressure, then gravitational seepage. Also, when shot in the chest, one cannot play dead because of involuntary hyperventilation. But the key was that this "bench-blood-DNA" could never be proved as Billy's to match with anyone. **Forensic DNA matching requires "reference DNA," meaning DNA obtained with absolute certainty from the individual in question.** The hoaxers were actually claiming the counterpart of finding a random finger print, and having no finger prints of the individual in question to compare with it to determine its identity. Ultimately, it would emerge that the forensic lab the hoaxers were using for their fake "forensics," did not even test for blood, so none could be shown as present on the bench! And their samples from claimed bench areas (which were likely rust stains) yielded no DNA anyway. So all this was kept secret.

Since the "Billy the Kid Case" was a hoax, these realities fazed none of the performing clowns, including their forensic expert, Dr. Henry Lee, who made blood claims himself.

And the hoaxers then lied that they had the bench-blood-DNA-of-Billy-the-Kid to justify digging up John Miller for "DNA identity matching; and also tried to dig up "Brushy Bill," In fact, they had nothing, and were just creepy clowns trying to invade graves of dead past clowns, Miller and "Brushy."

CHAPTER 3
"BILLY THE KID CASE" HOAX'S LEGAL FILINGS

CLOWNING THE DEATH SCENE

To attain their desired exhumations, the "Billy the Kid Case" clowns created legal documents faking a death scene, and concealing the Coroner's Jury Report, to justify their exhumation petitions and to create fake TV documentaries.

The Lincoln County Sheriff's Department murder Case No. 2003-274 against Pat Garrett, was created by its Sheriff, Tom Sullivan, and his deputized Mayor of Capitan, Steve Sederwall.

In the De Baca County Sheriffs Department, the same investigation was filed as No. 03-06-136-01 under its Sheriff, Gary Graves. The imposter-backing Historian for the U.S. Marshals Service, named David Turk, helped create documents, and filed one of his own with them.

Then the next Lincoln County Sheriff, Rick Virden, deputized Sullivan and Sederwall for the case. And the illegal Arizona exhumation of John Miller (and a random man buried beside him, named William Hudspeth) was done during his tenure.

And the hoaxers' attorneys, Sherry Tippett, Bill Robins III, and Mark Acuña, created exhumation petitions with the hoaxed claim of prosecuting Garrett as a murderer.

CAPITAN "MAYOR'S REPORT" OF STEVE SEDERWALL

Lincoln County Sheriffs Department Deputy Steve Sederwall was first in announcing the "Billy the Kid Case" murder case in his capacity as Capitan Mayor in his May, 2003, *Capitan Village Hall News* "Mayor's Report." His focus was on pretenders, with emphasis on "Brushy Bill." Low in hoax hierarchy, Sederwall was hardworking, claiming to have written the major hoax document: the "Probable Cause Statement" for Pat Garrett as a murderer.

And his later association with "Brushy"-backing author, W.C. Jameson, apparently inspired Jameson's continuation of the "Billy the Kid Case" hoax in his 2018 book, *Cold Case Billy the Kid.* As to the death scene, Sederwall's "Mayor's Report" used "Brushy Bill" and his faked shot victim, Billy Barlow. It stated:

> This investigation came about after Sheriff Sullivan and I talked about a man by the name of Brushy Bill Roberts. In 1950 Roberts came to the Governor of New Mexico with his attorney [sic - William Morrison, not an attorney]; saying he was Billy the Kid. He said that Pat Garrett shot a man by the name of Billy Barlow and buried his body claiming to be that of Billy the Kid. Roberts said he lived out a life within the bounds of the law under an assumed name and wanted a pardon that was promised to him by Governor Wallace.
>
> **[AUTHOR'S NOTE: This is the hoax's first known reference connecting the "Billy the Kid" hoax's claim that Garrett did not kill the Kid, to the "Brushy Bill" Roberts hoax.]**
>
> On the surface of this story you would say "so what?" But if you look at this man's claim he is saying our Sheriff Pat Garrett is a murderer. Garrett knew the Kid and killed someone else. **What this says also is that Pete Maxwell who said the body is of The Kid is a co-conspirator in a murder**. There is no statute of limitations on Murder [sic], so the Lincoln County Sheriff's Office has opened a case to pursue the investigation. If Brushy Bill Roberts is Billy the Kid then history changes. But if he is lying, we need to clear Garrett's name.
>
> **[AUTHOR'S NOTE: Confirmed is the case as a filed murder investigation against Pat Garrett, with a "Brushy" emphasis. Though avoiding mention of the Coroner's Jury Report, it is referenced by claiming that its witness, Peter Maxwell, lied about Billy being the victim. Also, it is untrue that there was no New Mexico Statute of Limitations for murder. For Pat Garrett it had expired in 1891! (See pages 22-23 above) Also, the sly double-talk that would characterize the hoax is used. Here, the absurd claim is made that the murder case against Pat Garrett was being done to clear his name of murder - though the hoaxers were his only accusers, and murder cases are not done to prove someone innocent!]**

I feel this investigation will put a positive light on the county, our town and the state in whole. Tom Sullivan and I have been in touch with the Governor's office and he is behind us. People who are conducting DNA on victims of the World Trade Center have agreed to complete DNA tests for us on remains of persons believed to be Billy the Kid. We have a filmmaker creating a made-for-TV story about this investigation. We have recruited some of the best investigators in the country from other states to assist in this investigation. The Sheriff and I feel this should not only clear up a 122-year-old mystery but also bring money into our village ...

Tom Sullivan and I know it is a crazy idea but won't it be fun.

"PROBABLE CAUSE STATEMENT" FOR PAT GARRETT AS A MURDERER

The key to the "Billy the Kid Case" hoax was getting access to graves to fabricate self-serving DNA matches. That meant filing a real murder investigation with a "Probable Cause Statement" which established, with probability, Pat Garrett's guilt.

That required manufacturing a fake murder motive for Garrett and a fake murder scene. Denied was William Bonney's Coroner's Jury Report, and the multiple additional corpse identifications. Resorted to were hearsay post-death Billy the Kid sightings, as used in the John Miller and "Brushy Bill" hoaxes.

The December 31, 2003 "Probable Cause Statement for Lincoln County Sheriff's Department Case No. 2003-274" is 11 pages of single-spaced footnoted text, combining double-talk, lies, and mock erudition. Though Deputy Steve Sederwall claimed to have written it, Attorney Bill Robins III may contributed, since he used the same wording a month before its December signing in reporter Louie Fecteau's November 19, 2003 *Albuquerque Journal's* "No Kidding: Governor Taps Lawyer for Billy." Robins stated: "[I]t was hard to tell who the good guys were." The "Probable Cause Statement" has: "[I]t was hard to tell who the good guys were." Also fellow hoaxer, U.S. Marshals Service Historian David Turk, provided fake research and an Addendum.

The "Statement" had two thrusts to establish Pat Garrett as a murderer of an "innocent victim" on July 14, 1881. The first used fabricated "suspicions," misinformation, and false forensic DNA claims, to claim Garrett's guilt.

The second thrust was fabrication of a murder motive for Garrett by a sub-investigation of Billy Bonney's jailbreak murder of his deputy guards, James Bell and Robert Olinger. Used were meaningless "what-ifs": *If* Garrett gave Billy the revolver used for the jailbreak, he and Billy *might* have been friends. And *if* they were friends, Garrett *might* again have helped Billy escape in Fort Sumner by killing an innocent victim. But the ifs" had no evidence. And there was no historical friendship between Garrett and Billy. So substituted were only old-timers' malarkey of post-death sightings of Billy. In fact, Garrett had no motive to assist Billy's jailbreak, and was not in Lincoln that day.

Subsequently, when I was litigating against the hoaxers, this sub-investigation was switched by them to the *total* Case 2003-274 to hide their Garrett attack and its connected DNA records. Also, this sub-investigation had its own fake forensics with DNA claims about "Deputy Bell's blood" on courthouse floorboards.

But for the "Probable Cause Statement," Sederwall and Sullivan claimed that Garrett was guilty, as would be proven by DNA comparisons of remains in Billy the Kid's and his mother's graves (to show Garrett's innocent victim lay in Billy's grave).

Added was a two page affidavit by a Homer Overton, addressed to Sheriff Sullivan, swearing that Garrett had not shot the Kid; but crumbling under Overton's made-up dates.

The upshot is that the "Probable Cause Statement" failed. It presented no reason, or probable cause, to indicate that Pat Garrett had not killed Billy Bonney. One can guess that, expecting no opposition, the hoaxers had written it for their complicit and beholden judges - just appointed by Richardson to join his hoard of clowns - who were supposed to rubber-stamp their exhumations, but might have wanted documentation to bear scrutiny.

Importantly, it would much later emerge, as I pursued the hoaxers with my open records investigations, that there had been a first and rejected "Probable Cause Statement," titled "Lincoln County Sheriff's Office, Lincoln County New Mexico, Case: William H. Bonney, a.k.a. William Antrim, a.k.a. The Kid, a.k.a. Billy the Kid: An Investigation into the events of April 28, 1881 through July 14, 1881 - seventy-seven days of doubt." Its authorship was uncertain. But it overtly promoted "Brushy Bill," gave his murder scene, and was apparently rejected in lieu of Sederwall's and Sullivan's more circumspect treatment. Importantly, that one used John Miller as a back-up pretender.

The official "Probable Cause Statement" follows.

LINCOLN COUNTY SHERIFF'S DEPARTMENT

CASE # 2003-274

Probable Cause Statement

In the struggle dubbed the "Lincoln County War" investigators [Sullivan and Sederwall] soon learned that nothing was as seemed.

[AUTHOR'S NOTE: For lack of any evidence, this is the familiar "suspicion" used by Billy the Kid imposters' authors.]

As they poured through the volumes of information, documents, paperwork, reports, county records, books and examined newly discovered evidence, it became apparent no clear lines could be drawn as to who was working with or for whom. What first appeared to be clear quickly became clouded as new information was uncovered,

[AUTHOR'S NOTE: No new evidence is ever presented.]

it's difficult to judge who the "good guys" and the "bad guys" were. One would think that the Lincoln County Sheriff''s Department would be on the side of the law. However, it was a duly sworn posse of Lincoln County Deputies that shot and killed John Tunstall, in what investigators in clean conscience can only cauterize [sic] as an unprovoked murder.

[AUTHOR'S NOTE: Tunstall's murder is irrelevant. It occurred when William Brady was Sheriff of Lincoln County; and was 3½ years before Garrett killed the Kid. Of course, Brady's dishonesty is irrelevant to Garrett as a murderer.]

Evidence shows that posse-men, Hill and Morton

[AUTHOR'S NOTE: Error: Tom Hill was not Brady's official posseman; he was in Jessie Evans's outlaw gang. Brady, in writing, swore he used no known outlaws on that posse.]

committed murder when "*Hill called to him* (Tunstall) *to come up and that he would not be hurt; at the same time both Hill and Morton threw up their guns, resting their stocks on their knees; that after Tunstall came nearer, Morton fired and shot Tunstall through the breast, and then Hill fired and shot Tunstall through the head ...*" [1]([1]Deposition of Albert Howe, Angel Report) Although these deputies were acting under the color off the law they were not acting within the law. This behavior permeates the Lincoln County War and investigators will not make judgments on that behavior but rather uncover the facts and present the facts without varnish.

[AUTHOR'S NOTE: Repeating that lawman can be dishonest, is irrelevant to proving Garrett a murderer.]

No one from the Governor to the District Attorney to the Sheriff of Lincoln County is beyond suspicion of deception and covering up the true facts in this case.

[AUTHOR'S NOTE: Vague "suspicion" is irrelevant to Garrett.]

This can be seen in a number of examples. In a letter to Riley and Dolan of the Murphy-Dolan faction from District Attorney W. L. Rynerson of the 3rd Judicial District, the attorney clearly demonstrates he himself plays a part in the hostile actions when he writes, "*Shake that McSween outfit up until it shells out and squares up and then shake it out of Lincoln. I will aid to punish the scoundrels all I can.*"[2] ([2]Rynerson letter to Riley and Dolan, Feb. 7 [sic], 1878, University of Arizona Special Collection)

[AUTHOR'S NOTE: Error: The letter is dated February 14, 1878; is about murdering Tunstall; and is irrelevant to Garrett.]

When investigators began to look at the murder of Deputy Sheriff J.W. Bell and Deputy Robert Olinger on April 28, 1881, it was found that much of the information we now know as "history" came from Pat F. Garrett's book, "The Authentic Life of Billy the Kid" published in 1882.

[AUTHOR'S NOTE: Error: Bell/Olinger eye-witness murder information was not claimed by Garrett, who was away at White Oaks; but was from, Gottfried Gauss, the caretaker.]

Investigators learned that much of this history is flawed for the reason historian Robert Utley writes: "*Although not many copies of the Authentic Life were sold, it nevertheless had a decisive impact on the Kid's image. More than any other single influence, the Garrett-Upson book fed the legend of Billy the Kid. As the legend blossomed, writers turned to the Authentic Life for details. Ash Upson's fictions became implanted in hundreds of " histories" that followed. For more than a century, only a few students thought to question the wild fantasies that flowed from Ash's imagination. In the evolution of the Kid's image, the Authentic Life is a book of enormous consequence.*"[3] ([3]Robert M. Utley. Billy the Kid a short and violent life. University of Nebraska Press, 1989.)

[AUTHOR'S NOTE: Utley is merely describing evolution of the legend, not history. And Garrett's book confirms his shooting of Billy. All subsequent scholarly historians, including Utley, confirmed that Garrett fatally shot Billy the Kid.]

On March 23 [sic – 17], 1879, Governor Lew Wallace met with William Bonney (Kid) in Lincoln. In this meeting it is demonstrated that Wallace convinced the Kid that it would be to his advantage to work for the government.

[AUTHOR'S NOTE: Wrong. Billy proposed to Wallace, by a letter of about March 13, 1879, to give eye-witness Grand Jury testimony against the murderers of Huston Chapman in exchange for Wallace's annulling his Lincoln County War indictments. But a straw man argument is being set up.]

The Kid becomes, what would be referred to in today's terminology as a "Confidential Informant." In Governor Wallace's hand we read "Statements made by Kid, Made Sunday night March 23, 1879."[4] ([4]Statements by Kid, Lew Wallace Collection, Indiana Historical Society Library) It was through this meeting Wallace devised a plan and attempted to deceive when he and the Kid entered into an agreement where by the Kid would appear to have been arrested.

[AUTHOR'S NOTE: Claiming attempt "to deceive" is a misleading switcheroo. The hoaxers admitted Billy's confidential informant status. The arrest plan was devised by both Wallace and Billy to prevent his being killed before his testimony against Chapman's murderers. But the hoaxers are still pumping the irrelevant claim that everyone was deceptive. Of course, that was irrelevant to Garrett as murderer.]

The Kid later talks of this and says he was allowed to wear his guns and he left when he wanted to leave.

David S. Turk, Historian for the United States Marshals Service has discovered other such deceptions in his study of official records.

[AUTHOR'S NOTE: Referring to "other such deceptions" is fake. Turk's "other deceptions" are never given. And Turk, an active "Billy the Kid Case" hoaxer, contributed his own fake Probable Cause addendum to the hoax. (See pages 201-204 below]

It is commonly believed

[AUTHOR'S NOTE: Misstatement: It is a *known*.]

that Lincoln County Sheriff Pat F. Garrett arrested the Kid in December of 1880 in Stinking Springs near Fort Sumner. But the records show that Garrett was elected in November of 1880 and did not take office until January of 1881.[5] ([5]Lincoln County Commissioners Records, November 8, 1880).

[AUTHOR'S NOTE: This leads to a fake claim that he did not have proper authority to capture Billy.]

He went to Fort Sumner as a Deputy United States Marshall, but even that Commission and authority are now questioned. Secret Service Special Operative Azariah F. Wild of New Orleans writes in his daily logs "*I this day went to Lincoln to meet Capt. Lea & Garrett who are to organize the Posse Comatatus (sic) to make a raid on Fort Sumner to arrest counterfeiters.*"[6] ([6]Report of Azariah F. Wild, November 11, 1880, Record Group 87, National Archives) Garrett shot and killed Charles Bowdre and Tom O'Folliard during the chase and arrested the Kid. Later, Secret Service Special Operative Azariah F. Wild writes to his superior and admits he was deceptive in his commission of Garrett. "*I will respectfully state that I applied to Marshall Sherman to appoint P.F. Garrett as a Deputy Marshall to which he paid no attention. I was in great need of Mr. Garrett [sic – Mr. Garrett's aid] at that time and took one of the Commissions Sherman sent to John Hurley (he having sent two) and substituted P.F. Garrett the very man who has rendered the Government such a valuable service in killing and arresting these men who I was in pursuit.*"[7] ([7]Report of Azariah F. Wild, January 4 [sic -3], 1881, Record Group 87, National Archives)

[AUTHOR'S NOTE: This fakes doubt about Garrett's commission. In fact, Wild, needing Garrett's aid, got paperwork from U.S. Marshal John Sherman; but two commissions were for John Hurley. So he crossed out Hurley's name on one, and added Garrett's. It was not done secretly, since Wild put it in his daily report to Secret Service Chief James Brooks. And it was accepted. Also, Sederwall recycled this fakery in W.C. Jameson's 2018 book titled *Cold Case Billy the Kid.]*

No one in 122 years has been able to speak with clear certainty where the gun came from that William Bonney used to kill Deputy J.W. Bell.

[AUTHOR'S NOTE: A switch to a sub-investigation begins to fake Garrett as Billy's escape accomplice.]

With the information investigators have seen they question Garrett's involvement in the Kid obtaining a weapon.

[AUTHOR'S NOTE: What follows is just fake "what-ifs": *If* Garrett was Billy's friend, he helped him escape. *If* he did that, he would later kill the victim to help Billy escape again.]

It would go to reason that if the body in Fort Sumner is anyone other than William Bonney then Garrett no doubt had a hand in allowing the Kid to escape on July 14, 1881.

[AUTHOR'S NOTE: This is fakery. No one says anyone but Billy was buried. It is just hoaxing.]

If the body at Fort Sumner is anyone other than William Bonney, then Garrett, whether by accident or design, is responsible for homicide of the person resting in that grave.

[AUTHOR'S NOTE: Here are more meaningless "what ifs."]

If it is not Bonney in the grave at Fort Sumner it would also go to reason that Garrett would be looked at as a suspect in furthering the escape of the Kid on April 28, 1881 when the two Lincoln County Sheriffs were murdered.

[AUTHOR'S NOTE: Here is the switcheroo. Now the fake "what-ifs" are used as fact: that Garrett helped Billy escape. THIS FAKERY IS THE HOAXERS' SOLE PROBABLE CAUSE FOR GARRETT AS A MURDERER. In fact, no evidence has been given; and none exists. And Pat and Billy were not friends.

[AUTHOR'S NOTE: What follows next is built on the hoaxers' lying that (1) they established Garrett's murder motive, and that (2) they established need to check Billy's grave for Garrett's "innocent victim."]

Although the investigation will deal with what happened in the Lincoln County court house on April 28, 1881, this writing will deal with the alleged shooting of William Bonney at Fort Sumner on the night of July 14, 1881.

[AUTHOR'S NOTE: Do not let this fast-one slip by. The deputy murders "sub-investigation" at the courthouse consisted merely of: (1) firing a gun inside to test if it could be heard across the street; and (2) bringing in a forensic consultant, Dr. Henry Lee, whose finding of "blood" on the upstairs hallway floorboards was a hoaxer lie. Lying more, the hoaxers said the "blood" was Bell's. Olinger was left out. Also left out is that this "investigation" has nothing to do with the gun used to shoot Bell. And, even if it did, that would have nothing to do with whether Garrett gave it to Billy, or whether Garrett murdered an innocent victim 2 ½ months later. The "upstairs blood," though irrelevant, will be debunked later with the rest of the fake forensic claims.]

[AUTHOR'S NOTE: At this point, the hoaxers abandon the deputy murders and the Garrett murder motive. But they pretend that they: (1) established Garrett's Billy friendship; (2) Garrett's escape weapon involvement; (3) Garrett's murder motive; and (4) Garrett's murder of the innocent victim.]

This writing will set forth probable cause as to why investigators question who is in the grave in Fort Sumner and seek DNA from Catherine Antrim.

[AUTHOR'S NOTE: Probable cause of Garrett as a murderer has not been established. But this double exhumation is the hoaxers' goal.]

[AUTHOR'S NOTE: What follows is the hoaxers' attempt to fake that someone other than William Bonney was shot by Garrett. It is back to "what-ifs": *If* there was any inconsistency in reporting of events around the murder, something is "suspicious;" ergo, Garrett killed someone else. But the hoaxers only fabricate some "inconsistencies."]

The detractors of this investigation hold up the statements of Lincoln County Sheriff Pat F. Garrett, Deputy Sheriff John W. Poe, and the Coroner's Jury report as proof it is William H. Bonney that Sheriff Garrett shot and killed on July 14, 1881 and that the Kid is buried in Ft. Sumner.

[AUTHOR'S NOTE: Hidden are the multiple additional corpse identifications. Later, in this document, in slip-ups, the hoaxers accidentally present more of them!]

Historian Philip J. Rash [sic - Rasch] tells the story history puts forth about the shooting of the Kid in the following manner:

Garrett led them to the mouth of Taiban Arroyo, arriving after dark on 13 July. When Brazil failed to appear, Poe, who was unknown in the area, agreed to ride into fort Sumner the next morning to see what he could learn. Finding the inhabitants suspicious and uncommunicative, he proceeded to Sunnyside, about seven miles north, to visit Milnor Rudolph, the postmaster and an old friend of Garrett's. Rudolph was nervous and evasive. He denied all knowledge of the Kid's whereabouts, but Poe was sure he was concealing something.[8] ([8] Poe, John W. *The Death of Billy the Kid.* New York: Houghton Mifflin Company, 1933) *There is a curious story that while the officer was on the way to Sunnyside, John Collins (Abraham Gordon Graham), a former member of Billy's gang, headed to Lobato's camp to warn the outlaw that officers were in the vicinity. On the way he met the Kid, bound for Fort Sumner. "Billy," he warned, "don't go down there. I just saw Poe, and no doubt Pat Garrett and a posse are around town looking for you."*

[AUTHOR'S NOTE: Recall that Poe was unknown to the locals; so this irrelevant hearsay further lacks credibility.]

The Kid merely laughed and answered, "Oh, that's O.K. I'll be alright," and rode on, leaving Collins badly puzzled."[9] ([9]Ben Kemp. *Dead Men, Who Rode Across the Border.* Unpublished. No date.)

That night Poe rendezvoused with Garrett and McKinney at La Punta de la Glorietta [sic], four miles north of Fort Sumner. Poe's report of both his failure to learn anything definite and his suspicions that there was so much smoke there must be some fire only increased the sheriff's skepticism. After some discussion he commented that the Kid was a frequent visitor to the house of Celsa Gutierrez (sister of Pat's wife Polineria [sic] *Gutierrez) and suggested that they watch her home. Their vigil proved fruitless. As midnight approached Garrett and Poe decided that there was only one other possible source of information - Peter Maxwell, the town's most prominent citizen.*

The officers arrived at his home about 12:30 AM on Friday, the 15th [sic]. *Pat instructed Poe and McKinney to wait outside while he went in to talk to Maxwell. Sitting down on the edge of the bed, he asked in a low voice whether the Kid was on the premises. Maxwell became very agitated, but answered that he was not. At that point a bare headed, bare footed man in his shirt sleeves, carrying a butcher's knife in his left hand and a revolver in his right sprang through the door and asked Maxwell who the two men outside were.*

Maxwell whispered, "That's him."

[AUTHOR'S NOTE: Note the hoaxer slip-ups in presenting this source: (1) *This* Garrett cannot recognize Billy, though they claimed he and Billy were such good friends that Garrett killed for him; and (2) Maxwell identifies the victim as Billy!]

Sensing a third person in the room, the intruder backed toward the door, at the same time demanding, "Quien es? Quien es?"

Pat jerked his gun and fired twice.[10] [11] *([10]Las Vegas Daily Optic, July 18, 1881. [11]Santa Fe Daily New Mexican, July 21, 1881) As the man fell Maxwell plunged over the foot of the bed and out the door, closely followed by the sheriff. Maxwell would surely have been shot by Poe if Garrett had not struck the latter's gun down saying, "Don't shoot Maxwell." He added, "That was the Kid that came in there onto me, and I think I have got him."*

[AUTHOR'S NOTE: This is Peter Maxwell's second dead Billy identification; and is not contradicting Garrett's statement.]

Poe was not so sanguine. "Pat," he answered, "the Kid would not come to this place, you shot the wrong man." All was quiet inside. After some persuasion Maxwell brought a tallow candle and placed it on the outside of the window sill. By its light the body of a man could be seen. Deluvina Maxwell, a Navajo servant, entered the room, examined the body, and found that it was indeed the Kid's.

[AUTHOR'S NOTE: This is a third identification of Billy! And Deluvina knew him, as he hoaxers later confirm themselves. She also reported his killing in a June 24, 1927 interview by J. Evetts Haley. And Poe's quote, in his 1933 book, *The Death of Billy the Kid*, expressed initial disbelief of Billy's coming there – and he did not know him. It does not disprove the victim.]

Garrett's first shot had struck him in the left breast just above the heart; the second had gone wild. Later it was learned that Billy had been staying at the house of Juan Chavez.

[AUTHOR'S NOTE: A fourth Billy identification!]

Becoming hungry, he had gone to Maxwell's to slice a steak from a yearling Pete had killed that morning.

The corpse was taken to a carpenter's shop and laid on the work bench.

[AUTHOR'S NOTE: The carpenter's bench would later became the hoaxers' focus for faking DNA claims.]

Fearing an assault from Billy's friends, the officers remained awake and on guard the rest of the night. However, it passed without incident.

[AUTHOR'S NOTE: The townspeople join the list confirming the body as Billy's, and are called "Billy's friends." Note also that Garrett does not try to conceal the body of the supposed innocent victim of his "murder."]

When morning came, Justice of the Peace Alejandro Segura convened a jury, with Rudolph as president.

[AUTHOR'S NOTE: The Justice of the Peace convened the Coroners Jury. Later the hoaxers will switch this fact.]

They rendered a verdict that William Bonney, Alias "Kid," had been killed by Garrett and were "unanimous in the opinion that the gratitude of the whole community is due the said Garrett for his act and that he deserves to be rewarded".

[AUTHOR'S NOTE: Note that the job of a Coroners' Jury was to identify the body. They did. Billy was known to them. The hoaxers already quoted historian Philip Rasch saying Rudulph was nervous when interviewed by Poe - indicating he knew Billy, and knew he was in the area. Crucial also is that the Coroner's Jury declared the killing justifiable homicide. That closed the case legally. Re-opening it is double jeopardy.]

That afternoon Jesus Silva and Vincente Otero dug a grave for the outlaw in the old military cemetery.[12] ([12]Philip Rasch. *Trailing Billy the Kid* by Philip J. [sic - Rasch] Outlaw-lawman research series Volume 1, University of Wyoming, Laramie, Wyoming, 1993.)

On face value this looks to be the truth. However, if you study the statements of the eye witness [sic] and the documents they do not match up and both can not be true.

[AUTHOR'S NOTE: This is to fake "inconsistencies."]

Deputy John Poe says the following:

It was understood when I left my companions in the morning that in case of my being unable to learn any definite information in Fort Sumner, I was to go to the ranch of Mr. Rudolph (an acquaintance and supposed friend of Garrett's) whose ranch was located some seven miles north of Fort Sumner at a place called "Sunnyside," with the purpose of securing from him, if possible, some information as to the whereabouts of the man we were after. Accordingly I started from Fort Sumner about the middle of the afternoon for Rudolph's ranch,

[AUTHOR'S NOTE: Remember "in the middle of the afternoon." It will later be switched to Poe leaving for Rudulph's at night.]

arriving there sometime before night. I found Mr. Rudolph at home, presented the letter of Introduction which Garrett had given me, and told him that I wished to stop overnight with him.[13] ([13]Poe, John W. Billy the Kid. Privately published by E.A. Brininstool. Los Angeles, CA.)

[AUTHOR'S NOTE: With this unpublished, Brininstool source - and reasonable assumption of its unavailability to readers – the hoaxers are about to construct a fake argument.]

In this part of Deputy Poe's statement he tells us he was sent to Rudulph's ranch by Garrett because Rudulph was "*an acquaintance and supposed friend of Garrett's,*" that the ranch was located seven miles north of Ft. Sumner, at Sunnyside. Poe also tells Rudulph he is going to spend the night at the ranch.

[AUTHOR'S NOTE: The fakery here is leaving out part of the quote. Brininstool information is as follows: There was no "Brininstool book." Poe wrote his account, including the Rudulph episode, for Charles Goodnight in 1917. In 1919; and an Edward Seymour in New York contacted Goodnight for information on the Kid. Goodnight referred him to Poe. Poe sent his account of Billy's death to Seymour, who sent it to Brininstool, who published it in British *Wild World Magazine*, in December of 1919, later making it a brochure. It was also used in in Poe's book, *The Death of Billy the Kid*, which the hoaxers

earlier cited. On its page 22, Poe states he declined the invitation to spend the night. But the hoaxers omitted its pages 25-26. There, Poe states: "Darkness was now approaching, and I said to Mr. Rudulph that inasmuch as myself and my horse were by this time pretty well rested, having had a good meal, I had changed my mind, and instead of stopping with him, would saddle up and ride during the cool of the evening to meet my companions. This I accordingly did, much, I thought, to the relief of Rudulph." So there was no inconsistency]

In Sheriff Garrett's statement he gives about the same facts of where he was headed and how far it was from Ft. Sumner. Garrett differs with Poe in one area when he says he "arranged with Poe to meet us that night at moonrise" rather then spend the night with Rudulph, as can be seen below:

[AUTHOR'S NOTE: This is to fake Garrett as making contradictions. But Poe *did not* spend the night. The hoaxers merely hid Poe's quote saying that he did not spend the night.]

I advised him (Poe) *also, to go to Sunnyside, seven miles above Sumner, and interview M. Rudolph Esq. In whose judgment and discretion I had great confidence. I arranged with Poe to meet us that night at moonrise, at La Puenta de la Glorietta, four miles north of Fort Sumner.*[14] ([14]Garrett, Pat F. The Authentic Life of Billy the Kid. University of Oklahoma Press, Norman. Oklahoma. 2000)

[AUTHOR'S NOTE: That was it: the hoaxers' alleged inconsistency: whether Poe did or did not spend the night at Milnor Rudulph's! But both Poe and Garrett agree that Poe did not. There was no inconsistency. Nevertheless, this hoaxer flimflam is later repeated on the same subject.]

Deputy Poe then gives his account of when he says he first saw the Kid when he writes:

I observed that he was only partly dressed, and was both bare-headed and bare-footed - or rather, had only socks on his feet, and it seemed to me that he was fastening his trousers as he came toward me art a very brisk walk.

As Maxwell's was the one place in Fort Sumner that I considered above suspicion of harboring "The Kid," I was entirely off my guard, that thought coming into my mind that the man approaching was either Maxwell

[AUTHOR'S NOTE: This quote dovetails with Poe's question about the correct man, since he could not identify Billy. Also note Poe's lack of alarm. It will be misstated by the hoaxers.]

or some guest of his who might have been staying there. He came on until he was almost within arm's length of where I sat before he saw me, as I was partly concealed from his view by the post of the gate. Upon his seeing me he covered me with his six-shooter as quick as lightening, sprang onto the porch, calling out in Spanish, "Quien es?" (Who is it?), *at the same time backing away from me toward the door through which Garrett only a few seconds before had passed, repeating his query, "Quien es?" in Spanish several times. At this I stood up and advanced toward him, telling him not to be alarmed: that he should not be hurt, and still without the least suspicion that this was the very man we were looking for.*

This statement raises many questions with investigators. Poe says he sees a man "*partially dressed, and was bare-headed and bare-footed - or rather, had only socks on his feet, and it seemed to me that he was fastening his trousers as he came toward me art a very brisk walk.*" Then the man covers him with his six shooter. Where did the man put the "*six-shooter*" when he was "*fastening his trousers*"?

[AUTHOR'S NOTE: This is an accidentally hilarious hoaxer contrivance of the impossibility of doing two things at once! Actually, one can hold a revolver and button one's pants. And Billy was a gunman and ambidextrous, so even more able! Amazingly, this silliness would be repeated by Sederwall for W.C. Jameson's 2018 book, *Cold Case Billy the Kid.*]

He did not stop and lay it down because Poe says he "*he came toward me art a very brisk walk.*"

[AUTHOR'S NOTE: Triple tasking!]

Another question that investigators struggle with is would it not go without saying Poe would have had a description of the Kid as he ventured into Ft. Sumner to scout around and gather information. It is beyond reason that he would go searching for a man without at least having a description of the man for whom he was searching?

[AUTHOR'S NOTE: It is not beyond reason. Garrett was not an experienced lawman. And Poe's task was not to search for Billy, but to find out from locals about Billy's whereabouts.]

In a town of about 200 people, many of which were Hispanic would Poe be unable to recognize the Kid from this description as he claims?

[AUTHOR'S NOTE: What description? It seems Poe had none. Also, this is racist. Many people of Hispanic background could be as fair as Billy.]

Deputy Poe continues his statement with these words:

As I moved toward him trying to reassure him, he backed up into the doorway of Maxwell's room, where he halted for a moment, his body concealed by the thick adobe wall at the side of the doorway, from whence he put his head out and asking in Spanish for the fourth or fifth time who I was. I was within a few feet of him when he disappeared into the room.

When the Kid asks Poe who he is in Spanish and has his pistol pointed at the deputy, what is Deputy McKinney doing at this time? Why is he not shouldering his rifle, and at least deploying to the side to cover his partner Deputy Poe from this very real threat? Today the shooting policy for police officers is tight and narrow: in 1881 a shooting policy was non-existent. Investigators believe the deputies had to have a description for whom they were searching. With a threat such as Poe describes, a man with a gun, added to the description of the most wanted man in New Mexico, there would have been cause for both deputies to have fired on the suspect.

[AUTHOR'S NOTE: Here comes fakery. Who says Poe had the description, or thought the gun was a threat? Back then, most men were armed. Poe even shows lack of alarm by reassuring the stranger. This fakery was repeated by Sederwall for W.C. Jameson's 2018 book, *Cold Case Billy the Kid.*]

Even if the deputies chose not to fire, would they have allowed the man who was threatening their lives with a gun

[AUTHOR'S NOTE: Note this switcheroo from a fake claim of alarm at "threatening their lives," to making it a fact.]

to walk in on the unaware Sheriff in the dark? If they chose to allow the man with a gun to walk in on the Sheriff would these seasoned lawmen

[AUTHOR'S NOTE: Kip McKinney was just a hog farmer.]

not at least have warned the Sheriff of the danger?

[AUTHOR'S NOTE: No danger is established.]

In Garrett's statement he relates the following:

From his step I could perceive he was either barefooted or in his stocking feet and held a revolver in his right hand and butcher knife in his left.

He came directly towards me. Before he reached the bed, I whispered, "Who is it Pete?"

[AUTHOR'S NOTE: If Garrett cannot recognize Billy, there goes the hoaxers' best-buddies-murder-plot case centerpiece! Note also that Maxwell provides another Billy identification!]

But I received no response for a moment. It struck me that it might be Pete's brother-in-law. Manuel Abrea, who had seen Poe and McKinney and wanted to know their business. The intruder came close to me, leaned both hands on the bed, his right and almost touching my knee, and asked in a low tone: "Who are they, Pete?" At the same moment Maxwell whispered to me, "That's him!" Simultaneously the Kid must have seen, or felt, the presence of a third person at the head of the bed. He raised quickly his pistol, a self cocker, within a foot of my breast. Retreating rapidly across the room he cried: "Quien es? Quien es? (Who's that? Who's that?) All this occurred in a moment. Quickly as possible I drew my revolver and fired, threw my body aside, and fired again. The second shot was useless: The Kid fell dead ..."

Investigators find it hard to believe that Garrett could see a 6 inch knife in the Kid's hand.

[AUTHOR'S NOTE: That night had a bright moon. When Billy opened the door, a held weapon would have been visible.]

Yet the Kid could not see a six foot, five inch man.

[AUTHOR'S NOTE: It was dark in the room. Note that at this half-way point in the Probable Cause Statement, with killing done, nothing indicates the victim was not Billy.]

Deputy Poe talks about what happened after the shooting of the Kid. He writes:

Within a very short time after the shooting, quite a number of the native people had gathered around, some of them bewailing the death of their friend,

[AUTHOR'S NOTE: From Poe's *The Death of Billy the Kid*, comes this hoaxer slip-up: These people, who can recognize Billy, will later be given his body to lay out.]

while several women pleaded for permission to take charge of the body, which we allowed them to do. They carried it to the yard to a carpenter's shop, where it was laid on a workbench, the women placing candles lightened around it, according to their ideas of properly conducting a "wake" for the dead.

[AUTHOR'S NOTE: By this point, there are profuse eye-witness identifications of Billy!]

Investigators keep Deputy Poe's statement in mind as they studied the Coroner's Jury Report:

Greetings:

On this 15th day of July, A.D. 1881, I, the undersigned, Justice of the Peace of the above named precinct, received information that a murder had taken place in Fort Sumner, in said precinct, and immediately upon receiving said information I proceeded to the said place and named Milnor Rudolph, Jose Silva, Antonio Sevedra, Pedro Antonio Lucero, Lorenzo Jaramillo and Sabal Gutierres a jury to investigate the case and the above jury convened in the home of Luz B. Maxwell and proceeded to a room in the said house where they found the body of William Bonney alias "Kid" with a shot in the left breast and having examined the body they examined the evidence of Pedro Maxwell, which evidence is as follows: "I being in my bed in my room, at about midnight on the 14th day of July, Pat F. Garrett came into my room and sat down. William Bonney came in and got close to my bed with a gun in his hand and asked me "who is it" and then Pat F. Garrett fired two shots at the said William Bonney and the said William Bonney fell near my fire place and I went out of the room and when I came in again about three or four minutes after the shots the said William Bonney was dead."

[AUTHOR'S NOTE: This is a definitive Jury, plus Maxwell , making identifications of the victim as William Bonney.]

The jury has found the following verdict: We the jury unanimously find that William Bonney has been killed by a shot on the left breast near the region of the heart, the same having been fired with a gun in the hand of pat F. Garrett and our verdict is that the deed of said Garrett was justifiable homicide and we are unanimous in the opinion that the gratitude of all the community is due to the said Garrett for his deed and is worthy of being rewarded.

M. Rudolph, President *Anto, Sevedra(signature)*
Pedro Anto. m. Lucero (signature)
Jose Silba (x) *Sabal Gutierrez (x)* *Lorenzo Jaramillo (x)*

All said information I place to your knowledge.

Alejandro Segura Justice of the Peace (signature)

[AUTHOR'S NOTE: This is a legally binding document confirming victim identification. To reopen the case is double jeopardy. Further confirmation of jurymen's certainty, is that no murder indictment was later made with the District Attorney of the First Judicial District Attorney against Garrett.]

Investigators remembered Deputy Poe's statement and Sheriff Garrett's statement as to where Poe had been that night.

[AUTHOR'S NOTE: The hoaxers hope the reader believed their faked contention that Poe spent the night at Rudulph's. What follows is more fakery to manufacture "inconsistencies."]

Earlier that evening

[AUTHOR'S NOTE: The time was afternoon, as quoted by the hoaxers earlier, and tagged by me to prepare for this switcheroo where they need night for their fake argument.]

Garrett had dispatched Deputy Poe to interview M. Rudulph in Sunnyside, seven miles north of Fort Sumner. Poe says he left Rudulph and rode to meet Garrett and McKinney. All records show that the shooting took place about midnight and Historian Philip I. Rash [sic] sets the time at 12:30 AM on July 15th. If this were true then the time does not allow for the statement of Poe and the coroner's jury report to both be true.

[AUTHOR'S NOTE: Their hoaxers' time switcheroo is done to discredit the Coroner's Jury Report: their bugbear. But, even if granted them, it does not work because of the length of the ride. Poe could cover the 7 miles to Sunnyside in 1½ hours. Puenta de la Glorietta was 4 miles north of Fort Sumner on the way. So Poe's return journey to meet his companions was only 3 miles, or about 45 minutes: easy to meet them by evening: a fact he and Garrett confirmed. No time inconsistency exists.]

If, after the shooting, Garrett had to get some order to the scene, locate a rider to ride to Sunnyside to get Rudulph,

[AUTHOR'S NOTE: The above Coroner's Jury Report clearly states that the appointment - and contacting - of Rudulph was a legal duty performed by the appropriate official: Justice of the Peace, Alejandro Segura; certainly <u>not</u> Garrett, then a suspect as to his legality in Billy Bonney's killing.]

and the rider then had to get his horses [sic] caught, saddled and ready to go all of which would take the better part of an hour,

[AUTHOR'S NOTE: Timing here is faked. Maxwell had a stable and workers. A horse could be readied quickly.]

the time would be 1:30 am.

[AUTHOR'S NOTE: The hoaxers are faking time "inconsistency. Yet they know that the Coroner's Jury met sometime during daytime of the 15th. There was no need for extreme urgency; and no evidence that it occurred.]

It would take a rider who was in shape, on a good horse, and riding fast, an hour and a half to cover the seven miles to Rudulph's ranch, putting the time at 2:30 am. Adding an hour for the rider to wake Rudulph up and for Rudulph to catch his horse and saddle the horse the time would be 3:30 am. If Rudulph was in good shape, on a good horse it would be another hour and a half on the return trip to Fort Sumner putting the time at 4:30 am. Add another hour to put together a jury, and the time is now 5:30 am. This is if everyone worked smoothly.

In the jury's report we find the words:

... a jury to investigate the case and the above jury convened in the home of Luz B. Maxwell and proceeded to a room in the said in said house where they found the body of William Bonney alias "Kid"...

Either the jury found the Kid in the Maxwell's home, or he was not given to the women to put on the carpenters workbench as Poe says, or the jury report is deceptive.

[AUTHOR'S NOTE: The hoaxers hope they convinced readers of that conclusion to fake an inconsistency. But there was enough time to carry the corpse from the Maxwell house, across about 300 yards of parade ground, to the carpenter's shop. In the morning, it could be returned to the Maxwell's house for the jurymen. This fakery was recycled by Sederwall for W.C. Jameson's 2018 book, *Cold Case Billy the Kid.*]

Deputy Poe also says:

The next morning we sent for the justice of the peace,

[AUTHOR'S NOTE: Here is undone the fakery of the night riding by giving this quote about the next morning.]

who held an inquest over the body, the verdict of the jury being such as to justify the killing, and later, on the same day, the body was buried in the old military burying ground at Fort Sumner.

If the Kid's body was taken to the carpenter shop then the jury did not find the body at Maxwell's house as stated and makes investigators wonder why they would lie in the report.

[AUTHOR'S NOTE: This fabrication leads to a "lie" accusation. But nothing indicates that the body was not brought to the house from the carpenter's shop. But the hoaxers are still trying to discredit the Coroner's Jury Report by fake

"contradictions;" though, of course, that is irrelevant to establishing the victim's identity.]

Deputy Poe says something else that raised investigators suspicions when he writes about the shooting itself:

[AUTHOR'S NOTE: This switcheroo distracts from the sly misstatements slipped past. And though the hoaxers never say what is "suspicious" in Poe's quote – which is merely repeating Garrett's description - they are setting the stage for their fake "investigation" to be described next.]

An instant later a shot was fired in the room, followed immediately by what everyone within hearing distance thought was two shots fired, the third report, as we learned afterward, being caused by the rebound of the second bullet which had struck the adobe wall and rebounded against the headboard of the wooden bedstead.

[AUTHOR'S NOTE: Let us take stock now. Nothing so far indicates a victim other than profusely identified Billy Bonney. Nor are there any "contradictions." Later, when exhumations were blocked, the hoaxers contradicted this document: stating Billy *was* shot, laid out on the bench, but played dead to bleed as a source of DNA, before evil Garrett switched him with the murdered innocent victim!]

[AUTHOR'S NOTE: Note that the second bullet hit the headboard. But the hoaxers will do fake forensics on a washstand instead! So next is a faked CSI-style investigation.]

On August 29, 2003, Deputy Sederwall of the Lincoln County Sheriff''s Department

[AUTHOR'S NOTE: Sederwall calls himself a deputy; years later, when hiding the case's DNA documents from my open records case, he would lie that he did the case as his "hobby!"]

located the carpenter bench where the Kid's body was placed on July 14, 1881.

[AUTHOR'S NOTE: Error: earliest morning of July 15th]

On September 13, 2003, investigators located all the furniture that was in Pete Maxwell's bedroom the night of the shooting, July 1881.

[AUTHOR'S NOTE: Though this information is irrelevant to the claim of whether Billy was Garrett's victim, this Maxwell furniture - including the carpenter's bench - became pivotal to the survival of the hoax after exhumations were blocked. But the furniture's connection to the historical scenes is not iron-clad. Maxwell family sold Fort Sumner at public auction on January 15, 1884 to Lonny Horn, Sam Doss, Daniel Taylor and

John Lord in partnership with the New England Cattle Company, which transferred its operations there. The Maxwell house (with the fateful bedroom) was torn down about 1887, and some of the timber was used to build the Pigpen Ranch south of Melrose, New Mexico.

Pete Maxwell died in 1898, Luz Maxwell in 1900. One of their daughters, Odile Maxwell married a Manuel Abreu, and settled outside the town. Odelia may have taken family furniture. In about 1925, Odile's and Manuel's then 15 year old daughter, Stella, made a little "Billy the Kid Museum" in a shack to cater to tourists. She labeled some furniture and a carpenter's bench as from that history. It closed in 1936. In about 1940, she and her husband, Kenneth Miller, displayed the furniture in their Santa Rosa, New Mexico gas station. Later in the decade, they moved to Albuquerque, but stored the furniture until bringing what remained to their converted back-yard chicken coop in 1959. Her youngest son, Mannie Miller, showed it to the hoaxers. He died on March 20, 2011, and it was sold to a collector. So all one can say is that about 44 years after Billy's killing, Stella Abreu assembled some alleged Billy the Kid-related furniture for profit.]

Among these items is the headboard of the bed that was in Maxwell's room that night. There is no bullet hole in the headboard.

[AUTHOR'S NOTE: That finding, though irrelevant to the victim, is part of the hoaxers fake forensics and was created to contradict Poe's eye-witness statement that the headboard was hit. The fakery omitted mention that Stella Abreu's museum's headboard was just a thin frame around a huge opening of the missing headboard. There is no place for a bullet hole! This fakery would be recycled by Sederwall in W.C. Jameson's 2018 book, *Cold Case Billy the Kid.*]

In a statement made by Deluvina Maxwell she says the following:

… There was a washstand with a marble top in Pete Maxwell's bedroom, which Garrett had seen in the moonlight and shot at, thinking it was Bonney trying to get up.

[AUTHOR'S NOTE: This is a faked Deluvina quote. Its footnote states: "[15]Deluvina Maxwell's story <u>as related to Lucien B. Maxwell grandchildren</u>, unpublished." This is just hearsay, without even a source. It is being used to fake legitimacy of the hoaxers' claim that the washstand was shot by Garrett.]

It was an old Spanish custom that the night before the burial of a person, people would take turns staying with the body and reciting prayers. William Bonney had a proper funeral. The people took turns and stayed through the night.

[AUTHOR'S NOTE: Another body identification as Billy!]

He was buried in the old government cemetery in Fort Sumner. For many years Deluvina left flowers on his grave in the summer time.[15]

[AUTHOR'S NOTE: This third person statement again shows the quote was not Deluvina. But she did lay flowers for decades, proving the body was Billy's!]

Deluvina lends credibility to the story of the Kid's body being laid on the carpenter bench.

[AUTHOR'S NOTE: Here is a hoaxer slip that ends their case: Billy's corpse on bench! And it ends "Brushy's" hoax too! To get out of that problem, the hoaxers later fabricated that Billy was just "playing dead!"]

In the items investigators located on September 13, 2003 was that wash stand.

[AUTHOR'S NOTE: This washstand is unsubstantiated as from Pete Maxwell's bedroom - as is the rest of the furniture from Stella Abreu's Billy the Kid Museum. And this washstand is implausibly toy-sized. Furthermore, eye-witness Poe said the headboard was hit. But what follows is a fake "crime scene investigation" using the unsubstantiated washstand.]

The was stand was dark in color and 29 1/2 inches wide, with a splash board on the back that measured 5 inch at the middle and tapered down to the ends in a decorative curve. From front to back the wash stand measured 16 inches. It stood 29 inches with three drawers with rusted locks on each drawer. There was what appeared to be a bullet hole through the stand.

Deputy Sederwall removed a .45 caliber pistol round from his deputy weapon and noticed the round was just a little bit bigger than the hole. The night of the shooting Sheriff Garrett was shooting a Colt Single Action Army Revolver, Serial Number 55093, caliber .44/40.[16] ([16]Typed letter from P.F. Garrett dated April 16, 1906. James H. Earl Collection, from County Clerk's office, El Paso, Texas.)

[AUTHOR'S NOTE: Note that there is no bullet, just holes. Claiming .44/40 ammunition is fakery to match Garrett's known weapon's caliber. Actually, there is no link to Garrett or to Maxwell's bedroom. There is even no link to anyone being shot, since accidental discharges happened in New Mexico where owning guns was common from the 19th century to the present – the time frame for "shooting" the tiny washstand!]

The bullet pierced the left side of the washstand, both sides of the drawer and exited out the right side of the stand.

The bullet struck the left side of the stand 22 1/4 inches on the center up from the bottom and 6 1/2 inches on the center of the back of the stand. The bullet exited to the right side 20 1/2 inches on the center up from the bottom and 6 1/2 inches on center from the back of the washstand. On the inside of the left side panel the wood was somewhat splintered indicating that was where the bullet entered the stand. On the right side panel the outside of the panel was splintered indicating the exit of the bullet.

The owner of the washstand, whose name investigators do not wish to release at this time

[AUTHOR'S NOTE: The hoaxers later named Mannie Miller.]

says it was inherited along with the bed from Maxwell's bedroom. The discovery of this evidence makes Deluvina's statement believable.

[AUTHOR'S NOTE: Historically real or not, the furniture examination is irrelevant to Garrett's victim's identity.]

Many questions remain. Why would the coroner's jury report and the eye witness reports be so at odds?

[AUTHOR'S NOTE: They are not at odds. The hoaxers simply made up some "discrepancies." But the hoaxers were heading to additional fakery, once again to attach the hated Coroner's Jury Report that undid their hoaxing.]

A hint can be found in a document discovered in July of 1989 by Joe O. Bowlin.

[AUTHOR'S NOTE: This is a low blow to a dead man. Joe Bowlin, with his wife Marlyn, founded the Billy the Kid Outlaw Gang to "preserve, protect, and promote the history of Billy Bonney and Pat Garrett." This hoax would have been anathema to Joe Bowlin. What follows misstates a book Bolin published posthumously for its old-timer author, A.P. "Paco" Anaya.]

The document is a story, according to Louis Anaya of Clovis, New Mexico as told to his father, Paco Anaya, a friend of Billy the Kid.

[AUTHOR'S NOTE: Note the admitted friendship of Paco Anaya and Billy. It will catch the hoaxers in another slip-up about the victim being Billy.]

This story was translated from Spanish and then printed in book form. In this transcript you will find the following:

Also, I will have to tell you a lot in reference to the reports that Pat Garrett made about the sworn declaration that appears in the records of the Secretary of State and more, concerning what he said about the

Coroners Jury that investigated the death of Billy the Kid when Pat killed Billy.

In this report, I find that the Coroners Jury that investigated the death of Billy the Kid when he was dead is not part of the same report that acted as a Coroners Jury, neither the form or the verdict of the Coroners Jury. The verdict is recorded in the office of the Secretary of State in Spanish, and they (the jury) are not the same men. There are two that did not even live in Fort Sumner.[17] ([17]Anaya, A. P. *I Buried Billy.* Creative Publishing Company. 1991.)

Paco Anaya goes on to list the members of the Jury that he remembered holding the inquest over the body. They are not the same as the jury report as is held up as proof that Garrett killed the Kid.

[AUTHOR'S NOTE: This is the two coroner's jury report claim made-up by windbag "Paco" Anaya, spewing malarkey for his manuscript devoid of historical knowledge. He was used first as an "expert" in the "Brushy Bill" hoax; and subsequently recycled as a staple in all Billy the Kid imposter hoax books to follow – including W.C. Jameson's *Cold Case Billy the Kid*]

One of the differences is Illeginio Garcia [sic - poor legibility - unclear spelling] as the Jury President and not M. Rudulph.

Paco Anaya says that Garrett wrote the first version in English himself. Anaya says that Garrett later came back and wrote another report in Spanish with the help of "Don Pedro Maxwell and Don Manuel Abrea," [sic - Abreu] Maxwell's brother-in-law.

This makes the investigators ask, if Garrett wrote the verdict is that why the words are found, "*...we are unanimous in the opinion that the gratitude of all the community is due to the said Garrett for his deed and is worthy of being rewarded"?*

It should be noted that in the Coroners Jury Report that Garrett puts forth

[AUTHOR'S NOTE: Note the switcheroo. Garrett did not "put forth" the Coroner's Jury Report. It was a legal document done by authority of Justice of the Peace, Alejandro Segura. Garrett was the *subject* of their investigation. The document was available to him after he was cleared of wrongdoing, to send to District Attorney William Breeden. And it surely was not available to humble citizen Anaya. But the hidden punch line is that Anaya's posthumously published manuscript was titled *I Buried Billy*, confirming the body as Billy Bonney's.]

it is interesting to note that two of those listed were in Garrett's wedding, Sabal Gutierrez is his brother-in-law, and Garrett admits in his statement that Rudulph is a close friend.

[AUTHOR'S NOTE: Note the lie. Garrett did not pick the jurymen; the Justice of the Peace did. All the fakery has done nothing to show that Garrett murdered anyone but Billy.]

[AUTHOR'S NOTE: Next is the hoaxer' last try: using fellow hoaxer, David Turk, for useless hearsay and his fancy title.]

David Turk, Historian for the United States Marshal's Service has pointed out other documents

[AUTHOR'S NOTE: Only one document is presented; though Turk came to New Mexico in December of 2003, possibly to assist in writing this Probable Cause Statement.]

bringing into question Garrett's involvement in the Kid's escape.

[AUTHOR'S NOTE: Note the switcheroo. Who said Billy escaped? He was dead.]

Mr. Turk has produced a Works Progress Administration, Federal Writer's Project interview where the following statement was taken:

The people around Lincoln

[AUTHOR'S NOTE: The killing was 150 miles from Lincoln; and Turk's old-timer reports are useless hearsay. He also supplied the hoax with his own slip-shod and pretender-oriented booklet titled "U.S. Marshals Service and Billy the Kid."]

say Garrett didn't kill Billie (sic) the Kid. John Poe was with Garrett the night he was supposed to ... said that he didn't see the man that Garrett killed.

[AUTHOR'S NOTE: Besides the fact that Poe's statements all refer to seeing the victim, Poe did not know Billy.]

I can take you to the grave in Hell's High Acre, an old government cemetery, where Billie (sic) was supposed to be buried and show you the grave.

The cook at Pete Maxwell's was always putting flowers on the grave and praying at it. This woman thought a lot of Billie (sic), but after Garrett killed the man at Maxwell's home her grandson was never seen again

[AUTHOR'S NOTE: No "grandson" was part of this history.]

and Billie (sic) was seen by Bill Nicholi an Indian scout. Bill saw him in Mexico.[18] ([18]Frances E. Tolly [Totty], comp. "Early Days in Lincoln County," Charles Remark Interview. February 14, 1938, Works Progress Administration, Federal Writer's Project, Folklore-Life Histories, Manuscript Division. Library of Congress.)

[AUTHOR'S NOTE: So this sole "evidence" that Garrett did not kill Billy is old-timer malarkey 57 years later, by someone unconnected to the event, and titled as "folklore."]

[AUTHOR'S NOTE: Next comes the conclusion pretending they proved their contentions.]

Discovering the headboard of Maxwell's bed that does not have a bullet hole in it, as Deputy Poe says it did, leads investigators to question if Poe was in fact in the room after the shooting of William Bonney as he said.

[AUTHOR'S NOTE: Omitted is that the headboard is just an empty frame. And claiming if it was not shot, Poe was not in the room" is absurd; and also irrelevant to victim identity.]

However, the discovery of the Maxwell wash stand with the bullet hole through it indicates someone was shot in Maxwell's room on the night of July 14, 18821.

[AUTHOR'S NOTE: Why? A shot washstand does not mean a shot person - or anything at all about who Garrett shot.]

The question remains as to who is in William H. Bonney's grave at Fort Sumner.

[AUTHOR'S NOTE: No question remains. This is all fakery.]

Investigators believe with the conflicts of Sheriff Pat F. Garrett and Deputy John Poe and the fact that these statements are at odds with the Jury Report as shown above,

[AUTHOR'S NOTE: This is fakery. The "conflicts" do not exist; and had nothing to do with whom Garrett shot.]

coupled with the evidence discovered by deputies,

[AUTHOR'S NOTE: There has been no legitimate evidence.]

probable cause exist [sic] to warrant the court to grant investigators the right to search for the truth in criminal investigation 2003-274 through DNA samples obtained from Catherine Antrim.

[AUTHOR'S NOTE: Without any probable cause of a murder, the hoaxers, contrived their objective: exhumation of Billy and his mother.]

[AUTHOR'S NOTE: Signatures follow; typed and written.]

Steven M. Sederwall: Deputy Sheriff, Lincoln County (12/31/03)

Tom Sullivan: Sheriff Lincoln County (12/31/03)

THE OVERTON AFFIDAVIT

Attached to the "Probable Cause Statement" was a two page, typed, old-timer Affidavit prepared for Sheriff Tom Sullivan by a Homer Overton in the mold of the fake identity Affidavits used by William V. Morrison for *Alias Billy the Kid.*. To be noted is that Overton is lying, for whatever reason. It should be noted that Pat Garrett's widow, Apolinaria Gutierrez Garrett, died in 1936, four years *before* Overton's alleged conversation with her in 1940 (b.1861 - d.1936)! She is buried in the Masonic Cemetery in Las Cruces, New Mexico, where Pat Garrett also lies.

Overton's windbag malarkey includes fabrications of a Pat Garrett report to Texas Rangers, a corpse with blasted face, and, of course, Garrett's murder of someone other than Billy the Kid.

Overton's claims also insult Pat Garrett's widow's reverential protection of Garrett's legacy. After Garrett's death in 1908, she even legally fought and reclaimed from a saloonkeeper his revolver used to kill Billy the Kid. She was the last person in the world to tell random, nine year old child, Homer Overton, that Pat had not shot the Kid - even if she had not been four years dead! Homer Overton wrote:

December 22, 2003

Tom Sullivan
Lincoln County Sheriff
P.O. Box 278
Carrizozo, NM 88301

Tom,

It was good talking to you on the phone and, as promised, I am sending this letter as promised to present this Statement of Facts.

Fact: I was born in Pecos, Texas in the year 1931 and lived there until the later [sic] part of 1941. In the summer of 1940, I was invited to spend the summer with Bobby Talbert and his mother, who had moved from Pecos to Las Cruces, New Mexico earlier that year.

[AUTHOR'S NOTE: Time specificity of Overton's age plus the date fixes Overton in Las Cruces in 1940 - not earlier.]

The time I spent there was wonderful, but one thing happened that summer that made the summer unforgettable.

Bobby's next door neighbor was a lady who introduced herself as Mrs. Garrett, the widow of Pat Garrett. Mrs. Garrett would invite us over to have iced tea with mint leaves in it, and told us stories about her life with Pat. I recall her having a parrot that had belonged to Pat which she said was very old. She told us some parrots live to be over 100 years.

That afternoon, she brought out a gun to show us and said it had belonged to Pat. As I recall, the gun appeared to be a Colt single action revolver. At that point I asked her if that was the gun used to kill Billy the Kid. At this point she got an unusual look on her face and stated that she was going to tell us something we would have to promise to keep a secret, and never to tell anyone. We both promised, and until this day I have never told anyone but my immediate family.

Mrs. Garrett proceeded to tell us the following facts concerning her husband and Billy:

Mrs. Garrett said, "Pat did not shoot Billy". She said there was a very close relationship between Pat and Billy, almost like a father and son relationship. She further stated that the night Pat was supposed to kill Billy, that they were in Ft. Sumner and had made a plan to make it look like Pat killed Billy so Billy could go to Mexico and live with no one looking for him any more. She said that Pat had seen a drunk Mexican lying in the street on his way to talk to Billy. So they planned to use the Mexican and claim that he was in fact Billy the Kid. She didn't state if the Mexican was dead or not, but said that they shot him in the face so he couldn't be recognized. They dressed him in Billy's clothes and Pat signed a paper for the Texas Rangers stating that he had killed Billy the Kid and that this was his body. The Mexican was then buried in Fort Sumner and identified as Billy.

Mrs. Garrett struck me as being very sincere when she told us this and she stated that she had never told anyone before. I have kept this secret for sixty-three years and feel it is time to disclose this story. I hope it will be helpful to you in your quest to find the truth about Billy, as I believe what Mrs. Garrett told us that day was the absolute truth.

All that I have told you is as I recall it related to me sixty-three years ago when I was nine years old. It made such an impression on me that I have remembered it in detail these sixty-three years.

Sincerely,
Homer D. Overton
AKA: Homer D. Kinsworthy
CONTACT INFORMATION

Witnessed by: Jerry Raffee, NOTARY
on December 27th 2003

SEAL AFFIXED

THE ABANDONED "SEVENTY-SEVEN DAYS OF DOUBT" DOCUMENT

A document which the lawmen hoaxers hid, and I got by my open records litigation against them, revealed the pretender core of the "Billy the Kid Case" hoax; which the hoaxers had worked hard to conceal to fake their circus as a real investigation.

Likely created around April of 2003, it is a draft of a never-used "Probable Cause Statement" for Pat Garrett as the murder suspect. "LATEST" is handwritten on its front page, as if drafts were attempted. It was titled: "Lincoln County Sheriff's Office, Lincoln County New Mexico, Case: William H. Bonney, a.k.a. William Antrim, a.k.a. The Kid, a.k.a. Billy the Kid: An Investigation into the events of April 28, 1881 through July 14, 1881 - seventy-seven days of doubt." I nick-named it the "Seventy-Seven Days of Doubt Document." Typed-in for future signatures are its lawmen: "Tom Sullivan: Sheriff, Lincoln County Sheriff's Office; and Steven M. Sederwall: Deputy Sheriff, Lincoln County Sheriff's Office."

The document's intent was incriminating Garrett as a murderer by portraying survival of Billy the Kid and killing of an innocent victim. Featured was "Brushy Bill" as Billy the Kid. His fake death scene was used as "survival" "evidence," or probable cause, for accusing Pat Garrett of murdering innocent victim, Billy Barlow. Nevertheless, the other pretender clown, John Miller, was also covered, showing he was always in these modern clowns' sights.

The "Seventy-Seven Days of Doubt" version is merely fake conspiracy theorizing, where "Brushy" is king, and John Miller is fleetingly appears for "survival suspicion." And like "Brushy's" believers, it used his quotes from his original taped interviews with his huckster promoter as proof!

But its actual author is unclear. The person was ignorant of real history; for example, calling Paulita (Peter Maxwell's sister), his "teenage daughter." Mere guesses for authoring are amateur historian Attorney Bill Robins III, since needed was a "Brushy"-believer. Or it could have been "Brushy" author, W.C. Jameson; or David Turk, who contributed his own big "Brushy"-oriented Addendum to the case.

Importantly, the "Seventy-Seven Days of Doubt Document" uses the imposter hoaxers' method of faking a death scene and hiding the Coroner's Jury Report. The document stated:

LINCOLN COUNTY SHERIFF'S OFFICE
LINCOLN COUNTY, NEW MEXICO

Case: ***William H. Bonney,*** *a.k.a.* **William Antrim,**
a.k.a. **The Kid,** ***a.k.a.*** **Billy the Kid**

An Investigation into the events of April 28, 1881 through July 14, 1881 - seventy-seven days of doubt.

Just minutes after twelve, noon, on April 28, 1881, two lawmen lay dead, in the yard of the courthouse in Lincoln, New Mexico, from gunshot wounds. In less time then [sic] it took the New Mexico breeze to clear the gunsmoke, history was clouded with the myth of the shooting and escape of William H. Bonney, a.k.a. Billy the Kid from the make-shift jail, where he awaited a date with the hangman.

The following is a thumbnail sketch of the most widely excepted [sic] account of the events of the escape, capture and shooting death of William H. Bonney a.k.a. Billy the Kid.

The Last Days of William H. Bonney

On August 17, 1877, in George Atkin's cantina near Camp Grant, Arizona, William H. Bonney, who answered to "The Kid" found himself in an altercation with Francis P. "Windy" Cahill over cards or Cahill's woman, no one is quite sure as newspapers report both. It's reported that Windy Cahill called The Kid a "pimp", and in response The Kid dubbed Cahill a "sonofabitch". Infuriated, Cahill reportedly grabbed the Kid and The Kid shoved his pistol into Cahill's stomach, sending a hot round into his belly. With Cahill on the floor, The Kid fled on a stolen horse. Cahill died the next day. A coroner's jury headed by Miles Wood found the shooting by The Kid to be "*criminal and unjustifiable*". The Kid now being a bona fide outlaw drifted across the line into New Mexico's Lincoln County where he signed on as a cowboy working for London born rancher John Tunstall.

Tunstall and his lawyer friend Alexander McSween had decided to challenge the chock-hold [sic] monopoly L.G. Murphy & Company had on Lincoln County. Murphy and his associates, with the backing of the "Santa Fe Ring" ran Lincoln County as they pleased and verticality [sic] unchecked until Tunstall's challenge. The Santa Fe Ring, with their powerful political and financial backing and through Murphy controlled the sheriff, maintained a buddy-buddy relationship with the military and appropriated by means both legal and illegal most of the government money out of the Mescalero Apache Indian Agency near Fort Stanton. When Tunstall wouldn't back down and his challenge became to [sic] powerful for the Murphy faction to turn their heads to, Tunstall was killed. His death on February 18, 1878 fanned the spark that raged into the white-hot flame that became the famed and bloody Lincoln County War.

As history goes Bonney was insignificant as a man, but there exist [sic] no better example of how legends of the west are born and continue to grow. By participating in a number of bloody shootouts, included [sic] the assassination of Lincoln County Sheriff William Brady and one of his deputies, on April 1, 1878, Bonney was catapulted from his status of an unknown drifter to the undisputed leader of the Tunstall-McSween faction and into history becoming bigger the [sic] life.

[AUTHOR'S NOTE: Though starting when Bonney was 17 ½ (not his last days!), the intent is to feign "historical knowledge, and fails. Billy was never the leader of the Tunstall-McSween faction. The fakery intentionally blurs history and "legend," to pretend that actual history *was* legend, to segue to the fakery that history was not as written. But all this is irrelevant to any probable cause of Pat Garrett murdering an innocent victim.]

After newly elected Lincoln County Sheriff Pat Garrett captured Bonney at Stinking Springs, east of Fort Sumner, just before Christmas 1880, Bonney was held in the jail in Santa Fe for several months and then taken to La Mesilla, New Mexico for trial.

The Dona Ana County, District Court records reveal on April 13, 1881, William H. Bonney was convicted of the April 1, 1878 murder of Lincoln County Sheriff William Brady. United States District Judge, Warren Henry Bristol, of the Third Judicial District, sentenced Bonney to be confined in Lincoln County until Friday, May 13, 1881. Looking down from the bench, the judge proclaimed, "*between 9 a.m. and 3 p.m., William Bonney, alias Kid, alias William Antrim, be taken from such prison to some suitable and convenient place of execution within said county of Lincoln, by Sheriff of such county and that then and there, on that day and between the aforesaid hours thereof, by the sheriff of said county of Lincoln, he, the said William Bonney, alias Kid, alias William Antrim, be hanged by the neck until his body be dead.*"

On April 21, 1881, Bonney was transported back to Lincoln under heavy guard. Because Lincoln had no adequate jail Bonney was incarcerated in the upstairs of the old Murphy-Dolan store, recently bought by the county to be used as the courthouse. A staircase led up to a hallway that ran north to south across the middle section of the building. The room ahead and to the left of the hallway was being used as the sheriff''s office. Off the sheriff''s office, with access only through the sheriff''s office was the room where Bonney was confined.

With no bars on the windows of this room, Sheriff Garrett had special leg shackles made, and Bonney was chained to the hardwood floor at all times. In addition, Garrett assigned Lincoln County Sheriffs Deputy J.W. Bell and Deputy United States Marshall [sic] Bob Olinger, to guard the prisoner twenty-four hours a day. On the floor Bonney's guards drew a chalk line across the center of the room, a line which Bonney was forbidden to cross or he would be shot by the guards.

On Wednesday, April 27, 1881 Sheriff Pat Garrett left Lincoln on a tax-collecting mission to White Oaks, New Mexico. Just after twelve, noon, the next day, Thursday, April 28, Deputy United States Marshall [sic] Olinger escorted all the prisoners with the exception of Bonney to the Wortley Hotel, across the street from the courthouse, for their midday meal, leaving Deputy Sheriff Bell in charge of Bonney.

No eye witness record can be found of the escape of Bonney with the exception of the following statement made by the courthouse caretaker Gottfried Gauss, published in the *Lincoln County Leader* on January 15, 1890, nearly a decade later.

I was crossing the yard behind the courthouse, when I heard a shot fired then a tussle upstairs in the courthouse, somebody hurrying downstairs, and deputy sheriff Bell emerging from the door running toward me. He ran right into my arms, expired the same moment, and I laid him down, dead. That I was in a hurry to secure assistance, or perhaps to save myself, everybody will believe.

When I arrived at the garden gate leading to the street, in front of the courthouse, I saw the other deputy sheriff Olinger, coming out of the hotel opposite, with the four or five other county prisoners, where they had taken their dinner. I called to him to come quick. He did so, leaving his prisoners in front of the hotel. When he had come up close to me, and while I was standing not a yard apart, I told him that I was just after laying Bell dead on the ground in the yard behind. Before he could reply, he was struck by a well-directed shot fired from a window above us, and fell dead at my feet. I ran for my life to reach my room and safety, when Billy the Kid called to me: "Don't run, I wouldn't hurt you – I am alone, and master not only of the courthouse, but also of the town, for I will allow nobody to come near us." "You go," he said, "and saddle one of Judge (Ira) Leonard's horses, and I will clear out as soon as I have the shackles loosened from my legs." With a little prospecting pick I had thrown to him through the window he was working for at least an hour, and could not accomplish more than to free one leg. He came to the conclusion to wait a better chance, tie one shackle to his waistbelt, and start out. Meanwhile I had saddled a small skittish pony belonging to

Billy Burt (the county clerk), as there was no other horse available, and had also, by Billy's command, tied a pair of red blankets behind the saddle ...

When Billy went down the stairs at last, on passing the body of Bell he said, "I'm sorry I had to kill him but I couldn't help it." On passing the body of Olinger he gave him a tip with his boot, saying, "You are not going to round me up again." And so Billy the Kid started out that evening, after he had shaken hands with everybody around and after having a little difficulty in mounting on account of the shackle on his leg, he went on his way rejoicing.

There are numerous theories about the killing of Deputy J.W. Bell. One is that he was coming up the stairs when shot. Another theory is Bell was running down the stairs and was at the bottom of the stairs and heading to the doorway when Bonney shot him. Garrett's testimony seems to be the most solid. Garrett says, "*Bell was hit under the right arm, the bullet passing through his body and coming out under the left arm. The ball had hit the wall on Bell's right, caromed passed through his body, and buried itself in an adobe (wall) on the left. There was no other proof besides the marks on the walls.*"

Garrett later said of Olinger, that he was "*hit in the right shoulder, breast and side. He was literally riddled by thirty-six buckshot.*" Each pellet weighed four grams - nearly a quarter pound of lead in all hit Olinger.

It's hard to determine how many shots were fired at Bell from Bonney's pistol. In the 1920's Maurice G. Fulton saw the building and states there were "*any number of bullet holes*". Fulton had a photograph taken in the 1930's prior to the restoration, which shows three.

With only two people on the stairway that day numerous versions of what happened have been brought forth, and debated. One theory in the Kid's escape is that he slipped his irons, which were double the usual weight, over his small wrists and hands. He turned on Bell striking the deputy over the head with the irons and grabbing the deputy's pistol. This theory could have come from the following article.

In the *Grand County Herald's*, May 14, 1881 edition an article appeared quoting an "anonymous bystander" as testifying about the Kid's escape. *He had at his command eight revolvers and six guns. He stood on the upper porch in front of the building and talked with the people who were in Wortley's, but he would not let anyone come towards him. He told the people that he did not want to kill Bell but, as he had to. He said he grabbed Bell's revolver and told him to hold up his hands and surrender; that Bell decided to run and he had to kill him. He declared he was "standing pat" against the world; and while he did not wish to kill anybody, if anybody interfered with his attempt to escape, he would kill him.*

In this statement the "anonymous bystander" claims Bonney says he took Bell's pistol from him and used it to kill the deputy. In Garrett's book *The Authentic Life of Billy the Kid,* Garrett writes this about the escape:

From circumstances, indications, information from Geiss (also spelled Gauss – the courthouse caretaker) and the Kid's admissions, the popular conclusion is that:

At the Kid's request, Bell accompanied him down stairs and to the back corral. As they returned, Bell allowed the Kid to get considerably in advance. As the Kid turned on the landing of the stairs, he was hidden from Bell. He was light and active, and with a few noiseless bounds, reached the head of the stairs, turned to his right, put his shoulder to the door of the room used as an armory (thought locked, this door was well known to open by a firm push), entered, seized a six-shooter, returned to the head of the stairs just as Bell faced him on the landing of the staircase, some twelve steps beneath, and fired. Bell turned, ran out into the corral and towards the little gate. He fell dead before reaching it. The Kid ran to the window at the south end of the hall, saw Bell fall, then slipped his handcuffs over his hands, threw them at the body, and said: "Here, damn you, take these, too."

Garrett's account seems to have to [sic] many holes to be taken as truth in this matter. At the beginning of Chapter XXII, where this account is found Garrett begins, *On the evening of April 28, 1881, Olinger took all the other prisoners across the street to supper, leaving Bell in charge of the Kid in the guard room.* It is a known fact that the escape did not happen in the evening as Garrett writes but just after noon.

Frederick Nolan, in his commentary notes at the side of the page in this book, points out the following: *The "popular" conclusion set forth here - that Bell would have allowed the Kid latitude and time he needed to perform these maneuvers - has already been examined. That he could have moved "noiselessly" when wearing manacles and leg irons defies belief. And would Billy have waited until after killing Bell before he "slipped his handcuffs over his hands?" Either the Kid struck Bell over the head with his handcuffs, grabbed Bell's gun and killed him with it, or, far more plausibly, someone hid a pistol in the outhouse privy, which Billy retrieved and, when they got inside, killed Bell with it.*

When Garrett describes The Kid shooting Olinger he says that ... *Olinger appeared at the gate leading into the yard, as Geiss appeared at the little corral gate and said, "Bob, The Kid has killed Bell." At the same instant the Kid's voice was heard above: "Hello, old boy," said he. "Yes, and he's killed me too," exclaimed Olinger, and fell dead with eighteen buckshot in his right shoulder and breast and side.*

It is doubtful that Olinger would have time to say the words that Garrett contributes [sic] to him before the Kid cut him down, making Garrett's account difficult to be taken as true accounting of the events.

[AUTHOR'S NOTE: Though lacking crafty finesse of the final Probable Cause Statement, this author likewise uses Garrett's ghostwritten, dime-novel-style book to try to discredit him. But it remains irrelevant to Garrett as a murderer.]

Garrett also says about The Kid in his account – *He took deliberate aim and fired the other barrel, the charge taking effect in nearly the same place as the first; then breaking the gun across the railway of the balcony, he threw the pieces at Olinger, saying: "Take it, damn you, you won't follow me any more with that gun."*

This doubtful this happened. [sic] The account of The Kid breaking Olinger's shotgun on the balcony is not found elsewhere. Added to the fact that Olinger's shotgun was a Whitney, serial number SN903, and is now on loan to the *Texas Ranger Hall of Fame* in Waco, Texas from the James H. Earl Collection; the shotgun is in tact [sic].

[AUTHOR'S NOTE: Error. Deputy Bob Olinger's Whitney double-barreled shotgun there is broken at its waist, and repaired, at some unknown time, by a wrapping of copper wire. Its curator at the Texas Ranger Museum, attesting to the description, is Don Agler. This is another irrelevant attempt to discredit Garrett.]

The version which seems the more popular, is that Bonney, retrieved a pistol that had been hidden in the outhouse by a "friend." History has theories but no firm answers to the identity of the "friend" who put the pistol in the outhouse.

[AUTHOR'S NOTE: Error. This seems to be a confusion of the Bell killing with Olinger's, for which the Whitney was used.]

After the Kid shot and killed both of his guards he gather [sic] weapons, and left Lincoln about 3 p.m. on a stolen horse. The Kid's whereabouts from the date of his escape until just before his death, as nearly every aspect of the case, is still debated. The Kid later showed up in Ft. Sumner, New Mexico. **Pete Maxwell's teenage daughter, Paulita,**

[AUTHOR'S NOTE: Error. Paulita was Peter Maxwell's sister. Also, using Paulita contradicts the "love tales" of "Brushy Bill" (Celsa) and John Miller (Isadora), and eliminates them as Billy contenders!. But revealed is the writer's historical ignorance.]

was supposedly in love with the Kid and he with her, which seems to be the most likely motive for him to return to Ft. Sumner.

On the night of July 14, 1881, after searching the area around Ft. Sumner Lincoln County Sheriff Pat Garrett and his deputies John Poe and Thomas C. "Kip" McKinney were about to ride back to Lincoln. Before leaving they thought it a good idea to check with Pete Maxwell. In Garrett's account of this he takes credit for wanting to check with Maxwell before giving up the chase, Deputy Poe differs with Garrett. In Deputy Poe's account written in 1919 we see the events through his eyes.

Garrett seemed to have but little confidence in our being able to accomplish the object of our trip, but said that he knew the location of a certain house occupied by a woman in Fort Sumner which the Kid had formerly frequented, and that if he was in or about Fort Sumner, he would most likely be found entering or leaving this house some time during the night. Garrett proposed that we go to a grove of trees near the town, conceal our horses, then station ourselves in the peach orchard at the rear of the house, and keep watch on who might come or go. This course was agreed upon, and we entered the peach orchard about nine o'clock that night, stationing ourselves in the gloom or shadow of the peach trees, as the moon was shining very brightly. We kept up a fruitless watch here until some time after eleven o'clock, when Garrett stated that he believed we were on a cold trail; that he had very little faith in our being able to accomplish anything when we started on the trip. He proposed that we leave the town without letting anyone know that we had been there in search of the Kid.

I then proposed that, before leaving we should go to the residence of Peter Maxwell, a man who up to that time I had never seen, but who, by reason of his being a leading citizen and having a large property interest should, according to my reasoning, be glad to furnish such information as he might have aid us [sic] *in ridding the country of a man who was looked on as a scourge and curse by all law-abiding people.*

Garrett agreed to this, and there-upon led us from the orchard by circuitous by-paths to Maxwell's residence, which was a building formerly used as officers' quarters during the days when a garrison of troops had been maintained at the fort. Upon our arriving at the residence (a very long, one-story adobe, standing end to the flush with the street, having a porch on the south side, which was the direction from which we approached, the premises all being enclosed by a paling fence, one side of which ran parallel to and along the edge of the street up to and across the end of the porch to the corner of the building). Garrett said to me, "This is Maxwell's room through the open door (left open on account of the extremely warm weather), while McKinney and myself stopped on the outside. McKinney squatted on the outside of the fence, and I sat on the porch.

It should be here that up to this moment I had never seen Billy the Kid, nor Maxwell, which fact in view of the events transpiring immediately afterward, placed me at an extreme disadvantage.

It was probably not more than thirty seconds after Garrett had entered Maxwell's room, when my attention was attracted, from where I sat at the little gateway, to a man approaching me on the inside of and along the fence, some forty or fifty steps away. I observed that he was only partially dressed and was both bareheaded and barefooted, or rather had only socks on his feet, and it seemed to me that he was fastening his trousers as he came toward me at a very brisk walk.

As Maxwell's was the one place in Fort Sumner that had considered above suspicion of harboring the Kid, I was entirely off my guard, the thought coming to my mind that the man approaching was either Maxwell or some guest of his who might be staying there. He came on until he was almost within arm's length of where I sat, before he saw me, as I was partially concealed from his view by the post of the gate.

Upon seeing me, he covered me with his six-shooter as quick as lightening, sprang onto the porch, calling out in Spanish "Quien es" (Who is it?) - at the same time backing away from me toward the door through which Garrett only a few seconds before had passed, repeating his query, "Who is it?" in Spanish several times.

At this I stood up and advanced toward him, telling him not to be alarmed, that he should not be hurt; and still without the least suspicion that this was the very man we were looking for. As I moved toward him to reassure him, he backed up into the doorway of Maxwell's room, where he halted for a moment, his body concealed by the thick adobe wall at the side of the doorway, form [sic] *whence he put his head and asked in Spanish for the fourth time who I was. I was within a few feet of him when he disappeared into the room.*

After this, and until after the shooting, I was unable to see what took place on account of the darkness of the room, but plainly heard what was said on the inside. An instant after the man left the door, I heard a voice inquire in a sharp tone, "Pete, who are those fellows on the outside?" An instant later a shot was fired in the room, followed immediately by what anyone within hearing distance thought were two shots. However, there were only two shots fired, the third report, as we learned afterward, being caused by the rebound of the second bullet, which had struck the adobe wall and rebounded against the headboard of a wooden bedstead.

I heard a groan and one or two gasps from where I stood in the doorway, as of someone dying in the room. An instant later, Garrett came out, brushing against me as he passed. He stood by me close to the wall at the side of the door and said to me, "That was the Kid that came in there onto me, and I think I got him". I said, "Pat, the Kid would not come to this place; you have shot the wrong man".

Upon saying this, Garrett seemed to be in doubt himself as to whom he had shot, but quickly spoke up and said, "I am sure it was him, for I know his voice to [sic] *well to be mistaken". This remark of Garrett's relieved me of considerable apprehension, as I had felt almost certain that someone whom we did not want had been killed.*

The next day Billy the Kid was buried in Fort Sumner. Or was it the Kid in the grave?

[AUTHOR'S NOTE: Poe's initial uncertainty about Billy's identity, is this writer's only "evidence" of victim identity doubt. Omitted are all witnesses, the Coroner's Jury, and Poe's acceptance.]

What Happen [sic] to William H. Bonney a.k.a. Billy the Kid?

Soon after the shooting in Maxwell's home on July 14, 1881, the rumor took life that Garrett shot the wrong man and that he knew he shot the wrong man but covered it up.

[AUTHOR'S NOTE: This "Seventy-Seven Days Document" is transparently tailored to fit the pretenders.]

Some even say that Garrett had an empty coffin buried the next day in Fort Sumner. Some say Garrett wrote the book *The Authentic Life of Billy the Kid*, in which he demonizing [sic] Billy the Kid, to prop up his waning popularity that was being eroded by the rumor that he killed The Kid in less than a fair fight or that he did not kill The Kid at all.

[AUTHOR'S NOTE: These contentions, without sources, appear made-up, and are not evidence.]

To this day the rumor still has life that Billy the Kid never died that night.

[AUTHOR'S NOTE: Nothing has been presented to support that "rumor."]

Most everything we know about William H. Bonney a.k.a. Billy the Kid is what is know [sic] about him in during the last three years of his life. The date and place of his birth, who his father was, where he lived, as a child is still a mystery. Most of what we do know and what we call history is flawed by myth. Even where he is buried is the subject of controversy these 122 years later.

[AUTHOR'S NOTE: This "what-if" illogic tries to make Bonney's death uncertain, by manufacturing "uncertainties" in his earlier history.]

In England is a grave with the name William H. Bonney on the headstone, where is it said [sic] Billy the Kid is buried. The story is that the Tunstall family, in apparition [sic] of his help and loyalty to John Tunstall, brought the Kid back to England where he lived a long life dying of old age.

[AUTHOR'S NOTE: This is so bizarre, it seems a delirium, rather than an argument. It does indicate the author lacks ability to sort fact from fiction.]

[AUTHOR'S NOTE: The case for Garrett's murder of an innocent victim ends here without proof; and segues to the pretenders.]

John Miller

[AUTHOR'S NOTE: At this preliminary stage - years before the hoaxers needed John Miller's exhumation to keep their hoax afloat - he was of minimal interest; their focus being "Brushy Bill." This disinterest is reflected in the following cursory text - whose negative presentation was kept secret when the hoaxers headed with backhoe to John Miller's grave, suddenly claiming *he* was Billy the Kid to drum up a media circus and TV program.]

In 1993 Helen Airy published a book by Sunstone Press entitled *What* [sic- Whatever] *Happened to Billy the Kid.* In this book the claim is made that a John Miller who died on November 7, 1937, at six-thirty in the evening, in the Pioneer [sic] Home in Prescott, Arizona and was buried in the Prescott Pioneer home cemetery [sic], was Billy the Kid. In Airy's book Miller is quoted as saying, "*there was a Mexican shot and buried in the coffin that is supposed to be the Kid.*"

In her book *What* [sic- Whatever] *Happened to Billy the Kid* these accounts are found:

Page 162 paragraph 2 - *Ann Storrer of Belen writes: "My father, Charlie Walker, grew up around Fort Sumner during the early 1900's. A Mexican he used to work for told him that he saw Billy the Kid at the bullfights in Mexico long after he was supposed to be dead. The rumor around Fort Sumner was that Pat Garrett and Bill [sic] the Kid were good friends and Garrett tried to stop everyone from killing Billy. My father believed there was never a body in the grave.*

Page 162 paragraph 3 and 4 - *Arleigh Nation of Albuquerque supplied the Following story; "A man by the name of Trujillo, who died in 1935 at the age of ninety-five told Nation he worked for Pete Maxwell at the time Billy the kid was supposed to have been killed. He said the day before the shoot-out they dressed up an Indian, who had died the night before, to look like the Kid. The Indian was buried in the grave that was said to have been the Kid's.*

Nation, who is a Billy the kid Buff, also said a neighbor of his who lived in Lincoln, Mrs. Syd Boykin, told him that the kid stayed as [sic] her home in Lincoln many times after he was supposed to have been dead.

Airy states that a John Collins claimed to have been a friend of Billy the Kid. Collins says that he helped bury the corpse of the man Garrett killed on July 14, 1881, and it was not Billy the kid.

Arley Sanches interviewed Nadine Brady, of Adelino, New Mexico, and whose grandfather was Sheriff William Brady, who was shot by the Kid, for a story, which appeared in the *Albuquerque Journal* on September 8, 1990. Nadine says one old timer told her Garrett didn't shoot Bonney. He told her Garrett and Bonney were friends and Garrett invented a story to help his friend escape. A wanderer was killed and buried, and Garrett told everyone he had shot Billy the Kid.

Airy says Frank Coe, a friend of Billy the Kid during the Lincoln County War, believed to the day of his death that Billy was still alive, and spent a great deal of time tracing reports that he had been seen.

The El Paso Herald Post, June 29, 1926 reported a story that a "government official" re[ported that "Billy the Kid and Garrett framed an escape" from Lincoln, New Mexico. The government official claimed the Kid was still alive in this article.

The El Paso Times, July 26, 1964, reported that retired Immigration and Naturalization Service Inspector, Leslie Traylor of San Antonio, Texas claimed Billy the Kid was a man named Henry Street Smith. Traylor said he traced Smith and believes him to be buried under the name of John Miller who died in 1935 in Prescott, Arizona.

[AUTHOR'S NOTE: Airy's John Miller hoax was debunked above. The writer here, however, does not appear to argue for Miller as Billy. And no death scene is presented, that being the purpose of a probable cause statement for a murder case!]

William Henry Roberts a.k.a. Brushy Bill Roberts

[AUTHOR'S NOTE: Next is the attempt to establish Oliver "Brushy Bill" Roberts as Billy the Kid. Noteworthy is use if his fake "William Henry" from *Alias Billy the Kid.* Though he surfaced throughout the hoax, it was given as "survival suspicion," not the case's goal. The very fact that this "Seventy-Seven Days of Doubt Document" was kept secret, indicated hiding of that motive. Apparently, it was intended to have that conclusion arise from the fake forensic DNA matchings. But the effusions that follow here show the "Brushy" bias as well as access to the transcript of "Brushy's" Morrison interviews. And the contradiction of his non-bench death scene, presented in detail below, was not yet anticipated; since the hoaxers expected the Billy and mother exhumations to go through, followed by a faked match to "Brushy." So switching to the bench scenario for "blood DNA" was unanticipated.]

Before Sheriff Pat Garrett could clean his pistol the bogus Billy the Kid's began to crop up everywhere. Some were too ridiculous to take notice of and some convinced a few people but were forgotten with the passage of time. Out of all the men to come forward to claim they are Billy the Kid the one that caused the most stir and gained national and even worldwide attention was Brushy Bill Roberts.

To this day Roberts' claim is being taken seriously by many. In Hamilton, Texas, where William Roberts is buried there stands a sign that proclaims that his grave is "The Authentic Grave Site of Billy the Kid." A plaque states that he spent the last part of his life attempting to get a "promised pardon" from the New Mexico Governor. Just weeks before Roberts death he and his attorney [sic - William Morrison, not an attorney] approached the Governor of New Mexico and asked for a pardon for the Kid, who Roberts claimed to be. Dubious of Roberts claims the Governor granted no pardon.

[AUTHOR'S NOTE: This "Brushy" pardon focus exposes the otherwise inexplicable linking of DNA to pardon in the hoax. Making "Brushy" Billy by the fake match, would then lead to a pardon for an alleged long law-abiding life as Billy the Kid.]

The story goes that in 1948, William V. Morrison was working as an investigator for a law firm. Morrison was a graduate attorney **[Morrison fabricated being an attorney, and was a traveling salesman]** and it was said that he had a "good nose for evidence". He was a member of the Missouri Historical Society and a descendant of Ferdinand Maxwell, the brother of Lucien Bonaparte Maxwell and uncle of Pete Maxwell. Because of this, Morrison possessed a keen interest in New Mexico history.

During this time Morrison was sent to Florida to investigate an inheritance claimant by the name of Joe Hines. Hines' brother, in North Dakota, had passed away and Hines claimed to be the sole inheritor of some property. As Morrison interviewed the old man the story did not match with the facts Morrison possessed. After more questions Joe Hines told Morrison his name, Hines, was an alias. Hines claimed his real name was Jesse [sic] Evans and he was a survivor of the Lincoln County War.

[AUTHOR'S NOTE: This is the pure "Brushy" hoax, straight from *Alias Billy the Kid.* Indicated is that the writer was a true-believer, like Bill Robins III or W.C. Jameson, or an opportunistic copier, merely seeking publicity and profit from winning.]

Morrison being proud of his ancestral connection to New Mexico history mentioned to Hines (Evans) that Billy the Kid worked for the Maxwells at one time

[AUTHOR'S NOTE: Morrison's fake claim about Billy.]

and added that the Kid was shot and killed in Maxwell's house on July 14, 1881. To that Hines replied, "Garrett did not kill the Kid on July 14, 1881, or any other time." Hines went on to say, "In fact Billy was still living in Texas last year. The reason that I know is that a friend of mine, now living in California stops over to visit with me here every summer. He and Billy and me are the only warriors left of the old Lincoln County bunch.

[AUTHOR'S NOTE: Besides the total fakery, real outlaw-murderer-rustler Jessie Evans would not have called himself a Lincoln County War "warrior."]

Later that year Morrison became acquainted with another man in Missouri who said he knew who all the parties were and gave Morrison an address of a man named O.L. Roberts who lived in Hamilton, Texas. In June of 1948 Morrison drove to Hamilton, Texas and met Roberts. On their first meeting Roberts told Morrison that the Kid was his half brother and was still alive in Old Mexico. The next day Morrison came back to Roberts home and Roberts sent his wife to a neighbor's house saying he and Morrison had business to discuss.

After Mrs. Roberts left the house Morrison claims Roberts pointed his finger at him and said, "Well, you've got your man. You don't need to look any farther. I'm Billy the Kid. But don't tell anyone. My wife doesn't know who I am. She thinks my half brother is Billy the Kid, but he died in Kentucky many years ago. I want a pardon before saying anything about this matter. I don't want to kill anyone anymore, but I'm not going to hang." Morrison goes on to write that Roberts told his story and tears coursed down his cheeks, as he said, "I done wrong like everyone else did in those days. I want to die a free man. I do not want to die like Garrett and the rest of them, by the gun. I have been hiding so long and they have been telling so many lies about me that I want to get everything straightened out before I die. I can do it with some help. The good Lord left me here for a purpose and I know why He did. Now will you help me out of this mess."

Morrison wanted proof that Roberts claims were true and knew the scars the Kid would have on his body. Morrison had Roberts strip and from the scars on Roberts' body Morrison was convinced that he was talking to the true William H. Bonney.

Roberts tells Morrison in detail how he escaped death at the hands of Sheriff Pat Garrett the night of July 14, 1881. In a statement Roberts records the following:

[AUTHOR'S NOTE: To follow are "Brushy's" words from pages 105-117 of W.C. Jameson's and Frederick Bean's 1998 *The Return of the Outlaw Billy the Kid.* They claimed to have gotten the transcript from "Brushy's" step-grandson, Bill Allison. Thus, indicated is possible participation of W.C. Jameson.]

[AUTHOR'S NOTE: Do not miss the attempted validation of "Brushy" that this document represents. His words are being used as "evidence" in *a real law enforcement case* to show probable cause that Garrett was a murderer, since *he* survived; ergo, Garrett *must have murdered innocent Billy Barlow*.]

I rode into Fort Sumner from Yerby's a few days before Garrett and his posse rode in. When they rode in that day, I had spent the day with Garrett's brother-in-law, Saval Gutierrez. Nearly all the people in this country were my friends and they helped me. None of them liked Garrett. It was dark that night, but there was enough moonlight to make shadows. Me and my partner Billy Barlow, rode up to Jesus Silva's house when we reached Fort Sumner. We had been staying at the Yerby Ranch laying low for a while. Word was all around that Pat Garrett and a posse were after me. Pat's wife was a sister to my friend Saval Gutierrez, and Saval told me that Pat was after me, that he heard it from his sister.

Things were mighty hot in Lincoln County for me right about then, but I wasn't running from it. I meant to have a talk with Pat Garrett and set things straight between us if I could. We used to be friends ... We hid our horses in the barn and walked up to Jesus' back door. Barlow was nervous about being in Fort Sumner with me and I couldn't blame him much. Jesus came to the back door when I tapped on it with the barrel of my six-shooter. When he saw that it was me, he grinned and let us in. I told Jesus we were hungry. We'd been out in the hills all day, scouting around Fort Sumner for any sign of Garrett and his posse. "I have nothing but cold frijoles, compadre," Jesus whispered as he closed the door. Barlow made a sour face. "I want some meat," he said, "we have been living on beans and tortillas all week. Ain't you got any beef?

According to Roberts statement Jesus Silva told Barlow that Pete Maxwell had some meat hanging on his porch. Barlow wanted to get the beef to cook but Roberts told him it was too dangerous and they should not move from the house. Barlow would not listen. According to Roberts statement Barlow took a butcher knife and left the house to head to Maxwell's to get the beefsteak. While Roberts and Jesus were lighting the wood stove they hear [sic] gunfire in the direction of Pete Maxwell's place. Roberts' statement goes on to describe the following events:

I pulled one of my .44's and ran through the door, trying to see in the dark. Two more shots came from a shadow beside the Maxwell house. I couldn't find a target to shoot at. It was too dark to see. *I ran toward Maxwell's back porch. I heard another gunshot and felt something hit me in the jaw. I stumbled and kept on running with a broken tooth rolling around my tongue. I tasted blood and spit the mess out of my mouth as I started emptying my six-shooter at the shadow where I saw the muzzleflash. From the corner of my eye I saw a body lying on the back porch ... I knew it had to be Barlow.*

My partner had walked right into a trap, and the trap had likely been set for me. I pulled my other .44 and ran toward the porch to check on Barlow, but I ran into a wall of gunfire. I knew I wasn't going to make it to my partner. Too many guns were shooting at me. I didn't have a chance. I turned for a fence across the back of Maxwell's yard and dove for it when a bullet caught me in the left shoulder. I jumped over the fence and landed hard on the far side, with the echo of gunshots all around me, ringing in my ears. I staggered into an alley that ran behind the house, firing my .44 over my shoulder until it clicked empty. My mouth and shoulder were bleeding and I lost track of where I was, but I knew I had to get away from Maxwell's before they killed me. I heard a shout and another gunshot. Something passed across my forehead like a hot branding iron. I was stunned. I lost footing and fell on my face in the darkness. I knew I was hurt bad and wondered if I would make it out of this scrape alive.

I forced myself up again, wiping the blood from my eyes with my shirtsleeve as I stumbled headlong down the ally. I didn't know how bad the head wound was, only that it was bleeding and I couldn't see. It wouldn't matter if the found me in the alley just then, they were bent on killing me, to be sure. If I fell again I knew they'd find me and finish the job, so I kept running down the ally as hard as I could, barely able to see where I was going. I heard them shouting to each other behind me, arguing over something, but I was too woozy to think about what they were saying and too frightened to care. The gunshot to my head had knocked me senseless. I kept on staggering and running down the alley, trying to get away. Blood was pouring into my eyes; I couldn't see a thing. I ran past a little adobe shack down the alley from Pete Maxwell's. I supposed all the shooting woke everybody up, because a door opened just a crack when I ran behind the adobe and I could see a lantern light spilling from the doorway across the alley.

I stumbled toward the light not knowing what else to do. I needed help and the open door was the only place I could find, hurt like I was. A Mexican woman pulled me inside. She saw the blood on my face and threw her hands over her mouth. She closed the door quickly and helped me to a chair. I sleeved the blood from my eyes, watching her, loading my Colts.

In Roberts' statement he identifies the woman as Celsa Cutierriz [sic - Gutierrez] who he had known previously. Ms. Cutierriz [sic] helped Roberts and kept him at her home that night. Roberts says that later Ms. Cutierriz [sic] had Frank Lobato saddle his horse and bring it around in the alley so he can [sic] escape. Before Roberts was able to leave Ms. Cutierriz [sic] told him it was rumored about Fort Sumner that Sheriff Garrett was telling everyone he had killed the Kid.

Roberts says, *I started puzzling over what Celsa told me. Garrett was trying to pass off Barlow's body as that of Billy the Kid. I wondered how he figured to get away with it. Garrett knew by now that he'd killed the wrong man in the dark. Billy Barlow looked a lot like me, the same general description, with blue eyes like mine. But in the daylight, a lot of folks who knew me would know they had the wrong body. I couldn't figure it, unless Garrett realized his mistake and was making a try at collection [sic] the reward money that was out on me anyway ...*

Roberts says it was 3 a.m. when Celsa brought his horse up to the house. He says he left with Frank Lobato. Roberts stayed in a camp south of Fort Sumner until his wounds healed and the first of August he rode to El Paso, Texas.

[AUTHOR'S NOTE: "Brushy's" expansive dialogue demonstrates the floridness of his lies and imagination. Noteworthy for the "Billy the Kid Case" hoaxers, however, is that his death scene with back-porch-Barlow points to an early phase of their own faking, where they were not yet concealing the major discrepancies between his "death scene" tale and their own.]

Questions About the Case

There seems [sic] to be problems with every account of the escape of Billy the Kid from the make shift [sic] jail in Lincoln and the shooting at Fort Sumner by Pat Garrett. In every account there remain questions as to what really happened.

[AUTHOR'S NOTE: The above used the hoaxers' fakery of "vague, though unfounded, suspicions" instead of actual evidence - which they lacked. What follows are fake "what-ifs" to make unwarranted leaps to hoaxed conclusions – called by the writer "Questions." It represents the writer's last chance to fake a link of Garrett to a "probable cause" of murder.]

[AUTHOR'S NOTE: For clarity, the illogical transitions are put in boldface. The breath-taking leap of the scam is seen when the "what-ifs" of the outhouse version, lead to a fake, implied accusation that Garrett reported the gun from armory version to hide that *he* was the pistol-giving "friend."]

1. In the historical account of the escape of Billy the Kid, from the courthouse in Lincoln, **it's believed** that a "friend" placed a pistol in the outhouse for Billy to use in his escape. The identity of the "friend" who placed the pistol in the outhouse has gone nearly unasked. **If** this version is true, and a "friend" left a pistol in the outhouse to aid in Bonney's escape that "friend" is a coconspirator to the murder of Bell and Olinger. This "friend" also should have been charged with two counts of homicide but remained at large. **Why** didn't Sheriff Garrett pursue the question of the idenenty [sic] of the "friend" who hid the pistol? Garrett says the Kid took the pistol from the armory. **If** the story of the pistol in the outhouse is true did Garrett have a reason to say it was from the armory?

2. **If** Roberts account and claim about the night of July 14, 1881, is to be believed then Lincoln County Sheriff Pat Garrett was not the hero that history portrays him as. Instead, he becomes a murderer who killed Billy Barlow and covered up that killing and passed off Barlow's body as that of Billy the Kid. With the sign in at [sic] Brushy Bill's grave site claiming to the [sic] grave site of Billy the Kid they are in short saying Pat Garrett lied. Did Garrett lie?

[AUTHOR'S NOTE: This earliest version of the "Billy the Kid Case" hoax relies heavily on "Brushy;" later discrepancies between the evolving hoax and "Brushy's" tales would be concealed by the hoaxers. Here, certainty of winning without bearing scrutiny, apparently yielded a devil-may-care attitude.]

[AUTHOR'S NOTE: This earliest version of the hoax also is unabashedly vicious in accusing Garrett of heinous crimes. Later, under scrutiny, the hoaxers would lie that the case was to protect Garrett's honor against "others" who had accused him!]

3. **If** Roberts claims are believed, it beings up other questions? [sic] He claims in his statement when talking about Pat Garrett, "*we use* [sic] *to be friend*" [sic]. **If** Garrett and Roberts were friends did Garrett and Garrett [sic] allowed The Kid out of friendship to escape from Fort Sumner, *did he also* arrange his escape from Lincoln? Did Garrett question why **his friend, the Kid**, with all the others involved in all the killing was the only one to be convicted and sentenced to hang? The Kid **mentions this** in an interview that was published in the *Mesilla News* on April 15, 1881 when he said, *Think it hard that I should be the only one to suffer the extreme penalties of the law."*

[AUTHOR'S NOTE: Here, "Brushy" is the authority, with "what-ifs" that fabricate Garrett as Billy's "friend" and "accomplice." In addition, lied is that Billy's mention had anything to do with Garrett, rather than to his own sense of injustice.]

4. **Did** Garrett arrange having the pistol put in the outhouse by the "friend" **and is this** why he did not search for the coconspirator to the murder of the two lawmen? **If this is the case then** Garrett is also a coconspirator in the murder of those two lawmen.

[AUTHOR'S NOTE: More meaningless "what-ifs."]

5. In the Lincoln County Courthouse Caretaker Gauss' statement he quotes Bonney as saying about Bell, "*I'm sorry I had to kill him but couldn't help it.*" This statement must raise the question did Bonney, when he produced the pistol he retrieved from the outhouse

[AUTHOR'S NOTE: Sly switcheroo from "what-ifs" to using the outhouse as a fact.]

order Bell to surrender? Did Bell panic and instead of throwing up his hands, turn and run causing Bonney to shoot him?

[AUTHOR'S NOTE: This parrots the historically accepted version. Later in the hoax, for fake forensics, it would be switched to Billy striking Bell with a shackle to cause "blood" on the hallway.]

6. Other questions come to mind in this investigation, some about Gauss. It should be noted that Gauss had worked with Tunstall, so had Bonney. Gauss and Bonney shared the same table as they took meals, slept on the same floor and spent a great deal of time together when Bonney was in the courthouse under guard. It goes to reason that Gauss was sympathetic towards Bonney . With that in mind it could be pointed out that there

were a number of things missing from Gauss's account. Gauss made no reference to how Bell was killed, and leaves out the fact that Bonney used Olinger's own shotgun to kill him. If Bonney retrieved a pistol from the outhouse it had to be prearranged with Bonney and the "friend" as to what date and where to place the pistol in order for Bonney to find it. Since Gauss spent so much time with Bonney would he not have heard something about the plot?

[AUTHOR'S NOTE: This is failed hoaxing! With Gauss as the accomplice, Garrett is innocent - undoing the scam!"]

7. Since the caretaker Gauss worked outside it is not outside the realm of possibility that he saw who put the pistol in the outhouse?

[AUTHOR'S NOTE: The historical reality of Gauss being the accomplice never made it to the final hoax.]

8. It is known that Bonney ate his meals at the courthouse and the only time he was allowed to leave was to use the outhouse. Bell and Olinger took turns escorting the prisoners to the hotel for lunch, leaving the other in charge of Bonney. Bonney as well as the others would have known that Olinger would be escorting the prisoners to lunch that day. Bonney was aware that out of the two guards Bell was the one to make his escape move on since Bell was easy going and seemed to get along with him. Bonney also knew that Olinger had killed men in the past and had threatened to kill him. **Had Garrett and the Kid discussed this and chose Bell** as the deputy for Bonney to make his move thinking Bell would just give up giving the Kid an hour to escape while Olinger was eating?

[AUTHOR'S NOTE: "What-if" blather with a fake conclusion.]

9. **If** Garrett was part of the plot for the Kid's escape **is that why** he rode to White Oaks on a "tax collecting" trip, to give himself an alibi?

[AUTHOR'S NOTE: More 'what-if" fakery.]

10. **If Garrett were part of the plot to allow the Kid to escape he would have reason to chase the Kid. He could not afford for the Kid to tell of his involvement in the two killings of the lawmen. Garrett also has a weak link in the plot, that being the "friend" who put the pistol in the outhouse. If Roberts' story is true, is Billy Barlow the one who put the pistol in the outhouse under orders of Garrett? In Roberts' accounting he shows up at Fort Sumner with no one but Barlow. Did he meet Barlow after he rode out of Lincoln and move on [sic] to Fort Sumner?**

[AUTHOR'S NOTE: The culmination of "what-if" fakery.]

11. **If** Garrett shot Billy Barlow in the dark, by mistake, on July 14, 1881, and Barlow was the only one who could tell the story of Garrett's involvement other than the Kid, would Garrett not know the Kid would run to keep from hanging?

[AUTHOR'S NOTE: This incoherent reverie, appears to contradict the Pat-Billy friendship on which this hoax relies.]

12. In Deputy John W. Poe's statement as he lays out the shooting in Maxwell's house on July 14, 1881, he says "... Garrett came out, brushing against me as he passed. He stood by me close to the wall at the side of the door and said to me, That was the Kid that came in there onto me, and I think I got him.' I said, "Pat, the Kid would not come to this place; you have shot the wrong man.' Upon my saying this, Garrett seemed to be in doubt himself as to whom had shot ..." Did Garrett kill the wrong man by mistake and cover it up?

[AUTHOR'S NOTE: The writer forgot that backing "Brushy" means no bedroom murder scene – but a Barlow-on-back-porch one. Also forgotten is that "Brushy's" scene had enough gunfire to rival the Alamo.]

[AUTHOR'S NOTE: Similar to the final "Probable Cause Statement," this "question" hides the multiple identifications of Billy, following this moment of doubt in a darkened room.]

13. Most researchers and historians have accepted without much question, the statement that Billy the Kid was born Henry McCarty, in New York on November 23, 1859. It should be noted that the first time this information comes to light is in Pat Garrett's book *The Authentic Life of Billy the Kid.*

[AUTHOR'S NOTE: Error. This was outlaw myth press in Billy's lifetime, while he was pursued by Garrett and Secret Service Agent Azariah Wild. It was in "Outlaws of New Mexico. The Exploits of a Band Headed by a New York Youth. The Mountain Fastness of the Kid and His Followers - War Against a Gang of Cattle Thieves and Murderers." December 27, 1880. *The Sun.* New York. Vol. XLVIII, No. 118, Page 3, Columns 1-2.]

In the book the evidence for this claim is sited [sic] to have come from a birth announcement that appeared in the on November 25, 1859. In 1950 William Morrison the attorney **[AUTHOR'S NOTE: Morrison was not an attorney]** for William (Brushy Bill) Roberts claims he asked the *New York Times* about the announcement and the Times replied that no information about birth announcements appeared in that issue. A ghostwriter by the name of Marshall Asmon [sic - Ashmun] Upson is credited with writing Garrett's book. It might also be worth mentioning the date November 23, is the birth date of Marshall Asmon [sic - Ashmun] Upson. Is it by chance that Upson and the Kid have the same birthday or by design?

[AUTHOR'S NOTE: Irrelevant, but a clumsy manufacturing of fake "suspiciousness," instead of evidence.]

14. As stated above most believe Billy the Kid was born in New York. This information also appeared for the first time in Garrett's book. **[AUTHOR'S NOTE: See *New York Sun* 1880 article reference above.]** It is also believed that Billy the Kid was shot and killed in 1881 at the age of 21. However, according to the United States Bureau of Census, 1880 census, Fort Sumner, San Miguel County, William Bonney says differently. Between June 17 and 19, 1880, while taking census records at the Fort, Lorenzo Labadie, a former Indian Agent, noted the vital statistics of one William Bonney, who was living next to Charlie Bowdre and his wife Manuela, leaving us to believe this to be the William Bonney of Lincoln County fame. What is interesting about the entry is that he gave his age as twenty-five, and his place of birth not New York but Missouri.

[AUTHOR'S NOTE: This fakes "suspicions. Also, it is believed that Manuela Bowdre gave the interview's incorrect information.]

The attorney Morrison asked Roberts why Garrett would say he was born in New York. Roberts told him that is what the told the "Coe boys" when he first came to New Mexico. Roberts went on to say he never saw New York until he was a grown man.

[AUTHOR'S NOTE: Morrison was not an attorney. And this is irrelevant, since "Brushy" was not Billy.]

Conclusion

If history is correct and William H. Bonney a.k.a. Billy the Kid was shot and killed by Lincoln County Sheriff Pat Garrett on July 14, 1881, at the house of Pete Maxwell in Fort Sumner, and was buried the next day in Fort Sumner, then Brushy Bill Roberts is a fake and nothing more than a story teller of the first order.

[AUTHOR'S NOTE: Again, this early document points to "Brushy" as Billy; which would later be more hidden.]

However, if it is not the body of William H. Bonney buried in Fort Sumner then Lincoln County Sheriff Pat Garrett killed the wrong man on July 14, 1881. He covered up that killing with help from others such as Pete Maxwell. If it is not Bonney buried at Fort Sumner then Garrett is a murderer and Maxwell is a knowing coconspirator to that homicide.

[AUTHOR'S NOTE: This is an early hoax attempt at a conspiracy theory. Instead of the "Garrett friendship," is presented "Brushy's" accidental killing of the innocent victim version. And Maxwell is added as a cover-up conspirator, without motive or evidence – or truth.]

If Brushy Bill Roberts were William H. Bonney then one would have to assume that the body in the grave is that of Billy Barlow as Robert's claims. If that is true Sheriff Garrett could quite possibly be a coconspirator of the double murder of two lawmen that occurred during the Kid's escape from Lincoln.

[AUTHOR'S NOTE: This illogical jump even leaves "Brushy" behind, since he never claimed Garrett as a jailbreak accomplice, or a "friendship" with Garrett to explain not being killed on July 14, 1881 to enable escape.]

The Lincoln County Sheriff''s Department believes, with the unanswered question as to who is buried in Fort Sumner

[AUTHOR'S NOTE: This is fakery. The victim is not doubted.]

there remains serious doubt as to what involvement Sheriff Pat Garrett played in the escape of Billy the Kid from Lincoln that resulted I the deaths of two lawmen.

[AUTHOR'S NOTE: This is fakery. There is no evidence that Garrett assisted the jail escape of Bonney, though it is an early version of the final "Probable Cause Statement's" fake Deputy Bell killing sub-investigation.]

If the body of William H. Bonney is buried in Fort Sumner the claims of William Roberts'' and others alleging to have been Billy the Kid are unfounded and the name of Pat Garrett is cleared of any wrong doing in this incident. It is the duty of the Lincoln County Sheriff''s Office to clear this mystery and possible crime off the books of history in a professional manner and to allow the guilt to fall where it belongs.

[AUTHOR'S NOTE: The imposters are easily debunked without exhumations. And no one is accusing Garrett, except imposters and hoaxers – and without basis.]

Billy the Kid's mother is buried in Silver City, New Mexico. To exhume her body could provide the DNA to solve this 122-year-old mystery. Her DNA would hold the key to the true answer as to where William Bonney is buried and if Pat Garrett was a murderer or a Sheriff doing his duty.

If those in Hamilton, Texas believe Roberts is in fact Roberts [sic] this DNA should prove their claim. If he is not the town of Hamilton,

Texas needs to take down the signs that the grave of Roberts is "The Authentic Grave Site of Billy the Kid." However, if Roberts is William Bonney then history should be rewritten showing what really happened in Lincoln County and Fort Sumner.

If Bonney is buried in Fort Sumner the History stands and the name of Sheriff Pat Garrett would be cleared and he did not kill some incendet [sic] person in Fort Sumner and would appear he had no hand in the escape of William Bonney from Lincoln and the death of Olinger and Bell.

Lincoln County Sheriff, Tom Sullivan and the Lincoln County Sheriff''s Office believe it our duty to put this mystery to rest after 122 years of doubt. Since these questions continue to nag at our conscience, and since there is no statute of limitations on Murder we feel this investigation should answer the question of "is Pat Garrett a murderer?" or a Sheriff doing his duty and wrongly accused of a crime?

[AUTHOR'S NOTE: No probable cause has been established to implicate Pat Garrett of murder of the innocent victim - the purpose of this document. But much evidence was revealed that the "Billy the Kid Case" hoax was a modernized version of the "Brushy Bill" hoax. And it is a lie about no Statute of Limitations. New Mexico's Statute of Limitations on murder ended the time for prosecution of Garrett to 1891.]

In Pat Garrett's book *The Authentic Life of Billy the Kid* he pens these words - "*Again I say that the Kid's body lies undisturbed in the grave - and I speak of what I know.*"

It is the intention of the Lincoln County Sheriff''s Office to prove one way or the other if these words are true.

____
Tom Sullivan: Sheriff
Lincoln County Sheriff''s Office

____
Steven M. Sederwall: Deputy Sheriff
Lincoln County Sheriff''s Office

____
Date

U.S. MARSHALS SERVICE HISTORIAN DAVID TURK'S PROBABLE CAUSE ADDENDUM

A secret "Billy the Kid Case" participating clown was Washington, D.C., based U.S. Marshals Service Historian David Turk, involved in the hoax from its 2003 start, and coming to New Mexico to help the hoaxers attack Pat Garrett's reputation. To put his participation in perspective, as the Marshals Service Historian, he was attacking its most famous Old West Deputy U.S. Marshal by declaring him a willful murderer of an innocent victim, with "Brushy Bill" as a possible surviving Billy the Kid.

Turk was the only historian backing Case 2003-274 in its "Probable Cause Statement;" with his fake "proof" being an old-timer's hearsay claim about a post-death Billy the Kid sighting. Also, since the "Statement's" footnotes were obscure National Archive documents on microfilm (like Azariah Wild's Secret Service reports), Turk may have provided them.

Later, in the forensic DNA scam being conducted by Dr. Henry Lee with the old carpenter's bench, Turk used his title as expertise to fake its "validation" as the one on which Billy was laid out.

Turk must have known he was a subversive, since he hid his participation in the "Billy the Kid Case;" and I only got his secret Addendum to its "Probable Cause Statement" by my open records litigation against its lawmen promulgators.

Its cover had a galloping Old West rider with a big marshal's badge. Its date was December 2003: the signing date of the "Probable Cause Statement." It was titled: "United States Marshals Service Executive Services Division: Research Report, Submitted by David S. Turk." Page one stated: "Research Report: The U.S. Marshals Service and Billy the Kid. **To Be Added in Its Present Entirety, with Exhibits, to Lincoln County, New Mexico Case # 2003-274**." It had nine pages of text; bibliographic "Endnotes;" and "Exhibits" consisting of a Turk article titled "How much did it cost to find Billy the Kid?;" a "National Police Gazette" May 21, 1881 article on Billy's escape; and a May 30, 1881 letter from Attorney Sidney Barnes (one of Billy's Mesilla prosecutors) about Billy's Mesilla trial and his later escape.

So David Turk had added to the "Billy the Kid Case's Probable Cause Statement," using his U.S. Marshals Service Historian title and taxpayers' money to defame one of the most famous Deputy

U.S. Marshals for a hoax! And he had contributed his own, major hoax document! And its style implied him as possibly assisting the actual "Probable Cause Statement," besides contributing a meaningless hearsay old-timer quote. And it indicates that he was supplying National Archive documents for the hoax.

For his own document, providing no historical evidence, Turk backed the "Billy the Kid Case" hoax's faked death scene, with Pat Garrett as the murderer of an innocent victim. William Bonney's Coroner's Jury Report is concealed, as are the multiple other corpse eye-witnesses. For filler, discussed are U.S. Marshals in the Lincoln County War period (including Garrett). But abruptly, based on a few WPA hearsay interviews from the 1930's (of people unconnected to the event), Turk concluded that Billy the Kid's killing "fueled speculation over the precise outcome."

The only parts of Turk's "Research Report" that also appear in the "Probable Cause Statement" are his Frances E. Totty, WPA quote about "Billie" being seen after the death date; and his "Endnote" sources, like Secret Service Operative Azariah Wild's reports. But Turk's report - that he tried so hard to hide - was part of the 2003-274 case file, as "probable cause" of a death scene in which Pat Garrett murdered an innocent victim, instead of killing Billy the Kid. Below is the report that Turk hid (with the irrelevant general U.S. Marshals' history omitted).

Research Report:
The U.S. Marshals Service and Billy the Kid

Submitted by David S. Turk, Historian
December 2003

"Research Report: The U.S. Marshals Service and Billy the Kid. To Be Added in its Present Entirety, with Exhibits, to Lincoln County, New Mexico Case # 2003-274."

Purpose of Research [Page 1]

There is renewed interest in examining the crimes and final resting place of William H. Bonney, also known as Henry Antrim, Henry McCarty, or Billy the Kid.

[AUTHOR'S NOTE: The only "renewed interest" was from the "Billy the Kid Case" hoax and loony conspiracy theorists.]

Two Sheriffs' Offices in New Mexico reopened an investigation, with the approval of the Governor of New Mexico. In September 2003 Steve Sederwall, Mayor of Capitan, and Deputy Sheriff, Lincoln County, New Mexico, contacted me on research matters relating to the Lincoln County War.

[AUTHOR'S NOTE: Turk claims Sederwall as contact.]

Given the integral role of the U.S. Marshals Service, and the dual roles between our two institutions during the time of Billy the Kid, and further that Pat Garrett was a Deputy U.S. Marshal during the pursuit of the Kid, and that another Deputy U.S. Marshal (and Lincoln County officer), Robert Olinger, was shot and killed by the Kid during his escape, it is relevant to the agency's historical interest to research those portions of the case pertinent to it to ensure accuracy.

[AUTHOR'S NOTE: The report gives no information to doubt conventional history. It does not "ensure accuracy!"]

The primary investigation of Lincoln County, New Mexico State No. 2004-274 [sic] is being conducted by Lincoln County Sheriff Tom Sullivan, De Baca County Sheriff Gary Graves, and Steve Sederwall, but the following findings add significantly to the data being collected in revisiting Billy the Kid.

[AUTHOR'S NOTE: No reason is given for "revisiting Billy the Kid," except hearsay death rumors 56 years after the event.]

Overview of Research Focus [Page 1]

The following research relates to the prominent roles of the U.S. Marshals Service in the Lincoln County War ... Finally, there is a study on the deaths of Deputy Marshal Olinger and Lincoln County Officer J.W. Bell, followed by Billy the Kid's subsequent escape. The Works Progress Administration interviewed several Lincoln residents during the late 1930's in this regard ...

[AUTHOR'S NOTE: The oddness of this statement is easy to miss; but each part is irrelevant to the others. Out of nowhere, will come Turk's "suspicions" that the Kid was not Garrett's murder victim.]

Deputy U.S. Marshal Garrett and His Agency Status [Page 4]

[AUTHOR'S NOTE: This page, about Garrett's U.S. Marshal status has Secret Service Agent Azariah Wild's praise of Garrett to his Chief. All is irrelevant to Garrett's murder victim.]

<u>**Key Event: Billy the Kid's Escape and the Deaths of Bell and Olinger**</u> [Page 8]

On April 28, 1881, [sic - missing word] made his famous escape from Lincoln. Accounts of the events were recalled later by witnesses. A contemporary news account from *The National Police Gazette* dated May 21, 1881, followed a generally accepted recollection pattern with some minor inconsistencies. Deputy U.S. Marshal Olinger and guard J.W. Bell ... were holding the Kid in the jail. Olinger dined at a local establishment, and during his absence the shackled prisoner hit Bell with handcuffs. He then grabbed Bell's revolver and shot him in the chest ... Just as he [Olinger] entered a small gate leading through the jail fence, the Kid shot him with a double-barreled gun, filling his breast of shot and killing him.

[AUTHOR'S NOTE: Note that the *National Police Gazette*, published in New York, was merely a dime novel tabloid, and not a legitimate historical source. Also, Turk presents Billy the Kid's escape without Garrett's participation.]

<u>**Differing Accounts on Death of Billy the Kid**</u> [Pages 8 - 9.]

Deputy U.S. Marshal and Lincoln County Sheriff Pat Garrett pursued Billy the Kid for several months after the deaths
[AUTHOR'S NOTE: About 2 ½ months.]

of Deputy Olinger and J.W. Bell. The end of the chase appeared to be at Pete Maxwell's ranch on July 15 [sic], 1881.

[AUTHOR'S NOTE: This is "Brushy" hoax-style sly innuendo of "suspicion" without evidence. And the date was July 14, 1881.]

What occurred at the Maxwell Ranch fueled speculation over the precise outcome. There appears [sic] to be many questions to answer.

[AUTHOR'S NOTE: This is full-blown, hoax conspiracy theory, with vague "suspicion." No evidence is given.]

According to the WPA interview of Francisco Trujillo in May 1937, Garrett was negotiating capture of the Kid with Pete Maxwell himself. Josh Brent's father was one of the Sheriff''s deputies, stating that Garrett said "that he sure hated to kill the boy, but he knew it was either his life or the boy's life."

[AUTHOR'S NOTE: The "Billy the Kid Case" hoaxers omitted this hearsay from their "Probable Cause Statement."

Yet another resident stated,

> The people around Lincoln say Garrett didn't kill Billie [sic] the Kid. John Poe was with Garrett the night he was supposed to ... [sic] said that he didn't see the man that Garrett killed. Ican [sic] take you to the grave in Hell's Half Acre, a old government cemetry [sic], where Billie [sic] was supposed to be buried to show you the grave.
>
> The cook at Pete Maxwell's was always putting flowers on the grave and praying at it. This woman thought a lot of Billie [sic], but after Garrett killed the man at Maxwell's home her grandson was never seen again and Billie [sic] was seen by Bill Nicoli? And indian scout. Bill saw him in old Mexico.

[AUTHOR'S NOTE: This hearsay was put in the "Probable Cause Statement" with attribution to Turk.]

The recollections took a legendary bent, even extending to events that occurred after those at the Maxwell ranch. Josh Brent stated that Garrett told his father that after he killed the Kid, "that a fellow from the east wrote him and said that he would pay $5000.00 for the trigger finger of the boy."

[AUTHOR'S NOTE: Irrelevant pseudo-historical filler like in the "Probable Cause Statement."]

<u>Other Related Fact</u> [Page 9.]

A sidelight from this period was the debunking of one widely-held story that Billy the Kid killed twenty-one men by the age of twenty-one. U.S. Attorney Barnes stated in a letter to the Attorney General, dated May 30, 1881, that while the Kid "has killed fifteen different men & is only twenty one years of age."

[AUTHOR'S NOTE: This irrelevant hearsay by one of Billy's Mesilla prosecutors, who had no way of knowing; was used to fake historical savvy, as in the "Probable Cause Statement."]

So U.S. Marshals Service Historian David Turk was a "Billy the Kid Case" hoaxer, abusing the prestige of his federal title, to present a fake death scene in Fort Sumner, and to conceal the definitive Coroner's Jury Report.

EXHUMATION PETITIONS

Since the exhumation petitions for Billy the Kid and his mother, Catherine Antrim, required a law enforcement murder case against Pat Garrett for justification, necessitated was a non-historical murder scene with his murdering an innocent victim. So that is what the hoaxers' attorneys presented, with the petitioners being Sheriff's Tom Sullivan and Gary Graves, and Deputy Sheriff Steve Sederwall. Demonstrating their lawman status and the faked murder scene, is their exhumation petition of July 26, 2004 for Billy the Kid. By their attorney, Mark Acuña, it was titled "County of De Baca, State of New Mexico, Tenth Judicial District. In the Matter of William H. Bonney A/K/A 'Billy the Kid.' Cause No. CV-04-00005." Acuña wrote:

PETITIONER'S [sic] RESPONSE TO THE VILLAGE OF FT. SUMNER'S MOTION TO DISMISS

COME NOW Petitioners Sullivan, Sederwall and Graves by and through their attorneys of record The Jaffe Law Firm (Mark Anthony Acuña, Esq.) and for their response to the Village of Fort Sumner's Motion to Dismiss sate as follows:

INTRODUCTION

Tom Sullivan, Steve Sederwall and Gary Graves are law enforcement officers. Prior to the filing of the Petition for Exhumation of the Remains of Billy the Kid, a.k.a. William H. Bonney, Sullivan, Sederwall, and Graves acting in their capacity as law enforcement officers initiated Investigation No. 2004 [sic] –274 filed in Lincoln County and Case No. 03-06-136-01 filed in De Baca County. **The principle purpose of opening the investigation and the case was to determine the guilt or innocence of sheriff Pat Garrett in the death of Billy the Kid.**

Initially, as part of their on-going investigation, Sederwall, Sullivan, and Graves, in their capacity as law enforcement officers petitioned the Sixth Judicial District Court for exhumation of the remains of Billy the Kid's mother, Katherine [sic] Antrim. As a part of the on-going investigation, the Petition to Exhume Katherine [sic] Antrim was intended to obtain DNA samples for purposes of comparing those DNA samples with DNA samples that were hoped to be obtained upon the exhumation of the remains of what are thought to be that of Billy the

Kid. After filing of the Petition to Exhume the remains of Katherine [sic] Antrim, a second petition was filed in the Tenth Judicial Court for purposes of the exhumation of Billy the Kid's remains and for purposes of obtaining DNA samples to compare with those samples obtained from the remains of Katherine [sic] Antrim. Sederwall, Sullivan, and Graves, all joined in on the Petition to Exhume the remains of Billy the Kid as Co-Petitioners and in their capacity as **law enforcement officers** engaged in an on-going investigation.

Petitioners assert that they maintain standing in the instant action as law enforcement officers engaged in the investigation of criminal violations, namely, the alleged killing of Billy the Kid by the legendary Sheriff, Pat Garrett. Moreover, Petitioners assert that as law enforcement officers they are duly authorized to investigate the death of Billy the Kid to determine 1) the guilt or innocence of sheriff Pat Garrett, and 2) to determine whether or not foul play was involved if there were violations of criminal statutes or laws. Acting in their capacity **as law enforcement officers** on behalf of the public and the public's best interest, Petitioners further assert that they are the real parties in interest to this suit and, therefore, maintain proper standing to prosecute these claims.

ARGUMENT

Petitioners are Law Enforcement Officers Currently Conducting Active Investigations Regarding the Death of Billy the Kid and, therefore, they have Standing.

New Mexico Rule of Civil Procedure 1-017 states in pertinent part that "every action shall be prosecuted in the name of the real party in interest ... for a party authorized by statute may sue in that person's own name without joining the party for whose benefit the action is brought; and when a statute of the state so provides, an action for the use or benefit for another shall be brought in the name of the state.

Moreover, Section 29-1-1 states impertinent [sic] part that ...

> "It is hereby declared to be the duty of every Sheriff, Deputy Sheriff, Constable and every other peace officer to investigate all violations of the criminal laws of the state which are called to the attention of any such officer or which he is aware, and it is also declared the duty of every such officer to diligently file a complaint or information, if the circumstances are such to indicate to a reasonably prudent person that such action should be taken, and it is also declared his duty to cooperate with and assist the Attorney General, District Attorney or other prosecutor, if any, if any in all reasonable ways ... Failure to perform his duty in any

material way shall subject such officer to removal from the office and payment of all costs of prosecution."

In the instant case, Petitioners Sullivan, Sederwall, and Graves acting in their capacity as law enforcement officers pursuant to Section 29-1-1, were not only authorized to commence the investigation into the death of William H. Bonney, a.k.a. Billy the Kid, but were duty-bound to fulfill their responsibilities as law enforcement officers to investigate the circumstances surrounding the death of Billy the Kid. Indeed, Petitioners initiated the investigations into the death of Billy the Kid based upon inconsistent and incongruous facts and information surrounding the death of Billy the Kid and raising suspicion as to the truth of the circumstances surrounding the killing of Billy the Kid. Under the circumstances, Petitioners had a duty to investigate or be subject to removal of office subject to Section 29-1-1.

Furthermore, pursuant to Rule 1-017, Petitioners acting in their capacity as law enforcement officers, are real parties in interest to the instant causes of action. Plaintiffs are authorized by statute, that is, Section 29-1-1, to being this action in their own names on behalf of and for the benefit of the public in their capacities of investigating law enforcement officers.

CONCLUSION

Therefore, based upon all the foregoing, it is clear that the Petitioners acting in their capacity as law enforcement officers and engaged in an active investigation regarding the death and alleged killing of Billy the Kid by Sheriff Pat Garrett, and of standing in this case and are real parties in interest.

Wherefore, Petitioners respectfully request that the court issue its order denying the Village of Ft. Sumner's Motion to Dismiss as against Petitioners; that the court allow Petitioners to remain in the instant action and for such other further and proper relief as the Court deems just and proper."

Respectfully submitted by:
The Jaffe Law Firm
Mark Anthony Acuña
Attorneys for Petitioners Sullivan,
Sederwall & Graves

BILLY THE KID AS PETITIONING FOR HIS OWN EXHUMATION FOR A FAKED DEATH SCENE

The "Billy the Kid Case" hoax's most out-of-control clowned death scene came from its likely intended beneficiary: Attorney Bill Robins III. His first public entry in the" Billy the Kid Case" may have been forced: to take-over from the hoaxers' faltering Silver City attorney, Sherry Tippet, losing to my attorneys opposing exhumations. And Robins was not circumspect about "Brushy Bill." On November 19, 2003, an AP internet article for Silver City, titled "Lawyer Appointed to Represent Dead Outlaw," quoted him: "Robins says he's excited to represent the Kid. His first duty as Billy's lawyer will be to intervene in the Silver City case to exhume the body of Billy's mother, Catherine Antrim. DNA testing is supposed to show whether Antrim was related to Ollie "Brushy Bill" Roberts. If Antrim is related to Roberts, that would mean Billy the Kid is buried in Hico [sic - Hamilton], Texas – not Fort Sumner."

After replacing Sherry Tippett, Robins led the exhumation attacks on both the mother's and Billy's graves. But an attorney needs a client to appear in a court. The client Robins chose proved his scorn of the law, the public, and the sanctity of graves. **His client was dead Billy the Kid, "co-petitioner" with the lawmen for his own exhumation! The circus was in town!**

Robins, of course, ignored that a corpse, as a non-existent being, has no legal standing to appear in a court of law. But for Governor Bill Richardson's complicit judges - Henry Quintero in Silver City and Ted Hartley in Fort Sumner - Robins channeled "Billy the Kid" and spoke for him (or "Billy" spoke through him) without their objection in their clown courts!

And "Billy the Kid," of course, wanted his mother and himself dug up to protect his "legacy." And the "legacy" dead "Billy the Kid" was "protecting" was the imposter hoaxes' fake death scene: that an innocent victim, not himself, had been killed by Pat Garrett in Fort Sumner on July 14, 1881.

And dead "Billy the Kid," channeled through Robins's mouth, claimed in Grant and De Baca County District Courts that "he" had led a long and law-abiding life after the death scene, so deserved a posthumous pardon from Governor Bill Richardson as "Brushy Bill" Roberts or as John Miller.

BILLY THE KID'S PRE-HEARING BRIEF

To corrupt clowning Silver City Judge, Henry Quintero, Attorney Bill Robins III presented his January 5, 2004's "In the Matter of Catherine Antrim, Billy the Kid's Pre-Hearing Brief."

It revealed, for the first time, the "Billy the Kid Case" hoax's attaching DNA matching to the pardon, as linked to the faked death scene and imposter survival claims, themselves linked to denying existence of the Coroner s Jury Report.

So, for his clown act, Robins's "Brief" had his client, dead Billy the Kid, as a co-petitioner for exhumation of his own mother, joining Sheriffs Tom Sullivan and Gary Graves, and Deputy Steve Sederwall, and as backing the pretenders as legitimate! Robins wrote:

> [T]he very question of [Billy the Kid's] life and death will be impacted by the results of the Petitioners' [lawmen's] investigation [into the Garrett murder and DNA].
>
> B. *The Planned Request For Pardon Confers Standing Here*
>
> Undersigned counsel intends to ask Governor Richardson that he pardon Billy the kid for the murder conviction of Sheriff Brady on several known bases including the fact that then Territorial Governor Lew Wallace reneged on his promise to pardon the Kid. There were at least two individuals that laid claim to Billy the Kid's identity years after his alleged shooting by Garrett. **Both of them apparently led long and peaceful and crime-free lives** ...
>
> The reasons that the exhumation is sought is to disinter the remains of Billy the Kid's mother for the extraction of Mitochondrial DNA.
>
> As such, Ms. Antrim presents the only source of such DNA. Should the exhumation be denied, Billy the Kid will be forever denied the opportunity to make use of modern technology to shed light on his life and death. **Should the DNA extracted from Ms. Antrim confirm that one of the potential Kids was in fact Billy the Kid, undersigned counsel will be able to make an even stronger argument for pardon by citing to the long years of law abiding life.**

Convinced he was above law or decency this smug rogue presented the following examples of fakery in his "Billy the Kid's Pre-Hearing Brief;" writing:

(1) COMES NOW, Bill Robins, III and David Sandoval, of the law firm of Heard, Robins, Cloud, Lubel & Greenwood, LLC, and on the behalf of the estate of William H. Bonney, aka "Billy the Kid."

[AUTHOR'S NOTE: The first claim is representation of Billy's "estate." First of all, Billy had no estate - meaning posthumous property for probate court. Secondly, property has nothing to do with exhuming his mother. Thirdly, this cover of something that sounds legal - like an estate - will next be switched to Billy talking for himself through Robins. Note that Attorney Sandoval was present to provide the New Mexico law license which Robins lacked, making him complicit in the hoax.]

(2) This is an interesting proceeding in that the relief sought here is not exclusively judicial. "[N]ormally a district court would not become involved in such matters unless a protesting relative or interested party files an injunction or takes some other legal action to halt the autopsy or disinterment,"

[AUTHOR'S NOTE: Robins's Brief is not "judicial" at all. It is pseudo-historical rambling with an irrelevant idea of a pardon. And its legal citations are all irrelevant filler.]

(3) Petitioners [Lincoln County Sheriff Tom Sullivan and his Deputy, Steve Sederwall] should thus be commended for bringing this Court into the picture.

[AUTHOR'S NOTE: Robins is trying to legitimize fellow hoaxers. Note also their law enforcement titles.]

(4) As will be shown clearly, Billy the Kid's interests are real, legitimate, proper for consideration, and we respectively ask the Court to recognize them as such.

[AUTHOR'S NOTE: Segueing into speaking for Billy, Robins does a switcheroo from "estate" to "interests." But a dead person has no interests, being dead - meaning legally non-existent.]

(5) To the extent that the Court remains concerned **with the presence of Billy the Kid in this litigation**, it is a matter that can be more properly addressed pursuant to legal requirements of standing and intervention, which the discussion below shows the Kid satisfies.

[AUTHOR'S NOTE: This is now the switcheroo point for Billy himself entering the courtroom. Robins even claims that Billy has "standing," meaning the legal right to be present in court.]

(6) The governor has the "power to grant reprieves and pardons." Undersigned counsel intends on seeking a pardon for Billy the Kid.

Certainly Governor Richardson is within his inherent appointment power to hire counsel to advise him on the merits of such a pardon.

[AUTHOR'S NOTE: Tricky Robins omits that pardon advising gives him no legal justification to be in this court seeking exhumation of Catherine Antrim. He has no real client.]

(7) Counsel's appointment here is in the nature of an appointment as a public defender

[AUTHOR'S NOTE: Now cagy Robins makes up that he was appointed by Richardson as a "public defender" for Billy. But only the judge can legally appoint an attorney for an indigent client in court - and, obviously, the client has to be alive.]

(8) Billy the Kid's interest here is his legacy. As noted in previous briefing the very question of his life and death will be impacted by the results of the Petitioners' investigation.

[AUTHOR'S NOTE: Here, dead Billy has "told" channeling Robins that *he* cares about "his legacy." Besides being absurd, that is not what "interest" means: which is legal justification for a case, not sentimentality of an historical nature.]

(9) Undersigned counsel intends to ask Governor Richardson that he pardon Billy the kid for the murder conviction of Sheriff Brady on several known bases including the fact that then Territorial Governor Lew Wallace reneged on his promise to pardon the Kid.

[AUTHOR'S NOTE: The pardon issue, though irrelevant to exhuming Catherine Antrim, is here segueing into "Brushy Bill" territory with "several known bases" that will apply to "Brushy" and not to Billy Bonney.]

(10) There were at least two individuals that laid claim to Billy the Kid's identity years after his alleged shooting by Garrett. Both of them apparently **led long and peaceful and crime-free lives**.

[AUTHOR'S NOTE: Here is the jump to "Brushy." And the "several known bases" for pardon are his long, peaceful, and crime-free life. The second pretender, John Miller, was added by the hoaxers to obscure their "Brushy" focus.]

(11) The reasons that the exhumation is sought is to disinter the remains of Billy the Kid's mother for the extraction of Mitochondrial DNA. As such, Ms. Antrim presents the only source of such DNA. Should the exhumation be denied, Billy the Kid will be forever denied the opportunity to make use of modern technology to shed light on his life and death.

[AUTHOR'S NOTE: Now Billy is himself in court, pleading, through Robins's mouth, for modern technology to help him. But do not miss the greater absurdity: this is a pretender argument by channeled "Brushy," wanting *his* life and death vouched for as Billy the Kid. And "Brushy's" real problem is hidden by Robins: mitochondrial DNA proves a mother relationship; "Brushy" *denied* she was his mother!]

(12) Should the DNA extracted from Ms. Antrim confirm that one of the potential Kids was in fact Billy the Kid, **undersigned counsel will be able to make an even stronger argument for pardon by citing to the long years of law abiding life.**

[AUTHOR'S NOTE: This was the sentence that proved to me that the "Billy the Kid Case was a "Brushy Bill" hoax, along with its plot: claim a match by faking DNA, then pardon "Brushy" as Billy the Kid. Note again the fakery that neither "Brushy" nor John Miller claimed Ms. Antrim was their mother – so mitochondrial DNA matching was meaningless unless the results' claims were faked.]

(13) This Court has allowed the intervention of the Town of Silver City in this matter. The municipal politicians there have apparently authorized the Town's Mayor to oppose the exhumation. Billy the Kid acknowledges the existence of case law that accords standing to the owners of the cemetery concerned in such proceedings.

[AUTHOR'S NOTE: Do not miss that speaking, channeled, dead Billy Bonney even has legal expertise on "case law" about court standing!]

(14) What is of interest here, is that such standing is often given to the cemetery owner because it may be the only entity that can represent the wishes of the deceased, an element typically considered in whether to order an exhumation ...

As expected, the Mayor here opposes the exhumation and is positioned to present evidence in support of its objection. Whether or not that truly represents the interests of Ms. Antrim can never be known. Given the identity of the decedent and the time that has passes since her death, the Mayor cannot possibly have any direct evidence of Ms. Antrim's wishes. As such, the evidence that is presented by the Mayor can be viewed as best, supposition, or at worst, utterly unreliable.

[AUTHOR'S NOTE: Do not miss the bizarreness of this argument. The Mayor, whose legal duty is to protect remains in a cemetery under his authority, according to Robins, needs to mind-read corpse Catherine to find out if *she* wants to be dug up. But Attorney Robins, the channeler, is about to come to the rescue and speak for the dead woman also!]

(15) One is left to question why such a party with such a remote interest and lack of express knowledge about the decedent's wishes is conferred standing while the interests of Billy the Kid go unheard if this Court denier him standing. Allowing such a party to appear and present evidence while denying the same opportunity to a party that has been appointed to represent the interests of the decedent's son does not seem prudent nor fair

[AUTHOR'S NOTE: This argument is so crazy that a reader might be tempted to rationalize that it cannot be as crazy as it sounds. Attorney Robins is saying that dead Billy has more credibility to let his wishes be known than the live Mayor, whose obligation it is to protect the cemetery. And Robins can speak for the exact wishes of the dead, unlike the more supernaturally limited Mayor.]

(16) 1st Factor Public Interest, Billy the Kid's name is forever tied to New Mexico and to that of another legendary figure of the Old West, Sheriff Pat Garrett. **A commonly held version** of history paints a picture of an ambush in which Garrett killed the Kid in Ft. Sumner where most believe the Kid still lies at rest. **This version has been questioned. It is the investigation into whether Garrett killed the Kid that has prompted these investigators to seek exhumation**.

[AUTHOR'S NOTE: This is pure "Brushy Bill" hoaxing. Only "Brushy's" believers question Pat Garrett's killing of Billy. Since "Brushy" was not Billy, there is no "public interest," meaning public value in the case. There are only the self-serving motives of the hoaxers, and the "Brushy" goal of puppeteer Robins.]

(17) 2nd Factor, the Decedents wishes. In spite of Silver City's position to the contrary, we simply do not know what the decedent's wishes would be. Given the present circumstances, however, where her remains could possibly provide critical evidence to be used by modern day advocates to clear her son's name, one might easily surmise that Silver City's dogged attempt to resist exhumation would not be appreciated by Ms. Antrim.

[AUTHOR'S NOTE: Now Robins is channeling Billy's mother enough to know that Silver City's blocking her exhumation would "not be appreciated" by her! For Robins, she is a "Brushy"-believer too! And she is angry! And corrupt Judge Henry Quintero never objected at all to Robins's making a mockery of his court. He was just basking in his undeserved Richardson appointment for a desired judgeship.]

(18) 3rd Factor, Surviving Relatives Wishes. There are no relatives of Ms. Antrim currently before the Court ... The closest party currently

before the Court is in fact Billy the Kid as represented by the undersigned counsel. As is apparent from the arguments set forth in this brief, the kid's [sic] interests would be furthered by the exhumation.

[AUTHOR'S NOTE: Here is Robins channeling dead Billy again to say that he wants his mother dug up as part of his agenda!]

(19) **Billy the Kid believes that the evidence adduced at the exhumation hearing will certainly support an order of exhumation here.**

[AUTHOR'S NOTE: Robins has crossed into the "Exorcist" movie's territory. He has disappeared. Only dead Billy is talking now through Robins's mouth. And *he* is "Brushy." The creepy thought is that Robins might not be faking. He may really think he *is* "Brushy Bill" incarnate.]

20) The foregoing has established that the undersigned counsel may legally and properly appear in these proceedings on behalf of, and to represent the interests of Billy the Kid.

[AUTHOR'S NOTE: Robins has established nothing whatsoever to justify his being in court as a channeler of dead Billy; nor has he established any reason for exhumations. But he has proved New Mexico's intractable corruption of collusive cronyism.]

(21) Respectfully submitted this 5th day of January, 2004.
Heard, Robins, Cloud, Lubel & Greenwood, L.L.P.

Bill Robins III
David Sandoval
Address and Telephone Numbers
ATTORNEYS FOR BILLY THE KID

SPEAKING FOR BILLY IN FORT SUMNER

On February 26, 2004, Attorney Robins, with Attorneys David Sandoval and Mark Acuña, filed the "Tenth Judicial Court of De Baca County Case No. CV-2004-00005, Petition for the Exhumation of Billy the Kid's Remains." Dead Billy was listed as a co-petitioner with the hoax's lawmen: "Gary Graves, Sheriff of De Baca County, Tom Sullivan, (Sheriff) and Steve Sederwall (Deputy Sheriff) of Lincoln County, New Mexico. (hereinafter the 'Sheriff-Petitioners')."

For digging up Billy, Robins used hoaxer-style of vague suspicion, like: "This was also a time whose history was not accurately nor completely written." Or, as he made-up: "For generations now, the life of Billy the Kid has been the subject of historical debate. Perhaps the most significant lingering question involves whether Billy the Kid was indeed shot by Sheriff Pat Garrett in an ambush."

Both "Brushy Bill" and John Miller were introduced in Section "IV. Historical Background." Robins stated: "The debate has been sparked at various times in the past by at least two individuals who laid claim to his identity. Ollie "Brushy Bill" Roberts resided in Hico, Texas and claimed to be Billy the Kid. **John Miller, in Arizona also died still claiming he was Billy the Kid. Co-Petitioners are in the initial phases of pursuing exhumations of these individuals as well."**

"Brushy" was emphasized with Attorney Robins's true-believer plug of deserving a pardon for his reformed long life.

To justify exhumation of Billy Bonney, Robins called the July 14, 1881 killing of Billy the Kid an "historical quandary" – but it was only a "quandary" for "Brushy" believers! He stated: "The investigation ["Billy the Kid Case"] has renewed questions as to whether Billy the Kid lies buried at the fabled grave-site in Ft. Sumner. Allowing the exhumation of the remains at Ft. Sumner grave site for extraction of DNA to be compared with that of Ms. Antrim's will likely finally provide definitive answers to this **historical quandary**."

Robins's lying becomes clear when one recalls that the month before, on January 9, 2004, the New Mexico Office of the Medical Investigator (OMI) had issued the Affidavits of its head, Dr. Ross Zumwalt and its forensic anthropologist, Dr. Debra Komar, stating that the graves of Billy Bonney and Catherine Antrim were invalid for DNA recovery by their uncertain location. And Robins himself had participated in the Komar deposition of January 20, 2004, in which she repeated that forensic truth. Obvious is the intent of the hoax to fake results, since real ones were impossible - and the hoaxers knew that.

Also, contemplate this clowning around when contemplating Attorney Bill Robins III's filings: When he was channeling dead Billy the Kid, he was actually channeling dead, talking "Brushy Bill" Roberts! So dead 'Brushy" was seeking *his own* pardon, while *still pretending* to be real Billy Bonney, by using demon-possessed Attorney Bill Robins's tongue in Silver City and Fort Sumner courts to fake a death scene with Garrett killing an innocent victim, namely the Billy Barlow of his own hoax!

So Robins now had Billy the Kid (secretly as "Brushy Bill" Roberts) request his own exhumation from Richardson's pocket-judge, Ted Hartley, based on using the imposters' hoaxed death scene, while concealing the Coroner's Jury Report.

As will be seen, it would be proof of the hoaxing clowns' desperation that, by 2005, they abandoned this neatly arranged scam to then claim that John Miller was actually Billy the Kid, and to dig him up for no reason other than keeping their circus on the road.

CHAPTER 4
"BILLY THE KID CASE" HOAX TV PROGRAM WITH FAKE DEATH SCENE

HOAX HISTORIAN, PROFESSOR PAUL HUTTON, MAKES A TV DOCUMENTARY

University of New Mexico history professor, Paul Hutton, was appointed by Governor Bill Richardson as the hoax's official historian. This clown fulfilled his role by making the hoax's key clowning media contacts: Bill Kurtis of Bill Kurtis Productions, and forensic expert, Dr. Henry Lee. And he wrote, narrated, and co-produced, with Bill Kurtis, the "Billy the Kid Case" hoax's 2004 TV documentary titled 'Investigating History, Billy the Kid."

"INVESTIGATING HISTORY: BILLY THE KID" ON TV

The first, in the hoaxers' intended TV series of "Billy the Kid Case" fake forensics with exhumations, was Paul Hutton's 2004 History Channel documentary titled "Investigating History: Billy the Kid." It united the major hoaxing clowns as its talking head participants. They declared the "Billy the Kid Case" hoax's tenets: the historical death scene was untrue; Pat Garrett assisted Billy the Kid's jailbreak because they were friends; Garrett murdered an innocent victim, not Billy the Kid in Fort Sumner; the body was kept secret; there was no Coroner's Jury Report; and tourist interests blocked truth-seeking exhumations for DNA. Stressed was that "Brushy Bill" Roberts was plausibly Billy the Kid. Added was that the "investigation" was to assist Governor Bill Richardson's decision as to pardoning Billy, with "Brushy" implied as the recipient. John Miller was not yet needed.

HUTTON'S PROFITEERING PLOT

From the start, Hutton saw the program as his cash cow: the first in his series. He boastfully confirmed it to a *University of New Mexico Campus News* reporter, Carolyn Gonzales, for her February 16, 2004 article titled "Hutton Writes Wild Frontier Stories for History Channel." Gonzalez wrote: "His role has evolved into fulltime scriptwriting for "Investigating History" ... Hutton pitched **the idea of the series** to the History Channel after working with Governor Bill Richardson to try to verify the Kid's identity through a DNA comparison with his mother ... Richardson, who dubbed Hutton "Doc," appointed him historian on the Billy the Kid issue."

For it, Hutton also created a hoax mantra: "the mystery of Billy's murder." When interviewed on April 24, 2004 by a Rick Nathanson for the *Albuquerque Journal* weekly television guide, "Entertainer," Hutton was quoted: "[P]eople are always intrigued by mystery, and this has always been one of the great mysteries of the Old West. **The great mystery in this case is, of course, who is buried in Billy the Kid's grave in Fort Sumner**." Setting up Garrett as murder of an innocent victim, Hutton called him "Billy's good friend." He also straddled the fence, stating: "I'm pretty sure that Pat Garrett shot Billy the Kid that night at Pete Maxwell's house." Left out was that his program claimed the opposite.

HUTTON'S PROGRAM'S OVERVIEW

In his error-filled, "Brushy"-backing program, proving his ignorance of real history, Hutton had Richardson as an "historical investigator" using "experts" as a "pardon team" for Billy the Kid. They were fellow hoaxers: Sheriff Tom Sullivan, Deputy Steve Sederwall, *True West* magazine Editor-in-Chief Bob Boze Bell; and "Brushy"-believers, Bill Robins III and W.C. Jameson. In the credits, Hutton listed "Frederick Nolan;" though, Nolan told me it was without his participation or knowledge.

Hutton narrates, as the cover of "Brushy's" book, *Alias Billy the Kid*, looms: "Over the years that story has gained some credence." W.C. Jameson lies that the "Coroner's Jury Report was never found," and "no evidence jurymen saw the body." Steve Sederwall adds, "If "Brushy Bill" is Billy the Kid, it comes down to this ... Garrett had to have let him escape in Fort Sumner."

Hutton states: "New Mexico Governor Bill Richardson is ready to make things right." Richardson himself says: "I might pardon him." But *that* will be based on [Attorney] Robins's "investigation."

Since I had been exposing their exhumation-seeking hoax in district courts, Hutton switched the "Billy the Kid Case" from Pat Garrett murdering the innocent victim, to an investigation" to see if Billy the Kid "deserved" a pardon for *his own* killings.

Faking hoaxers' expertise, Hutton has Sheriff Sullivan "discover" Billy's promised Lew Wallace pardon; has himself and Bob Boze Bell as the "Governor's pardon team historians;" and has Bill Robins III doing pardon legalities. Deputy Sederwall is a Capitan Mayor wondering if "Brushy" was Billy. And Richardson declares commitment to "science," "tourism," and New Mexico.

RE-ENACTING THE FAKE DEATH SCENE

Hutton's presentation, built on "Brushy Bill" and "Billy the Kid Case" hoaxes, seeks to cast doubt on the Fort Sumner death scene; to make Pat Garrett a liar; and to denigrate legitimate historians.

The film starts with Billy approaching the Maxwell house, while Hutton intones: "This is one of the most controversial moments in the history of the Old West: history's version of the last seconds of Billy the Kid ... Pat Garrett fires into the darkness ... Billy the Kid is dead when he hits the floor - or is he?" He then doubts a successful shot in the dark; and sneers: "The story is almost too good ... that the Kid ... would come strolling into this room unarmed and right into the hands of the law enforcement official ... is just too bizarre." **[But Billy was armed; and was likely sent to the ambush, since he was just going to the opposite side of the house to cut meat from a side of beef.]**

Concealing all corpse identifications, Hutton calls the killing "a mystery;" quotes Deputy John Poe's initial doubt, as if denying corpse identity; calls the killing "Garrett's version;" and lies that eye-witness, Pete Maxwell, "never gave his version." He concludes that it was "unlikely" that Billy the Kid was shot.

Hutton proclaims: "Some suggested that it was more likely that Pat Garrett, Billy's friend, let him go ... burying someone else in his place" **[hoaxing friendship and innocent victim]**. Boze Bell (titled as "Editor, True West Magazine") sneers that: "Friends of Pat Garrett conducted what they called an autopsy, took no photographs, and wanted Garrett rewarded. **[Jurymen were not Garrett's friends; they identified the body as Billy's; nobody had a camera, and Garrett qualified for reward.]** Boze Bell says Garrett killed in "secrecy," burying the body the next day. **[The body had a vigil and legal inquest.]**

Hutton calls history "Garrett's version;" says that the only eye-witness was Pete Maxwell, "who was never interviewed" **[hiding Maxwell's Coroner's Jury testimony for the Coroner's Jury Report - which is also concealed - and hiding the 200 townspeople's corpse vigil]. Hutton** lies that Deputy Poe "contradicted" Garrett's statement. **[Poe was merely initially unsure that Garrett had shot Billy, whom he did not know and could not recognize; as he wrote in his 1933 book: *The Death of Billy the Kid.* All the identifications of the corpse left him with no doubt Billy had been killed.]**

But the most egregious and most damaging part of Hutton's TV fraud is his "Billy the Kid Case" hoax re-enactment with Garrett, as Billy's friend and deputy murder accomplice, placing the revolver in the courthouse-jail's outhouse to enable Billy's killing of the deputy guards. No one, before this "Billy the Kid Case" hoax, had accused Garrett of this horrific crime of being the accomplice to the murder of his own deputies and assisting escape of his condemned prisoner. Debased clown Hutton contaminated public awareness irrevocably real by this faked scene.

In conclusion, "Investigating History: Billy the Kid" was "Billy the Kid Case" hoaxing, with its covert "Brushy Bill" pardon thrust. But it set the stage for any pretender by faking that legitimate doubt existed about the killing of Billy Bonney on July 14, 1881.

CHAPTER 5
"BILLY THE KID CASE" HOAX FAKE FORENSICS WITH DR. HENRY LEE

DR. LEE WAS THE PERFECT DNA MATCH

Dr. Henry Lee, the forensic expert recruited for the "Billy the Kid Case's" fake forensics, had national name recognition from assisting O.J. Simpson walk free in his 1996 murder trial. As to reputation for veracity, that was another story.

Prosecutor, Vincent Bugliosi, in his book, *Outrage: The Five Reasons Why O.J. Simpson Got Away With Murder*, called Henry Lee "nothing short of incompetent." Bugliosi was avoiding "liar." An example from *Outrage* was Lee's testifying that "crime-scene" shoe "imprints" on murder victim Nicole Simpson's walkway did not match O.J. Simpson's incriminatory, "size-12 Bruno Magli bloody shoe prints" - also at the scene. But the smaller "prints" Lee used, according to Bugliosi, had been hardened into the concrete during its laying "ten years earlier!"

Helpful Dr. Lee resurfaced for the 2007 murder trial defense for music impresario, Phil Spector; accused, and ultimately convicted, of fatally shooting actress, Lana Clarkson. But Attorney Sara Caplan - in Spector's first defense team - testified to the judge, Larry Paul Fidler, that, at the crime scene, Lee bottled dead Clarkson's torn-off fingernail, which indicated possible struggle - not Spector's defense's claim of her committing suicide. Then that fingernail disappeared. Judge Fidler declared destruction of evidence. The CNN.com AP headline of May 25, 2007 was: "Famed expert's credibility takes a hit at Spector trial."

Lee's involvement in a 2016 documentary, "The Case of JonBenet Ramsey," which accused her then nine year old brother, Burke Ramsey of murdering her, resulted in now grown-up Burke's $750 million defamation suit, which included Lee. On January 5, 2019, Dailymail.com reporter Maxine Shen wrote:

"CBS and the brother of JonBenet Ramsey settle their $750m defamation lawsuit to the 'satisfaction of both parties.' " It stated: "Beyond CBS and the documentary production company Critical Content, LLS, Burke's lawsuit named **forensic scientist Henry Lee** and forensic pathologist Werner Spitz among several others who appeared in the broadcast."

Dr. Lee made the news again on June 25, 2019, with reporter Lauren Fruen's DailyMailOnline article titled: "Celebrity forensic scientist who worked on trials of O.J. Simpson, Phil Spector and Michael Peterson, and helped investigate JonBenet Ramsey's murder is accused of botching evidence in multiple murder cases." It stated that: "his evidence is now being questioned after a 1989 conviction was overturned [when a] court found two men were convicted based on part on false testimony from Lee. He is now accused of giving incorrect testimony in at least three other cases. These include trial of Phil Spector and murders of two women. Prosecutor Christopher Darden says Dr. Lee 'stretched' the truth in the O.J. trial. Lee says he has 'never been accused of wrongdoing' in more than 8,000 cases." (As to never accused of wrongdoing, Lee conveniently "forgot" my 2006 complaint to the American Academy of Forensic Sciences Ethics Committee about his fake forensics for Lincoln County Sheriff's Department's Case 2003-274 leading to exhumations in its "Billy the Kid Case" hoax. And the unethical Ethics Committee had covered up his clowning.)

As to the specifics of reporter Fruen's article: "Ralph 'Ricky' Birch and Shawn Henning were convicted based in part on false testimony about blood stains on a towel by Lee that were later proven not to be blood." (And he would likewise fake blood for the "Billy the Kid Case" hoax.) For the O.J. Simpson trial, Fruen wrote that prosecutor, Chris Darden, stated that Lee made-up that "something was wrong" with the blood sample given in evidence by the Los Angeles Police Department to support the defense claim that the sample was tampered. (And he would likewise make-up whatever crime scene the "Billy the Kid Case" hoaxers wanted.) Fruen brought up his alleged "hiding evidence or giving incorrect testimony." The Phil Spector case's lost fingernail is cited. In a case of the murder of a Janet Myers, Lee got her husband, Kerry Myers convicted based on her blood being on his pants. But that blood was later questioned. And released Kerry Meyers was quoted: "It's frustrating that he's still doing it, and nobody is questioning him." And in a case of a murdered teenager named Joyce Stochmal, reporter Lauren Fruen wrote: "Dr. Lee is said to have testified that a substance found on suspect David Weinberg's knife was blood. He admitted at the time there was no way to know if it was human." Fruen stated that tests had proved it was not human before Lee made his statement. And "Weinberg was convicted."

So Henry Lee was the perfect "expert" to hide that no verifiable DNA of Billy the Kid existed on the planet - and "find" some. He also sham-tested for "blood" wherever he was pointed; and made up crime scene scenarios however he was directed - as long as the hoaxers' TV production company kept filming and paying him.

DR. LEE JOINS THE CIRCUS

After I had legally blocked the exhumations of Billy Bonney and his mother, Dr. Henry Lee entered the "Billy the Kid Case" in 2004, at its Version II of the hoax, with playing-dead-shot-Billy-bleeding-on-the-carpenter's-bench-for-DNA.

Deputy Steve Sederwall had contacted him through the "Billy the Kid Case's" official historian, Paul Hutton; as Sederwall testified in his June 26, 2012 deposition for my open records litigation against the lawmen: "Paul Hutton wanted me to be on some investigative history ... I said, "You know, I'm looking at bringing Henry Lee out here ... Tell Kurtis I'll let him film it if he wants to, or whatever, if he can get Henry out here." So [Hutton] jumped on it."

Sederwall had also alluded to Hutton's setting up the "deal" with Bill Kurtis; stating in my litigation's January 21, 2011 Evidentiary hearing that: "I got a call from Paul Hutton, a historian up in Albuquerque, teaches at the University. He was writing a deal for Bill Curtis [sic]. He wanted us [Sederwall and Sullivan] to interview with Bill Curtis [sic] ... Paul and I were friends ... So Curtis [sic] contacted us and wanted to know if he could follow the investigation ... That's when Bill Curtis [sic] got involved, and **Curtis [sic] paid to bring Dr. Lee to New Mexico**." [Transcript 1/21/11, pp. 164, 168]. It soon emerged that Lee and Kurtis were partners in producing TV documentaries.

As forensic expert, Lee brought in his lab, Orchid Cellmark. On August 9, 2004, I had contacted its then director, Mark Stolorow, explaining the "Billy the Kid Case" hoax. He was amused. On August 18th, we spoke again. He was defensive. Orchid Cellmark, he told me, was under a "gag order" on the case. Dr. Lee was in charge! Three months later, Orchid Cellmark was caught faking DNA computer data on another case. That scandal appeared on November 18, 2004, in "TalkLeft.com," as "Fraud alleged at Cellmark, DNA Testing Firm." It stated: "This is shocking to the forensic community which has always believed that raw data cannot be electronically manipulated." It concluded: "Bottom line: A lot of defendants will be seeking retesting by an independent lab when the prosecution is relying on results by Cellmark."

Orchid Cellmark was reduced to one lab in Farmers Branch, Texas. And Mark Stolorow was replaced as director by Dr. Rick Staub. Unlike Stolorow, Staub seemed indifferent to scandal. And, as will be seen, though his lab found **no DNA at all** in Henry Lee's eventual bench specimens, it did not stop him and the hoaxers from exhuming John Miller, with the claim of having Billy the Kid DNA from bench blood for identity matching!

Also, though Lee would be seeking blood - as the only DNA source the hoaxers could think of after exhumations of Billy and his mother were blocked by me - it was kept secret that Orchid Cellmark does not test for blood!

One can even surmise that Lee and his lab would also have participated in Version I one of the hoax, and claimed DNA from the likely empty graves of Billy and his mother, and presented whatever results were desired - with "Brushy" added in.

Lee's joining the "Billy the Kid Case" was announced by hoax-backing *Albuquerque Journal* reporter, Rene Romo. On August 2, 2004, Romo splashed, "Forensic Expert on Billy's Case: Questions Remain on Outlaw's Fate" Romo declared: "Dr. Henry Lee, one of the nation's leading forensic scientists ... has added the Billy the Kid slaying to his case files ... "This is an extremely interesting case of some historical importance,' Lee said in an interview ... 'That's why I agreed to spend some of my own time to work with them ... **It's basically a worthwhile project and legitimate**."

So famous Dr. Lee called the "Billy the Kid Case" "a worthwhile project and legitimate." What else was the public to think? And Romo confirmed: "Lee's expenses were paid by Illinois-based Kurtis Productions, headed by Bill Kurtis, host of the History Channel series 'Investigating History.' "

Lee's profit motive was further elucidated in the August 12, 2004 *Lincoln County News* article by Doris Cherry: "Forensics 101 for 'Billy." She quoted Sheriff Tom Sullivan: "Along with Sullivan and Lee were a crew from Curtis [sic] Production Company filming for the History Channel and Court T.V. **Dr. Lee also has a show produced by Curtis [sic] Production**."

So Billy the Kid DNA exhumations and "matchings" were to be churned out by Lee and Kurtis for their enterprise. No wonder Lee called the project "worthwhile." He was intending an exhumation franchise.

But the public was fed a different bill of goods via the hoaxers. By April 13, 2006, deceived reporter, Leo W. Banks of the *Tucson Weekly*, in "The New Billy the Kid?" had Lee pleading; as in: "Everybody wants a piece of the Kid, even a celebrity like Henry Lee ... when he heard about the Kid dig-up efforts, **he called Sederwall to volunteer his services**."

The "Billy the Kid Case" hoaxers plugged Lee extravagantly. Rene Romo's August 2, 2004 *Albuquerque Journal* article even used their "Probable Cause Statement's" fellow hoaxer: "You're getting the top guy ... I think that will go a long way to finding out what happened in Lincoln," said **David S. Turk**, historian with the U.S. Marshals Service ... who is cooperating on the case."

DR. LEE AND FAKE BENCH "BLOOD" OF BILLY THE KID

When presented with the carpenter's bench, a legitimate forensic expert would have checked its validity for the "crime scene" and checked if "reference DNA" of Billy the Kid existed for identity matching if DNA was found on it. And there was none.

And the bench had no forensic validity either. It first appeared in 1926, 45 years after Billy's shooting, when a teenaged Maxwell relative named Stella Abreu, for tourists, made a Fort Sumner Billy the Kid Museum in a shack. And, knowing Billy had been laid out on a bench, she asked a local man for one for her display (according to historian, Jerry Richard Weddle). After her museum closed in 1937, that likely fake bench's storage was nil for blood. As stated in the "Probable Cause Statement," the hoaxers found it in the Albuquerque converted chicken coop of Stella's descendant, with her other alleged Maxwell family furniture.

But claiming "blood" - not necessarily *real* blood - was the hoaxers' only bench concern. So they faked it. On August 14, 2004, for the *Lincoln County News*, reporter Doris Cherry's "Forensics 101 for 'Billy,'" quoted Steve Sederwall: "The bench has been in the Maxwell family descendents **since 1881** and has been stored out of weather, protecting the blood evidence ... **Only once was the blood exposed to the elements, when a family member who took the bench without family approval returned it to the Maxwell family home in Fort Sumner and left it outside to get rained on once.** So the odds of finding blood evidence were very good."

The "rained on" part was not good for blood! It got worse. For an October 6, 2005 *RuidosoNews.com* article, hoax loyalist, Julie Carter, wrote "Follow the Blood: In the Billy the Kid Case, Miller

Exhumed." She stated: "The Maxwell compound and everything in it was reportedly washed away in a flood of 1906. The photo of the bench was taken in 1926 by historian Maurice Fulton ... Since 1959, they [Maxwell family] had stored the historical furniture and household items in an old chicken coop." Flooded out and unknown location from 1881 to 1926 were also bad! And another gap was from being photographed in Stella's Museum in 1926, to transport in 1959 to the Albuquerque, back yard chicken coop.

To fake its "validation," fellow hoaxers were used. On April 19, 2006, hoax-backing Julie Carter, in *RuidosoNews.com*, reported in "Digging up Bones": "UNM History professor Paul Hutton and U.S. Treasury [sic - Marshals Service] historian Dave Turk have both authenticated the bench." The hoaxers were back in business with hoax Version II and new exhumation hopes.

When Henry Lee examined the bench, he, of course, found "blood" too. Rene Romo's August 2, 2004, *Albuquerque Journal's* "Forensic Expert on Billy's Case" stated: "Lee, assisted by Calvin Ostler [his assistant] ... performed tests on the bench that Sederwall believes to be the one on which the Kid's body was laid out after Garrett gunned him down. Preliminary results indicated **trace evidence of blood**, but, without further testing, it is not certain whether the blood was human, Lee said."

In fact, there was no certain blood at all! I had seen the old bench. It had a few rust-colored discolorations - as expected.

But the hoaxer clowns, as P.T. Barnum disciples, know that "Advertising is like learning - a little is a bad thing." So they went into overdrive promoting their fake blood.

On August 12, 2004, reporter Doris Cherry, for her *Lincoln County News*, "Forensics 101 for 'Billy,' " wrote: "Dr. Lee proved the good odds by utilizing a laser to bore into the wood of the bench to take samples and he took scrapings from the top and underneath of the bench. **'Then he swabbed it with the chemical that changes color to indicate the presence of blood,' Sullivan said**."

The clowns were just hoaxing. Lee stated in his report - which I got after years of open records litigation against the record-hiding lawmen - that the had tested with Luminol, a non-specific chemical that fluoresces with *any iron-containing substance* - like rust, more likely on a carpenter's bench than blood. **And no other testing would *ever be done* to verify blood, or to connect it to Billy (which was impossible).**

But the clowns were performing for the press. Romo's original **"trace,"** in his August 2, 2004, "Forensic Expert on Billy's Case," started bleeding like stigmata for Doris Cherry's "Forensics 101 for Billy": **Sullivan declared that Lee "found a lot of blood**."

Julie Carter, for her October 6, 2005, *RuidosoNews.com* article "Follow the Blood: In the Billy the Kid Case, Miller Exhumed," quoted showman Steve Sederwall: "**We witnessed a large amount of blood." And he creatively lied that it proved "an upper chest wound**." That clown added the hoax punch-line: "Whoever was laid on that [bench], whether it was Billy the Kid or not," said Sederwall, "he left his DNA." The investigators said the amount of blood found on the bench indicated that whoever was on that bench must have been still alive. **"Dead men don't bleed," explained Sederwall. "and we witnessed a large amount of blood."**

By April 13, 2006, "blood" was almost dripping off the bench. Leo Banks of the *Tucson Weekly*, in "The New Billy the Kid," reported that **Sederwall said the bench was "saturated!"**

I got Lee's February 25, 2005 report on January 31, 2012 in my open records litigation. It was titled "Forensic Research & Training Center Forensic Examination Report," as ""Requested by: Lincoln County Sheriff's Office, New Mexico; Investigation History Program, Kurtis Production." "Local Case No." was "2003-274." The "Report To:" was Steve Sederwall, Lincoln County Sheriff's Office, New Mexico." The "forensic investigation team" had: "Calvin Ostler, Forensic Consultant, Riverton, Utah;" "Tom Sullivan, Sheriff, Lincoln County, New Mexico;" "Steve Sederwall, Deputy Sheriff, Lincoln County;" and "David Turk, US Marshall [sic], United States Marshall [sic] Service." The carpenter's bench was reported under "Item # 1 Workbench." Lee concluded:

> After a detail examination of the evidence and review of all the results of field testing, the following conclusion was reached.
>
> 1. Brownish dark stains were observed on different areas of the workbench. These areas were subjected to chemical presumptive blood tests. Some of those samples give a positive reaction. These results indicate the presence of Heme or Peroxidase like activity with those stains testing positive, **which suggest that those stains could be bloodstains**. Further DNA testing could reveal the nature and identity of these blood-like stains.

Hoaxing Lee hid more likely rust, and that Orchid Cellmark did not test for blood. And he hid that finding DNA would not even connect it to the stains, since he did no controls from non-stained areas. Nor were controls taken from everyone present at his testing to check for *their* contaminating DNA (think sneeze!). Lastly, he was lying that "[f]urther DNA testing could reveal the nature and identity of these blood-like stains," since there was no "reference DNA" of Billy the Kid to test their "identity."

But Orchid Cellmark Lab was hyped. Reporter, Doris Cherry, in her August 12, 2004, "Forensics 101 for 'Billy' " stated: "Each swab and all scrapings from the bench were sealed in preparation to shipping to the Orchard Selmark [sic - Orchid Cellmark] Lab in Dallas. Sullivan said Dr. Lee uses the lab for most of his work."

Ultimately, by open records litigation and subpoena of Orchid Cellmark Lab, on April 20, 2012, I got Lee's carpenter's bench DNA results. Its October 15, 2004's "Laboratory Report, Forensic Identity, Mitochondrial Analysis, Results and Conclusions" for its Case 4444-001B-004B (for Case 2003-274) **[APPENDIX: 1] SHOWED LEE'S BENCH SPECIMENS HAD NO DNA! THE HOAXERS HAD LIED ABOUT HAVING BENCH-BLOOD-DNA OF BILLY THE KID FOR DNA MATCHINGS!** And they knew it by October 15, 2004. There was no justification to dig up anyone at all in their fake "investigation!" But they did anyway!

DR. LEE DEFAMES PAT GARRETT WITH A WASHSTAND, A HEADBOARD, AND A MADE-UP DEATH SCENE

What the hoaxers really wanted was a death scene incriminating Garrett as a bad guy capable of killing the innocent victim, then lying that the victim was Billy the Kid. So they must have told Dr. Henry Lee. With no Maxwell house in existence since about 1887 to investigate for a "crime scene," and with the uncertain furniture of Peter Maxwell's bedroom from Stella Abreu's Museum, he, of course, obliged with his fake forensics and flaunted expertise as cover for clowning.

Lee started with a washstand from Stella's Museum, which was not part of the historical death scene, and which further lacked credibility as being the size of a toy, not an actual washstand. (Its eventual measurements by Lee were: 28¾" x 16", x 30" high.) **[FIGURE: 3]**

But it had two bullet holes in it; though there was no bullet, and no record of when it was shot! But the lawmen had it, as stated in their "Probable Cause Statement": "On September 13, 2003, investigators located all the furniture that was in Pete Maxwell's bedroom the night of the shooting, July 1881. In the items investigators located on September 13, 2003 was that wash stand."

Their "Probable Cause Statement" had used it to fabricate Garrett as a liar, since he claimed his second shot hit Maxwell's **headboard, and never mentioned a washstand**. In his 1933 *The Death of Billy the Kid*, Poe had reported that: "[A] shot was fired in the room, followed immediately by what everyone within hearing distance thought were two other shots. However, there were only two shots fired, the third report, as we learned afterward, being caused by the rebound of the second bullet, which had struck the adobe wall and **rebounded against the headboard of a wooden bedstead**." So, by their fake "what-if" reasoning, the lawmen had made-up that *if* Garrett lied about not hitting the washstand, then he lied about the corpse's identity!

So obliging Dr. Lee recycled their washstand-headboard scam as a "forensic investigation" to incriminate Garrett as a liar, by faking a crime scene for them, then saying Garrett must have lied because it was not the shooting scene *he* gave!

Hoax-helping reporter, Rene Romo, presented Lee's "washstand" fakery in his August 2, 2004 *Albuquerque Journal*'s "Forensic Expert on Billy's Case." stating:

> Lee and the investigators [Sullivan, Sederwall, and Calvin Ostler] also examined a washstand that was purportedly struck by a bullet when Garrett shot the Kid in a bedroom of the outlaw's friend, Pete Maxwell, in Fort Sumner ... Lee and the investigators used laser technology Saturday to determine the trajectory of the bullet as it entered the left side of the washstand and exited the right at a downward angle. Given the washstand's likely location in the room, the investigation has already cast some doubt on Garrett's account of the fatal shooting, Sederwall and [Calvin] Ostler said.
>
> 'The evidence we are seeing does not corroborate the popular legend,' Ostler said. 'Something's askew' ...
>
> **One simple explanation that Lee offered is that Garrett may have shot defensively at the Kid as he fled and struck the washstand from the side instead of head on. Garrett's official story may have omitted that embarrassing detail. "You don't want to paint yourself as a chicken," Lee suggested.**

So Lee made-up this scene with no bullet for dating, and no provable relationship of the washstand to Garrett or to Billy or to Peter Maxwell or to the shooting. And Lee fabricated his groveling Garrett from the little box being toy-sixed, so being near the floor.

Item # 2 Washstand

This Washstand measures approximately 28 ¾" long by 16" deep by 30" tall. Figure 6 is a sketch diagram of the washstand. This washstand is made of wood with a black color finish on it.

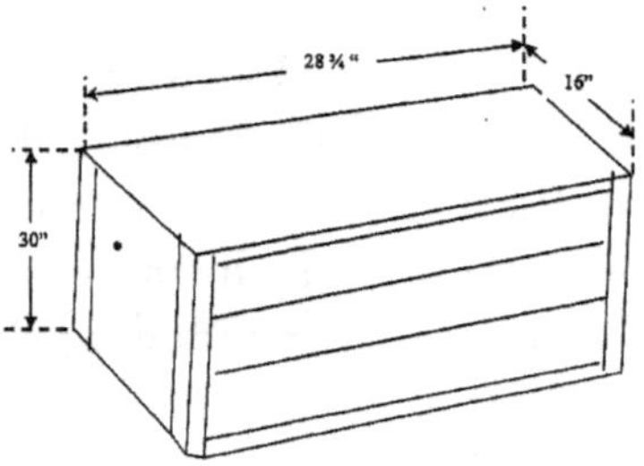

Figure 6, Washstand

Photograph # 3 shows the left side panel of the washstand and photograph # 4 depicts a view of the
Visual examination of the external s
holes, one single hole in each end of
examination of these holes indicates
bullet holes.

Page 10 o

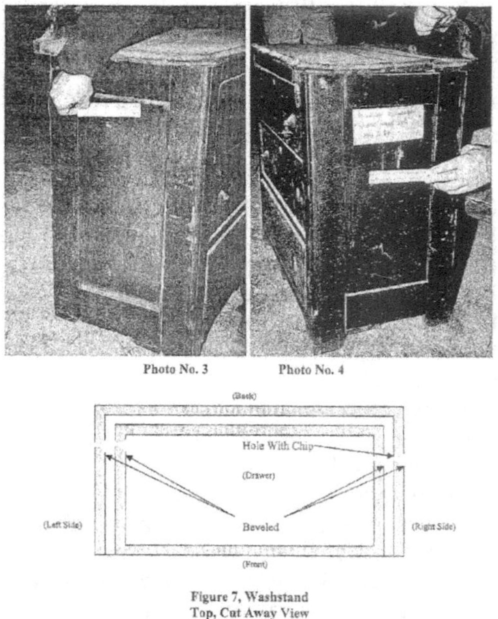

Photo No. 3 Photo No. 4

Figure 7, Washstand
Top, Cut Away View

Figure 7 is a cut away diagram of the washstand. This diagram depicts the relative locations of the two holes on the side panels of the washstand.

The hole on the left side panel is round and well defined. The hole on the right side panel is chipped and beveled. The left side panel hole is consistent with a bullet entrance hole.

Page 11 of 25

FIGURE: 3. "Washstand" from Stella Abreu's Fort Sumner Billy the Kid Museum, 1926-1936

For his February 25, 2005 report titled "Forensic Research & Training Center Forensic Examination Report" - which I got through my open records litigation against the hoaxing lawmen - under "Item # 2 Washstand," Lee babbled his fabrication:

> The angles produced in the examination tell us two things: First, the bullet was fired from no more than 41" from the floor given the reported limitations of the room. The room was reported to be 20' by 20'; the maximum distance is assumed to be 20'. If the firearm was a maximum of 41" off the floor it is unlikely that the shooter was standing. It is more likely the shooter was kneeling, squatting, or close to the floor. Second, the horizontal angle is such that if the Washstand was positioned so that the back was against the wall, the shot could not have been fired from more than approximately 40 inches from the Washstand, because the wall would have been in the way. The angle of trajectory intersects the back plane of the Washstand at approximately 45 3/16", and no more than 46". Lee's conclusion reflected his well-known caution about putting his lies in writing: "Two bullet holes were located on the side panels of the Washstand. The hole on the left side panel is consistent with a bullet entrance hole while the hole on the right side panel is consistent with a bullet exit hole. However, it is not possible to determine when those bullet holes were produced at this time.

The lawmen also gave Dr. Lee Stella's Museum's headboard to "investigate." Important for their fake argument of Garrett as a liar, was claiming it had no bullet hole as claimed by him and Poe. So that is what Lee gave them.

Lee's February 25, 2004 "Forensic Research & Training Center Forensic Examination Report," under its topic, **"Item # 2 Headboard;"** stated:

> **No bullet hole and no observable damage, no sign of bullet ricocheted type of defects were found on the Headboard. No blood or biological materials were observed on the Headboard.**

What Lee slyly omitted, is that Stella's "headboard" is just a rim around empty space. **[Figure: 4]** *There is no headboard to have the hole!* But Lee's assistant, Calvin Ostler, lied to Rene Romo for his August 2, 2004 *Albuquerque Journal*'s "Forensic Expert on Billy's Case" by stating: "The evidence we are seeing does not corroborate the popular legend" [meaning real history].

FIGURE: 4. Headboard lacking a center from Stella Abreu's Fort Sumner Billy the Kid Museum, 1926-1936 (Courtesy of Kenny Miller)

Deputy Steve Sederwall was soon spouting Dr. Lee's Garrett-is-a-liar fable in Julie Carter's October 2005, "Follow the Blood": "Using high-tech lasers and other modern crime scene methods, investigators learned that the shooting of the Kid in Pete Maxwell's bedroom was not in the way history has portrayed it. Tests indicate that Garrett fired his second shot from the doorway while on his knees and with his left hand on the floor, firing back over his shoulder ... Being blinded by his first shot, it appears he was in a great hurry to get out of the room and fell to the floor.' [Sederwall] added: 'To find the furniture from Maxwell's bedroom was great. But to have Dr. Lee recover usable evidence was truly a historical find.' "

In fact, this Garrett-washstand-headboard fabrication is merely an example of the hoaxing clowns' colluding to fake a death scene. All were just performing for their media circus.

BIG PICTURE FOR DR. HENRY LEE'S FAKE "BILLY THE KID CASE" FORENSICS

Dr. Henry Lee, though hoaxing, was self-protective. The hoaxers feared his forensic report would reveal their lies. And they knew that his Orchid Cellmark Lab got no DNA from his carpenter's bench samples, ending their claimed "bench-DNA-of-Billy-the-Kid" to fake justification of exhumations.

So they hid Lee's and Orchid Cellmark's records from my open records case against them. And, during its litigation, Steve Sederwall also forged Lee reports to fake the case as his own private hobby, while removing Lee's conclusions. This forging was punitively sanctioned in Judge George Eichwald's May 15, 2014 "Findings of Fact and Conclusions of Law and Order of the Court."

In fact, Dr. Henry Lee's so-called forensic investigation was just his own fictions built on the hoaxers' fictional death scene. And even if he got bench DNA, there was no "reference DNA" of Billy Bonney to match with it to prove it was his.

But their lie that they had Billy-the-Kid's-bench-blood-DNA would be used in a year as justification for digging-up John Miller (with William Hudspeth thrown in), and for trying to dig up "Brushy Bill" Roberts - all based on those two imposters' faked death scenes of Pat Garrett's killing of an innocent victim ("Brushy's" Billy Barlow and Miller's Indian friend), and the denial of the existence of the Coroner's Jury Report that put an end to all their clown acts.

CHAPTER 6
ILLEGALLY EXHUMING JOHN MILLER AND WILLIAM HUDSPETH FOR A MEDIA CIRCUS

CLOWNS AND CRIMINALITY

Disciples of Barnum & Bailey circus's P.T. Barnum, the "Billy the Kid Case" hoaxers heeded his admonition: "Without promotion something terrible happens: Nothing!"

By 2005, their hoax was in big trouble. With my blocking their fake exhumations of Billy and his mother, there was no fodder for their press or their tabloid-level "history's mysteries" TV "documentaries." That was when the most ludicrous clown of all, John Miller, was turned to as their savior.

So, in death, John Miller became the most successful Billy the Kid pretender, if being the only dug-up one marks fame. He certainly got the three-ring media circus that he never attained - or did not want - in his lifetime. And he got the most dramatic treatment of all the pretenders: his remains stolen and pulverized for no reason except his harmless clowning-around in life.

But he had posthumously met the dark clowns who wanted to use him to kill history. Since the "Billy the Kid Case" was a publicity stunt, its drive was for *any* publicity. "Brushy Bill" as Billy the Kid may have been its covert goal, but any exhumation keeping the TV cameras rolling sufficed. And John Miller's grave in the Prescott, Arizona Pioneers' Home Cemetery, was available for desecration because it was state-owned. That meant it was under the auspices of corrupt Governor Janet Napolitano, apparently willing to do a favor for her corrupt New Mexico counterpart, Bill Richardson. She merely needed to look away from backhoeing her cemetery's bodies for a publicity stunt.

Since the hoaxers knew by Miller's May 19, 2005 exhumation that they had no DNA of Billy the Kid from Dr. Henry Lee's carpenter's bench specimens, exhumation would be straightforward willful and wanton desecration of John Miller's grave, with grave-robbing to hand over his dismembered bones to Orchid Cellmark Director Rick Staub - present to be included in Bill Kurtis Productions' filming - and to carry them back to Texas.

There was worse. The Arizona Pioneers' Home Cemetery had unmarked graves. So uncertain of John Miller's location, and out-of-control, the hoaxers would ultimately dig up an adjoining grave of a random man named William Hudspeth, and steal his remains too, to fill up Dr. Rick Staub's bone bags!

SHERIFF RICK VIRDEN LED THE CIRCUS

After Lincoln County Sheriff Tom Sullivan's term ended in 2004, his Undersheriff, Rick Virden, a "Billy the Kid Case" hoax peripheral participant, was elected Sheriff. Virden immediately deputized Tom Sullivan and past Deputy Steve Sederwall to continue his Case No. 2003-274.

From the 2003 start of their "Billy the Kid Case," the hoaxers had kept John Miller half-heartedly in their sights, as was seen in their already-cited "Seventy-Seven Days of Doubt" initial draft of a "Probable Cause Statement" for their Lincoln County Sheriff's Department Case No. 2003-274. There, Miller's brief presence was for "survival suspicion" to prove Pat Garrett had not killed the Kid," and as a foil for "Brushy Bill." (See pages 186-187 above)

By 2005, having only a faltering hoax and the lie of possessing bench-DNA-of-Billy-the-Kid, John Miller became a necessity as their "Billy the Kid." So they hid his 10-years-too-old age. They also hid that he had no playing-dead-on-the carpenter's-bench scene - and *even denied being present on July 14, 1881, for his own fabricated Garrett-killing-an-Indian-friend tale.*

Nonetheless, scorning their audience as idiots, with P.T. Barnum's supposed dictum, "There's a sucker born every minute," they reversed course once again, claiming their (non-existent) blood-of-playing-dead-Billy-on-the-bench-DNA, gotten by famous forensic expert Dr. Henry Lee, would prove Miller was the Kid.

So lacking any basis, by history or by DNA, to justify John Miller's exhumation, the hoaxers proceeded with paranoid secrecy, though with a special report to feign legitimacy of the exhumation by its being part of Virden's Case No. 2003-274.

So before they got caught for the Miller-Hudspeth exhumations' illegalities and lied that they had not been involved in the exhumations, the lawmen prepared the "Lincoln County Sheriff's Department Supplemental Report for Case No. 2003-274 for the Exhumation of John Miller." I got it from Prescott Police Department. Signed by Steve Sederwall on Sheriff Rick Virden's official form, it began like this:

LINCOLN COUNTY SHERIFF'S DEPARTMENT SUPPLEMENTAL REPORT

Case # : 2003-274
Date: Thursday, May 19, 2005
Subject: Exhumation of John Miller
Location: Arizona Pioneers' Cemetery, Prescott, Arizona
Report By: Steven M. Sederwall

On Thursday, May 19, 2005, at approximately 1:00 pm the following met at the Arizona Pioneers' Cemetery at Prescott, Arizona.

Investigators:

Steven M. Sederwall, Lincoln County Deputy Sheriff

Following Sederwall, was Tom Sullivan as "Sheriff of Lincoln County, Retired," then Dale Tunnell as an "Arizona State Investigator." In line was "**Dr. Rick Staub, Orchid Cell Mark** [sic], DNA," proving the lab head himself was there for the bones.

The remaining "Investigators" were listed as: "Mike Poling, Yavapai County Sheriff''s Deputy [a random lawman who merely arrived to give forensic expert, Laura Fulginiti, specimens from another case, but was slyly added to fake presence of Arizona authority; and was later faked by the hoaxers as responsible for the exhumation!]; Laura Fulginiti, Forensic Scientist - Anthropologist; Kristen Hartnett, Forensic Scientist - Archeologist; Misty Rodarte, Arizona Pioneers' Administration."

Then came "Others Present," mostly Arizona Pioneers' Home staff, with addition of Deputy Tom Sullivan's wife, Pat.

Lastly, under "Bill Kurtis Productions," were cameraman, Joel Sapatori; and the soundman, Greg Gricus – the only real motive for the fake exhumation.

FAKING JOHN MILLER BELIEVERS: FELLOW HOAXERS, DALE TUNNELL AND TOM SULLIVAN

The hoaxers' problem with John Miller as Billy the Kid was that he had no believers. So, the year after his exhumation, fellow hoaxer, Dale Tunnell, became his fan, via Helen Airy's 1993 *Whatever Happened to Billy the Kid?* That was when the clowns were being investigated for felonious assault on his grave.

A March 13, 2006 Internet article about Tunnell, on helenair.com, by a Robert Struckman, was "Bitterroot man hopes to uncover the truth about Billy the Kid." The article demonstrated yet another hoax rewrite, apparently in response to my open records requests to the lawmen hoaxers as public officials. They now *denied being lawmen*, and claimed to be "amateur historians" owning private records, immune to the open records act. For Struckman, Tunnell became an "amateur historian" too. So Struckman wrote: "[Tunnell] would like to confirm the story put forth by Airy. **Like him, she was an amateur historian who bucked the official story.** Academics scoffed at her account. 'I'd like to prove her correct,' he said."

Also calling himself a "forensic criminologist," Tunnell tried to upgrade imposter, John Miller. Struckman recorded:

> Tunnell's interest in the famous outlaw was piqued when he read a 1993 book by Helen Airy entitled, "Whatever Happened to Billy the Kid" ...
>
> "Even if it [DNA matching] comes back positive, there will be more work to do," Tunnell said. He hopes to find conclusive documentation placing Miller at or near Fort Sumner in July of 1881 or connecting his wife, Isadora, to a relationship there ...
>
> Tunnell has found enough material to poke holes in the official histories, he said ...
>
> "I want to set the record straight. If Billy the Kid , from 1881 to 1937, lived the life of an honest man, a hardworking fool, then I say he paid his debt to society," Tunnell said.

For Struckman, Tunnell portrayed himself as owning a company named Forensitec, having "a Ph.D. in forensic criminology ... pursuing a second doctorate in general psychology; being a "retired federal investigator," "a deputy sheriff in 1974 in Lincoln County," an "investigator with the Arizona Department of Corrections," and "a federal agent with the U.S. Department of Interior."

On the Internet, Forensitec was, at the time, listed as: "Forensitec - Forensic Psycholinguistic Patterning." Tunnell is listed its "President and founder." As to his "Ph.D.," he called himself "a doctoral learner in General Psychology," and the "World's Foremost Authority in Forensic Language Analysis." This apparently meant he read psychology books and thought he could tell if people were lying (ironic given his hoax participation, and apparently being no "doctor," as he claimed). There was no Ph.D. Later, when the exhumation was a matter for the Prescott Police Department, he was listed as a 15 year friend of Steve Sederwall.

All Tunnell's fakery left a credibility gap. Hiding their "Billy the Kid Case's" Pat Garrett murder case, made exhumation seem like just a favor to Miller: setting *his* record straight! So hapless Tunnell became confused by the hoax's tangled lies and made an unintentionally funny comment to Struckman: ""It's possible," Tunnell said, "that Garrett conspired with Billy to fake the death. Maybe **Billy never laid, wounded, on the carpenter's bench**. Maybe another body was buried in Billy's place." Oops, "Doctor" Tunnell! Without Billy on the bench, there goes Lee's blood-DNA-of-Billy-the-Kid." There goes digging up John Miller solely for a DNA match to it!!!

Tunnell concluded his interview with the hoaxers' full scheme:

> After **getting permission [questionable]** to exhume Miller's body, DNA samples were taken. The DNA analysis will be done by Dr. Henry Lee, founder of the Forensic Science Program at the University of New Haven and chief emeritus of the Connecticut State Police, Sullivan said.
>
> What if the DNA matches the wooden bench?
>
> "We'll change history. I don't know. Arizona would have the real Billy the Kid," Sullivan said.

Struckman ended his article with hoaxing Deputy Tom Sullivan, who had also just become a John Miller believer:

> After getting permission [no legitimate permit for exhumation for DNA matching was obtained] to exhume Miller's body, DNA samples were taken. The DNA analysis will be done by Dr. Henry Lee, founder of the Forensic Science Program at the University of New Haven and chief emeritus of the Connecticut State Police, Sullivan said.
>
> What if the DNA matches the wooden bench?
>
> "We'll change history. I don't know. Arizona would have the real Billy the Kid," Sullivan said.

THE SECRET FRENZIED DIG OF MAY 19, 2005

John Miller's eternal rest at the Arizona Pioneers' Home Cemetery ended on May 19, 2005, when the hoaxers secretly and violently backhoed his coffin and grave, frantically grabbing bones into the night, and handing them to on-site Orchid Cellmark Lab Director, Dr. Rick Staub, who, with them, was being filmed by Bill Kurtis Productions for another of his fake forensics programs - presumably his "Investigating History" series, in partnership with Dr. Henry Lee, who had created the fake bench DNA.

Present with the hoaxers was moonlighting, Maricopa County, forensic anthropologist, Dr. Laura Fulginiti, who had been nervously added by them to feign forensic credibility (taking no chances with Dale Tunnell's Forensitec and Ph.D. tales). She, however, ultimately presented a problem by being honest, and dutifully recording everything they did.

RECONSTRUCTING THE DIGGING

My open records requests in 2006 to Governor Janet Napolitano's office revealed more about the illegal exhumations. Emboldened by their huge umbrella of two governors, Sullivan and Sederwall had relied on an apparent loophole in Arizona exhumation law: the supervisor of a state cemetery could approve an exhumation *to identify remains.* But its statutory intent was to *ensure correct grave markers* - not investigating a deceased person's delusional identity claims. Adding to criminality, of course, was having no valid DNA to justify any exhumation. But to advance their scheme, the hoaxers had added more clowns.

PIONEERS' HOME SUPERVISOR JEANINE DIKE

The role of "supervisor of a state cemetery" as permission-granter would be assumed by Jeanine Dike, the Supervisor of the Arizona Pioneers' Home and Cemetery in 2005. The rumor was that the hoaxers were directed to her by Governor Janet Napolitano's office. Steve Sederwall and Dale Tunnell took her on; with Tunnell as a forensic expert from Forensitec, Sederwall as a cop. Dispensing with the name, "John Miller," they told her they had to dig up "William Bonney!"

That they landed Jeanine Dike hook, line, and sinker is seen by her chummy e-mail of May 3, 2005 to Tunnell - as "Dale" - signed as "Superintendent," with "Subject: Disinterment of Wm Bonney": "I am so glad for you that things are coming together for the forensic study on Wm Bonney. I am asking Dale Sams to contact Mountain View Cemetery and make arrangements for the disinterment and reinterment to take place on May 19, 2005 at 10 AM ... I wish you the best and I hope your anticipated results are correct. It has been a pleasure working with you."

The next day, May 4, 2005, dazzled Dike cleared the way with her employee, Dale Sams, e-mailing him to make arrangements for "disinterment and reinterment." For billing, she provided Tunnell's Forensitec address. (Another later e-mail from the Pioneer Home's next Supervisor, Gary Olson, to Napolitano's Office, stated that Tom Sullivan had paid the exhumation bills. Three years later, under oath in a deposition, Sullivan revealed who did pay - Bill Richardson.)

The same May 4, 2005, Dale Sams, on their Pioneers' Home's official letterhead with "Governor Janet Napolitano" under Arizona's state seal, contacted a George Thompson, at an adjoining cemetery. The subject was "Disinterment." Sams wrote: "George: An excavator wants to disinter William Bonney on May 19 at 10 am at the Pioneers' Home Cemetery ... Please have someone there to dig up Mr. Bonney. I'm not sure where he's located but this company believes he's there."

One can add lyrics for these merry clowns: "Hi-ho, hi-ho, it's off to dig we go,/ Without a clue who is buried where,/ and without having DNA to compare!"

ADDING DR. LAURA FULGINITI

Maintaining the Billy the Kid Case hoax's forensic veneer, the hoaxers, for facsimile forensic validation, or for Bill Kurtis Productions film impact, had hired moonlighting, Maricopa County, forensic anthropologist, Dr. Laura Fulginiti. Another dreamboat for hoaxers, she took their word about "permission" without checking, shrugged off plowing into an additional and random grave, and noticed nothing amiss by their slipshod and breakneck single day's digging (to maintain secrecy).

Tucson Weekly's reporter, Leo W. Banks, in his April 13, 2006 "The New Billy the Kid?" noted that the graves were in an unmarked field. And none other than Dale Tunnell had done the locating! And they dug up two bodies! Banks wrote:

The Miller exhumation began about 1 p.m. on May 19 last year, and didn't end until about 7:30 that night, with investigators examining the last of the remains by flashlight. A backhoe did most of the heavy labor, after which the diggers worked by hand to avoid damaging the coffins or the remains.

But they soon learned that the coffins had already collapsed with age, which had also made the bones extremely fragile. Each piece was carefully photographed, measured and cleaned, then placed on a white sheet on the ground.

Dr. Laura Fulginiti, a well-known forensic anthropologist from Phoenix, supervised the dig. She describes the atmosphere as collegial and charged with excitement as they removed the tobacco-colored bones from the ground.

"At one point, they were holding up the skull and comparing it with pictures of Billy," Fulginiti says. "They recited the story to each other, and when we found something that matched, like the scapula (shoulder) fracture, they were like little kids. They were really invested in this, and that added to the enthusiasm."

But the effort was anything but clear-cut.

In the first place, Miller's grave held no marker or headstone, and neither did the grave closest to his. To determine where Miller's plot should be, the investigators used a map provided by the Pioneers' Home, which pinpointed the location to within 20 square feet.

As Tunnell acknowledges, ground shift and weather patterns can sometimes move bodies underground, and Miller had been 6 feet under almost 70 years. How certain were they of digging in the right place? "Probably upwards of 90 percent," says Tunnell.

Dr. Laura Fulginiti, neither scholarly or meticulously ethical like New Mexico's Office of the Medical Investigators, Drs. Ross Zumwalt and Debra Komar, ruminated to Leo Banks: "Was it respectful to Miller to dig him up? Part of me says it wasn't, given that the information we had wasn't the best ... From the beginning, I assumed it was another of these Wild West goose chases."

But Fulginiti's June 2, 2005 report to "Dale L. Tunnell, Ph.D., Forensitec," titled "Re: Exhumation, Pioneer [sic] Home Cemetery, Prescott, Arizona," was invaluable. No hoaxer, she ponderously recorded the absurd. (See pages 258-259, 319-322 below)

And, as will be seen, she inadvertently hoaxbusted the "Billy the Kid Case" clowns' lies intended to make John Miller Billy the Kid. And she also made clear random man, William Hudspeth's, undeniably illegal exhumation. This was her big picture:

- For grave location she relied only on "Dr." Tunnell and his associates (presumably Sullivan and Sederwall).
- She documented two, unmarked, separate, adjacent graves, which she named "South" and "North."
- The North Grave, she concluded, was not Miller's. (It was William Hudspeth's.) It had a *right* scapula with "extensive healed traumata;" and she denied the hoaxers' on-site claim of a bullet hole. For the press, it would become the hoaxers' *left* scapula of *John Miller* with a *bullet hole*.")
- The John Miller, South Grave's skull was "edentulous" (toothless). For the press, the hoaxers would lie that he had "buck teeth."

But lax Dr. Fulginiti even permitted a Yavapai County Deputy named Mike Poling - delivering specimens to her from another case of hers - to use his metal detector for casket location with those unmarked and uncertain graves. Deputy Poling would later prove to have been another lucky break for the hoaxers.

ADDING PERPETRATORS AND WITNESSES

The Lincoln County Sheriff's Department Supplemental Report for Case #: 2003-274, lists the perpetrator as that Department; and adds profuse witnesses, and the filming by Bill Kurtis Productions. Later, this report would make Virden the main defendant in my open records litigation.

SWEARING THE CLOWNS TO SECRECY

Sullivan and Sederwall built-in a delay in exposing the John Miller exhumation with their accumulating troop of clowns as they struggled to decide whether to ditch John Miller for the real prize: faking "Brushy Bill" Roberts as Billy the Kid. So they swore everyone to secrecy! And, apparently, no one wondered why.

Everyone complied, as seen in an e-mail sent by Sederwall on July 6, 2005, to Misty Rodarte, present at the dig, and the Arizona

Pioneers' Home Administrator. The subject was "Billy the Kid." In his full-bore "martyr for truth" mode, Steve Sederwall stated:

> Thanks for calling the other day. It is too funny how these people react to someone looking for the truth. Thanks for not talking to anyone about it that is just what we are doing [sic].
>
> Here is the update: Rick from the lab called me the other day. They have recovered DNA from the grave to the right as you stand at the foot of the graves. They are working on the grave on the left now. When they recover DNA from that grave they will compare them both with the work bench we recovered last year. I will keep you up to speed on it and we will not wait. Tell all the wonderful folks out there we said hello.

By August 18, 2005, the new and uneasy Arizona Pioneers' Home Supervisor, Gary Olson, e-mailed Napolitano's Office: "Representatives from APH [Arizona Pioneers' Home] were in attendance during the process - some were asked to sign a confidentiality agreement and asked to remain silent by Sullivan and Sederwall. We have no copy of this form."

THE SECRECY ENDS

The secrecy worked. Not till 2006 did the Arizona digging emerge. Sullivan and Sederwall were interviewed by reporter Leo Banks for his April 13, 2006's *Tucson Weekly* "The New Billy the Kid?" Their fables showed they had decided not to risk legal scrutiny which had stopped them in New Mexico. Banks recorded:

> "People at Fort Sumner wouldn't allow us to exhume Billy's remains, because they're not sure he's there," says the 65-year-old Sullivan, still smarting from the criticism. "Everybody lawyered up, and we ran into a lot of legal B.S."
>
> **So Sullivan and Sederwall stole into Arizona on stocking feet, working quietly to get Miller's bones out of his grave at Prescott's state-run Arizona Pioneers' Home, snag some DNA and head back home.**
>
> "We slipped in there and slipped out fast," Sullivan told the *Weekly*.
>
> "We all stayed at the same hotel, sort of to keep it quiet. If the media got word, our critics would've gotten together to lawyer the whole thing up, serve people with papers and temporary restraining orders, and all that crap."

Again, their Pat Garrett as murderer fabrication tripped easily off their lying tongues at Leo Banks's leading question:

Was Sheriff Garrett, a **known friend of the Kid**, outraged at Billy's conviction in the Brady trial and somehow involved in helping Billy escape justice?

"From a law-enforcement perspective, nothing fits," says Sullivan ...

Sederwall points with suspicion to the last line of the coroner's report on Billy. "It says Garrett deserves the reward money for killing him," he says. "I've never seen that in a coroner's report before."

They even made-up a return to the Silver City mother's grave, by lying about Judge Henry Quintero's stipulation that they could only return to his court if they got DNA from Billy the Kid's remains in Fort Sumner for matching with the mother. But these clowns stated: "The judge in Silver City said you can't exhume Catherine, because you have nothing to compare her DNA to," says the former sheriff ... They told us to come back if we found more evidence. Then we got DNA from the bloody workbench ..."

Unaware of their ricochet validation trick, Banks used their fellow hoaxer, *True West* editor, Bob Boze Bell, who heralded their next hoped-for grave, saying he supported using science to find out if Billy ("Brushy Bill") was buried in Hico [sic - Hamilton], Texas.

But Leo Banks also quoted legitimate historian Frederick Nolan, who called the "Billy the Kid Case" a "disgraceful charade."

THE NEW CLOWN ACT

Using hoax-backing reporters, the hoaxing clowns then rewrote the "Billy the Kid Case" hoax around their John Miller as Billy the Kid exhumation.

Hoax-backing reporter, Julie Carter, wrote her October 6, 2005 *RuidosoNews.com* article, "Follow the Blood: In the Billy the Kid Case, Miller Exhumed." For it, Steve Sederwall posed for a trophy photo holding John Miller's (or William Hudspeth's) skull.

Carter quoted bombastic Sederwall: "In the light of the evidence, we see that the history of Billy the Kid will change. Those with monied interest in history remaining the same will not be happy ... As a cop I know when people fight to keep you from looking at something, they are always trying to hide something. The Lincoln County War is still going on." So Julie Carter gave the new version of the ever-changing hoax, now with John Miller as king. She wrote:

One established absolute fact to date in the ongoing

saga of the legend of Billy the Kid is that he is dead. That fact can be written without question because 145 [sic - 146] years since he was born would make it so.

The looming question today is, Where is he dead? Currently, investigators are waiting to see if the DNA taken from a carpenter's work bench last summer (July 2004) matches the DNA taken in May from the exhumed body of John Miller, one of two who claimed to be William H. Bonney aka Billy the Kid.

[AUTHOR'S NOTE: This is hoaxing to introduce John Miller and his secret exhumation. In fact, there existed no bench-DNA-of-Billy-the-Kid for matchings. And, as will be seen, it is uncertain that DNA was gotten from Miller's bones.]

The carpenter's work bench is reportedly the one the Kid was laid on by friends in the Maxwell compound in Ft. Sumner after he was shot.

[AUTHOR'S NOTE: This uses Version II of bleeding-Billy-on-the-bench-for-DNA.]

Retired Lincoln County Sheriff Tom Sullivan and retired federal cop and Capitan Mayor Steve Sederwall continue to pursue the official investigation they began in 2003.

[AUTHOR'S NOTE: The hoaxers were concealing their active deputyships under Sheriff Rick Virden because they were hiding case records from my open records investigations.]

Seeing too many holes in the Billy the Kid legend and knowing that science could now prove fact from century old supposition, the pair set out to do just that.

On April 28, 2003, the 122 anniversary of the escape of Billy the Kid from the Lincoln County Court-house, Sullivan and Sederwall opened Lincoln County Case # 2003-274 into the deaths of Bob Olinger and J.W. Bell whose murders were never investigated or prosecuted.

[AUTHOR'S NOTE: Fake switcheroo of case to deputy murders from their Garrett as murder filing, also to evade my open records requests.]

Investigators fired off two black powder rounds to see if the shots inside of the courthouse could be heard from the hotel and as far down the street as the Ellis Store.

[AUTHOR'S NOTE: This is the Deputy Bell murder sub-investigation.]

Later joined by De Baca County Sheriff (Ft. Sumner) Gary Graves, the trio launched a probe into the Kid's escape that led to his slaying in July 1881 in Ft. Sumner. The aim of the investigation has always been to use forensic science and modern police techniques to clear up questions about the Kid's escape and death.

Joining Sederwall and Sullivan in the search for the facts is Bill Kurtis, executive producer of A&E Channel's Cold Case Files, American Justice and Investigative Reports. Kurtis has had cameras running to document the progress of the investigation including the scraping of material in the bench that has revealed human DNA and **a blood pattern consistent with an upper chest wound** such as the one the Kid was said to have received from Garrett on July 14, 1881.

[AUTHOR'S NOTE: Fabrication of chest wound.]

"Whoever was laid on that, whether it was Billy the Kid or not," said Sederwall, "he left his DNA." The investigators said the amount of blood found on the bench indicated that whoever was on that bench must have been still alive. **"Dead men don't bleed," explained Sederwall. "and we witnessed a large amount of blood."**

[AUTHOR'S NOTE: Here is the switch to shot Billy.]

When the lab called and said the DNA was human and it was the same DNA on the three-board-wide bench, Sederwall and Sullivan decided it was time to start looking at the John Miller story a little harder.

[AUTHOR'S NOTE: THIS IS LYING, SINCE NO DNA WAS OBTAINED FROM THE BENCH. IT IS JUST FAKING MILLER AS BILLY.]

With both Sederwall and Sullivan present, the exhumation of Miller took place on May 21 in Prescott, Ariz., where he was buried in the cemetery of the Pioneer Home ...

This case has not failed to amaze us at every turn, said Sederwall. John Miller even held some surprises for us. He had buck teeth just as history tells us the Kid had. But we were shocked to see that Miller sported a very old bullet wound that entered the left chest and exited the shoulder blade, the same wound Garrett claimed to have inflicted on the Kid the night in July 1881.

[AUTHOR'S NOTE: As will be seen, this is hoaxing. Miller's skull was toothless. <u>William Hudspeth's</u> *right* scapula had an imperfection – denied as gunshot by on-site forensic expert, Dr. Laura Fulginiti.]

Miller's samples have been sent to an unnamed laboratory in Texas to extract DNA ...

[AUTHOR'S NOTE: Here, Orchid Cellmark Lab is concealed because of my open records case seeking its DNA records.]

In his investigation Sederwall found a photo of the carpenter work bench originally thought to be lost. The Maxwell compound and everything in it was reportedly washed away in a flood of 1906. The photo of the bench was taken in 1926 by historian Maurice Fulton.

Our thinking was, said Sederwall, that if they took a picture of it, it was important and someone still has the bench. We also noticed that the museum in Ft. Sumner had a piece of tapestry that was the same tapestry shown in the window of the bench photo. If the tapestry survived the flood, so did the bench.

Tracing down through the generations of the Maxwell family tree, Sederwall found not only a 1936 written reference to the items from the bedroom where the Kid was said to be shot, but in Albuquerque in August 2003 he found direct descendents of the Pete Maxwell family. Since 1959, they had stored the historical furniture and household items in an old chicken coop. The carpenter's workbench was intact as was the entire bedroom set including the washstand said to be pierced by Garrett's second bullet shot in the dark at the Kid.

Enter Dr. Henry Lee.

Dr. Lee is one of the nation's leading forensic scientists with case names attached to his including O.J. Simpson, JonBenet Ramsey and Lacy Peterson. Lee was anxious to aid Billy the Kid to his resume and called the investigators to offer his services.

[AUTHOR'S NOTE: Lie: Lee was paid by Bill Kurtis to do the case, and partnered with him for "Investigating History" TV series.]

The director of the Connecticut State Police Forensic Laboratory traveled to Lincoln County in July 2004 to conduct tests in both the Lincoln County Courthouse and in Albuquerque on the workbench and wash stand.

Using high-tech lasers and other modern crime scene methods, investigators learned that the shooting of the Kid in Pete Maxwell's bedroom was not in the way history has portrayed it.

Tests indicate that Garrett fired his second shot from the doorway while on his knees and with his left hand on the floor, firing back over his shoulder, recounted Sederwall. Being blinded by his first shot, it appears he was in a great hurry to get out of the room and fell to the floor.

[AUTHOR'S NOTE: This is Lee's fake "crime scene."]

He added: "To find the furniture from Maxwell's bedroom was great. But to have Dr. Lee recover usable evidence was truly a historical find."

[AUTHOR'S NOTE: Lie: No DNA was obtained.]

No digging in New Mexico

Attempts to obtain permission to exhume the Kid's body from his Ft. Sumner grave and the body of his mother buried in a Silver City cemetery were blocked by municipal officials in both towns. Investigators had hoped to use modern forensics to scientifically prove or disprove the claims made by Brushy Bill Roberts and John Miller that they were the Kid. Their stories offered the possibility that the Kid did not die on July 14, 1881, in Ft. Sumner.

[AUTHOR'S NOTE: Hidden is the OMI's denying them exhumation permits for uncertain gravesites.]

A judge in Silver City told the investigators to come back if they had enough evidence to warrant the need for Catherine Antrim's (the Kid's mother) DNA. With the DNA results from the blood on the table and soon the results of Miller's DNA, investigators will likely move to take the judge up on that offer.

[AUTHOR'S NOTE: This misstates Grant County Judge Henry Quintero's stipulation that to dig up the mother required was DNA from the Fort Sumner Billy the Kid grave.]

In the light of the evidence, we see that the history of Billy the Kid will change. Those with monied interest in history remaining the same will not be happy, stated Sederwall.

As a cop I know when people fight to keep you from looking at something, they are always trying to hide something. The Lincoln County War is still going on.

[AUTHOR'S NOTE: Example of the false, but grandiose, pronouncements characterizing hoax press.]

The next month, more promoting of John Miller's as the Kid was done by hoax-backing reporter, Rene Romo, for November 6, 2005's *Albuquerque Journal's* "Billy the Kid Probe May Yield New Twist." And Romo had secretly worked with Governor Napolitano's office and Pioneer's Home Supervisor Gary Olson to hide illegality of the Miller-Hudspeth exhumations. Romo wrote:

LAS CRUCES - An ongoing investigation into the fate of Henry McCarty, alias William Bonney, alias Billy the Kid, could still yield a surprising twist in the controversial case.

Without any fanfare, former Lincoln County Sheriff Tom Sullivan and Steve Sederwall last May obtained DNA from the remains of a cowboy, John Miller. Before dying in the 1930's Miller told friends and a son that he was really Billy the Kid.

Miller's remains were exhumed from the cemetery of the Pioneer [sic] Home, a state-owned nursing home in Prescott, Ariz. His DNA is to be examined by a Dallas-based laboratory.

If Miller's DNA matches that of blood traces taken from a 19th century bench purportedly from the Maxwell Ranch in Fort Sumner, Sederwall and Sullivan say they could have a break that upends accepted historical accounts of the Kid's life and death.

The old bench was discovered last year at the Albuquerque home of Maxwell descendents. It is believed to be the one on which the Kid's body was placed after he was shot by Lincoln County Sheriff Pat Garrett on July 14, 1881, in a darkened bedroom of the Maxwell Ranch.

"Wouldn't it be a coincidence if someone we dug up in Arizona, and who died in 1934 and claimed to be Billy the Kid, bled on the bench? That's like winning the lottery," Sederwall said.

"That would be so coincidental, I would challenge anyone to prove it's not him (Billy the Kid)."

Sederwall acknowledges that what started out as an effort to defend the honor of Garrett against claims that the famous Lincoln County sheriff did not kill the Kid may have taken a new direction.

[AUTHOR'S NOTE: Under my investigation and litigation, the hoaxers hid their "Probable Cause Statement" accusing Garrett of murder, to claiming absurdly that they were investigating him for murder to prove him innocent!]

Sullivan and Sederwall began their investigation in 2003 when Sullivan was sheriff and Sederwall a reserve deputy. But they were rebuffed in their 2003 and 2004 attempts to exhume the Kid's remains in Fort Sumner and those of the outlaw's mother in Silver City.

The Lincoln County investigators wanted to use the DNA from the Kid's grave, or that of his mother, to validate the widely accepted story of Garrett's killing of Billy the Kid.

But critics in Fort Sumner and Silver City, as well as history buffs around the country, lambasted Sullivan and Sederwall, saying that the Kid's death and burial in De Baca County was well established.

Fort Sumner officials, in particular, fretted that the investigation would undermine the value of the Kid's grave there as a tourist destination.

[AUTHOR'S NOTE: Hoaxing blamed local officials and "tourism," instead of the truth: no DNA.]

In the decades after the Kid's demise, several old men emerged claiming they were Billy the Kid. One would-be Billy was Ollie P. "Brushy Bill" Roberts of Hico, Texas. Another was John Miller, the subject of a book called "Whatever Happened to Billy the Kid" by Helen Airy.

While Sederwall and Sullivan have both been commissioned as special deputies by current Lincoln County Sheriff Rick Virden, Sederwall said their investigation does not use county funds.

Sederwall said he expected the analysis of Miller's DNA to be completed by the end of the year or January.

If Miller's DNA matches what is presumed to be the Kid's on the bench, the news will be publicized by Bill Kurtis, anchor of the A&E Network weekly series "American

Justice," Sederwall said.

He said Kurtis, head of Chicago-based Kurtis Productions, has an "exclusive deal" to publicize the news because Kurtis helped to pay for some costs associated with the investigation.

Sederwall, who is also the mayor of Capitan and a history buff, said Miller's skeletal remains were intriguing. He said Miller had buck teeth, like the Kid, and an old bullet wound that entered his upper left chest and exited through the scapula.

[AUTHOR'S NOTE: As will be seen, this hoaxed skeleton is contradicted by the forensic report of on-site forensic expert, Dr. Laura Fulginiti. Miller's skull had no teeth. And it was William Hudspeth skeleton that had a healed right –not left – scapula, with no bullet damage.]

If that DNA matches the work bench, I think the game is over," Sederwall said.

If not, he said, investigators will try to obtain permission to exhume the remains of Roberts, who is buried in Hamilton, Texas.

The tales told by the hoaxers to their complicit reporters show how close old clown John Miller came to being Billy the Kid.

CHAPTER 7
CAUGHT IN THEIR CLOWN COSTUMES

THE CLOWN-CATCHER, DAVID SNELL

Legitimate investigative reporter, Leo Banks, had revealed the hoaxers' stealth and their exhumation of an additional man in the John Miller exhumation in his April 13, 2006 *Tucson Weekly's* "The New Billy the Kid?"

But there had been an even greater threat to the hoaxing clowns. Accustomed to corrupt Governor Bill Richardson's shielding in their fake New Mexico exhumation cases, the hoaxers were caught by surprise when an outraged Arizona citizen, amateur historian, David Snell, pressed criminal charges.

Having heard rumors about the intended exhumation, he had repeatedly checked the Arizona Pioneers' Home Cemetery, until he discovered its open field rutted with tire tracks of the desecrating participants and camera crew.

So he first called Arizona Pioneers' Home Supervisor Jeanine Dike to inquire. She lied: denying any exhumation. The next Arizona Pioneers' Home Supervisor, Gary Olson, did the same. His boss was Governor Janet Napolitano. It had been a crime. Olson knew it. Napolitano knew it. Snell knew it.

David Snell's dramatic role as a whistleblower was described in an April 12, 2006 article by a Joanna Dodder in *The Daily Courier* of Prescott. Its headline was "Officials could face charges for digging up alleged Billy the Kid." Dodder quoted Snell: "This is some kind of good o ' boy back-slappin' beer-drinkin' crusade ... He's [Billy's] buried in Ft. Sumner, where he's always been."

And on March 11, 2006 - just two days before Dale Tunnell's article about being an amateur-historian-forensic-expert-John-Miller-believer - Snell filed his criminal complaint. For it, he wrote to Shiela Polk, the Yavapai County Attorney - the county of the Arizona Pioneers' Home Cemetery exhumation as a crime. Snell stated:

> I feel it is my duty to report to you that grave robbers are plying their trade in Yavapai County. There individuals' crimes are being committed openly, knowingly, and with contempt for state and county law regarding exhumations. In the course of their nefarious activities, these parties have compromised and ultimately corrupted various officials and public employees. To date, all the parties involved in these crimes have been exempted from any sort of criminal investigation, let alone prosecution ...
>
> Now that these circumstances have been brought to your personal attention, I have every confidence that the good citizens of Yavapai County, and Arizona, can be assured of timely and effective action against these ghoulish scofflaws who loot our people's final resting places for personal gain.

Next stop was the Prescott Police Department; then the Prescott City Attorney, Glenn Savona. Dodder's article stated:

> Now Prescott City Prosecutor Glenn Savona is trying to figure out whether someone violated the law and whether the city or state has jurisdiction since the State of Arizona owns the Pioneers' Home Cemetery.
>
> Complicating matters is the fact that the person who apparently gave Sullivan permission to dig up the grave, former Pioneers' Home Superintendent Jeanine Dike, is away on a Mormon mission until June 2007 ...
>
> Dike apparently agreed to let Sullivan and others dig up Miller's unmarked remains under a relatively new state law that allows the action without a court order and permit if it's for "internal management," according to a Prescott Police Department report.
>
> "It doesn't look like the request came for an internal issue," Savona said. That law doesn't allow people to take the remains, either, he added ...
>
> The only other way to legally disinter the body is to get a permit from the Yavapai County Community Health Services Department after getting a court order or family permission
>
> Fulginiti and others told police that Tunnell assured them he had permission to conduct the dig.

So it emerged that the hoaxers had intended to claim "permission" came from Superintendent Jeanine Dike.

For reporter Joanna Dodder, Tom Sullivan and Steve Sederwall, facing dire charges, ditched their Tunnell-generated "amateur historian" identities and shape-shifted back to Lincoln County Deputy Sheriffs investigating murderer, Pat Garrett:

> Former Lincoln County Sheriff Tom Sullivan said he and the others plan to compare DNA from Miller's bones with DNA from blood that came from a bench on which Billy the Kid lay after Lincoln County Sheriff Pat Garrett shot him on July 14, 1881, in Ft. Sumner, N.M. ...
>
> Sullivan and former Capitan, N.M., mayor Steve Sederwall now are commissioned as Lincoln County deputies, Sullivan said. They are in the midst of a 3-year- old investigation into whether Billy the Kid actually is buried in Ft. Sumner ...
>
> Sullivan and his fellow former lawmen are on a mission to find the real Billy using modern-day technology.

And, apparently hoping discovery trumped criminality, and, for self-preservation, ditching their "Brushy Bill" as Billy the Kid directive from Governor Richardson, they wildly lied to reporter Joanna Dodder that their Arizona exhumation had *yielded proof that Miller was Billy the Kid*!

What evidence? Their fake "DNA matching" of John Miller (with William Hudspeth kept secret) to the fake bench-Billy-the-Kid-DNA was supposedly months away. They had to work with what they had: a pile of stolen bones.

So Tom Sullivan, now as a Lincoln County Deputy, gave Joanna Dodder a quote faking a link of the exhumation to the "Billy the Kid Case's" Garrett-as-murderer hoax. He was quoted: "**A shoulder bone from Miller's grave already indicates damage consistent with that of a gunshot wound that The Kid suffered ... The skeleton's protruding teeth and small stature also are consistent with Billy** ... Since Garrett was friends with The Kid, he might have shot him and then let him escape."

And their buddy, Dale Tunnell, was shape-shifted to their forensic expert who had hired another one, a Dr. Laura Fulginiti, to be *on site*. So they repeated that fake skeleton claim from Rene Romo's November 6, 2005, *Albuquerque Journal's*, "Billy the Kid Probe May Yield New Twist."

PILTDOWN MAN HOAX REDUX

The desperately lying "Billy the Kid Case" hoaxers were inadvertently rerunning the most famous skeleton hoax of all: Piltdown man. Between 1908 and 1912, an amateur anthropologist named Charles Dawson, claimed to have found Charles Darwin's coveted "missing link" between apes and men in and near Piltdown gravel quarry in East Sussex, England. Possible, though unproved, hoaxer, Dawson, hoped his discovery would yield him a fellowship in the British Royal Society. He had "discovered" parts of a human-like skull, an ape-like jawbone, a hominid-seeming canine tooth; plus an ivory tool and Stone Age animal teeth - for a Stone Age touch. "Museum experts" assembled the skull and jawbone into a creature they named *Eanthropus dawsoni*, to honor Dawson. Popularly called "Piltdown Man," it held its spot in humans' family tree for over 40 years.

In 1953, Sir Kenneth Oakley, using a new fluorine absorption test, proved Piltdown Man was a fake composite of a medieval human skull and an antique orangutan's jawbone - all stained to match. And the ape's jawbone's teeth were filed to fit the skull.

For their own Piltdown Man hoax, the "Billy the Kid Case" hoaxing lawmen tried to seduce Arizona reporter, Leo Banks, by: "We're giving Arizona Billy the Kid!" For his April 13, 2006 *Tucson Weekly* article, "The New Billy the Kid?" Deputy Tom Sullivan, as a John Miller fan and Helen Airy convert, was quoted: "Helen Airy's book triggered it for me ... It made a lot of sense. I read it and thought, 'We have another Billy the Kid.' "

And Sederwall and Sullivan performed their "high-tech forensic" routine, flaunting famous Dr. Lee and the carpenter's bench - now "saturated with blood." Banks quoted: "When we found the bench and the other evidence, we thought, 'Let's forget about these other bodies,' " says Sullivan, referring to Catherine Antrim and the Kid. "Let's do Miller. And if that doesn't work, we'll go down to Texas and do Brushy Bill."

But reporter, Leo Banks had researched the "Billy the Kid Case," and had discovered their digging up of random man, William Hudspeth. So he snidely called their roving extravaganza "airship Billy." And he exposed that Sullivan's and Sederwall's "Billy the Kid" skeleton claims were made by mixing up Miller's and the random man's bones! Banks had interviewed Dr. Laura Fulginiti. She denied their skeletal claims! Banks wrote:

Fulginiti says the first body she studied had buck teeth and the scapula fracture that caused such a commotion with investigators.

As Sederwall told the *Weekly*, "We were shocked when we got him up. He had buck teeth just like the Kid and a bullet hole in the upper left chest that exited the shoulder blade."

Sullivan made a similar statement, suggesting this might be the man Garrett shot the morning of July 14, 1881.

But when contacted by the *Weekly*, Fulginiti didn't support their enthusiasm. "There was evidence of trauma on the scapula, but I couldn't tell whether it was from a gunshot wound or not," she said.

Honest Dr. Fulginiti also told Banks that the buck teeth were from the corpse that Banks named "Scapula Man" (William Hudspeth), from his non-shot, but damaged *right* scapula! And Fulginiti stated that John Miller's skull had no teeth at all! Fulginiti had researched Miller as dying of a broken hip. So Banks called him "Hip Man."

Dutiful reporter, Banks, also contacted Orchid Cellmark Lab, discovering: "**The DNA expert present at the exhumation, Dr. Rick Staub, of Orchid Cellmark Labs in Dallas, was unable to extract useable DNA from Hip Man [John Miller]. But he did get a usable sample from Scapula Man [William Hudspeth]**."

This constituted Dr. Staub's admission that John Miller's bones had yielded no DNA!

When confronted by all this obviously incriminating information by Leo Banks for his article, Sullivan and Sederwall were left clumsily lying that Dr. Laura Fulginiti, their forensic expert hired specifically to validate the exhumation, was wrong. And simply ignored was that Miller's bones had yielded no DNA to use for faking their claim that he was Billy the Kid.

Nevertheless, it was now obvious that, for their own Piltdown Man hoax, the hoaxers had assembled a "John Miller as a Billy the Kid" from William Hudspeth's bones (Banks's "Scapula Man"). That was how random man, William Hudspeth, with dismembered corpse, and bones stolen by Dr. Rick Staub of Orchid Cellmark for meaningless DNA extraction - became part of Billy the Kid's history.

THE INCRIMINATING FULGINITI REPORT

Dr. Laura Fulginiti had reported it all. Duped into thinking Dale Tunnell was a forensic expert doing the exhumation, as "Dr. Tunnell," she had titled her June 2, 2005 report: "Re: Exhumation, Pioneer Home Cemetery, Prescott, Arizona for "Dale L. Tunnell, Ph.D. [sic – no Ph.d.], Forensitec." I got its copy from the Prescott Police Department. **[APPENDIX: 2]** In it, Fulginiti described the scene of the hoaxers' feverish digging to avoid being caught red-handed. She had written:

On May 19, 2005 at approximately 1230 hours I am asked to assist in the exhumation of the remains of an individual known as Mr. John Miller by Dr. Dale Tunnell, President, Forensitec. The purpose of my involvement is to aid in the exhumation process as well as to assess any skeletal remains recovered. The exhumation takes place at the Arizona Pioneer [sic] Home Cemetery, Iron Springs Road in Prescott Arizona in the presence of Dr. Tunnell, several of his associates, members of the Arizona Pioneer Home staff and Kristen Harnett M.A., AMSU graduate student.

[AUTHOR'S NOTE: The unmarked grave first exhumed was later called the South Grave, and was John Miller's.

Dr. Tunnell located the alleged gravesite of Mr. Miller prior to our arrival on the scene … At approximately 1400 hours, a backhoe began to remove the sod overlying the alleged grave, which was oriented in an East-West direction, with the head to the West. When fragments of wood began to be removed, the grave was excavated using a shovel … The left femoral shaft, minus the head, was removed, examined, and packaged for DNA analysis [the role of Rick Staub, Director of Orchid Cellmark].

[AUTHOR'S NOTE: Tunnell then changed his mind, and they dug up the adjacent, North Grave of William Hudspeth]

Dr. Tunnell, in consultation with the cemetery staff and his other associates determined that the adjacent grave to the North was likely that of Mr. Miller and excavation shifted to that gravesite … The backhoe removed the overlying sod until fragments of wood began to be unearthed. The excavation shifted to shovels and the top of the casket was identified. Excavation proceeded using trowels and hand tools until various aspects of the skeleton were identified and cleared … Skeletal elements were measured for depth and location, removed from the grave and examined ... **There were extensive healed traumata on the right scapula** ... The remains were photographed, samples were harvested for DNA (tooth and femur) [Note and the skull had teeth] remains were returned to the grave and reburied.

[AUTHOR'S NOTE: Fulginiti then had doubts about the North Grave's remains, with bad scapula, being John Miller's.]

Anecdotal historical information suggested that Mr. John Miller had died from complications of a fractured hip while recuperating in the Arizona pioneer Home. The individual in the north grave, while having extensive pathological conditions, particularly in the upper body, did not have discernible pathology of the *os coxae* [pelvis].

[AUTHOR'S NOTE: The North Grave's body had no broken hip like John Miller. So they hit the South Grave again.]

The south grave was excavated by shovel to the point where the remnants of the casket lid were identified. Excavation resumed using trowels and hand tools until the left femoral head was identified.

The head of the femur was misshapen with bony remodeling, suggesting an **antemortem injury** ... The ischium [part of the pelvis] tapered to a point with lack of union to the pubis [another part of the pelvis], suggesting a healing fracture of the ischiopubic ramus. **This evidence led the team to believe that the individual in the south grave was, in fact, more consistent with the known facts regarding the Medical history of Mr. John Miller and additional DNA samples were recovered (femur, scalp [?], matter from inside the braincase).**

[AUTHOR'S NOTE: The South Grave had Miller's broken hip.]

The maxillae and mandible were recovered but were edentulous [had no teeth at all].

[AUTHOR'S NOTE: So Miller had NO TEETH. Random man Hudspeth had the "buck teeth" claimed as Billy the Kid's!"]

This was how Fulginiti revealed that the body in the North Grave its the bad scapula and alleged buck teeth was not Miller's! That was how she revealed that William Hudspeth had been dug up also. And the bad scapula and buck teeth were his! And his damaged scapula was the right one, not the left! And its damage was not from a bullet! So the hoaxers were switching "Scapula Man" (William Hudspeth) for John Miller ("Hip Man") for their fables to the press; a well as switching his right scapula as a left one!

WILLIAM HUDSPETH COMES A'HAUNTING

Things got worse for the hoaxing clowns. On May 13, 2006, Mark Shaffer of the *Arizona Republic* wrote, for the Internet, "N.M. pair may face charges in grave case." In it, he was first to name the second corpse: William Hudspeth. For Shaffer, Sullivan and Sederwall shape-shifted into tourism promoters - albeit Arizona's. And their buddy, Dale Tunnell, became a "forensic scientist." But the perpetrators were obvious to Shaffer:

> Last year, a pair of former New Mexico law enforcement officers had the body of Miller and a man identified as William Hudspeth, who was interred next to him, exhumed from the Pioneers' Home Cemetery. Bones and teeth were taken to a Dallas laboratory for DNA analysis.
>
> The Yavapai County Attorney's Office is reviewing a Prescott Police Department investigation to determine if criminal charges will be filed in the exhumation of Miller and Hudspeth because a permit was not obtained.
>
> Dennis McGrane, chief deputy Yavapai County attorney, said Friday that his office is seeking outside legal help in the case ...
>
> Former Lincoln County, N.M., Sheriff Tom Sullivan and his partner, former federal officer and Capitan, N.M., Mayor Steve Sederwall, don't believe that Sheriff Pat Garrett ambushed and killed Billy the Kid in Fort Sumner, N.M., on a July night in 1881. They contend the Kid could have lived out his years peacefully using the alias John Miller.
>
> Sullivan and Sederwall sold the History Channel on their theory and camera operators from the channel filmed the exhumation.
>
> Sullivan said that he came up with the bloody bench that the outlaw purportedly died on "through good police work," and now it's just a matter of making a DNA match.

Deputy Sullivan and "forensic scientist" Tunnell then offered Arizona the Kid as a lure:

> "It's a believable story," Sullivan said. "You look at the likenesses in those pictures and the fact that they were both good with a gun, had blue eyes, were good dancers and expert horsemen and made frequent trips to Mexico. I look at Brushy Bill and say, 'Uh, I don't know about him,' but I think a good case can be made about John Miller.' "

Sullivan said he hopes to have DNA results on the bodies and bench by this summer while pushing for more exhumations.

Dale Tunnell, a forensic scientist who assisted in Miller's exhumation, said New Mexico has staked a good chunk of its tourism future on Bonney being buried in Fort Sumner and "a group of people there have banded together to protect that gravesite at all costs.

"If someone can prove that William Bonney is not buried there, they can turn out the lights of that town. And I'm thinking Prescott could be the big beneficiary of that," Tunnell said.

CHAPTER 8
CLOWNS CHASING CLOWNS

CLOWN CRIMINALS

Great effort went into blocking the criminal investigation for desecration of graves and grave-robbing begun by David Snell. Honest Yavapai County's Prescott City Prosecutor Glenn Savona had pointed out that the "internal management" statute of the Pioneers' Home did not apply; nor did any law allow taking remains out of state to Texas. He added that there had been no necessary court order from Yavapai County Community Health Services Department or family permission. He indicated felonies.

So the hoaxing clowns got out of Yavapai County. They lied that Deputy Mike Poling, who had delivered to Dr. Fulginiti specimens from another case, then lent his metal detector at their request, was responsible for the exhumation! That meant that Yavapai County might have to prosecute *him*: making a conflict of interest. So the case was transferred to Maricopa County!

Since I was providing information at each stage, I was informed of the other ploy used by the hoaxers. They also claimed that Arizona Pioneers' Home Supervisor Jeanine Dike and Dale Tunnell were responsible for the digging. So Maricopa County opened Case No. 2006020516 against them! But I was assured that the names were just a filing formality. In actuality, it would emerge that Governor Bill Richardson and Governor Janet Napolitano were pressuring Maricopa County's Chief Prosecutor Andrew Thomas to stop the case.

Unaware, from June 9, 2006 to October 17, 2006, I supplied the assigned Maricopa County Prosecutor, Deputy Attorney Jonnell Lucca, with hoax information; hoaxer names; lack of DNA to justify any exhumation; and, certainly, no right to dig up William Hudspeth. Nevertheless, this corrupt official wrote to me on October 17, 2006: "Dear Dr. Cooper: This letter is to inform you that the Maricopa County Attorney's Office has **declined to file charges against Jeanine Dike and Dale Tunnell** as there is no reasonable likelihood of conviction in this case. There is no further information regarding the decision. Thank you for your interest in the case." So she pretended Dike and Tunnell were the only suspects. And she hid the felonious desecration and grave-robbing of William Hudspeth.

She had folded under Richardson's Santa Fe Ring-style racketeering. I owned a telling e-mail (obtained from its Lincoln County public official recipient wanting anonymity), dated May 16, 2006, by gloating Steve Sederwall, feeling immune. It was signed with a smiley face symbol and "Steve." He stated:

> Well **we have the governor reaching out to the Arizona [sic- missing word, Prosecutor?]** to stop this investigation. They thought we had the DNA [sic - illegible word follows] and they tried to get the FBI to get John Millers bones back with a warrant and get the DNA. They think we are going to announce that John Miller is the kid in France [an upcoming secret trip promoting the hoax]. We will not give them a break. They are now trying to get is [sic - us?] worked up about grave robbery charges. But being good cops we have all the docs that show the state of Arizona did the dig not us. How funny. if [sic] they do something stupid and file on us we sue and Arizona well [sic] be the state of Tom and Steve.

But the hoaxers had miscalculated. Good ol' boy anti-intellectualism played poorly in Arizona. Leo Banks's April 13, 2006 *Tucson Weekly* article, "The New Billy the Kid?" was snidely subtitled: "The mad search for the bones of an American outlaw icon has come to Arizona."

And as the legal case loomed, Sederwall sulkily told hoax ally, Julie Carter, on April 19, 2006, for her blog, under "Digging up bones, Arizona may protest Miller exhumation," that they had returned the exhumed bones. Of course, that left out the illegality of taking them in the first place, and the fact that large amounts had been pulverized by Orchid Cellmark for its meaningless DNA extractions. Sederwall was quoted: " 'We have done absolutely nothing wrong. We did not violate any law whatsoever and made sure we had all the t's crossed and the i's dotted. We have documents to back up what we went to Arizona to do, **all the way to the state level**. We went there quietly to do this without any fan fare. It doesn't mean we did it without permission'... Sederwall said the return of the bones has been part of the deal from the very beginning and concurred with Sullivan that they had permission and assistance for their investigation at the cemetery."

COVER-UPS BY AND FOR CLOWNS

AT NAPOLITANO'S OFFICE

Steve Sederwall was a good judge of the morally deficient. On August 18, 2005, Governor Napolitano's Policy Advisor for Health, Anne Winter, panicked, e-mailing Alan Stephens, Napolitano's Chief of Staff, and Tim Nelson, Napolitano's General Counsel: "Re: Pioneer Home, Grave, Billy the Kid and DNA," with worrisome communication from Superintendent Olson:

> Hi - you both should be aware of this one. Tim, I've asked Gary the new Superintendent of the Pioneer Home for his contact at the AG office. Given that this home reports to the Governor's Office, what risks do we have? What level of involvement do we need? And, do you have direction for Gary. He's really terrific. He'll be in town Friday if you want to discuss this with him in person. Please advise. Thanks!
>
> ATTACHMENT:
>
> There is suspicion that a former resident of the Arizona Pioneers' Home (APH) who is buried in the Arizona Pioneers' Cemetery may be "Billy the Kid." In this, a couple of former sheriff officers from Lincoln County New Mexico visited APH approximately two years ago and requested information on John C. Miller (supposedly he had paid for a new tombstone for Billy the Kid's mother prior to his death, but had made no outward claim to be Billy the Kid) **[Author's Note: John Miller died in 1937. The new Catherine Antrim gravestone was installed in 1947.]** Subsequent to approval by then Superintendent Jeanine Dike, these two investigators were given the cemetery plot map and all hard copy and archived information on John C. Miller. **Approximately 6 months ago, Steve Sederwall (one of the investigators) and Tom Sullivan (current New Mexico Lincoln County Sheriff and financial support of this investigation) received permission from the Superintendent Jeanine Dike to exhume the body of Mr. Miller to do genetic testing for comparison analysis to find out if he was Billy the Kid (according to my understanding, Jeanine Dike felt she had the authority to authorize the release of the records and the exhumation of the body since there were no living heirs).**
>
> **[AUTHOR'S NOTE: Gary Olson shows no doubt that the exhumers were Tom Sullivan and Steve Sederwall.]**

Subsequent to Jeanine's retirement, APH received the call as to the date this exhumation would occur. This happened on 5/25/05 (between Jeanine's retirement and my arrival) [sic] - and was followed through with pursuant to the prior permission given to do so. **Representatives from APH were in attendance during the process - some were asked to sign a confidentiality agreement and asked to remain silent by Sullivan and Sederwall we have no copy of this form).**

In this exhumation it was discovered that the graves of Mr. Miller and another had combined through the shifting of the land - and so a sample was taken from each of the graves for the genetic testing.

[AUTHOR'S NOTE: Olson lied about "combined" graves in apparent cover-up attempt of the illegal second exhumation; contradicting on-site expert Dr. Laura Fulginiti's report that the graves were entirely separate.]

First of all, permission had only been given for Mr. Miller's remains - in this, it was discovered that Mr. Miller had no living relatives which is why permission had been given. However, no one had looked into relatives of the individual in the second grave until recently **(per the Attorney General's Office)**. To date, one of the grave remains has been analyzed with a negative result; the other result is not in yet ... The APH Cemetery is not considered a private cemetery via statutory definition because the APH Cemetery Statute was changed to allow APH to sell interment rights - making it a public cemetery. Public cemeteries require a permit for exhumations - no permit was obtained for the above exhumation.

The Attorney General's Office feels that Mr. Snell will not give up on this, and since the History Channel was allowed to film it may show up on TV at some point. **The AG's office is still working on this one** .

The problems are: an exhumation permit was not obtained if the APH is in fact a public cemetery; the relatives if any of the individual in the second grave were not contacted/informed and an authorization obtained from them; exhumation remains are somewhere in New Mexico or beyond being analyzed; do we need to get them back and does the Superintendent have the authority to release records and/or give permission for an exhumation if no heirs exist?

This was corrupt Arizona Governor (and future Secretary of Homeland Security under President Barack Obama, and then President of the University of California) Janet Napolitano's crooked cover-up of grave-robbing for fellow governor, Bill Richardson, in action.

AT YAVAPAI COUNTY DEPARTMENT OF COMMUNITY HEALTH

Another cover-up attempt came by letter, on March 30, 2006, to Governor Napolitano's in-house Policy Advisor for Health Anne Winter, on official stationary, as "Re: Disinterment of bodies at Arizona Pioneer's [sic] Cemetery, Prescott May 19, 2005." It was from a Marcia M. Jacobson. Anne Winter stated:

> As Director of Yavapai County Department of Community Health Services, I am the appointed local registrar with the responsibility and authority to issue disinterment-reinterment permits pursuant to A.R.S. Title 36, Article 2, and 36-327. A concerned citizen recently brought a matter to my attention that warrants report to you as Governor Napolitano's Policy Advisor for Health and the official responsible for oversight of the Arizona Pioneer's Home and Cemetery in Prescott ...
>
> As reported to me and confirmed through our independent review, a disinterment was conducted May 19, 2005 to a body at Arizona Pioneer's Cemetery pursuant to authorization granted by then Superintendent Jeanine Dike. This authorization was granted without having first obtained a disinterment-reinterment permit from my office pursuant to A.R.S. 36-327. The disinterment was reportedly conducted with some publicity as the purpose of the operation was apparently to confirm or disprove that the remains were that of William H. Bonney a/k/a "Billy the Kid."
>
> Irregularities in the disinterment process were compounded when another body was uncovered and, rather than stop and seek any type of authorization for disinterment for a second body, work continued and specimens of unknown quantity or type were removed from each of the two bodies for scientific testing. It is unclear at that point who was responsible for allowing that disinterment of the second body proceed [sic]. It is our understanding that Jeanine Dike had retired as Superintendent sometime prior to the disinterment operation and the current Superintendent, Gary Olson, had not yet commenced his service. Our review of the matter has confirmed the foregoing through the attached correspondence and other related documents including an interview with the **Yavapai County Sheriff's Office Detective Mike Poling, who was at the site for the primary purpose of delivering specimen to Dr. Laura Fulginiti for her examination and testing in a completely unrelated matter.**

> While this matter technically constitutes a violation punishable as a Class 1 misdemeanor through A.R.S. 36-344 and would be punishable as a Class 4 felony through A.R.S. 32-1364(B) if committed with malice or wantonness, my responsibility lies primarily in fulfilling my responsibility and authority to issue disinterment-reinterment permits and not necessary to insure that criminal prosecution or enforcement be initiated ... I, however, would recommend that appropriate policies or procedures are implemented to ensure that such incidents do not recur at a later time.
>
> **With this notification, I will consider this matter closed.**

But determined and brave David Snell had foiled Marcia Jacobson. The "matter" had not been "closed."

COVER-UP BY ARIZONA PIONEER'S HOME

Rumors about David Snell's not backing off, and Snell's badgering of Arizona Attorney General Terry Goddard for the truth, broke through the Sullivan-Sederwall confidentiality agreement's cover-up. Arizona Pioneers' Home Supervisor Gary Olson communicated with Snell in an October 3, 2005 letter:

> You recently asked the Arizona Pioneers' Home if a body in its cemetery had been exhumed for the purpose of determining whether the body could be identified as Billy the Kid. I understand that you have also been making inquiries to the Attorney General's Office.
>
> The purpose of this letter is to correct information previously provided to you by the Arizona Pioneers' Home. In our conversation, I told you that nothing of that nature had occurred since my arrival at the end of May. I further understand that another representative from the Arizona Pioneers' Home told you that no bodies had been exhumed. While I was not employed by the Arizona Pioneers' Home prior to the end of may, I understand that an exhumation at the Pioneers' Home cemetery did occur earlier this year for the purpose you noted.
>
> I apologize for the misinformation.

David Snell had smoldered, then sent his enraged letter to Yavapai County Attorney Shiela Polk on March 11, 2006, initiating the exhumations' criminal investigation.

CHAPTER 9
AFTER THE CIRCUS LEFT TOWN

THE RAVAGED GRAVES

Not until my open records litigation, with subpoena of Orchid Cellmark Lab's records, was the full of the Arizona Pioneers' Home Cemetery graves' ravishment revealed. The Lab's report for its Case No. 4444 (for Case 2003-274) for May 19, 2005, titled "Chain of Custody," confirmed Dr. Rick Staub as hand delivering dismembered John Miller (South grave) and William Hudspeth (North grave), as accessioned on May 23, 2005. **[APPENDIX: 3]**

Their bones had been torn from their skeletons for no reason other than to fill Dr. Rick Staub's bone-bags for their illegal transport back to Texas.

Stolen were: Miller's "skull and mummified brains," "jawbone," "pelvis," and "left femur." Stolen were: Hudspeth's "mandible and teeth," and "right femur." Even part of Miller's shattered casket had been taken. There was not much left in either man's grave. And DNA extraction destroys much of the bones to get results.

And the hoaxers would have known all along that they had no DNA of Billy the Kid to compare with anything. And all involved had to know that one of the two bodies represented straightforward desecration and grave-robbing of a random man (since there could not be two John Miller's)!

And Bill Kurtis's Production company was filming all along. But this time he documented a crime scene. I was told the rumor that he subsequently destroyed or hid his footage.

THE DNA TRAVESTY

Of course, the Orchid Cellmark records of the bones taken, of DNA extractions, and of any possible DNA matchings were hidden by the hoaxers and Dr. Rick Staub. But my open records litigation, with subpoena of Orchid Cellmark Lab's records, gave the results they had obtained from their horror-show circus exhumations.

Dr. Rick Staub, hiding that there was no Billy the Kid DNA for matching to justify any exhumations, had told reporter Leo Banks, for his April 13, 2006 *Tucson Weekly* article "The New Billy the Kid?" that no DNA had been obtained from the John Miller specimens, and the only DNA came from random man, William Hudspeth.

Nevertheless, by 2009, Orchid Cellmark claimed in a report that DNA had been extracted from John Miller's *and* William Hudspeth's femurs; meaning, by then, there had been a possible fix-up - like Orchid Cellmark's other DNA faking case: its scandal as reported in November 18, 2004's "TalkLeft.com," as "Fraud alleged at Cellmark, DNA Testing Firm," with illegal manipulation of data.

The Orchid Cellmark DNA results of the Miller/Hudspeth exhumations were in January 26, 2009's "Laboratory Report - Forensic Identity – Mitochondrial Analysis," using the subsets of its in-house Case 4444 (for its Case No. 2003-274 specimens). **[APPENDIX: 4]** Under its sample 4444-011, John Miller's left femur from the South Grave was reported as having "a mitochondrial DNA profile obtained." For William Hudspeth, sample 4444-012 of his North Grave's mandible and teeth yielded a useless mix of DNA: "Consequently no sequence data are reported … [P]rofiles are therefore inconclusive." However, random man, Hudspeth's, Case 4444-013 North Grave's right femur yielded the "mitochondrial DNA profile obtained," as originally admitted by Dr. Staub to reporter Leo Banks.

Of course, there was no Billy the Kid DNA anyway for determining identity matching (since the carpenter's bench yielded none, and could not be "reference DNA" anyway). So the "Billy the Kid Case" hoaxers had nothing.

Nevertheless, to Governor Napolitano, the clowns had made-up a DNA match for John Miller. It was a double-talk lie, claiming a match of 80%; which has no forensic meaning - a match is 100%, meaning identical. And it was merely submitted to her office; and I got it by open records request. It was not publicized.

The hoaxers had just been hedging their bets, and hoping against convictions. And they really had not wanted to make John Miller Billy the Kid anyway. And, as P.T. Barnum's disciples, these clowns knew: "There's no such thing as bad publicity."

CHAPTER 10
TAKING THE CIRCUS TO FRANCE

A GREAT STORY

As their Arizona troubles grew, the Billy the Kid Case hoaxers had concealed their media coup. It was finally announced by Steve Sederwall on April 24, 2006 in the blog of hoax-participating *True West* magazine Editor-in Chief Bob Boze Bell as follows:

> The Wild is back in the West. This past year a French film crew made a film about investigation #2003-274 'The Billy the Kid Investigation'. The film was selected for the Cannes Film Festival. The Film maker is taking (Tom) Sullivan and I to Cannes ... We may have put the Kid on the front pages of the New York times [sic] but now we have taking [sic] our bandit buddy to Cannes. We should blend in France. Does it get any funnier?

This giddy mood was for good reason.

Hoaxer mouthpiece, Julie Carter, on May 5, 2006, on her website, wrote: "Culture shock: The cowboys and the Kid go to France." The 90-minute French-made film was "Requiem for Billy the Kid;" was directed by an Anne Feinsilber, and would be shown at the Cannes Film Festival on May 19th.

Director Anne Feinsilber's inspiration, Carter said, had been the June 5, 2003 *New York Times* article! After contacting Sullivan and Sederwall, she had raised almost a million dollars for her Cargo Films production!

And Tom Sullivan had become an actor: he played Sheriff William Brady! (Julie Carter reported that Sullivan had spent nine months in 2004 - when sheriff - filming on taxpayer money when he was supposed to be Sheriff 24 hours per day. What "fun!")

FRENCH FILM FESTIVITIES

Sullivan and Sederwall made it legally unscathed from Arizona to the "Festival de Cannes" for the most prestigious film festival in the world. It ran from May 17th to the 28th of 2006. "Requiem for Billy the Kid" was one of twenty eight films under "hors compétition" (not for competition), right along with Al Gore's "An Inconvenient Truth" on global warming.

Screened on May 19th, it was listed as the first film for director-writer Anne Feinsilber. As narrator, was actor, Kris Kristofferson: the actor who played "Billy the Kid" in Sam Peckinpah's famous Western, "Pat Garrett and Billy the Kid."

Anne Feinsilber's message was pure Billy the Kid Case hoax: doubt existed about Billy's killing; and the pretenders might be real Billy. Arbiters of historical "truth" were now Deputy Tom Sullivan and Deputy Steve Sederwall - as they called themselves.

The catalogue stated: "The premise of the film is an investigation into the often-challenged circumstances that led to the death of the 21-year old outlaw in the hands of Sheriff Pat Garrett on July 14, 1881." Perched on this pedestal of "documentary cinema" were the fake "friendship" of Garrett and Billy, and "tens of thousands" visiting "Brushy's" rarely visited grave. Sullivan and Sederwall spun their murder case against Garrett as saving his honor.

"REQUIEM" SPELLS REQUIEM

Director Anne Feinsilber's film got wide and good publicity. And the arbiters of truth were hoaxing Sullivan and Sederwall.

On May 21st, from *Variety* magazine, came the review of "Requiem for Billy the Kid" by a Todd McCarthy. He wrote: "With Sam Peckinpah's Billy, Kris Kristofferson re-enlisted to portray the Kid delivering his account of what happened between him and Pat Garrett in 1881, pic goes on a photogenic search for the "truth" about the young killer. Seems there has always been a rumor that Billy escaped and lived to a ripe old age, and Tom Sullivan, who was sheriff of Lincoln County when pic was shot in the fall of 2004, describes his efforts to exhume the body of Billy's mother for DNA, efforts shot down by a judge whose motives Sullivan describes as baldly financial."

A May 25th review by Dave McCoy of MSN Movies, as "L 'Ouest Américain," said: "Feinsilber follows up on a rumor that Pat Garrett shot the wrong man and Billy the Kid actually isn't buried where it's said he is."

Anne Feinsilber's damage was further evidenced on a May 6, 2006 Internet version of *The Hollywood Reporter* in reviewer, Ray Bennett's, "Bottom line: A story well told." He wrote: "History has it that Sheriff Pat Garrett, a reformed villain, gunned down William Bonney, also known as Billy the Kid, at Fort Sumner, where his grave has a much-visited marker. Some say, however, that the friendship between Garrett and Bonney led the lawman to let the outlaw go and another man's body lies beneath his headstone. Could Billy the Kid have lived to see two world wars and driven a car? Feinsilber sets out to discover the truth and she finds several people in New Mexico whose grandparents were said to have known Bonney. Competing factions would like to exhume the bodies of Billy and his mother Catherine, who died of tuberculosis when Billy was 14, in order to prove once and for all when he died. Such myths fuel tourism, however, and the mystery has remained unsolved."

With this Billy the Kid Case hoax victory, Pat Garrett became a "reformed villain," the friendship between Garrett and Billy was real, a stranger's body very likely lay in Billy's grave, the exhumation would have solved the questions "once and for all," and the "mystery" was being left unsolved to "fuel tourism."

Anne Feinsilber, in one fell swoop, had arguably done more damage, than any other person in the world, to almost 80 years of historical work. Her total "research" seems to have been listening to Sullivan and Sederwall gabbing, talking to some addled old-timers, and hiring Hollywood actors.

Feinsilber's contagion of disinformation continued.

The hoaxers' reporter, Julie Carter, enthused on June 9, 2006 for *RuidosoNews.com* under "The cowboys are back in town, film in six months." "Producers hope to host a film debut and make a county event of its first American showing. Sullivan said after that it will probably be released to PBS and then followed by DVD sales. Sederwall and Sullivan gifted the director with their black cowboy hats before they left.

Carter's article demonstrated that, by June 9th, the hoaxers' euphoria had swelled to grandiosity. Their spin of "doing it for New Mexico tourism," had inflated to "doing it for the French economy!" Thus, Carter quoted: "Sederwall said he was amazed at the amount of money The Kid brought to France and to Cannes by the way of the film."

All the while, Frederick Nolan's telephone calls to the BBC to present historical truth as counterpoint to the hoax went ignored.

CHAPTER 11
THE CIRCUS TRAVELS TO TEXAS WITH SHOVELS

GOING AFTER "BRUSHY BILL"

Off the hook for the illegal exhumations by 2007, the hoaxers rolled their circus wagons to Texas and "Brushy Bill" Roberts's grave. That onslaught, like the Arizona one, was under Sheriff Rick Virden, using his Deputies, Tom Sullivan and Steve Sederwall. And they had another hurdle, compliments of me. In 2006, was my American Academy of Forensic Sciences Ethics Complaint against Dr. Henry Lee for hoaxing. Though his unethical Ethics Committee covered-up, he apparently stopped the hoaxers using his carpenter's bench DNA scam. So they could not claim possessing DNA to match with "Brushy's."

Nevertheless, Virden tried, writing in 2007 on his official stationery to Mayor Roy Rumsey, misspelling his name, but using lawman clout to try and get the job done. Virden wrote:

> Hamilton Texas
> Mayor Roy Ramsey
>
> Mayor Ramsey,
>
> This letter will inform you that Tom Sullivan and Steve Sederwall are both commissioned deputies with the Lincoln County New Mexico Sheriff's Department.
>
> They have been investigating case # 2003-274. Their investigation has been funded by them personally and has been conducted on their own time.
>
> Mr. Mayor, should you have any questions please do not hesitate to contact me.
>
> R.E. Virden
> Lincoln County Sheriff

Virden's double-talk tried to cover all hoax bases. The "funded by them personally," came from my years of open records exposure of their tax-dollar consumption. And, "their own time" was part of their new switcheroo that it was not a law enforcement case at all, but their private hobby! That scam was to hide the DNA records from me, since turn-over was only legally demanded of public officials, not private citizens. That left Virden absurdly telling Rumsey that he was sending his Deputies for his New Mexico murder case - which was really a hobby - but those Deputies could dig up "Brushy," though his jurisdiction was Lincoln County, New Mexico; and certainly not Texas!

Mayor Rumsey did not have to decipher this craziness, since I had already told him that the circus was coming to town. Deputy Steve Sederwall met with him. Rumsey told me that he told Sederwall: "If 'Brushy Bill' is Billy the Kid, I'm Pancho Villa."

Rumsey added for the press in a May 5, 2007 *Houston Chronicle* article titled "DNA could solve the mystery of Billy the Kid": "Roberts was 'just a big windbag who went around telling stories. Few people, if anybody, believed him."

Sederwall had floated the hoax's new spin. The *Roswell Daily Record*, using a Stephenville, Texas, article, wrote on May 2, 2007, "Billy the Kid Exhumation a Possibility." "Sederwall said if DNA is allowed to be obtained from Roberts, investigators will pursue exhuming the body of Catherine McCarty Antrim, who researchers have confirmed was Billy the Kid's mother." [Hidden is that this had already been blocked by Judge Quintero.]

On May 4th, for the hoax-backing *Albuquerque Journal's* "Manhunt for Real Billy the Kid Goes On: Deputy hopes DNA will finally reveal outlaw's true identity." Sederwall again blew smoke: "Those (Hamilton City) people want to know, they are not afraid ... You talk to Fort Sumner and they want to pull pistols on us. You talk to Hamilton City and they're like, 'Sure, we'd like to know.' "

On May 10, 2007, Hamilton's Town Council unanimously opposed exhumation; even though Texas's own "Brushy Bill" believer, Jannay Valdez - still pitching after his stint for Richardson for the June 5, 2003 *New York Times* - spoke for it.

But what if the hoaxers had gotten "Brushy's bones? Even Henry Lee might have returned with his fakery for that lure.

But one thing was certain: the hoaxers had abandoned their clown, John Miller, along with that circus's paraphernalia of extra corpse, William Hudspeth, and deserved felony prosecutions.

CHAPTER 12
EXPOSING THE "BILLY THE KID CASE" HOAX IN COURT

OPEN RECORDS SHOWDOWN

After I stopped the exhumations of Billy and his mother in 2003 to 2004 in District Courts, the rewritten hoax had featured Dr. Henry Lee's faked carpenter's bench "blood" and the exhumation of John Miller. From the start of their "Billy the Kid Case," the hoaxers had considered themselves clever in filing Lincoln County Sheriff's Department Case No. 2003-274 as a murder investigation of Pat Garrett, because it enabled exhumations to solve the "crime." But the hoaxers forgot it meant that its public official lawmen were subject to open records law.

So the next step in exposing the hoax was requesting these public official clowns' DNA records of Dr. Lee's bench investigation and his Orchid Cellmark Lab's DNA extractions and matchings for his case for the grave-robbed remains of John Miller and William Hudspeth.

By 2006, I began my records requests, and the hoaxers began their ever more desperate attempts to hide these incriminating records. As a measure of New Mexico's all-pervasive Santa Fe Ring-style corruption which had initiated the hoax, it took me seven years to get records available on the day I started. During litigation, five sets of my *own* attorneys tried to throw my case. Then I went *pro se* and won. But the judge and the state's high courts illegally rewrote open records law to remove the statute's intended penalty to the lawmen. The system was rigged for crooked clowns to protect crooked clowns.

But I got what I wanted: proof of no valid DNA, meaning illegality of their exhumations. So it was good old clowning John Miller that who helped bring down these creepy clowns.

SUMMARY OF OPEN RECORDS FIGHT

The details of my open records fight are covered in my 2014 book, *Cracking the Billy the Kid Case Hoax: The Strange Plot to Exhume Billy the Kid, Convict Sheriff Pat Garrett of Murder, and Become President of the United states*; and my 2019 book, *The Cold Case Billy the Kid Megahoax: The Plot to Steal Billy the Kid's Identity and Defame Sheriff Pat Garrett as a Murderer.*

In short, while the "Billy the Kid Case" hoaxers rewrote the hoax every time I blocked them, they also denied my open records requests from 2004 for their DNA documents. For that records hiding, they claimed that their Case 2003-274 was exempt as a criminal investigation. This was fakery, since that exception's intent is to prevent a suspect from escaping; and Pat Garrett, dead since 1908, was going nowhere. **(But remember their criminal investigation claim.)**

Afraid of assassination if the hoaxers realized I was behind all their opposition, to maintain my anonymity I first used a local journalist as my proxy. By 2006, under my name, I began my own records requests to the responsible records custodian, Sheriff Rick Virden. He used fellow hoaxer, Lincoln County Attorney Alan Morel, to respond. They tried to scare me off by claiming to report me as a terrorist! So, in 2007, I got a lawyer to do the requests.

Through Morel, Virden lied to my lawyer that he had no records whatsoever for Case 2003-274, and claimed Tom Sullivan and Steve Sederwall had them. Through Morel, Sullivan and Sederwall then **lied, claiming it was never a law enforcement case, but was their private hobby** (immune to the public records act), and its records were their private "trade secrets;" thereby brazenly reversing the law enforcement exception they had used for years to deny me records through my proxy!

Improper withholding of public records triggers litigation, so, in October of 2007, my lawyer filed "Sandoval District Court Case No. D-1329-CV-2007-1364, Gale Cooper et al v. Rick Virden, Lincoln County Sheriff and Custodian of the Records of the Lincoln County Sheriff's Office; and Steven M. Sederwall, Former Lincoln County Deputy Sheriff; Department; and Thomas T. Sullivan, Former Lincoln County Sheriff and Former Lincoln County Deputy Sheriff.

Demanded were the DNA records of Case 2003-274. That meant Dr. Henry Lee's specimens from the carpenter's bench and courthouse floorboards sub-investigation of the Deputy James Bell killing; Dr. Rick Staub's bones from exhumed John Miller and William Hudspeth; Orchid Cellmark Labs' DNA extractions from the carpenter's bench, the floorboards, John Miller, and William Hudspeth; and Orchid Cellmark's matchings of Miller and Hudspeth DNA to bench DNA. My lawmen defendants - with unlimited tax dollars to pay for attorneys as public officials (while claiming to be hobbyists) - got two law firms, who split the case for apparent double billing (Virden with one, Sullivan and Sederwall with another).

Though the judge eventually declared them public officials and ordered records turn-overs, the lawmen, certain of immunity, ignored him; with Virden lying he did not know how to get them, and Sullivan and Sederwall still saying they were private.

Virden, however, did eventually turn-over his about 200 page Sheriff's Department file for Case 2003-274, though expurgated of DNA records, but having a "Contact List" for the other hoaxers - like Professor Paul Hutton - and having U.S. Marshals Service Historian David's secret Addendum to the Probable Cause Statement. (See pages 200-204 above) (Of course, that proved hoaxing Attorney Alan Morel's lying that the case had no records whatsoever!) And, contrary to a legitimate court, the judge did not hold them in contempt; instead, allowing their seven years of stonewalling, and their possibly double-billing lawyers pocking a half-million taxpayers' dollars in fees, for records available on day one for the cost of postage.

Then things got worse. The hoaxers did turn over Lee reports; except Steve Sederwall forged them to look like his private investigation to trick the judge, while removing Lee's conclusions which contradicted the hoax's more extreme claims about the bench blood of Billy the Kid. I caught them; so the judge again demanded turn-over. So, after five years, I got Lee's single report. But that was just his specimen recoveries.

The lawmen hid Orchid Cellmark Lab's records which proved their fraudulent claims and illegality of exhumations. But the ongoing litigation justified subpoenaing the records. So Orchid Cellmark turned over 133 pages, which documented no DNA recovery from the carpenter's bench, and useless DNA from John Miller and William Hudspeth. (Do not miss the outrage that this random man was callously and illegally pulverized for no reason.)

Then things got worse. The last of my attorneys betrayed my case, and I had to go *pro se* and fight alone. I prevailed. But the judge shielded the lawmen, removing all penalties for wrongful records withholding, to punish me by blocking my deserved near million dollars award. But he did sanction them for the forgeries.

I took the case to the state Court of Appeals and state Supreme Court, who not only upheld no penalties to the my undeniable records violators, but removed the one for their forgeries too! To understand this Santa Fe Ring-style collusion, note that the Chief Justice of the Supreme Court was Charlie Daniels: appointed by Richardson; a major Richardson political donor; and husband of Richardson's own Attorney Randi McGinn, who had participated in the "Billy the Kid Case" hoax herself!

"BILLY THE KID CASE" HOAX UPSHOT

John Miller was the main victim of the "Billy the Kid Case" hoax - if you leave out William Hudspeth, and the real history of Billy Bonney and Pat Garrett.

In its wake, this hoax left two documentaries disseminating its lies: 2004's "Investigating History: Billy the Kid," and 2006's "Requiem for Billy the Kid."

So it is not surprising that its unrepentant, unpunished, and unexposed clowns staged a come-back, 15 years after they started the "Billy the Kid Case" hoax, through "Brushy"-backing author, W.C. Jameson, in his 2018 book: *Cold Case Billy the Kid*. In it, John Miller, got another try for the gold ring of being Billy on the hoaxers' circus merry-go-round. And, as the only corpse trophy admitted to in their fake forensics, he got a come-back as "Billy the Kid," while towing many of the past "Billy the Kid Case" hoaxers into the present, as renamed "cold case investigators."

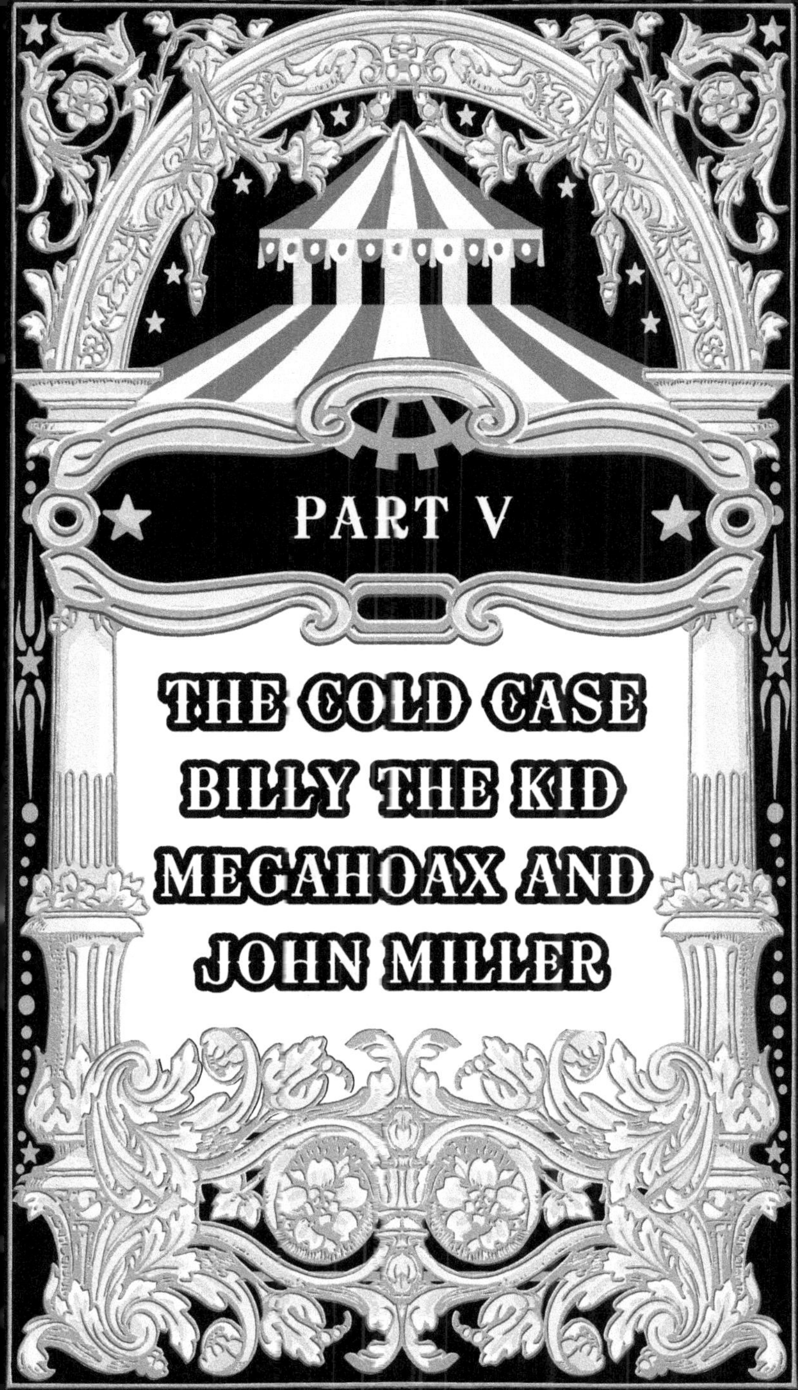

PART V

THE COLD CASE BILLY THE KID MEGAHOAX AND JOHN MILLER

CHAPTER 1
DEAD JOHN MILLER JOINS A MEHGAHOAX

RECRUITING THE SAME OLD CLOWN

Despite the obvious absurdity of John Miller's Billy the Kid identity claims, comedian George Carlin's warning must be heeded: "Just because you got the monkey off your back, doesn't mean the circus has left town."

The "Billy the Kid Case" hoaxers, after being blocked from exhuming Billy Bonney and his mother, having been threatened with prosecution for grave-robbing John Miller and William Hudspeth, and being exposed in my open records litigation as hiding all DNA records and forging Dr. Henry Lee reports, did not get off the back of Billy the Kid history. By 2018, their circus was back in town with a book by "Brushy Bill"-backer, W.C. Jameson, titled *Cold Case Billy the Kid*. And Jameson was so desperate to foist his hoax mantra - that history is not as written - that he had joined forces with past "Billy the Kid Case" hoaxers promoting their own circus of smoke-and-mirror lies.

That was how W.C. Jameson, those conniving clowns' dupe, became their narrator for Dr. Lee's-bench-blood-of-Billy-the-Kid fakery, Lee's Garrett-shooting-washstand-not-headboard-scam, and John-Miller-as-Billy-the-Kid-as-proven-by-his-exhumation lie.

So dead John Miller returned to the scene of his Billy the Kid clowning, as the centerpiece of yet another three ring circus.

Jameson's "Acknowledgements" had listed Tom Sullivan, Gary Graves, Dr. Henry Lee, Rick Staub, Dale Tunnell, and Dave Turk. (Page 181) Sullivan's 2013 death, proves Jameson's long association with these clowns. And featured is Dr. Lee's reports' forger himself, erstwhile Deputy and self-proclaimed "Probable Cause Statement" author, Steve Sederwall. (Page 181)

Duped Jameson, as their narrator, show-cased Sederwall; writing: "Hi s tenacity and thoroughness when taking on the study of historical topics is exceeded by no one I have ever encountered." Impressed by his cowboy costuming and 6'5" height, Jameson advertised him vaguely as a "cop," a U.S. government investigator, and a worker of crime scenes, with his own "investigative agency" for "western cold cases." (Page vi) And kept secret was the entire "Billy the Kid Case" and Sederwall's participation in it. And the only whiff of me and my years of litigations exposing Sederwall and the rest of the hoax, was Jameson's acceptance of his martyr for the truth scam. As Jameson wrote: **"[H]e was once hauled into court by one of the rabid embracers of the status quo."** (Page x)

But even Jameson's title was a hoax. *Cold Case: Billy the Kid* had no cold case! There was just the imposters' fables; with "Brushy Bill's" having Pat Garrett kill a fictional Billy Barlow; with the "Billy the Kid Case's" lie that Garrett killed an innocent victim to save Billy after shooting him to "play dead;" and John Miller's fiction of not being there, and having an Indian friend as Garrett's victim. The rest of Jameson's book is as unreal, with known events rewritten by fabricated evidence as "crime scene investigations;" accepted information given as the hoaxers' discoveries; "Brushy Bill" Roberts being a quoted authority for events he never knew about; and John Miller being proven as Billy the Kid by his skeleton.

I debunked Jameson's *Cold Case Billy the Kid* in my 2019 *The Cold Case Billy the Kid Megahoax: The Plot to Steal Billy the Kid's Identity and Defame Pat Garrett as a Murderer*. For this book, the focus is just on that hoax's claiming the Fort Sumner death scene was in doubt, claiming that Dr. Henry Lee's forensics got blood from the carpenter's bench and cast doubt on Garrett's version of the death scene, and claiming that John Miller's remains matched Billy the Kid.

CHAPTER 2
COLLECTED CLOWNS FAKING DEATH SCENE DOUBTS

THE CLOWN ACT UNDER THE BIG TOP

The Jameson-Sederwall duo (presumably assisted by the acknowledged additional hoaxers) present their hoax's make-or-break July 14, 1881 death scene in chapters "Shooting at Fort Sumner" (Pages 131-134) and "Discrepancies." (Pages 135-163)

Concealed is that the tales of "Brushy Bill," John Miller, and the "Billy the Kid Case" do not match each other. The "Brushy" hoax had Billy Barlow accidentally killed by Garrett as mistaken by him on the dark night (it was actually bright moonlight) on the Maxwell house's back porch. John Miller had his Indian friend accidentally shot by Garrett in an uncertain location as mistaken for him. The "Billy the Kid Case" hoax had super-friend Garrett shooting willing Billy to play dead on the carpenter's bench (to bleed for future fake DNA); then murdering the innocent victim to switch with Billy for burial.

Concealed, obviously, is the Coroner's Jury Report of William Bonney identifying him as the victim; as well as the multiple other corpse identifications, including the 200 townspeople at the night vigil.

Concealed also, is zero evidence supporting any of the pretender hoaxes. So the duo rely on fake "discrepancies," fake "investigations," and Dr. Henry Lee's fake carpenter's bench and washstand forensics. The result is a megahoax, that disproves "Brushy's" and Miller's fakery by mismatch with the carpenter's bench scenario, and exposes its creators by its ridiculous lies.

Their hoaxed claim is that "researchers never noted the obvious and glaring discrepancies" in Pat Garrett's and John W. Poe's accounts of the shooting. There were none, but the Jameson-

Sederwall duo propose to show them by breaking the death scene shooting to five parts: arrival of participants to Maxwell's room, shooting, post-shooting removal of body, the "inquests" [sic - there was just one] and burial. (Page 135)

Since the only relevant fact is the profuse identification of the body as Billy Bonney's - as was obviously omitted by these clowns - the meaninglessness of their scam is obvious from the start. Important, however, are additions to the hoaxes by this magahoax's new fake "cop investigations" by Steve Sederwall.

FAKING DISCREPANCIES

Discrepancies are faked using Pat Garrett's 1882 *Authentic Life of Billy the Kid* and John W. Poe's *The Death of Billy the Kid*, to pretend they proved events did not occur. So the duo conclude that this "incident [shooting in the bedroom] as the two lawmen described it never took place." (Page 141) Examples follow:

1) DEPUTIES OUTSIDE: The duo claim it was suspicious for Garrett to enter the Maxwell's bedroom, while leaving his deputies outside, because it was too careless for searching for "the most dangerous outlaw in New Mexico." (Page 138)

FAKING EVIDENCE: Omitted is that Garrett did not believe that Billy was in Fort Sumner, and was merely checking with Maxwell. Omitted is another possibility, that a trap was being set, with Billy being sent to Maxwell's bedroom for ambush. In that case, it was strategic to have the deputies outside in case Billy escaped out of the room.

2) IN SOX AND BUTTONING PANTS: The approach of the stranger, in sox and buttoning his pants, is tackled by "cop" Sederwall, recycling this absurdity from his (concealed) Case No. 2003-274's "Probable Cause Statement" about it being too hard to hold a gun and a knife and button your pants; plus gravel would hurt your sensitive stockinged feet! (Page 139)

FAKING EVIDENCE: Billy apparently could multi-task! And apparently he could tackle gravel too! Sederwall's silliness in the "Probable Cause Statement" stated:

> **[Poe stated]** ***At this I stood up and advanced toward him, telling him not to be alarmed ... and still without the least suspicion that this was the very man we were looking for.***

This statement raises many questions with investigators. Poe says he sees a man "*partially dressed, and was bare-headed and bare-footed - or rather, had only socks on his feet, and it seemed to me that he was fastening his trousers as he came toward me art a very brisk walk.*" Then the man covers him with his six shooter. Where did the man put the "*six-shooter*" when he was "*fastening his trousers*"?

He did not stop and lay it down because Poe says he "*he came toward me art a very brisk walk.*"

3) SPEAKING SPANISH: Sederwall cogitated that if approaching Billy said, "Quien es?" and non-Spanish-speaking Poe responded in English to reassure him, then bi-lingual Billy would have reverted to English. So Sederwall concludes that left just two possibilities: it was not Billy; or Poe lied! (Page 140)

FAKING EVIDENCE: Omitted is that Billy was the most hunted man in the Territory. Speaking Spanish to a stranger was his disguise. Furthermore, he probably used the language commonly, as he would with bi-lingual Peter Maxwell in the next a moment. And the disguise worked! Poe assumed he was a Maxwell worker. Sederwall's two "possibilities" are absurd.

4) LETTING BILLY ENTER THE BEDROOM: Sederwall claimed it was unimaginable that two deputies let a man with a knife and a gun walk into the bedroom with Garrett, without shouting a warning. And he imagines that Billy would have been more cautious, or even shot the deputies. (Pages 140-141)

FAKING EVIDENCE: Fantasizing is not evidence.

In fact, neither Poe nor McKinney knew Billy, and thought he was a Maxwell worker. Billy's gun was attributed to strangers alarming him, and could as easily be construed as a worker being protective of Maxwell, and rightly asking them in Spanish, "Who are you?" And none of the lawmen were expecting Billy to turn up at Maxwell's house, so were not alarmed. As Poe stated in his book: "As Maxwell's was the one place in Fort Sumner I considered above suspicion of harboring the Kid, I was entirely off my guard." (Poe, Page 34)

As to Billy being incautious, he was known for fearlessness. That is how he ended up in Fort Sumner, instead of hightailing it to Old Mexico after his jailbreak.

And Fort Sumner had strangers passing through. It is absurd to think that he would automatically shoot them!

5) ENTERING THE BEDROOM: Garrett's statement that the person "sprang quickly into the door" is contrasted with Poe describing Billy backing towards the door, to claim Billy never entered the room! (Page 132)

FAKING EVIDENCE: Actually, the manner of entering is merely vantage. In his 1933 book, Poe described Billy as "backed up into the doorway of Maxwell's room, where he halted for a moment, his body concealed by the thick adobe wall at the side of the doorway." (Poe, Page 35) So Poe could not have seen Billy's final turn to enter the room face-forward as Garrett saw. There is no discrepancy.

6) THE VICTIM'S IDENTITY: After the shooting, Maxwell is presented as running out; Garrett as doubtful, saying, "**I think I have got him;**" and Poe being doubtful. (Page 133)

FAKING: Garrett did not say, "I think I have got him." In his book, he was certain: "I told my companions that I had got the Kid. They asked if I had not shot the wrong man. I told them I made no mistake, for I knew the Kid's voice too well." He explained the Deputies' doubt: "Seeing a bareheaded, bare-footed man, in his shirt sleeves, with a butcher knife in his hand, and hearing his hail in excellent Spanish, they naturally supposed him to be a Mexican and an attaché of the establishment, hence their suspicion that I had shot the wrong man." (Garrett, Page 217)

As to Poe, *he* is the one who gave quote the duo called Garrett's: " 'I think I have got him' ... I said, 'Pat, the Kid would not come to this place; you have shot the wrong man ...' Upon my saying this, Garrett seemed to be in doubt himself as to whom he shot, but quickly spoke up and said, 'I am sure that was him, for I know his voice too well to be mistaken.' " (Poe, Pages 37-38) And Poe confirmed: Upon examining the body, we found it to be that of Billy the Kid." (Page 41) There was no discrepancy.

FAKING A MAXWELL BEDROOM DOOR DISCREPANCY

This new hoax of Maxwell's bedroom having no outside door - also in Jameson's 2016 *Pat Garrett: The Man Behind the Badge* - is to destroy the historical death scene in one fell swoop, since all participants recounted it. A diagram is given and labeled "Floor plan of the Maxwell house," and has no door. And the building is called a one-story adobe. (Page 137) **[FIGURE: 5]**

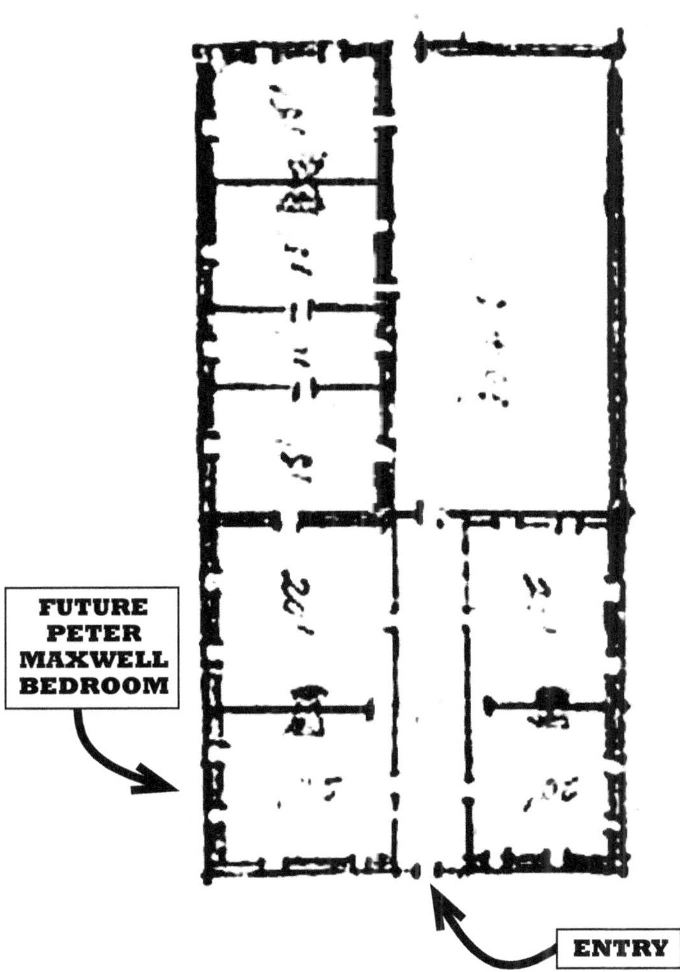

FIGURE: 5. Falsely used by the hoaxers as "Floor plan of Maxwell house" from the "National Archives" (Page 137); this diagram is from the National Archives and is "Commanding Officer's Quarters, Fort Sumner, New Mexico Territory;" and its copy, so labeled, is at the Fort Sumner State Monument

To claim that Garrett lied about the door, the hoaxers state: "**Garrett wrote, '[Billy] 'stepped onto the porch and entered Maxwell's room through the open door left open on account of the extremely warm weather**.' " (Page 131) And Poe's witnessing Billy enter through that door is cited as to his lying also. (Page 140) Added is that if there was a door, it was not open, as Garrett said, because scary animals could get in. (Page 138) So the duo conclude that Garrett and Poe were lying about the entire scene to conceal that Billy the Kid was never shot.

FAKED INVESTIGATION: <u>The claimed "floor plan" is not Maxwell's bedroom, but is the original Fort Sumner Commanding Officer's quarters for the Bosque Redondo Indian Reservation from 1863 to 1868</u>. Since its National Archives and at Fort Sumner State Monument sources label it as such, the hoaxers are faking its identification.

Omitted is that in 1870, when Lucien Maxwell bought Fort Sumner, he rebuilt it as his family home. As Robert Mullin wrote on the back of the Maxwell house photo: "*Pete Maxwell's House Fort Sumner ... Originally 1 Story Flat Roof, Officers Quarters. 2nd Floor Added By Maxwell.*"

The actual Maxwell house floor plan shows the outside door. [Figure: 6] And the Maxwell house photograph, also shows that door in Maxwell's bedroom. [Figure: 7]

And to claim, as did the hoaxing duo, that the door was not left open, is meaningless fantasizing.

And the Garrett quote is faked. He actually wrote: "When we reached the porch in front of the building, I left Poe and McKinney at the end of the porch, and about twenty feet from the door of Pete's bedroom, while I myself entered it." (Garrett, Page 215) The quote is actually distorted from Poe's book; stating: "'You fellows wait here while I go in to talk to [Maxwell].' Thereupon he stepped onto the porch and entered Maxwell's room through the open door (left open on account of the extremely warm weather), while McKinney and myself stopped on the outside." (Poe, Page 31)

Also, **Poe described the further role of that outside door when he almost shot Maxwell: "A moment after Garrett came out of the door, Pete Maxwell rushed squarely onto me in a frantic effort to get out of the room." (Poe, Page 38) This contradicts the hoaxers' walking through the house fakery.**

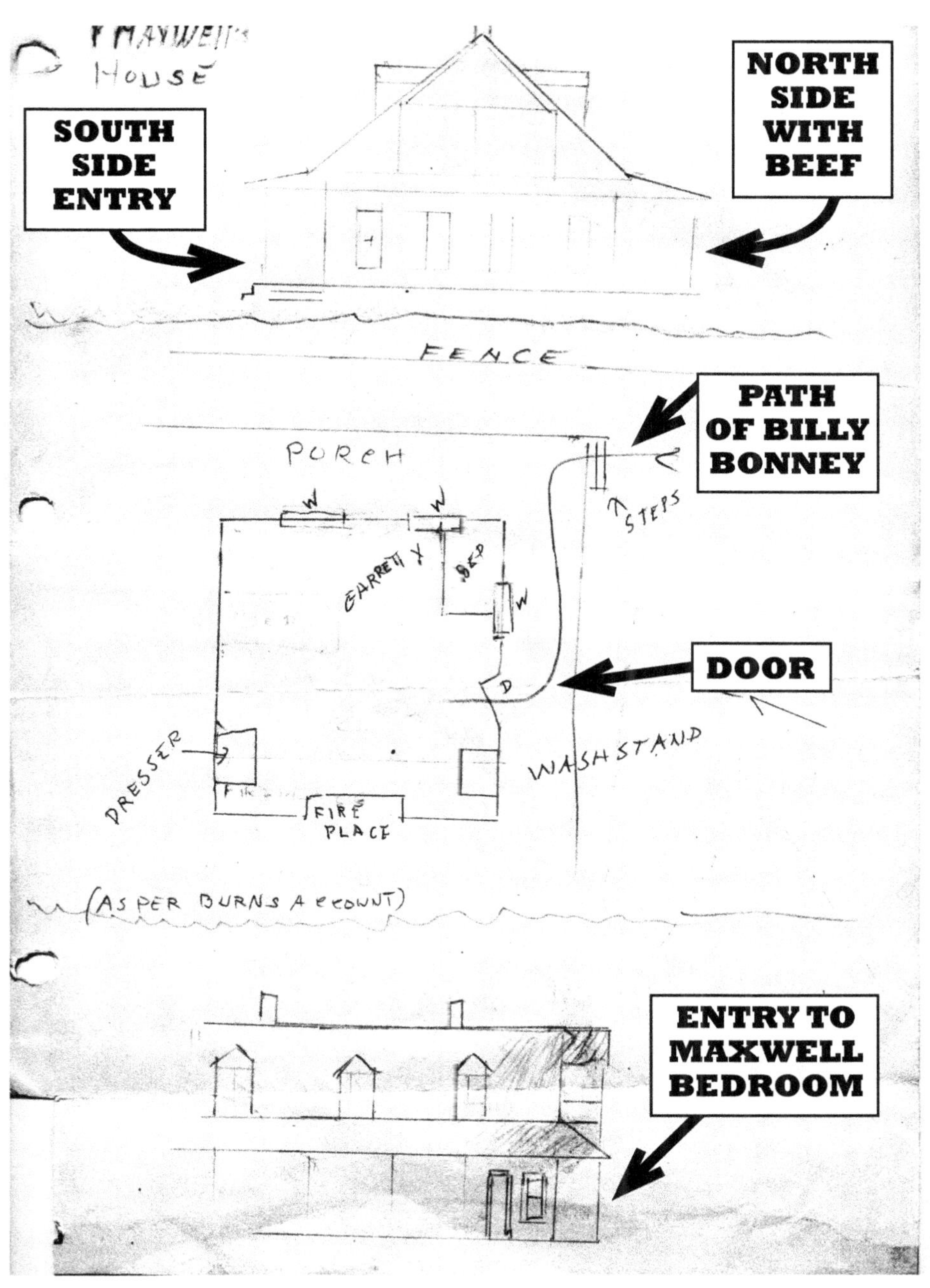

FIGURE: 6. Diagrams by Maurice Garland Fulton of the Maxwell's house, with Peter Maxwell's bedroom, and Billy Bonney's entry through its outside door. From the Midland, Texas, Haley Library, Robert N. Mullin Collection.

FIGURE: 7. Photograph of the Maxwell house showing Peter Maxwell's bedroom with a door to the outside. From the Midland, Texas, Haley Library, Robert N. Mullin Collection.

SOURCE FOR FAKE DOOR INVESTIGATION: This "investigation's" no door claim was lifted from an undated article by an unknown author (erroneously named as Gregory Scott Smith) titled "The Death of Billy the Kid: A New Scenario?" now in the Fort Sumner State Monument files. It used the John L. McCarty papers of an October 22, 1942 interview titled "Kid Dobbs Interviews: An Interview with Garrett H. 'Kid' Dobbs at Farmington, New Mexico," on September 12, 1942, with Mel Armstrong and John McCarty, Thursday Morning, October 22, 1942, In the Presence of Mrs. Dobbs and Pat Flynn. J.D. White, Amarillo, Heard Part of the Final Statements of this Interview Re. Billy the Kid's Death."

Garrett H. "Kid" Dobbs merely spouted old-timer windbag malarkey. His fabrication, with the usual claim of knowing Billy the Kid, began with: "Billy told me ... he came from San Francisco, California, and had killed a chinaman out there for insulting his mother." Here is Dobbs's Lincoln County War Battle: "Once when a friend of Billy the Kid was killed, Billy went to Chisholm [sic] and volunteered to lead the Chisholm party at war ... They made a fight and Murphy's men set fire to McSwain's [sic] house ... Billy had killed four of Murphy's men during the fight ... [During the escape] McSwain [sic] was killed by Murphy. Mrs. McSwain [sic] yelled for her trunk in the house and Tom O'Folliard went back in and got it but burnt his whiskers."

For the death scene, Dobbs's fakery continued:

> Billy was hiding out in Pete Maxwell's house ...
>
> Maxwell wrote Garrett a letter saying he would turn over Billy to him. Garrett thought it might be a trick to trap him for Billy. <u>Pat had Frank Poe and Jim McIntosh, two deputies with him</u>. [Note ignorance of even of the famous deputies.] He told them he was afraid this was a trap and wasn't going up there until he spoke with Maxwell ... Garrett wrote a note to Maxwell and sent it to him by a Mexican boy telling him to meet them at the Mexican plaza 6 miles below Fort Sumner ...
>
> Garrett told Pete if it was a trap he would kill him too. He told Pete he was coming up that night.
>
> They arrived ay Maxwell's early before Billy came in from his daylight hiding and [Pat] told his deputies to bed down in one corner of Maxwell's yard. Pat went in to the house and waited in Maxwell's bedroom.

> When Billy came in that night he saw the men in the yard and asked the cook who they were. The cook said they were some of Pete's sheepherders ...
>
> In the meantime Maxwell had told the cook not to save any cold meat ... so the Kid would have to fix his own supper.
>
> Billy asked the cook where the knife was ... Garrett could hear every word in the bedroom.
>
> Then the Kid asked where the meat was and the cook said he guessed it was in the meat box. The Kid told him it wasn't. The cook told Billy it must be in Pete's bedroom then as Pete had brought some new meat out from town. [Note that Dobbs did not even know that Fort Sumner *was* the town.]
>
> The Kid had the knife in his left hand and started to the bedroom to get some meat. [Note that Billy walks through the house to get to the bedroom.] There was a broken-rock walk way just large enough for two to pass in the hall way from the kitchen to the bedroom. There was a dining room between the kitchen and bedroom. Garrett could hear the Kid coming on those rocks. He was sitting on the foot of the bed [The interviewer here explains that the hall "ran east and west; and Pete's room was on the west] ...
>
> It was warm weather and the bedroom window was open ... The door opened and Billy saw Pat move off the bed. Billy said: Como estes? (What's that) ...
>
> Garrett ... fired and as Billy fell he fired over Pat's head and the bullet went in the ceiling ... Pat's shot went under Billy's heart ...
>
> Pat and Pete ... told me how it happened many times as did the deputies.

For "The Death of Billy the Kid: A New Scenario?" the unknown author used this junk and added his/her ignorant research by attaching the National Archives floor plan. It was called "the original layout of the officers' quarters buildings, one of which became the Maxwell house [provided to show no outside door]. Taken in conjunction with the Dobbs interview [Billy walking through the house], it raises a whole new series of questions as to exactly how Billy the Kid was killed on that July night in 1881." This author was unaware that Lucien Maxwell rebuilt the house as two stories and added the outside door to what would be Peter's bedroom. And the equally ignorant hoaxers used that diagram for *Cold Case Billy the Kid*. (Figure: 5 above). So the ignorant author concluded:

"We can posit an alternative scenario, based partly on what Dobbs said and partly on common sense. If the Kid was really after a hunk of steak he would have gone to the kitchen or the 'cool box' either in the storage or dining area or even outside in the courtyard, because it beggars belief that Maxwell would have a side of beef hanging in his bedroom. However, if the Kid was either going to or just leaving [his lover] Paulita either from the room next to Dona Luz - which would then require him to use the hallway just as Dobbs describes it – or alternatively from one of the two rooms on the northern side of the house, he would as he reached the front (eastern) doorway [believed by Smith, and used by the hoaxers, as the only entrance] – either from the inside or out – have seen the two strangers and acted just as Poe and Garrett described – skipping through the door [here an inside door] into Pete's bedroom to find out who they were – and Garrett was there waiting for him."

HOAXERS' PAST FAKE DOOR GAMBIT": Sederwall had also used this no outside door scam for fellow "Billy the Kid Case" hoaxer and editor, Bob Boze Bell, for Bell's August, 2010's *True West's* "Caught with his Pants Down? Billy the Kid vs Pat Garrett, One Door Closes."

For it, Sederwall was a **"retired lawman"** giving "CSI" evidence that Billy was in Paulita's bedroom, **"across from Pete's, when he heard two men (Poe and McKinney) talking outside."** Using Dobbs's no outside door, Sederwall has Billy enter the bedroom from the hall. And his "CSI" proof is none other than hoaxing Dr. Henry Lee's Case 2003-274 fake washstand forensics, with Sederwall making-up his own version that **"laser lines up perfectly with the hole [sic] in the washstand"** if Garrett shot Billy, then ran out the inside door, and on his knees fired back in, hitting the washstand!

So Bob Boze Bell concluded: **"[C]onventional wisdom is often misinformed, which I found out when Gregory Smith [the erroneously listed author of the article] discovered the original 1863 floor plans ... Apparently, windows, not doors, were located alongside these rooms. Lucien ... might have created doorways when he and his family moved in. Yet if Pete's room did not have an outside door, historians will certainly be forced to look at the event with new eyes."**

To be noted is that opportunistic clown Sederwall here backs the victim being Billy Bonney!

FAKING SHOOTING SCENE DOUBTS

The historical shooting scene is given, with Garrett's sitting on Peter Maxwell's bed when Billy entered; with Maxwell identifying him; and with Garrett shooting twice. Doubts are presented about Garrett's claim that Billy had a gun and knife, and the possibility he was unarmed. (Pages 142-143)

OMITTED EXPLANATIONS: Omitted are historically postulated explanations for Garrett's description of the shooting. His telling of a surprise encounter with Billy was likely to shield Peter Maxwell from accusation of complicitness. It was possible that Maxwell played traitor, setting up the ambush with Garrett, who was hiding in the dark room, with his deputies outside to shoot in case Billy escaped. With Billy's popularity in the town, it would have been a great risk to Maxwell if this had been revealed. This is supported by Poe's book, in which he described almost shooting Maxwell when he ran out the door; which would have only occurred if Poe was anticipating an escaping Billy, and was prepared to shoot him. (Poe, Page 39) And Poe reported the danger from Billy's partisans: "We spent the remainder of the night on the Maxwell premises, keeping constantly on our guard, was we were expecting to be attacked by friends of the dead man." (Poe, Page 44)

A further possibility is presented in Frederick Nolan's 1992 *The Lincoln County War: A Documentary History*. "Garrett found the Kid in bed with Paulita Maxwell and shot him *in flagrante delictu*; the authored version [given by Garrett] ... was then cooked up to protect the girl's reputation." (Nolan, Page 425) This was Sederwall's likely source for his fable.

Obviously, Garrett's possible need to protect other killing participants, has nothing to do with an unwarranted leap that the corpse was not Billy's.

Questioned are whether two or three shots were fired.

OMITTED EVIDENCE: Poe provided the explanation for the sound of three shots in his book: "An instant later a shot was fired in the room, followed immediately by what everyone within hearing distance thought were two other shots. However, there were only two shots fired, the third report, as

we learned afterward, being caused by the rebound of the second bullet, which had struck the adobe wall and rebounded against the headboard of a wooden bedstead." (Poe, Pages 36-37) **Garrett also addressed it in his book as first thinking Billy had fired one shot to his two. But Billy's revolver showed no shot fired. Garrett stated: "We searched long and faithfully – found both my bullet marks but no other."** (Garrett, Page 218) **And eye-witness Peter Maxwell testified on July 15, 1881 for the Coroner's jurymen: "*Pat F. Garrett fired two shots at the said William Bonney and the said William Bonney fell near my fire place.*"**

Omitting that the actual second strike involved Maxwell's headboard, given is Dr. Henry Lee's fake washstand forensics, with his positioning of Garrett on the floor and shooting. A Homeland Security "expert" is used to claim physiologic alterations in a shooter causing "fight or flight mode" and flinching, supposedly as confirmation of Lee's positioning to claim Garrett lied by reporting it differently. Also claimed is that Garrett also lied by leaving out the washstand. (Pages 144-146)

MAJOR HOAXING: This fakery uses the "Billy the Kid Case" hoax as evidence to call Garrett a liar, by its substitution of the unsubstantiated washstand for the shot headboard; and use of Dr. Henry Lee's fake crime scene reconstruction based on it. (See page 229 above) In fact, Deputy Poe confirmed that: "[T]he second bullet, which had struck the adobe wall ... [had] rebounded against the headboard of a wooden bedstead." (Poe, Pages 36-37)

FAKING THE BODY'S REMOVAL

Little is said about taking Billy Bonney's body from Peter Maxwell's bedroom to the carpenter's shop to avoid admitting to the townspeople's multiple identifications of Billy.

Instead, a quote is taken from Garrett's July 15, 1881 "letter to the territorial governor": "It was my desire to have been able to take him alive, but his coming upon me so suddenly and unexpectedly led me to believe that he had seen me enter the room, or had been informed by someone of the fact, and that he had come there armed with pistol and knife expressly to kill me if he could." (Page 147)

Trying to fake a discrepancy, there followed a convoluted rendition of Deputy Poe's stating that the room was too dark to make things out. And Poe is claimed to have had to go through the house to get to the bedroom. (Page 147)

FAKING EVIDENCE: Hiding numerous identifications of the corpse as Billy Bonney's, this is mere blather about Garrett's description, and Poe's blocking entry to the bedroom based on the already faked claim of the lack of its outside door.

But Garrett's quoted letter of July 15, 1881 to Acting-Governor William Ritch (as reprinted in the Las Cruces *Rio Grande Republican* as "Kid the Killer Killed, Wm. Bonney alias Antrim, alias Billy the Kid, Fatally Meets Pat Garrett, the Lincoln County Sheriff" (see pages 12-13 above) actually debunked the Jameson-Sederwall duo's fakery by giving the historical shooting scene, and reprinting the Coroner's Jury Report's identifying the body and confirming justifiable homicide.

Written to get the promised reward, Garrett may have added his necessity of killing to address Lew Wallace's offers on December 22, 1880's Las Vegas *Daily Gazette*, and May 3, 1881's *Daily New Mexican*, which both stated: "I will pay $500 reward to any person or persons who will capture William Bonney, alias The Kid, <u>and deliver him to any sheriff of New Mexico</u>. Satisfactory proofs of identity will be required." It was not a dead-or-alive notice. So killing, instead of capture, had to be addressed. So Garrett did. Noteworthy is that this is also the letter confirming he sent the original Coroner's Jury Report to District Attorney William Breeden. And Breeden agreed to justifiable homicide, and assisted in processing Garrett's reward. This alone destroyed the hoaxing duo's lies.

Next was quibbling about the body lying on its back or front, with Jesus Silva, Maxwell's foreman, quoted from Miguel Otero's **1936** book, *The Real Billy the Kid*, as the body being face down. So the duo questioned whether Silva entered first (Page 148)

FAKING EVIDENCE: With Garrett's shooting Billy from the front, he was likely knocked backwards, landing supine. Also, the hoaxers admit the room was next lit, and the body examined. And it could have been turned over then.

The Jesus Silva story came from an *Alias Billy the Kid* prompt footnote: a July, 1936 *Frontier Times* interview of a Leslie Traylor of Galveston, Texas, titled "Facts Regarding the Escape of Billy the Kid." Traylor, a history buff, interviewed old-timers in Lincoln and Fort Sumner in 1933 and 1935; including Jesus Silva about Garrett's shooting of Billy. He wrote: "Silva said he was at home when he heard the shot, and they sent for him, that when he arrived they were afraid to go into the room, and as he knew the Kid well and was not afraid, he went in with a light and found him dead, lying face downward with a pistol in one hand and a butcher knife in the other." So the real issue for the hoaxers to wrangle with is not face-up or down, but that Jesus Silva was yet another witness identifying the corpse as Billy Bonney's!

And Miguel Otero was a meaningless hearsay source, who wrote his book 55 years after the shooting!

There was no discrepancy.

And, by now, the hoaxers had presented the multiple body identifications as Billy: Garrett, Peter Maxwell, Jesus Silva, Deluvina, the townspeople's vigil, and the Coroner's Jury Report in the Garrett article's letter. Thus Garrett killed Billy. Thus, no pretender was Billy. End of story.

FAKING A "PETER MAXWELL"

A key death scene witness was Peter Maxwell, with it occurring in his bedroom and with his Coroner's Jury testimony stating: *"Pat F. Garrett fired two shots at the said William Bonney and the said William Bonney fell near my fire place and I went out of the room and when I came in again about three or four minutes after the shots the said William Bonney was dead."*

So "cop" Sederwall tried to discredit Maxwell's fatal and untouchable testimony. To do so, he cited a 1978 article by a "Bundy Avants" [sic] (in an unreferenced publication) titled: "The Bundy Avants [sic] Story." In it, that old-timer claimed to have spoken to Peter Maxwell years after the shooting, with Maxwell telling him information contradicting the death scene as: Billy was not shot; Poe was not there; the body was of a Mexican; and Garrett kept it all secret. (Page 136)

FAKE EVIDENCE: The Bundy Avant article is from a May-June, 1978 *True West* magazine interview with old-timer Avant, spouting malarkey. In 1894, as a child, he came with his cattle ranching family from Texas to Roswell, New Mexico; then moved to Capitan, when he was eight; then White Oaks in 1905 for farming. Avant's Billy the Kid-related tall tales begin with George Coe, who, he made-up, told him he had retrieved murdered John Tunstall's body. Name-dropping, Avant faked John Chisum's brand as the "Long S," when it was the "Long Rail." He babbled that "Colonel Henry Fountain" was a family friend; when Fountain's name was Albert Jennings, and his little son, murdered with him, was Henry.

For his Peter Maxwell fabrication, Avant had himself meeting an old man named "Pete," a cook at a ranch near the San Andres Mountains. This pseudo-Pete says: "I've takin a likin' to you" ... I sensed he had something on his mind which had bothered him for a long time and he felt he had found someone to confide in." Avant says the man told him he was Pete Maxwell, and would tell Avant a secret, if he promised not to tell it "to a living sole as long as I'm alive." Pete then tells him, "Billy is not dead; I can take you to where he lives and has a nice family ... I'll tell you how it was ... There was no light in the house and Pat and I were in the dark when we heard someone come in. We both thought it was Billy. So when the man came in and sensed someone else was there beside me, he said, 'Quien es?' and Pat just fired. We heard the man fall. But when we struck a match and looked at him, we saw it was not the Kid ... Pat was pretty well shook up, as he didn't want it said he had killed the wrong man. It was a Mexican and we decided he was a drifter who would never be missed ... I agreed to keep quiet, too, as I could see it would give Billy a chance to slip away and start a new life, which he had been talking of doing." Avant says it must be true, because Maxwell would know.

In fact, Peter Maxwell lived near Fort Sumner until his death on June 21, 1898. [FIGURE: 8] His death, as a "Las Vegas" item, in June 28, 1898's *The Albuquerque Citizen*; stated: "By parties arriving from Fort Sumner it was learned Saturday that Peter Maxwell died at his home near that place , an the morning of the 21st, and was buried on the following day. He leaves a wife and one child. Peter Maxwell was the son

of Lucien B. Maxwell, the original owner of the celebrated Maxwell land grant lying in Colorado and New Mexico. Peter Maxwell is well remembered in Las Vegas, where he was a frequent visitor in years past." Also, the coarse vernacular Bundy Avant faked for his pseudo-Pete is incompatible with that sophisticated and bi-lingual man born to Luz Trotier de Beaubien of Hispanic aristocracy, and Lucien Bonaparte Maxwell, of the prosperous Menard family.

FIGURE: 8. Peter Maxwell's house near Fort Sumner, where he lived after the town was sold; discrediting Bundy Avant's claim that he lived as a cook in a San Andres Mountains cow camp; from Midland, Texas, Haley Library, Robert N. Mullin Collection

Avant continued his Billy the Kid related lies with a meeting with John W. Poe at Roswell at a later date. Poe asks him what he thought of Garrett, and Avant "didn't think too highly of him." This pseudo-Poe, who was not present at the killing scene, tells Avant that he had been Garrett's deputy when Garrett killed Billy in Fort Sumner, but since "Pat Billy, and I were good friends at one time," he wanted to pay his last respects [with Avant unaware that Poe had never met Billy until moments before the killing]. So Poe used two horses to ride to Fort Sumner that night. Avant says Garrett then refused to let Poe see the body; so Poe suspected foul play and turned in his badge. Avant concluded: "This made the second time in a period of three years that I had been told by two men, who of all people should know the facts, that Billy was not killed by Pat Garrett." (Avant, Pages 47-48)

This Bundy Avant fakery replicated Billy the Kid fakery of old-timer Homer Overton's fake Affidavit used as evidence in 2003 by then "Billy the Kid Case" hoaxer, Sheriff Tom Sullivan, for an addendum to his Case No. 2003-274's "Probable Cause Statement." (See pages 174-175 above) And it revealed the current fakery of the Jameson-Sederwall duo by using the same kind of junk as "evidence."

NOTHING BUT CLOWNING

The Jameson-Sederwall clowning, though adding more hoaxing to the original hoaxes, added no actual evidence that Pat Garrett did not kill Billy the Kid. One is left wondering what these hoaxers were trying to accomplish, besides the well-worn, hollow, meaningless, and failed history-is-not-as-written mantra of their respective hoaxes; along with Steve Sederwall showing off his fake "investigations" and faking Lincoln County Sheriffs Department's Case 2003-274 "Billy the Kid Case" as his own private pursuit.

CHAPTER 3
FAKING NO INQUEST

CLOWNS VERSUS CORONER'S JURY REPORT

To face the July 15, 1881 Coroner's Jury Report, the Jameson-Sederwall duo had only their faked discrepancies, fake "investigations," and fake conspiracy theories.

Recycled was Steve Sederwall's "Billy the Kid Case" hoax's "Probable Cause Statement," with his made-up time discrepancies for Justice of the Peace Alejandro Segura's contacting Sunnyside's Milnor Rudulph to fabricate that the Jury never even convened. (See debunking in pages 159-160 above)

As in that "Probable Cause Statement," the body's location was questioned because the Report said: "*[T]he above jury convened in the home of Luz B. Maxwell and* ***proceeded to a room in the said house where they found the body of William Bonney alias "Kid."*** But the body was taken to the carpenter's shop vigil. So the location is called a lie. (Page 149)

FAKERY: It is obvious that, after that wake, the body was returned to the Maxwell house for the inquest.

It is claimed that Justice of the Peace Segura "instructed Rudulph to assemble a coroner's jury and serve as foreman." (Page 149)

WRONG: Segura appointed Rudulph and the five jurymen, as he himself stated in the Coroner's Jury Report: "*I, the undersigned, Justice of the Peace ... immediately upon receiving said information I proceeded to the said place and named Milnor Rudolph, Jose Silva, Antonio Sevedra, Pedro Antonio Lucero, Lorenzo Jaramillo and Sabal Gutierres a jury to investigate the case.*"

The Report, as written by Milnor Rudulph, about "gratitude of the community" being owed to Garrett, is called "suspicious" to "cop" Sederwall, because it praises; but Fort Sumner people would have been angry at the killing, not grateful. (Pages 150-151)

FALSE INTERPRETATION: Sederwall seems unaware that Rudulph, as discussed above, was a Ringite. (See page 304 above) Rudulph would have praised Garrett for stamping out the last anti-Ring rebel. And the jurymen, presumably terrified by this killing, would not have dared to object.

The Report's existence is next "doubted" by claiming its not being filed in San Miguel County; "Paco" Anaya claiming two reports; the inquest being speedy; William Keleher's photocopy in Spanish [in his 1957 *Violence in Lincoln County*] as being the "second coroner's report;" his translation meant the victim spoke English; and that some signers misspelled names. So the duo doubt that the jurymen even saw the body. (Pages 150-151)

HOAXING EVIDENCE: The Coroner's Jury Report is well documented. Its original was sent by Pat Garrett to First Judicial District Attorney William Breeden, with its copy to Acting-Governor William Ritch. As Breeden's, it was filed in his Santa Fe office; and later moved with other official papers to the State Capitol Building. It was located there in the basement 1932 by state employee, Harold Abbott. He made copies, later reproduced by historians, like William Keleher. (See pages 20-22 above)

Windbag "Paco" Anaya's "two reports" was fabrication, as was the rest of his posthumous book's Billy the Kid history. But, as stated, he did know one thing: Billy was killed by Pat Garrett; hence the title, *I Buried Billy*.

As to viewing the body, the Coroner's Jury Report confirmed it performed the inquest's legal duties: interviewing witness Peter Maxwell, identifying the body as Billy Bonney's, examining the wound, and concluding that the homicide did not require prosecution as being justifiable self-defense.

For their conclusion, the Jameson-Sederwall duo rely on their own clowning; and state that Garrett killed an innocent man, rushed through the inquest process to hide the body of the non-Billy victim by burial, and wrote the "second" [i.e., real] Coroner's Jury Report himself. And 'cop" Sederwall announces that "somebody (or somebodies) are lying" to hide the truth. (Pages 151 -152)

CHAPTER 4
THE RETURN OF THE FAKE FORENSICS

THE "BILLY THE KID CASE'S" HOAXED FORENSICS

Jameson and Sederwall, pretending they proved the corpse was unidentified (Pages 153-154), recycle Dr. Henry Lee's fake "Billy the Kid Case" forensics, while shape-shifting it as Sederwall's personal investigation; and, of course, hiding that Sederwall forged Lee's reports for my open records case. So Sederwall calls Fort Sumner an active crime scene (Page 154), echoing the book's title as a "cold case" involving Pat Garrett.

HOAXING: Fort Sumner was not Pat Garret's shooting's "crime scene" after the Coroner's Jury decision of July 15, 1881; stating: "*[O]ur verdict is that the deed of said Garrett was justifiable homicide.*" There was no crime.

FAKING CARPENTER'S BENCH FORENSICS

Steve Sederwall, as sole "investigator," of the pretend crime scene, presents Case 2003-274's carpenter's bench "investigation" as his own, and adds more lies. The bench is called an **important source of "bloodstains from the slain intruder"** (Page 155) - a new name for the innocent victim - **as a source of DNA**.

Research is claimed on Maxell house history (Pages 155-159), though it was never bench's location. Admitted is that the town was sold in 1884, and its buildings no longer stand. The furniture (bed, washstand, with added carpenter's bench) is traced to Peter Maxwell's sister Odelia, married to Manuel Abreu. Hilariously inserted is Bundy Avant's old-timer malarkey of meeting "Pete" in the San Andres mountains. (See pages 299-302 above) So Maxwell is portrayed as giving away his furniture after being reduced to "cooking for 'wagon outfits!' " It is then is traced to Odelia's and Manuel's daughter, Stella Abreu, for her "museum" (with a photograph of that shed-like building). The carpenter's bench photo by an unknown photographer from the Robert Mullin Collection is cited, but its date of about 1926 - 46 years after the shooting - is omitted. Given is Sederwall's tracing the bench to the Albuquerque home of Stella Maxwell's son, Mannie Miller, in his converted chicken coop. (Pages 158-160)

Dr. Henry Lee is introduced as contacted by Sederwall. Lied is that "**a number of locations" on the bench's top and bottom tested positive for blood** by "presumptive blood test reagents phenolphthalein and o-tolidine." **Sederwall makes-up "blood" from "two different human beings;"** claiming future **separation would identify the "slain intruder."** (Page 163) A Lee report is not cited, but one is in the Bibliography as: "Lee, Dr. Henry. Forensic Examination Report (Examination of Furniture From Pete Maxwell's of July 15, 1881) 22 May 2004." (Page 187)

FAKERY: Sederwall is lying. No blood was identified. Lee's sole report of February 25, 2005 merely hoaxed "blood-like" stains. And Orchid Cellmark Lab got no DNA from the bench. The useless mixed samples were from courthouse floorboards and William Hudspeth's jawbone - mixed simply meaning from *two or more* sources. [Appendix: 4]

The cited Lee report appears to be one of Sederwall's forged ones, with the date changed to May 22, 2004. The one he gave to the Court was titled "Forensic Research and Training Center Forensic Examination Report: "Examination of furniture from Pete Maxwell's of July 15, 1881," and dated February 25, 2005.

Sederwall made-up "bloodstains from the slain intruder," repeating the "Billy the Kid Case" hoax's lie about the bench having "mixed DNA" of two people bleeding on it: first playing-dead-Billy; next, switched shot innocent victim. In fact, the bench yielded no DNA.

IRRELEVANT: Offered was no proof that Garrett did not kill Billy. And debunked were "Brushy's" and John Miller's death scenes lacking the carpenter's bench scenario (to bleed for Dr. Lee's future fake DNA.)

FAKING "MAXWELL FURNITURE" FORENSICS

Steve Sederwall, as sole "investigator," next had Dr. Henry Lee examine the headboard and the washstand *for him*.

HOAXING THE HEADBOARD

Sederwall reminds the reader that Deputy Poe had said Garrett's second shot rebounded from the wall and hit the headboard of Maxwell's bed. But he states that Lee found "nothing resembling the impact of a bullet, even a scratch." So Poe is called a liar. (Pages 160-161) No mention is made of Lee's report, but the Bibliography cites "Lee, Dr. Henry. Forensic Examination Report (Examination of Furniture From Pete Maxwell's of July 15, 1881) 22 May 2004." (Page 187)

HOAXING: Sederwall is clowning, since the "headboard" is just a big empty hole with a frame, having no place for the bullet hit. But scorning readers' intelligence, he gives its photo. (Wily Dr. Lee had omitted a photo of it for his February 25, 2005 report's section on it.)

The Lee report in the Bibliography appears to be one of Sederwall's forged ones, with the date changed to May 22, 2004. The one Sederwall first presented to me was his fake "Forensic Research and Training Center Forensic Examination Report: "Examination of furniture from Pete Maxwell's of July 15, 1881," dated February 25, 2005. Its second forged version, with different font and deleted "Results and Conclusions," went to the Court as Exhibit E.

Lee's, actual report of February 25, 2005 had stated dishonestly: "No bullet hole and no observable damage, no sign of bullet ricocheted type of defects were found on the Headboard. No blood or biological materials were observed on the Headboard."

This is pure hoaxing by both Sederwall and Lee; as well as records forgery - as declared for Sederwall by my District Court's litigation Judge, George Eichwald.

IRRELEVANT: All this fakery had nothing to do with Garrett not killing Billy, or "Brushy" or John Miller being Billy the Kid.

HOAXING THE WASHSTAND

Sederwall also repeated Dr. Henry Lee's fake washstand forensics. (Pages 161-163) A photo of it (Page 162) differs from the one photographed and diagramed by Lee in his February 25, 2005 report, by having a raised back rim - with Lee's picture being only a box. Described are the washstand's two holes. Lee's bullet trajectory is presented, with his fake claim of Garrett shooting from the floor. No report is mentioned, but the Bibliography cites: "Lee, Dr. Henry. Forensic Examination Report (Examination of Furniture From Pete Maxwell's of July 15, 1881) 22 May 2004." (Page 187)

HOAXING: The toy-sized washstand used, is implausible as being one from Maxwell's bedroom; or he would have had to wash himself crouched on the floor - like Lee's faked shooting Garrett!

And neither Garrett nor Poe reported a washstand as struck by a bullet of Garrett's. So the alleged bullet trajectory is meaningless hoaxing of Garrett as shooting it, and of his position in the room.

The Lee report cited in the Bibliography appears to be one of Sederwall's forged ones, with date changed to May 22, 2004. It was given to me with a "Results and Conclusions" section absent.

Lee's actual report of February 25, 2005 was actually non-committal; stating: "Two bullet holes were located on the side panels of the Washstand. The hole on the left side panel is consistent with a bullet entrance hole while the hole on the right side panel is consistent with a bullet exit hole. However, it is not possible to determine when those bullet holes were produced at this time [meaning any time from the 1870's to 1926's Stella Abreu" Museum!]."

IRRELEVANT: All this was irrelevant to Garrett not killing Billy; or "Brushy" or John Miller being Billy the Kid.

CHAPTER 5
RETURN OF THE "BILLY THE KID CASE'S" JOHN MILLER EXHUMATION FAKERY

ATTACKING JOHN MILLER'S BONES AGAIN

John Miller made his hopefully last encore in W.C. Jameson's *Cold Case Billy the Kid* with Steve Sederwall flaunting the "Billy the Kid Case's" fake forensics of the John Miller exhumation. Jameson appeared to have the misguided hope that any denial of the historic death scene would help his "Brushy Bill" cause.

But unleashed Sederwall proclaimed that John Miller matched Billy the Kid! (To hell with "Brushy!") And Case 2003-274's exhumation became, in Sederwall's telling, just part of his personal "ongoing investigation." (Page 165) Of course, dug up random man, William Hudspeth, was concealed; as was the close call with criminal prosecution for the exhumations, and having no DNA from the carpenter's bench to compare with anyone!

FAKING THE JOHN MILLER EXHUMATION

Reflecting Sederwall's clowning, no background is given for John Miller: like being born in 1950, almost ten years before Billy; like knowing no Billy the Kid history at all; like dying soon after breaking a hip; and like being toothless. According to Sederwall, Miller's exhumation was now claimed to have been done on May 9, 2005 [sic - May 19] by an unnamed "forensic anthropologist" and "authorized by the state of Arizona."(Page 165)

HOAXING: Hidden is the report for that exhumation: "Lincoln County Sheriff's Department Supplemental Report," listing "Case # 2003-274, Date: Thursday, May 19, 2005, Subject: Exhumation of John Miller, Location: Arizona Pioneers' Cemetery, Prescott, Arizona, Report By: Steven M. Sederwall, On Thursday, May 19, 2005, at approximately 1:00 pm the following met at the Arizona Pioneers' Cemetery at Prescott, Arizona. Investigators: Steven M. Sederwall, Lincoln County Deputy Sheriff."

Hidden is that the hired Maricopa County forensic anthropologist was Dr. Laura Fulginiti, who denied all the hoaxers claims. Hidden is that the hoaxers had no Billy the Kid DNA to justify any exhumation at all for identity matching. Hidden is the wanton desecration of random man, William Hudspeth, buried beside Miller.

Sederwall repeated his and Tom Sullivan's Piltdown man-style hoax, originally used by them in 2006 after the exhumation to claim that Miller had buck teeth and a shot left scapula; when they were actually using *Hudspeth's skeleton* with its non-bullet damaged *right* scapula.

Now Sederwall stated: "**The right scapula of John Miller manifested a round hole. The anthropologist observed that it appeared to be a bullet hole that had healed" and the bullet entered the upper chest and exited his back**. He added that **Miller's right front incisor was placed somewhat in front of his left front incisor." So he concluded that this was Pat Garrett's bullet killing buck-toothed Billy the Kid**. (Page 165)

LYING: Sederwall was recycling and adding to his fakery to reporter, Rene Romo, in his November 6, 2006's *Albuquerque Journal's* "Billy the Kid Probe May Yield New Twist." Romo wrote: "Sederwall ... said Miller's skeletal remains were intriguing. He said Miller had buck teeth, like the Kid, and an old bullet wound that entered his upper left chest and exited through the scapula." Hidden, is that forensic expert, Dr. Laura Fulginiti, reported Miller having no teeth and no damaged scapula. Hidden is that Sederwall was faking the results from random man, William Hudspeth, who had a damaged *right*, not *left* scapula, with Dr. Fulginiti denying the damage was a bullet wound. (See pages 243, 247, 251, 257, 259 above and 320 below)

About Hudspeth's scapula damage, Fulginiti wrote in her forensic report of on the exhumations: "There were extensive healed traumata on the right scapula." She did not state that "The right scapula of John Miller manifested a round hole," or observe "that it appeared to be a bullet hole that had healed." or that the bullet entered the upper chest and exited his back. Sederwall was just clowning around.

After clowning Sederwall had given this Piltdown man-style hoax performance to hoax-backing reporter, Rene Romo, he juggled the same lies for hoax-backing reporter, Julie Carter, for her October 6, 2005 *RuidosoNews.com* article, "Follow the Blood: In the Billy the Kid Case, Miller Exhumed." She wrote: "This case has not failed to amaze us at every turn, said Sederwall. John Miller even held some surprises for us. He had buck teeth just as history tells us the Kid had. But we were shocked to see that Miller sported a very old bullet wound that entered the left chest and exited the shoulder blade, the same wound Garrett claimed to have inflicted on the Kid the night in July 1881."

Sederwall and Tom Sullivan later performed their Piltdown Man-style hoax duet for reporter Leo Banks's April 13, 2006 *Tucson Weekly* article, "The New Billy the Kid?" Banks wrote: "As Sederwall told the *Weekly,* 'We were shocked when we got him up. He had buck teeth just like the Kid and a bullet hole in the upper left chest that exited the shoulder blade.' Sullivan made a similar statement, suggesting this might be the man Garrett shot the morning of July 14, 1881."

Banks, who had treated their circus routines with the scorn they deserved, fact checked their claims. He wrote: "[W]hen contacted by the *Weekly,* Fulginiti didn't support their enthusiasm. 'There was evidence of trauma on [Hudspeth's] scapula, but I couldn't tell whether it was from a gunshot wound or not,' she said."

Sederwall then claimed he (as sole "investigator," got DNA from Miller's remains "sufficient to conduct a test." (Page 165)

HOAXING: Hidden was that they never had Billy the Kid DNA to match with Miller's, with their only lying about getting it from the carpenter's bench. Hidden was no need for DNA matching anyway, since Miller had no historical match to Billy.

Jameson was apparently unaware of the "Billy the Kid Case's" publicity, in which the conscienceless, profiteering clowns were willing to claim any remains as Billy the Kid's to keep Bill Kurtis's cameras rolling. For Julie Carter's October 6, 2005 "Follow the Blood," Sederwall had plugged Miller as Billy; crowing: ""In the light of the evidence, we see that the history of Billy the Kid will change. Those with monied interest in history remaining the same will not be happy ... As a cop I know when people fight to keep you from looking at something, they are always trying to hide something. The Lincoln County War is still going on."

For reporter Rene Romo's November 6, 2006's *Albuquerque Journal's* "Billy the Kid Probe May Yield New Twist," hoaxing Sederwall had plugged John Miller, as well as faking having DNA from the carpenter's bench; stating: "If that [John Miller] DNA matches the work bench, I think the game is over."

JOHN MILLER EXITS IN A CLOWN'S BLAZE OF GLORY

Imposter, John Miller, thus, ended his Billy the Kid run like a clown shot out of a cannon: with a big bang, signifying nothing. Reduced to a pile of destroyed bones, he had led his troop of dark and sleazy clowns through New Mexico and Arizona, with a side-trip to France, and into a new book that could deposit him anywhere.

P.T. Barnum, in an honest moment about himself, that also applied to that charlatan hoard promoting Miller, had stated: "I'm a showman by profession ... and all the gilding shall make nothing else of me." Indeed, gilding Miller and his bones hid not at all that he was as fake as his promoters and as the forensics done using him.

The take-home after John Miller's circus show - performed by him when alive or as a skeleton, was he and his troop of hoaxing clowns were all just con-artists floating a variation of P.T. Barnum's huckster scorn: "Nobody ever lost a dollar by underestimating the gullibility (Barnum said "taste") of the American public."

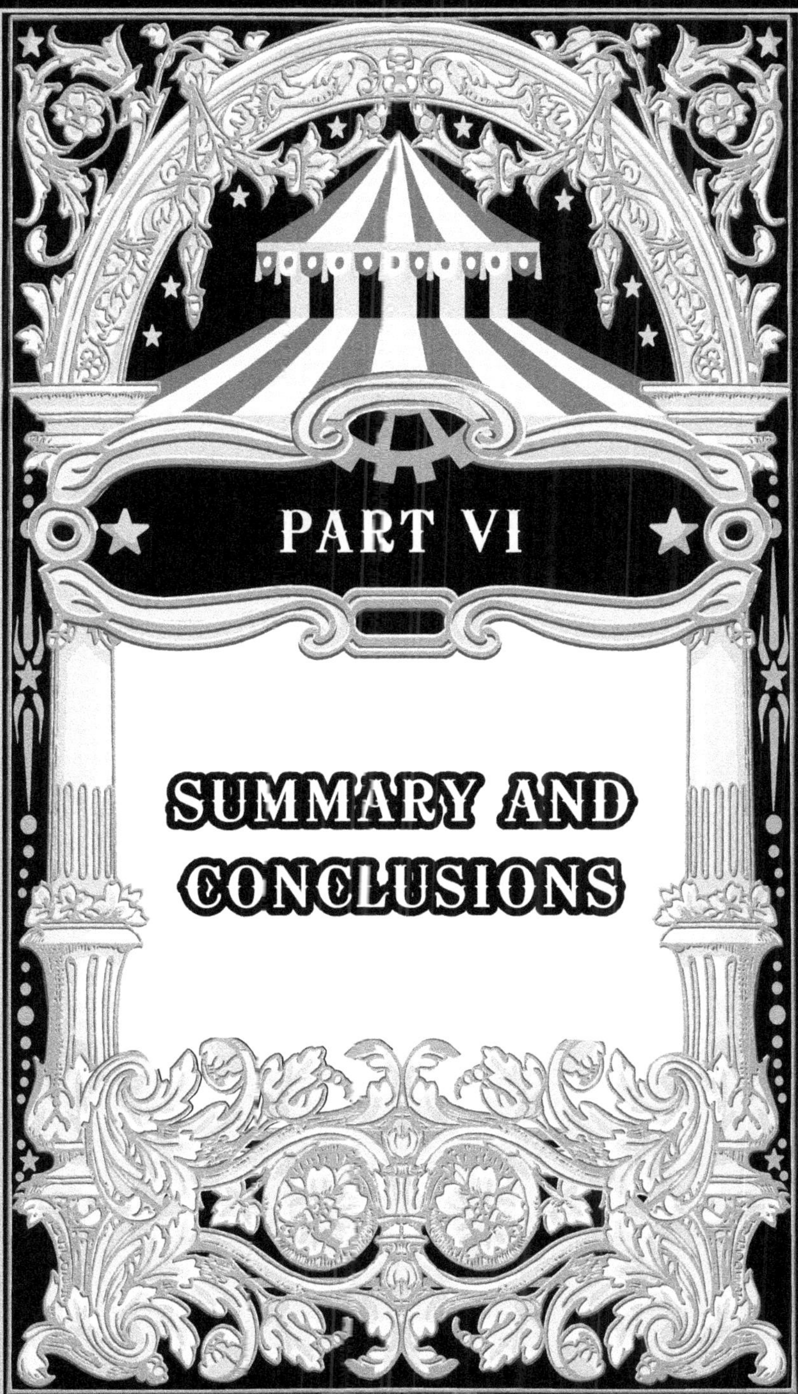

PART VI

SUMMARY AND CONCLUSIONS

CHAPTER 1
WILLIAM HUDSPETH GOT THE LAST WORD

IFS, WHYS, AND CLOWNS

John Miller presented no accurate autobiographical, physical, or historical evidence supporting his impersonating of Billy the Kid. And the "Billy the Kid Case" hoaxers and W.C. Jameson backed him just to keep their media circus on the road. For that show, all these clowns had to do for their three ring performance was to keep some big secrets from their public.

If John Miller was Billy Bonney, he would have been born almost a decade later; would not have made preposterous mistakes in telling his history; would have looked identical to him; and would have had his revolutionary zeal and multi-cultural world view instead of an outlaw myth script.

Why Miller could not "become Billy" had to do with bad timing: he lived too early, and missed the scholarly history books which could have better costumed his clowning.

Why Miller wanted to be the Kid is more fascinating. Possibly his tragic murdered parents and early life as an abduction victim attracted him to the violent mythology. And his multi-scarred body pointed to his rough life. It all could seem grand if he was famous Billy the Kid

Why becomes more cynical when it comes to "Billy the Kid Case" hoaxers. They were mere opportunists. Bill Richardson was after political fodder; the rest were gobbling profits in cash or kind in New Mexico's modern incarnation of the Santa Fe Ring. They shared John Miller's ambition to the extent that any claimed connection to Billy Bonney gilded their lackluster lives. And "Brushy Bill"-backer, W.C. Jameson, had merely hitched a ride on their fakery with his own "Cold Case Billy the Kid" megahoax, desperately hoping to promote his own fake agenda and himself by using John Miller as a vehicle for death scene doubts.

And despite all efforts at debunking, John Miller probably is now embedded, with at least a few dupes, as a real contender for Billy the Kid's identity.

So join in with Stephen Sondheim:

> But where are the clowns?
> Quick send in the clowns.
> Don't bother, they're here.

As 19th century German poet and man of letters, Heinrich Heine, wrote: "When the heroes go off stage, the clowns come on." John Miller, other Billy the Kid imposters like him, and their gaggle of hoaxing hucksters are all ridiculous clowns, trailing the main act of Billy Bonney's real history as its tragic-comic freak-show.

WILLIAM HUDSPETH'S REVENGE

The modern clowns who dragged old clown, John Miller, onto the world stage, can never escape his underground neighbor, William Hudspeth; reduced, like him, to a pile of dismembered bones, depleted by their theft to Texas for meaningless pulverizing for sham DNA.

Someday, William Hudspeth may get the last laugh, and justice may be served. He has the perfect case as being the only character in the long circus procession of imposters and fakers who was actually his real self: a random anyman with a bad scapula and buck teeth.

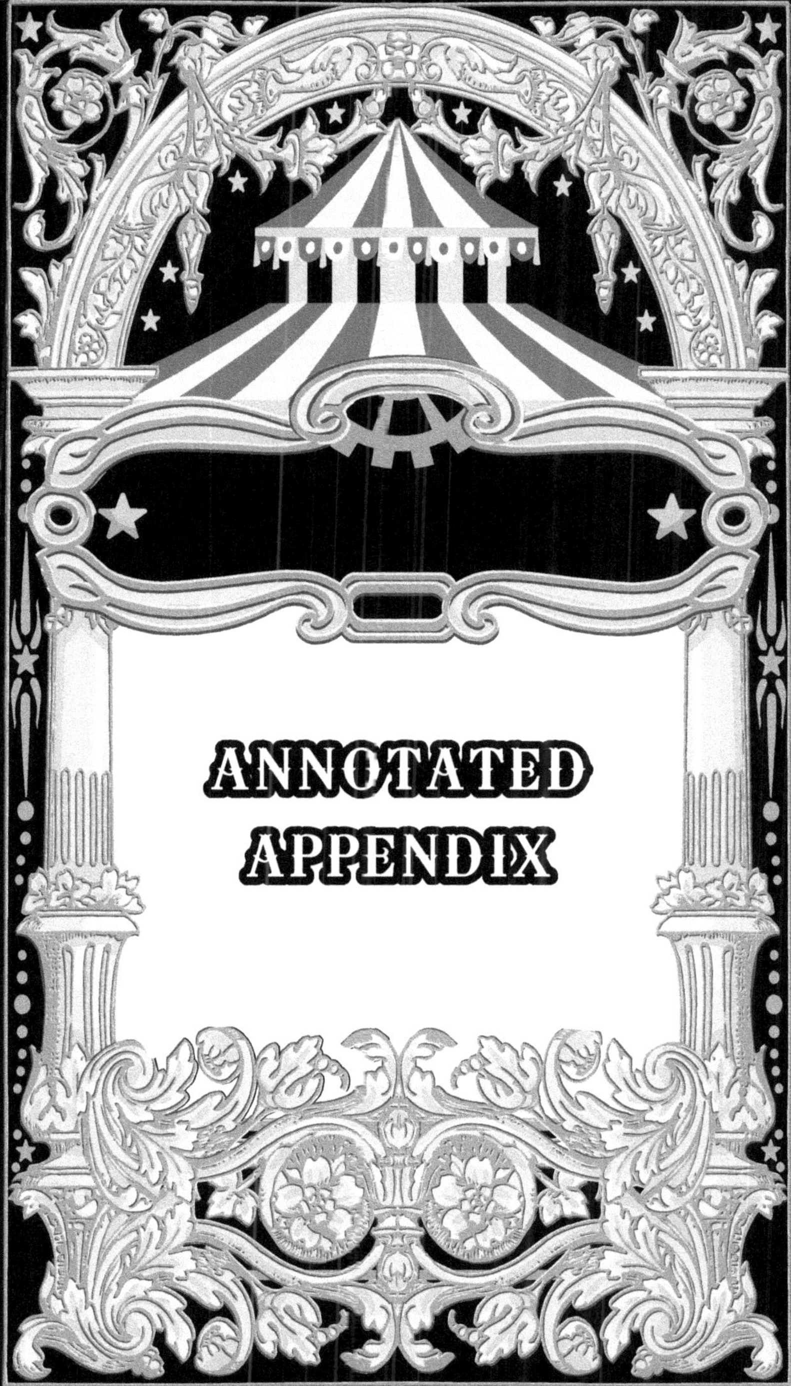

ANNOTATED APPENDIX

APPENDIX: 1. NO DNA FROM CARPENTER'S BENCH: Orchid Cellmark's October 15, 2004's "Laboratory Report, Forensic Identity, Mitochondrial Analysis, Results and Conclusions" for its Case 4444-001B-004B (for Case 2003-274's bench results).

[AUTHOR'S SUMMARY: Lee's carpenter's bench underside swabbings and shavings were labeled as evidence numbers 4444-001B, 4444-002B, 4444-003B, and 4444-004B. "Results" showed the specimens "failed to yield amplifiable DNA." "Conclusions" recorded: "no mitochondrial [DNA] sequence data were generated."

LABORATORY REPORT - FORENSIC IDENTITY – MITOCHONDRIAL ANALYSIS

CASE DATA:

Referring Agency: Calvin D. Ostler

Cellmark Case #: FOR 4444B

Agency Contact: Calvin D. Ostler

Report Date: October 15, 2004

1. Evidence Received:

Accession #	Sample Description	Receipt Date/ Method of Delivery
4444-001A	Wood shavings "Lincoln County Courthouse #1"	8/4/04 - FedEx
4444-002A	Wood shavings "Lincoln County Courthouse #2"	
4444-001B	Swabbing from "underside of bench #3"	
4444-002B	Swabbing from "underside of bench #4"	
4444-003B	Wood shavings "underside of bench #3"	
4444-004B	Wood shavings "underside of bench #4"	

DR. HENRY LEE'S CARPENTER'S BENCH SAMPLES:
4444-001B
4444-002B
4444-003B
4444-004B

2. **Results:**

Sequence data obtained from the swabbing from the underside of the bench (4444-001B) are inconclusive. As a result, no data from this sample are reported.

The swabbing from the underside of the bench (4444-002B) and wood shavings from the underside of the bench (4444-003B and 4444-004B) were extracted according to accepted mitochondrial extraction protocol; however, the swabbing and wood shavings (4444-002B, 4444-003B, 4444-004B) failed to yield amplifiable DNA. Therefore, no sequence data were generated for comparison to a reference specimen.

Procedures used in the analysis of this case adhere to the standards adopted by the DNA Advisory Board on DNA analysis methods.

3. **Conclusions:**

Sample 4444-001B provided an inconclusive mtDNA profile; therefore, no conclusions can be reached with regard to the origin of this sample.

Samples 4444-002B, 4444-003B and 4444-004B did not provide sufficient human mitochondrial DNA for sequencing. Since no mitochondrial sequence data were generated, no conclusions with regard to this sample can be reached.

4. **Disposition of Evidence:**

All evidence received in this case will be returned to the submitting agency.

Orchid Cellmark has maintained complete chain of custody documentation from receipt of evidence to disposition.

NO DNA RECOVERED:

3. Conclusions

Sample 4444-001B provided an inconclusive mtDNA profile; therefore, no conclusions can be reached with regard to the origin of this sample.

Samples 4444-002B, 4444-003B and 4444-004B did not provide sufficient human mitochondrial DNA for sequencing. Since no mitochondrial sequence data were generated, no condlusions with regard to this sample can be reached.

5. **Case Review:**

The individuals below have reviewed the results and conclusions described in this report.

Joseph Warren
Forensic Supervisor

Rick W. Staub, Ph.D.
Laboratory Director

Kristina Paulette
Forensic Analyst

SIGNED under oath before me this 15th day of October, 2004.

Notary Public

APPENDIX: 2. FULGINITI REPORT: Dr. Laura Fulginiti. "Re: Exhumation, Pioneer Home Cemetery, Prescott, Arizona for Dale L. Tunnell, Ph.D. [sic], Forensitec. June 2, 2005.

[AUTHOR'S NOTE: Report of moonlighting Maricopa County Office of the Medical Investigator's forensic anthropologist]

RE: EXHUMATION PIONEER HOME CEMETERY, PRESCOTT, ARIZONA FOR DALE L. TUNNELL, PhD, FORENSITEC. JUNE 2, 2005

On May 19, 2005 at approximately 1230 hours I am asked to assist in the exhumation of the remains of an individual known as Mr. John Miller by Dr. Dale Tunnell, President, Forensitec. The purpose of my involvement is to aid in the exhumation process as well as to assess any skeletal remains recovered. The exhumation takes place at the Arizona Pioneer [sic] Home Cemetery, Iron Springs Road in Prescott Arizona in the presence of Dr. Tunnell, several of his associates, members of the Arizona Pioneer Home staff and Kristen Harnett M.A., AMSU graduate student.

Dr. Tunnell located the alleged gravesite of Mr. Miller prior to our arrival on the scene. The gravesite was located using the line of headstones to the West of the target grave. A standard reference point was established as the headstone of Michael Clancy. At approximately 1400 hours, a backhoe began to remove the sod overlying the alleged grave, which was oriented in an East-West direction, with the head to the West. When fragments of wood began to be removed, the grave was excavated using a shovel. Once the top of the casket and a portion of femur were unearthed, the excavation relied on digging with trowels and by hand. The position of the femur indicated that the remains were supine, with the feet to the East and the skull to the West. The left femoral shaft, minus the head, was removed, examined, and packaged for DNA analysis.

Dr. Tunnell, in consultation with the cemetery staff and his other associates determined that the adjacent grave to the North was likely that of Mr. Miller and excavation shifted to that gravesite.

[AUTHOR'S NOTE: This unmarked North Grave was not John Miller's, as Dr. Fulginiti later proved; and was that of random man, William Hudspeth. His exhumation was a multi-felony crime, later covered-up by the Maricopa County prosecutor.]

The backhoe removed the overlying sod until fragments of wood began to be unearthed. The excavation shifted to shovels and the top of the casket was identified. Excavation proceeded using trowels and hand tools until various aspects of the skeleton were identified and cleared. The skeleton in this grave was also lying supine, head to the West and feet to the East. The casket had collapsed onto the body at some point prior to the exhumation process. **A metal detector on loan from the Yavapai County Sheriff''s Office and operated by Det. Mike Poling, YCSO, was used to locate metal items, including nails and casket fittings.** (These items were donated to the Arizona Pioneer Home for their museum).

[AUTHOR'S NOTE: Poling was accidentally present to deliver specimens to Laura Fulginiti; but the hoaxers later lied that he was the lawman responsible for the exhumation.]

Minimal historical artifacts, such as buttons, a possible rivet, portions of wood from the casket and casket fittings were identified as they were unearthed. Skeletal elements were measured for depth and location, removed from the grave and examined (see Forensitec report). Pathological conditions such as osteoarthritis, healed fractures and markers of occupation were noted as follows. The vertebrae exhibited signs of extreme osteoarthritis in the form of lipping of the vertebral bodies, collapse of some of the bodies and osteophytic activity. **There were extensive healed traumata on the right scapula**

[AUTHOR'S NOTE: So the <u>damaged right scapula</u> was in North Grave of William Hudspeth, and was not a shot left scapula of John Miller as the hoaxers later lied.]

and the left clavicle, a healed Colles' fracture of the right distal radius, a healed fracture of the second rib and a healed fracture of the left fourth metacarpal. The bone was dark brown in color, friable and dry. There was postmortem damage, both from the collapse of the lid of the casket onto the remains as well as from the removal process. The remains were photographed, samples were harvested for DNA (tooth and femur) and the remains were returned to the grave and reburied.

Anecdotal historical information suggested that Mr. John Miller had died from complications of a fractured hip while recuperating in the Arizona pioneer Home. The individual in the north grave, while having extensive pathological conditions, particularly in the upper body, did not have discernible pathology of the *os coxae.*

[AUTHOR'S NOTE: Fulginiti saw that the North Grave's remains did not have John Miller's broken hip; so the scapula was not his. She therefore concluded that the South Grave is Miller's; and it had the broken hip.]

At this point in the exhumation, a decision was made to exhume the *os coxae* of the individual in the south grave to confirm that we had indeed excavated the remains of Mr. John Miller from the north grave. The south grave was excavated by shovel to the point where the remnants of the casket lid were identified. Excavation resumed using trowels and hand tools until the left femoral head was identified.

The head of the femur was misshapen with bony remodeling, suggesting an antemortem [before death] injury. Additional excavation revealed the left innominate, which also had extensive remodeling of the acetabulum, ischium and pubis. The ischium tapered to a point with lack of union to the pubis, suggesting a healing fracture of the ischiopubic ramus. **This evidence led the team to believe that the individual in the south grave was, in fact, more consistent with the known facts regarding the Medical history of Mr. John Miller and additional DNA samples were recovered (femur, scalp?, matter from inside the braincase).**

[AUTHOR'S NOTE: Confirmation of South Grave as John Miller's because of broken hip.]

The maxillae and mandible were recovered but were edentulous.

[AUTHOR'S NOTE: Miller had NO TEETH AT ALL. The Hoaxers later lied that he had buck teeth like Billy the Kid's!]

There was limited pathology of the vertebrae, ribcage, clavicles and scapulae of the individual from the south grave. Mild osteoarthritis of the vertebral bodies was the only pathology of note. Photographs of the cranium and mandible were taken and the remains were returned to the grave and reburied.

Biological profiles of the two individuals are similar. Both were adult males, consistent with individuals of European (White) descent, and of advancing years. The nasal apertures on both were tall and narrow, with a sharp nasal sill, the malars were retreating and the cranial shape, while fragmentary, was round. The pubic symphyses exhibited characteristics of Suchey-Brooks Phase IV (36-86 years, mean 61.2 years).The symphyseal faces were flat and eroded with marked ventral ligaments. The sternal ends of the ribs; while fragmentary, exhibited long bony extensions, consistent with an Iscan, Loth stage 8 (65 plus). **The individual in the south grave was edentulous.**

[AUTHOR'S NOTE: Repeated is that Miller had NO TEETH.]

The scene was returned to a state approximating that prior to our arrival and was cleared shortly after sundown. Items of evidence collected were distributed to members of the Arizona Pioneer Home Cemetery staff and to Dr. Richard Staub (see Forensitec report).

Laura C. Fulginiti, Ph.D., D-ABFA
Forensic Anthropologist

[AUTHOR'S NOTE: Fulginiti Report Summary.]

1) DALE TUNNELL: "**located the alleged gravesite of Mr. Miller prior to [her] arrival on the scene**."
2) MILLER'S SOUTH GRAVE: "**The left femoral shaft, minus the head," was taken by DR. Staub "for DNA.**"
3) HUDSPETH'S NORTH GRAVE: "**Dr. Tunnell, in consultation with the cemetery staff and his other associates determined that the adjacent grave to the North was likely that of Mr. Miller and excavation shifted to that gravesite.**"
4) HUDSPETH'S NORTH GRAVE: "**A metal detector on loan from the Yavapai County Sheriff's Office and operated by Det. Mike Poling, YCSO, was used to locate metal items, including nails and casket fittings.**"
5) HUDSPETH'S REMAINS: "**There were extensive healed traumata on the right scapula and the left clavicle, a healed Colles' fracture of the right distal radius, a healed fracture of the second rib and a healed fracture of the left fourth metacarpal.**"
6) THE NORTH GRAVE IS IDENTIFIED AS NOT MILLER'S:: "**Anecdotal historical information suggested that Mr. John Miller had died from complications of a fractured hip while recuperating in the Arizona pioneer Home. The individual in the north grave ... did not have discernible pathology of the *os coxae*.**"
7) THE SOUTH GRAVE IS IDENTIFIED AS MILLER'S: "**The head of the femur was misshapen with bony remodeling, suggesting an antemortem injury ... The ischium tapered to a point with lack of union to the pubis, suggesting a healing fracture of the ischiopubic ramus. This evidence led the team to believe that the individual in the south grave was, in fact, more consistent with the known facts regarding the Medical history of Mr. John Miller and additional DNA samples were recovered ... The maxillae and mandible were recovered but were edentulous.**"

APPENDIX: 3. GRAVE-ROBBED REMAINS OF JOHN MILLER AND WILLIAM HUDSPETH: Orchid Cellmark Laboratory's May 19, 2005 "Chain of Custody" for the taken skeletal remains.

[AUTHOR'S SUMMARY: Stolen from Miller's South grave were his "skull and mummified brains," "jawbone," "pelvis," "left femur," and part of his casket. Stolen from Hudspeth's North grave were his "mandible and teeth," and "right femur."

ORCHID CELLMARK 2600 Stemmons Freeway · Suite 133 · Dallas, TX 75207 · 214.631.8152 · 800.752.2774 · 214.634.3322 Fax

FOR 4444

CHAIN OF CUSTODY

A CHAIN OF CUSTODY DOCUMENT MUST ACCOMPANY EACH FORENSIC CASE SUBMISSION

EVIDENCE RECEIPT

Signature: Rick W. Staub Date: 5.19.05 8:00 P.M.
Package Sealed?: YES Seal Intact: YES Signs of Tampering? NO
Method of Delivery: Hand delivered by RWS Received From:
Tracking Number: — Printed Name:

CASE INFORMATION

Shipping Agency: — Agency Ref. No.
Referring Agency: Offense:
Contact: Victim's Name(s):
Agency Address: Suspect's Name(s):
Phone Number: Fax Number:

ACCESSIONING LOG

Analyst: [illegible signature] Date: 5/23/05

Sample No.	Sample Description	Referring Agency ID
✓ 006	Jawbone - South grave	
✓ 007	Casket Wood - South grave	
✓ 008	Paper / Cloth material - South grave	
✓ 009	Skull and Mummified Brains - South grave	
✓ 010	Pelvis - South grave	
✓ 011	Left femur - South Grave	
✓ 012	Mandible + teeth - North grave	
✓ 013	Right femur - North grave	

EVIDENCE RETURN

Items Inspected By/Date: [signature] Date: 5/15/06
Evidence Returned By: Sonja Jones
Method of Shipment: Fed EX Tracking Number: 7909 2236 907
Evidence Released To: Date:
Printed Name: Time:

M:\Chain of Custody Form\Mito Chain of Custody (1 sign).doc Version: 08/11/03

Accredited by the American Society of Crime Laboratory Directors / Laboratory Accreditation Board

APPENDIX: 4. DNA EXTRACTIONS FROM JOHN MILLER AND WILLIAM HUDSPETH: Orchid Cellmark Laboratory's January 26, 2009 "Laboratory Report - Forensic Identity – Mitochondrial Analysis," for Case 4444 (for Case No. 2003-274)

[AUTHOR'S SUMMARY: Under "Results," DNA is listed for Miller's South grave's left femur, as specimen 4444-011, as "a mitochondrial DNA profile obtained." Under "Results," DNA is listed for Hudspeth's North Grave's right femur, as specimen 4444-013, as "mitochondrial DNA profile obtained." Under "Results," useless mixed DNA profile came from Hudspeth's "mandible and teeth" as specimen 4444-012.]

[AUTHOR'S NOTE: Useless mixed DNA came under "Results" from Hudspeth's "mandible and teeth" as specimen 4444-012, and from Dr. Lee's courthouse floorboard sample for the Deputy Bell's killing as specimen 4444-002A.]

LABORATORY REPORT - FORENSIC IDENTITY – MITOCHONDRIAL ANALYSIS

CASE DATA:

Referring Agency: Calvin D. Ostler
Cellmark Case #: FOR 4444
Cellmark Report #: FOR 4444C
Agency Contact: Calvin D. Ostler
Report Date: January 26, 2009

4444. Evidence Received:

Accession #	Sample Description	Receipt Date/Method of Delivery
4444-001A	Wood shavings "Lincoln County Courthouse #1"	8/4/04 FedEx
4444-002A	Wood shavings "Lincoln County Courthouse #2"	
4444-001B	Swabbing from "underside of bench #3"	
4444-002B	Swabbing from "underside of bench #4"	
4444-003B	Wood shavings "underside of bench #3"	
4444-004B	Wood shavings "underside of bench #4"	
4444-005	Reference hair - BTK?	1/31/05 USPS
4444-006	Jaw bone from south grave	5/19/05 Hand delivered to Orchid Cellmark (Stemmons Frwy) by Rick W. Staub (RWS)
4444-007	Casket wood from south grave	
4444-008	Paper/cloth material from south grave	
4444-009	Skull and mummified brains from south grave	
4444-010	Pelvis from south grave	
4444-011	Left femur from south grave	
4444-012	Mandible and teeth from north grave	
4444-013	Right femur from north grave	

NOTE: HAND-DELIVERED BY DR. STAUB

SOUTH GRAVE = JOHN MILLER

NORTH GRAVE = WILLIAM HUDSPETH

2. Results:

Mitochondrial DNA from specimen 4444-002A, 4444-005, 4444-011, 4444-012, and 4444-013 was amplified and sequenced at Hypervariable Regions I and II of the Mitochondrial Control Region. Sequence data are presented as variations from the Revised Cambridge Reference Sequence (rCRS). Bases not specifically listed are consistent with rCRS.

HVI (16024 – 16365)

	16153	16223	16266	16292
4444-011	•	T	•	T
4444-013	A	•	G	•
rCRS	G	C	C	C

(•) consistent with rCRS

4444-013: RANDOM MAN WILLIAM HUDSPETH'S FEMUR YIELDED MEANINGLESS DNA

HVII (73-340)

	73	189	204	207	263	309.1	315.1
4444-011	G	G	C	A	G	C	C
4444-013	•	•	•	•	G	303-340 INC	
rCRS	A	A	T	G	A	-	-

(•) consistent with rCRS (INC) inconclusive (-) no base present at this position

Samples 4444-002A, and 4444-012 indicate a mixture of two or more mitochondrial DNA profiles. Consequently, no sequence data are reported.

Specimen 4444-005 was extracted according to the accepted Mitochondrial DNA Extraction Protocol. No mitochondrial DNA was detected following amplification. Therefore, no sequence data were generated for comparison to reference specimens.

Procedures used in the analysis of this case adhere to the standards adopted by the DNA Advisory Board on DNA analysis methods.

4444-012: HUDSPETH MANDIBLE GAVE USELESS MIXED DNA

SOURCES

ANNOTATED BIBLIOGRAPHY

RELEVANT 19th CENTURY HISTORY

COMPREHENSIVE REFERENCES

Nolan, Frederick. *The War: A Documentary History*. Norman: University of Oklahoma Press. **1992.**

__________. *The West of Billy the Kid*. Norman: University of Oklahoma Press. **1998.**

HISTORICAL ORGANIZATIONS (PERIOD)

SANTA FE RING, 19th CENTURY

MODERN SOURCES

Brown, Richard Maxwell. *Strain of Violence: Historical Studies of American Violence and Vigilantism*. New York: Oxford University Press. 1975. (**New Mexico unique for assassination as part of political system**)

Caffey, David L. *Chasing the Santa Fe Ring: Power and Privilege in Territorial New Mexico*. Albuquerque, New Mexico: University of New Mexico Press. 2014.

__________. *Frank Springer and New Mexico: From the Colfax County War to the Emergence of Modern Santa Fe*. Texas A and M. University Press. 2007.

Cleaveland, Agnes Morley. *No Life for a Lady*. Boston: Houghton Mifflin. 1941.

__________. *Satan's Paradise: From Lucien Maxwell to Fred Lambert*. Boston: Houghton Mifflin Company. 1952.

Cleaveland, Norman, *Colfax County's Chronic Murder Mystery*. Santa Fe: New Mexico. The Rydel Press. 1977.

__________. *A Synopsis of the Great New Mexico Cover-up*. Self-printed. 1989.

__________. *Some Comments Norman Cleveland May Make to the Huntington Westerners on Sept. 19, 1987*. Unpublished.

__________. *Some Highlights of William R. Morley's Contribution to the Pioneer Development of the Southwest*. Self-printed. No Date.

__________. *The Great Santa Fe Cover-up*. Based on a Talk given Before the Santa Fe Historical Society on November 1, 1973. Self-printed. 1982.

Cleaveland, Norman and George Fitzpatrick. *The Morleys - Young Upstarts on the Southwest Frontier*. Albuquerque, New Mexico: Calvin Horn Publisher, Inc. 1971.

Cooper, Gale. *The Santa Fe Ring Versus Billy the Kid: The Making of An American Monster*. Albuquerque, New Mexico: Gelcour Books. 2018.

Klasner, Lilly. Eve Ball. Ed. *My Girlhood Among Outlaws*. Tucson, Arizona: The University of Arizona Press. 1972. Klasner, Lilly. Eve Ball. Ed. *My Girlhood Among Outlaws*. Tucson, Arizona: The University of Arizona Press. 1972. (**John Chisum's in jail write-up about Santa Fe Ring injustices to himself**)

Lamar, Howard Robert N. *The Far Southwest 1846 – 1912: A Territorial History*. New Haven and London: Yale University Press. 1966. (**Chapter 6 covers the Santa Fe Ring)**)

Meinig, D. W. *The Shaping of America. A Geographical Perspective on 500 Years of History. Vol. 3. Transcontinental America 1850 - 1915*. New Haven and London: Yale University Press. 1998. (**Pages 127 and 132 are on the Santa Fe Ring.**)

Montoya, María E. Translating Property. The Maxwell Land Grant and the Conflict Over Land in the American West, 1840-1900. Berkeley and Los Angeles: University of California Press. 2002.

Naegle, Conrad Keeler. *The History of Silver City, New Mexico 1870-1886.* University of New Mexico Bachelor of Arts thesis. Pages 30-60. Unpublished. 1943. Collection of the Silver City Museum, Silver City, New Mexico. (**Grant County rebellion**)

__________. "The Rebellion of Grant County, New Mexico in 1876." *Arizona and the West: A Quarterly Journal of History.* Autumn, 1968. Volume 10. Number 3. Tucson, Arizona: The University of Arizona Press. 1968. Pages 225-240. (**Grant County rebellion against Santa Fe Ring**)

Newman, Simeon Harrison III. "The Santa Fe Ring." *Arizona and the West.* Volume 12. Autumn 1970. Pages 269-288.

Otero, Miguel A. *My Life on the Frontier, 1882-1897: Incidents and Characters of the period when Kansas, Colorado, and New Mexico were Passing Through the Last of their Wild and Romantic Years.* New York: The Press of the Pioneers. 1935. Pages 232-233. (Quoted by Victor Westphall, *Thomas Benton Catron and His Era.* Page 188) (**Quote: "the 'Santa Fe Ring,' the real machine controlling the political situation in New Mexico."**)

Pearson, Jim Berry. *The Maxwell Land Grant.* Norman: University of Oklahoma Press. 1961.

Taylor, Morris F. *O.P. McMains and the Maxwell Land Grant Conflict.* Tucson, Arizona: The University of Arizona Press. 1979. (**Traces origins of the Santa Fe Ring**)

Theisen, Lee Scott. "Frank Warner Angel's Notes on New Mexico Territory, 1878." *Arizona and the West: A Quarterly Journal of History.* Winter 1976. Volume 18. Number 4. Pages 333-370. (**About the Angel notebook given to Lew Wallace and listing names of Santa Fe Ring members**)

Westphall, Victor. *Thomas Benton Catron and His Era.* Tucson, Arizona: University of Arizona Press. 1973. (**Ring-denier, who cites sources exposing the Ring**)

CONTEMPORARY SOURCES (CHRONOLOGICAL)

A.C.L. Editorial. "New Mexico, A Sorry Showing for a Would-be State, Tweed's Disciples Preying on the Populace, How the Territorial Ring is Run, Why the Territory Should Not Be Made a State. **March 13, 1876.** *The Boston Daily Globe.* Volume IX, Number 62. Newspaperarchive.com.

No Author. "A Contemplated Political Change." Grant County *Herald.* **September 16, 1876**. Quoted by Conrad Keeler Naegle in *The History of Silver City, New Mexico 1870-1886* doctoral thesis. Pages 39-40. (**Listing reasons to escape the Ring by annexing to Arizona Territory**)

Wallace, Lew. "Our mutual friend, M. Hinds, who will hand you this ..." Letter to A.H. Markland. **November 14, 1878**. Indiana Historical Society. Lew Wallace Collection. M0292. Box 3. Folder 17. (**Ring tries to remove him as governor**)

Leonard, Ira E. "When you left here I promised to write you concerning events transpiring here ..." Letter to Lew Wallace. **May 20, 1878 [sic - 79]**. Indiana Historical Society. Lew Wallace Collection. M0292. Box 4. Folder 10. (**Quote: "Santa Fe ring ... so long an incubus on the government."**)

Wallace, Lew. "I have the honor to inform you that the Legislature of this Territory adjourned ..." **February 16, 1880**. Letter to Carl Schurz. Indiana Historical Society. Lew Wallace Collection. M0292. Box 4. Folder 14. (**Key documentation of Catron as head of the Santa Fe Ring, and Wallace's Ring opposition**)

No Author. "White Cap's Proclamation." *Las Vegas Optic.* March 12, 1880. (**Manifesto against land-grabbing Catron and the Ring**)

No Author. "The Santa Fe Ring is the most corrupt combination that ever cursed any country or community." Las Cruces *Thirty-Four Newspaper.* **October 27, 1880**. From Victor Westphall, *Thomas Benton Catron and His Era.* Page 186.

No Author. "The Ring must soon discover that the time has passed in New Mexico when men can be herded like so many sheep ..." *Albuquerque Daily Democrat.* **March 4, 1884**. (Quoted by Victor Westphall, *Thomas Benton Catron and His*

Era. Page 191.) (**About Santa Fe Ring control of appointments to legislature**)

No Author. *Santa Fe Weekly New Mexican Review.* **March 13, 1884.** *Santa Fe Weekly New Mexican Review.* (**Accusation of Catron and the Ring of controlling grand juries and** bribery)

No Author. *Albuquerque Daily Democrat.* **March 15, 1884.** (**Oscar P. McMains "Memorial" against land-grabbing Ring**)

Valdez, Jose and Enrique Mares. "Scorching Letter, The Knights of Labor Send a Communication to Powderly! Politicians Arraigned! The Boldest Document Ever Issued in the Territory." **August 18, 1890.** *Las Vegas Democrat.* Volume 1. Center for Southwest Studies. Thomas B. Catron Papers, MSS 29, Series 102, Box 8, Folder 4. (**Gives history of Santa Fe Ring with T.B. Catron as head**)

No Author. *Los Angeles Times.* **1899.** Undated clipping, Laughlin Papers, State Records Center, Santa Fe, New Mexico. Quoted by Victor Westphall, *Thomas Benton Catron and His Era.* Page 285. (**Joking article about the Santa Fe Ring**)

EXPOSÉS Of (CONTEMPORARY)

COMPLAINT ABOUT TO PRESIDENT RUTHERFORD B. HAYES

Matchett, W.B. and Mary E. McPherson " W.B. Matchett and Mary E. McPherson 'Make certain charges against the U S. Officials in the Territory of New Mexico.' " Letter to President Rutherford B. Hayes. Received and filed **May 1, 1877**. Interior Department Papers 1850-1907; Appointments Division and Subsequent Actions. Microfilm File Case Number 44-4-8-3. Record Group 48. Microfilm No. M750. Roll 1. National Archives and Records Administration. U. S. Department of Justice. Washington, D.C. (**Sent to President Rutherford B. Hayes and Secretary of the Interior Carl Schurz.**)

McPherson, Mary and W.B. Matchett. "To the President. Please make the enclosed a part of the evidence in the case of "Charges Against New Mexican Officials" Letter to President Rutherford B. Hayes. **May 3, 1877**. McPherson, Mary E. Letters and Petitions to President Rutherford B. Hayes re: Removal Governor Axtell and the Santa Fe Ring. Interior Department Papers 1850-1907; Appointments Division and Subsequent Actions. Microfilm File Case Number 44-4-8-3. Record Group 48. Microfilm Roll M750. National Archives and Records Administration. U.S. Department of Justice. Washington, D.C. (**Addendum to their May, 1877 "Certain Charges Against U.S. Officials in New Mexico Territory."**)

__________. "The Secretary of the Interior, Sir – Accompanying please find copy of charges, &c., against S.B. Axtell, Governor, and Other New Mexican Officials ..." "Charges Against New Mexican Officials." Letter to Secretary of the Interior Carl Schurz. **May 5, 1877**. McPherson, Mary E. Letters and Petitions to President Rutherford B. Hayes re: Removal Governor Axtell and the Santa Fe Ring. Interior Department Papers 1850-1907; Appointments Division and Subsequent Actions. Microfilm File Case Number 44-4-8-3. Record Group 48. Microfilm Roll M750. National Archives and Records Administration. U.S. Department of Justice. Washington, D. C.

__________."*In the Matter of Charges vs. Gov. S.B. Axtell and Other New Mexico Officials. Submitted to the Departments of the Interior and Justice.* **August, 1877.** Printed as a 31 page booklet. No publisher listed. Indiana Historical Society. Lew Wallace Collection. M0292. Box 3. Folder 20. (**About the Santa Fe Ring, Catron, and Elkins; in Lew Wallace's personal possession**)

McPherson, Mary. "Please place before the Attorney General ..." Letter to President Rutherford B. Hayes. **August 23, 1877.** Interior Department Papers 1850-1907; Appointments Division and Subsequent Actions. Microfilm File Case Number 44-4-8-3. Record Group 48. Microfilm No. M750. Roll 1. National Archives and Records Administration. U. S. Department of Justice. Washington, D.C.

Springer, Frank. Deposition to Investigator Frank Warner Angel for the Departments of Justice and the Interior. **August 9, 1878**. Frank Warner Angel report titled *In the Matter of the Investigation of the Charges Against S.B. Axtell Governor of New Mexico*. October 3, 1878. Interior Department Papers 1850-1907; Appointments Division and Subsequent Actions. Microfilm Case File No. 44-4-8-3. Record Group 48. Microfilm Roll M750. National Archives and Records Administration. U.S. Department of Interior. Washington, D.C.

(SEE: Thomas Benton Catron; Frank Warner Angel, Legislature Revolt, Grant County Rebellion, Colfax County War, Lincoln County War)

NORTH CAROLINA REGULATORS, 18th CENTURY

Kars, Marjoline. *Breaking Loose Together: The Regulator Rebellion in Pre-Revolutionary North Carolina*. Chapel Hill and London: The University of North Carolina Press. 2002.

Maier, Pauline. *From Resistance to Revolution: Colonial radicals and the development of American opposition to Britain, 1765-1776*. New York and London: W.W. Norton & Company. 1991.

LINCOLN COUNTY REGULATORS, 19th CENTURY

Lody, William F. "Gold Bullet Sport; The Knights of the Overland". *Beadle's Dime New York Library*. 7(83). New York: Beadle & Adams, Publishers. December 17, 1874.

Cooms, Oll. "The Boy Ranger: or, The Heiress of the Golden Horn." *Pocket Series. No. 11.* New York: Beadle & Adams, Publishers. 1874.

Wheeler, Edward L. *The Deadwood Dick Library*. "A Tale of the Regulators and Road-Agents of the Black Hills. The Double Daggers; or, Deadwood Dick's Defiance." Beadles Half Dime Library. No. 20. Cleveland, Ohio: Arthur Westbrook Co. 1877.

__________."Deadwood Dick, The Prince of the Road: or The Black Rider of the Black Hills". *The Deadwood Dick Library. 1(1).* Cleveland, Ohio: The Arthur Westbrook Co. 1877.

No Author. "The Rover of the Forest." *Munro's Ten Cent Novels*. No. 42. New York: George Munro & Co. 1864.

LINCOLN COUNTY REGULATOR MANIFESTO (BY BILLY BONNEY)

Regulator. "Mr. Walz. Sir ..." Letter to Edgar Walz. July 13, 1878. Adjutant General's Office. File 1405 AGO 1878. (Quoted in Maurice Garland Fulton, *History of the Lincoln County War*. Tucson: University of Arizona Press. 1975. pages 246-247, and Frederick Nolan, *The Lincoln County War: A Documentary History*, page 310.)

NEW MEXICO TERRITORY REBELLIONS AGAINST THE SANTA FE RING (CHRONOLOGICAL)

LEGISLATURE REVOLT (1872)

No Author. *Journal of the House of Representatives of the Territory of New Mexico, Session of 1871-1872*. Santa Fe: A.P. Sullivan. **1872.** Pages 144-154. (**Confirms troops used by Ring to suppress the Legislature Revolt of 1872**)

No Author. "Our Own Dear Steve, How Elkins Made His Influence Felt in New Mexico – The Ring in Which a Judge Figured – Politics in 1870. *Las Vegas Daily Optic*. **September 2, 1884.** (Reprinted from the *Omaha Herald*) Front Page. Volume V,

Number 258, Column 4. Newspaperarchive.com. (**Exposing the Ring in the 1872 Legislature Revolt with Catron's and Elkins's corrupt alliance with Judge Joseph Palen**)

GRANT COUNTY REBELLION (1876)

MODERN SOURCES

Naegle, Conrad Keeler. *The History of Silver City, New Mexico 1870-1886*. University of New Mexico Bachelor of Arts thesis. Pages 30-60. Unpublished. 1943. Collection of the Silver City Museum, Silver City, New Mexico.

__________. "The Rebellion of Grant County, New Mexico in 1876." *Arizona and the West: A Quarterly Journal of History*. Autumn, 1968. Volume 10. Number 3. Tucson, Arizona: The University of Arizona Press. 1968. Pages 225-240. (**Rebellion against Santa Fe Ring**)

CONTEMPORARY SOURCES (CHRONOLOGICAL)

No Author. "Diario del Consejo der Territorio de Neuvo Mejico, Session de 1871-1872." *Santa Fe New Mexican*. **January 8, 1872**. Santa Fe: A.P. Sullivan. 1872. Pages 144-154. New Mexico Supreme Court Library. Santa Fe, New Mexico. (**A Ring expurgated document, with a copy found in 1942 by Conrad Naegle; confirming troops used by Ring to suppress Territorial legislature**)

No Author. "Diario del Consejo der Territorio de Neuvo Mejico, Session de 1871-1872. Las Cruces *Borderer*. **January 24, 1872**. Pages 110-113. (**Don Diego Archuleta, President of the Council, gives speech objecting to troops in legislature**)

No Author. "Ring influence [in the Territorial legislature is] being actively used against every measure that tends to do justice" [in Grant and Doña Ana Counties]." *Grant County Herald*. **August 8, 1875.** Quoted by Conrad Keeler Naegle in *The History of Silver City, New Mexico 1870-1886,* doctoral thesis. Page 39.

No Author. "A Contemplated Political Change." Grant County *Herald*. **September 16, 1876**. Quoted by Conrad Keeler Naegle in *The History of Silver City, New Mexico 1870-1886* doctoral thesis. Pages 39-40. (**Listing reasons to escape the Ring by annexing to Arizona Territory**)

No Author. [Grant County should not] "sort o' wait and hear from Santa Fe ... before taking action." Tucson *Arizona Citizen*. **September 23, 1876.** Quoted by Conrad Keeler Naegle in *The History of Silver City, New Mexico 1870-1886* doctoral thesis. Page 41. (**Arizona encourages escape from Santa Fe Ring**)

No Author. Grant County *Herald*. **September 23, 1876**. (**Need for school system stressed.**)

No Author. Grant County *Herald*. **September 30, 1876**. (**"Annexation Meeting" announced**)

No Author. "Proceedings of Grant County Annexation Meeting." Grant County *Herald*. **Saturday October 7, 1876**. Page 2. Columns 1 and 2. Collection of the Silver City, New Mexico, Museum. (**"Grant County Declaration of Independence"**)

No Author. Grant County *Herald*. " 'Petition to Remove Judge Bristol. We the undersigned citizens of the Third Judicial District of the Territory of New Mexico, without regard to party, would respectfully request and petition for the removal of Judge Warren Bristol ...' " No date. **1876 or 1877**.(Quoted in "W.B. Matchett and Mary E. McPherson 'Make certain charges against the U.S. Officials in the Territory of New Mexico.' " Letter to President Rutherford B. Hayes. Received and filed May 1, 1877. Interior Department Papers 1850-1907; Appointments Division and Subsequent Actions. Microfilm File Case Number 44-4-8-3. Record Group 48. Microfilm No. M750. Roll 1. National Archives and Records Administration. U.S. Department of Justice. Washington, D.C.) (**Anti-Santa Fe Ring article**)

(SEE: Santa Fe Ring; Thomas Benton Catron; Stephen Benton Elkins)

COLFAX COUNTY WAR (1877)

MODERN SOURCES

Caffey, David L. *Frank Springer and New Mexico: From the Colfax County War to the Emergence of Modern Santa Fe.* Texas A and M. University Press. 2007.

Cleaveland, Norman. *The Morleys - Young Upstarts on the Southwest Frontier.* Albuquerque, New Mexico: Calvin Horn Publisher, Inc. 1971.

Dunham, Harold H. "New Mexican Land Grants with Special Reference to the Title Papers of the Maxwell Grant." *New Mexico Historical Review.* (January 1955) Vol. 30, No. 1. pp. 1 - 23.

Keleher, William A. *The Maxwell Land Grant. A New Mexico Item.* Albuquerque, New Mexico: University of New Mexico Press. 1964.

Lamar, Howard Roberts. *The Far Southwest 1846 - 1912. A Territorial History.* New Haven and London: Yale University Press. 1966.

Montoya, María E. *Translating Property. The Maxwell Land Grant and the Conflict Over Land in the American West, 1840-1900.* Berkeley and Los Angeles, California: University of California Press. 2002.

Murphy, Lawrence R. *Lucien Bonaparte Maxwell. Napoleon of the Southwest.* Norman: University of Oklahoma Press. 1983.

Pearson, Jim Berry. *The Maxwell Land Grant.* Norman: University of Oklahoma Press. 1961.

Poe, Sophie. *Buckboard Days.* Albuquerque, New Mexico: University of New Mexico Press. 1964.

Taylor, Morris F. *O.P. McMains and the Maxwell Land Grant Conflict.* Tucson, Arizona: The University of Arizona Press. 1979.

CONTEMPORARY SOURCES (CHRONOLOGICAL)

No author. "Anarchy at Cimarron." *Santa Fe Weekly New Mexican.* **November 16, 1875. (Ringite backing of Axtell's use of troops in the Colfax County War)**

Dawson, Will. Editorial. *Cimarron News and Press.* **December 31, 1875. (Ring-biased editorial by temporary editor blaming citizens for unrest)**

No Author. Report on murder trial for Franklin Tolby. Pueblo, *Colorado Chieftain.* **May 25, 1876**. Quoting *Daily New Mexican,* May 1, 1876. From Morris F. Taylor. *O.P. McMains and the Maxwell Land Grant Conflict.* Tucson, Arizona: The University of Arizona Press. 1979. Page 49. **(Ring-biased jury instructions by Judge Henry Waldo to protect Ring murderers of Tolby)**

No Author. "Rejoicing at Cimarron," "Axtell's Head Falls at Last," "General Lew. Wallace Appointed Governor." *Cimarron News and Press.* **September 6, 1878.**

No Author. *Santa Fe Weekly New Mexican.* **September 21, 1878 and October 19, 1878. (Ring-biased accolades for removed Gov. Axtell)**

(SEE: Regulators, Santa Fe Ring; Thomas Benton Catron; Stephen Benton Elkins, Colfax County War, Lincoln County War)

LINCOLN COUNTY WAR (1878)

MODERN SOURCES

Cramer, T. Dudley. *The Pecos Ranchers in the Lincoln County War.* Orinda, California: Branding Iron Press. 1996.

Fulton, Maurice Garland. Robert N. Mullin. Ed. *History of the Lincoln County War.* Tucson, Arizona: The University of Arizona Press. 1997.

Jacobsen, Joel. *Such Men as Billy the Kid. The Lincoln County War Reconsidered.* Lincoln and London: University of Nebraska Press. 1994.

Keleher, William A. *The Fabulous Frontier: Twelve New Mexico Items.* Albuquerque, New Mexico: The University of New Mexico Press. 1962.

___________. *County 1869-1881*. Albuquerque, New Mexico: University of New Mexico Press. 1957.

Mullin, Robert N. Re: Frank Warner Angel Meeting with President Hayes. August, 1878. Binder RNM, VI, M. Midland, Texas: Nita Stewart Haley Memorial Library and J. Evetts Haley History Center. (Unpublished).

Nolan, Frederick W. *The Life and Death of John Henry Tunstall*. Albuquerque, New Mexico: The University of New Mexico Press. 1965.

___________. *The Lincoln County War: A Documentary History*. Norman: University of Oklahoma Press. 1992.

___________. *The West of Billy the Kid*. Norman: University of Oklahoma Press. 1998.

Rasch, Philip J. *Gunsmoke in Lincoln County*. Laramie, Wyoming: National Association for Outlaw and Lawmen History, Inc. with University of Wyoming. 1997.

___________. Robert K. DeArment. Ed. *Warriors of Lincoln County*. Laramie: National Association for Outlaw and Lawmen History, Inc. with University of Wyoming. 1998.

Utley, Robert M. *High Noon in Lincoln. Violence on the Western Frontier*. Albuquerque, New Mexico: University of New Mexico Press. 1987.

Wilson, John P. *Merchants, Guns, and Money: The Story of Lincoln County and Its Wars*. Santa Fe, New Mexico: Museum of New Mexico Press. 1987.

No Author. "Disturbances in the Territories, 1878 - 1894. Lawlessness in New Mexico." Senate Documents. 67th Congress. 2nd Session. December 5, 1921 - September 22, 1922. pp. 176 - 187. Washington, D.C.: Government Printing Office. 1922.

CONTEMPORARY SOURCES (CHRONOLOGICAL)

No Author. "Brady Inventory McSween Property." **February, 1878**. Herman B. Weisner Papers, ca. 1957-1992. New Mexico State University Library at Las Cruses. Rio Grande Historical Collections. Accession No. Weisner Ms 0249. Box 10. Folder M15. Folder Name. "Will and Testament A. McSween."

No Author. "Amnesty for Matthews and Long in the Third Judicial Court April Term 1879." **April, 1879**. Herman B. Weisner Papers, ca. 1957-1992. New Mexico State University Library at Las Cruces. Rio Grande Historical Collections. Accession No. Ms 0249. Box 1. Folder 4. Folder Name. "Amnesty."

No Author. "Charges against Jessie Evans and John Kinney." Doña Ana County Civil and Criminal Docket Book. **August 18, 1875 to November 7, 1878**. Herman B. Weisner Papers, ca. 1957-1992. New Mexico State University Library at Las Cruces. Rio Grande Historical Collections. Accession No. Ms 0249. Box 13. Folder V 3. Folder Name. "Venue, Change Of."

No Author. "Dismissal of Cases Against Dolan, Matthews, Peppin, October 1879 District Court." **October, 1879**. Herman B. Weisner Papers, ca. 1957-1992. New Mexico State University Library at Las Cruces. Rio Grande Historical Collections. Accession No. Ms 0249. Box 13. Folder V3. Folder Name: "Venue, Change Of."

No Author. "Killers of Tunstall. February 18, 1879." Herman B. Weisner Papers, ca. 1957-1992. New Mexico State University Library at Las Cruses. Rio Grande Historical Collections. Accession No. Ms 0249. Box 12. Folder T1. Folder Name: "Tunstall, John H."

No Author. "Lincoln County Indictments July 1872 - 1881." Herman B. Weisner Papers, ca. 1957-1992. New Mexico State University Library at Las Cruces. Rio Grande Historical Collections. Accession No. Ms 0249. Box 8. Folder L11. Folder Name. "Lincoln Co. Indictments."

(SEE: William H. Bonney, John Henry Tunstall, Alexander McSween, Samuel Beach Axtell, Frank Warner Angel, Nathan Augustus Monroe Dudley)

HISTORY OF WILLIAM HENRY BONNEY (WILLIAM HENRY McCARTY, HENRY ANTRIM, AKA BILLY THE KID)

BIOGRAPHICAL SOURCES

Abbott, E.C. ("Teddy Blue") and Helena Huntington Smith. *We Pointed Them North: Recollections of a Cowpuncher.* Norman, Oklahoma: University of Oklahoma Press. 1955. (**Billy the Kid's multi-culturalism, Page 47.**)

Anaya, Paco. *I Buried Billy.* College Station, Texas: Creative Publishing Company. 1991.

Ball, Eve. *Ma'am Jones of the Pecos.* Tucson, Arizona: The University of Arizona Press. 1969.

Bell, Bob Boze. *The Illustrated Life and Times of Billy the Kid.* Cave Creek, Arizona: Boze Books. 1992. (Frank Coe quote about the Kid's cartridge use, Page 45.)

Bell, Bob Boze. *The Illustrated Life and Times of Billy the Kid.* Second Edition. Phoenix, Arizona: Tri Star-Boze Publications, Inc. 1996.

Burns, Walter Noble. *The Saga of Billy the Kid.* Stamford, Connecticut: Longmeadow Press. 1992. (Original printing: 1926, Doubleday.)

__________. *"I also know that the Kid and Paulita were sweethearts."* Unpublished letter to Jim East. June 3, 1926. Robert N. Mullin Collection. File RNM, IV, NM, 116-117. Nita Stewart Haley Memorial Museum, Haley Library. Midland, Texas.

Coe, George with Doyce B. Nunis, Jr. Ed. *Frontier Fighter. The Autobiography of George Coe Who Fought and Rode With Billy the Kid.* Chicago: R. R. Donnelley and Sons Company. 1984.

Cooper, Gale. *Billy the Kid's Writings, Words, and Wit.* Gelcour Books: Albuquerque: New Mexico. 2012.

__________. *Billy and Paulita: The Saga of Billy the Kid, Paulita Maxwell, and the Santa Fe Ring.* Gelcour Books: Albuquerque: New Mexico. 2012.

__________. *The Lost Pardon of Billy the Kid: An Analysis Factoring in the Santa Fe Ring, Governor Lew Wallace's Dilemma, and a Territory in Rebellion.* Gelcour Books: Albuquerque: New Mexico. 2017.

__________. *The Santa Fe Ring Versus Billy the Kid: The Making of an American Monster.* Gelcour Books: Albuquerque: New Mexico. 2018.

Garrett, Pat F. *The Authentic Life of Billy the Kid The Noted Desperado of the Southwest, Whose Deeds of Daring and Blood Made His Name a Terror in New Mexico, Arizona, and Northern Mexico.* Santa Fe, New Mexico: New Mexico Printing and Publishing Co. 1882. (Edition used: Edited by Maurice Garland Fulton. New York: The Macmillan Company.)

Hendron, J. W. *The Story of Billy the Kid. New Mexico's Number One Desperado.* New York: Indian Head Books. **1994**.

Hoyt, Henry. *A Frontier Doctor.* Boston and New York: Houghton Mifflin Company. 1929. (**Describes Billy's superior abilities. Pages 93-94, including fluency in Spanish.**)

Jacobsen, Joel. *Such Men as Billy the Kid. The Lincoln County War Reconsidered.* Lincoln and London: University of Nebraska Press. **1994**.

Kadlec, Robert F. *They "Knew" Billy the Kid. Interviews with Old-Time New Mexicans.* Santa Fe, New Mexico: Ancient City Press. **1987**.

Keleher, William A. *The Fabulous Frontier: Twelve New Mexico Items.* Albuquerque, New Mexico: The University of New Mexico Press. **1962**.

__________.*Violence in Lincoln County 1869-1881.* Albuquerque, New Mexico: University of New Mexico Press. **1957**.

Koop, W.E. *Billy the Kid: The Trail of a Kansas Legend.* Self Published. **1965**.

McFarland, David F. Reverend. *Ledger: Session Records 1867-1874. Marriages in Santa Fe New Mexico. "Mr. William H. Antrim and Mrs. Catherine McCarty."*

March 1, 1873. (Unpublished). Santa Fe, New Mexico: First Presbyterian Church of Santa Fe.

Meadows, John P. "Billy the Kid to John P. Meadows on the Peñasco, May 1-2, 1881." *Roswell Daily Record*. **February 16, 1931**. Page 6.

__________. Ed. John P. Wilson. *Pat Garrett and Billy the Kid as I Knew Them: Reminiscences of John P. Meadows*. Albuquerque: University of New Mexico Press. **2004**.

Mullin, Robert N. *The Boyhood of Billy the Kid*. Monograph 17, Southwestern Studies 5(1). El Paso, Texas: Texas Western Press. University of Texas at El Paso. 1967.

Poe, John W. *The Death of Billy the Kid*. (Introduction by Maurice Garland Fulton). Boston and New York: Houghton Mifflin Company. 1933.

__________. "The Killing of Billy the Kid." (a personal letter written at Roswell, New Mexico to Mr. Charles Goodnight, Goodnight P.C., Texas) July 10, 1917. Earle Vandale Collection. 1813-946. No 2H475. Center for American History. University of Texas at Austin.

Rakocy, Bill. *Billy the Kid*. El Paso, Texas: Bravo Press. 1985.

Rasch, Phillip J. *Trailing Billy the Kid*. Laramie, Wyoming: National Association for Outlaw and Lawman History, Inc. with University of Wyoming. 1995.

Russell, Randy. *Billy the Kid. The Story - The Trial*. Lincoln, New Mexico: The Crystal Press. 1994.

Scanland, John M. (Foreword) using Patrick F. Garrett, Patrick F. *Billy the Kid: The Outlaw. Authentic Story of Billy the Kid by Pat F. Garrett. Greatest Sheriff of the Old Southwest*. New York: Atomic Books Inc. **1946**. Oberlin College Library Special Collections, Pop Culture. Walter F. Tunks Collection. Number 2344. (**Pirated edition of Pat Garrett's *Authentic Life of Billy the Kid* featuring apocryphal outlawry of Billy the Kid**)

Siringo, Charles A. *The History of Billy the Kid*. Santa Fe: New Mexico. Privately Printed. 1920.

Tuska, Jon. *Billy the Kid. His Life and Legend*. Westport, Connecticut: Greenwood Press. 1983.

Utley, Robert M. *High Noon in Lincoln. Violence on the Western Frontier*. Albuquerque, New Mexico: University of New Mexico Press. 1987.

__________. *Billy the Kid. A Short and Violent Life*. Lincoln and London: University of Nebraska Press. 1989.

Weddle, Jerry. *Antrim is My Stepfather's Name. The Boyhood of Billy the Kid*. Monograph 9, Globe, Arizona: Arizona Historical Society. 1993.

No Author. "The Prisoners Who Saw the Kid Kill Olinger." April 28, 1881. Herman B. Weisner Papers, ca. 1957-1992. New Mexico State University Library at Las Cruces. Rio Grande Historical Collections. Accession No. Ms 0249. Box 30 T. Folder 8.

WORDS OF (CHRONOLOGICAL)

SPENCERIAN PENMANSHIP

Spencer, Platt Rogers. *Spencerian Penmanship*. New York: Ivison, Phinney, Blakemont Co. **1857.**

__________________. *Spencerian System of Practical Penmanship*. New York: Ivison, Phinney, Blakemont Co. **1864.** (Reprinted by Milford, Michigan: Mott Media, Inc. 1985.)

Spencer, H.C. (Prepared for the "Spencerian Authors) *Spencerian Key to Practical Penmanship*. New York: Ivison, Phinney, Blakemont, Taylor & Co. **1874**.

__________________. (Prepared for the "Spencerian Authors) *Theory of Spencerian Penmanship for Schools and Private Learners Developed by Questions and Answers with Practical Illustrations. Designed to Be Used by Pupils in Connection With the Use of Spencerian Copybooks*. New York: Ivison, Phinney, Blakemont, Taylor & Co. **1874**.

Spencerian Authors. *Theory of Spencerian Penmanship for Schools and Private Learners Developed by Questions and Answers with Practical Illustrations: Designed to Be Used by Pupils in Connection With the Use of Spencerian Copybooks.* (New York: Ivison, Phinney, Blakemont, Taylor & Co. 1874.) Reprinted and modified by Milford, Michigan: Mott Media, Inc. **1985. (Page 30 describes forming "the capital stem;" pages 2-7 describe "position" and "hand-arm movements;" and page 45 describes the pen and "shading;" all used by Billy Bonney)**

Sull, Michael, *Spencerian Script and Ornamental Penmanship.* Prairie Village: Kansas. (Unpublished, undated, modern manual).

Cooper, Gale. *Billy the Kid's Writings, Words, and Wit.* Albuquerque, New Mexico: Gelcour Books. **2012**.

HOYT BILL OF SALE

Bonney, W H. "Know all persons by these presents ..." Thursday, **October 24, 1878.** Collection of Panhandle-Plains Historical Museum, Canyon, Texas. Item No. X1974-98/1. (**Hoyt Bill of Sale**)

LETTERS TO LEW WALLACE

Bonney, W H. "I have heard you will give one thousand $ dollars for my body which as I see it means alive ..." **March 13(?), 1879**. Fray Angélico Chávez Historical Library, Santa Fe, New Mexico. Lincoln County Heritage Trust Collection. (AC481).

__________. "I will keep the keep the appointment ..." **March 20, 1879**. Indiana Historical Society. M0292.

__________. "... on the Pecos." ("Billie" letter fragment). **March 24(?), 1879**. Indiana Historical Society. Lew Wallace Collection. M0292. Box 4. Folder 7.

__________. "I noticed in the *Las Vegas* Gazette a piece which stated that 'Billy the Kid' ..." **December 12, 1880**. Indiana Historical Society. Lew Wallace Collection. M0292.

__________. "I would like to see you ..." **January 1, 1881**. Indiana Historical Society. Lew Wallace Collection. M0292.

__________. "I wish you would come down to the jail and see me ..." **March 2, 1881**. Fray Angélico Chávez Historical Library, Santa Fe, New Mexico. Lincoln County Heritage Trust Collection. (AC481).

__________. "I wrote you a little note day before yesterday ..." **March 4, 1881**. Indiana Historical Society. Lew Wallace Collection. M0292.

__________. "For the last time I ask ..." **March 27, 1881**. Indiana Historical Society. Lew Wallace Collection. M0292.

(SEE: Lew Wallace response letters to)

LETTER TO SQUIRE WILSON

Bonney, W H. "Friend Wilson ..." **March 18, 1879**. Indiana Historical Society. Lew Wallace Collection. M0292. (**For pardon negotiation with Lew Wallace**)

LETTER TO EDGAR CAYPLESS

Bonney, W H. "I would have written before ..." **April 15, 1881**. Copy in William Kelleher's *Violence in Lincoln County;* originally reproduced in Griggs *History of the Mesilla Valley*. (**Original lost**)

REGULATOR MANIFESTO LETTER

Regulator. "Mr. Walz. Sir ..." Letter to Edgar Walz. **July 13, 1878**. Adjutant General's Office. File 1405 AGO 1878. (Quoted in Maurice Garland Fulton, *History of the Lincoln County War*. Tucson: University of Arizona Press. 1975. Pages 246-247.)

DEPOSITION OF

Bonney, William Henry. Deposition to Frank Warner Angel. **June 8, 1878**. Frank Warner Angel report, Pages 314-319 from *In the Matter of the Examination of the Causes and Circumstances of the Death of John H. Tunstall a British Subject.* Report filed October 4, 1878. Angel Report. Records of the Justice Department. Record Group 60. Class 44 Litigation Files. Container 21. National Archives and Records Administration. U.S. Department of Justice. Washington, D.C. or Angel Report in Interior Department Papers 1850-1907; Appointments Division and Subsequent Actions. Microfilm File Case Number 44-4-8-3. Record Group 48. Microfilm No. M750. Roll 1. National Archives and Records Administration. U.S. Department of Justice. Washington, D.C.

COURT TESTIMONY OF

Rynerson, William. "The Grand Jurors for the Territory of New Mexico taken from the body of the good and lawful men of the County of Lincoln ..." Indictments of the April, Lincoln County Grand Jury. **April 28, 1879**. Herman B. Weisner Papers, ca. 1957-1992. New Mexico State University Library at Las Cruces. Rio Grande Historical Collection. Accession No. Ms 0249. Box 4/39. Folder E-Z. Folder Name: "Jessie Evans Accessory to Murder." **(Billy's testimony for pardon bargain)**

Bonney, William Henry. Testimony in Court of Inquiry for N.A.M. Dudley. **May 28-29, 1879**. *Proceedings of a Court of Inquiry in the Case of Lt. Col. N.A.M. Dudley (May 2,1879 – July 5, 1879).* File No. QQ1284. (Boxes 3304, 3305, 3305A); Court Martial Files 1809-1894. Records of the Office of the Judge Advocate General - Army. Record Group 153. Old Military and Civil Branch. National Archives and Records Administration. Washington, D. C.

INTERVIEW WITH LEW WALLACE OF

Wallace, Lew. "Statements by Kid, made Sunday night **March 23, 1879**." (Cover sheet reads: "Fort Stanton, March 20, 1879. William Bonney ("Kid") relative to arrangement with him." Indiana Historical Society. Lew Wallace Collection. M0292. Box 4. Folder 6.

NEWSPAPER INTERVIEWS BY

Wilcox, Lucius "Lute" M. (city editor, owner, J.H. Koogler). "The Kid. Interview with Billy Bonney The Best Known Man in New Mexico." *Las Vegas Gazette.* **December 27, 1880**.

__________. Interview, at train depot. *Las Vegas Gazette.* **December 28, 1880. (Has Billy Bonney's "adios" quote.)**

No Author. "Something About the Kid." *Santa Fe Daily New Mexican.* **April 3, 1881. (Quote: "two hundred men have been killed ... [I] did not kill all of them.")**

No Author. "I got a rough deal ..." *Mesilla News.* **April 15, 1881**.

Newman, Simon N. Ed. Interview with "The Kid." *Newman's Semi-Weekly*. **April 15, 1881**.

__________. Departure from Mesilla. *Newman's Semi-Weekly.* **April 15, 1881**.

No Author. "Advise persons never to engage in killing." *Mesilla News.* **April 16, 1881. (Billy Bonney's quote)**

FEDERAL INDICTMENT OF

Catron, Thomas Benton. "Case No. 411. The United States vs. Charles Bowdry [Bowdre], Doc Scurlock, Henry Brown, Henry Antrim alias "Kid," John Middleton, Stephen Stevens, John Scroggins, George Coe and Frederick Waite." **June 21, 1878**. Herman B. Weisner Papers, ca. 1957-1992. New Mexico State University Library at Las Cruces. Rio Grande Historical Collections. Accession No. Ms 0249. Box 1. B-Folder 4. Name: Andrew Roberts Indictment.

GENERAL LETTERS ABOUT

Kimbrell, George. "I have the honor to request that you will furnish me a posse ..." Letter to Lieutenant Millard Filmore Goodwin. **February 20, 1879**. Indiana Historical Society. Lew Wallace Collection. Box 4, Folder 3. (**For pursuit of William Bonney and Yginio Salazar**)

Goodwin, Millard Filmore. ""I have the honor to submit the following report regarding my duties performed ..." Letter to Fort Stanton Post Adjutant John Loud. **February 23, 1879**. Indiana Historical Society. Lew Wallace Collection. Box 4. Folder 3. (**Assisting pursuit of William Bonney and Yginio Salazar**)

Dudley, Nathan Augustus Monroe. "I enclose herewith report of 2nd Lieut. M.F. Goodwin ..." Letter to Acting Assistant Adjutant General at Headquarters. **February 24, 1879**. Indiana Historical Society. Lew Wallace Collection. M0292. Box 4, Folder 3. (**Documents military pursuit of William Bonney**)

Leonard, Ira. "The air is filled tonight with 'rumors of wars ... Letter to Lew Wallace. **April 20, 1879**. Indiana Historical Society. Lew Wallace Collection. M0292. Box 4. Folder 9. (**About DA Rynerson: "He is bent on going for the Kid"**)

Hoyt, Henry F. "This time it is me who is apologizing for the long delay in answering ..." (Letter to Lew Wallace Jr.) **April 27, 1927**. Indiana Historical Society. Lew Wallace Collection. M0292. Box 14, Folder 11. (**About Billy Bonney's Bill of Sale to him**)

__________. "Copy of a bill of sale written by Wm H. Bonney ..." Letter to Lew Wallace Jr. **April 27, 1927**. Indiana Historical Society. Lew Wallace Collection. M0292. Box 14, Folder 11. (**Calls Billy Bonney "a natural leader of men"**)

SECRET SERVICE REPORTS ABOUT

Wild, Azariah F. "Daily Reports of U. S. Secret Service Agents, Azariah F. Wild." Microfilm T-915. Record Group 87. Rolls 308 (July 1, 1879 - June 30, 1881) National Archives and Records Department. Department of the Treasury. United States Secret Service. Washington, D. C.

LEW WALLACE WRITINGS TO AND ABOUT

WALLACE'S LETTERS TO (CHRONOLOGICAL)

Wallace, Lew. "Come to the house of Squire Wilson ..." Letter to W H. Bonney. **March 15, 1879**. Indiana Historical Society. Lew Wallace Collection. M0292. Box 4. Folder 6.

__________. "The escape makes no difference in arrangements ..." Letter to W.H. Bonney. **March 20, 1879**. Indiana Historical Society. Lew Wallace Collection. M0292. Box 4. Folder 6.

WALLACE'S LETTERS ABOUT (CHRONOLOGICAL)

Wallace, Lew. "I have just ascertained that 'The Kid' is at a place called Las Tablas ..." Letter to Edward Hatch. **March 6, 1879**. Indiana Historical Society. Lew Wallace Collection. Box 9, Folder 10. (**Written on dead John Tunstall's stationery**)

__________. "I beg to submit to you a list of persons whom it is necessary, in my judgment, to arrest ..." Letter to Henry Carroll. **March 11, 1879**. Indiana Historical Society. Lew Wallace Collection. M0292. Box 4. Folder 5. (**Sherman outlaw list with "The Kid" – William Bonney**)

__________. "I enclose a note for Bonney." Letter to John "Squire" Wilson. **March 20, 1879**. Indiana Historical Society. Lew Wallace Collection. M0292. Box 4. Folder 6.

__________. "My time has been so constantly occupied in getting my work into operation ..." Letter to Carl Schurz. **March 21, 1879**. Indiana Historical Society. Lew Wallace Collection. M0292. Box 4. Folder 7. (**Progress report with**

multiple enclosures; one listing "The Kid -William Bonney in anti-outlaw campaign of "taking the head off the evil.")

__________. "To day I forwarded a telegram to you, with another to the President ..." Letter to Carl Schurz. **March 31, 1879**. Indiana Historical Society. Lew Wallace Collection. M0292. Box 4. Folder 7. **(Mention of "precious specimen nicknamed 'The Kid' ")**

REWARD NOTICES FOR

Wallace, Lew. "Be good enough to prepare a draft of proclamation of reward $500 for the capture and delivery of William Bonney, alias the Kid ..." Letter to Territorial Secretary William Ritch. **December 13, 1880**. Herman B. Weisner Papers, ca. 1957-1992. New Mexico State University Library at Las Cruces. Rio Grande Historical Collections. Accession No. Ms 0249. Box W3. Folder 13. Folder Name: "Wallace, Gov. N.M." From Lew Wallace Papers. New Mexico State Records Center. Santa Fe, New Mexico. **(Wallace's first reward for Billy the Kid)**

__________. "Billy the Kid: $500 Reward." *Las Vegas Gazette*. **December 22, 1880**.

__________. "Billy the Kid. $500 Reward." **May 3, 1881**. *Daily New Mexican*. Vol. X, No. 33. Page 1, C 3.

REWARD POSTERS FOR

Greene, Chas. W. "To the New Mexican Printing and Publishing Company." **May 20, 1881**. Indiana Historical Society. Lew Wallace Collection. M0292. Box 4, Folder 17. **(Printer's bill to Lew Wallace for Reward posters for "Kid")**

__________. "I enclose a bill ..." Letter to Lew Wallace for "Kid" wanted posters. **June 2, 1881**. Indiana Historical Society. Lew Wallace Collection. M0292. Box 4, Folder 18.

DEATH WARRANT FOR

Wallace, Lew. "To the Sheriff of Lincoln County, Greeting ..." **April 30, 1881**. Indiana Historical Society. Lew Wallace Collection. M0292. Box 9, Folder 11.

CORONER'S JURY REPORT FOR

Rudulph, Milnor, Pedro Lucero, Jose Silba, Sabal Gutierrez, Lorenso Jaramillo. Coroner's Jury Report for William Bonney alias "Kid." **July 15, 1881**. Original in Spanish. Indiana Historical Society. Lew Wallace Collection. M0292. Box 9. Folder 11. **(Certified photocopy donated by Maurice Garland Fulton in 1951 of Spanish Coroner's Jury Report. July 15, 1881 - matches photo in William Kelleher's *Violence in Lincoln County*, Pages 306-307)**

Rudulph, Milnor, Pedro Lucero, Jose Silba, Sabal Gutierrez, Lorenso Jaramillo. Coroner's Jury Report for William Bonney alias "Kid." **July 15, 1881**. English translation. The Mullin Collection. RNM, VI, J - Legal Papers and Documents. Midland, Texas: Nita Stewart Haley Memorial Library and J. Evetts Haley History Center.

Rudulph, Milnor, Pedro Lucero, Jose Silba, Sabal Gutierrez, Lorenso Jaramillo. Coroner's Jury Report for William Bonney alias "Kid." **July 15, 1881**. English translation. William A. Keleher. *Violence in Lincoln County 1869-1881*. Pages 343-344.

Ritch, William G. "In the matter of the application by Patrick F. Garrett for a reward claimed to have been offered May-1881 for the capture of Wm Bonney alias "the Kid." *Executive Record Book Number 2*. July 25, 1867-November 8, 1882. **July 21, 1881**. Pages 533-535. New Mexico Secretary of State Records. Collection 1971-001, Series 1; Records of the Secretary of the Territory. (Accessed from Albuquerque Public Library Microfilm, Territorial Archives of New Mexico, Roll 21.) **(Acting-Governor Ritch agreed with the reward, and citing the Coroner's Jury Report's identification of William Bonney)**

No Author. *Executive Record Book Number 2.* July 25, 1867-November 8, 1882. **July 21, 1881.** Pages 533-535. New Mexico State Records Center and Archives, Santa Fe. New Mexico Secretary of the State Records Series 1. Records of the Secretary of the Territory. (**About granting Garrett's reward, citing copy of Coroner's Jury Report**)

No Author. "Kid the Killer Killed, Wm. Bonney alias Antrim, alias Billy the Kid, Fatally Meets Pat Garrett, the Lincoln County Sheriff." Las Cruces *Rio Grande Republican.* **July 23, 1881**. Page 2. Volume 1, Number 10. NewspaperArchive.com. (**Copy of Pat Garrett's letter to Acting Governor William Ritch confirming that the original Coroner's Jury Report was sent to District Attorney of the First Judicial District, and copy of it was included in this letter to the Governor**)

King, Frank M. *Wranglin' the Past: Reminiscences of Frank M. King.* "Chapter xix, The Kid's Exit." Pasadena, California: Trail's End Publishing Company. **1935 and 1946.** (**Describes recent location of Pat Garrett's report to the Governor about the killing of Billy the Kid, with confirmation of Coroner's Jury Report, Page 171**)

Keleher, William A. *Violence in Lincoln County 1869-1881.* Albuquerque, New Mexico: University of New Mexico Press. **1957.** (**Photocopy of Spanish Coroner's Jury Report, July 15, 1881. Pages 306-308; Kelleher's English translation, Pages 343-344.**)

OUTLAW MYTH ARTICLES ABOUT (CHRONOLOGICAL)

GENERAL ARTICLES (CHRONOLOGICAL)

No Author. Grant County *Herald.* **May 10, 1879**. Results of the Lincoln County Grand Jury. (**Also published in the Mesilla *Thirty Four.* Confirmation of the William Bonney testimony and James Dolan and Billy Campbell murder indictments, from Page 224 of William Kelleher, *Violence in Lincoln County.***)

Koogler, John H. Editorial. "Desperadoe's Stronghold, An Organized Gang Assisted by Nature and Defiantly Reckless, Who Terrorize the Country to the East of Us." *Las Vegas Morning Gazette.* **December 3, 1880**. Volume 2, Number 120. https://chroniclingamerica.loc.gov. (**Calling Billy Bonney an outlaw leader; motivating his denial letter of December 12, 1880 to Governor Lew Wallace.**)

No Author. "Outlaws of New Mexico, The Exploits of a Band Headed by a New York Youth, The Mountain Fastness of the Kid and His Followers - War Against a Gang of Cattle Thieves and Murderers - The Frontier Confederates of Brockway, the Counterfeiter." *The Sun.* New York. **December 22, 1880**. Vol. XLVIII, No. 118, Page 3, Columns 1-2.

No Author. "A Big Haul! Billy Kid, Dave Rudabaugh, Billy Wilson and Tom Pickett in the Clutches of the Law." *The Las Vegas Daily Optic.* Monday, **December 27, 1880**. Volume 2, Number. 45. Page 4, Column 2. chroniclingamerica.loc.gov.

No Author. "A Bay-Mare. Everyone who has heard of Billy 'the kid' has heard of his beautiful bay mare." *Las Vegas Morning Gazette.* Tuesday, **January 4, 1881**.

No Author. "The Kid. Billy 'the Kid' and Billy Wilson were on Monday taken to Mesilla for Trial." *Las Vegas Morning Gazette.* Tuesday, **March 15, 1881**.

Newman, Simon. "In the Name of Justice! In the Case of Billy Kid." *Newman's Semi-Weekly.* Saturday, **April 2, 1881**.

No Author. "Billy the Kid. Seems to be having a stormy journey on his trip Southward." *Las Vegas Morning Gazette.* Tuesday, **April 5, 1881**.

No Author. "The Kid." *Santa Fe Daily New Mexican.* **May 1, 1881**. Volume X, Number 32, Page 1, Column 2.

No Author. "Billy Bonney. Advices from Lincoln bring the intelligence of the escape of 'Billy the Kid.' " *Las Vegas Daily Optic.* Monday, **May 2, 1881**.

No Author. "The Kid's Escape." *Santa Fe Daily New Mexican.* Tuesday Morning, **May 3, 1881**. Volume X, Number 33, Page 1, Column 2.

No Author. "The above is the record of as bold a deed ..." *Santa Fe Daily New Mexican.* **May 4, 1881. (About Billy's great escape jailbreak)**

No Author. "Dare Devil Desperado. Pursuit of 'Billy the Kid' has been abandoned." *Las Vegas Daily Optic.* **May 4, 1881**.

No Author. "More Killing by Kid, When But a Short Distance From Lincoln, He Meets one of His Old Enemies, and Kills Him and His Companion. Two More Victims." Editorial. *Santa Fe Daily New Mexican.* **May 4, 1881**. Volume X, No. 34, Page 1, Column 2. Newspaperarchive.com. **(Claims Kid killed Billy Matthews)**

No Author. No headline. "Anything that the imagination can concoct ..." *Santa Fe Daily New Mexican.* **May 5, 1881**. Volume X. Page 4, Column 1. Newspaperarchive.com. **(Claims Kid was in Albuquerque)**

No Author. No headline. Mr. Richard Dunham says ..." *Santa Fe Daily New Mexican,* **May 5, 1881**, Volume X. Page 4, Column 3. Newspaperarchive.com. **(Claims Kid was in Stinking Springs)**

No Author. "Richard Dunham's May 2, 1881 encounter with Billy the Kid.", *Santa Fe Daily New Mexican,* **May 5, 1881**, Page 4, Column 3. (private collection)

No Author. "The question if how to deal with desperados who commit murder has but one solution - kill them." *Las Vegas Daily Optic.* Tuesday, **May 10, 1881**.

No Author. "Billy 'the Kid.' " *Las Vegas Gazette.* Thursday, **May 12, 1881**.

No Author. "The Kid was in Chloride City ..." *Santa Fe Daily New Mexican.* **May 13, 1881**. Page 4, Column 3.

No Author. "Billy 'the Kid' is in the vicinity of Sumner." *Las Vegas Gazette.* Sunday, **May 15, 1881**.

No Author. "The Kid is believed to be in the Black Range ..." *Santa Fe Daily New Mexican.* **May 19, 1881**. Page 4, Column 1.

No Author. "Billy the Kid was last seen in Lincoln County ..." *Santa Fe Daily New Mexican.* **May 19, 1881**. Page 4 Column 1.

No Author. (O.L. Houghton's Conversation with Lew Wallace, before May 26, 1881), *The Las Vegas Daily Optic*, **May 26, 1881**, p.4, c.4. Indiana Historical Society. Lew Wallace Collection. M0292.

No Author. " 'Billy the Kid' has been heard from again." *Las Vegas Daily Optic.* Friday, **June 10, 1881**.

No Author. " 'Billy the Kid,' He is Reported to Have Been Seen on Our Streets Saturday Night." *Las Vegas Daily Optic.* Monday Evening, **June 13, 1881**. Vol. 2, No. 188, Page 4, Column 2

Wilcox, Lute, Ed. "Billy the Kid would make an ideal newspaper-man in that he always endeavors to 'get even' with his enemies." *Las Vegas Daily Optic.* Monday Evening, **June 13, 1881**. Volume 2, Number 188, Page 4, Column 1.

No Author. "Land of the Petulant Pistol "Scenes" where Life and Land are Cheap ... 'Billy the Kid' as a Killer." *Las Vegas Daily Optic.* Wednesday Evening, **June 15, 1881.** Front Page. 1, Volume 2, Number 190, Columns 1-2. (Possibly contributed to by Lew Wallace, who published with a similar title in the Crawfordsville *Saturday Evening Journal* on June 18, 1881)

No Author. "Barney Mason at Fort Sumner states the 'Kid' is in Local Sheep Camps." *Las Vegas Morning Gazette.* **June 16, 1881**.

No Author. "The Kid." *Santa Fe Daily New Mexican.* **June 16, 1881**. Volume X, Number 90, Page 4, Column 2.

No Author. "Billy the Kid." *Las Vegas Daily Optic.* Thursday, June 28, 1881.

No Author. " 'The Kid' Killed." *Las Vegas Daily Optic.* **July 18. 1881**.

No Author. No title. **Thursday, July 28, 1881.** Pueblo, Colorado, Colo*rado Chieftain.* www.coloradohistoricnewspapers.org. **(Quoting from the New York *Tribune* on killing of "Tiger in human form known as "Billy the Kid")**

Gauss, Gottfried. Interview with *Lincoln County Leader.* **November 21, 1889. (About Billy Bonney's Lincoln jailbreak)**

LEW WALLACE'S ARTICLES

Koogler, John H. "Interview with Governor Lew Wallace on 'The Kid.'" *Las Vegas Gazette*. **April 28, 1881**.

No Author. "The Thug's Territory. Stage Robbers and Cut-Throats Have Things Their Own Way in New Mexico. Gen. Lew Wallace Anxious to Punish the Crime That is So Prevalent – A Chapter About 'Billy the Kid' – The Governor has a Narrow Escape From Being Spanked." *St. Louis Daily Globe-Democrat*. Monday Morning, **May 16, 1881**. Page 2, Columns 5 and 6. (private collection)

No Author. (Lew Wallace interview) "Billy the Kid. General Wallace Tells Why the Young Desperado of New Mexico Wanted to Kill Him, A Dashing and Daring Career in the Land of the Petulant Pistol." (Lew Wallace interviewed on June 13, 1881), Crawfordsville *Saturday Evening Journal*, **June 18, 1881**. Indiana Historical Society. The Papers of Lew and Susan Wallace. Microfilm Edition. Indianapolis, Indiana: Indiana Historical Society Press. 2008.

No Author. (Lew Wallace interview) "Lew Wallace's Foe. Threatened by 'Billy the Kid.' The Writing of 'Ben Hur' Interrupted. An Incident of the Soldier-Author's Career in New Mexico. *San Francisco Chronicle*. December 10, 1893. Indiana Historical Society. Lew Wallace Collection. M0292. Box 14. Folder 11. (Lew Wallace creating outlaw myth of outlaw Billy the Kid")

No Author. "Street Pickings," Weekly *Crawfordsville Review - Saturday Edition*, **January 6, 1894**. Indiana Historical Society. The Papers of Lew and Susan Wallace. Microfilm Edition. Series I. Reel 27. Indianapolis, Indiana: Indiana Historical Society Press. 2008.

No Author. "An Old Incident Recalled." Crawfordsville *Weekly News-Review*. **December 20, 1901**. Indiana Historical Society. The Papers of Lew and Susan Wallace. Microfilm Edition. Series I. Reel 27. Indianapolis, Indiana: Indiana Historical Society Press. 2008.

Lewis, E.I. "Gen. Wallace's Feud with Billy the Kid, When the General Was Governor of New Mexico and Billy Bonne Was the Most Dangerous Western Outlaw. He Was a Waif and Was Reared in Indiana. *The Indianapolis Press*. Saturday, **June 23, 1900**. Page 7. Lew Wallace Collection. Indiana Historical Society. M0292. Box 14. Folder 11. (photocopy) (Original article is in OMB 23, Box 1. Folder 5) (**Creating self-serving myth of outlaw Billy the Kid"**)

Wallace, Lew. "General Lew Wallace Writes a Romance of 'Billy the Kid' Most Famous Bandit of the Plains: Thrilling Story of the Midnight Meeting Between Gen Wallace, Then Governor of New Mexico, and the Notorious Outlaw, in a Lonesome Hut in Santa Fe." *New York World Magazine*. Sunday, **June 8, 1902**. Lew Wallace Collection. Indiana Historical Society. M0292. . Box 14. Folder 11.

OTHER HISTORICAL FIGURES (PERIOD)

ANGEL, FRANK WARNER

LETTERS BY

Angel, Frank Warner. "I am in receipt of your favor of the 12th ..." Letter to Samuel Beach Axtell. **August 13, 1878**. Interior Department Papers 1850-1907; Appointments Division and Subsequent Actions. Microfilm Roll M750. National Archives and Records Administration Record Group 48. Microfilm Case Number 44-4-8-3. U.S. Department of Interior. Washington D.C.

__________. "I enclose copies of letters received by me from Gov Axtell ..." Letter to Secretary of the Interior Carl Schurz. **August 24, 1878**. (Enclosing copy of letter to him from Governor S.B. Axtell of August 12, 1878; and Angel's response to Axtell of August 13, 1878.) Microfilm File Case Number 44-4-8-3. Record Group

48. Microfilm No. M750. Roll 1. National Archives and Records Administration. U.S. Department of Justice. Washington, D.C.

__________. "I have just been favored by a call from W.L. Rynerson ..." Letter to Secretary of Interior Carl Schurz **September 6, 1878**. Microfilm File Case Number 44-4-8-3. Record Group 48. Microfilm No. M750. Roll 1. National Archives and Records Administration. U.S. Department of Justice. Washington, D.C.

REPORTS BY

Angel, Frank Warner. *Examination of charges against F. C. Godfroy, Indian Agent, Mescalero, N. M.* **October 2, 1878**. (Report 1981, Inspector E.C. Watkins; Cited as Watkins Report). M319-20 and L147, 44-4-8. Record Group 075. National Archives and Records Administration. U.S. Department of Justice. Washington, D. C.

__________. *In the Matter of the Investigation of the Charges Against S.B. Axtell Governor of New Mexico. Report and Testimony.* **October 3, 1878.** Angel Report. Interior Department Papers 1850-1907; Appointments Division and Subsequent Actions. Microfilm Case File No. 44-4-8-3. Record Group 48. Microfilm Roll M750. National Archives and Records Administration. U.S. Department of Interior. Washington, D.C. (**Mentions Santa Fe Ring**)

__________. *In the Matter of the Examination of the Causes and Circumstances of the Death of John H. Tunstall a British Subject.* Report filed **October 4, 1878**. Angel Report. Interior Department Papers 1850-1907; Appointments Division and Subsequent Actions. Microfilm File Case Number 44-4-8-3. Record Group 48. Microfilm No. M750. Roll 1. National Archives and Records Administration. U.S. Department of Justice. Washington, D.C.

__________. *In the Matter of the Lincoln County Troubles. To the Honorable Charles Devens, Attorney General.* **October 4, 1878**. Angel Report. Microfilm Case File No. 44-4-8-3. Record Group 48. Microfilm Roll M750. National Archives and Records Administration. U.S. Department of Justice. Washington, D.C.

NOTEBOOK ON SANTA FE RING MEMBERS BY

Angel, Frank Warner. "To Gov. Lew Wallace / Santa Fe, N. M., 1878." Notebook. **1878**. Indiana Historical Society. Lew Wallace Collection. M0292. Microfilm No. F372. (**Original missing, copy on microfilm; Notebook prepared for Lew Wallace listing names of Santa Fe Ring members**)

Theisen, Lee Scott. "Frank Warner Angel's Notes on New Mexico Territory, 1878." *Arizona and the West: A Quarterly Journal of History*. Winter 1976. Volume 18. Number 4. Pages 333-370. (**About the Angel notebook**)

AXTELL, SAMUEL BEACH

CONTEMPORARY SOURCES (CHRONOLOGICAL)

No author. "Anarchy at Cimarron." *Santa Fe Weekly New Mexico*. **November 16, 1875**. (**Ring-biased article justifying Governor S.B. Axtell calling in troops in the Colfax County War after murder of Reverend Franklin Tolby**)

Axtell, Samuel B. "The Legislature to Assess Property. *Message of Gov. Samuel B. Axtell to the Legislative Assembly of New Mexico, Twenty-second Session.* Page 4. Manderfield & Tucker, Public Printers: Santa Fe, New Mexico. **1875 or 1876**. Interior Department Papers 1850-1907; Appointments Division and Subsequent Actions. Microfilm File Case Number 44-4-8-3. Record Group 48. Microfilm No. M750. Roll 1. National Archives and Records Administration. U.S. Department of Justice. Washington, D.C.

Elkins, Stephen B. "I trouble you to say a word in behalf of Gov. Axtell ..." Letter to President Rutherford B. Hayes. **June 11, 1877**. Interior Department Papers 1850-

1907; Appointments Division and Subsequent Actions. Microfilm Roll M750. National Archives and Records Administration Record Group 48. Microfilm Case Number 44-4-8-3. U. S. Department of Interior. Washington D. C. (**Trying to prevent Axtell's removal as governor**)

Axtell, Samuel B. "I have today mailed to you a reply to the charges on file in your Dept against me." Letter to Secretary of the Interior Carl Schurz. **June 15, 1877**. Interior Department Papers 1850-1907; Appointments Division and Subsequent Actions. Microfilm Roll M750. National Archives and Records Administration Record Group 48. Microfilm Case Number 44-4-8-3 U.S. Department of Interior. Washington D.C. (**Refuting charges made in Colfax County**).

Isaacs, I. and G.N. Coe. "Charges Against S.B. Axtell, Governor of New Mexico." **June 22, 1878**. Interior Department Papers 1850-1907; Appointments Division and Subsequent Actions. Microfilm File Case Number 44-4-8-3. Microfilm No. M750. Roll 1. National Archives and Records Administration. Record Group 48. U.S. Department of Justice. Washington, D.C.

Schurz, Carl. "I transmit herewith an order from the President ..." **September 4, 1878**. Letter to Lew Wallace. Indiana Historical Society. Lew Wallace Collection. M0292. Box 3. Folder 14. (**Suspension of Governor S.B. Axtell and Wallace's appointment as new Governor**)

Elkins, Stephen Benton. "To the President. Referring to a conversation had with you last week ..." Letter to President James Abram Garfield. **March 17, 1881**. (Received Executive Mansion April 6, 1881). Interior Department Papers 1850-1907; Appointments Division and Subsequent Actions. Microfilm Roll M750. National Archives and Records Administration Microfilm Roll M750. National Archives and Records Administration Record Group 48. Microfilm Case Number 44-4-8-3. U.S. Department of Interior. Washington D.C. Microfilm Case Number 44-4-8-3. U.S. Department of Interior. Washington D.C. (**Request for re-appointment of Axtell as Territorial New Mexico Governor**)

BONNEY, WILLIAM HENRY

(See History of William Henry Bonney)

BRADY, WILLIAM

BIOGRAPHICAL SOURCE

Lavash, Donald R. *Sheriff William Brady. Tragic Hero of the Lincoln County War.* Santa Fe, New Mexico: Sunstone Press. 1986.

CONTEMPORARY SOURCES (CHRONOLOGICAL)

Brady, William. Affidavit of **July 2, 1876** concerning appointment as Administrator for the Emil Fritz Estate. Copied from the original District Court Record. (private collection)

__________. Affidavit of **August 22, 1876** documenting business debts to L. G. Murphy and Co. pertaining to the Emil Fritz Estate. Copied from the original District Court Record. (private collection)

__________. Affidavit of **July _, 1876** of Resignation as Emil Fritz Estate Administrator. Copied from the original District Court Record. (private collection.)

__________. Affidavit of **August 22, 1876** confirming giving Alexander McSween the books of the L.G. Murphy Company for the purpose of making business debt collections. Copied from the original District Court Record. (private collection)

Tunstall, John Henry. "A Taxpayer's Complaint ... January 18, 1878." Mesilla *Independent*. **January 26, 1878. (Exposé of William Brady embezzling tax money to buy cattle for "The House;" and Catron then paid that bill)**

Dolan, James J. "Answer to A Taxpayer's Complaint." Mesilla *Independent*. **January 29, 1878. (Response to J.H. Tunstall's exposé)**

Bristol, Warren. "Action of Assumpsit to command Sheriff Brady of Lincoln County to attach goods of Alexander A. McSween." **February 7, 1878**. District Court Record. (private collection).

__________. Preprinted form for "Writ of Attachment" (Printed and sold at the office of the Mesilla News) filled out to command the Sheriff of Lincoln County to attach goods of Alexander McSween for a suit of damages for ten thousand dollars. **February 7, 1878**. District Court Record. (private collection).

Brady, William. "List of Articles Inventoried by Wm Brady sheriff in the suit of Charles Fritz & Emilie Scholand vs A.A. McSween now in the dwelling house belonging to A.A. McSween." (undated, but in **February of 1878**) (private collection)

BRISTOL, WARREN HENRY

CONTEMPORARY SOURCES (CHRONOLOGICAL)

Bristol Warren. "Writ of Embezzlement." **December 21, 1877**. Herman B. Weisner Papers, ca. 1957-1992. New Mexico State University Library at Las Cruces. Rio Grande Historical Collections. Accession No. Ms 0249. Box 10. Folder M-13. Folder Name. "Will and Testament A. McSween." (**Emilie Fritz Scholand's sworn complaint against Alexander McSween**)

__________. "Action of Assumpsit to command Sheriff Brady of Lincoln County to attach goods of Alexander A. McSween." **February 7, 1878**. District Court Record. (private collection).

__________. Preprinted form for "Writ of Attachment" (Printed and sold at the office of the Mesilla News) filled out to command the Sheriff of Lincoln County to attach goods of Alexander McSween for a suit of damages for ten thousand dollars. **February 7, 1878**. District Court Record. (private collection).

__________. "My reasons for not holding October term of Court ..." Telegram to U.S. Marshal John Sherman. **October 4, 1878**. Indiana Historical Society. Lew Wallace Collection. M0292. Box 3. Folder 15. (**Claiming outlawry, but shielding of the murderers of John Tunstall**)

__________. *Instructions to the Jury*. District Court 3rd Judicial. District Doña Ana. Filed **April 9, 1881**. Writ of Embezzlement. New Mexico State University Library at Las Cruces. Rio Grande Historical Collection. Accession No. Ms 0249. Box 1. Folder 14C. Folder Name: "Billy the Kid Legal Documents." (**Forcing the jurymen in Billy Bonney's Mesilla trial to convict him of first degree murder**)

CATRON, THOMAS BENTON

BIBLIOGRAPHICAL SOURCES

Cleaveland, Norman, *A Synopsis of the Great New Mexico Cover-up*. Self-printed. 1989.

__________. *The Great Santa Fe Cover-up. Based on a Talk given Before the Santa Fe Historical Society on November 1, 1978*. Self-printed. 1982.

__________. *The Morleys - Young Upstarts on the Southwest Frontier*. Albuquerque, New Mexico: Calvin Horn Publisher, Inc. 1971. (**Page 93 gives Catron's vindictive indictment of Cleaveland's grandmother, Ada Morley, for mail theft as revenge denying him use of a Maxwell Land Grant buggy.**

Dodge, Andrew R., and Betty K. Koed, eds. *Biographical Directory of the United States Congress 1774-2005*. Washington, D.C.: United States Government Printing Office. 2005

Dunham, Harold H. "New Mexican Land Grants with Special Reference to the Title Papers of the Maxwell Grant." *New Mexico Historical Review*. (January, 1955) Vol. 70. No. 1. pp. 1 - 23.

Hefferan, Vioalle Clark. *Thomas Benton Catron*. Albuquerque, New Mexico: University of New Mexico. Zimmerman Library. Unpublished Thesis for the Degree of Master of Arts. 1940. .(**In praise of Catron; includes railroad involvement, Page 35; First National Bank stockholder from 1871 to 1907, Page 28**)

Keleher, William A. *The Maxwell Land Grant. A New Mexico Item*. Albuquerque, New Mexico: University of New Mexico Press. 1964.

Klasner, Lilly. Eve Ball. Ed. *My Girlhood Among Outlaws*. Tucson, Arizona: The University of Arizona Press. 1972.

Lamar, Howard Robert N. *The Far Southwest 1846 – 1912: A Territorial History*. New Haven and London: Yale University Press. 1966. (**Chapter 6 covers the Santa Fe Ring)**)

Montoya, María E. *Translating Property. The Maxwell Land Grant and the Conflict Over Land in the American West, 1840-1900*. Berkeley and Los Angeles: University of California Press. 2002.

Mullin, Robert N. "A Specimen of Catron's Dirty Work. Sworn Affidavit of Samuel Davis." October 1, 1878. Binder RNM IV, EE. (Unpublished). Midland, Texas: Nita Stewart Haley Memorial Library and J. Evetts Haley Historical Center.

__________. "Catron Embarrassed Throughout His Life by an Affliction." (Date Unknown). Binder RNM, IV, M. (Unpublished). Midland, Texas: Nita Stewart Haley Memorial Library and J. Evetts Haley Historical Center. Robert Mullin Papers. Binder RNM IV, EE (Unpublished).

__________. "Prior to Lincoln County War Catron Had Defended Colonel Dudley." (No Date). Notes from "Lincoln County War Cast of Characters." Midland, Texas: Nita Stewart Haley Memorial Library and J. Evetts Haley Historical Center.

Murphy, Lawrence R. *Lucien Bonaparte Maxwell. Napoleon of the Southwest*. Norman: University of Oklahoma Press. 1983.

Otero, Miguel A. *My Life on the Frontier, 1882-1897: Incidents and Characters of the period when Kansas, Colorado, and New Mexico were passing through the last of their Wild and Romantic Years*. New York: The Press of the Pioneers. 1935. Pages 232-233. (Quoted by Victor Westphall, *Thomas Benton Catron and His Era*. Page 188*)* (**Quote: "the 'Santa Fe Ring,' the real machine controlling the political situation in New Mexico."**)

Pearson, Jim Berry. *The Maxwell Land Grant*. Norman: University of Oklahoma Press. 1961.

Sluga, Mary Elizabeth. *Political Life of Thomas Benton Catron 1896-1912*. Albuquerque, New Mexico: University of New Mexico. Zimmerman Library. Unpublished Thesis for the Degree of Master of Arts. 1941. (**Thesis in praise of Catron for an M.A.**)

Taylor, Morris F. *O.P. McMains and the Maxwell Land Grant Conflict*. Tucson, Arizona: The University of Arizona Press. 1979. (**Traces origins of the Santa Fe Ring with T.B. Catron and S.B. Elkins**)

Westphall, Victor. *Thomas Benton Catron and His Era*. Tucson, Arizona: University of Arizona Press. 1973.

__________. "Fraud and Implications of Fraud in the Land Grants of New Mexico." *New Mexico Historical Review*. 1974. Vol. XLIX, No. 3. 189 - 218.

Wooden, John Paul. *Thomas Benton Catron and New Mexico Politics 1866-1921*. Albuquerque, New Mexico: University of New Mexico. Zimmerman Library. Unpublished Thesis for the Degree of Master of Arts. 1959. (**M.A. thesis praising Catron**)

GENERAL CONTEMPORARY EXPOSÉS OF(CHRONOLOGICAL)

Middaugh, Asa F. Deposition. **March 31, 1876**. "Exhibit B" in the August 9, 1878 deposition of Frank Springer to Investigator Frank Warner Angel. Frank Warner Angel report titled *In the Matter of the Investigation of the Charges Against S.B. Axtell Governor of New Mexico*. October 3, 1878. Interior Department Papers 1850-1907; Appointments Division and Subsequent Actions. Microfilm Case File No. 44-4-8-3. Record Group 48. Microfilm Roll M750. National Archives and

Records Administration. U.S. Department of Interior. Washington, D.C. (**About Catron's malicious prosecution of Ada McPherson Morley**)

Springer, Frank. Deposition to Investigator Frank Warner Angel. **August 9, 1878**. Frank Warner Angel report titled *In the Matter of the Investigation of the Charges Against S.B. Axtell Governor of New Mexico*. October 3, 1878. Interior Department Papers 1850-1907; Appointments Division and Subsequent Actions. Microfilm Case File No. 44-4-8-3. Record Group 48. Microfilm Roll M750. National Archives and Records Administration. U.S. Department of Interior. Washington, D.C. (**Mentions Catron, Elkins, and the Santa Fe Ring, and provided Exhibits of letters exposing Catron's evil.**)

No Author. "The Santa Fe Ring is the most corrupt combination that ever cursed any country or community." Las Cruces *Thirty-Four Newspaper*. **October 27, 1880**. From Victor Westphall, *Thomas Benton Catron and His Era*. Page 186. (**Article summarizing Ring abuses in urging voters to oppose Ring candidates**)

No Author. "The Ring must soon discover that the time has passed in New Mexico when men can be herded like so many sheep ..." *Albuquerque Daily Democrat*. **March 4, 1884**. Quoted by Victor Westphall, *Thomas Benton Catron and His Era*. Page 191. (**About Santa Fe Ring control of appointments to legislature**)

Valdez, Jose and Enrique Mares. "Scorching Letter, The Knights of Labor Send a Communication to Powderly! Politicians Arraigned! The Boldest Document Ever Issued in the Territory." **August 18, 1890.** *Las Vegas Democrat*. Volume 1. Center for Southwest Studies. Thomas B. Catron Papers, MSS 29, Series 102, Box 8, Folder 4. (**Gives history of Santa Fe Ring with T.B. Catron as head**)

No Author. "Catron and the Laboring Men." Unknown newspaper. **1892?** University of New Mexico Library. Center for Southwest Studies. Thomas B. Catron Papers, MSS 29, Series 401, Box 1, Folder 3. (**Opposition to Catron as Delegate to Congress as "the biggest corporation man in New Mexico"**)

Victory, John P. "No Consistent Democrat Should Vote for T.B. Catron, John P. Victory in Forcible and Cogent Language Gives Answerable Reasons." **No month, 1895.** Printed broadside. University of New Mexico Library. Center for Southwest Studies. Thomas B. Catron Papers, MSS 29, Series 409, Box 1, Folder 3.

Wallace, Lew. "I have your several letters, including the last one of the 3rd inst." Letter to Eugene Fiske. **November 6, 1897**. Indiana Historical Society. Lew Wallace Collection. AC233. Box 1. Folder 7. (part of 1981 addition) (**About Catron's control over New Mexicans**)

Cutting, Bronson. "Catron was the boss of the Territory ..." Letter to James Roger Addison. **December 11, 1911**. Cited by Victor Westphall in *Thomas Benton Catron and His Era* from his citation: Lincoln County Manuscripts Division. Box 12. Courtesy of David Stratton. (**Catron as head of the Santa Fe Ring**)

Johnson, E. Dana. "[H]e ruled with a rod of iron ..." Editorial. *Santa Fe New Mexican*. **May 16, 1921**. Catron Papers 801, Box 1. Quoted by Victor Westphall, *Thomas Benton Catron and His Era*. Pages 394-395. (**Tactics of "boss" Catron without using the words Santa Fe Ring**)

(SEE: Santa Fe Ring; Frank Warner Angel)

FEDERAL INDICTMENT OF REGULATORS BY

Catron, Thomas Benton. "Case No. 411. The United States vs. Charles Bowdry [Bowdre], Doc Scurlock, Henry Brown, Henry Antrim alias "Kid," John Middleton, Stephen Stevens, John Scroggins, George Coe and Frederick Waite." **June 21, 1878.** Herman B. Weisner Papers. ca. 1957-1992. New Mexico State University Library at Las Cruces. Rio Grande Historical Collections. Accession No. Ms 0249. Box 1. Folder B-4. Folder Name: Andrew Roberts Indictment.

RESIGNATION AS TERRITORIAL U.S. ATTORNEY BY

Elkins, Stephen Benton. "Elkins – Telegraph Cipher, Cipher with Catron." Sent to T.B. Catron. ___ **1878?** University of New Mexico Library. Center for Southwest Studies. Thomas B. Catron Papers, MSS 29, Series 108, Box 1, Folder 4. (**Ring code-cipher key about T.B. Catron's resignation as U.S. Attorney**)

__________. "Asking delay of action upon charges against U.S. Atty. Catron ..." **September 24, 1878**. Angel Report. Microfilm File Case No. 44-4-8-3. Record Group 48. National Records and Archives Administration. Microfilm No. M750. Roll 1. U.S. Department of Justice. Washington, D. C.

__________. "Regarding Attorney General's decision on T.B. Catron." Letter. **September___, 1878**. Angel Report. Microfilm File Case No. 44-4-8-3. Record Group 48. National Records and Archives Administration. Microfilm No. M750. Roll 1. U.S. Department of Justice. Washington, D.C.

Catron, Thomas Benton. "In accordance with a purpose long entertained ...." Letter to Charles Devens. **October 10, 1878.** Angel Report. Microfilm File Case No. 44-4-8-3. Record Group 48. National Records and Archives Administration. Microfilm No. M750. Roll 1. U.S. Department of Justice. Washington, D.C. (**Resignation as U.S. Attorney**)

Devens, Charles. "Your resignation of the office of United States Attorney ..." Letter to T.B. Catron. **October 19, 1878**. Angel Report. Microfilm File Case No. 44-4-8-3. Record Group 48. National Records and Archives Administration. Microfilm No. M750. Roll 1. U.S. Department of Justice. Washington, D. C.

Catron, Thomas Benton. "Please change my resignation ...." **November 4, 1878.** Telegram to Charles Devens. Angel Report. Microfilm File Case No. 44-4-8-3. Record Group 48. National Records and Archives Administration. Microfilm No. M750. Roll 1. U.S. Department of Justice. Washington, D. C. (**Resignation as U.S. Attorney**)

Devens, Charles. "Your resignation of the office of United States Attorney ..." Letter to T.B. Catron. **November 12, 1878**. Angel Report. Microfilm File Case No. 44-4-8-3. Record Group 48. National Records and Archives Administration. Microfilm No. M750. Roll 1. U.S. Department of Justice. Washington, D.C.

Elkins, Stephen Benton. "Relative to resignation of T. B. Catron U. S. Attorney." Letter to Charles Devens. **November 10, 1878**. Angel Report. Microfilm File Case No. 44-4-8-3. Record Group 48. National Records and Archives Administration. Microfilm No. M750. Roll 1. U.S. Department of Justice. Washington, D.C.

Devens, Charles. "To honorable S. B. Elkins re. T. B. Catron continuing to act as U.S. Attorney ..." Letter to Stephen B. Elkins. **November 12, 1878**. Angel Report. Microfilm File Case No. 44-4-8-3. Record Group 48. National Records and Archives Administration. Microfilm No. M750. Roll 1. U.S. Department of Justice. Washington, D.C.

Barnes, Sidney M.. "I Sidney M. Barnes do solemnly swear ..." Swearing in as U.S. Attorney. **January 20, 1879**. Angel Report. Microfilm File Case No. 44-4-8-3. Record Group 48. National Records and Archives Administration. Microfilm No. M750. Roll 1. U.S. Department of Justice. Washington, D.C. (**Catron replaced by Ringite attorney Sidney Barnes**)

Elkins, Stephen Benton. "I have waited some time to reply to your lengthy letter ..." Letter to T.B. Catron. **August 15, 1879**. West Virginia & Regional History Center. West Virginia University Libraries, Morgantown, W. Va. Stephen B. Elkins Papers (A&M 53). Box 1. Folder 1. (**Reveals he prevented Catron's dismissal and indictment from Angel's report, allowing the resignation to prevent exposure**)

PECOS RIVER COW CAMP OF (CHRONOLOGICAL)

Riley, John H. Letter to N.A.M. Dudley. **May 19, 1878.** (**Fabricated Regulator theft of Catron's cattle from the Dolan Pecos Cow Camp**) Cited by Victor Westphall, Page 87.

Catron, Thomas Benton. Catron letter to Governor S. B. Axtell to intervene in Lincoln County. **May 30, 1878**. Midland, Texas: Nita Stewart Haley Memorial Library and J. Evetts Haley Historical Center. Robert Mullin Papers. Binder RNM IV, EE (Unpublished). (**Fabricated attack of Regulators on his cow camp workers**) Cited by Victor Westphall, Page 89-90.

OWNERSHIP FILING ON CARRIZOZO CATTLE COMPANY BY

Catron, Thomas Benton.. Statement of sole ownership of Carrizozo Ranch in Tax Dispute Case. No date. Herman B. Weisner Papers, ca. 1957-1992. New Mexico State University Library at Las Cruces. Rio Grande Historical Collections. Accession No. Ms 0249. Box. 2. Folder C-8. Folder Name "T.B. Catron Tax Troubles." (**One of Catron's Lincoln County holdings**)

CHAPMAN, HUSTON INGRAM

CONTEMPORARY SOURCES (CHRONOLOGICAL)

Wallace, Lew. "I enclose you a copy of a letter from Las Vegas ..." Letter to Edward Hatch. **October 28, 1878**. Indiana Historical Society. Lew Wallace Collection. M0292. Box 3. Folder 16. (**Forwards Chapman's letter to Hatch**)

__________. "In a communication, dated October 28. inst., I requested, for reasons stated, a safe-guard for Mrs. McSween ..." Letter to Edward Hatch. **November 9, 1878**. Indiana Historical Society. Lew Wallace Collection. M0292. Box 3. Folder 17.

No Author. (signed E.). "Death of Chapman." *Las Vegas Gazette.* **March 1, 1879**. From *Proceedings of a Court of Inquiry in the Case of Lt. Col. N.A.M. Dudley (May 2,1879 – July 5, 1879)*. File No. QQ1284. (Boxes 3304, 3305, 3305A); Court Martial Files 1809-1894. Records of the Office of the Judge Advocate General – Army. Record Group 153. Old Military and Civil Branch. National Archives and Records Administration. Washington, D. C.

Chapman, W.W. "Yours of the 1st inst. came ..." Letter to Ira E. Leonard. **March 20, 1879**. Indiana Historical Society. Lew Wallace Collection. M0292. Box 4. Folder 6.

Rynerson, William. "The Grand Jurors for the Territory of New Mexico taken from the body of the good and lawful men of the County of Lincoln ..." Indictments of the April, Lincoln County Grand Jury. **April 28, 1879**. Herman B. Weisner Papers, ca. 1957-1992. New Mexico State University Library at Las Cruces. Rio Grande Historical Collection. Accession No. Ms 0249. Box 4/39. Folder E-Z. Folder Name: "Jessie Evans Accessory to Murder." (**Billy's testimony indicts J.J. Dolan, Billy Campbell, and Jessie Evans fulfilling his pardon bargain**)

Chapman, W.W. "Since receiving yours of the 1st March ..." Letter to Ira Leonard. **May 8, 1879**. Indiana Historical Society. Lew Wallace Collection. M0292. Box 4. Folder 10.

LETTERS BY

Chapman, Huston I. "You will please pardon me for presuming so much upon your kindness ..." Letter to Lew Wallace **October 24, 1878**. Indiana Historical Society. Lew Wallace Collection. M0292. Box 3. Folder 16. (**Makes clear N.A.M. Dudley's danger to Susan McSween**)

__________. *'You attach much importance to the awe-inspiring influence of the military ...*" Letter to Lew Wallace. **November 25, 1878**. From Frederick Nolan, *The Lincoln County War*, p. 359.

__________. "You must pardon me for so often presuming upon your kindness ..." Letter to Lew Wallace. **November 29, 1878**. Indiana Historical Society. Lew Wallace Collection. M0292. Box 3. Folder 18.

CHISUM, JOHN SIMPSON

Hinton, Harwood P., Jr. "John Simpson Chisum, 1877-84." *New Mexico Historical Review* 31(3) (July 1956): 177 - 205; 31(4) (October 1956): 310 - 337; 32(1) (January 1957): 53 - 65.

Klasner, Lilly. Eve Ball. Ed. *My Girlhood Among Outlaws.* Tucson, Arizona: The University of Arizona Press. 1972. (**Contains John Chisum's in jail write-up about Santa Fe Ring injustices to himself**)

COE FAMILY

BIOGRAPHICAL SOURCES

Coe, George. Doyce B. Nunis, Jr. Ed. *Frontier Fighter. The Autobiography of George Coe Who Fought and Rode With Billy the Kid.* Chicago: R. R. Donnelley and Sons Company. 1984.

Coe, Wilbur. *Ranch on the Ruidoso. The Story of a Pioneer Family in New Mexico, 1871 - 1968.* New York: Alfred A. Knopf. 1968.

DEDRICK BROTHERS

BIOGRAPHICAL SOURCES

Upham, Elizabeth. (Related by marriage to Daniel Dedrick). Personal interviews. 1998.

Upham, Marquita. (Relative by marriage to Daniel Dedrick). Personal interview. 1998.

CONTEMPORARY SOURCES (CHRONOLOGICAL)

Dedrick, Dan. "I have been under an arrest for six days ..." **April 5, 1879**. Letter to Lew Wallace. Indiana Historical Society. Lew Wallace Collection. M0292. Box 4. Folder 8. (**Says he was not told his arrest charges**)

No Author. "Arrests of Dedricks. Legal Documents." Herman B. Weisner Papers, ca. 1957-1992. New Mexico State University Library at Las Cruces. Rio Grande Historical Collections. Accession No. Ms 0249. Box 1. Folder B-8. Folder Name: "Lincoln County Bonds."

DOLAN, JAMES JOSEPH

BIOGRAPHICAL SOURCE

Slates, Thomas. "The James J. Dolan House, Lincoln New Mexico." *New Mexico Architecture* 11. 8/9 (1969). pp. 17-20.(**With Dolan biography**)

CONTEMPORARY SOURCES BY AND ABOUT (CHRONOLOGICAL)

Tunstall, John Henry. "A Tax-payer's Complaint, Office of John H. Tunstall, Lincoln, Lincoln Co., N.M., January 18, 1878, 'The Present Sheriff of Lincoln County Has Paid Nothing During His Present Term of Office.' Governor's Message for 1878." Mesilla *Independent.* **January 26, 1878**. Volume 1, Number 32. NewspaperArchive.com. (**Exposé of William Brady and John Riley for embezzling tax money to buy cattle; T.B. Catron then paid that bill**)

Dolan, James J. "Answer to A Taxpayer's Complaint." Mesilla *Independent.* **January 29, 1878**. (**Response to J.H. Tunstall's exposé of embezzlement of tax money to buy cattle**)

McSween, Alexander. "It looks as though the agent were the property of J.J. Dolan & J.H. Riley, known here as Dolan & Co." Letter to Secretary of Interior Carl

Schurz. **February 11, 1878**. From Frederick Nolan. *The Life and Death of John Henry Tunstall*. Albuquerque, New Mexico: The University of New Mexico Press. 1965. Page 266.

Rynerson, William. "Friends Riley & Dolan, Lincoln N.M. I have just received letters from you mailed 10th inst." **February 14, 1878**. Letter to James Dolan and John Riley. Copy as Exhibit B in June 6, 1878 deposition of Alexander McSween. Frank Warner Angel report. *In the Matter of the Examination of the Causes and Circumstances of the Death of John H. Tunstall a British Subject.* Report filed October 4, 1878. Frank Warner Angel report. Interior Department Papers 1850-1907; Appointments Division and Subsequent Actions. Microfilm File Case Number 44-4-8-3. Record Group 48. Microfilm No. M750. Roll 1. National Archives and Records Administration. U.S. Department of Justice. Washington, D.C. (James J. Dolan Deposition. June 20, 1878. Pages 235-247.) (**Implying planned killing of J.H. Tunstall**)

Wilson, John, George B. Barker, Robert M. Gilbert, John Newcomb, Samuel Smith, Benjamin Ellis. "We the undersigned Justice of the Peace and Coroners Jury who sat upon the inquest held this 19th day of February 1878 on the body of John H. Tunstall ..." Coroner's Jury Report for John Tunstall. **February 19, 1878. (Naming as murderers, among others, James Dolan, Frank Baker, Jessie Evans, William Morton, and George Hindman**)

Rynerson, William. "The Grand Jurors for the Territory of New Mexico taken from the body of the good and lawful men of the County of Lincoln ..." Indictments of the April, Lincoln County Grand Jury. **April 28, 1879**. Herman B. Weisner Papers, ca. 1957-1992. New Mexico State University Library at Las Cruces. Rio Grande Historical Collection. Accession No. Weisner MS 249. Box 4/39. Folder E-Z. Folder Name: "Jessie Evans Accessory to Murder." (**Billy Bonney's testimony indicts J.J. Dolan, Billy Campbell, and Jessie Evans for pardon bargain**)

Purington, George Augustus. "The District Court adjourned on Thursday ..." **May 3, 1879**. Indiana Historical Society. Lew Wallace Collection. M0292. Box 4. Folder 10. (**Letter to Adjutant General on Grand Jury indictments of the Murphy-Dolans - including Dolan for the H.I. Chapman murder - and N.A.M. Dudley; copy sent to Lew Wallace**)

Wild, Azariah F. "Daily Reports of U. S. Secret Service Agents, Azariah F. Wild." Microfilm T-915. Record Group 87. Rolls 307 (January 1,1878 - June 30, 1879) and 308 (**July 1, 1879 - June 30, 1881**). National Archives and Records Department. Department of the Treasury. United States Secret Service. Washington, D. C. (**Dolan as an informer against "the Kid gang"**)

DUDLEY, NATHAN AUGUSTUS MONROE

BIOGRAPHICAL SOURCES

Heitman, Francis B. *Historical Register and Dictionary of the United States Army, From Its Organization, September 29, 1789, to March 2, 1903.* (Entry for Galusha Pennypacker, Pages 782-7830.) Washington, D.C.: Government Printing Office. 1903.

Kaye, E. Donald. *Nathan Augustus Monroe Dudley: Rogue, Hero, or Both?* Parker, Colorado: Outskirts Press, Inc. 2007.

Oliva, Leo E., *Fort Union and the Frontier Army in the Southwest.* Southwest Cultural Resource Center, Professional Papers No. 41, National Park Service, 1993, Pages 488-489, 550, 574, 624-626, 656-659 are on Dudley. (**Quoted to E. Donald Kaye from the now-lost letter of Amos Kimball: "I guess you heard that Dudley made Colonel. The army bureaucracy is like a giant cesspool, where the biggest chunks rise to the top."**)

MILITARY COURT OF INQUIRY FOR

Leonard, Ira E. "*Charges and specifications against Lieutenant Colonel N.A.M. Dudley, Commander at Fort Stanton, New Mexico.*" **March 4, 1879**. Letter to Secretary of War George McCrary. *Proceedings of a Court of Inquiry in the Case of Lt. Col. N.A.M. Dudley (May 2,1879 - July 5, 1879).* File No. QQ1284. (Boxes 3304, 3305, 3305A); Court Martial Files 1809-1894. Records of the Office of the Judge Advocate General - Army. Record Group 153. Old Military and Civil Branch. National Archives and Records Administration. Washington, D. C. (**Charges against Dudley for murders and arson**)

No Author. *Proceedings of a Court of Inquiry in the Case of Lt. Col. N.A.M. Dudley **(May 2,1879 – July 5, 1879)***. File No. QQ1284. (Boxes 3304, 3305, 3305A); Court Martial Files 1809-1894. Records of the Office of the Judge Advocate General - Army. Record Group 153. Old Military and Civil Branch. National Archives and Records Administration. Washington, D. C.

OTHER CONTEMPORARY SOURCES FOR (CHRONOLOGICAL)

Dudley, Nathan Augustus Monroe. "I am in receipt of a copy of letter written by one H.I. Chapman, calling himself the Attorney ..." **November 9, 1878**. Letter to Lew Wallace. From *Proceedings of a Court of Inquiry in the Case of Lt. Col. N.A.M. Dudley (May 2,1879 – July 5, 1879).* File No. QQ1284. (Boxes 3304, 3305, 3305A); Court Martial Files 1809-1894. Records of the Office of the Judge Advocate General – Army. Record Group 153. Old Military and Civil Branch. National Archives and Records Administration. Washington, D.C. (**Forwarding the Susan McSween affidavits in answer to the charges made by Chapman**)

Wallace, Lew. "I am in receipt of Col. Dudley's reply to the charges against him ..." Letter to Edward Hatch. **November 14, 1878**. Indiana Historical Society. Lew Wallace Collection. M0292. Box 3. Folder 17. (**Has quote: "the "reply is perfectly satisfactory"**)

__________. "I am constrained to request that Lieut Col. N.A.M. Dudley, Commanding at Fort Stanton, be relieved ..." Letter to Edward Hatch. **December 7, 1878**. Indiana Historical Society. Lew Wallace Collection. M0292. Box 3. Folder 18. (**Removal of Dudley requested**)

Dudley, Nathan Augustus Monroe. "An Open Letter, By Lieut. Col. N.A.M. Dudley, 9th Cavalry, to His Excellency Governor Lew Wallace." Letter to Lew Wallace. Santa Fe *Weekly New Mexican*. **December 14, 1878**. Reprinted in *Mesilla News*. December 21, 1878. As Exhibit 13 from *Proceedings of a Court of Inquiry in the Case of Lt. Col. N.A.M. Dudley (May 2,1879 – July 5, 1879).* File No. QQ1284. (Boxes 3304, 3305, 3305A); Court Martial Files 1809-1894. Records of the Office of the Judge Advocate General – Army. Record Group 153. Old Military and Civil Branch. National Archives and Records Administration. Washington, D.C. (**Attacks Wallace's Amnesty Proclamation as applying to the military**)

__________. "I have the honor to repeat the request made on a former occasion that Lt. Col. N.A.M. Dudley be relieved of the command ..." Letter to Edward Hatch. **March 7, 1879**. Indiana Historical Society. Lew Wallace Collection. M0292. Box 4, Folder 4.

Hatch, Edward. "Lieutenant Colonel N.A.M. Dudley is hereby relieved from command and duty ..." Special Field Order 2. **March 8, 1879**. Indiana Historical Society. Lew Wallace Collection. M0292. Box 4, Folder 4. (**Wallace succeeds in removing Dudley**)

Wallace, Lew. "I have official information that a court of inquiry for Col. Dudley has been ordered ..." Letter to Carl Schurz. **April 4, 1879**. Indiana Historical Society. Lew Wallace Collection. M0292. Box 4. Folder 8.

Purington, George Augustus. "The District Court adjourned on Thursday ..." **May 3, 1879**. Indiana Historical Society. Lew Wallace Collection. M0292. Box 4. Folder 10. (**Indictments of the Murphy-Dolans and N.A.M. Dudley**)

No Author. Verdict on Civil Cause 298 for arson of Susan McSween's house. *Mesilla News*. **December 6, 1879**. Unpublished. personal communication from Frederick Nolan. July 29, 2005. (**Dudley exonerated**)

ELKINS, STEPHEN BENTON

BIOGRAPHICAL SOURCES (CHRONOLOGICAL)

Lambert, Oscar Doane. *Stephen Benton Elkins. American Foursquare.* Pittsburgh, Pennsylvania: University of Pittsburg Press. **1955**.

Cleaveland, Norman, *The Morleys - Young Upstarts on the Southwest Frontier.* Albuquerque, New Mexico: Calvin Horn Publisher, Inc. **1971**.

Westphall, Victor. *Thomas Benton Catron and His Era.* Tucson, Arizona: University of Arizona Press. **1973.**

Taylor, Morris F. *O.P. McMains and the Maxwell Land Grant Conflict.* Tucson, Arizona: The University of Arizona Press. **1979**. (**Traces origins of the Santa Fe Ring with T.B. Catron and S.B. Elkins**)

Cleaveland, Norman. *The Great Santa Fe Cover-up. Based on a Talk given Before the Santa Fe Historical Society on November 1, 1978.* Self-printed. **1982.**

__________. *A Synopsis of the Great New Mexico Cover-up.* Self-printed. **1989.**

EVANS, JESSIE

BIOGRAPHICAL SOURCE

McCright, Grady E. and James H. Powell. *Jessie Evans: Lincoln County Badman.* College Station, Texas: Creative Publishing Company. 1983.

FOUNTAIN, ALBERT JENNINGS

BIBLIOGRAPHICAL SOURCE

Gibson, A. M. *The Life and Death of Colonel Albert Jennings Fountain.* Norman: University of Oklahoma Press. 1965.

FRITZ FAMILY (EMIL AND CHARLES FRITZ AND EMILIE FRITZ SCHOLAND)

Fritz, Charles. Affidavit of **September 18, 1876** claiming that Emil Fritz had a will. Probate Court Record. (private collection)

__________. Affidavit of **September 26, 1876** Authorizing Alexander McSween to Receive Payments for the Emil Fritz Estate. Probate Court Record. (private collection)

Scholand, Emilie and Charles Fritz. Affidavit of **September 26, 1876** appointing McSween to collect debts for the Emil Fritz Estate. Copied from the original District Court Record. (private collection)

Fritz, Charles. Affidavit of **December 7, 1877** to order Alexander McSween to pay the Emil Fritz insurance policy money. Probate Court Record. (private collection)

Scholand, Emilie. Affidavit of **December 21, 1877** Accusing Alexander McSween of Embezzlement. Copied from the original District Court Record. (private collection)

Bristol Warren. "Writ of Embezzlement." **December 21, 1877**. Herman B. Weisner Papers, ca. 1957-1992. New Mexico State University Library at Las Cruces. Rio Grande Historical Collections. Accession No. Ms 0249. Box 10. Folder M-13. Folder Name. "Will and Testament A. McSween." (**Emilie Fritz Scholand's sworn complaint against Alexander McSween**)

Fritz, Charles. Affidavit sworn before John Crouch, Clerk of Doña Ana District Court, for Writ of Attachment issued against property of Alexander A. McSween. Probate Court Record. **February 6, 1878**. (private collection)

__________ and Emilie Scholand. Attachment Bond sworn before John Crouch, Clerk of Doña Ana District Court, against Alexander A. McSween for indebtedness to them. **February 6, 1878**. (private collection).

No Author. Diagram showing parcels of land to each of the heirs of Emil Fritz. Herman B. Weisner Papers, ca. 1957-1992. New Mexico State University Library at Las Cruces. Rio Grande Historical Collections. Accession No. Ms 0249. Box P1. Folder 11. Folder Name. "Charles Fritz Estate."

GARRETT, PATRICK FLOYD

BIBLIOGRAPHICAL SOURCES

Metz, Leon C. *Pat Garrett. The Story of a Western Lawman.* Norman: University of Oklahoma Press. 1974.

Mullin, Robert N. "Killing of Joe Briscoe." Letter to Eve Ball. January 31, 1964. (Unpublished). Binder RNM, VI, H. Nita Stewart Haley Memorial Museum. Haley Library. Midland, Texas.

__________. "Pat Garrett. Two Forgotten Killings." *Password.* X(2) (Summer 1965). pp. 57 - 65.

__________. "Skelton Glen's Manuscript Entitled 'Pat Garrett As I Knew Him on the Buffalo Ranges.'" (1890, Unpublished). Binder RNM, III B, 20. Nita Stewart Haley Memorial Museum. Haley Library. Midland, Texas. (**The killing of Joe Briscoe is recounted**)

AUTOBIOGRAPHICAL SOURCES

Garrett, Pat F. *The Authentic Life of Billy the Kid The Noted Desperado of the Southwest, Whose Deeds of Daring and Blood Made His Name a Terror in New Mexico, Arizona, and Northern Mexico.* Santa Fe, New Mexico: New Mexico Printing and Publishing Co. 1882. (Edition used: Edited by Maurice Garland Fulton. New York: The Macmillan Company. 1927)

REWARD FOR KILLING BILLY THE KID

No Author. No title. *Santa Fe Daily New Mexican.* **July 21, 1881.** Volume X, Number 120, Page 4. Column 1. NewspaperArchive.com. (**Pat Garrett's meeting with Acting Governor Ritch about the Billy the Kid reward.**)

Ritch, William G. "In the matter of the application by Patrick F. Garrett for a reward claimed to have been offered May-1881 for the capture of Wm Bonney alias "the Kid." *Executive Record Book Number 2.* July 25, 1867-November 8, 1882. **July 21, 1881**. Pages 533-535. New Mexico Secretary of State Records. Collection 1971-001, Series 1; Records of the Secretary of the Territory. (Accessed from Albuquerque Public Library Microfilm, Territorial Archives of New Mexico, Roll 21.) (**Presentation of Garret's bill for the reward, showing that Acting-Governor Ritch agreed with the reward, but legal opinion from Attorney General William Breeden necessitated getting a legislative act to convert Wallace's private reward to Territorial**)

No Author. "Kid the Killer Killed, Wm. Bonney alias Antrim, alias Billy the Kid, Fatally Meets Pat Garrett, the Lincoln County Sheriff." Las Cruces *Rio Grande Republican.* **July 23, 1881**. Page 2. Volume 1, Number 10. NewspaperArchive.com. (**Copy of Pat Garrett's letter to Acting Governor William Ritch confirming that the original Coroner's Jury Report was sent to District Attorney of the First Judicial District, and copy of it was included in this letter to the Governor**)

Sheldon, Lionel. "In the Matter of the Claim of Sheriff Pat Garrett." Letter to the Legislature. **February 14, 1882**. Territorial Archives of New Mexico. Microfilm Roll 5, Frame 765. (**As Governor, approving Garrett's reward and stating**

he would have granted it outright had it not already been sent to the Legislature by Acting-Governor Ritch for an act)

No Author. "An Act for the Relief of Pat. Garrett." *1882 Acts of the Legislative Assembly of the Territory of New Mexico, Twenty-Fifth Session. Convened at the Capitol, at the City of Santa Fe, on Monday, the 2d day of January, 1882, and adjourned on Thursday, the 2d day of March, 1882.* **February 18, 1882**. Chapter 101. Page 191. **(Granting Pat Garrett's reward for Billy the Kid, confirming it had been withheld on a technicality)**

Fulton, Maurice Garland. "I think I have solved the puzzle of the reward offers ..." October 28, 1951. Letter to Robert N. Mullin. Nita Stewart Haley Memorial Library and J. Evetts Haley History Center, Midland, Texas. Mullin Collection. Series RNM, VI, J, Legal Papers and Documents. "William Bonney, Reward for Death, Lincoln Notes." **(Confirming Attorney General's opinion to Acting Governor William Ritch about conversion of reward by legislative act)**

__________. "The rewards for the Kid give a clue to Catron's participation ..." **November 26, 1951.** Letter to Robert N. Mullin. Nita Stewart Haley Memorial Library and J. Evetts Haley History Center, Midland, Texas. Mullin Collection. Series RNM, VI, J, Legal Papers and Documents. "William Bonney, Rewards." **(Contemplating Catron's participation for the reward)**

__________. "Ritch was governor for the time-being ..." **March 15, 1953.** Letter to Robert N. Mullin. Nita Stewart Haley Memorial Library and J. Evetts Haley History Center, Midland, Texas. Mullin Collection. Series RNM, VI, J, Legal Papers and Documents. "William Bonney, Rewards." **(Confirming Attorney General's opinion to Acting Governor William Ritch about conversion of reward by legislative act)**

OTHER CONTEMPORARY SOURCES (CHRONOLOGICAL)

No Author. "Garrett Exonerates Maxwell." *Santa Fe Daily New Mexican.* **July 21, 1881**. Volume X, Number 120. NewspaperArchive.com. **(Confirming Pat Garrett's killing of Billy the Kid)**

Wild, Azariah F. "Daily Reports of U. S. Secret Service Agents, Azariah F. Wild." Microfilm T-915. Record Group 87. Roll 308 **(July 1, 1879 - June 30, 1881)**. National Archives and Records Administration. Department of the Treasury. United States Secret Service. Washington, D. C. **(Using Garrett to capture Billy Bonney)**

GAUSS, GOTTFRIED

Gauss, Gottfried. Interview with *Lincoln County Leader*. **November 21, 1889. (About Billy Bonney's Lincoln jailbreak)**

HOYT, HENRY F.

AUTOBIOGRAPHICAL SOURCE

Hoyt, Henry. *A Frontier Doctor.* Boston and New York: Houghton Mifflin Company. 1929. **(Describes Billy Bonney's superior abilities, pp. 93-94.)**

CONTEMPORARY SOURCES (CHRONOLOGICAL)

Bonney, William H. Bill of Sale to Henry Hoyt. **October 24, 1878**. Collection of Panhandle-Plains Historical Museum. Canyon, Texas. (Item No. X1974-98/1)

Hoyt, Henry F. "This time it is me who is apologizing ..." Letter to Lew Wallace Jr. (Lew Wallace's grandson) **April 27, 1927**. Indiana Historical Society. Lew Wallace Collection. M0292. Box 14, Folder 11.

__________. "Copy of a bill of sale written by Wm H. Bonney ..." Letter to Lew Wallace Jr. **April 27, 1927**. Indiana Historical Society. Lew Wallace Collection. M0292. Box 14, Folder 11.

LEONARD, IRA E.

BIOGRAPHICAL SOURCE

Nolan, Frederick. Biography and photograph of Ira Leonard. Unpublished. personal communication. July 29, 2005.

COURT OF INQUIRY OF N.A.M. DUDLEY BY (SEE: Nathan Augustus Monroe Dudley Court of Inquiry)

LETTERS TO AND FROM

LEW WALLACE TO AND FROM

Leonard, Ira E. "Dear Gov. You have undoubtedly learned ere this of the assassination ..." Letter to Lew Wallace. **February 24, 1879**. Indiana Historical Society. Lew Wallace Collection. M0292. Box 4. Folder 3. (**On Chapman murder.**)

Wallace, Lew. "It is important to take steps to protect the coming court ..." Letter to Ira Leonard. **April 6, 1879**. Indiana Historical Society. Lew Wallace Collection. M0292. Box 4. Folder 8.

Leonard, Ira. "The air is filled tonight with 'rumors of wars ... Letter to Lew Wallace. **April 20, 1879**. Indiana Historical Society. Lew Wallace Collection. M0292. Box 4. Folder 9. (**About District Attorney Rynerson: "He is bent on going for the Kid"**)

__________. "When you left here I promised to write you concerning events transpiring here ..." Letter to Lew Wallace. **May 20, 1878 [sic - 79]**. Indiana Historical Society. Lew Wallace Collection. M0292. Box 4. Folder 10. (**Has quote on the Murphy-Dolan party as: "part and parcel of the Santa Fe ring that has been so long an incubus on the government of this territory.")**

__________. "I write to you with pencil because I am laboring for breath ..." Letter to Lew Wallace. **May 23, 1879**. Indiana Historical Society. Lew Wallace Collection. M0292. Box 4. Folder 11. (**With quote "we are pouring the 'hot shot' into Dudley." (With enclosed letter of May 20, 1879**)

__________. "Dudley commenced on the defense Thursday afternoon ..." Letter to Wallace. **June 6, 1879**, Indiana Historical Society. Lew Wallace Collection. M0292. Box 4. Folder 11. (**About disgust at corrupt Court."**)

__________. "Yours of the 7th inst reached me ..." Letter to Lew Wallace. **June 13, 1879**. Indiana Historical Society. Lew Wallace Collection. M0292. Box 4. Folder 11. (**about Court of Inquiry corruption**)

MAXWELL, DELUVINA

Maxwell, Deluvina. "I came here after Lucien Maxwell was already here...." Letter to J. Evetts Haley. June 24, 1927. Nita Stewart Haley Memorial Library and J. Evetts Haley History Center, Midland, Texas. J. Evetts Haley Collection, JEH, J-I – Maxwell, Deluvina. (**Debunking that Peter Maxwell's bedroom had no door to the outside, and that Pat Garrett did not kill Billy the Kid**)

MAXWELL FAMILY

Cleaveland, Agnes Morley. *No Life for a Lady*. Boston: Houghton Mifflin. 1941.

__________. *Satan's Paradise: From Lucien Maxwell to Fred Lambert*. Boston: Houghton Mifflin Company. 1952.

Cleaveland, Norman. *The Morleys - Young Upstarts on the Southwest Frontier*. Albuquerque, New Mexico: Calvin Horn Publisher, Inc. 1971.

Dunham, Harold H. "New Mexican Land Grants with Special Reference to the Title Papers of the Maxwell Grant." *New Mexico Historical Review*. (January 1955) Vol. 30, No. 1. pp. 1 - 23.

Freiberger, Harriet. *Lucien Maxwell: Villain or Visionary*. Santa Fe, New Mexico: Sunstone Press. 1999.

Keleher, William A. *The Maxwell Land Grant. A New Mexico Item*. Albuquerque, New Mexico: University of New Mexico Press. 1964.

Lamar, Howard Roberts. *The Far Southwest 1846 - 1912. A Territorial History*. New Haven and London: Yale University Press. 1966.

Miller, Kenny. Descendant of Lucien Bonaparte Maxwell. Personal communication. 2011 to 2012.

Montoya, María E. *Translating Property. The Maxwell Land Grant and the Conflict Over Land in the American West, 1840-1900*. Berkeley and Los Angeles, California: University of California Press. 2002.

Murphy, Lawrence R. *Lucien Bonaparte Maxwell. Napoleon of the Southwest*. Norman: University of Oklahoma Press. 1983.

Pearson, Jim Berry. *The Maxwell Land Grant*. Norman: University of Oklahoma Press. 1961.

Poe, Sophie. *Buckboard Days*. Albuquerque, New Mexico: University of New Mexico Press. 1964.

Taylor, Morris F. *O. P. McMains and the Maxwell Land Grant Conflict*. Tucson, Arizona: The University of Arizona Press. 1979. (**Origins of Santa Fe Ring**)

No Author. "Mrs. Paula M. Jaramillo, 65 Died Here Tuesday." *The Fort Sumner Leader*. Official Newspaper County of De Baca. December 20, 1929. No. 1158, Page 1, Column 1. (**Billy Bonney's sweetheart, Paulita Maxwell**)

COMMANDING OFFICER'S QUARTERS BEFORE MAXWELL FAMILY CONVERSION

Diagram. "Commanding Officer's Quarters Fort Sumner, New Mexico Territory." National Archives, Microfilm RG 98, Consolidated Files Quartermaster General; with copy in Fort Sumner, New Mexico, State Monument. (**Faked in *Cold Case Billy the Kid* as being the Maxwell house itself**)

MAXWELL FAMILY HOUSE IN FORT SUMNER

Drawing. "As per Burns account." Maxwell family house, and diagram of Peter Maxwell's bedroom with external door. Nita Stewart Haley Memorial Library and J. Evetts Haley History Center, Midland, Texas. Mullin Collection. Series RNM, IV, Y, Notebook: Places and Events, A-O. (**Debunking *Cold Case Billy the Kid* hoax that Peter Maxwell's bedroom had no door to the outside**)

Photograph. "Pete Maxwell's House Fort Sumner." Annotated on back by Robert N. Mullin. **Undated.** Nita Stewart Haley Memorial Library and J. Evetts Haley History Center, Midland, Texas. Mullin Collection. Series RNM, IV, A, 161.0. (**Maxwell family house showing external door in Peter Maxwell's bedroom debunking *Cold Case Billy the Kid* that the Maxwell house was one story and that Maxwell's bedroom had no door to the outside**)

Mullin, Robert N. "Pete Maxwell's House Fort Sumner, Prior to Erection of New Home 2 ½ Mi. S.E.[after sale of town]; Originally 1 Story Flat Roof, Officers Quarters. 2nd Floor Added By Maxwell." Annotation on back of photograph of Maxwell house. **Undated.** . Nita Stewart Haley Memorial Library and J. Evetts Haley History Center, Midland, Texas. Mullin Collection. Series RNM, IV, A, 161.0. (**Making clear the distinction between the Officer's Quarters and the later Maxwell house**)

MAXWELL FAMILY FURNITURE

Blythe, Dee. "Billy the Kid Landmarks Fast Vanishing: Historic Spots Hard to Find; Markers Needed." *Clovis, New Mexico Evening News-Journal*. **May 31, 1937** Volume 9. Number 2. Section E. Monday,. (**Photo and article about Maxwell family furniture**)

Weddle, Jerry. "The Kid at Old Fort Sumner." *The Outlaw Gazette: Billy the Kid Outlaw Gang New Mexico.* **December, 1992. (Louisa Beaubien Barrett, Luz Maxwell's niece, error-filled history as recorded by her daughter Marian Barrett, including the claim that Pat Garrett's second shot went through a washstand; later used in the "Billy the Kid Case" hoax)**

__________. Statement that he interviewed Stella Abreu Maxwell in Albuquerque in her old age, and she stated she got the carpenter's bench from a man in Fort Sumner for her 1925 Billy the Kid Museum. Author's interview. February 5, 2018. (**The bench had not been kept by the family**)

McSWEEN, ALEXANDER

Bristol Warren. "Writ of Embezzlement." **December 21, 1877**. Writ of Embezzlement. New Mexico State University Library at Las Cruces. Rio Grande Historical Collections. Lincoln County Papers. New Mexico State University Library at Las Cruces. Rio Grande Historical Collections. Accession No. Ms 0249. Box No. 10. Folder M-13. "Will and Testament A. McSween."

Fritz, Charles. Affidavit sworn before John Crouch, Clerk of Doña Ana District Court, for Writ of Attachment issued against property of Alexander A. McSween. Probate Court Record. **February 6, 1878**. (private collection).

Bristol, Warren. Action of Assumpsit to command Sheriff of Lincoln County to attach goods of Alexander A. McSween. **February 7, 1878**. District Court Record. (private collection).

__________. Preprinted form in his name for "Writ of Attachment" filled out to command the Sheriff of Lincoln County to attach goods of Alexander McSween for a suit of damages for ten thousand dollars. **February 7, 1878**. (private collection).

McSween, Alexander. "It looks as though the agent were the property of J.J. Dolan & J.H. Riley, known here as Dolan & Co." Letter to Secretary of Interior Carl Schurz. **February 11, 1878**. From Frederick Nolan. *The Life and Death of John Henry Tunstall.* Albuquerque, New Mexico: The University of New Mexico Press. 1965. Page 266.

__________. "Will and Testament A. McSween." **February 25, 1878**. Herman B. Weisner Papers, ca. 1957-1992. New Mexico State University Library at Las Cruces. Rio Grande Historical Collections. Accession No. Ms 0249. Box 10. Folder M15. Folder Name. "Will and Testament A. McSween."

__________. Deposition to Frank Warner Angel. **June 6, 1878**. Pages 5-183 of Frank Warner Angel report *In the Matter of the Examination of the Causes and Circumstances of the Death of John H. Tunstall a British Subject.* Report filed **October 4, 1878**. Angel Report. Microfilm File Case Number 44-4-8-3. Record Group 48. Microfilm No. M750. Roll 1. National Archives and Records Administration. U.S. Department of Justice. Washington, D.C. (**Reports secret**

Angel, Frank Warner. *In the Matter of the Lincoln County Troubles. To the Honorable Charles Devens, Attorney General.* **October 4, 1878**. Angel Report. Microfilm File Case Number 44-4-8-3. Record Group 48. Microfilm No. M750. Roll 1. National Archives and Records Administration. U.S. Department of Justice. Washington, D.C.

McSWEEN, SUSAN

BIOGRAPHICAL SOURCE FOR

Chamberlain, Kathleen P. *In the Shadow of Billy the Kid: Susan McSween and the Lincoln County War.* Albuquerque: University of New Mexico Press. 2013.

CONTEMPORARY SOURCES ABOUT (CHRONOLOGICAL)

Dudley, Nathan Augustus Monroe. "I am in receipt of a copy of letter written by one H.I. Chapman, calling himself the Attorney ..." **November 9, 1878**. Letter to Lew

Wallace. From *Proceedings of a Court of Inquiry in the Case of Lt. Col. N.A.M. Dudley (May 2,1879 – July 5, 1879).* File No. QQ1284. (Boxes 3304, 3305, 3305A); Court Martial Files 1809-1894. Records of the Office of the Judge Advocate General - Army. Record Group 153. Old Military and Civil Branch. National Archives and Records Administration. Washington, D.C. (**Answer to charges, with attached defamatory affidavits against Susan McSween**)

McSween, Susan. Testimony in Court of Inquiry for Lieutenant Colonel N.A.M. Dudley. **May 23-24, 26, 1879**. *Proceedings of a Court of Inquiry in the Case of Lt. Col. N.A.M. Dudley (May 2,1879 – July 5, 1879).* File No. QQ1284. (Boxes 3304, 3305, 3305A); Court Martial Files 1809-1894. Records of the Office of the Judge Advocate General – Army. Record Group 153. Old Military and Civil Branch. National Archives and Records Administration. Washington, D.C.

No Author. Verdict on Civil Cause 298 for arson of Susan McSween's house. *Mesilla News*. **December 6, 1879**. Unpublished. personal communication from Frederick Nolan. July 29, 2005. (**Dudley exonerated**)

MEADOWS, JOHN P.

Meadows, John P. "Billy the Kid to John P. Meadows on the Peñasco, May 1-2, 1881." *Roswell Daily Record*. February 16, 1931. Page 6.

Meadows, John P. Ed. John P. Wilson. *Pat Garrett and Billy the Kid as I Knew Them: Reminiscences of John P. Meadows*. Albuquerque: University of New Mexico Press. 2004.

MURPHY, LAWRENCE GUSTAV

Murphy, Lawrence G. "Will of Lawrence G. Murphy." Herman B. Weisner Papers, ca. 1957-1992. New Mexico State University Library at Las Cruces. Rio Grande Historical Collections. Accession No. Ms 0249. Box 11. Folder P15. Folder Name: "Murphy, Lawrence G."

PEPPIN, GEORGE

No Author. "Old Citizen Gone." *Capitan News*. **September 23, 1904.** Volume 5. Number 29. Page 4. Center for Southwest Research. Microfilm AN2.L52a.

POE, JOHN WILLIAM

Poe, John W. "The Killing of Billy the Kid." (a personal letter written at Roswell, New Mexico to Mr. Charles Goodnight, Goodnight P.C., Texas) July 10, 1917.

__________. *The Death of Billy the Kid*. (Introduction by Maurice Garland Fulton). Boston and New York: Houghton Mifflin Company. 1933.

Poe, Sophie. *Buckboard Days*. Albuquerque, New Mexico: University of New Mexico Press. 1964.

RILEY, JOHN HENRY

CONTEMPORARY SOURCES ABOUT

Tunstall, John Henry. "A Tax-payer's Complaint, Office of John H. Tunstall, Lincoln, Lincoln Co., N.M., January 18, 1878, 'The Present Sheriff of Lincoln County Has Paid Nothing During His Present Term of Office.' Governor's Message for 1878." Mesilla *Independent*. **January 26, 1878**. Volume 1, Number 32. NewspaperArchive.com. (**Exposé of William Brady and John Riley for embezzling tax money to buy cattle; and T.B. Catron then paid that bill**)

Dolan, James J. "Answer to A Taxpayer's Complaint." Mesilla *Independent*. **January 29, 1878**. (**Response to J.H. Tunstall's exposé**)

McSween, Alexander. "It looks as though the [Indian] agent were the property of J.J. Dolan & J.H. Riley, known here as Dolan & Co." Letter to Secretary of Interior Carl Schurz. **February 11, 1878**. From Frederick Nolan. *The Life and*

Death of John Henry Tunstall. Albuquerque, New Mexico: The University of New Mexico Press. 1965. Page 266.

RUDuLPH, MILNOR

Keleher, William A. *Violence in Lincoln County 1869-1881*. Pages 350-351. Albuquerque, New Mexico: University of New Mexico Press. 1957.

(SEE: Coroner's Jury Report of William Bonney)

RYNERSON, WILLIAM LOGAN

BIOGRAPHICAL SOURCES

Miller, Darlis A. "William Logan Rynerson in New Mexico. 1862-1893." *New Mexico Historical Review* 48 (April 1973) pp. 101-131.

No Author. "A Brief History of the Rynerson House." Las Cruces: Del Valle Design & Imaging. No copyright. https://delvalleprintinglc.com/rynerson-house/.

CONTEMPORARY SOURCES BY AND ABOUT (CHRONOLOGICAL)

Rynerson, William L "Indictments of the April, Lincoln County Grand Jury." **April 28, 1879**. Herman B. Weisner Papers, ca. 1957-1992. New Mexico State University Library at Las Cruces. Rio Grande Historical Society Collection. Accession No. Ms 0249. Box 4/39. Folder E-Z. Folder Name: "Jessie Evans Accessory to Murder." **(Indictments of Dolan, Campbell, and Evans)**

___________. "Friends Riley & Dolan, Lincoln N.M. I have just received letters from you mailed 10th inst." Letter to James Dolan and John Riley. **February 14, 1878**. Copy as Exhibit B in June 6, 1878 deposition of Alexander McSween. Frank Warner Angel report. *In the Matter of the Examination of the Causes and Circumstances of the Death of John H. Tunstall a British Subject*. Report filed October 4, 1878. Interior Department Papers 1850-1907; Appointments Division and Subsequent Actions. Microfilm File Case Number 44-4-8-3. Microfilm No. M750. Roll 1. National Archives and Records Administration. U.S. Department of Justice. Washington, D.C. (James J. Dolan Deposition. June 20, 1878. Pages 235-247.) **(Planned killing of J.H. Tunstall)**

Angel, Frank Warner. "I have just been favored by a call from W.L. Rynerson ..." Letter to Secretary of Interior Carl Schurz. **September 6, 1878**. Microfilm File Case Number 44-4-8-3. Record Group 48. Microfilm No. M750. Roll 1. National Archives and Records Administration. U. S. Department of Justice. Washington, D.C.

Rynerson, William. Venue Change. **April 21, 1879**. Herman B. Weisner Papers, ca. 1957-1992. New Mexico State University Library at Las Cruces. Rio Grande Historical Collection. Accession No. Ms 0249. Box 1. Folder 14-D. Folder Name: "Billy the Kid Legal Documents." **(Change of Billy Bonney's trial venue from Lincoln County to Doña Ana County to insure a hanging trial by prevent Lincoln County citizens knowledgeable about the War being jurors)**

SALAZAR, YGINIO

Salazar, Joe. (Grandson of Yginio Salazar). Personal Interviews 1999-2001. **(My interviews about Ygenio)**

TUNSTALL, JOHN HENRY

BIOGRAPHICAL SOURCES

Nolan, Frederick W. *The Life and Death of John Henry Tunstall*. Albuquerque, New Mexico: The University of New Mexico Press. 1965.

CONTEMPORARY SOURCES (CHRONOLOGICAL)

Tunstall, John Henry. "A Tax-payer's Complaint, Office of John H. Tunstall, Lincoln, Lincoln Co., N.M., January 18, 1878, 'The Present Sheriff of Lincoln County Has Paid Nothing During His Present Term of Office.' Governor's Message for 1878." Mesilla *Independent*. **January 26, 1878**. Volume 1, Number 32. NewspaperArchive.com. **(Exposé of William Brady and John Riley for embezzling tax money to buy cattle; and T.B. Catron then paid that bill)**

Dolan, James J. "Answer to A Taxpayer's Complaint." Mesilla *Independent*. **January 29, 1878. (Response to J.H. Tunstall's exposé of embezzlement of tax money to buy cattle)**

Rynerson, William. "Friends Riley & Dolan, Lincoln N.M. I have just received letters from you mailed 10th inst." Letter to James Dolan and John Riley. **February 14, 1878**. Copy as Exhibit B in June 6, 1878 deposition of Alexander McSween. Frank Warner Angel report. *In the Matter of the Examination of the Causes and Circumstances of the Death of John H. Tunstall a British Subject.* Report filed October 4, 1878. Interior Department Papers 1850-1907; Appointments Division and Subsequent Actions. Microfilm File Case Number 44-4-8-3. Record Group 48. Microfilm No. M750. Roll 1. National Archives and Records Administration. U. S. Department of Justice. Washington, D.C. (James J. Dolan Deposition. June 20, 1878. pp. 235-247.) **(Planned killing of J.H. Tunstall)**

Wilson, John, George B. Barker, Robert M. Gilbert, John Newcomb, Samuel Smith, Benjamin Ellis. "We the undersigned Justice of the Peace and Coroners Jury who sat upon the inquest held this 19th day of February 1878 on the body of John H. Tunstall ..." Coroner's Jury Report for John Tunstall. **February 19, 1878. (Naming Tunstall's murderers)**

Springer, Frank. "I hope you have received a full account of the Troubles in Lincoln County from your nephew ..." Letter to Senator Rush Clark. **April 9, 1878**. Herman B. Weisner Papers, ca. 1957-1992. New Mexico State University Library at Las Cruces. Rio Grande Historical Collections. Accession No. Ms 0249. Box 4/39. Folder D-6. Folder Name "Frank Springer Letter to Rush Clark." **(Links Santa Fe Ring to murder of J.H. Tunstall)**

(SEE: Frank Warner Angel)

WALLACE, LEW

AUTOBIOGRAPHICAL AND BIOGRAPHICAL SOURCES

Governor of Territorial New Mexico 1878-81." *New Mexico Historical Review. 59(1)* (January, 1984).

Morsberger, Robert E. and Katherine M. Morsberger. *Lew Wallace: Militant Romantic.* New York: McGraw-Hill Book Company. 1980.

Wallace, Lew. *An Autobiography. Vol. I.* New York and London: Harper and Brothers Publishers. 1997.

___________. *An Autobiography. Vol. II.* New York and London: Harper and Brothers Publishers. 1997.

COLLECTED PAPERS OF

Wallace, Lew. Collected Papers Microfilm Project Sponsored by the National Historical Publications Commission. Microfilm Roll No. 99. Santa Fe, New Mexico: State of New Mexico Records Center and Archives. 1974.

___________. Lew and Susan Wallace Collection. Indiana Historical Society. M0292.

___________. Collected Papers. Lilly Library. Bloomington, Indiana.

SECRET ANGEL NOTEBOOK ON SANTA FE RING FOR

Angel, Frank Warner. "To Gov. Lew Wallace, Santa Fe, N. M., 1878." Notebook. **1878**. Indiana Historical Society. Lew Wallace Collection. M0292. Microfilm No. F372. (**Original missing, copy on microfilm; secret notebook prepared for Lew Wallace listing names for Lincoln County and the Santa Fe Ring**)

Theisen, Lee Scott. "Frank Warner Angel's Notes on New Mexico Territory, 1878." *Arizona and the West: A Quarterly Journal of History*. Winter 1976. Volume 18. Number 4. Pages 333-370. (**About the Angel notebook**)

AMNESTY PROCLAMATION OF

Wallace, Lew. "Proclamation by the Governor." **November 13, 1878**. Indiana Historical Society. Lew Wallace Collection. M0292. Box 3. Folder 17. (**Amnesty Proclamation for Lincoln County War fighters, but excluding those already indicted, like Billy Bonney**)

DUDLEY COURT OF INQUIRY TESTIMONY BY

Wallace, Lew. Testimony in Court of Inquiry for Lieutenant Colonel N.A.M. Dudley. **May 12-15, 1879**. *Proceedings of a Court of Inquiry in the Case of Lt. Col. N.A.M. Dudley (May 2,1879 – July 5, 1879)*. File No. QQ1284. (Boxes 3304, 3305, 3305A); Court Martial Files 1809-1894. Records of the Office of the Judge Advocate General – Army. Record Group 153. Old Military and Civil Branch. National Archives and Records Administration. Washington, D.C.

INTERVIEW NOTES ON BILLY BONNEY BY (SEE: William H. Bonney)

REWARD NOTICES AND POSTERS FOR WILLIAM BONNEY BY (SEE: William H. Bonney)

LETTERS BY AND TO

TO AND FROM WILLIAM BONNEY

(SEE: History of William H. Bonney)

TO SHERIFF PATRICK F. GARRETT

Wallace, Lew. "To the Sheriff of Lincoln County, New Mexico, Greeting ..." **April 30, 1881**. Indiana Historical Society. Lew Wallace Collection. M0292. Box 9. Folder 11. (**Death Warrant for William Bonney after his Mesilla trial and before his Lincoln jailbreak**)

TO AND FROM IRA E. LEONARD (SEE: Ira Leonard)

TO AND FROM JUSTICE OF THE PEACE JOHN B. WILSON

Wallace, Lew. "I hasten to acknowledge receipt of your favor of the 11th Jan. ult. ..." **January 18, 1879**. Indiana Historical Society. Lew Wallace Collection. M0292. Box 4. Folder 1. (**Lincoln County as carrying on a revolution**)

Wallace, Lew. "I enclose a note for Bonney." Letter to John "Squire" Wilson. **March 20, 1879.** Indiana Historical Society. Lew Wallace Collection. M0292. Box 4. Folder 6. (**The pardon negotiation for Billy Bonney**)

Wilson, John B. Signed JBW. **April 8, 1879**. Indiana Historical Society, Lew Wallace Collection. M0292. Box 4, Folder 8. (**Notes on rustling**)

__________. Letter to Lew Wallace. **May 18, 1879**. Indiana Historical Society. Lew Wallace Collection. M0292. Box 4, Folder 5.

ARTICLES ABOUT WILLIAM BONNEY BY (SEE: William H. Bonney)

WILD, AZARIAH

BIOGRAPHICAL SOURCES

Brooks, James J. *1877 Report on Secret Service Operatives.* "On Azariah Wild." **September 26, 1877**. Page 392. Department of the Treasury. United States Secret Service. Washington, D.C.

Nolan, Frederick. "Biography of Azariah Wild." Unpublished and personal communications, June 11, 2005 and October 9, 2005.

CONTEMPORARY SOURCES (CHRONOLOGICAL)

Wild, Azariah F. "Daily Reports of U. S. Secret Service Agents, 1875-1937." Record Group 87. Microfilm T-915. Microfilm Rolls 306 (June 15, 1877 - December 31, 1877), 307 (January 1,1878 - June 30, 1879), 308 (July 1, 1879 - June 30, 1881; October 4, 1880, Pages 330-333; October 5, 1880, Pages 336-339; November 11, 1880, Pages 484-488), 309 (July 1, 1881 - September 30, 1883), 310 (October 1, 1883 - July 31, 1886). National Archives and Records Department. Department of the Treasury. Secret Service Division. Washington, D.C.

WILSON, JOHN B. "SQUIRE"

CORONER'S JURY REPORT FOR JOHN H. TUNSTALL BY

Wilson, John, George B. Barker, Robert M. Gilbert, John Newcomb, Samuel Smith, Benjamin Ellis. "We the undersigned Justice of the Peace and Coroners Jury who sat upon the inquest held this 19th day of February 1878 on the body of John H. Tunstall ..." Coroner's Jury Report for John Tunstall. **February 19, 1878**. (**Naming as murderers, among others, James Dolan, Frank Baker, Jessie Evans, William Morton, and George Hindman**)

LETTERS FROM

Wilson, John B. Letter to Lew Wallace. Unsigned but noted as from "Sqr. Wilson by Wallace. Undated, but likely **March, 1879**. Indiana Historical Society. Lew Wallace Collection. M0292. Box 4, Folder 7. (**On Lady Liberty stationery**)

__________. Affidavit of John Wilson. **March ?, 1879**. Indiana Historical Society. Lew Wallace Collection. M0292. Box 4, Folder 7.

__________. Signed JBW. **April 8, 1879**. Indiana Historical Society, Lew Wallace Collection. M0292. Box 4, Folder 8. (**Notes on rustling**)

__________. Letter to Lew Wallace. **May 18, 1879**. Indiana Historical Society. Lew Wallace Collection. M0292. Box 4, Folder 5.

LETTERS TO

Bonney, W H. "Friend Wilson ..." **March 18, 1879**. Indiana Historical Society. Lew Wallace Collection. M0292 (**For mediating his pardon negotiation with Lew Wallace**)

Wallace, Lew. "I enclose a note for Bonney." Letter to John "Squire" Wilson. **March 20, 1879.** Indiana Historical Society. Lew Wallace Collection. M0292. Box 4. Folder 6. (**The pardon negotiation for Billy Bonney**)

OLIVER "BRUSHY BILL" ROBERTS BILLY THE KID IMPOSTER HOAX

SOURCES TO DEBUNK CLAIMS IN "BRUSHY BILL" HOAX, IN ADDITION TO CITED SOURCES FOR WILLIAM BONNEY'S REAL HISTORY (CHRONOLOGICAL)

HOAX-BACKING BOOKS (CHRONOLOGICAL)

Sonnichsen, C.L. and William V. Morrison. *Alias Billy the Kid*. Albuquerque, New Mexico: University of New Mexico Press. **1955**. (**Portraying "Brushy Bill" Roberts as Billy the Kid**)

Jameson, W.C. and Frederic Bean. *The Return of the Outlaw Billy the Kid*. Plano, Texas: Republic of Texas Press. **1998**. (**Backing Roberts as Billy the Kid**)

Jameson, W.C. and Frederic Bean. *The Return of the Outlaw Billy the Kid*. Plano, Texas: Republic of Texas Press. **1998**. (**Backing Roberts as Billy the Kid**)

__________. *Billy the Kid: Beyond the Grave*. Boulder, Lanham, Maryland: Taylor Trade Publishing. **2005**. (**A repeat of the "Brushy Bill" imposter hoax**)

__________. *Billy the Kid: The Lost Interviews*. Clearwater, Florida: Garlic Press Publishing. **2012.** (Reprint 2017). (**Forged rewriting of the 1949 Morrison transcript of "Brushy" to fake dialogue to update the hoax**)

__________. *Pat Garrett: The Man Behind the Badge*. Boulder, Colorado: Taylor Trade Publishing. **2016**. (**Defamation of Pat Garrett as murdering an innocent victim instead of Billy the Kid**)

__________. *Cold Case Billy the Kid: Investigating History's Mysteries*. Guilford, Connecticut: Twodot. **2018.** (**Fusing the "Brushy" hoax and "Billy the Kid Case" hoax to argue for "Brushy" as Billy the Kid**)

DEBUNKING SOURCES

No Author. Roberts family members. Federal Census for Arkansas, Sebastian County, Bates Township. **June 1, 1880.** Lines 27-33. (**Cited in Don Cline's *Brushy Bill Roberts: I Wasn't Billy the Kid* to show "Brushy" was 10 months old at the census – 20 years too young to be Billy Bonney**)

Rudulph, Milnor. Coroner's Jury Report for William Bonney alias "Kid." **July 15, 1881.** Indiana Historical Society. Lew Wallace Collection. M0292. Box 9. Folder 11. Accession Number 1951.0104 from Maurice G. Fulton. (**Photostatic copy of original Spanish Coroner's Jury Report, certified on January 18, 1951, donated by Maurice Garland Fulton - matches photo in William Kelleher's *Violence in Lincoln County* copy**)

Ritch, William G. "In the matter of the application by Patrick F. Garrett for a reward claimed to have been offered May-1881 for the capture of Wm Bonney alias "the Kid." *Executive Record Book Number 2*. July 25, 1867-November 8, 1882. **July 21, 1881**. Pages 533-535. New Mexico Secretary of State Records. Collection 1971-001, Series 1; Records of the Secretary of the Territory. (Accessed from Albuquerque Public Library Microfilm, Territorial Archives of New Mexico, Roll 21.) (**"Brushy Bill" hoax fakes that reward was withheld from Garrett for no Coroner's Jury Report and proof of body**)

No Author. "Kid the Killer Killed, Wm. Bonney alias Antrim, alias Billy the Kid, Fatally Meets Pat Garrett, the Lincoln County Sheriff." Las Cruces *Rio Grande Republican*. **July 23, 1881**. Page 2. Volume 1, Number 10. NewspaperArchive.com. (**Copy of Pat Garrett's letter to Acting-Governor Ritch confirming that the Coroner's Jury Report was sent to District Attorney of the First Judicial District, and copy to him**)

No Author. " 'The Kid' Killed! He Meets His Death at the Hands of Sheriff Pat Garrett, of Lincoln County. The Particulars of the Affair as Poured into the Ears of Eager Reporters. *The Las Vegas Daily Optic.* **July 18, 1881**. Volume 2, Number 217. NewspaperArchives.com. (**Confirming Pat Garrett's killing of Billy the Kid**)

No Author. *Executive Record Book Number 2.* July 25, 1867-November 8, 1882. **July 21, 1881.** Pages 533-535. New Mexico State Records Center and Archives, Santa Fe. New Mexico Secretary of the State Records Series 1. Records of the Secretary of the Territory. (**About granting Garrett's reward; "Brushy" hoax faked an irregularity**)

No Author. "Garrett Exonerates Maxwell." *Santa Fe Daily New Mexican.* **July 21, 1881**. Volume X, Number 120. NewspaperArchives.com. (**Confirming Pat Garrett's killing of Billy the Kid**)

No Author. No title. *Santa Fe Daily New Mexican.* **July 21, 1881.** Volume X, Number 120, Page 4. Column 1. (**Pat Garrett's presentation to Acting-Governor Ritch of his reward request, with Ritch willing to pay**)

No Author. "Words of Commendation and Encouragement." *Las Vegas Daily Gazette.* **July 22, 1881.** Volume 3. Number 15. Newspapers.com. (**Confirming Pat Garrett's killing of Billy the Kid**)

Ashenfelter, Singleton M. "Exit 'The Kid', The Fugitive Murderer Hunted Down and Killed by Sheriff Garrett." *The New Southwest, And Grant County Herald.* **July 23, 1881.** Number 30. University of New Mexico. Zimmerman Library. Microfilm AN2 G71. (**Apocryphal description of Billy the Kid's body, but confirmation of the killing**)

No Author. "The Life of Billy the Kid. His Name Was Billy McCarthy, and He was Born in New York." *The New York Sun.* (From *The St. Louis Globe-Democrat*) **August 10, 1881.** Volume XLIII, Number 314. Newspapers.com. (**Confirming Pat Garrett's killing of Billy the Kid**)

Glen, Skelton. "Pat Garrett As I Knew Him on the Buffalo Ranges." (**1890**, Unpublished). Binder RNM, III B 20. Nita Stewart Haley Memorial Museum. Haley Library. Midland, Texas. (**The killing of Joe Briscoe is recounted, but was unknown to "Brushy" who garbled it from a John Meadows article**)

Taeger, Mary Nell. "Severo Gallegos Tells His Story and of His Family's Friend, 'Billy the Kid.' " *Ruidoso News.* **July 30, 1948.** Front page, Page 6. Volume II, Number 11. NewspaperArchive.com. (**A Billy the Kid history confabulator, used by Morrison as a prompt for "Brushy's" jailbreak tale. Gallegos was then used give a fake affidavit that "Brushy" was Billy**)

___________. No Author. "Severo Gallegos Tells His Story and of His Family's Friend, 'Billy the Kid.' " (continued) *Ruidoso News.* **August 6, 1948.** Page 3. Volume II, Number 12. NewspaperArchive.com. (**A Billy the Kid history confabulator used for "Brushy Bill" hoax**)

No Author. "Fort Sumner Jury Thought the Kid Had Been Killed." *Alamogordo News.* **November 30, 1950.** Volume 53, Number 48. .NewspaperArchive.com. (**Finding the Coroner's Jury Report; ignored in *Alias Billy the Kid***)

No Author. Will A. Keleher, History Student, Sure Kid Was Shot." *Albuquerque Journal.* **December 1, 1950**. Volume illegible, Number 61. Newspaperarchive.com. (**Debunking "Brushy's" claim to be Billy the Kid**)

No Author. "Notorious Character is Buried." *Hico News Review.* **January 5, 1951.** Front Page. Volume LXV, Number 34. Texas Tech University Library. Southwest Collections/Special Collections Library. Microfilm H626 Hico (Texas) News Review 1929-1974 Reel 8. (**Obituary of "Brushy Bill" Roberts**)

Morrison, William V. Letter to Philip Rasch. **April 12, 1954.** Rio Grande Historical Collections./Hobson Huntslinger University Archives. New Mexico State University, Las Cruces. (**Lying that he was being backed for "Brushy" by many people, including William Keleher**)

Keleher, William A. *Violence in Lincoln County 1869-1881.* Albuquerque, New Mexico: University of New Mexico Press. **1957**. (**Photocopy of Spanish Coroner's Jury**

Report, July 15, 1881. Pages 306-308; Kelleher's English translation, Pages 343-344.)

Pittmon, Geneva Roberts. "Dear Sir: the reason you are not finding my family ..." **December 16, 1987.** Letter to Joe Bowlin. In collection of Old Fort Sumner Museum, Fort Sumner, New Mexico. (**Roberts's niece using family Bible to prove Roberts was not Billy the Kid**)

__________. "I don't know of any job he held ..." Letter to Don Cline. **April 27, 1988. (Cited in Don Cline's *Brushy Bill Roberts: I Wasn't Billy the Kid* to show "Brushy" was a mentally disabled farm hand in his real life.**)

Cline, Don. *Brushy Bill Roberts: I Wasn't Billy the Kid.* **Undated [1988 or 1989?].** Unpublished manuscript. New Mexico Commission of Public Records. State Records Center and Archives. Santa Fe. MS Donald Cline Collection. Subseries 5.2, Folder 138. Box 10421. Serial No. 9560 Santa Fe NMSRCA. (**Debunking "Brushy's" Billy the Kid claims**)

__________. Interview with "Brushy's" brother, Tom's daughter, Mary June Roberts. January 28, 1988. (**Denying "Brushy's" genealogical claims**)

Anaya, Paco. *I Buried Billy.* College Station, Texas: Creative Publishing Company. 1991. (**Eye-witness claim of burying Billy Bonney**)

Nolan, Frederick. *The West of Billy the Kid.* Norman: University of Oklahoma Press. **1998**. (**See Page 7 for quote on the Eugene Cunningham hoaxed photo of Catherine Antrim, which "Brushy" confabulated as his aunt, Kathleen Bonney**)

Johnson, Jim. *Billy the Kid: His Real Name Was ...*" Denver, Colorado: Outskirts Press, Inc. **2006**. (**Debunking Roberts as Billy the Kid**)

Haws, Roy L. *Brushy Bill: Proof That His Claim to Be Billy the Kid Was a Hoax.* Santa Fe: Sunstone Press. **2015**. (**Roberts relative debunking him as Billy the Kid**)

No Author. "Memorials." *El Paso Post-Herald.* **September 9, 1977.** Volume XCVII, Number 216. Page 24, Column 5. Newspaperarchive.com (**Obituary for William V. Morrison, showing he was not an attorney**)

Cooper, Gale. *The Cold Case Billy the Kid: Megahoax: The Plot to Steal Billy the Kid's Identity and Defame Sheriff Pat Garrett as a Murderer.* . Albuquerque, New Mexico: Gelcour Books. **2019**.

__________. *The Billy the Kid Imposter Hoax of Brushy Bill Roberts.* Albuquerque, New Mexico: Gelcour Books. **2019**.

(See William H. Bonney's Coroner's Jury Report)

ABOUT REJECTED PARDON OF (CHRONOLOGICAL)

Humphreys, Sexton. "Pardon Me, I'm Alive," Says Billy the Kid." *Indianapolis News.* **November 25, 1950**. Page 9. Indiana Historical Society. Lew Wallace Collection. M0292. Box 14. Folder 12.

Morgan, Art. "Billy the Kid Only a Phony It Turns Out." *Santa Fe New Mexican.* **November 30, 1950**. Issue 6. Front page, Page 3. NewspaperArchive.com.

No Author. "Mabry Terms "Billy" Outright Imposter." *Clovis News Journal.* **November 30, 1950.** Volume 22, Number 208. Newspaperarchive.com. (**Thursday, when interview was held**)

Smylie, Vernon. "Billy the Kid Flunks in Talk With Governor." *El Paso Herald Post.* **November 30, 1950.** Volume LXX, Number 285. Front Page, Page 13. Newspaperarchive.com. (**Thursday, when interview was held**)

United Press. "Pardon Mt 6-Shooters. Billy the Kid? Governor to Decide." *The Indianapolis News.* **November 30, 1950.** Indiana Historical Society. Lew Wallace Collection. M0292. Box 14. Folder 12.

No Author. " 'Billy the Kid' Bubble Bursts as Gov. Mabry Rejects Oldster's Claim." *Albuquerque Journal.* **December 1, 1950.** Volume [illegible], Number 61. Front Page, Page 4. Newspapers.com.

No Author. "Will A. Keleher, History Student, Sure Kid Was Shot." *Albuquerque Journal.* **December 1, 1950.** Volume [illegible], Number 61. Front Page. Newspaperarchive.com. **(Supports Governor Mabry calling "Brushy Bill" a Billy the Kid imposter)**

No Author. "Billy the Kid is Called Imposter by New Mexico Chief." *Lubbock Morning Avalanche.* **December 30, 1950.** Page 12. Newspaperarchive.com.

WILLIAM V. MORRISON'S PROMPTING RESEARCH FOR PARROTING BY "BRUSHY" FOR INTERVIEW TAPING AND FOR THE PARDON INTERVIEW (CHRONOLOGICAL)

BILLY THE KID'S WRITINGS FROM LEW WALLACE COLLECTION AT THE INDIANA HISTORICAL SOCIETY

Morrison, William V. "Urgent need of photostatic copies correspondence ..." **October 6, 1950.** Telegram to Indiana Historical Society, The William Henry Smith Memorial Library. Indiana Historical Society. Collection Number RG6. Box 17, Folder 11.

Dunn, Caroline. "We have microfilm of Bonney-Wallace correspondence ..." Letter to William V. Morrison. **October 7, 1950.** Letter to William V. Morrison. Indiana Historical Society, The William Henry Smith Memorial Library. Collection Number RG6. Box 17, Folder 11.

Morrison, William V. "Upon my return from Lincoln, N.M., today I have your telegram ..." **October 9, 1950. Letter** to The William Henry Smith Memorial Library. Collection Number RG6. Box 17, Folder 11.

Dunn, Caroline. "Your letter of the 9th received ..." **October 13, 1950.** Letter to William V. Morrison. Indiana Historical Society. Collection Number RG6. Box 17, Folder 11.

Morrison, William V. "Your letter of the 13th received ..." **October 17, 1950.** Letter to Caroline Dunn of The William Henry Smith Memorial Library. Indiana Historical Society. Collection Number RG6. Box 17, Folder 11.

No Author. Bill for $9.78 for "17 sheets photostats, Lew Wallace Collection. **October 25, 1950.** Telegram to Indiana Historical Society Memorial Library. Indiana Historical Society. Collection Number RG6. Box 17, Folder 11.

Dunn, Caroline. "Enclosed are the photostats of the documents in the Lew Wallace collection, with certification ..." **October 25, 1950.** Letter to William V. Morrison. Indiana Historical Society. Collection Number RG6. Box 17, Folder 11.

Morrison, William V. "This will serve to acknowledge receipt ..." **October 28, 1950.** Letter to Caroline Dunn of The William Henry Smith Memorial Library. Indiana Historical Society. Collection Number RG6. Box 17, Folder 11.

No Author. Bill for $2.61 for "6 Pstat neg." **October 30, 1950.** Telegram to Indiana Historical Society Memorial Library. Indiana Historical Society. Collection Number RG6. Box 17, Folder 11.

Wallace, Lew Jr. "A photostatic copy is being prepared of the letter in my possession from William H. Bonney ..." **October 30, 1950 .** Letter to William V. Morrison. Indiana Historical Society. Lew Wallace Collection. M0292. Box 8. Folder 3. **(Received a copy of actual Billy Bonney pardon plea letter of March 13, 1879)**

___________. "Your letter of November 2 confuses me ..." **November 10, 1950.** Letter to William V. Morrison. Indiana Historical Society. Lew Wallace Collection. M0292. Box 8. Folder 3. **(Expressing suspicion about a Billy the Kid imposter)**

Dunn, Caroline. "In my letter to you of November 5 I said I was returning the transcripts ..." **November 14, 1950.** Letter to William V. Morrison. Indiana Historical Society. Collection Number RG6. Box 17, Folder 11.

ALIAS BILLY THE KID'S PROMPT FOOTNOTES' SOURCES OF WILLIAM V. MORRISON AND C.L. SONNICHSEN (CHRONOLOGICAL)

BOOKS CITED

Walter Noble Burns's 1926 *The Saga of Billy the Kid.* (**fictionalized account using Pat Garrett's 1882 edition of *The Authentic Life of Billy the Kid***)

Garrett, Pat F. *The Authentic Life of Billy the Kid The Noted Desperado of the Southwest, Whose Deeds of Daring and Blood Made His Name a Terror in New Mexico, Arizona, and Northern Mexico.* Santa Fe, New Mexico: New Mexico Printing and Publishing Co. 1882. (Edition used: Edited by Maurice Garland Fulton. New York: The Macmillan Company. 1927)

Coe, George with Doyce B. Nunis, Jr. Ed. *Frontier Fighter. The Autobiography of George Coe Who Fought and Rode With Billy the Kid.* Chicago: R. R. Donnelley and Sons Company. 1934. (**multiple references**)

Siringo, Charles A. *History of Billy the Kid.* Printed by Charles A. Siringo. 1920. Page 32. (**largely fictionalized, using Garrett's *The Authentic Life of Billy the Kid*, by a Garrett posseman not involved in capturing Billy, for claim that Billy worked for Murphy and Dolan. Also, it contained the Jim East letter used by "Brushy" to confabulate a story about giving an "Indian girl" the Billy the Kid tintype**)

Poe, John W. *The Death of Billy the Kid.* Boston and New York: Houghton Mifflin Company. **1933**. Page 21. [sic- Page 31 in *Alias Billy the Kid*]. (**cited by Sonnichsen for fake argument that Fort Sumner residents would have hidden Billy's survival of the Garrett shooting**)

Miguel Otero. *The Real Billy the Kid.* Rufus Rockwell Wilson, Inc. 1936. Page 37. (**for Pat Garrett's statement that Billy tried to shoot Billy Matthews at Sheriff Brady's ambush, then repeated verbatim by "Brushy"**)

Hudson, Bell. Ed. Mary Hudson Brothers. *Billy the Kid.* Farmington, New Mexico: The Hustler Press. **1949**. Page 47. (**for Billy staying in sheep camps near Fort Sumner and a scene of encountering Barney Mason in one**)

LETTERS CITED

Jim East. "At the time of the capture of Billy, the Maxwell family were living at Fort Sumner ..." Letter to W.H. Burgess. **May 20, 1926. (source for the Jim East name, but its key mention of Paulita Maxwell as Billy's love was missed; identified as copy from Burgess supplied by Sonnichsen, who also had a copy of Walter Noble Burns's June 3, 1926 reply to Burgess that Paulita was Billy's "sweetheart"**) (Page 38)

Roberts, Oliver P. "Brushy Bill." "She said she had three affidavits that people knew me in 1887 ..." **May 24, 1949**. Letter to William V. Morrison. Footnote in *Alias Billy the Kid.* (Page 59)

JOURNAL/MAGAZINE ARTICLES CITED

Adams, Ramon F. "Billy the Kid's Lost Years: Cyclone Denton Tells of Bonney's Life as a Cowboy in Arizona." *The Texas Monthly.* 4.2. (**August-December, 1929**). Pages 205-211. (Scan courtesy of Cornette Library at West Texas A&M. (**source for claiming falsely that Billy worked at the Gila Ranch in Arizona**)

Smith, Wilbur. Interview. "The Amigo of 'Billy the Kid': The Man Who Fought Side by Side With Lincoln County's Outlaw Character Tells About the Days of 'Judge Colt's Rule.' " *New Mexico Magazine* article interview of **April, 1933**. Pages 26-49. University of New Mexico, Albuquerque. Zimmerman Library. Center for Southwest Research Anderson. Call Number F 791 N45. (**gives names of people hoping that Billy was alive, including Ygenio) Salazar**)

Traylor, Leslie. "Facts Regarding the Escape of Billy the Kid." *Frontier Times*. **July, 1936.** Pages 506-513 (on Page 509). FrontierTimesMagazine.com. (**About Billy the Kid's jailbreak being aided by Sam Corbett placing a gun in the latrine, based on a hearsay interview by Traylor in Lincoln in 1933 and 1935; also in article are his Jesus Silva interview on identifying Billy's body and his confirming the erroneous identification of Billy's gravesite in the Fort Sumner cemetery in 1935**)

Ball, Eve. "Billy Strikes the Pecos." *New Mexico Folklore Record*, IV. **1949-50.** Pages 7-10. University of New Mexico, Albuquerque. Zimmerman Library. Call Number GR 1 N 47, Volume 4. (**source for Billy Bonney's crossing the Guadalupe Mountains on foot to the Seven Rivers Jones family**)

Fulton, Maurice Garland. "Billy the Kid in Life and Books." *The New Mexico Folklore Record*. Volume IV, **1949-1950**. Pages 1-6. University of New Mexico, Albuquerque. Zimmerman Library. Call Number GR 1 N 47, Volume 4. (**source for the Greathouse shooting of Jim Carlyle, for the Mesilla trial being unjust,, for alleged photo of Billy's mother as "Mrs. Antrim"**)

NEWSPAPER ARTICLES CITED

Hunter's Frontier Times Magazine. "A Story of 'Billy the Kid.' " July, 1943, Pages 217-218. (quoting *Laredo Times* for **August 10, 1881).** frontiertimesmagazine.com/. (**source for claiming falsely Billy's demanding $5 per day payment from John Chisum**)

No Author. *Las Vegas Gazette* December 24, 1880, and the *Santa Fe New Mexican* of May 7, 1881. (**straw man argument for no reward made by Sonnichsen by citing editions with wrong dates for Lew Wallace's Billy the Kid reward notices**)

Wallace, Lew. *New York World Magazine*. "General Lew Wallace Writes a Romance of 'Billy the Kid' Most Famous Bandit of the Plains: Thrilling Story of the Midnight Meeting Between Gen Wallace, Then Governor of New Mexico, and the Notorious Outlaw, in a Lonesome Hut in Santa Fe." **June 8, 1902**. Lew Wallace Collection. Indiana Historical Society. M0292. . Box 14. Folder 11.(**"Brushy's" source for pardon bargain misinformation and for "pardon in your pocket" quote**) Cited by Sonnichsen, but identified as from the Indiana Historical Society, meaning Morrison's research.

No Author. "Billy the Kid, Alive Is Ridiculed by Oldtimers." El Paso *Herald*. **June 23, 1926**. Page 7. Newspapers.com. (**contradicting hearsay reports that Garrett had not killed the Kid, but used by hoax to quote those hearsay reports**)

John Meadows "John Meadows Tells of His Association With Pat Garrett." [sic - "My Association With Pat Garrett, Peace Officer of New Mexico."] *Alamogordo News*, **March 8, 1936**. Pages 1, 4. University of New Mexico, Albuquerque. Zimmerman Library. Zimmerman New Mexico Microfilm AN2, A46. (**source of error for Garrett killing his buffalo hunter partner, when he actually killed Joe Briscoe**)

No Author. "Frontiersmen Track Reports 'Kid' Is Alive." El Paso *Herald-Post*. **June 22, 1938.** NewspaperArchive.com. and El Paso *Times*. **November 10, 1937. (article about Pawnee Bill's searching for a Billy the Kid as alive – but not searching for "Brushy")**

COURT, MILITARY, AND LEGISLATIVE RECORDS CITED

U.S. District Court Minute Book B, Third Judicial District, Indictment 411 for killing "Buckshot" Roberts **[1878,]**, Page 76, quashed.

Lincoln County Grand Jury Minute Book B for **April, 1879**, for Indictments 243, 244; Pages 92-93, 298-299 (**misread and confused with Billy's 1880 Mesilla hanging trial**) (Page 34)

Adjutant General's files from the State Library in Austin, Texas, about Jessie Evans's **July 7, 1880** capture near Fort Stockton, Texas. (**about Jessie Evan's 1880 capture in Texas**)

Doña Ana County Court Minutes, "Instructions to the Jury," Cause No. 532. Pages 100-103; (**indictment for Brady ?**)

Doña Ana County Court Minute Book D for Cause No. 532 (verdict and sentence), killing of William Brady. **[1881]** Page 406. (**listing attorney as Simon B. Newcomb**)

No Author. *Executive Record Book Number 2.* July 25, 1867-November 8, 1882. **July 21, 1881.** Pages 533-535. New Mexico State Records Center and Archives, Santa Fe. New Mexico Secretary of the State Records. Records of the Secretary of the Territory. (**About granting Garrett's reward; used by Sonnichsen to fabricate irregularity**)

INTERVIEWS CITED

Mullin, Robert N. cited as having copies of reminiscences of Louis Abraham about Silver City and Billy. No date. (**noted by Sonnichsen as showing the murder at 12 as fictitious, but rest of information was ignored**) (Page 77)

Anaya, A.P. "Paco." Interview given to a George Fitzpatrick. Undated. (**Used to claim that he claimed two coroner's jury reports, but not knowing that he also claimed in a manuscript, published in 1991, that he buried Billy Bonney**)

Sonnichsen, C.L. Interview With Jack Fountain. April 15, 1944. (**A.J. Fountain's fake hearsay account of Garrett telling him he killed Billy to get a $10,000 reward, and that the side of beef was beside Maxwell's bedroom**)

Morrison, William V. Interviews with Oliver "Brushy Bill" Roberts. 1949-1950. (Unpublished)

Morrison, William V. Miscellaneous hearsay interviews of non-historical people for claims of Garrett not killing Billy, or identifying "Brushy" as Billy.

ADDITIONAL SOURCES CITED IN W.C. JAMESON'S THE RETURN OF THE OUTLAW BILLY THE KID (CHRONOLOGICAL)

Ashenfelter, Singleton M. "Exit 'The Kid', The Fugitive Murderer Hunted Down and Killed by Sheriff Garrett." *The New Southwest, And Grant County Herald.* **July 23, 1881.** Number 30. University of New Mexico. Zimmerman Library. Microfilm AN2 G71. (**Apocryphal description of Billy the Kid's body**)

Morrison, William V. Letter to Robert N. Mullin. **July 12, 1955.** (**Claiming "Brushy" could not read, so could not have studied sources**)

Branch, Louis Leon. From manuscript of Charles Frederick Rudulph. *"Los Billitos": The Story of "Billy the Kid" and His Gang: As Told by Charles Frederick Rudulph – a Member of Garrett's Historical Posse.* New York: Carleton Press. **1980.** (**Hearsay claim that the body of Billy the Kid was left in the Maxwell bedroom overnight for the coroner's Jury**)

Haws, Eulaine Emerson. Genealogical papers provided to Martha Vada Roberts Heath. Tyler, Texas. No date. Unpublished. (**Fake "Brushy Bill" genealogy debunked by Eulaine Roberts's son, Roy L. Haws**)

Tunstill, William A. *Billy the Kid and Me Were the Same: A Documentary on the Life of Billy the Kid.* Roswell, New Mexico: Western History Research Center. 1988. (**"Brushy"-backer faking a genealogy**)

Acton, Scott. Unpublished results of computerized pattern recognition system comparing facial images of William Henry Roberts and Billy the Kid. **1990.** (**Fake photo-matching of "Brushy Bill" and Billy Bonney**)

Kyle, Thomas G. "Computers, Billy the Kid, and Brushy Bill: The Verdict Is In." *True West.* **July, 1990.** Pages 16-19. (**No "Brushy" photo-match**)

Sonnichsen, Charles Leland. Interview. Oklahoma City, Oklahoma. **1991.** (**With claim that "Brushy" was Billy Bonney**)

JOHN MILLER BILLY THE KID IMPOSTER HOAX (CHRONOLOGICAL)

No Author. "Man Raised by Indians Passes." *Prescott Evening Courier*. **November 8, 1937**. Volume LV. Number 266. Page 3. Column 6. https://news.google.com/newspapers via https:// www.dcourier.com/pre-website-archives/ **(Showing zero match to history of Billy Bonney)**

No Author. "Brief Items in the Daily Life of Prescott." *Prescott Evening Courier*. **November 9, 1937**. Number 266. Page 2. **(Obituary of John Miller. Gives date of birth as December, 1850, showing no match to Billy Bonney or being a "kid")** https://www.dcourier.com/pre-website-archives/

Huff, J. Wesley. "Did Sheriff Pat Garrett Kill Billy the Kid? Herman Tecklenburg Says No; Billy Lived on Ranch at Ramah 35 Years Ago and Visited Him." *The Gallup Independent*. **August 9, 1944**. Volume 55, Number 185. Section Four. Pages 19, 23. Newspapers.com. **(Tecklenburg's Billy the Kid fables)**

Kyle, Thomas G. "Computers, Billy the Kid, and Brushy Bill: The Verdict Is In." *True West*. **July, 1990.** Pages 16-19. **(No John Miller photo-match)**

Airy, Helen L. *Whatever Happened to Billy the Kid?* Santa Fe, New Mexico: Sunstone Press. **1993**. **(John Miller as Billy the Kid)**

Johnson, Jim. *Billy the Kid: His Real Name Was ...* Denver, Colorado: Outskirts Press, Inc. **2006**. **(Debunking evidence for John Miller as Billy the Kid, and providing his dates of arrival and death at the Arizona Pioneers' home cemetery, and his obituary)**

Sams, Dale. Arizona Pioneers' Home and Cemetery Administrator. Personal communication. January 12, 2010. **(Confirmed that records list John Miller's DOB as December, 1850; and birthplace as Fort Sill, Texas)**

(SEE: "Billy the Kid Case" hoax)

"BILLY THE KID CASE" HOAX LINCOLN COUNTY SHERIFF'S DEPARTMENT CASE NO. 2003-274

RELEVANT BOOKS

Althouse, Bill. *Frozen Lightening: Bill Richardson's Strike on the Political Landscape of New Mexico*. Buckman, New Mexico: Thinking Out Loud Press. **2006**.

Bugliosi, Vincent. *Outrage: The Five Reasons Why O.J. Simpson Got Away With Murder*. New York and London: W.W. Norton & Company. **1996**. **(Exposé of Dr. Henry Lee faking forensics in legal cases, Pages 47-49)**

Cline, Donald. *Alias Billy the Kid: The Man Behind the Legend*. Santa Fe: New Mexico: Sunstone Press. **1986**. **(Historian cited by the hoaxers as backing them; apparently unaware of his 1988 manuscript: *Brushy Bill Roberts: I Wasn't Billy the Kid*)**

Cooper, Gale. *Billy the Kid's Pretenders: Brushy Bill and John Miller*. Albuquerque, New Mexico: Gelcour Books. **2012**.

__________. *Billy the Kid's Writings, Words, and Wit*. Albuquerque, New Mexico: Gelcour Books. **2012**.

__________. *MegaHoax: The Strange Plot to Exhume Billy the Kid and Become President*. Albuquerque, New Mexico: Gelcour Books. **2012**.

__________. *Cold Case Billy the Kid: The Plot to Steal Billy the Kid's Identity and Defame Sheriff Pat Garrett as a Murderer.* Albuquerque, New Mexico: Gelcour Books. **2019**.

__________. *Cracking the Billy the Kid Case Hoax: The Strange Plot to Exhume Billy the Kid, Convict Sheriff Pat Garrett of Murder, and Become President of the United States.* Albuquerque, New Mexico: Gelcour Books. **2014**.

__________. *The Billy the Kid Imposter Hoax of Brushy Bill Roberts.* Albuquerque, New Mexico: Gelcour Books. **2019**.

__________. *The Famous Coroner's Jury Report of Billy the Kid: An Inquest That Made History.* Albuquerque, New Mexico: Gelcour Books. **2019**.

Garrett, Pat F. *The Authentic Life of Billy the Kid The Noted Desperado of the Southwest, Whose Deeds of Daring and Blood Made His Name a Terror in New Mexico, Arizona, and Northern Mexico.* Santa Fe, New Mexico: New Mexico Printing and Publishing Co. **1882**. (Edition used: Edited by Maurice Garland Fulton. New York: The Macmillan Company. 1927)

Metz, Leon C. *Pat Garrett. The Story of a Western Lawman.* Norman: University of Oklahoma Press. **1974**.

Nolan, Frederick. *The West of Billy the Kid.* Norman: University of Oklahoma Press. **1998**. **(Page 7 for quote on the Eugene Cunningham hoaxed photo of Catherine Antrim)**

Palast, Greg. *Armed Madhouse.* New York: Penguin Group USA. **2007**. **(Bill Richardson exposé)**

Poe, John W. *The Death of Billy the Kid.* (Introduction by Maurice Garland Fulton). Boston and New York: Houghton Mifflin Company. **1933**.

Richardson, Bill, with Michael Ruby. *Between Worlds: The Making of an American Life.* New York: G.P. Putnam's Sons. **2005**. **(Bill Richardson autobiography)**

Siringo, Charles. *The History of Billy the Kid.* Santa Fe: New Mexico. Privately Printed. **1920**. **(Reproduces the Jim East letter on pages 96-107)**

(SEE: William H. Bonney; Oliver "Brushy Bill" Roberts Billy the Kid Imposter Hoax; John Miller Billy the Kid Imposter Hoax; *Cold Case Billy the Kid* Megahoax

CORONER'S JURY REPORT FOR WILLIAM H. BONNEY (SEE WILLIAM H. BONNEY)

PAT GARRETT'S PROSECUTION IMMUNITY "BILLY THE KID CASE" BY STATUTE OF LIMITATIONS

No Author. "An Act to Provide the Limitation of Criminal Actions." *Acts of the Legislative Assembly of the Territory of New Mexico, Twenty-Second Session, Convened at the Capitol. at the City of Santa Fe on Monday the 6th Day of December, 1875, and Adjourned on Friday the 14th day of January, 1876.* Santa Fe, New Mexico: Manderfield & Tucker, Public Printers. **1876**. Hathitrust Digital Library. **(Providing for a 10 year statute of limitations on murder; so Garrett could not be prosecuted in 2003 for the 1881 killing of Billy Bonney, since that expired in 1891)**

No Author. Ed. L. Bradford Prince. *The General Laws of New Mexico.* "Limitations of Criminal Actions. "Limitation of Criminal Actions, Acts of the Legislative Assembly of the Territory of New Mexico, Twenty-Second Session, Convened at the Capitol, at the City of Santa Fe on Monday the 6th day of December, 1875, and Adjourned on Friday the 14th day of January, 1876." Chapter 13, Section 1. **1882. (Providing for a 10 year statute of limitations on murder; so Garrett could not be prosecuted in 2003 for the 1881 killing of Billy Bonney)**

PAMPHLETS FOR (CHRONOLOGICAL)

Turk, David S. Historian U.S. Marshals Service. "Research Report: The U.S. Marshals Service and Billy the Kid. To Be Added in its Present Entirety, with Exhibits, to Lincoln County, New Mexico Case # 2003-274." U.S. Marshals Service Executive Services Division." **December, 2003. (a major hoax document by "Billy the Kid Case" participant as an addendum to the "Probable Cause Statement"**)

Madrid, Patricia A. Attorney General. *Inspection of Public Records Act Compliance Guide. Fourth Edition. The "Inspection of Public Records Act" NMSA 1978, Chapter 14, Article 2: A Compliance Guide for New Mexico Public Officials and Citizens.* Santa Fe: Office of the Attorney General. **January, 2004. (For open records compliance and litigation**)

PRESS RELEASE FOR (GOVERNOR BILL RICHARDSON)

Richardson, Bill. "Governor Bill Richardson Announces State Support of Billy the Kid Investigation." **June 10, 2003. (Announcement at State Capitol of state backing of case # 2003-274 and listing of the participants: Tom Sullivan, Steve Sederwall, Gary Graves, Sherry Tippett, and Paul Hutton)**

__________. "Gov. Bill Richardson Appoints Criminal Defense Lawyer to NM Supreme Court." **November 2, 2007. (Corrupt Charles Daniels, husband of Richardson's attorney Randi McGinn**)

__________. "Governor Bill Richardson to Consider Billy the Kid Pardon Petition." Press release. **December 16, 2010. (The Randi McGinn pardon petition for "Billy the Kid"**)

__________. "Governor Richardson to Announce his decision on Billy the Kid Pardon Request Tomorrow." Press release. **December 30, 2010.**

LETTERS ABOUT

Kurtis, Bill. "This letter is provided as official verification ..." Letter to Steve Sederwall. **October 4, 2010.** Entered by Sederwall's Defense Attorney as Exhibit A in Sandoval District Court Case No. D-1329-CV-2007-1364 Hearing on January 17, 2012. (**Paying for Dr. Henry Lee's forensics**)

E-MAILS ABOUT

Saar, Meghan. To Gale Cooper. "BTK Hoax Article." E-Mail To Gale Cooper. **January 31, 2006. (Hoax-backing *True West* magazine rejecting my article proposal to expose the "Billy the Kid Case" hoax**)

Ford, Simon. "Subj. Questions regarding Orchid-Cellmark." E-mail to Gale Cooper. **January 31, 2011. (Consultation on mixed DNA samples and DNA separation costs**)

Miller, Kenny. Personal communication to author about family history and showing Maxwell family objects - including the carpenter's bench, bedstead, and wash stand - and providing photos of them to author. **2011 to 2012. (Information from Maxwell family descendant**)

BLOGS ABOUT

No author. "Fraud Alleged at Cellmark, DNA Testing Firm. TalkLeft: The Politics of Crime. http://www.talkleft.com./new_archives/008809.html. **November 18, 2004.**

Boze Bell, Bob. "The Wild is back in the West." BBB's Blog. **April 24, 2006. (Announcement of invitation of Sullivan and Sederwall to Cannes Film Festival.**) http://www.truewestmagazine.com/weblog/blogger1.htm

WEBSITE FOR:

Sederwall, Steve. "billythekidcase.com" Website. From **October (?) 2010 to 2012(?). (For $25.00 membership selling Case 2003-274 records)**

TELEVISION DOCUMENTARIES PERPETRATING

History Channel. "Investigating History: Billy the Kid." Week **of April 24, 2004 and May 2, 2004.(Co-Producer, writer, narrator was "Billy the Kid Case" hoaxer Paul Hutton)**

National Geographic International Discovery ID Channel. "History Mysteries." **2010. (Sederwall presenting the fake Dr. Lee Deputy James Bell top-of-the-stairs murder "investigation")**

ARTICLES ABOUT (CHRONOLOGICAL)

Humphreys, Sexson. "Pardon My 6-Shooters: Billy the Kid? Governor to Decide; 'Pardon Me, I'm Alive,' Says Billy the Kid." *The Indianapolis News*. Thursday, **November 30, 1950**. Indiana Historical Society. Lew Wallace Collection (M292). Box 14. Folder 12.

Hutton, Paul Andrew. "Dreamscape Desperado." *New Mexico Magazine*. Volume 68. Number 6. Pages 44-58. **June, 1990.**

Janofsky, Michael. "122 Years Later, the Lawmen Are Still Chasing Billy the Kid." *The New York Times*. **June 5, 2003**. Vol. CLII, No. 52,505. Pages 1 and A31. **(First national announcement of Billy the Kid Case)**

No Author. "Lincoln County deputy sheriff sends his own letter to governor." *Silver City Daily Press*. **June 25, 2003**. Pages 1, 13.

DellaFlora, Anthony. "State Not Kidding Around: Governor won't mind if probe of the notorious 19th century N.M. outlaw boosts tourism." *Albuquerque Journal*. **June 11, 2003**. No. 162. Pages 1 and A1. **(First big New Mexico announcement of Billy the Kid Case)**

Bommersbach, Jana. "Digging Up Billy: If Pat Garrett didn't kill the Kid, who's buried in his grave?" *True West*. **August/September 2003**. Volume 50. Issue 7. P. 42-45.

No Author. AP. "Authorities call for exhumation of Billy the Kid's mother to solve mystery." *Silver City Sun News*. **October 11, 2003**.

Bommersbach, Jana. "From Shovels to DNA: The inside story of digging up Billy." *True West*. **October/November, 2003.** Volume 50. Issue 7. Pages 42-45.

Jameson, W.C. and Leon Metz. "Was Brushy Bill Really Billy the Kid? Experts face off over new evidence." *True West*. **November/December, 2003**. Volume 50. Issue 10. Pages 32-33.

Murphy, Mary Alice. "Billy the Kid 'Hires' a Lawyer." *Silver City Daily Press Internet Edition*. http://www.thedailypress.com/NewsFolder/11.17.2.html. **November 17, 2003**.

Boyle, Alan. "Billy the Kid gets a lawyer: 122 years after shootout, attorney to gather information for a pardon." msnbc.com. **November 18, 2003**.

Fecteau, Louie. "No Kidding: Governor Taps Lawyer For Billy." *Albuquerque Journal*. Page 1, A6. **November 19, 2003**.

No Author. AP. "Lawyer Appointed to Represent Dead Outlaw." *Silver City Sun News*. http://www.krqe.com/expanded.asp?RECORD_KEY%5bContent. **November 19, 2003. (Bill Robins III's appointment by Richardson)**

No Author. "Lawmakers Consider Posthumous Pardon for Billy the Kid." *abqtrib.com News*. **November 21, 2003**.

Boyle, Alan. "Billy the Kid's DNA Sparks Legal Showdown: Sheriffs and mayors face off over digging up remains from the Old West." *msnbc.com*. **November 21, 2003**.

Romo, Rene. "Kid's Mom May Stay Buried: Silver City wins round to block exhumation for outlaw's DNA." *Albuquerque Journal*. **December 9, 2003**. Section D3.

Janna Bommersbach. "Breaking Out More Shovels: Fort Sumner's Sheriff Gary Graves commits to digging up Billy the Kid's Grave." *True West.* **January/February, 2004**. Volume 51. Issue 1. Pages 46-47 **(Hoax-backing article)**

Benke, Richard. AP. "N.M. Re-Opens Case of Billy the Kid." Yahoo! News. **January 13, 2004**.

__________. "Billy the Kid's Life and Death May Be Put to DNA Test: Officials want to examine the body of the outlaw's mother to test a Texas man's claim that he was Bonney. If so, Pat Garrett didn't kill the Kid." *The Nation.* **January 18, 2004. (Uses fake Overton Affidavit given by Attorney Sherry Tippett)**

No Author. AP. "Billy the Kid hearing delayed for months: Sheriffs need more time to prepare arguments for exhuming remains of outlaw's mother." **January 23, 2004**.

Miller, Jay. "Digging Up the Latest on Billy the Kid." *Las Cruces Sun-News.* **February 3, 2004**.

Gonzales. Carolyn. "Hutton writes wild frontier stories for History Channel." *University of New Mexico Campus News.* **February 16, 2004**. Volume 39. No. 12. **(Hoaxer Hutton's TV program announced)**

Miller, Jay. "The Billy the Kid Code." *Las Cruces Sun-News.* **March 29, 2004**.

Nathanson, Rick. "Grave Doubts: 'Investigating History' series tries to clear up the mysteries surrounding Billy the Kid." *Albuquerque Journal Weekly TV Guide: Entertainer.* **April 24, 2004**. Pages 3 5.

Murphy, Mary Alice and Melissa St. Aude. "Sederwall, Sullivan uninvited to ball." *Silver City Daily Press Internet Edition.* **June 10, 2004**.

Hill, Levi. "Billy the Kid Stirring Up Dust in Silver City." *Las Cruces Sun-News.* **June 12, 2004**. Section 5A. Pages 1, A2.

No Author. "Attorney Refuses Judge's statements concerning exhumation." *thedailypress.com.* **June 15, 2004. (Attorney Tippett lies about the OMI)**

Richardson, Bill. "Verbatim: I have to decide whether to pardon him. But not right away – after the investigation, after the state gets more publicity." *Time.* **June 21, 2004**. Vol. 163. No. 25. Page 17.

Romo, Rene. "Back off on Billy, Gov. Asked: Silver City says inquiry into death of Kid would harm state tourism. *Albuquerque Journal.* **June 23, 2004**. Section B-1, B-5.

Miller, Jay. "Inside the Capitol. Bizarre case of Billy the Kid." *Roswell Daily Record.* **July 2, 2004**. Page A4.

Romo, Rene. "Forensic Expert on Billy's Case: Questions Remain on Outlaw's Fate." *Albuquerque Journal.* **August 2, 2004**. Page 1. **(Falsely claims blood on bench; says "trace blood")**

No Author. "Forensic expert joins Billy the Kid inquiry in New Mexico." *AP SignOnSanDiego.com.* **August 2, 2004. (Announcing Dr. Henry Lee)**

Miller, Jay. "Inside the Capitol. Sheriffs slippery on Billy the Kid Case." *Roswell Daily Record.* **August 9, 2004**. Page A4.

Cherry, Doris. "Forensics 101 for 'Billy'." *Lincoln County News.* **August 12, 2004**. Pages 2, 10. **(Quotes Sullivan's lie: "a lot" of blood on bench)**

Miller, Jay. "Inside the Capitol. Expert questions Kid probe." *Roswell Daily Record.* **August 20, 2004**. Page A4.

__________. "Inside the Capitol. Hat dance on probe funding." *Roswell Daily Record.* **September 1, 2004**. Page A4.

__________. "Inside the Capitol. Three sheriffs push Kid Case." *Roswell Daily Record.* **September 5, 2004**. Page A4.

__________. "Inside the Capitol. Sheriffs hoax is world-class." *Roswell Daily Record.* **September 8, 2004**. Page A4.

__________. "Inside the Capitol. Kid gets day in court Sept. 27." *Roswell Daily Record.* **September 12, 2004**. Page A4.

__________. "Inside the Capitol. Kid probe making us think." *Roswell Daily Record.* **September 13, 2004**. Page A4.

Stinnett, Scot. "De Baca County Citizens' Committee Files Petition for Recall of Sheriff Gary Graves." *De Baca County News.* **September 14, 2004**.

Miller, Jay. "Inside the Capitol. Who is Attorney Bill Robins?" *Roswell Daily Record.* **September 15, 2004**. Page A4.

Green, Keith. "Mountain Asides: Billy's restless bones are stirred up once again. *RuidosoNews.com.* **September 16, 2004.**

Miller, Jay. "Inside the Capitol. Kid Case: David fights Goliath." *Roswell Daily Record.* **September 17, 2004**. Page A4.

__________. "Inside the Capitol. Many reasons to dig up Kid." *Roswell Daily Record.* **September 19, 2004**. Page A4.

__________. "Inside the Capitol. Nothing to worry about." *Roswell Daily Record.* **September 20, 2004**. Page A4.

Stallings, Dianne. "Showdown in the County Seat." *RuidosoNews.com* **September 21, 2004. (Commissioner Leo Martinez's meeting threatening recall of Sheriff Sullivan for perpetrating a hoax)**

Miller, Jay. "Inside the Capitol. Who speaks for Pat Garrett?" *Roswell Daily Record.* **September 22, 2004**. Page A4.

Stallings, Dianne. "Showdown in the County Seat: shouting match erupts at County Commissioners meeting Tuesday over investigation of Billy the Kid." *Ruidoso News.* **September 22, 2004.**

Cherry, Doris. "Lincoln County 'War' Heats Up Over 'Billy: Capitan Mayor Tracks His Kind of '---' To County Commission Meeting. Tells Jay Miller where to go: wonders why commissioner has his panties in a wad." *Lincoln County News.* **September 23, 2003**. Vol. 99. No. 38. Pages 1-3. **(Commissioner Martinez stops the hoaxers' exhuming Billy the Kid)**

Miller, Jay. "Inside the Capitol. Is there a new Santa Fe Ring?" *Roswell Daily Record.* **September 24, 2004**. Page A4.

Stinnett, Scott. "Rest in Peace, Billy! Exhumation case dismissed." *De Baca County News.* **September 30, 2004**. Vol. 104. No. 2. Pages 1, 5, 6.

Miller, Jay. "Inside the Capitol. Fort Sumner celebrates win." *Roswell Daily Record.* **October 1, 2004**. Page A4.

No author. "Fraud Alleged at Cellmark, DNA Testing Firm. TalkLeft: The Politics of Crime. http://www.talkleft.com./new_archives/008809.html. **November 18, 2004. (Dr. Henry Lee's lab fakes DNA results)**

Jana Bommersbach. "Kid Exhumation Nixed: Billy and his mom to rest in peace. *True West.* **January/February 2005**. Volume 52. Issue 1. Pages 68-69.

Carter, Julie. "Follow the Blood: In the Billy the Kid Case, Miller Exhumed." *RuidosoNews.com.* **October 6, 2005. (Sederwall lies about blood on bench; gives "dead men don't bleed" quote; has the Lonnie Lippman photo of him holding John Miller/William Hudspeth skull)**

Sullivan, Tom. "Letters: Your Opinion." *RuidosoNews.com.* **October 21, 2005. (Sullivan letter to the editor: "Why are they so afraid of the truth?")**

Carter, Julie. "Billy the Kid in Prescott? *New Mexico Stockman.* **November, 2005**. Pages 38, 39, 76.

Romo, Rene. "Billy the Kid Probe May Yield New Twist. *Albuquerque Journal. ABQ Journal.com.* **November 6, 2005. (Claims Sullivan and Sederwall have John Miller's DNA)**

Struckman, Robert. "Bitterroot man hopes to uncover truth about Billy the Kid." http://www.helenair.com/articles/2006/03/13/montana/a05031306_01.txt (Missoulian) **March 13, 2006. (Hoaxer Dale Tunnell backing John Miller as Billy the Kid**

Dodder, Joanna. "Officials could face charges for digging up alleged Billy the Kid." *The Daily Courier of Prescott Arizona.* **April 12, 2006. (Sullivan claims DNA in "two months," and fakes Hudspeth skeleton as John Miller's and makes up a left scapula bullet wound)**

Banks, Leo W. "The New Billy the Kid? The mad search for the bones of an American outlaw icon has come to Arizona." *Tucson Weekly.* http://www.tucsonweekly.com/gbase/Currents/Content?oid=oid:81013 **April 13,**

2006. (**Sullivan lies that bench is "saturated with blood; Dr. Rick Staub says DNA extracted from William Hudspeth not John Miller**)

Carter, Julie. "Digging up bones, Arizona may protest Miller exhumation." jcarter@tularosa.net. **April 19, 2006**.

Dodder, Joanna. "Officials could face charges for digging up alleged Billy the Kid." *The Daily Courier of Prescott Arizona*. **April 12, 2006**. (**Sullivan claims DNA in "two months," and fakes Hudspeth skeleton as John Miller's with buck teeth and a left scapula bullet wound**)

Banks, Leo W. "The New Billy the Kid? The mad search for the bones of an American outlaw icon has come to Arizona." *Tucson Weekly*. http://www.tucsonweekly.com/gbase/Currents/Content?oid=oid:81013 **April 13, 2006**. (**Sullivan lies that bench is "saturated with blood; Dr. Rick Staub says DNA extracted from William Hudspeth not John Miller**)

Carter, Julie. "Digging up bones, Arizona may protest Miller exhumation." jcarter@tularosa.net. **April 19, 2006**.

Carter, Julie. "Culture Shock: The cowboys and the Kid go to France. jcarter@tulerosa.net. **May 5, 2006**. (**Sullivan worked on movie 9 months**)

Shafer, Mark. "N.M. pair may face charges in grave case." **May 13, 2006**. markshafer @ArizonaRepublic.com. http://www.azcentral.com/arizonarepublic/local/articles/0513billythekid0513.html

Myers, Amanda Lee. "New Mexicans Dig Up Trouble in Arizona." *Albuquerque Journal, New Mexico and the West*. **May 14, 2006**. Page B4. (**Also in gulfnews.com; states Dallas lab" is doing DNA comparisons**)

___________."Billy the Kid Still 'Wanted.' " **May 16, 2006**. gulfnews.com. http://archive.gulfnews.com/articles/06/05/16/10040234.html.

No author. "Festival de Cannes, **May 17-28, 2006**. Requiem for Billy the Kid." http://www.festival-cannes.fr/films/fiche_film.php?langue=4355535. (**Cannes Film Festival synopsis**)

No author. "Out of Competition/Cannes Classics: Requiem for Billy the Kid. Festival de Cannes May 17-28, 2006." http://www.festival-cannes.fr/films/fiche_film.php?langue=4355535. **May 20, 2006**. (**Sullivan and Sederwall called two sheriffs**)

McCarthy, Todd. "Requiem for Billy the Kid." **May 21, 2006**. Variety.com. http://www.variety.com/review/VE1117930570?categoryid=2220&cs=1&nid=2562.

McCoy, Dave. "L 'Ouest Américain." **May 25, 2006**. MSN Movies. http://movies.msn.com/movies/canneso6/dispatch8.

Bennett, Ray. "Requiem for Billy the Kid." TheHollywoodReporter.com. **May 26, 2006**. (**Demonstration of hoax damage to history**)

Carter, Julie. "The cowboys are back in town, film in six months." jcarter@tulerosa.net. **June 9, 2006**. (**Describes plans for more programs**)

Dodder, Joanna. "Back at Rest: Bones of Billy the Kid return to Prescott." *The Daily Courier*. **July 9, 2006**. http://prescottdailycourier.com/print.asp?ArticleID=40353&Section ID=1&SubSectionID=1

No Author. AP. "Prescott, Ariz. - Prosecutors won't seek charges against two men who exhumed the remains of a man who claimed to be the outlaw Billy the Kid." AOL News. **October 23, 2006**.

___________. AP. "Billy the Kid Case Dropped." *Albuquerque Journal. Metro.* D3. **October 24, 2006**.

___________. AP. "Men Who Exhumed Billy the Kid Won't Be Charged." **October 24, 2006.** *New York Sun*. http://www.nysun.com/article/42176. (**Claims Sullivan and Sederwall did Arizona exhumation, have Miller DNA, and sent to Orchid for matchings to bench DNA**)

___________. AP. "Arizona: No Charges Sought for Exhuming Remains." *New York Times*. A-26. **October 24, 2006**. http://www.nytimes.com/2006/10/24/us/24brfs-002.html?r=1&oref=slogin. (**Cover-up Miller/William Hudspeth exhumations**)

Turk, David S. "Billy the Kid and the U.S. Marshals Service." *Wild West.* **February, 2007**. Volume 19. Number 5. Pages 34 – 41. (**Turk's expurgated "U.S. Marshals Service and Billy the Kid"**)

Jason Strykowski. "A Tale of Two Governors ... And one Kid." *True West.* **May, 2007**. Vol. 54. Issue 5. Page 64.

No Author. AP. "Billy the Kid Exhumation a Possibility." *Roswell Daily Record.* **May 2, 2007**. **From Stephenville, Texas AP on "Brushy Bill" exhumation attempt; Sederwall claims has John Miller's DNA**)

Carter, Julie. "Brushy Bill targeted for DNA testing; Billy the Kid workbench goes on display." *Ruidoso News.* **May 3, 2007**.

__________. AP. "Manhunt for Real Billy the Kid Goes On: Deputy hopes DNA will finally reveal outlaw's true identity." *Albuquerque Journal.* **May 4, 2007**. B3.

Zorosec, Thomas. "DNA could solve mystery of Billy the Kid." Chron.com - Houston Chronicle. **May 5, 2007**. (**From Hamilton, Texas; "Brushy Bill" exhumation attempt**)

Carter, Julie. AP. "Texas town denies request to exhume Billy the Kid claimant." *Houston Chronicle.* **May 11, 2007**.

__________. "Evidence Hidden in Spector Trial." BBC Internet News. May 24, 2007. (**Dr. Henry Lee alleged as destroying evidence**)

__________. AP. "Famed experts credibility takes a hit at Spector trial." CNN.com law center. **May 25, 2007**. (**Dr. Henry Lee allegedly destroyed evidence**)

Stallings, Dianne. "Billy the Kid case straps county for insurance." *RuidosoNews.com.* **August 13, 2008**.

Carter, Julie. "Lincoln County deputies resign commissions for Kid case." *Ruidosonews.com.* **August 16, 2007**. (**Start of ploy calling Case 2003-274 a "hobby"**)

Romo, Rene. "Seeking the Kid, Minus Badges. Deputies Resign to Hunt for Billy." *Albuquerque Journal.* **August 18, 2007**. No. 230. pp. 1-2.

Concerned Citizens of Lincoln County. "Should Lincoln County Have Grave Concerns Over A Person Like Steve Sederwall Running for Sheriff? *Lincoln County News.* **October 16, 2008**. Page 6.

Miller, Jay. "Kid's Pardon a Publicity Stunt." "Inside the Capitol" syndicated column "Inside the Capitol" and blog, insidethecapitol.blogspot.com. **June 23, 2010**.

Stinnett, Scot. "Billy the Kid historian says pardon all part of the hoax." *De Baca County News.* Pages 3, 9. **June 24, 2010**. (**Reprint of my Jay Miller article without commentary**)

No Author. "Billy the Kid 'to be pardoned.' " *Press Trust of India* (*Hindustan Times*) and Pakistan *Daily Express.* **July 11, 2010**. (**Pardon for "Brushy Bill"**)

Romo, Rene. "Gov. Weighs Pardon for Billy the Kid." *Albuquerque Journal. Saturday,* No. 205. Front page, and A6. **July 24, 2010**.

Licón, Adriana Gómez. "Pardon form New Mexico governor unlikely for Billy the Kid." *El Paso Times.* **July 29, 2010**.

Massey, Barry. Associated Press. Santa Fe. "Billy the Kid To Be Pardoned, 130 Years Later? Lawman's Grandchildren Outraged; 'Would You Issue A Pardon For Someone Who Made His Living As A Thief?' National, international, and internet publications. **July 30, 2010**.

Gardner, David. Los Angeles. "Pat Garrett's family plan showdown over plans to finally pardon Billy the Kid." London's *Daily Mail Online.* **July 31, 2010**.

Boardman, Mark. "The Lunacy of Billy the Kid." *True West.* **August, 2010.** Volume 57. Issue 8. Pages 42-47. (**Defamatory article about me**)

Massey, Barry. Associated Press. Santa Fe. "NM gov meets with lawman Pat Garrett's descendants." **August 4, 2010**. www.wthr.com/global/story.asp?s=12926188.

Vaughn, Chris. "Texas Town seeks New Mexico pardon for Billy the Kid." *Fort Worth Star-Telegram.* **August 14, 2010**. (**Bid for "Brushy Bill" Roberts pardon.**)

Lacey, Marc. "Old West Showdown Is Revived. *New York Times.* **August 15, 2010**. (**Richardson shape-shifted to "amateur historian."**)

No Author. "A Tale of Two Billys." *New English Review: The Iconoclast.* (Internet). **August 15, 2010.**

Gordon, Bea. "Examining Legend: The Pardoning of Billy the Kid.. New Mexico Gov. Bill Richardson's talking about exonerating the state's most famous outlaw. But at what cost?" www.newwest.net/topic/article/29850/C37/L37/ **August 17, 2010.**

Massey, Barry. Associated Press. Santa Fe. " 'Billy the Kid' pardon effort draws Wild West showdown." Wilkes-Barre, Pennsylvania. *The Times Leader.* **August 21, 2010. (Introduction of William N. Wallace and Indiana Historical Society opposition. In starpress.com of east central Indiana as "Should Billy the Kid Be Pardoned?")**

Miller, Jay. "When is a promise not a promise?" *Inside the Capitol.* **August 30, 2010.**

(Sides, Hampton. "Not-So-Charming Billy." *NY Times Opinion Section Op-Ed Contributor.* September 6, 2010.

Richardson, Bill. "Governor Bill Richardson to Consider Billy the Kid Pardon Petition." Press release. **December 16, 2010. (Floating the Randi McGinn petition)**

Martinez, Edecio. "Billy the Kid to be Pardoned 130 Years Later." CBSNEWS.com. **December 27, 2010.**

Guarino, Mark. "Outgoing New Mexico Gov. Bill Richardson is considering a pardon for celebrated outlaw Billy the Kid. An informal e-mail poll shows support. But time is running out." Associated Press. **December 29, 2010.**

Levy, Glen. "Will Billy the Kid Be Pardoned? Governor Has Until Friday." TIME NewsFeed.com. **December 29, 2010.**

Richardson, Bill. "Governor Richardson to Announce his decision on Billy the Kid Pardon Request Tomorrow." Press release. **December 30, 2010.**

Burke, Kelly David. "Billy the Kid Pardon?" FoxNews.com. **December 30, 2010.**

Hopper, Jessica. "Gov. Bill Richardson 'I've Decided Not to Pardon Billy the Kid.' " ABCNEWS.com. **December 31, 2010.**

Rojas, Rick. "No Pardon for Billy the Kid. New Mexico Gov. Bill Richardson says, 'The Romanticism appealed to me ... but the facts and evidence did not support it." *Los Angeles Times.* **December 31, 2010.**

Watson, Kathryn. "Alas, no pardon for Billy the Kid: New Mexico's Richardson says close call." washingtontimes.com. **December 31, 2010.**

No Author. "Richardson Declines to Pardon Outlaw Billy the Kid." FoxNews.com. **December 31, 2010.**

Lacey, Marc. "For 2nd Time in 131 Years, Billy the Kid is Denied Pardon." *New York Times.* Page A10. **January 1, 2011.**

Romo, Rene. "Fight Won, Questions Remain: Billy the Kid DNA Report Released." *Albuquerque Journal.* Front Page and Page B1. **April 29, 2012.**

Sandlin, Scott. "Billy the Kid case costs taxpayers nearly $200K: Billy the Kid lives on in battle of public records." *Albuquerque Journal.* Front Page, Page A2, Page A8. No. 162. **June 11, 2013 (Fakes blood on carpenter's bench)**

Cherry, Doris. "Modern Billy the Kid 'Cases' Cost Public Plenty: County Shells Out Bucks for Failing to Release Information." *Lincoln County News.* **June 27, 2013.** Volume 109. Number 6. Front Page and Pages 7-8. **(Based on my June 18, 2013 letter to the Lincoln County Commissioners)**

Stallings, Dianne. "Former Lincoln County sheriff dies in Texas: Tom Sullivan died Saturday in Texas." **October 22, 2013.** ruidosonews.com.

"BILLY THE KID CASE" LEGAL DOCUMENTS (BY LOCATION)

CAPITAN, NEW MEXICO (FIRST ANNOUNCEMENT OF CASE NO. 2003-274)

Sederwall, Steve, "Mayor's Report, **May 5, 2003.**" *Village of Capitan: Capitan Village Hall News.* Capitan, New Mexico. **(Announces filed Case 2003-274)**

ALBUQUERQUE, NEW MEXICO (OPPOSITION OF THE OMI TO EXHUMATIONS)

Zumwalt, Ross E. "Affidavit of Ross E. Zumwalt, MD. In the Matter of Catherine Antrim. Case No. MS 2003-11 Sixth Judicial Court, County of Grant, State of New Mexico. **January 9, 2004. (Exhumation refused based on invalid DNA)**

Komar, Debra. "Affidavit of Debra Komar, PhD. In the Matter of Catherine Antrim. Case No. MS 2003-11 Sixth Judicial Court, County of Grant, State of New Mexico. **January 9, 2004. (Exhumation refused based on invalid DNA)**

Snead, William E. Attorney for Office of Medical Investigator." "In the Matter of Catherine Antrim: Response of Office of Medical Investigator to Petition to Exhume Remains of Catherine Antrim." Case No. MS 2003-11. Sixth Judicial Court, Grant County. **January 13, 2004. (Opposition of OMI to exhumation)**

Komar, Debra. "Deposition of Debra Komar, Ph.D. In the Matter of Catherine Antrim. Case No. MS 2003-11." Sixth Judicial Court, County of Grant, State of New Mexico. Taken by Adam S. Baker, Attorney for Town of Silver City. Signed: Debra Komar, Ph.D. **January 20, 2004. (Exhumation refused based on invalid DNA in Billy the Kid's and mother's graves)**

LINCOLN COUNTY, NEW MEXICO (LINCOLN COUNTY SHERIFF'S DEPARTMENT CASE NO. 2003-274, "BILLY THE KID CASE")

Virden, R.E. Lincoln County Undersheriff report. "I participated in the investigative reconstruction ..." **April 28, 2003. (Participation in Case # 2003-274.)**

Sullivan, Tom. Lincoln County Sheriff. "Lincoln County Sheriffs Department is currently conducting an investigation ..." Letter to Charles Ryan, Director Arizona Department of Corrections. **April 30, 2003. (Describes Garrett as murderer and planned exhumations of John Miller and "Brushy Bill" Roberts)**

__________. "Denial Letter." Pre-printed form to my attorney, Randall M. Harris. **October 8, 2003. (Open records denial for the Probable Cause Statement using exception of ongoing law enforcement investigation.)**

Sullivan, Tom. Sheriff, Lincoln County Sheriff's Office, and Steven M. Sederwall. Deputy Sheriff, Lincoln County Sheriff's Office. "Lincoln County Sheriff's Office, Lincoln County, New Mexico, Case: William H. Bonney, a.k.a. William Antrim, a.k.a. The Kid, a.k.a. Billy the Kid: An Investigation into the events of April 28, 1881 through July 14, 1881 – seventy-seven days of doubt." **No Date. (Rejected Probable Cause Statement for Case No. 2003-274. In Lincoln County Sheriff's Department case file for 2003-274.)**

__________. "Lincoln County Sheriff's Department Case #2003-274 Probable Cause Statement." Filed in Lincoln County Sheriff's Department. Carrizozo, New Mexico. **December 31, 2003. (Became publicly available as "Plaintiff Exhibit 1 in Petitioner's Attorney Sherry Tippett's Silver City "Brief in Chief in Support of the Exhumation of Catherine Antrim." Case No. MS 03-011." Sixth Judicial Court, County of Grant, State of New Mexico." January 5, 2004)**

Overton, Homer D. aka Homer D. Kinsworthy. "Affidavit for Lincoln County Sheriff's Department Case #2003-274 Probable Cause Statement." **December 22, 2003. (Fake swearing that Garrett's widow –dead in 1936 - told him in 1940 that Garrett did not kill the Kid. Became publicly available as "Plaintiff Exhibit 1 in Petitioner's Attorney Sherry Tippett's Silver City "Brief in Chief in Support of the Exhumation of Catherine Antrim." Case No. MS 03-011." Sixth Judicial Court, County of Grant, State of New Mexico." January 5, 2004)**

No Author. "Contact List, William H. Bonney Case # 2003-274, Lincoln County Sheriff's Office & Investigators." No Date. **Probably 2003. (In Lincoln County Sheriff's Department Case file for 2003-274)**

Virden, Rick, Lincoln County Sheriff "Deputy Sheriff Commission [Card] to Tom Sullivan." **January 1, 2005.**

__________. "Deputy Sheriff Commission [Card] to Steven Sederwall." **February 25, 2005.**

Sederwall, Steven M., Lincoln County Sheriff's Deputy Investigator. "Lincoln County Sheriff's Department Supplemental Report, Case #2003-274. Subject: Exhumation of John Miller. Location: Arizona Pioneers' Cemetery, Prescott, Arizona." **May 19, 2005. (Arizona exhumations John Miller and William Hudspeth)**

Virden, R.E. Lincoln County Sheriff. letter to Jay Miller. "We are interested in the truth surrounding Billy the Kid and are continuing the investigation ..." **November 28, 2005. (Virden confirms continuing Billy the Kid case and deputizing Sullivan and Sederwall for it.)**

Virden, R.E. Lincoln County Sheriff. To Hamilton, Texas, Mayor Roy Ramsey [sic]. "This letter will inform you that Tom Sullivan and Steve Sederwall are both commissioned deputies ..." **No date, but around May 2007. (Virden's attempt to exhume "Brushy" with Sullivan and Sederwall as the Deputies)**

Lee, Henry, Dr. Letter to Jay Miller. "In response to your letter dated March 27, 2006 ..." **May 1, 2006. (Lee confirms sending his carpenter's bench and floorboard report to Lincoln County Sheriff's Department.)**

"Jordan, Wilma" aka Gale Cooper. To David Turk, Historian U.S. Marshals Service. "Looking for the truth is good ..." **June 15, 2006. (Attempt to get the Turk's "U.S. Marshal's Service and Billy the Kid " pamphlet for Case 2003-274.)**

Turk, David. Historian U.S. Marshals Service. To "Wilma Jordan." "Thank you for your thoughtful and thorough letter ..." **July 3, 2006. (Tracked "Wilma's" address; refuses to give his "U.S. Marshal's Service and Billy the Kid "pamphlet.)**

Sederwall, Steve. "billythekidcase.com." Sederwall's pay for view website with Case 2003-274 records. **October, 2010. (Selling public records online.**

SILVER CITY, NEW MEXICO (EXHUMATION ATTEMPT ON CATHERINE ANTRIM)

Tippett, Sherry. Attorney. To Richard Gay, Assistant to the Chief of Staff, Governor Richardson's Office. "Memorandum, RE: Exhumation of Catherine Antrim." **July 11, 2003. (Tippett's lie of OMI backing exhumation.)**

Tippett, Sherry. Attorney for Petitioners Sullivan, Sederwall, and Graves. "In the Matter of Catherine Antrim: Petition to Exhume Remains." Case No. MS 03-011. Sixth Judicial Court, County of Grant, State of New Mexico. **October 3, 2003. (Start of exhumation attempts; perjury about permission from OMI)**

Kennedy, Paul J., Adam S. Baker, Thomas F. Stewart, Robert L. Scavron, Attorneys for Mayor Terry Fortenberry on Behalf of the Town of Silver City. "In the Matter of Catherine Antrim: Motion to Intervene." Case No. MS 03-011. Sixth Judicial Court, County of Grant, State of New Mexico. **October 31, 2003. (Start of my exhumation opposition)**

__________. "In the Matter of Catherine Antrim: Response in Opposition to the Petition to Exhume Remains." Case No. MS 03-011. Sixth Judicial Court, County of Grant, State of New Mexico. **October 31, 2003.**

Tippett, Sherry J. Attorney for Petitioners. "State of New Mexico, County of Grant, Sixth Judicial District Court, In the Matter of Catherine Antrim, No. MS. 2003-11. Petitioner's Response in Opposition to the Town of Silver City's Motion to Intervene." (Unfiled) **No Date.**

Baker, Adam S. Attorneys for Mayor Terry Fortenberry on Behalf of Silver City. "In the Matter of Catherine Antrim: Request for Hearing." Case No. MS 03-011. Sixth Judicial Court, County of Grant, State of New Mexico. **November 4, 2003.**

Foy, Jim, District Judge. "In the Matter of Catherine Antrim: Notice of Recusal." Case No. MS 03-011. Sixth Judicial Court, County of Grant, State of New Mexico. **November 14, 2003. (Honest Judge Foy removes himself)**

Miranda, Velia C., District Court Clerk. "In the Matter of Catherine Antrim: Notice of Assignment/Designation of District Judge H.R. Quintero." Case No. MS 03-011. Sixth Judicial Court, County of Grant, State of New Mexico. **November 14, 2003. (Entry of Richardson appointee judge)**

Tippett, Sherry J. Attorney for Petitioners Sullivan, Sederwall and Graves. "In the Matter of Catherine Antrim: Petitioner's Response in Opposition to the Town of Silver City's Motion to Intervene." No. MS. 2003-11. State of New Mexico, County of Grant, Sixth Judicial District Court. (Unfiled) **No Date.**

Robins, Bill III and David Sandoval, Attorneys for Billy the Kid. "In the Matter of Catherine Antrim: Billy the Kid's Unopposed Motion for Intervention and Request for Expedited Disposition." Case No. MS 2003-11. Sixth Judicial Court, County of Grant, State of New Mexico. **November 26, 2003. (First petition with dead Billy the Kid as co-Petitioner to Sullivan, Sederwall, and Graves.)**

Kennedy, Paul J., Adam S. Baker, Thomas F. Stewart, Robert L. Scavron, Attorneys for Mayor Terry Fortenberry on Behalf of the Town of Silver City. "In the Matter of Catherine Antrim: Reply in Support of the Town of Silver City's Motion to Intervene." Case No. MS 2003-11. Sixth Judicial Court, County of Grant, State of New Mexico. **December 8, 2003. (Justifying need to protect Antrim grave)**

Tippett, Sherry J. Attorney for Petitioners Sullivan, Sederwall and Graves. "In the Matter of Catherine Antrim: Petitioners Response in Opposition to the Town of Silver City's Motion to Intervene." Case No. MS 2003-11. Sixth Judicial Court, County of Grant, State of New Mexico. **December 8, 2003. (Tippett lies by saying town has no "legal interest" to intervene)**

Quintero, H.R. District Judge. "In the Matter of Catherine Antrim: Order." Case No. MS 03-011. Sixth Judicial Court, County of Grant, State of New Mexico. **December 9, 2003. (Rescheduling hearing from January 6, 2004 to January 27, 2004.)**

Baker, Adam S. Attorneys for Mayor Terry Fortenberry on Behalf of the Town of Silver City. "In the Matter of Catherine Antrim: Intervenor Town of Silver City's Brief on Petition to Exhume." Case No. MS 03-011. Sixth Judicial Court, County of Grant, State of New Mexico. **January 5, 2004. (Arguing 1962 precedent case of Lois Telfer blocking exhumation)**

Tippett, Sherry J. Attorney. To Mayor Steve Sederwall, Sheriff Tom Sullivan, Sheriff Gary Graves. "In the Matter of Catherine Antrim: Petitioners Brief in Chief in Support of Exhumation." Case No. MS 2003-11. Sixth Judicial Court, County of Grant, State of New Mexico. **January 5, 2004. (Using Probable Cause Statement and Homer Overton Affidavit as Plaintiff exhibits)**

Robins, Bill III and David Sandoval. Attorneys for Billy the Kid. "In the Matter of Catherine Antrim: Billy the Kid's Pre-Hearing Brief." Case No. MS 2003-11. Sixth Judicial Court, Grant County. **January 5, 2004. (Linking exhumation and pardon with "Brushy Bill" Roberts as Billy – CRACKED THE HOAX as a "Brushy Bill" scam by using "Brushy's" dark night for July 14, 1881)**

Tippett, Sherry. Attorney for law enforcement Petitioners Tom Sullivan, Steve Sederwall, Gary Graves. "In the Matter of Catherine Antrim: Petitioner's [sic] Brief in Chief in Support of Exhumation." Case No. MS 2003-11. Sixth Judicial Court, Grant County. **January 5, 2004.**

Kennedy, Paul J., Adam S. Baker, Thomas F. Stewart, Robert L. Scavron, Attorneys for Mayor Terry Fortenberry on Behalf of the Town of Silver City. "In the Matter of Catherine Antrim: Response in Opposition to Petitioners' Brief in Chief." Case No. MS 2003-11. Sixth Judicial Court, County of Grant, State of New Mexico. **January 21, 2004.**

__________. "In the Matter of Catherine Antrim: Silver City's Response in Opposition to Petitioners' Motion for Continuance." Case No. MS 2003-11. Sixth Judicial Court, County of Grant, State of New Mexico. **January 21, 2004.**

Tippett, Sherry J. Attorney. To Mayor Steve Sederwall, Sheriff Tom Sullivan, Sheriff Gary Graves. "Attached is a copy of Judge Quintero's Order of December 9, 2003, ruling on our Hearing ..." **December 17, 2003. (States that they will win on January 27, 2004; urges completing the Probable Cause Statement)**

Quintero, H.R. District Judge, Division 1. "Order of Continuance. In the Matter of Catherine Antrim. Case No. MS 03-011." Filed **January 23, 2004**. Sixth Judicial Court, County of Grant, State of New Mexico. Filed January 23, 2004. **(Tippett sanctioned to pay airfare for witness, Frederick Nolan for changing the hearing date on short notice)**

Robins, Bill III and David Sandoval. Attorneys for Billy the Kid. "In the Matter of Catherine Antrim: Billy the Kid's Brief on the Question of Ripeness." Case No. MS 2003-11. Sixth Judicial Court, Grant County. **February 24, 2004. (Setting up Quintero's sending the exhumation to Fort Sumner)**

Acúna, Mark Anthony and Sherry J. Tippett. Attorneys for Petitioners Sullivan, Sederwall and Graves. "In the Matter of Catherine Antrim: Petitioners' Brief on the Question of Ripeness." Case No. MS 2003-11. Sixth Judicial Court, Grant County. **February 24, 2004.**

Baker, Adam S. and Thomas F. Stewart, Robert L. Scavron, Attorneys for Silver City and Joani Amos-Staats. "In the Matter of Catherine Antrim: Silver City's and Joani Amos-Staats' [sic] Joint Motion to Dismiss on Grounds of Ripeness." Case No. MS 2003-11. Sixth Judicial Court, County of Grant, State of New Mexico. **February 24, 2004.**

Acúna, Mark Anthony. Attorney for Petitioners Sullivan, Sederwall and Graves. "In the Matter of Catherine Antrim: Entry of Appearance." Case No. MS 03-011. Sixth Judicial Court, County of Grant, State of New Mexico. **February 26, 2004. (Replacing Tippett for law enforcement Petitioners)**

Robins, Bill III and David Sandoval. Attorneys for Billy the Kid. "In the Matter of Catherine Antrim: Response to Motion to Dismiss." Case No. MS 2003-11. Sixth Judicial Court, Grant County. **March 10, 2004.**

Quintero, Henry R. "In the Matter of Catherine Antrim: Decision and Order." Case No. MS 03-011." Sixth Judicial Court, County of Grant, State of New Mexico. **April 2, 2004. (Stipulation that case is not ripe, and requires DNA from Fort Sumner Billy the Kid grave first before trying to exhume Catherine Antrim)**

Fortenberry, Terry D, Mayor; Thomas A. Nupp Councilor District 2; Steve May, Councilor District 4; Gary Clauss, Councilor District 3; Judy Ward, Councilor District 1; Alex Brown, Town Manager; Cissy McAndrew, Executive Director Chamber of Commerce; Frank Milan, Director Silver City Mainstreet Project; Susan Berry, Director Silver City Museum. "Open Letter to Governor Bill Richardson." **June 21, 2004. (Request to cease "Billy the Kid Case" exhumations)**

FORT SUMNER, NEW MEXICO (EXHUMATION ATTEMPT ON WILLIAM H. BONNEY)

De Baca County Commissioners Special Meeting." Minutes. (Powhatan Carter III, Chairman; Joe Steele; Tommy Roybal; Nancy Sparks, County Clerk. To whom it may concern. "The De Baca County Commissioners are in full support of Village of Fort Sumner's stand against exhuming the body of Billy the Kid." **September 25, 2003. (Voted against exhumation of Billy the Kid)**

Robins, Bill III and David Sandoval, Mark Acuña, Attorneys for Co-Petitioner Billy the Kid and Sheriff-Petitioners. "In the Matter of William H. Bonney, aka 'Billy the Kid': Petition for the Exhumation of Billy the Kid's Remains." Case No. CV-04-

00005. Tenth Judicial District, County of De Baca, State of New Mexico. **February 26, 2004. (Robins joins Acuña to exhume the Kid)**

Robins, Bill III and David Sandoval, Attorneys for Co-Petitioner Billy the Kid. "In the Matter of William H. Bonney, aka 'Billy the Kid': Notice of Excusal." Case No. CV-2004 [sic]-00005. Tenth Judicial District, County of De Baca, State of New Mexico. **March 5, 2004. (Petitioners' removal of honest Judge Ricky Purcell from hearing the case.)**

Jimenez Maes, Petra, Chief Justice. "In the Matter of William H. Bonney, aka 'Billy the Kid': Order Designating Judge." Case No. CV-2004-00005. Tenth Judicial District, County of De Baca, State of New Mexico. **April 1, 2004. (Richardson's corrupt judge appointee, Ted Hartley, is appointed to case)**

Baker, Adam S. and Herb Marsh, Jr., Attorneys for the Village of Fort Sumner. "In the Matter of William H. Bonney, aka 'Billy the Kid': Village of Fort Sumner's Unopposed Motion to Intervene." Case No. CV-04-00005. Tenth Judicial District, County of De Baca, State of New Mexico. **April 12, 2004.**

__________. "In the Matter of William H. Bonney, aka 'Billy the Kid': Response in Opposition to the Petitioners for the Exhumation of Billy the Kid's Remains. In the Matter of William H. Bonney, aka 'Billy the Kid.' " Case No. CV-04-00005. Tenth Judicial District, County of De Baca, State of New Mexico. **April 12, 2004.**

Hartley, Teddy L. "In the Matter of William H. Bonney, aka 'Billy the Kid': Order." Case No. CV-04-00005. Tenth Judicial District, County of De Baca, State of New Mexico. **April 20, 2004. (Intervention of Village of Fort Sumner granted)**

Baker, Adam S. and Herb Marsh, Jr., Attorneys for the Village of Fort Sumner. "In the Matter of William H. Bonney, aka 'Billy the Kid': Response in Opposition to the Petition for the Exhumation of Billy the Kid's Remains." Case No. CV-04-00005. Tenth Judicial District, County of De Baca, State of New Mexico. **May 6, 2004.**

__________. "In the Matter of William H. Bonney, aka 'Billy the Kid': Village of Fort Sumner's Motion For Proof of Attorneys' Authority To Act On Behalf Of William H. Bonney." Case No. CV-04-00005. Tenth Judicial District, County of De Baca, State of New Mexico. **June 24, 2004. (Confronting Attorney Bill Robins III's fakery of representing Billy the Kid based on dead Billy not being real so he cannot have a lawyer)**

__________. "In the Matter of William H. Bonney, aka 'Billy the Kid': Village of Fort Sumner's Motion to Dismiss Against Petitioners Sullivan, Sederwall, and Graves for Lack of Standing." Case No. CV-04-00005. Tenth Judicial District, County of De Baca, State of New Mexico. **June 24, 2004. (Invalid murder case because Pat Garrett properly killed Billy the Kid)**

Hartley, Teddy L. District Judge. "Notice of Hearing. "In the Matter of William H. Bonney, aka 'Billy the Kid': Notice of Hearing." Case No. CV-04-00005. Tenth Judicial District, County of De Baca, State of New Mexico. **July 6, 2004. (Hearing set for September 27, 2004)**

Acuña, Mark Anthony, Attorney for the Petitioners Sullivan, Sederwall and Graves. "In the Matter of William H. Bonney, aka 'Billy the Kid': Petitioner's Response to the Village of Ft. Sumner's Motion to Dismiss." Case No. CV-04-00005." Tenth Judicial District, State of New Mexico, County of De Baca. **July 29, 2004.(Acuña argues Sheriff-petitioners' Sullivan, Graves, and Sederwall's standing based on law enforcement as Sheriffs and Deputy Sheriff; later Sullivan and Sederwall would lie that they had done the case as private hobbyists to avoid the open records act for public officials to hide their fake DNA documents)**

Robins, Bill III and David Sandoval; Attorneys for the Billy the Kid; and Adam S. Baker and Herb Marsh, Jr., Attorneys for the Village of Fort Sumner. "In the Matter of William H. Bonney, aka 'Billy the Kid': Stipulation of Dismissal." Case No. CV-04-00005. Tenth Judicial District, County of De Baca, State of New Mexico. **August 23, 2004. (Fake dead Billy the Kid petition dismissed with prejudice)**

"In the Matter of De Baca County Sheriff Gary Graves. Petition for Order Allowing Recall Vote." Case No. CV-04-00019. Tenth Judicial District Court, State of New Mexico, County of De Baca. **September 13, 2004. (Recall starts against Sheriff Gary Graves, separate from the exhumation case.)**

Acuña, Mark Anthony and Adam S. Baker, Attorneys for Petitioners Graves, Sullivan and Sederwall; and the Village of Fort Sumner. "In the Matter of William H. Bonney, aka 'Billy the Kid': Stipulation of Dismissal With Prejudice." Case No. CV-04-00005. Tenth Judicial District, County of De Baca, State of New Mexico. **September 24, 2004. (Petitioners withdraw with prejudice at Fort Sumner. Definitive victory against Billy the Kid exhumation.)**

ARIZONA: YAVAPAI (PRESCOTT) AND MARICOPA COUNTIES (EXHUMATIONS OF JOHN MILLER AND WILLIAM HUDSPETH)

Sederwall, Steven M., Lincoln County Sheriff's Deputy Investigator. "Lincoln County Sheriff's Department Supplemental Report, Case #2003-274. Subject: Exhumation of John Miller. Location: Arizona Pioneers' Cemetery, Prescott, Arizona." **May 19, 2005. (Arizona exhumations John Miller and William Hudspeth)**

Cahall, Anna, Detective Prescott Police Department. "CASE REPORT 0600012767." **April 5, 2006. (Concerning the John Miller exhumation)**

Tunnell, Dale. To Jeanine Dike. "Subject: RE: Disinterment of Wm Bonney." **May 3, 2005.**

Dike, Jeanine. To Dale Tunnell. "Subject: Disinterment of Wm Bonney." **May 3, 2005.**

___________. To Dale Sams. "Subject: FW: Disinterment Wm Bonney." **May 3, 2005.**

___________. To Dale Sams. "Subject: FW: Disinterment Wm Bonney." **May 4, 2005.**

Sams, Dale. To George Thompson. "Subject: Disinterment." **May 4, 2005. (Confirms Sams has no idea where the Miller grave is located.)**

Sederwall, Steven M., Lincoln County Sheriff's Deputy Investigator. "Lincoln County Sheriff's Department Supplemental Report, Case #2003-274. Subject: Exhumation of John Miller. Location: Arizona Pioneers' Cemetery, Prescott, Arizona." **May 19, 2005. (Arizona exhumations John Miller and William Hudspeth)**

Fulginiti, Laura C. Ph.D., D-ABFA. Forensic Anthropologist. To Dale L. Tunnell, Ph.D. "RE: Exhumation, Pioneer Home Cemetery, Prescott, Arizona." **June 2, 2005. (Report of the Miller-Hudspeth exhumations revealing fake hoaxer claims of buck teeth and bullet wound to left scapula of John Miller.)**

Sederwall, Steven. To Misty Rodarte. "Subject: Billy the Kid." **July 6, 2005.**

Winter, Anne. "To: Tim Nelson; Alan Stephens. Subject: Pioneer Home, Grave, Billy the Kid and DNA." **August 18, 2005. (Has attachment of Pioneers' Home Supervisor Gary Olson's cover-up letter to her and implied internal cover-up. Also states that Sullivan paid for the exhumation.)**

___________. "To: Tim Nelson; Alan Stephens. Subject: Billy the Kid." **September 8, 2005. ("80% DNA match" with Miller claimed)**

Olson, Gary. Superintendent Arizona Pioneers' Home. To David Snell. "You recently asked the Arizona Pioneers' Home if a body in its cemetery had been exhumed ..." October 3, 2005. **(Confirms original cover-up of John Miller exhumation.)**

Winter, Anne. "To Gary Olson. Subject: RE: the kid." **October 17, 2005. (Requesting any DNA results yet to him.)**

Olson, Gary. "To Anne Winter. Subject: RE: the kid." **October 17, 2005. (Reporting on no DNA results yet to him.)**

Winter, Anne. "To: Jeanine L'Ecuyer. Subject: FW: the kid." **October 17, 2005. (Reporting on no DNA results yet to Olson.)**

Olson, Gary. "To: Anne Winter. Subject: FW: re. John Miller." **October 20, 2005. (Cover-up `planned for Romo. "I thought you and the Governor may want to know about this request.")**

Winter, Anne. "To: Tim Nelson; Alan Stephens. Subject: FW: re. John Miller. **October 20, 2005. (Cover-up plan for reporter Rene Romo's *Albuquerque***

***Journal* article stating: "Remember there was the legal issue that they dug up two bodies.")**

__________. "To: Jeanine L'Ecuyer. Subject: FW: re. John Miller." **October 25, 2005. (Planning cover-up for media requests.)**

Sederwall, Steven. "To: Barbara J. Miller; Steve McGregor; Rick Staub; Misty Rodarte; Emily Smith; Bob Boze Bell. Subject: in the Albuquerque Journal." **November 6, 2005. (Copy Romo article.)**

Olson, Gary. "To Anne Winter, Mark Wilson. Subject: FW: in the Albuquerque Journal." **November 7, 2005. (Copy Romo article.)**

Winter, Anne. "To: Jeanine L'Ecuyer; Tim Nelson; Alan Stephens. Subject: Billy the Kid. **November 7, 2005. (About Gary Olson's cover-up in KPNX interview.)**

Snell, David. To Shiela Polk. Yavapai County Attorney. "I feel it is my duty to report to you that graverobbers are plying their trade ..." **March 11, 2006. (Arizona citizen starting criminal investigation of Miller/Hudspeth exhumations.)**

Jacobson, Marcia. "To Anne Winter, Policy Advisor for Health, Office of the Governor, and Chief Randy Oaks, Prescott Police Department. Re: Disinterment of bodies at Arizona Pioneer's [sic] Home Cemetery." **March 30, 2006. (Attempted cover-up of John Miller and William Hudspeth exhumations.)**

Cahall, Anna, Detective Prescott Police Department. "CASE REPORT 0600012767." **April 5, 2006. (Interviews with Sullivan, Sederwall, Tunnell)**

Savona, Glenn A. Prescott City Prosecutor. To Shiela Sullivan Polk, Yavapai County Attorney. "Re: Police Department DR# 2006-12767 Arizona Pioneers' Home Cemetery." **April 13, 2006. (Calls exhumations potential felonies)**

Cooper, Gale. To Detective Anna Cahall. Prescott Police Department. "Re: Exhumation of John Miller and adjacent grave for pursuing the New Mexico Billy the Kid Case." **April 13, 2006.**

__________. To Detective Anna Cahall. Prescott Police Department. "Re: Pertinent articles regarding exhumation of John Miller and remains from adjacent grave for alleged promulgation of the New Mexico Billy the Kid Case, a murder investigation." **April 17, 2006.**

__________. To Deputy County Attorney Steve Jaynes and County Attorney Dennis McGrane. (via fax) "Re: Information on the New Mexico Billy the Kid Case pertinent to the Arizona John Miller exhumations." **May 2, 2006.**

Sederwall, Steve. To confidential recipient. "Well we have the governor reaching out to the Arizona to stop this investigation." **May 16, 2006.**

Cooper, Gale. To Attorney Jonnell Lucca (via fax). "Re: Case # CA20006020516. Follow-up to our telephone conversation of June 9, 2006, to address the issue of Permit for the exhumations of John Miller and the remains from an adjacent grave for promulgation of the New Mexico Billy the Kid Case, a murder investigation." **June 12, 2006.**

__________. To Attorney Jonell Lucca (via fax). "Re: Case # CA20006020516. Follow-up to my fax of June 12, 2006, to address additional issues pertinent to the exhumations of John Miller and William Hudspeth, done for promulgation of the New Mexico Billy the Kid Case, an alleged murder investigation." July 11, 2006.

Sams, Dale. Arizona Pioneers' Home Administrator. To Gale Cooper. Confirming approximate date of John Miller's birth as 1850. **August 8, 2006.**

Cooper, Gale. To Attorney Jonell Lucca (via fax). "Re: Case # CA20006020516. Follow-up to my fax of July 11, 2006, to address issues pertinent to the promulgators of the New Mexico Billy the Kid Case (which resulted in the exhumations of John Miller and William Hudspeth); with added focus on its alleged forensic experts and co-participants." **August 11, 2006.**

__________. To Attorney Jonell Lucca. "Re: Enclosed reference copy of Freedom of Information Act (FOIA) to Governor Janet Napolitano regarding her possible participation in the Prescott, Arizona exhumations of John Miller and William Hudspeth, and their legal issues related to Maricopa County Prosecutor's Office Case # CA20006020516." **September 22, 2006.**

__________. To Attorney Jonell Lucca. "Re: Information pertaining to Case # CA20006020516 (exhumations of John Miller and William Hudspeth) - American Academy of Forensic Science Ethics and Conduct Complaint against Dr. Henry Lee." **October 2, 2006.**

Lucca, Jonell L. To Dr. Gale Cooper. "This letter is to inform you that the Maricopa County Attorney's Office has declined to file charges ..." **October 17, 2006. (Corrupt claim that the only suspects were Jeanine Dike and Dale Tunnell to shield Sullivan and Sederwall)**

Cooper, Gale. To Attorney Jonell Lucca. "Re: Maricopa County Case # CA20006020516." **October 30, 2006. (Confirmation of getting her case termination letter, and asking why she changed suspects. Never answered.)**

Cooper, Gale. To Detective Anna. Prescott Police Department. "Re: Freedom of Information Act Request for Records of Prescott Police Department Case No. 06-12767. **September 11, 2008. (No response)**

HAMILTON, TEXAS (EXHUMATION ATTEMPT ON "BRUSHY BILL" ROBERTS)

Virden, R.E. Lincoln County Sheriff. To Hamilton, Texas, Mayor Roy Ramsey [sic]. "This letter will inform you that Tom Sullivan and Steve Sederwall are both commissioned deputies ..." **No date, but around May 2007. (Virden's attempt to exhume "Brushy Bill" Roberts.)**

Cooper, Gale. "RE: Lincoln County Sheriff's Department's 2007 attempt to exhume Oliver "Brushy Bill" Roberts. Faxed letter to Hamilton, Texas, Mayor Roy Rumsey. **September 11, 2008.**

Rumsey, Roy. Hamilton Mayor. "RE: Lincoln County Sheriff's Department's 2007 attempt to exhume Oliver Roberts." Faxed letter to Gale Cooper. **September 12, 2008. (Confirmation that the case is closed)**

PAST ATTEMPT TO EXHUME WILLIAM H. BONNEY

"Motion to Intervene. In Re Application of Lois Telfer, Petitioner for the Removal of the Body of William H. Bonney, Deceased, From the Ft. Sumner Cemetery in Which He is Interred for Reinterment in the Lincoln, New Mexico, Cemetery. Case No. 3255." **December 5, 1961.** In the District Court of the Tenth Judicial District Within and For the County of De Baca. Signed: Victor C. Breen and John Humphrey, Jr., Attorneys for Louis A Bowdre. **(Louis Bowdre was the relative of Charles Bowdre whose grave is contiguous to William Bonney's.)**

Breen, Victor C. and John Humphrey, Jr., Attorneys for Louis A Bowdre. "Motion to Intervene. In Re Application of Lois Telfer, Petitioner for the Removal of the Body of William H. Bonney, Deceased, From the Ft. Sumner Cemetery in Which He is Interred for Reinterment in the Lincoln, New Mexico, Cemetery." Case No. 3255. In the District Court of the Tenth Judicial District, County of De Baca. **December 5, 1961. (Louis Bowdre was the relative of Charles Bowdre whose grave is contiguous to William Bonney's.)**

Kinsley, E.T. District Judge. "Decree. In Re Application of Lois Telfer, Petitioner for the Removal of the Body of William H. Bonney, Deceased, From the Ft. Sumner Cemetery in Which He is Interred for Reinterment in the Lincoln, New Mexico, Cemetery." Case No. 3255." In the District Court of the Tenth Judicial District Within and For the County of De Baca. **April 6, 1962. (Petition for exhumation Billy the Kid denied on basis that his grave could not be located and the search would disturb Bowdre's remains. That precedent was ignored by the current Petitioners and their attorneys.)**

MY OPEN RECORDS REQUESTS (CHRONOLOGICAL)

RECORDS REQUESTS BY JAY MILLER AS MY PROXY

Miller, Jay. To Steve Sederwall, Mayor of Capitan and Deputy Sheriff of Lincoln County. "FOIA/IPRA." **May 13, 2004.**

__________. To Village of Capitan Records Custodian. "I would like to inspect and copy the following documents of Steve Sederwall ..." **May 13, 2004.**

__________. To County Clerk of Lincoln County/Records Custodian, Lincoln County Courthouse. "Re: I would like to inspect the following documents of Tom Sullivan, elected Sheriff of Lincoln County." **May 13, 2004.**

__________. To County Clerk of DeBaca County/Records Custodian. "Freedom of Information Act Request: Inspect and copy records pertaining to Gary Graves, elected sheriff ..." **May 13, 2004.**

Morel, Alan P. Lincoln County Attorney. To Jay Miller. "RE: Freedom of Information Act Request dated May 13, 2004." **May 19, 2004.**

Grassie, Anna Gail. (For Village of Capitan and Mayor Steve Sederwall). To Jay Miller. "Reference: Freedom of Information Request from Jay Miller dated May 13, 2004." **May 25, 2004.**

Miller, Jay. To Michael Cerletti, Secretary, Department Tourism. "RE: FOIA/IPRA on Billy the Kid Case promulgators and Department of Tourism." **May, 28, 2004.**

__________. To Attorney Alan P. Morel. "Re: Response to your letter dated May 19, 2004 on behalf of the County Clerk of Lincoln County and Lincoln County Sheriff Tom Sullivan." **June 1, 2004.**

__________. To Mayor Steve Sederwall. "FOIA/IPRA on Steve Sederwall as Mayor of Capitan and Deputy Sheriff of Lincoln County." **June 1, 2004.**

Morel, Alan P. Lincoln County Attorney. To Jay Miller. "RE: Response to your letter dated May 19, 2004 on behalf of the County Clerk of Lincoln County and Lincoln County Sheriff Tom Sullivan. **June 1, 2004.**

Sederwall, Steven: Mayor. To Jay Miller. "I am in receipt of your letter dated June 1, 2004." **June 3, 2004.**

Morel, Alan P. Lincoln County Attorney. To Jay Miller. "RE: Freedom of Information Act Request June 1, 2004." **June 4, 2004.**

Cerletti, Mike.. To Jay Miller. "Reply to your freedom of information request." **June 7, 2004. (Denied participation of Tourism Department in Billy the Kid Case)**

Miller, Jay. To Lincoln County Attorney Alan Morel. "Copy all documents relevant to David Turk, historian for the U.S. Marshals Service ..." **June 9, 2004.**

__________. To Mayor of Capitan and Deputy Sheriff of Lincoln County Steve Sederwall. "Evade response by claiming that you were being addresses solely in your capacity as Mayor ..." **June 9, 2004.**

__________. To Sheriff Gary Graves and Nancy Sparks, De Baca County Clerk. "Freedom of Information Act Request: I would like to inspect any and all documents relevant to David Turk ..." **June 9, 2004.**

Sederwall, Steven M. To Jay Miller. "This office has no records ..." **June 10, 2004.**

Miller, Jay. To Mayor Steve Sederwall. "FOIA/IPRA on Steve Sederwall as Mayor of Capitan and Deputy Sheriff of Lincoln County." **June 10, 2004.**

____________. To Attorney General Patricia Madrid. "Re: Follow-up on FOIA/IPRA Request to Lincoln County Sheriff Tom Sullivan." **June 14, 2004. (No response)**

Sparks Nancy. (Clerk for Sheriff Gary Graves). To Jay Miller. "Re: FOIA/IPRA request for records of De Baca County Sheriff Gary Graves." **June 14, 2004.**

Miller, Jay. To Mayor of Capitan and Deputy Sheriff of Lincoln County Steve Sederwall. "Thank you for your prompt response to my letter of June 1, 2004 ... " **June 21, 2004.**

___________. To Attorney General Patricia Madrid. RE: Follow-up on FOIA/IPRA Requests to Steve Sederwall, Mayor of Capitan and Deputy Sheriff of Lincoln County." **June 21, 2004.**

__________. To Lincoln County Attorney Alan Morel. "I would like to inspect and copy any and all documents relevant to your client Tom Sullivan, Sheriff of Lincoln County with regard to a statement made by his attorney Sherry Tippett ..." **June 23, 2004.**

__________. To Mayor of Capitan and Deputy Sheriff of Lincoln County Steve Sederwall. "To inspect and copy all records relevant to your attorney, Sherry Tippett's, claims ..." **June 23, 2004.**

__________. To Michael Cerletti, Secretary Tourism. "Thanks for your response ..." **June 23, 2004.**

Lama, Albert J. Assistant Attorney General. To Jay Miller. "Concerning an alleged violation of the Inspection of Public Records Act by the Lincoln County, De Baca County, and Village of Capitan." **June 24, 2004.**

Miller, Jay. To Attorney General Patricia Madrid. "Re: Follow-up on FOIA/IPRA Requests to Steve Sederwall, Mayor of Capitan and Deputy Sheriff of Lincoln County." **June 21, 2004.** (**Instead of answering, they closed the case**)

Graves, Gary W. De Baca County Sheriff. To Jay Miller. "I am writing in response to your request ..." **June 22 2004.** (**Denies information on David Turk**)

Miller, Jay. To Sheriff Gary Graves. "Freedom of Information Act Request: Inspect and copy all records relevant to your attorney, Sherry Tippett ..." **June 23, 2004.**

__________. To Sheriff Gary Graves and Nancy Sparks. "Re: FOIA/IPRA request for records." **June 25, 2004.**

Graves, Gary W. De Baca County Sheriff. To Jay Miller. "I do not maintain requests for travel reimbursements ..." **June 29, 2004.** (**His clerk did send records!**)

__________. To Jay Miller. "As per your FOIA/IPRA Request on **June 23, 2004** ..." June 29, 2004. (**Denies records on Attorney Sherry Tippett.**)

__________. To Jay Miller. "I do not maintain or have any records in reference to Sherry Tippett ..." **June 29, 2004.**

Miller, Jay. To Attorney Alan Morel. "Re: Deputizing of Capitan Mayor Steve Sederwall as referenced in your letter dated June 4, 2004 on behalf of Lincoln County Sheriff Tom Sullivan." **July 1, 2004.**

Morel, Alan P. Attorney for Lincoln County. To Jay Miller. "Re: Deputizing of Capitan Mayor Steve Sederwall as referenced in your letter dated June 4, 2004 on behalf of Lincoln County Sheriff Tom Sullivan." **July 1, 2004.**

__________. To Jay Miller. "RE: Freedom of Information Act/Inspection of Public Records Act Request dated June 2[illegible], 2004." **July 2, 2004.**

Sparks, Nancy. De Baca County Clerk. "I have sent you everything I have on Sheriff Graves ..." July 2, 2004.

Prelo, Marc. Attorney for Village of Capitan. To Jay Miller. "RE: Village of Capitan/Freedom of Information Act - Inspection of Public Records Request. **July 5, 2004.** (**Response for Sederwall to Jay Miller**)

Miller, Jay. To Assistant AG Mary Smith. "Re: Response to your letter of June 24, 2004." **July 8, 2004.**

__________. To Sheriff Gary Graves. "Re: Follow-up on your responses to my prior FOIA/IPRA requests." **July 8, 2004.**

Morel, Alan P. Lincoln County Attorney. To Jay Miller. "RE: Freedom of Information Act Request dated July 1, 2004." **July 9, 2004.** (**Statutes justifying deputizing Sederwall**)

Smith, Mary H., Assistant Attorney General. To Jay Miller. "Re: Determination of Inspection of Public Records Act Complaint v Village of Capitan." **August 3, 2004.** (**Corrupt rejection of open records complaint.**)

__________. To Jay Miller "Re: Determination of Inspection of Public Records Act complaint v De Baca County." **August 3, 2004.** (**Corrupt rejection of open records complaint.**)

Miller, Jay. To Sheriff Tom Sullivan. "Re: David Turk, Historian for the U.S. Marshals Service." **August 5, 2004.**

__________. To Office of General Counsel - FOIA REQUEST, Attn. Arleta Cunningham, U.S. Marshal's Service. "Re. David Turk, historian for U.S. Marshal's Service, FOIA on Sederwall/Sullivan/Graves/ Billy the Kid Case." **August 5, 2004.**

__________. To Assistant AG Mary Smith. "Re. Response to your letter of August 3, 2004 about determination of my IPRA complaint v Mayor of Capitan Steve Sederwall, who also represents himself as Deputy Sheriff of Lincoln County; and the Village of Capitan." **August, 10, 2004.**

Sullivan, Tom, Lincoln County Sheriff. "In response to your 'Inspection of Public Records Act" request dated August 5, 2004." **August 18, 2004. (Denies open records request on David Turk based on ongoing criminal investigation)**

Morel, Alan P. Lincoln County Attorney. To Jay Miller. "In response to your "Information Act Request dated August 5, 2004." **August 18, 2004.**

Miller, Jay. To Deputy Attorney General Stuart Bluestone. "Re: Complaint and appeal for assistance with regard to non-compliance with FOIA/IPRA requests made to Capitan Mayor Steve Sederwall, who represents himself as Deputy Sheriff of Lincoln County and the Village Clerk of Capitan." **August 28, 2004. (No response)**

__________. To Deputy Attorney General Stuart Bluestone. "Re: Complaint and appeal for assistance with regard to non-compliance with FOIA/IPRA requests made to Lincoln County Sheriff Tom Sullivan and Lincoln County Clerk." **September 4, 2004. (No response)**

Utley, Robert M. "Billy Again." **September 16, 2004. (Sent to Jay Miller and forwarded to me regarding Paul Hutton in Billy the Kid Case.)**

Smith Mary. Assistant Attorney General. To Jay Miller. "Re: Inspection of Public Records Act complaint v Steve Sederwall, Mayor of Capitan and Lincoln County Deputy Sheriff." **May 17, 2005. (Nine months later: Rejection of complaint)**

Bordley, William E. To Jay Miller. "Freedom of Information/Privacy Act Request No. 2004USMS7634, Subject: David Turk, Historian U.S. Marshals Service, FOIA on Sederwall/Sullivan/Graves/Billy the Kid Case." June 22, 2005.

Miller, Jay. To William E. Boardley, Associate General Counsel/FOIPA Officer, U.S. Marshal's Service. "Follow-up on your response titled Freedom of Information Act Request No. 2004USMS7634 Subject: David Turk, Historian U.S. Marshal's Service, FOIA on Sederwall/Sullivan/Graves/Billy the Kid Case." **July 25, 2005.**

DeZulovich, Mavis. FOI/PA Liaison, Office of Public Affairs. To Jay Miller. "This letter is in response to your Freedom of Information/Privacy Act Request No. 2004USMS7634 in reference to David Turk. **August 24, 2005. (States Turk is not Probable Cause Statement author, but references his pamphlet.)**

Virden, R.E. Lincoln County Sheriff. Letter to Jay Miller. "We are interested in the truth surrounding Billy the Kid and are continuing the investigation ..." **November 28, 2005. (Confirms deputizing Sullivan and Sederwall for "Billy the Kid Case")**

Miller, Jay. To Paul Hutton. "As a journalist following the Billy the Kid Case ..." **February 6, 2006.**

__________. To Attorney General Patricia Madrid. "Re: Follow-up on non-response by Attorney General to my September 4, 2004 Complaint and Appeal for assistance with regard to non-compliance by past Lincoln County Sheriff Tom Sullivan with my FOIA/IPRA Requests." **March 20, 2006.**

__________. To Paul Hutton. "Repeat of one sent to you on February 6, 2006, because I received no response to it." **March 20, 2006.**

__________. To Sheriff Rick Virden. "Inspection of Public Records Act/Freedom of Information Act request." **March 27, 2006.**

__________. To Attorney Marc Prelo. "Re: Follow-up on Freedom of Information Request response dated July 5, 2004." **March 27, 2006. (Requests information on taxpayer money for Sederwall's Billy the Kid Case participation)**

Prelo, Marc Attorney. To Jay Miller. "RE: Village of Capitan/Freedom of Information Act – Inspection of Public Records Request." **Match 31, 2006. (Confirms his use of taxpayer money for Sederwall's Billy the Kid Case participation)**

Morel, Alan P. Lincoln County Attorney. To Jay Miller. "RE: Freedom of Information Act/Inspection of Public Records Act request dated March 27, 2006, to Lincoln County Sheriff Rick Virden. **April 3, 2006.**

___________. To Jay Miller. "Re: Follow-up on Freedom of Information Act Request Responses Dated May 19, 2004 and June 4, 2004." **April 17, 2006. (Confirms his use of taxpayer money for Sullivan's Billy the Kid Case participation)**

Miller, Jay. To Attorney General Patricia Madrid. "Re: Follow-up on FOIA/IPRA Request to Lincoln County Sheriff Tom Sullivan." **May 6, 2006. (No response)**

___________. To Assistant Attorney General Mary Smith. "Re. Response to your letter of May 17, 2005 rejecting my IPRA complaint against then Mayor of Capitan Steve Sederwall, who also represented himself as Deputy Sheriff of Lincoln County." **May 6, 2006. (No response.)**

Miller, Jay. To Assistant Attorney General Mary Smith. "Re. Response to your letter of May 17, 2005 rejecting my IPRA complaint against then Mayor of Capitan Steve Sederwall, who also represented himself as Deputy Sheriff of Lincoln County." **June 13, 2006. (Repeat complaint with new information. No response.)**

___________. To Paul Hutton. "Re. Clarification of my letter to you dated March 20, 2006, and reframing of it as a FOIA/IPRA Request." **June 13, 2006.**

___________. To Attorney Mark Acuña. "Re. Follow-up on your legal participation in the New Mexico Billy the Kid Case and participation of the Jaffe Law Firm in the New Mexico Billy the Kid Case." **June 22, 2006. (No response.)**

___________. To Attorney General Patricia Madrid. "Re. FOIA/IPRA Request with regard to your relationship with Attorney Bill Robins III and/or his law firm Heard, Robins, Cloud, Lubel & Greenwood LLP." **August 8, 2006.**

___________. To Attorney Mark Acuña.. "Re. Follow-up on my unanswered letter of June 22, 2006 with regard to your legal participation in the New Mexico Billy the Kid Case and the participation of your Jaffe Law Firm in the New Mexico Billy the Kid Case." **August 8, 2006. (No response).**

___________**.** To Mavis DeZulovich. FOIA/PA Liaison U.S. Department of Justice. "Re: Follow-up to your August 24, 2005 response to my Freedom of Information Act request No. 2004USMS7634 in reference to David Turk, Historian for the U.S. Marshals Service." **August 8, 2006. (Request for Turk's pamphlet)**

Hutton, Paul "I was never the 'state historian' ..." . Letter to Jay Miller. **June 20, 2006. (Central "Billy the Kid Case" hoaxer lies about his role)**

Miller, Jay. To Attorney Mark Acuña. "Re. Follow-up on your legal participation in the New Mexico Billy the Kid Case and participation of the Jaffe Law Firm in the New Mexico Billy the Kid Case." **June 22, 2006. (No response.)**

___________. To Attorney General Patricia Madrid. "Re. FOIA/IPRA Request with regard to your relationship with Attorney Bill Robins III and/or his law firm Heard, Robins, Cloud, Lubel & Greenwood LLP." **August 8, 2006.**

___________. To Attorney Mark Acuña.. "Re. Follow-up on my unanswered letter of June 22, 2006 with regard to your legal participation in the New Mexico Billy the Kid Case and the participation of your Jaffe Law Firm in the New Mexico Billy the Kid Case." **August 8, 2006. (No response).**

___________. To Mavis DeZulovich. FOIA/PA Liaison U.S. Department of Justice. "Re: Follow-up to your August 24, 2005 response to my Freedom of Information Act request No. 2004USMS7634 in reference to David Turk, Historian for the U.S. Marshals Service." **August 8, 2006. (Requesting copy of David Turk's pamphlet on Billy the Kid and U.S. Marshals Service)**

___________. To Dr. Rick Staub, Director Orchid Cellmark Lab. "Re: The participation by you and Orchid Cellmark in the New Mexico Billy the Kid Case." **August 8, 2006. (No response.)**

Miller, Jay. To Attorney General Patricia Madrid. "RE: FOIA/IPRA request regarding Attorney Bill Robins III and/or his law firm Heard, Robins, Cloud, Lubel, and Greenwood." **August 24, 2006.**

Cedrick, Nikki. FOIA/PA Liaison U.S. Department of Justice. "Per your FOI request No. 2004USMS7634." **August 31, 2006. (Refuses to send copy of David Turk's pamphlet on Billy the Kid)**

Miller, Jay. To Attorney General Patricia Madrid. "Re: Second FOIA/IPRA Request with regard to documentation of financial relationship of Attorney General Patricia Madrid and/or her Office, and Attorney Bill Robins III and/or his law firm Heard, Robins, Cloud, Lubel, and Greenwood LLP." **September 1, 2006.**

____________. To Assistant Attorney General Mary Smith. "Re. Response to your letter of May 17, 2005 rejecting my IPRA complaint against then Mayor of Capitan Steve Sederwall, who also represented himself as Deputy Sheriff of Lincoln County." **September 1, 2006. (No response)**

____________. To Deputy Attorney General Stuart Bluestone. "Re: Follow-up on your recent telephone call to me about my current, repeated, FOIA/IPRA non-compliance complaints to Attorney General Patricia Madrid with regard to Tom Sullivan's and Steve Sederwall's participation in the Billy the Kid Case in their capacities as public officials." **September 1, 2006. (No response)**

Bordley, William E. Associate General Counsel/FOIPA Officer for U.S. Department of Justice. To Jay Miller. "Re: Freedom of Information/Privacy Act Request No. 2006USMS9782 Subject: Copy of Report Entitled *The U.S. Marshals Service and Billy the Kid.*" **September 5, 2006. (Refuses to send copy of David Turk's pamphlet on Billy the Kid)**

Kupfer, Elizabeth, Records Custodian. To Jay Miller. "Need additional time ..." **September 6, 2006.**

Miller, Jay. To Nikki Cedrick, FOIA/PA Liaison U.S. Department of Justice. "Re: Follow-up to your August 31, 2006 response to my Freedom of Information Act request No. 2004USMS7634 in Reference to David Turk, Historian for the U.S. Marshals Service; and request for clarification." **September 11, 2006.**

Smith, Glenn R., Deputy Attorney General and Elizabeth Kupfer, Custodian of Public Records. (For Attorney General Patricia Madrid). To Jay Miller." RE: Inspection of Public Records Request." **September 20, 2006.**

Bordley, William E. Associate General Counsel/FOIPA Officer for U.S. Department of Justice. To Jay Miller. "Re: Freedom of Information/Privacy Act Request No. 2006USMS9782 Subject: Copy of Report Entitled *The U.S. Marshals Service and Billy the Kid.*" **September 5, 2006. (Refuses copy of David Turk's pamphlet on Billy the Kid.)**

Kupfer, Elizabeth, Records Custodian. To Jay Miller. "Need additional time ..." **September 6, 2006.**

Miller, Jay. To Nikki Cedrick, FOIA/PA Liaison U.S. Department of Justice. "Re: Follow-up to your August 31, 2006 response to my Freedom of Information Act request No. 2004USMS7634 in Reference to David Turk, Historian for the U.S. Marshals Service; and request for clarification." **September 11, 2006.**

Smith, Glenn R., Deputy Attorney General and Elizabeth Kupfer, Custodian of Public Records. (For Attorney General Patricia Madrid). To Jay Miller." RE: Inspection of Public Records Request." **September 20, 2006.**

RECORDS REQUESTS BY GALE COOPER

"Jordan, Wilma" aka Gale Cooper. To David Turk, Historian U.S. Marshals Service. "Looking for the truth is good ..." **June 15, 2006. (Attempt to get the Turk's "U.S. Marshal's Service and Billy the Kid " pamphlet for Case 2003-274.)**

Turk, David. Historian U.S. Marshals Service. To "Wilma Jordan." "Thank you for your thoughtful and thorough letter ..." **July 3, 2006. (Creepy Turk traced a "Wilma Jordan's" address; refused to send his Billy the Kid pamphlet)**

Cooper, Gale. To Governor Bill Richardson and Records Custodian for FOIA/IPRA Requests. "Re: Freedom of Information Act (FOIA)/Inspection of Public Records Act (IPRA) request concerning participation of Governor Bill Richardson in the New Mexico Billy the Kid Case and related issues." **September 22, 2006**.

___________. To Governor Janet Napolitano. "Re: Freedom of Information Act (FOIA) request pertaining to the Prescott, Arizona exhumations of John Miller and William Hudspeth at the Arizona Pioneers' Home Cemetery on May 19, 2005." **September 22, 2006**.

___________. To Sheriff Rick Virden. "Re: Freedom of Information Act (FOIA)/New Mexico Inspection of Public Records Act (IPRA) request pertaining to Lincoln County Sheriff's Department Case # 2003-274 ("Billy the Kid Case") and to its May 19, 2005 Prescott Arizona exhumations of John Miller and William Hudspeth." **September 22, 2006**.

Morel, Alan P. Lincoln County Attorney. To Gale Cooper. "Re: Freedom of Information Act/Inspection of Public Records Act Request dated September 22, 2006, to Lincoln County Sheriff Rick Virden." **September 29, 2006**.

Sullivan, Tom and Steve Sederwall. To Lincoln County Attorney Alan Morel. "The Dried Bean. 'You Believin' Us or Them Lyin' Whores.' " **September 30, 2006. (Exhibit 4 in IPRA response to me of October 11, 2006 from Sheriff Rick Virden through Lincoln County Attorney Alan Morel.**)

Maestas, Marcie. Records Custodian for Governor Bill Richardson. To Gale Cooper, M.D. "Received your request to inspect certain records ..." **October 3, 2006**.

Morel, Alan P. Lincoln County Attorney. To Gale Cooper. "RE: Freedom of Information Act (FOIA)/New Mexico Inspection of Public Records Act (IPRA) to Lincoln County Sheriff Ricky [sic] Virden and the Lincoln County Records Custodian, dated September 22, 2006." **October 11, 2006**.

Maestas, Marcie. Records Custodian for Governor Bill Richardson. To Gale Cooper, M.D. "Response to your Inspection of Public Records request received by our office on September 28, 2006 ..." **October 13, 2006**. (**Denial of each item, but miscellaneous documents provided**)

Michael R. Haener. Deputy Chief of Staff to Governor Janet Napolitano. "Enclosed records responsive to your request ..." **November 13, 2006**.

Cooper, Gale. To Governor Janet Napolitano. "Re: Repeated Freedom of Information Act (FOIA) request pertaining to the Prescott, Arizona exhumations of John Miller and William Hudspeth at the Arizona Pioneers' Home Cemetery on May 19, 2005." **March 20, 2007**. (**Repeated because of no response**)

___________. To Governor Janet Napolitano's Records Custodian. "Re: Repeat submission of incompletely answered Freedom of Information Act request dated September 22, 2006. **March 21, 2007**.

Shilo Mitchell, Deputy Press Secretary for Governor Janet Napolitano. To Gale Cooper, M.D. ""We have no responsive documents from your last request ..." **August 2, 2007**.

Cooper, Gale. To January Contreras, Policy Advisor for Health for Governor Janet Napolitano. "Re: Non- response to my Freedom of Information Act request dated June 29, 2007." **August 10, 2007**.

___________. "Re: Freedom of Information Act request pertaining to New Mexico Governor Bill Richardson's Grand Jury investigation(s) concerning CDR Financial Products, Inc." To Attorney General Eric Holder. **May 25, 2010**.

___________. "Re: Freedom of Information Act request pertaining to New Mexico Governor Bill Richardson's Grand Jury investigation(s) concerning CDR Financial Products, Inc." To President Barak Obama. **May 25, 2010**.

___________. "Re: Freedom of Information Act request pertaining to New Mexico Governor Bill Richardson's Grand Jury investigation(s) concerning CDR Financial Products, Inc." To New Mexico U.S. Attorney Greg Fouratt Obama. **May 25, 2010**.

Hardy, David M. Section Chief, Record/Information Dissemination Section. "Subject: Bill Richardson, January 2008 – Present, FOIPA Request No.: 1149852-000."

To Gale Cooper. U.S. Department of Justice, Federal Bureau of Investigation. **June 28, 2010. (Refused records as being on a "third party")**

Stewart, William G. II. Assistant Director. "Subject of Request: Gov. Bill Richardson (grand jury investigation), Request Number 2010-2058." To Gale Cooper. U.S. Department of Justice. **July 14, 2010. (Refused based on "personal privacy")**

__________. "Subject of Request: Gov. Bill Richardson (grand jury investigation), Request Number 2010-2045." To Gale Cooper. U.S. Department of Justice. **July 28, 2010. (Refused information based on "personal privacy")**

INVESTIGATIONS OF DR. HENRY LEE AND ORCHID CELLMARK LAB (CHRONOLOGICAL)

BACKGROUND

Bugliosi, Vincent. *Outrage: The Five Reasons Why O.J. Simpson Got Away With Murder*. New York and London: W.W. Norton & Company. **1996. (Exposé of Dr. Henry Lee forensic scams, Pages 47-49.)**

No author. "Fraud Alleged at Cellmark, DNA Testing Firm." TalkLeft: The Politics of Crime. http://www.talkleft.com./new_archives/008809.html. **November 18, 2004.**

Shen, Maxine. "CBS and the brother of JonBenet Ramsey settle their $750m defamation lawsuit to the 'satisfaction of both parties' after he claimed their documentary implied he killed his sister." **January 5, 2019.** DailyMailOnline.com. **(Defamation case involving Dr. Henry Lee's forensics)**

Fruen, Lauren. "Celebrity forensic scientist who worked on trials of O.J. Simpson, Phil Spector and Michael Peterson, and helped investigate JonBenet Ramsey's murder is accused of botching evidence in multiple murder cases." **June 25, 2019.** DailyMail.com.

RECORDS REQUESTS BY JAY MILLER AS MY PROXY

Miller, Jay. To Dr. Henry Lee. "Re: Forensic consultation in the New Mexico Billy the Kid Case." **March 27, 2006. (Included all the articles with Lee's forensic claims)**

Lee, Henry, Dr. To Jay Miller. "In response to your letter dated March 27, 2006 ..." **May 1, 2006. (Says sent his single forensic report for Case No. 2003-274 to the Lincoln County Sheriff's Department directly)**

Miller, Jay. To Dr. Henry Lee. "Re: Follow-up on your letter of May 1, 2006 responding to my request of March 27, 2006 for information on your forensic consultation in the New Mexico Billy the Kid Case." **June 15, 2006.**

__________. To Dr. Henry Lee. "Re: Follow-up to my letter of June 15, 2006 with regard to your forensic consultation in the New Mexico Billy the Kid Case." **August 8, 2006.**

__________. To Dr. Rick Staub. "Re: The participation by you and Orchid Cellmark in the New Mexico Billy the Kid Case." **August 8, 2006. (No response)**

ETHICS COMPLAINT AGAINST

Cooper, Gale. To Haskell Pitluck, AAFS Ethics Committee Chairman and members of the AAFS Ethics Committee. "Re: Formal Ethics Complaint against Dr. Henry Lee for his work as a forensic expert in Lincoln County, New Mexico, Sheriff's Department Case # 2003-274 ('the Billy the Kid Case')." **October 2, 2006.**

Cooper, Gale. To Haskell Pitluck, AAFS Ethics Committee Chairman. "Re: Follow-up on my October 2, 2006 complaint on Dr. Henry Lee to the Ethics Committee of the American Academy of Forensic Sciences." **March 5, 2007.**

__________. To Dr. Bruce Goldberger. President AAFS. "Re: Informing of non-action to date on my American Academy of Forensic Sciences Ethics Committee complaint filed October 2, 2006 against Dr. Henry Lee." **April 10, 2007.**

Goldberger, Bruce. Dr. and President AAFS. To Gale Cooper. (via fax) "I have received the complaint today ..." **April 12,, 2007.**

__________. To Gale Cooper. (via fax) "You should receive a letter from Mr. Pitluck in the coming week or two ..." **May 4, 2007.**

Pitluck, Haskell M. AAFS Ethics Committee Chairman. To Gale Cooper, M.D. "Ethics Committee has completed its investigation ..." **May 9, 2007. (Corrupt denial)**

Cooper, Gale. To Haskell Pitluck, AAFS Ethics Committee Chairman. "Re: Follow-up on the May 9, 2007 AAFS response to my October 2, 2006 Ethics Complaint on Dr. Henry Lee. **May 30, 2007.**

__________. To Dr. Bruce Goldberger. President AAFS. "Re: Need for clarification in the May 9, 2007 AAFS Ethics Committee response to my AAFS Ethics and Conduct Complaint of October 2, 2006 against Dr. Henry Lee." **May 30, 2007.**

Pitluck, Haskell M. AAFS Ethics Committee Chairman. To Gale Cooper, M.D. "Ethics Committee has completed its investigation ..." **June 2, 2007. (Denial of any responsibility by Dr. Lee for "actions or statements of others.")**

Cooper, Gale. To Rene Romo. *Albuquerque Journal.* "Re: Attributions made by you in your August 2, 2004 *Albuquerque Journal* article titled 'Forensic Expert on Billy's Case: Questions Remain on Outlaws Fate.'" **June 19, 2007.**

__________. To Haskell Pitluck, AAFS Ethics Committee Chairman. "Re: Requested clarification of your responses of May 9, 2007 and June 2, 2007 to my October 2, 2006 AAFS Ethics Complaint against Dr. Henry Lee." **June 19, 2007.**

__________. To Den Slaney. Albuquerque Museum of Art and History. "Re: Information request for Dreamscape Desperado exhibit." **June 29, 2007. (Using fake carpenter's bench blood claim)**

Pitluck, Haskell M. AAFS Ethics Committee Chairman. To Gale Cooper, M.D. "Ethics Committee has completed its investigation ..." **July 6, 2007.**

Walz, Kent. Editor-in-Chief *Albuquerque Journal.* To Gale Cooper. "Response to your letter concerning Rene Romo's story of August 2, 2004." **August 13, 2007. (Stated Lee never denied the quotes attributed to him)**

OPEN RECORDS VIOLATION CASE:

Sandoval County District Cause No. D-1329-CV-2007-1364, Gale Cooper and De Baca County News, a New Mexico Corporation, PLAINTIFFS, vs. Rick Virden, Lincoln County Sheriff and Custodian of Records; and Steven M. Sederwall, Former Lincoln County Deputy Sheriff; and Thomas T. Sullivan, Former Lincoln County Sheriff and Former Lincoln County Deputy Sheriff, DEFENDANTS.

(CHRONOLOGICAL)

INSPECTION OF PUBLIC RECORDS ACT STATUTE

Madrid, Patricia A. Attorney General. *Inspection of Public Records Act Compliance Guide. Fourth Edition. The "Inspection of Public Records Act" NMSA 1978, Chapter 14, Article 2: A Compliance Guide for New Mexico Public Officials and Citizens.* Santa Fe: Office of the Attorney General. **January, 2004.**

King, Gary, Attorney General. "IPRA Guide: The Inspection of Public Records Act NMSA 1978, Chapter 14, Article 2; A Compliance Guide for New Mexico Public Officials and Citizens. Seventh Edition. **2012.**

RECORDS REQUEST PHASE

Cheves, Philip W. Barnett Law Firm. To Sheriff Rick Virden. "Re: Request for Inspection of Public Records." **April 24, 2007. (Start of my records requesting for the Dr. Henry Lee and Orchid Cellmark forensic DNA records)**

Morel, Alan P., Lincoln County Attorney. To Barnett Law Firm. "Re: Freedom of Information Act/Inspection of Public Records Act Request Dated April 24, 2007." **April 27, 2007. (Fakes Case 2003-274 as only deputy murder investigation.)**

Cheves, Philip W. Barnett Law Firm. To Sheriff Rick Virden. "Re: Request for Inspection of Public Records." **May 9, 2007**.

______________. To Alan P. Morel, Esquire. "Re: Request for Inspection of Public Records." **May 9, 2007**.

Morel, Alan P., Lincoln County Attorney. To Barnett Law Firm. "RE: Freedom of Information Act/Inspection of Public Records Act Request to Sheriff Rick Virden Dated May 9, 2007." **May 11, 2007**. **(Lies that Lincoln County have no Case 2003-274 records "whatsoever")**

______________. To Barnett Law Firm. "RE: Freedom of Information Act/Inspection of Public Records Act Request to Alan P. Morel, Esq., Dated May 9, 2007." **May 14, 2007**. **(Fakes "deputies too records" excuse)**

Cheves, Philip W., Barnett Law Firm. To Alan P. Morel, Esquire. "Re: Request for Inspection of Public Records." **June 8, 2007**.

Cheves, Philip W., Barnett Law Firm. "Re: Request for Inspection of Public Records" to Tom Sullivan. **June 14, 2007**.

______________. "Re: Request for Inspection of Public Records" to Steve Sederwall. **June 14, 2007**.

Morel, Alan P., Lincoln County Attorney. Thomas Stewart, Lincoln County Manager, and Rick Virden, Lincoln County Sheriff. To Tom Sullivan and Steve Sederwall. "Re: Request for Inspection of Public Records." **June 21, 2007**. **(This was attached to Morel's letter of June 22, 2007 as feigned records recovery)**

Sederwall, Steven M. and Thomas T. Sullivan. To Rick Virden, Lincoln County Sheriff. "Memorandum. Subject: Billy the Kid Investigation." **June 21, 2007**. **(Key hoax document attached to the Morel letter of June 22, 2007, blames Richardson and Robins for case, attaches $6,500 in "bribery" checks to Sullivan, and quitting as deputies)**

Morel, Alan P. Lincoln County Attorney. To Barnett Law Firm. "RE: Freedom of Information Act/Inspection of Public Records Act Request to Alan Morel, Esq., Dated June 8, 2007." **June 22, 2007**. **(Attached was the Sullivan-Sederwall June 21, 2007 "Memorandum.")**

Morel, Alan P., Lincoln County Attorney. To Barnett Law Firm. "RE: Freedom of Information Act/Inspection of Public Records Act Request to Alan P. Morel, Esq., dated June 8, 2007." **June 26, 2007**. **(Last response before litigation)**

RECORDS LITIGATION PHASE

Barnett, Mickey. "Verified Complaint for Declaratory Judgment Ordering Production of Certain Records and Information." **October 15, 2007**. **(Start of litigation for Cause No. D-1329-CV-2007-1364, repeats records in first request)**

__________. "Verified First Amended Complaint for Declaratory Judgment Ordering Production of Certain Records and Information." **November 1, 2007**. **(Removes Lincoln County as defendant, repeats records in first request)**

Zimitski, Dewayne. Process server for Steve Sederwall and Tom Sullivan. "Affidavit of DeWayne Zimitski for Cause No. D 1329 CV 2007-01364." **December 27, 2007**. **(Thuggish evasion by cursing Sullivan)**

Cooper, Gale. To Attorney General Gary King. "Re: Informing about an IPRA violation case: Sandoval County Thirteenth Judicial District Cause No. D1329-CV2007-1364." **January 22, 2008**.

___________. To Attorney Leonard DeLayo for FOG. "Re: Sandoval County Thirteenth Judicial District Court Cause No. D 1329 CV2007-1364; an IPRA violation case." **January 22, 2008**.

Werkmeister, Nicole. Attorney for Narvaez law firm. Cause No. D1329-CV-07-1364." Thirteenth Judicial District Court, State of New Mexico, County of Sandoval. March 5, 2008. "Motion to Dismiss Based on Improper Venue and Failure to State a Claim." **March 5, 2008**. **(Attorney for Rick Virden)**

Brown, Kevin M. Attorney for defendants Sullivan and Sederwall. To Barnett Law Firm. "Thomas T. Sullivan's Responses to Request for Production of Documents, No. D-1329-CV-2007-01364." **March 17, 2008. (Claims not public records, and defendant does not have them.**.)

___________. To Barnett Law Firm. "Steven M. Sederwall's Responses to Request for Production of Documents." **March 17, 2008. (Claims not public records, and defendant does not have them.**.)

Barnett, Mickey. "Plaintiffs' Response to the Motion of Defendant Rick Virden to Dismiss For Improper Venue and Failure to State Claim." **March 24, 2008.**

Shandler, Zachary. (For Attorney General Gary King). To Gale Cooper M.D. "RE: Gale Cooper and De Baca County News vs. Lincoln County et al., Cause No. D-1329-CV2007-1364." **April 3, 2008.**

Kent, Kerry. ML Claims Examiner. "Tom, I'm sending you a letter advising that the IJ $10,000 limit for attorneys fees is gone ..." E-Mail. **August 9, 2008. (Proving huge taxpayer costs of my IPRA litigation)**

Stewart, Tom. Lincoln County Manager. "Subject: FW: IJ 20282/Billy the Kid File. County Commissioners, For the first time I can recall as county manager, we have run out of insurance coverage on a case." E-Mail. **August 9, 2008. (Though proving taxpayer costs of my IPRA litigation, the defendants ignored the liability and ultimately incurred the huge plaintiffs' bill)**

Stinnett, Scot. To Gale Cooper. (via e-mail). "IPRA Case Updates." **August 12, 2008. (About FOG probably joining IPRA case**.)

Sullivan, Thomas T. "Deposition." **August 18, 2008. (Taken by Mickey Barnett)**

Sederwall, Steven M. "Deposition." **August 18, 2008. (Taken by Mickey Barnett)**

Barnett, Mickey. Attorney. To Gale Cooper. (via e-mail). "FOG is in." August 22, 2008.

Virden, Rick. "Deposition." **September 8, 2008. (Taken by David Garcia)**

Werkmeister, Nicole. "Re" Gale Cooper, et al, v. Rick Virden, et al. Thirteenth Judicial District Court Cause No. D-1329-CV-2007-01364." Attorney. Letter to Attorney Mickey D. Barnett. **September 3, 2008. (Virden turn-over by subpoena duces tecum of Sheriff's Department file for Case # 2003-274 – minus any forensic documents; calls case criminal investigation)**

Virden, Rick. Case 2003-274 file Turn-over. **September 3, 2008. (By subpoena duces tecum; 193 pages)**

Rogers, Patrick J. Attorney. "Docs for editing. To: Mickey Barnett; David A. Garcia." (via e-mail). Monday, **September 22, 2008.** (Forwarded to Gale Cooper on September 25, 2008.) **(Threat FOG to pressure for dismissing Virden)**

Cooper, Gale. From Attorney David Garcia. (via e-mail). "Re: FW: Docs for editing." **September 25, 2008.**

___________. "Subj. IPRA Case Communication for Review. To Attorneys Barnett and Garcia and Scot Stinnett." (via e-mail). **September 28, 2008. (Case overview, our legal relationship, and responses to the Rogers e-mail.**)

___________. To Attorney Leonard DeLayo. "Fwd: Response regarding IPRA Case." **September 29, 2008. (Case overview for Barnett of September 28, 2008 with responses to the Rogers e-mail.**)

Rogers, Patrick. Forwarded from Scot Stinnett. (via e-mail). "No Subject." **September 30, 2008. (A copy of an e-mail from corrupt Attorney Rogers to Attorney DeLayo pushing falsely for Sederwall as Records Custodian.)**

___________. "Re: Second Response To Your FOG Proposal." To Gale Cooper. (via e-mail) **October 1, 2008** 4:40:27 AM.. **(Attorney Rogers tries to coerce me by Sederwall as Records Custodian or he will withdraw FOG**)

Barnett, Mickey D. Attorney. "Re: Sullivan Sederwall Depositions. To Gale Cooper." (via e-mail). **October 1, 2008.**

Brown, Kevin M. Attorney. "Re: Cooper v. Lincoln County, et al. No. D-1329-CV-07-1364. To Patrick J. Rogers." **October 16, 2008.**

Cooper, Gale. To Attorney Pat Rogers. "Re: Response documents forwarded to me by e-mail on October 20, 2008 concerning NMFOG's actions in relation to my IPRA case No. D-1329-CV-1364." **October 27, 2008**.

Rogers, Patrick J. Attorney. Letter of withdrawal as the FOG attorney pertaining to my IPRA case. **November 10, 2008**. (**Corruptly trying to throw my case**)

Cooper, Gale. "Re: My response to your letter of October 16, 2008 to Attorney Pat Rogers, and my dissociation from the referenced Foundation For Open Government communications." Letter to Brown. **November 17, 2008**.

Threet, Martin E. Attorney and Attorney A. Blair Dunn." Plaintiffs' Motion for Summary Judgment. Gale Cooper and De Baca County News, a New Mexico Corporation, Plaintiffs, vs. Lincoln County and Rick Virden, Lincoln County Sheriff and Custodian of Records; and Steven M. Sederwall, Former Lincoln County Deputy Sheriff; and Thomas T. Sullivan, Former Lincoln County Sheriff and Former Lincoln County Deputy Sheriff, Defendants. No. D-1329-CV-07-1364." County of Sandoval , Thirteenth Judicial District Court. **July 31, 2009**.

Werkmeister, H. Nicole. Attorney. Defendant Rick Virden's Response to Plaintiff's [sic] Motion for Summary Judgment and Cross-Motion for Summary Judgment. Gale Cooper and De Baca County News, a New Mexico Corporation, Plaintiffs, vs. Lincoln County and Rick Virden, Lincoln County Sheriff and Custodian of Records; and Steven M. Sederwall, Former Lincoln County Deputy Sheriff; and Thomas T. Sullivan, Former Lincoln County Sheriff and Former Lincoln County Deputy Sheriff, Defendants. No. D-1329-CV-07-1364." County of Sandoval , Thirteenth Judicial District Court. **August 29, 2009**.

Brown, Kevin. Attorney. "Defendants Sederwall and Sullivan's Response to Motion for Summary Judgment. Gale Cooper and De Baca County News, a New Mexico Corporation, Plaintiffs, vs. Lincoln County and Rick Virden, Lincoln County Sheriff and Custodian of Records; and Steven M. Sederwall, Former Lincoln County Deputy Sheriff; and Thomas T. Sullivan, Former Lincoln County Sheriff and Former Lincoln County Deputy Sheriff, Defendants. No. D-1329-CV-07-1364." County of Sandoval , Thirteenth Judicial District Court. **September 2, 2009**.

Threet, Martin E. Attorney and Attorney A. Blair Dunn. "Plaintiffs' Reply and Motion to Exceed Page Limit For Exhibits. Gale Cooper and De Baca County News, a New Mexico Corporation, Plaintiffs, vs. Lincoln County and Rick Virden, Lincoln County Sheriff and Custodian of Records; and Steven M. Sederwall, Former Lincoln County Deputy Sheriff; and Thomas T. Sullivan, Former Lincoln County Sheriff and Former Lincoln County Deputy Sheriff, Defendants. No. D-1329-CV-07-1364." County of Sandoval, Thirteenth Judicial District Court. **September 29, 2009**. (**Attempt to enter my extensive evidence into court record**)

__________. Motion for Summary Judgment. **January, 2010**.

Eichwald, George P. Hearing for "Plaintiffs' Motion for Summary Judgment." Transcript. **November 20, 2009**. (**Plaintiffs' Motion for Summary Judgment Granted.**)

__________. "Summary Judgment" granted for Plaintiffs. January, 2010.

Brown, Kevin. "I am enclosing the document Mr. Sederwall received from Dr. Lee ..." Letter. **February 18, 2010**. (**Unrequested Lee floorboard report**)

Lee, Henry and Calvin Ostler. "Forensic Research and Training Center Forensic Examination Report: "Examination of Lincoln County Court House." **February 25, 2005**. (**Given to Plaintiffs on February 18, 2010 by Brown and on April 6, 2010 by Werkmeister as a requested Lee report – but was the fake Version I (9 pages) of an unrequested floorboard report**)

Threet, Martin E. "I am returning the Lee report ..." Letter to Brown. (Rejecting and returning the Lee floorboard report) **February 25, 2010**.

"Presentment Hearing." Transcript. **March 9, 2010**. (**Defendants give unrequested Lee floorboard report as fulfilling records turn-over; and lying that it is only the record in Sederwall's possession**)

Eichwald, George P., District Judge. "Order Granting Plaintiff's Motion for Summary Judgment and Denying Defendant Virden's Cross Motion for Summary Judgment and Order Granting Leave to File Interloculatory Appeal" **March 12, 2010. (Grants evidentiary hearing.)**

Werkmeister, Nicole. "Attached is the Forensic Examination Report From Dr. Henry Lee ..." Fax cover letter. **April 6, 2010. (Copy faxed of same unrequested (fake) Lee floorboard report from Brown was enclosed)**

Eichwald. George P., District Judge. "Order Granting Plaintiffs' Motion for Summary Judgment and Denying Defendant Virden's Cross-Motion for Summary Judgment and Order Granting Leave to File Interloculatory Appeal." **March 12, 2010. (Major Plaintiff victory)**

Threet, Martin E. "Take a look at this letter ..." Fax cover letter to me. **April 13, 2010. (Werkmeister sending fake floorboard Lee report to us)**

Threet, Martin E. "The time for interloculatory appeal having passed ..." Letter to Werkmeister and Brown. **May 3, 2010**

Hearing for "Mandatory Order of Disclosure and Production Hearing." Transcript. **September 9, 2010.**

Threet, Martin E. "Re: Billy the Kid. "Henry Narvaez has again repeated his assurance to me that if we will agree to dismiss Virden ..." Fax to me. **September 14, 2010. (Threet's attempt to trick me into dismissing Virden)**

__________. "Re: Plaintiff's response to letter from Sheriff Rick Virden. It is the position of my clients ..." Letter. **September 27, 2010.**

Virden, Rick. "It is my understanding that on May 22, 2004, Steve Sederwall ..." Letter to Henry Lee. **October 26, 2010. (sham recovery attempt to Dr. Henry Lee)**

__________. "It is my understanding that in the spring or summer of 2004, Steve Sederwall sent a blood sample(s) to Orchid Cellmark ..." Letter "To Whom It May Concern." **October 26, 2010. (Sham recovery attempt to Orchid Cellmark)**

Narvaez Law Firm. Billing to New Mexico County Insurance Authority. **October 31, 2010. (Listing secret meetings with Attorney Threet to dismiss Virden)**

Gulliksen, Joan., Orchid Cellmark Customer Liaison, Forensics. "Orchid Cellmark is in receipt of your letter requesting DNA documents ..." Letter to Virden. **November 2, 2010. (Orchid Cellmark response requesting client name to release records; Virden did not get the records)**

__________. "Orchid Cellmark, this is Joan ..." Transcript of telephone call from Virden. **November 2, 2010. (Virden did no follow-up)**

__________. "Orchid Cellmark, this is Joan ..." E-mail to Virden. **November 2, 2010. (Virden did no follow-up)**

Brown, Kevin. "Enclosed please find a copy of another report dated February 25, 2005 which deals with the examination of furniture by Dr. Lee." Letter to Threet. **November 10, 2010. (Sending Lee's forged bench report; different font than the first forged floorboard report)**

Lee, Henry and Calvin Ostler. "Forensic Research and Training Center Forensic Examination Report: "Examination of furniture from Pete Maxwell's of July 15, 1881." February 25, 2005. **(Given to Plaintiffs on November 10, 2010 as Lee bench report (16 pages) – but was its forged Version I)**

Werkmeister, Nicole. Letter to Threet. **November 4, 2010. (Shaming Virden recovery of Orchid Cellmark records; saying Lee did not respond)**

Lee, Henry. "This letter is in response to your letter ..." Letter to Virden. **November 12, 2010. (Lee confirms report; Virden never asked for it!)**

Werkmeister, Nicole. Letter to Threet. **November 22, 2010. (copies of Virden's sham Lee and Orchid Cellmark requests sent to Threet)**

Robins, Bill III. Deposition taken by Attorney Martin E. Threet. **January 6, 2011.**

"Evidentiary Hearing on Plaintiff's Motion for Mandatory Order of Disclosure and Production." Transcript. **January 21, 2011. (Defendants gave forged Lee Floorboard report (9 pages) Version II entered as Exhibit F; forged Lee bench report (16 pages) Version I entered as Exhibit E)**

Lee, Henry and Calvin Ostler. "Forensic Research and Training Center Forensic Examination Report: "Examination of furniture from Pete Maxwell's of July 15, 1881." February 25, 2005. **(Given to Court on January 21, 2011 as Lee bench report (16 pages), Exhibit E – but was its fake Version 1)**

Lee, Henry and Calvin Ostler. "Forensic Research and Training Center Forensic Examination Report: "Examination of Lincoln County Court House." February 25, 2005. **(Given to Court on January 21, 2011 as Lee floorboard report (9 pages), Exhibit F – but was its forged Version II)**

Brown, Kevin. "I represent Steve Sederwall ..." Letter to Dr. Staub. **February 3, 2011. (Sederwall's court-ordered bogus Orchid Cellmark recovery attempt)**

Cooper, Gale. "Re: Termination of legal services for Gale Cooper and the *De Baca County News* vs Lincoln County Sheriff Rick Virden et al case." Letter to Attorney Martin E. Threet. **February 12, 2011. (Termination of Threet)**

__________. "Subj: Change of Legal Representation for Virden et al." E-mail to Attorney Blair Dunn. **April 13, 2011. (Termination of Dunn)**

Brown, Kevin. Letter. **June 7, 2011. (Follow-up to Sederwall's court-ordered Dr. Lee report turn-over)**

"Presentment Hearing." Transcript. **September 23, 2011. (Plaintiffs presenting discrepancies in the Lee reports)**

Eichwald, George P., District Judge. "Order on Hearing of January 21, 2011." **September 28, 2011. (Joined the deputy killings and Kid killing investigations; calling them and records public)**

Riordan, William and Patrick Griebel. "Plaintiffs' Requested Findings of Fact and Conclusions of Law." **November 4, 2011.**

Cooper, Gale. "Re: Immediate termination of services for Sandoval District Court Cause No. D-1329-CV-07-1364." Letter to Attorney Griebel. **November 21, 2011.**

Griebel, Patrick and Jeremy Theoret. "Plaintiff's Motion for Payment of Damages, Costs and Fees." **December 12, 2011.**

__________. "Plaintiff's Reply in Support of Motion for Payment of Damages, Costs and Fees." **January 13, 2012.**

Hearing on "Plaintiffs' Motion to Supplement the Record and a Request for Sanctions, and Co-Plaintiff's Motion For Attorney Fees." **January 17, 2012. (Lee reports presented for sanctions as forged; and co-plaintiff Stinnett requests fees for past attorneys. Judge grants 100% fees)**

Brown, Kevin. Court-ordered turn-over of 25 page, "original" Lee report. **January 31, 2012. (Tutn-over of the authentic, 25 page, Lee report)**

Eichwald, George P., District Judge. "Order on Plaintiffs Motion to Supplement the Record and Request for Award of Sanctions against Defendants." **February 23, 2012. (Ordered Sederwall to produce original Lee report)**

Lee, Henry and Calvin Ostler. "Forensic Research and Training Center Forensic Examination Report." February 25, 2005. **(Court-ordered turn-over to Plaintiffs on January 31, 2012 as "original" Lee report (25 pages) combining bench, floorboards, and wash stand)**

Griebel, Patrick J. Attorney for Scot Stinnett. "Subpoena for Production or Inspection to Laboratory Corporation of America." **March 29, 2012. (Non-IPRA subpoena of records from Orchid Cellmark parent company)**

__________. "Reply in Support of Plaintiff's Motion for Order to Show Cause." **April 11, 2012. (Co-Plaintiff's attempt to get Sullivan and Sederwall "Private Donor Fund" checking account information))**

Hearing on "Plaintiffs' Second Motion to Supplement the Record and a Request for Sanctions." **May 31, 2012 (Forged Lee reports for sanctions)**

Brown, Kevin. Court-ordered turn-over of another 25 page, "original" Lee report. **June 7, 2012. (CD of same report as given on January 31, 2012, but with color photos and no signatures)**

Sederwall, Steven. Deposition. **June 26, 2012. (Admitted forgery as "massaging!")**

Virden, Rick. Deposition. **June 27, 2012.**

"Status Conference." Transcript. **September 21, 2012.**

Eichwald, George P., District Judge. "Order." For Status Conference of **September 21, 2012. (Court-ordered mediation and Evidentiary hearing)**

Eichwald, George P., District Judge. "Order." For Settlement Conference of **March 27, 2013. (Court-ordered mediation and Evidentiary hearing)**

STEVE SEDERWALL'S FORGED DR. HENRY LEE REPORTS

Brown, Kevin. "I am enclosing the document Mr. Sederwall received from Dr. Lee ..." Letter. **February 18, 2010. (Unrequested Lee floorboard report which was a forgery)**

Lee, Henry and Calvin Ostler. "Forensic Research and Training Center Forensic Examination Report: "Examination of Lincoln County Court House." February 25, 2005. **(Given to me on February 18, 2010 by Kevin Brown and on April 6, 2010 by Nicole Werkmeister as a requested Lee report – but was Version I (9 pages) of an unrequested and forged floorboard report)**

Threet, Martin E. "I am returning the Lee report ..." Letter to Brown. (Rejecting and returning the Lee floorboard report) **February 25, 2010. (Unrequested)**

"Presentment Hearing." Transcript. **March 9, 2010. (Defendants gave the judge the unrequested (forged) Lee floorboard report as fulfilling records turn-over; and lied that was the only record in Sederwall's possession)**

Werkmeister, Nicole. "Attached is the Forensic Examination Report From Dr. Henry Lee ..." Fax cover letter. **April 6, 2010. (Copy faxed of same unrequested (forged) Lee floorboard report from Brown)**

Brown, Kevin. "Enclosed please find a copy of another report dated February 25, 2005 which deals with the examination of furniture by Dr. Lee." Letter to Threet. **November 10, 2010. (Sending Lee's (forged) bench report; different font than the (forged) floorboard report)**

Lee, Henry and Calvin Ostler. "Forensic Research and Training Center Forensic Examination Report: "Examination of furniture from Pete Maxwell's of July 15, 1881." February 25, 2005. **(Given to me on November 10, 2010 as Lee bench report (16 pages) – but was forged)**

"Evidentiary Hearing on Plaintiff's Motion for Mandatory Order of Disclosure and Production." Transcript. **January 21, 2011. (Defendants gave forged Lee Floorboard report (9 pages) Version II as Exhibit F; and forged Lee bench report (16 pages) as Exhibit E)**

Lee, Henry and Calvin Ostler. "Forensic Research and Training Center Forensic Examination Report: "Examination of furniture from Pete Maxwell's of July 15, 1881." February 25, 2005. **(Given to Court on January 21, 2011 as Lee bench report (16 pages), Exhibit E – but was a forgery)**

Lee, Henry and Calvin Ostler. "Forensic Research and Training Center Forensic Examination Report: "Examination of Lincoln County Court House." February 25, 2005. **(Given to Court on January 21, 2011 as Lee floorboard report (9 pages), Exhibit F – but was its forged Version II)**

"Presentment Hearing." Transcript. September 23, 2011. **(I realized forgery was taking place and presented discrepancies in the Lee reports)**

Hearing on "Plaintiffs' Motion to Supplement the Record and a Request for Sanctions, and Co-Plaintiff's Motion For Attorney Fees." January 17, 2012 **(Sanctions against Defendants requested for forged reports; and co-plaintiff requested fees for past attorneys. Judge granted 100% fees)**

Eichwald, George P., District Judge. "Order on Plaintiffs Motion to Supplement the Record and Request for Award of Sanctions against Defendants." February 23, 2012. **(Ordered Sederwall to produce authentic Lee report)**

Lee, Henry and Calvin Ostler. "Forensic Research and Training Center Forensic Examination Report." February 25, 2005. **(Court-ordered turn-over to Plaintiffs on January 31, 2012 as "original," authentic, sole Dr. Henry Lee**

report, as (25 pages) combining bench, floorboards, and wash stand into a single report)

Hearing on "Plaintiffs' Second Motion to Supplement the Record and a Request for Sanctions." **May 31, 2012 (Sanctions requested for forged Lee reports)**

ORCHID CELLMARK RECORDS SUBPOENAED (RECEIVED 133 PAGES ON APRIL 20, 2012)

Griebel, Patrick J. Attorney for Scot Stinnett. "Subpoena for Production or Inspection to Laboratory Corporation of America." **March 29, 2012. (Non-IPRA subpoena of records from Orchid Cellmark parent company; got 133 pages of results of Lee's floorboards and bench, and Arizona exhumations; missing DNA matching results of bench to remains)**

SELECT RECORDS

Evidence Bag Photo. Chain of Custody Label: "Case No. 2003-274, Underside Bench 4. Date: 07,31,04." Below is written Orchid Cellmark Case and Specimen No. 4444-002B. **July 31, 2004. (Case 2003-274 was made Orchid Cellmark Case No. 4444)**

Ostler, Calvin D. "FedEx Mailing Envelope and tracking information to "Rick Staub, Orchid Cellmark." **August 3, 2004. (Specimens delivered August 4, 2004)**

"Orchid Cellmark Evidence Evaluation Worksheet Case No. 4444 A and B." **August 16, 2004. (Lee's floorboard and bench specimens)**

"Orchid Cellmark Evidence Evaluation Worksheet Case No. 4444." **April 13, 2006. (Listing specimens from John Miller-William Hudspeth exhumations.**

"Orchid Cellmark Chain of Custody for Case No. 4444." **May 19, 2005. (On date of John Miller exhumation and signed by Orchid Cellmark Director Rick Staub with the south and north grave specimens he collected listed)**

"Orchid Cellmark Laboratory Report - Forensic Identity - Mitochondrial Analysis for 4444." **January 26, 2009. (Listing specimens for reports requested by me: Lee's from bench and Orchid Cellmark's from the Arizona graves.)**

GALE COOPER AS PRO SE

Cooper, Gale. "Plaintiff Gale Cooper's Entry of Pro Se Appearance." **November 13, 2012.**

__________. "Plaintiff Gale Cooper's Pre-Evidentiary Hearing Brief." **November 14, 2012.**

__________. "Plaintiff Gale Cooper's Pre-Evidentiary Hearing Brief." **November 14, 2012.**

Narvaez, Henry, Attorney for Virden. "It is our position that those deposition [sic] and exhibits are not relevant to the subject matter of the hearing..." Letter to Gale Cooper. **November 20, 2012. (Trying to keep out June 26-27, 2012 incriminating depositions of Sullivan and Sederwall)**

Cooper, Gale. "Plaintiff Gale Cooper's Witness List for Evidentiary Hearing on December 18, 2012." **December 10, 2012.**

"Evidentiary Hearing." Transcript. **December 18, 2012. (Virden testifies)**

Cooper, Gale. "Plaintiff Gale Cooper's Motion to Compel Defendants' Production of the Requested Forensic DNA Records of Lincoln County Sheriff's Department Case No. 2003-274." **January 3, 2013.**

__________. "Plaintiff Gale Cooper's Motion for Expedited Hearing on Her Filed Motions for the February 4, 2013 Evidentiary Hearing." **January 14, 2013.**

"Evidentiary Hearing." Transcript. February 4, 2013. (**Sederwall and Morel testify**)

Cooper, Gale. "Notice of Filing of Attached Plaintiff Gale Cooper's Proposed Findings of Fact and Conclusions of Law." **February 27, 2013.**

__________. "Plaintiff Gale Cooper's Proposed Findings of Fact and Conclusions of Law." **February 27, 2013.**

Cooper, Gale. "Plaintiff Gale Cooper's Motion to Request Award of Her Costs and Damages From Defendants and to Request Award of Sanctions Against Defendants." **May 23, 2013.**

__________. "Affidavit of Gale Cooper." **May 22, 2013. (Sworn costs)**

__________. "Plaintiff Gale Cooper's Request for Hearing." **May 23, 2013.**

Cooper, Gale. "Re: Open letter to Lincoln County Commissioners about Lincoln County Sheriff's Department **Case No. 2003-274** and Sandoval County District Court **Cause No. D-1329-CV-1364**, Gale Cooper and De Baca County News vs. Rick Virden, Lincoln County Sheriff and Custodian of the Records of the Lincoln County Sheriff's Office; and Steven M. Sederwall, Former Lincoln County Deputy Sheriff; and Thomas T. Sullivan, Former Lincoln County Sheriff and Former Lincoln County Deputy Sheriff." **June 18, 2013. (Summary of "Billy the Kid Case" hoax, its litigation, and its costs; no response)**

__________. "Plaintiff Gale Cooper's Notice of Briefing Completion with Repeated Request for Hearing." **July 1, 2013.**

__________. "Addendum to Plaintiff Gale Cooper's Motion to Request Award of Her Costs and Damages From Defendants and to Request Award of Sanctions Against Defendants." **July 1, 2013.**

__________.Hearing for Plaintiff Gale Cooper's Motion to Request Award of Her Costs and Damages From Defendants and to Request Award of Sanctions Against Defendants." Transcript. December 18, 2013. **(I won!)**

Eichwald, George P. Judge. "Findings of Fact and Conclusions of Law and Order of the Court." **May 15, 2014. (Plaintiff Gale Cooper prevailed)**

__________ "Final Judgment." **March 8, 2017. (Plaintiff Gale Cooper prevailed)**

"COLD CASE BILLY THE KID" MEGAHOAX

THE JAMESON BOOKS (CHRONOLOGICAL)

Jameson, W.C. *Billy the Kid: Beyond the Grave.* Boulder, Lanham, Maryland: Taylor Trade Publishing. **2005. (A repeat of the "Brushy Bill" imposter hoax)**

__________. *Billy the Kid: The Lost Interviews.* Clearwater, Florida: Garlic Press Publishing. **2012.** (Reprint 2017). **(Forged rewriting of the 1949 Morrison transcript of "Brushy" to fake dialogue to update the hoax)**

__________. *Pat Garrett. The Man Behind the Badge.* Boulder, Colorado: Taylor Trade Publishing. **2016. (Defamation of Pat Garrett, "Brushy Bill" as a quoted authority, and "Billy the Kid Case" hoaxing as evidence to claim Garrett murdered an innocent victim instead of Billy the Kid)**

__________. *Cold Case Billy the Kid: Investigating History's Mysteries.* Guilford, Connecticut: Twodot. **2018. (Fusing the "Brushy" hoax and "Billy the Kid Case" hoax to argue for "Brushy" as Billy the Kid)**

SOURCES FOR DEBUNKING CLAIMS (CHRONOLOGICAL)

(SEE: "Billy the Kid Case" hoax)

RELEVANT TO DENYING WILLIAM H. BONNEY'S CORONER'S JURY REPORT'S EXISTENCE

(SEE: William H. Bonney, Coroner's Jury Report; and Patrick F. Garrett, Reward)

RELEVANT SOURCES HOAXERS CITED RELATED TO JOHN MILLER CLAIM (CHRONOLOGICAL)

Garrett, Pat F. *The Authentic Life of Billy the Kid.* Santa Fe, New Mexico: New Mexico Printing and Publishing Co. **1882.** (Edition used by me: Edited by Maurice Garland Fulton. New York: The Macmillan Company. 1927)

Poe, John W. *The Death of Billy the Kid.* (Introduction by Maurice Garland Fulton). Boston and New York: Houghton Mifflin Company. **1933.**

Otero, Miguel, *The Real Billy the Kid.* New York: Rufus Rockwell Wilson. **1936.** (**Claim that Jesus Silva for shot Billy Bonney face down. But Otero had no first-hand knowledge, and the book was 55 years after the event.**)

Klasner, Lilly. Eve Ball. Ed. *My Girlhood Among Outlaws.* Tucson, Arizona: The University of Arizona Press. **1972.**

Avant, Bundy. (Told to Arthur Clements). "The Bundy Avant Story: New Mexico in the days when a thin population was intent on bettering itself and each man could devise his own method for 'getting' while getting' was good.' " (Part One) *True West.* **May-June, 1978**, Volume 25, Number 5. (**Old-timer malarkey about a fake "Peter Maxwell" in the San Andres Mountains**)

Anaya, Paco. *I Buried Billy.* College Station, Texas: Creative Publishing Company. **1991.(Cited as claiming counterfeiting for Billy**)

Lee, Henry and Calvin Ostler. "Forensic Research and Training Center Forensic Examination Report: "Examination of Lincoln County Court House." February 25, 2005. (**Apparently the forged "Billy the Kid Case's floorboard report**)

Lee, Henry. "Forensic Examination Report (Examination of Furniture From Pete Maxwell's of July 15, 1881) 22 May 2004." From W.C. Jameson, *Cold Case Billy the Kid.* Page 187. (**Apparently the forged "Billy the Kid Case's" carpenter's bench, washstand, and headboard report**)

INDEX

www.ingramcontent.com/pod-product-compliance
Lightning Source LLC
Chambersburg PA
CBHW071402090426
42737CB00011B/1316

* 9 7 8 1 9 4 9 6 2 6 1 7 9 *